Solving the Assessment Puzzle Piece by Piece

Carolyn Coil
Dodie Merritt

Pieces of Learning

© 2001 Pieces of Learning
Cover by John Steele

www.piecesoflearning.com

CLC0261
ISBN 1-880505-98-3
Printed in the U.S.A.

Table of Contents

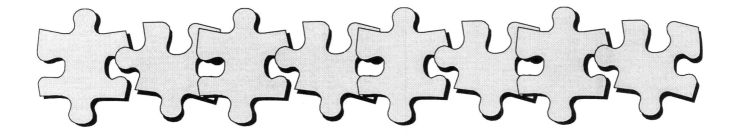

Acknowledgements

With appreciation for all of my DeKalb County, Georgia graduate students -
    For those who encouraged me to learn about assessment and teach the course *Educational Assessment and Measurement*

    For those who learned about rubrics and checklists, developed them and applied what they learned in their classrooms. You are my "living laboratory!"

    For those who wrote many of the teacher-created rubrics contained in this book

Special thanks to teachers with whom I have worked extensively, for together we have learned so much about assessment -

    Teachers and coordinators in Laredo ISD, Laredo, Texas

    Teachers, administrators and other educators throughout the state of Indiana

    Teachers and others in Wake County, North Carolina, especially teachers who attended my workshops for Academically Gifted or on the topic of Differentiated Curriculum

In appreciation and in recognition of -

    Kathy Wertz, Prairie Heights Middle School, La Grange, Indiana for sharing her method of using curriculum compacting in math

    Chris Kern, Avondale High School, Avondale Estates, Georgia for her unique final exam

    Colleagues in the Genoa-Kingston School District, Genoa, IL

    Jim Curry's English teacher who coined the term "NSH" or "Not So Hot"

    and

    to our families and friends for their love and support.

Chapter 1
Introduction
What does it all mean and why do we do it anyway?

Ms. Weeks was drowning in a sea of papers to grade. She knew her students would demand to know their grades immediately but she felt overwhelmed. Not only did she have to grade the papers, she also had to come up with numbers to reflect that grade in her grade book and the school's computerized grading program. "We live and die by numbers and points and scores," she thought, "not by what the kids actually learn."

The school principal, Mr. Vasquez, was worried about test scores. The standardized test the district had been using for several years had just been re-normed and the superintendent didn't want to see test scores drop. His school was successfully using many types of alternative assessments, but he didn't know how student progress might be reflected in the re-normed test. He did know that his school and all others in the district would be evaluated based on test scores. "Test scores are everything in this district," he told his teachers.

How, why and what we assess are some of the most pressing issues, questions and concerns in education today. Indeed, if assessment is the tail and curriculum the dog, we certainly often have a case of the tail wagging the dog! Many educators are deeply concerned about this issue yet feel lost or confused in the competing requirements, needs and demands they hear from students, parents, administrators, and the public at large.

This book is written for teachers, administrators and other practitioners who are not assessment experts but who need to know and understand the basics of assessment and what is being required of them. In this book, we take a broad look at assessment and what it means for today's educators. All facets of assessment, from assessment terminology to standardized tests, from portfolios to report cards, from rubrics to standards and benchmarks are considered. We hope it will clarify assessment issues for you and will make them easier to understand and deal with.

As a result of reading this book you will:

- Comprehend basic assessment terminology

- Understand the advantages and disadvantages of standardized tests and alternative assessment measures

- Know the purposes and functions of standards and benchmarks

- Know how to write rubrics and other forms of alternative assessments

- See numerous samples of rubrics written by classroom teachers

- Find out a variety of ways to report student progress

On the next page you will see the *Glass of Water* activity. I have used this activity in many of my assessment workshops in order to introduce four basic terms which are used over and over again (often interchangeably though they shouldn't be) when we discuss educational assessment issues. These are:

- Assess
- Measure
- Test
- Evaluate

This activity purposely does not directly relate to education and, in fact, is particularly helpful for that very reason. Sometimes when we step back from our area of concentration and expertise and see issues in a broader perspective, it helps us put them into focus more easily. That is what this activity is intended to do. You may do the activity by yourself, or you can discuss it in a group setting so that you can brainstorm together and debate different points of view.

Do the activity before looking at subsequent pages for explanations and a discussion of the four terms.

Glass of Water Activity

A glass of water can teach us a great deal about assessment and the terminology we use when discussing it. Get a glass of water and put it in front of you as you do this activity. Consider the glass of water as you discuss each of the following:

How would you:

1. Assess it?

2. Measure it?

3. Test it?

4. Evaluate it?

What are the differences in these four terms?

In educational assessment, what do you do when you measure something?

How can you assess <u>without</u> measuring?

Reproducible for teacher use.

Thinking About the Glass of Water Activity

Now that you've completed the *Glass of Water* activity, you might like to read my ideas and the ideas of other teachers as they did this activity.

Assess

> *I would use a variety of techniques to find out about distinct characteristics or properties of the liquid, such as quality, purity, density, clarity, composition. I would observe it using all of my senses. I'd taste it, smell it, stir it, look at it or use it. This would give me the opportunities I need to gather the data necessary to make a conclusion. -- Workshop participant*

Assessment is the broad term which encompasses all the others. Considering assessing a glass of water, we would need to collect and gather information and data from a wide variety of sources, settings and circumstances. We might observe and determine what its uses are.

We could design a checklist and look at as many different factors as possible, using the five senses to observe the properties of water and check them off. The checklist might include questions such as the ones below:

- Is it a liquid?
- What is its color and clarity?
- Is it hot or cold?
- What does it smell like?
- Is it safe to drink?
- Shall I taste it?
- What does it taste like?

In our process of assessment, we might want to analyze specific parts and qualities of the water, then combine and integrate our new findings with previous knowledge about the properties and characteristics of water. Then we would have the information we need to make a knowledgeable assessment.

Assessment can be any method through which one gathers information to find out about something. Assessing something means you may measure it or evaluate it. It means having a broad viewpoint and finding out much more information than test results can give. Assessment means using all the information and data gathered, along with previous knowledge, in order to make a decision about the whole.

Measure

> *I would determine how much is in the glass, how much it weighs, and the amount of each chemical in the water. Then I would systematically collect, quantify and make an ordered list of all the properties of the water.* -------
> *Middle school science teacher*

Measurement nearly always means expressing information in the form of a number. These numbers, in turn, provide specific data for assessments. Measurement quantifies learning. It is systematic and uses some type of predetermined standard with specific defined criteria.

Measurement includes factors such as a numerical score, quantitative analysis, knowing how many, and perhaps a percentage or percentile ranking. When you measure something, you examine specific parts or qualities, and then use a standard for determining some type of numerical value or rank.

When something is measured, it is important that everyone be in agreement regarding what the numbers actually mean. If I told you the score, rank or rating is 70 this would have no meaning unless I also told you the significance of the number. Is is a percentage? a percentile? a class ranking? a golf score? Numbers in and of themselves have no value and no purpose in measurement. It is only when the standard of measurement is known that numbers become important.

In the glass of water activity, we could measure the water in many ways. However, these measurements would tell us little if we didn't know the significance behind the numbers themselves. The same is true of the measurements we use in the classroom.

Test

> *You would most likely test the glass of water for specific properties, like its ph content or its chemical make-up. You could also test it to see if it is drinkable or not and whether it has harmful micro-organisms.*
> *--- Teacher, 5th grade*

When I've done this activity with my graduate students or in a workshop, this is the word that most people miss in terms of its real meaning and significance. The most important thing about any **test** is that it involves **taking a sample and assuming it is representative of the whole.**

To test the glass of water, we would need to use a formal standardized procedure to gather information in order to make comparisons between it and a standard glass of water with known properties. We would need to know the specific things we were looking for before we could test it. In other words, we would need to establish the specific purpose for the test.

After the purpose was established and the testing procedures set, we would go ahead and conduct the test. We might even do the same test several times in order to make sure our results were accurate. But one thing is certain. We would not pour the entire glass of water onto the microscope in order to conduct the test. We would take several samples but we wouldn't use the whole thing!

The same is true with medical tests. When someone goes to the doctor or hospital for a blood test, a few drops of blood or perhaps a few vials of blood are taken. It is a given that no one would go for a blood test if they were going to drain all the blood from your body in order to do the test!

When I look at the function of tests in schools, however, I feel this is exactly what is happening. Instead of the test being one sample of student work and one sample of students' learning of the curriculum, in many schools the test has *become* the entire curriculum! Many teachers are told that if it's not on the test it is not important to teach it. Teaching units and daily lesson plans are written based on test objectives. Important and enriching classroom activities are being eliminated because they aren't the things being tested. How did we get to the point in education where we assume the test drives the entire curriculum? This is not what a test is supposed to do!

When I was a classroom teacher, my students would sometimes come to me after a test and complain, "You didn't ask all the stuff I studied!" My response was always, "Did you know the answers to the questions I did ask?" Most of the time my students grudgingly admitted that they did. This was always my cue that my test was fair. I never wanted my test to test *everything they knew.* I did want it to be a fair sampling of what they studied and what they had learned. In my mind, this is the true function of a test, whether it is a teacher-made or a standardized test.

Evaluate

> *When evaluating, I would focus on forming a judgment about the experiment. In my evaluation I could ask several questions: Was it worth doing? Was it a valuable activity? What do the results tell me? Should I try to generalize what I've learned to other glasses of water? Do I want to repeat the process or the experiment? These and other similar questions would form the basis for my evaluation. ----- High school teacher*

To **evaluate** means to make a value judgment based on set or specific criteria. Evaluation is often done by integrating new data with what you already know. In our glass of water example, we might evaluate by making judgments and decisions about the nature of the water based on the knowledge we have gained through our tests, measurements and other assessments and based on what we know about water from our general knowledge and past experiences.

Many times, worth, value or quality is determined by comparisons and by the interpretation of results and data. Because of this, we would need to consider all the data in order to make a judgment or form an opinion about the water.

Because evaluation is a judgment call, it may be more subjective than the other three terms we have considered. This is particularly true in educational assessment. We are not evaluating an object such as a glass of water, but instead are evaluating human beings.

In an age of intense educational accountability it is important that we maintain a balance so that we don't go overboard quantifying everything by the numbers and evaluating every form of human behavior and interaction. At the same time, we have to make sure our value judgments are not clouded by bias, personal preference or undocumented assessments based on good intentions.

Similarities in and uses of the four terms

These four terms -- assessment, testing, measuring and evaluating -- overlap. They all depend on each other. It is very difficult to do one without eventually including the others. Testing and measurement are components of assessment. Evaluation is the process of making judgments and decisions using tests, measurements and other assessments as the basis of one's decision making.

When we measure something in educational assessment, we usually compare a score to a given standard by using a numerical grade which is often translated into a letter grade. While these letter grades are nearly universally understood, they may not always be. I remember my son declaring that he could easily get through school implementing the motto "*C for complete, D for done!*" We need to be sure our measurements and subsequent evaluations are understood by all who will examine them.

In schools we collect information and measurements in a variety of ways. We use multiple choice tests, teacher-made tests, standardized tests, and essay tests, each with a numerical scoring key. We use checklists, charts, graphs, teacher observations with numerical scales, classwork grades, homework grades and rubrics with numbers. All of these are necessary and important measurement tools.

As educators, we also assess without measuring. This type of assessment includes teacher observations, interaction with peers, performances and portfolios. We also use student products, question and answer sessions, data without numbers, and co-operative group discussions. We may have students work on problems involving real life situations and observe their ability to apply knowledge across the curriculum. With these assessments, we often rely on anecdotal records or verbal descriptions as alternatives to specific numeric measurements.

Why Assess?
If we assess it, everyone believes it's important!

> *Tracey, a fifth grade teacher, was feeling particularly discouraged after spending her whole weekend grading papers and creating a unit test to give her students during the upcoming week. "Why do I bother to assess my students anyway?" she thought. "Isn't it enough just to teach them without having to grade all those papers, give test after test, create rubrics for projects and then somehow count up all those points at report card time? I'd like to take this grade book and throw it away! Assessment is just a lot of unnecessary paperwork."*

10 Basic Purposes of Assessment
1. Selecting, clarifying and evaluating educational objectives

Objectives frequently become much clearer when educators deal with assessment issues. When we use assessment data well, we take a comprehensive look at student outcomes and then match our teaching objectives to the students' needs. We may ask ourselves, "What is really important for students to know and to be able to do? What are the essentials?" Our objectives must also be clearly stated to the students. This is best done before instruction begins. When we look at what we will assess, we know where our focus and emphasis should be.

2. Planning instruction

When used correctly, assessment can be a wonderful instructional tool. It can help us find out what our students already know. We can then use this information and plan instruction based on it. This involves pre-testing, identifying strengths and weaknesses and knowing when remediation or acceleration are needed and what they are needed for. Using assessment in this way can make our teaching more efficient and effective.

Assessment gives us the information we need to implement ongoing individualized instruction, curriculum compacting and flexible grouping. It allows us to evaluate student progress and plan instruction accordingly. By assessing our students' learning styles, modalities and multiple intelligences, we can plan a wider range of classroom activities and educational experiences to better meet all of their needs.

3. Evaluating student work

One of the most obvious purposes of assessment is that it gives us a way to evaluate students and make judgments about their work on a regular basis. Teachers struggle to find ways to do this fairly and accurately. Establishing specific criteria for evaluation is a critical first step. From this criteria we can determine more concrete assessment tools such as points, scores, percentages or letter grades. Student work, especially projects and performances, may also be evaluated using rubrics, checklists, observation logs, etc.

4. Reporting and comparing student progress

Parents want to know how well their child is doing. Most are interested in knowing their child's position relative to acceptable educational standards. They may also want to know how their child compares to others in the school, district, state or nation. School boards, administrators and the media often want to use student assessment to compare student progress between one year and another or between one school and another. Therefore, it's important that we find ways to inform students, their parents and others about student progress.

For individual students, the most efficient way to communicate this information seems to be grades on a progress report or report card. Report card grades, however, are more than just interesting information! They determine grade point averages and class rankings which are unbelievably significant to many students and their parents. Yet we need to remember that grades are just one indicator of student progress.

For a more generalized look at student progress, we tend to use standardized test scores. They provide one view of students' positions as they relate to educational standards. From these scores, comparisons can be made from year to year, from student to student or from school to school.

Other assessment methods may provide different perspectives about student progress. Student led conferences, parent-teacher conferences, portfolios of student work which demonstrate progress over time, weekly or monthly progress reports, videos of student performances, student journals and learning logs are some examples. Assessing students in all of these ways can help us ascertain a student's standing and lead us to the next step by showing what that student can do to improve or to maintain progress.

5. Counseling

Students constantly need guidance in the academic realm as well as in their personal growth and affective skills. Some have severe social or emotional problems while others may struggle academically. Assessment instruments give us a way to identify which students are contending with emotional or psychological problems and can help us determine how to best help these students. Psychological tests, vocational preference tests, checklists assessing strengths and weaknesses and student questionnaires are just some of the instruments we can use to help us deal with these problems and counsel students effectively.

Student self assessment is an excellent counseling tool. It helps students assess their own strengths and weaknesses in the context of academics, career planning and personal growth. Students who are aware of their own strengths and weaknesses learn to make adjustments and choices which are beneficial for their development throughout their lives.

6. Motivating and encouraging students

Assessments provide motivation and encouragement for many students. Procrastinators need due dates and an assurance their work will be examined and graded by the teacher. If work was never assessed and everyone was guaranteed to receive the same grade no matter what work they had done, many students would stop working as hard and some would stop working altogether!

Without some type of assessment, most students would think, "Why bother?" Others would become very resentful because they were working so much harder than others, yet did not get any particular credit or recognition for doing so. The Communist economic system collapsed for similar reasons. Perhaps it is human nature to be motivated by getting rewards for hard work. Assessment serves this purpose for many students.

Assessment also serves as a motivator when students can see their progress and accomplishments. For a student who is discouraged and feels unmotivated, looking at past performance and seeing how much improvement has been made can be a great encourager. Assessment makes this progress more readily observable, quantifiable and obvious.

Finally, assessment helps us predict future performance. Students are often motivated by goals for the future, and various types of assessments help point the way to future possibilities. This can be a tremendous inspiration to some students.

7. Giving special recognition to students

Assessments give us the data to use when choosing students to recognize for outstanding accomplishments. Selecting students for special honors such as membership in Beta Club or the National Honor Society includes assessing them in a number of different ways based on established criteria. This assures that the selection process is fair and unbiased.

Special recognition is often given to students for outstanding products or performances. Science fair winners, first chair in band, first place in a writing contest and the like are all chosen through various types of project or performance assessments. Gathering assessment data helps us be fair evaluators so that appropriate recognition can be given.

8. Selecting students for special programs or instruction

In general, the criteria for entry into special programs are set by district, state or federal regulations. The data from various assessment instruments helps us see which students meet the criteria so that they can be placed in appropriate learning environments. Identification procedures for gifted or special education students generally require that students be assessed in specific ways. This is significant because accurately assessing and selecting students for special programs allows them to interact with others that are functioning on the same ability level as well as receive targeted and appropriate instruction.

9. Evaluating program effectiveness

Assessment can be used to improve a program or to judge its worth and effectiveness. It is a good way to make sure a program is meeting student needs and its stated goals and objectives. Assessments often give validity to programs by documenting innovative teaching strategies and techniques, student growth, parental involvement, changes in student attitudes, etc.

Peer review is sometimes a feature of this type of evaluation. Programs may be evaluated by teachers from another district in the same state. Teachers may be evaluated by their peers based on standards developed by teachers and the school district. When done well, this type of review and evaluation helps us make positive changes and encourages us to keep doing the things that are working well.

10. Holding schools accountable

How good a job **are** you doing? is the central question of accountability, but this is often fraught with questions and misunderstandings. Accountability includes standards, standardized tests, performance indicators such as dropout rates, school attendance, etc., rewards and sanctions. Test scores, student outcomes and the other factors mentioned above are valuable information but are not automatic verdicts of good or poor teaching. Should teachers be held accountable for their students' performance or only for providing good teaching?

The feeling is out there that somehow schools are not as good as they used to be or as they need to be to compete in the 21st century. In many states, performance goals have been set so high that nearly all schools fail. This creates the false impression that kids are getting dumber and teachers are doing worse than ever.

Teachers, principals and school districts are under more pressure than ever before to show results that will prove to the public that they are effective. Local newspapers regularly publish test scores broken down by school and by subject. When states set an arbitrary standard, there is no modification for factors such as high poverty or student mobility. This makes accountability more difficult for teachers who work in disadvantaged schools. This becomes an issue of fairness.

The current accountability movement sometimes limits teachers' control over curriculum and instruction and at times seems distrustful of teachers' professional ability to assess student performance and growth. However, using assessment data to hold schools accountable can serve many positive purposes. It can help teachers target skills and outcomes. It gives us specific standards and benchmarks to work toward. In any case, assessment data should not be used to punish teachers, administrators and schools who are working as hard as they can, sometimes under extremely difficult circumstances.

Why Assess?
Teacher Reflection Page

1. Read over the 10 purposes for assessment listed and discussed in this chapter. In the space below, write the top three for you and a sentence or two explaining why these three are particularly important. If possible, discuss your top three with a colleague.

    1. _____

    2. _____

    3. _____

2. What other purposes do you see for assessment?

3. Tracey, the teacher quoted at the beginning of this section, says: *"Assessment is just a lot of unnecessary paperwork."* Do you agree or disagree? Why?

Reproducible for teacher use.

Chapter 2
Assessment Terminology
45 Terms to Understand So You Can Talk Like an Assessment Expert

This chapter establishes a common language for this book and should be useful in any discussions you have about assessment. Its purpose is to acquaint those of you who are not familiar with assessment terminology with the words used both by experts in the field as well as by those who think they understand educational assessment but often do not. Terms mean different things to different people. Misunderstandings caused by misinterpreting the meanings of specific terms may result in confusion and conflict. Uses of assessment data for purposes for which it was not intended become clear when you understand what the terminology actually means. The definitions have been written in an understandable, user-friendly fashion with a minimum of jargon. Make sure you fully comprehend each of these terms. This will be a great advantage to you in any discussion you have about educational assessment, measurement or testing.

1. **accountability** - Responsibility for student learning based on agreed-upon criteria such as rubrics or test scores. It includes being responsible for and being able to document results. In most systems of educational accountability, teachers are responsible for what they teach and what the child learns. When curriculum is diverse and flexible and involves higher level thinking skills it is more difficult to measure accountability via standardized testing.

2. **achievement test** - A type of test that measures what has been taught and learned and the extent to which an individual has achieved or mastered a set of defined objectives or learning outcomes, usually acquired as the result of instruction or schooling. This test should be administered after the program, unit of work or experience has been completed. Often it is a written standardized test which measures the information, knowledge or skills acquired in certain subject areas, and is used to judge specific academic abilities. These tests are more valid and reliable when the test objectives are aligned with what has actually been taught. When this type of test is based on grade level work, it may not show the actual achievement of gifted and high ability students because these students often hit the test ceiling and there is no way to measure how high their achievement really is. Examples: Iowa Test of Basic Skills, California Achievement Test, many state developed standardized tests given at various grade levels.

3. **aptitude** - A combination of natural and acquired talents, interests and/or abilities that a student may innately possess or that he/she may have learned. These usually indicate ability to learn more and develop proficiency in a given area, subject or skill.

4. **aptitude test** - A test that measures a person's abilities in something he has not been taught. It generally measures or predicts what a student will be able to do in the future and the likely effects of future learning experiences. Thus it

may predict future behavior, achievements or performance by measuring general abilities, knowledge and problem solving skills. These tests are often used to measure general intelligence or mental ability and to predict the likelihood of an individual's benefiting from a certain type of educational or training program. Examples include IQ tests which predict how well a student will do in school and SAT's, ACT's, and GRE's which predict success in college or graduate school.

5. **assessment** - A broad general term used to describe any systematic approach or plan for gathering, using, synthesizing and evaluating data to find out more about a student, establish effectiveness of curriculum, instruction and program, determine strengths and weaknesses, appraise ability and performance and/or to see what has been learned.

6. **average** - Mathematically, the sum of a group of numbers divided by the amount of numbers. This term is also used to describe the center, the normal or the general level of knowledge which is minimally acceptable. On report cards, a grade of 'C' usually indicates average. In schools, the desire is often expressed to be above average.

7. **battery** - A set of tests that were normed or standardized on the same group of students so that the results of each test can be compared to one another. Often these tests measure similar kinds of abilities and skills. Also used to indicate any series of tests given together; each test in the series gives different types of information.

8. **benchmarks** - A progression showing the steps, guideposts or reasonable expectations indicating what students are capable of learning and what they should know and be able to do at different ages and grade levels in regard to standards. They often provide the framework for teaching and assessing key concepts and skills because they are usually more specific and concrete than standards.

9. **bias** - A leaning or inclination giving an unfair advantage or disadvantage. An undesirable characteristic of tests in which factors unrelated to the test influence the scores. Therefore, the content of test items discriminates in favor of or against certain students or groups of students because of their experiences, race, gender, cultural exposure, economic status, etc. An error in content, administration and/or interpretation built into the system which contributes to a statistical difference between groups or types of people.

10. **ceiling** - The upper limit that can be measured by a given test or assessment. Individuals are said to have reached this point when their abilities exceed the highest performance level at which the test can make reliable discriminations. Test ceilings create problems in measuring the progress of gifted/high achieving students who may hit the ceiling before beginning a unit of study or a school year.

11. consistency - Doing the same thing every time. Accuracy and predictability in measurement over a period of time with different students and different scorers in different environments.

12. content validity - Describes the degree to which a given test measures what it says it is measuring.

13. correlation - A relationship, correspondence or connection between any two things. This is not a cause and effect relationship; two items may be strongly correlated without one causing the other.

14. criterion-referenced - An assessment which measures progress toward mastery of a given set of objectives, outcomes or skills. This measurement does not compare one person's score to the scores of the rest of the group. Instead, it is an objective measure of mastery tied to specific skills and objectives which are measured based on predetermined standards or criteria. Each individual is judged on how well he achieves the criteria, with an emphasis on performance relative to an absolute standard.

15. deviation - The extent to which a score differs from a certain reference point, usually the norm, midpoint or average.

16. diagnostic test - Test which assesses specific skills to determine specific individual strengths and weaknesses, usually in reading and/or math. This type of test should be used by teachers to guide them in planning instruction based on student needs. Such tests should be tied to curriculum and content objectives.

17. evaluation - Process of gathering and using qualitative and quantitative data to make a judgment of value, worth, merit or effectiveness. This can be for an individual student, group, class, grade level, department, school, school district or program.

18. formative evaluation - Information and data gathered along the way which is used to improve, modify or revise a program, curriculum or unit of instruction in order to enhance student learning. This type of evaluation is helpful in guiding ongoing classroom instruction.

19. grade equivalent - Theoretically, an average score at a given grade level. This score relates a student's raw score to the average scores obtained by norming groups at different grade levels. This score is often greatly distorted because there are so many variations in what is actually taught at each grade level.

20. high stakes test - The results of this test will have a significant impact on the life of the student, teacher, administration and/or school. Often the scores determine eligibility for programs, school admission, etc. Examples include graduation tests, the SAT and ACT tests, end of grade tests, tests at the end of selected grades which indicate whether a student will be retained or promoted to the next grade.

21. intelligence quotient (IQ) - A number which indicates the ratio of one's mental age to his/her chronological age. The average IQ is thought to be 100. An IQ score is no longer thought to be the sole measure of intelligence, nor is it always a fixed number throughout a person's life. IQ scores can change over time due to a person's ability to learn from experience, respond quickly in new situations and use reasoning and logic to solve problems.

22. Likert scale - A numeric rating scale of attitudes or values indicating most to least, strongly agree to strongly disagree, etc. The respondent uses this scale to indicate attitudes about people, places, ideas, concepts, activities or objects. It is useful in putting a numeric measurement onto qualitative ideas and other things that are hard to measure objectively.

23. mastery test - A criterion-referenced test which shows the extent to which a student has mastered a given set of objectives or skills. This assessment gives the teacher information about what the student already knows, what he has learned in a given amount of time and what he still needs to know.

24. measurement - The process of gathering data and quantifying something according to a numerical scale or standard and assigning numbers to processes, events and objects.

25. mean - The average of a set of scores or numbers; the sum divided by the number of scores. Extremes in scores skew the mean. For instance, giving a student a zero has a major effect on his average.

26. median - The middle number; the point where there are one-half above and one-half below thus dividing the group into two equal parts; the 50th percentile.

27. mental age - The age for which a given score on an intelligence test is considered average or normal.

28. norm-referenced - Includes both standardized and specially constructed intelligence and achievement tests which compare students to one another. Performance of others is the standard by which the student is measured. Scores are put in rank order and are used to measure one person's results as compared to another's. Students who compete with one another for selection when there are a limited number of places may compete via norm-referenced tests.

29. norms - Statistics developed by test makers to represent specific populations and how the average person in that population would do on a specific test. Norms may include grade, age, percentile or standard score and provide a basis for comparison.

30. objectivity - Consistency in scoring no matter who the scorer is. As such, it precludes differences of opinion among scorers as to whether responses are to be scored right or wrong. This is much easier to accomplish with a test that has a given correct answer for each item.

31. percentage - The number of points or a given part out of 100. The score on many classroom tests as well as report card grades are based on the percentage a student has gotten correct.

32. percentile - One of the points on a 99 point scale. Each point reflects the distribution of ranked scores and shows a person's relative standing within a particular group. Your position on the percentile scale shows the percentage of those above and those below you. The percentiles of any given group will therefore show half above the 50th percentile and half below the 50th percentile. Though many people get the terms confused, *percentile* is not the same as a *percentage*. For example, a student could score 95% on a test and be in any percentile depending on the scores of the others in the group.

33. performance assessment - Any systematic, evaluative appraisal of a student's ability to perform tasks or do something. Examples include demonstrations, dance recitals, oral reports, cheerleader tryouts, work samples.

34. portfolio assessment - A collection and evaluation of student products and performances selected for inclusion based on agreed-upon criteria. Portfolios generally illustrate a range of abilities and special talents showing growth, self reflection and achievement. They may be composed of the student's best work or work that shows improvement over time.

35. quartile - The division of achievement distribution into four equal parts. The quartile scale is 0-25, 26-50, 51-75 and 76-100. The number of persons per quartile is the same.

36. range - The difference between the highest score and the lowest score plus 1.

37. reliability - The extent to which scores, tests, programs or assessments are accurate, dependable, stable, consistent and free from error over a period of time. This includes the way they are administered, implemented and scored.

38. rubric - A teacher-constructed list of characteristics used as criteria for ranking the quality of students' work along with some type of guide for scoring or grading. Usually this guide describes the criteria along with a numerical range or scale to indicate the degree of quality or mastery shown by the work. There are many different types of rubrics all of which are useful for project or performance assessment.

39. standard deviation - A statistical measure of the dispersion in a set of scores, beginning with the mean or average. Usually the standard deviation is a 15 point range. It is used to indicate what percent of scores are higher and lower than the mean.

40. standardized test - A systematic sample of student performance obtained under prescribed conditions such as time allotted, verbal instructions required, etc. Such tests are usually developed for state or national use and are norm-referenced in order to provide accurate and meaningful information regarding a student's level of performance relative to others at the same age or grade level. Many of these tests are high stakes tests and their scores may be the sole criterion upon which students, teachers or administrators are judged. Because of this, such tests often take on great importance resulting in curriculum and instruction being aligned to test items and objectives.

41. standards - Agreed-upon values used to measure levels of attainment that students should work toward in content, process, performance or lifelong learning. Specific indicators of what students should know and be able to do as a result of their education.

42. stanine - A type of standardized score based on a scale of nine equal units that range from a high of 9 to a low of 1. In general, stanines 1-3 are considered below average, 4-6 are average and 7-9 above average.

43. summative evaluation - The use of some type of assessment to determine the effectiveness of a unit, course of study or program after it has been completed. An example is a final exam or the test at the end of a unit of study. It should be reliable and generally allows for comparisons among students. It is often used as a means of grading students but may also be used for future planning of curriculum and instruction.

44. test - A sample obtained from some systematic procedure which is assumed to have all the characteristics of the whole. Tests are used for gathering data, making comparisons and recording progress.

45. validity - The extent to which a test does the job for which it is used and measures what it is supposed to measure.

Assessment Terminology
Teacher Reflection Page

1. Review the 45 terms defined in this chapter. Categorize them using the chart below.

Very Familiar with	Somewhat familiar with	Totally new term to me

2. Identify any terms you feel are misused or misunderstood in your school, school district, state or by the media. Discuss these with a colleague and make a plan to help others understand them better.

3. What other assessment terms do you hear or use frequently? List them below. If you are not sure what they mean, or if you think they may have different meanings to different people, clarify their meanings.

Reproducible page for teacher use.

Chapter 3
Standards and Benchmarks
How do we know what our students need to know?

Not long ago, the United States launched a rocket carrying an unmanned vehicle to explore part of the planet Mars. Many of us listened intently to the news hoping to hear about the expected landing and what might be found during this mission. But the vehicle never landed. It was lost in space, they finally admitted, because some of the scientists and engineers were using the metric scale while others had used feet and inches! The measurements were not <u>standardized</u> and the mission ended in failure.

I'm a Macintosh computer user. I love my Mac and have always used Apple computers. However, this causes me lots of problems. While the computer industry is still evolving, the standard most people are using for personal computers is based on the PC format. Yet, rapid technological change has left us with no definitive <u>standards</u> for hardware, software or peripherals.

The 2000 Presidential election was one of the most bizarre and unusual in American history. No doubt this election will be studied for years! Many of the problems were a result of having no national or state <u>standards</u> regarding which votes counted and which did not, no <u>standard</u> method of voting, no <u>standard</u> voting machines and no <u>standard</u> voter registration procedures. Many of the controversies in this election would not have occurred if known and universally accepted standards were in place.

Ms. Bennett's third graders filed into her classroom on the first day of school. They were an incredibly diverse group in terms of race, ethnicity, experiences, learning styles, readiness, ability levels, talents, parental involvement and languages spoken. In fact, the only thing 'standard' about them was that they were all in third grade. "How can I ever teach these kids using one set of standards?" Ms. Bennett thought. "And why should I want to? After all, they're individual human beings to be nurtured not inanimate objects to be put in one mold."

Standards: Why are They Necessary?

Standards play an important role in our everyday lives. From the measurements we use in cooking or travel to the results we get in scientific discoveries or national elections, standards are important and necessary. It makes sense, then, to assume that some standards are needed in the education of American children. The issue is not so much whether we **need** educational standards, but what these standards should be and how they should affect classroom teaching.

First and foremost, educational standards must have broad support among teachers and the general public. This type of ownership is crucial. Because of this, standards have been presented to the public as a whole by addressing two primary concerns:

1. American competitiveness

First is the worry that America might be losing its competitiveness. The underlying fear is that if this happens, our economy and our country as a whole will suffer in the long term. Many feel that the way to regain (or retain) top status is to demand more from each child and each school. This concern comes mostly from international studies of achievement where American students do not typically score near the top. Some think that the way to address this problem is through establishing educational standards at every level. They believe this can lead to a rigorous and challenging course of study for all students.

Those who are apprehensive about this issue believe that we need to push students to learn more and learn it faster than ever before. They feel that our students can't compete because they are poorly prepared. Ironically, there is little, if any, evidence to support a relationship between economic productivity and high test scores in schools. Nevertheless, this seems to be a persuasive argument for politicians and policy makers to use.

2. Gap in achievement levels

The second concern is the gap between the achievement of high and middle income students as compared to the achievement of lower income students. Part of the thinking behind the standards movement is the desire for this gap to be closed.

To address the disparity between high and low achieving students, federal laws, especially Title I laws, state that all students should be held to the same high standards. The assumption is that raising standards for all students, teachers and schools will improve education for poor and minority children. Embedded in this is the belief that high expectations lead to high performance.

Authentic, standards-based reform has the potential to promote rich, high level teaching for all students and high levels of support to help all students meet the standards. The reality is that while all students are held to the same standards, all students and all schools don't actually have equal levels of support or access to the same resources needed to meet these standards. When standards are used to hold students and schools accountable, it seems reasonable that resources such as funding, fully qualified teachers, and necessary materials and equipment should be equally available to all schools and all teachers. Unfortunately this is sometimes not the case.

Beyond the two concerns discussed above is the larger goal of developing an increasing number of students who can function and succeed in an Information Age economy and society. In many schools in low socio-economic areas, students are not meeting the standards and are not receiving the quality of education needed for success in our rapidly changing world. In fact, in spite of our best efforts to raise student achievement, during the 1990's the gap in achievement between high achieving and low achieving students actually grew larger. Doing something about this is definitely one of the reasons the push for high standards continues.

Benefits of Educational Standards

Developing and implementing high educational standards has many benefits. Such standards:

1. Help teachers pay more attention to clear expectations for all students.

2. Determine basic concepts and key learnings along with developmentally appropriate levels to attain these learnings.

3. Involve teachers, administrators and parents in developing and defining them so there is ownership at all levels.

4. Reflect shared norms and knowledge about what all students should know.

5. Break down teacher isolation and call for teacher collaboration around a common set of educational guidelines.

6. Have the potential to increase student achievement.

7. Provide a consistent way to talk about what is going on in the classroom.

8. Establish an excellent list of skills and expectations that can serve as a beginning point for curriculum compacting.

9. Provide guidelines for curriculum and teaching to ensure that students will have access to the knowledge needed for their later success.

10. May highlight student performance and point the way to improving instruction.

11. Give the message that all students need and deserve a high quality education.

12. Change the focus from quantity (such as how many days a child has attended school) to quality (such as what important concepts did that child learn during that time) and results.

13. Encourage ongoing high quality professional development for teachers.

Potential Problems with Standards

Standards-based reform also has a number of problems. Some of these are listed below.

1. The sheer number of standards often leads to "drill and kill" content coverage where kids learn loads of facts but little more.

2. Tests on the standards may drive the entire curriculum. "Test prep" has become the defacto curriculum in many schools.

3. Standards often create lots of extra paperwork which becomes more important than teaching and learning.

4. Defining what is important for all students to know is a difficult task when knowledge is increasing and changing so rapidly.

5. In-depth learning and critical/creative thinking often get lost in the push for standards.

6. Some students have already met the age appropriate benchmarks in skills and knowledge yet must sit through instruction focused on standards they already know.

7. Some standards are unrealistic and seem designed to prevent students from passing or graduating.

8. Students who can't meet the standards may become dropouts.

9. Teachers may have no time to explore topics that interest them and their students but aren't related to what is tested or listed in the standards.

10. Standards may encourage rote memorization without higher level thinking.

11. Standards may give some people the impression that all students in a grade begin at the same starting point. This is almost never true.

12. Students are not standardized. It may not be realistic to hold a 14-year-old immigrant child who speaks little English and has never attended school before to the same standards as a native English speaking middle class student who began preschool at age 3 and has been read to since birth!

Standards and Curriculum

As can be seen from the above lists, educational standards are neither a cure-all nor a disaster. They can be beneficial if we use them in a way that does not cause us to abandon good curriculum design and effective instructional strategies.

A standards-based curriculum can define a challenging course of study and set a minimum level of achievement, proficiency or competency for all students. Standards are useful when there is a tremendous disparity among teachers of the same subject in terms of how long they spend on a particular topic or skill. Additionally, they can help when there is a great lack of uniformity in what is taught from one classroom to another and little consistency in the knowledge and skills covered in any given course or subject area.

Standards are being used more and more as the basis for designing the curriculum. They help us define what should be taught and then provide the link between what is expected, what is taught and what is assessed. The essential question of standards is *What should our students be taught?* This deals with the fundamentals of curriculum. As important as the questions of *Who learns what?* and *When do they learn it?* are the questions of *What new knowledge belongs in the curriculum?* and *What content can we eliminate if we include new things?* Standards furnish us with some guidelines to help answer all of these questions.

There seem to be three contradictory theories about what students should learn:

1) Give students as much knowledge as possible about as many facts and as many things as possible.

2) Present a few major ideas in depth.

3) Teach process rather than content.

We are facing an information explosion unprecedented in human history. Even if we try to teach as (1) above suggests, in a school year we still can teach only a minute portion of all the knowledge and information that is out there. Keeping the status quo with the same list year after year of what students should know and be able to do is probably not a valid practice in an age of information explosion. The implication is that standards should not be static, but have to constantly be revisited and revised as knowledge grows and changes.

Usable standards for students in the 21st century should focus on major ideas, skills and processes. The factual content may change as our knowledge base and views about what it means to be an educated person change. When standards are used in this way, they are valuable tools for educators. At the same time, there are some important guidelines about what we should **not** do with standards:

- Prescribe the curriculum to only fit the standards

- Make the curriculum a list of skills from the standards to be covered

- Pace the curriculum so that every standard is covered for every student with no thought for differentiation

- Ignore the learning needs of students who have already met the grade level standards

Types of Standards

Standards should be clear to everyone, including teachers, parents and students. Standards should address only the essentials and not be a laundry list of everything that is to be taught. They should not prescribe teaching methods, devise classroom strategies, or become lesson plans. Standards are the ends, not the means, thus the choice of means should be left to the school or the teacher.

Most experts recommend that standards should be rigorous and world class. Students should be assessed based upon known standards and criteria, not compared to each other. Because we are in the era of the 'standards movement,' numerous sets of standards have been developed by states, educational organizations and the federal Department of Education. A summary of the types of standards is below:

National Standards
- Have been developed by many different organizations.

- Some are very general while others provide specific benchmarks.

- Basic concepts and key learning components tend to be similar from state to state.

- Standards can be used as guideposts for all educators.

State Standards
- Almost all states now have state educational standards in most academic subjects.

- Most are tied to statewide standardized high stakes tests.

- Teachers use standards documents to align curriculum and instruction.

Content Standards (What students are expected to know)
- Describe skills and abilities students should have.

- Describe goals for individual students.

- Tell the knowledge and understandings students are expected to know.

- Often are measured by tests.

Performance Standards (What students are expected to be able to do)
- Emphasize use and application of knowledge.

- Include higher level thinking skills.

- Action and problem-solving oriented.

- Can be done at different levels or degrees of competency.

- Often are measured by rubrics.

Benchmarks

Benchmarks are guideposts that identify realistic expectations of how most students should progress through the standards at certain ages and/or grade levels. They are usually developed from a set of standards in some form of a grade level or K-12 continuum. Some type of assessment is usually present to document progress through the various benchmarks.

Benchmarks can be:

- Specific information and skills to be learned.
- Performance activities or tasks the student should know how to do.

Benchmarks are often more helpful to classroom teachers than the standards themselves because they are tied more directly to grade level and classroom practice.

For Teacher Reflection

Which standards and benchmarks am I most familiar with?

How have I used standards as guidelines in my teaching?

How have they improved the day-to-day instruction in my classroom?

In what ways have they been detrimental to my students or my teaching?

What is the difference between teaching to the standards and teaching to the test?

Standards and Assessment

Standards imply assessment. However, there are many questions surrounding the issue of standards and how to assess them. Who decides what the standards should be? Precisely what standards should be tested? Should they reflect facts or concepts? What assessments will be used to determine whether students are reaching the standards? Must standards always be assessed using standardized tests or can they be assessed in other ways? These and many other similar questions make this a very complex problem and concern.

Standards-based reform is about setting higher standards and measuring the attainment of those standards in criterion-referenced ways. As students progress through the school system, the standards for performance rise steadily, and accountability is directly tied to these standards. With standards, everyone knows what is expected and no allowances are made for substandard performance.

The public looks to tests as a way of measuring how well students have met the standards. If standards and accountability are to improve schools and help children learn rather than punish teachers, schools and students, we must ensure that 1) the standards are appropriate, 2) ways to assess them are valid, relevant, fair and unbiased, and 3) the implementation is reasonable. High standards and high stakes testing are not necessarily the same thing, though many perceive that they are.

Good standards-based assessment is not always a test. It is not always paper/pencil and is not always from the book. Other alternate forms of assessment which can be used to determine achievement of the standards include:

- Interviews
- Open-ended questions
- Student explanations of why and how
- Real life problem solving
- Rubrics
- Student activities tied to the standards

All students may not meet a given standard but many may be working toward it. We need to document where they are and what they still need to do to meet it. Portfolios are one means of assessment that can help us keep track of students' progress over time.

Mandatory standards are supposed to make lazy teachers and students change their ways. With this viewpoint, the source of failure may be seen as the student's lack of motivation to take tough courses and work hard in school. The remedy often becomes a demand that students achieve the standards -- or else! Sometimes this strategy backfires. Ironically, teachers in low performing schools drill students on the standards, teach to the standards (or to the test), and practice test taking skills. However, many assign little or no homework or in-depth study because the kids won't do it.

Meanwhile, many high performing schools have geared up even more to meet the standards, piling on more homework than ever and teaching difficult subjects and courses at earlier grade levels than they did a generation ago. Students in these schools have lots of homework, take tough courses and get into the best colleges in the world. These students probably didn't need higher standards in the first place! By contrast, students in poor urban or rural schools who have to meet equivalent standards often drop out or fail the high stakes tests.

Motivation is more complex than telling students they must pass a high stakes exam or be retained in school. High quality instruction, the energy and enthusiasm of good teachers and individualized support are all needed to help struggling students reach the higher standards. When current test scores are all that matter, motivation to meet the standards fades. These test scores usually don't help us show individual student growth toward mastering the standards. Yet one strategy to motivate struggling students might be to show them how much progress they have made toward the final goal.

We need to use standards and the assessment of those standards more as a motivator and less as a punishment. Fallout from low scores can wear out well-meaning teachers and administrators. Harsh sanctions aimed at students, teachers and schools who don't meet the standards don't seem to be the best or most educationally sound approach. We need to find ways to improve schools, not punish them. Standards should be used to help each child improve, not to punish those who cannot possibly bridge the gap between where they are educationally and where they are supposed to be according to tough standards and benchmarks.

Assisting Students Who Don't Meet the Standards

As indicated above, not every student enters school with the same background experiences and abilities. There is some concern that having higher standards and having universal standards may be contradictory educational goals, and doubts about all students meeting the highest standards are widespread. It seems obvious that provisions should be made to assist students in meeting the standards. As educators we need to ask ourselves how we can best help students who have difficulty doing this. What assistance will students who fail to reach the standards receive and how will schools prepare teachers to teach them?

Standards do not have to be tied to age and grade level, but in most American schools they are. In meeting the standards, we must allow for the fact that students are at different starting points and learn in different ways. Many children need more time to master basic skills which lead to mastery of the standards and benchmarks.

There are a number of pro-active strategies we can use to help all students meet the standards.

- Giving individual attention and extra help
- Teaching these students in different ways (for example using differing modalities or the multiple intelligences in curriculum planning)
- Providing more time to meet the standards
- Offering remediation, including prevention and intervention
- Organizing tutoring and small group instruction
- Analyzing assessment results, determining strengths and weaknesses and designing instruction accordingly, linking it to academic standards
- Aligning curriculum to the standards
- Providing teacher training to support using standards and assessment to improve instruction
- Using resources which are based on benchmarked content standards

Standards and Creative Teaching

Creative teaching should be the goal in every school. At the same time, meeting specific benchmarks and standards is also necessary. These two goals do not need to contradict one another. Engaging kids creatively may bring a better mastery of the standards than 'drill and kill' activities do.

Learning facts is not inherently bad or uncreative! Actually, understanding a subject almost always begins with building a knowledge base, including factual information. Learning the facts by using them to do critical and creative thinking may be one of the best strategies for meeting the standards. This allows students to successfully do inquiry-based learning when they use the facts to figure out their own strategies for solving problems.

Standards sometimes make teachers rely on a schedule of instruction to make sure they cover all the standards rather than pacing instruction to meet individual student needs. Standards usually establish a minimum level of learning, but often this minimum becomes the maximum. Kids who have already mastered the information are forced to go over it again and again instead of learning new material or creatively exploring other topics of interest that are not included in the standards.

In a creativity-oriented standards-based classroom, inventive and creative strategies should be encouraged. Conceptual understanding and higher level thinking should be valued more than memorization of facts. Students should learn that there are often multiple ways to solve the same problems and should be inspired to create their own strategies when problem solving. Instructional activities should encourage creative communication, with thought provoking questions, speculations and investigations as the norm.

In an ideal world educational standards might not be necessary. If every child had a gifted teacher who could individualize and teach to every learning style, all students would finish school completely competent. But we live and teach in a less than perfect world. Because of this, it is helpful not to look at the ideal, but rather to look at best practices. The list on the next page will help you formulate some practical ideas about implementing standards.

Best Practices for Implementing Standards

1. Meet in small groups to study the standards, review them in light of current curriculum, and put them in a format which will be helpful for ongoing planning of curriculum and instruction.

2. Look at test scores and other data about student achievement to see which areas students are strong in and which areas need more work.

3. Translate the standards into clear and doable instructional goals and objectives.

4. Align your curriculum to the standards in such a way that you focus on key concepts and ideas.

5. Develop or revise instructional units based on groups of standards. Earmark priority instructional units or topics. Borrow units other districts have developed that meet your priorities.

6. Use district level or school-based resource personnel or outside consultants to help find and/or develop high level instructional materials.

7. Find ways to integrate science, math, language arts, technology and other subject areas.

8. Use learning theories such as learning modalities, learning styles, brain compatible learning, and multiple intelligences as tools to help you assist all students in meeting the standards. (See Teaching Tools for the 21st Century by Carolyn Coil, Pieces of Learning, Marion Illinois, for more information.)

9. Give professional feedback to others and seek it for your own teaching. Analyze your own effectiveness and use the feedback to continuously improve your own instructional practice.

10. Focus on what the students need to know and need to be able to do to meet the standards. Then brainstorm ways to help them do these things.

11. Examine student work with other teachers and come to consensus on criteria for quality work and the meaning of grades.

12. Encourage students to be active, self-directed learners who can construct their own knowledge base.

13. Engage students in self-assessment, teach them ways to look at their own learning and have them share the responsibility for learning.

14. Allow students to work in groups frequently, sharing knowledge and learning to problem solve together.

15. Become more of a facilitator and less of an information giver.

Using Standards to Integrate Curriculum, Instruction and Assessment

> *Standards can provide us with excellent guidelines for examining and integrating curriculum, instruction and assessment. Below are some recommended strategies you may wish to try in your classroom.*

1. Integration of standards from two or more subject areas

2. Cooperative learning and flexible grouping

3. Active communication between students

4. Innovative questioning techniques

5. Active learning

6. Teacher as facilitator

7. Problem solving

8. Integration of technology

9. Reflective thinking (metacognition)

10. Student responsibility for learning

For Teacher Reflection

1. Which of the Best Practices listed on the previous page seem feasible for my school and situation? Share this list with other teachers in your grade level, teaching team or department. Together make an implementation plan based on the Best Practices and other ideas you may have.

2. Look at the list at the top of this page. Brainstorm practical ways you could accomplish some of these ideas in your classroom.

Chapter 4
Standardized Tests
The Good, The Bad and The Ugly!

I do not spend an inordinate amount of time preparing my students for standardized tests. I do use our curriculum alignment to make sure I am covering the skills that are necessary for them to know at test time. I do some timed math computation to give them experience with this type of testing. I feel if I do the best job I can do in my classroom, for the most part my students will be successful on the tests. -- 2nd grade teacher

Why the Emphasis on Testing?

Accountability is a part of life in most of today's jobs and professional endeavors. Thus, it should not be surprising that it is emphasized in education as well. The teacher quoted above seems quite comfortable with her abilities as a teacher and her students' abilities to succeed on the tests. Other teachers I interviewed were not nearly as relaxed about the issue of standardized testing.

This emphasis on test taking definitely increases pressure on schools and teachers. Norm-referenced tests seek to sort and rank students. This results in teachers being concerned about how they will look if their children do poorly. Many principals, especially those in low performing schools, worry about their own jobs.

Pressure about testing can create tension in high performing schools as well. When students score at the 99-98 percentile on standardized tests, it is impossible for teachers to meet the district goal of improving test scores by 5 points the following year! Yet this is what some teachers are being asked to do.

This does not mean that tests do not have important and positive purposes in schools. High stakes testing does make us pay attention to all students, especially those who might otherwise do poorly and fall between the cracks. Test results can serve a variety of diagnostic functions which may well be their most important use in terms of instruction. When tests are used as diagnostic tools, they help us determine specific strengths and weaknesses in individual students and in our teaching.

Educational accountability generally consists of looking at average scores for an entire school on national or state tests. Yet testing is often handled in such a way that reliable long-term data about a particular student or group of students is difficult to obtain.

It seems evident that accountability using test scores as the sole criterion for success often fails to take into account differences among students and schools. A teacher must work with the students and families he or she is given. A teacher in a school with an upper middle class student population can easily look fine if judged by standardized tests, because these students will usually do well. On the other hand, that same teacher may not look nearly as good in a school with a different student population.

The public as a whole puts a great deal of emphasis on testing. Therefore, politicians and school officials have come to think that test scores are the most important thing (or the only important thing) in looking at student learning. Educational accountability should be about more than test scores. However, in most districts, students' test scores are used by top administrators to hold principals accountable and are sometimes used in decisions about teacher hiring, firing, promotion and transfer.

Sometimes teachers cover the objectives which will be tested while leaving out some worthwhile objectives or information which are not on the tests. The result of gearing instruction only toward tested objectives is that it may produce a very narrow curriculum and hamper flexibility and creativity in both teachers and students.

Uses of Standardized Test Scores

In spite of the fact that American students are among the most tested in the world, we rarely use test results to help us produce better and more able students. Most often test scores are used to sort and select students or to punish students, teachers, schools and/or school districts.

Standardized test scores are often used to rank schools and teachers. In some cases, parents use test results to determine the qualifications of a teacher. This seems a bit unfair. In fact, if a standardized test is the only measurement that holds teachers accountable, then we are in trouble! A teacher, like each and every student, is so much more than a standardized test!

At best, standardized test scores (as well as many other types of assessments) should have a variety of uses. They may:

1. be used as diagnostic tools
2. furnish data for setting educational goals
3. serve as a guide in planning for improvement
4. provide a variety of ways to measure student performance
5. help teachers evaluate programs, curriculum and instruction
6. be a means to compare and rank schools and students
7. determine eligibility for funding

Let's look at some of these uses in more detail.

Tests can be used as **diagnostic tools** as teachers plan for remediation, or to help a teacher, school or grade level to look at how they are teaching certain skills or certain aspects of the curriculum. It should be a guide to show teachers what they are doing right, what they need to change and what works best for students. When tests are used in this fashion, they can help teachers in planning classroom instruction and in forming flexible groups for learning.

Standardized tests are used because they **provide data** and a results orientation that are essential to improvement. Test results can be used to provide educators with a common instructional focus. They also encourage teachers to abandon ineffective practices.

Teachers need to look at test scores to see if a student has **improved** or regressed in performance. We need to use tests to determine whether our instruction was effective, to find out what our students have learned and which students need additional help. We should use test results to help us guide students and show them how to take what they have learned and use it in a variety of ways. When we do this, what is learned in school can become a tool for our students in life outside of the classroom.

Students can use tests to see if their study skills are paying off. The structure provided by tests may be limiting, but many students need some structure in order to learn, and many teachers need this structure in order to plan effective curriculum and instruction. Test scores help both teachers and students target steps for **improvement.**

When test results are used as a **basis for comparison**, students are compared to others who have taken the same test. This may be those in the same class, the same grade, the same school, the same school district, or students all across the nation. A problem in using tests for comparison is that we often end up comparing 'apples and oranges!' It doesn't work to look at test scores for a grade level one year and plan for next year's students based on those scores. Next year's class will have entirely different students with different strengths, weaknesses, learning styles, problems and home lives.

Many people believe that administering more and harder tests will pave the way to better, more effective schools. This would have us believe that a successful school is always one that enrolls large numbers of students who pass the standardized tests. The problem schools, then, are those that enroll the greatest percentage of students who fail. Unfortunately, looking at test scores in this way takes no note of home, environmental or socioeconomic factors which may affect how students do.

Educators often respond to the pressure for good test scores in two ways. Some try "quick fix" strategies designed to raise test scores. Others try a range of instructional strategies that do not focus so much on test scores as they do with increasing the number of students who can function productively in the Information Age of the 21st century.

Higher test scores and reaching higher levels of learning are not necessarily the same thing. Some students say that real learning is being shoved aside to raise test scores. Students often learn to write essays only in the boilerplate format favored by test scorers.

One problem with computer-scored assessments is that they do not take into account the test taker's thought process. They do not fully measure students' critical and inventive powers. Yet tests should be reflections of how students are thinking! Tests are much more valuable when students can show why they were thinking a certain way and then are allowed to go back and revise or correct the mistakes they made. When this happens, testing becomes an excellent instructional tool.

Helping Students Become Good Test Takers

Standardized high stakes tests help to decide issues such as grade placement, retention, college admissions, graduate school admissions, special education placement and admission to special programs as well as to diagnose strengths and weaknesses. Yet these tests do not tell the whole story. Many students who are not totally successful on tests are still very successful as students.

However, until we as a nation move away from the heavy emphasis currently placed on standardized testing, perhaps we have no choice but to teach our students how to be good test takers. We want them to maximize their ability to transpose their knowledge and skills on a test. If they do not understand the techniques they need to use to maximize this transfer, students will underperform and not do as well as they should on tests.

Some specific strategies to teach test taking skills are:

- Send home practice packets to prepare for the test.
- Explain the format of the test.
- Set up classroom assessments in the same format as the test.
- Give practice tests.
- Practice listening skills all year.
- Teach the content of the test.
- Give practice sessions and do daily activities which use the skills tested.
- Show students how to use the process of elimination.
- Practice completing the easier questions first.
- Give the same amount of time to complete a classroom assignment as the time allowed to complete a portion of the test.
- Point out key words and phrases in test questions.
- Teach how to read for details, listen and follow directions.
- Ask students to repeat the directions back to you.
- Teach students to think in a logical and problem solving manner.
- Do problems of the day to increase abilities in problem solving and mental math.

Students not only need to have practice in test taking, they also need to develop strategies to avoid being stressed during the testing period. We can help by giving them opportunities to gain confidence as test takers. Giving them lots of positive feedback is a beginning step in building self confidence. Because they need to believe they are capable of answering correctly, self confidence is important. Presenting

©2001 Pieces of Learning

skills and concepts in a way that requires higher order thinking will help the students feel confident about their ability to solve the simpler problems presented on the test.

Teachers are often told to help their students relax during the testing period and to work on ways to calm students during testing situations when there is a lot of anxiety. This seems a rather difficult task in a media-hyped testing environment. A special section about school testing was enclosed in a recent edition of a local newspaper. Twelve full pages were devoted to describing the importance of the high stakes tests in one local school district within the region. The test environment is described as follows:

> *On the days students are scheduled to take the exam, they won't be allowed to bring textbooks, scrap paper or book bags to their classrooms. They'll also be prohibited from carrying anything out of the classroom after they finish their tests. Finally, students will be under constant supervision while the test is being administered.*

It seems it would be almost impossible for anyone, students or teachers, to relax in such a punitive environment! Why would anyone think this is good for student learning or a good environment to find out what students know and can do?

One area of test taking in which students generally need practice is in developing the ability to work rapidly enough to finish the timed portion of the test. Students need practice in order to learn how to budget their time to complete all the questions. They also need help in proofreading and in learning how to go back to completed test questions to verify their answers. Some students have problems with looking at all choices before making a decision. They learn early that tests are based on time, so they choose the first answer they read that looks like it might be correct.

Teachers should spend time building all of these test taking skills, but this should not be the entire curriculum! Especially important is not to keep endlessly drilling and drilling students who already know the answers and are comfortable with the test format.

Time spent in testing and test preparation

> *Students hate these tests. The tests are too long. No matter what we do, they produce too much anxiety because parents and the outside world place so much importance on them. We are a nation who wants to assess, test and evaluate everything because the general public seems to think that is the way to make education better. --- 6th grade teacher*
>
> *My students will have 13 days of standardized testing between January and March. They get so tired of it! I dislike it most of all when I think about all of the instructional time that is lost in test practice and test taking. --- 8th grade teacher*

One problem in using standardized tests as such an important measure of learning is that too much time can be spent in test preparation and too much focus is sometimes put on test scores. Teachers who do this are not really able to "teach." They are too busy making sure their test scores are acceptable. We certainly need to **periodically** check students' learning, but we don't need to inundate students with tests! Even the most successful students can be drowned by tests and get lost in them.

Sometimes students just get tired of all the test taking, including taking the practice tests. The result is that they may not bother to do their best because of test burnout.

Too much time spent in preparation for testing can limit a student's comprehensive education. It can drain the energy, excitement and life from any classroom. Instead of test preparation, teachers should be spending most of their time creating an environment in which students are excited about learning. If we can sustain this enthusiasm for learning throughout the school years, we will create lifelong learners.

As discussed in the section above, one of our goals needs to be to encourage students to be good test takers because tests will be around for a long time, and students should be prepared for them. However, there should be other ways to assess achievement besides standardized tests. We shouldn't be spending most of the school year preparing students for tests!

For Teacher Reflection

1. Do test-prep workbooks help students learn broad content and skills or do they just help students get higher test scores?

2. What long term benefits, if any, do you see in test practice or in having students take sample tests before they take the "real thing?"

3. What strategies do you think are most effective in helping students do well on high stakes tests?

4. In your experience, does test preparation take too much time away from other types of instruction?

Connections between what is taught and test content

> *The pressure to raise test scores may ultimately lower the quality of education after teachers, feeling the pressure, limit their teaching to the skills and content tested. --- 3rd grade teacher*
>
> *Not all of the material that needs to be taught is covered on the high stakes standardized test. For example, if only mammals and insects are covered in the science portion, does that mean that we don't teach the children about other types of animals? That would seem to be nonsense, but that is how many teachers are now teaching. If it isn't written down as a test objective, it isn't considered important to teach it. --- 1st grade teacher*

In many school districts across our country, the entire curriculum is aligned to standardized tests. Often, teachers' lesson plans must indicate test objectives for every lesson that is taught. If there is true aligning of the curriculum to meet testing standards, this can be beneficial because the standards are more likely to be taught and learned. However, it is not beneficial when teachers simply teach to the test.

Aligning curriculum and instruction to the test can help teachers pace their instruction. It helps them make sure they teach the areas that the test covers. It also focuses their attention on important material that may not be covered in the curriculum or textbook. However, tests should reflect only a *sampling* of what students have learned and should serve merely as guidelines for our planning and teaching. A *test sample* is only a portion of what needs to be learned and should never be looked upon as the *whole*. Unfortunately, we often look at test scores as the only thing that is important!

Many districts are aligning their curriculum to the test in one of two ways. Both ways are described below along with comments about each.

1. Establishing the curriculum first, then developing the test

- Local control of the curriculum is more feasible.

- Customizing the curriculum to meet the needs of the children is easier.

- Individual districts may find this task time consuming and expensive.

- Committees may get bogged down and take years trying to do this.

- Even within a district, various schools have various needs so one test won't reflect the curriculum each student should have.

2. Establishing the test first, then aligning the curriculum to cover the test

- There is 100% alignment because the test provides the basis of the curriculum.

- Control of the curriculum is in the hands of the test developers.

- Many teachers end up teaching checklists of test objectives, usually with kids memorizing lots of trivial information.

- Teachers teach to the test and don't teach anything else.

- The content of a minimum standards test becomes the curriculum so the curriculum has a floor but no ceiling.

- If it is a state or national test, the needs of individual schools, districts or classrooms are not considered.

Because standardized testing comes mostly from state mandates, tests are usually statewide. Thus, most curriculum alignment is done after the test is established (#2 above).

Teaching only test objectives carries with it the risk of not expanding students' knowledge beyond the basics. When curriculum is totally aligned to the test, important things which are not on the test will not be taught. In many school districts, elementary students are tested just in reading and math. One outcome of this is that science and social studies are being almost totally ignored. Does this mean that science and social studies are no longer important for elementary students to know?

If teachers just teach to the test, students' individual needs, learning styles and creativity aren't addressed. When teachers try to teach only the objectives on the test, they do not enrich or expand the curriculum. Teachable moments are often lost due to these factors. A stressful environment can be the result, and students are the losers.

In the past few years students seem to be less creative. Perhaps a reason for this is that the pressure to get through the curriculum leaves less time for creative projects. This could cause an additional problem. Will first rate teachers who view effective teaching as a creative art more than test preparation begin to feel limited, stifled and discouraged in a field they once felt was exciting and energizing? Will these teachers leave teaching and take with them the creative spark so necessary for superb teaching and student motivation? Only time will tell.

Clearly, standardized testing is a mixed bag. Certainly there are beneficial aspects to this type of testing. There are also harmful effects for students and for teachers. Both points of view are summarized below.

Beneficial Aspects of Standardized Tests

1. High stakes testing draws more attention to the state curriculum. If a teacher teaches to the test, he or she is most likely teaching the grade level curriculum objectives.

2. Tests establish and assess respectable standards for literacy and numeracy and give schools focus in improving and refining instructional practices particularly in reading, writing and math.

3. Tests and testing standards can be used to help plan curriculum to best meet the needs of students.

4. Tests expose students to material that may be used to determine their academic futures.

5. Students who take standardized tests are more likely to be exposed to what others are learning across the country. It may give them a more global perspective.

6. Tests usually lead to greater standardization across schools in terms of what is taught and when.

7. Tests clarify what students are expected to learn. Test scores form objective criteria and minimum standards for student learning. They can provide numerical and intelligible data on both performance and improvement.

8. Testing emphasizes the need to bring all students to a basic proficiency level.

9. Testing provides the means to show mastery of specific skills.

10. Testing makes students realize that they are accountable for the information that is taught in class. It provides a measure to show them what they have learned.

11. Tests can help teachers diagnose individual strengths and weaknesses so they can remediate and direct students in a more individual manner.

12. Students can use test scores to see their own strengths and weaknesses and to set goals for improvement.

13. Test scores can give vital information about patterns of strengths and weaknesses in a classroom, school or district.

14. Test scores may give us an unbiased comparison of student achievement which can be used to show growth from year to year and as a diagnostic tool for future learning and educational programming.

15. When students do well or improve in an area, test scores can be very encouraging because they show improvement in an objective way. If they understand the scale and know what the numbers mean, it is a solid way for them to look at their own educational accomplishment.

16. Testing may encourage students to achieve goals and have a strong work ethic. Students are proud when they score well.

17. Accountability measured by test scores may give both teachers and students higher expectations for student performance.

18. Test scores can lead to more support and help for low-performing students and schools.

19. Developing test taking skills can help students learn to read for details, think logically, and devise strategies for problem solving.

20. If the test incorporates higher level thinking skills, it may encourage teachers to include problem solving and critical thinking in their curriculum and daily lessons.

Harmful Aspects of Standardized Tests

1. Too much emphasis on test results can make the entire curriculum choppy.

2. There is a minimum of time to incorporate hands-on problem solving and student projects. In-depth study, extension, and enrichment activities are lost when the focus is teaching to the test.

3. Many tests do not promote creative and critical thinking. Testing limits teacher creativity and teachers may lose the joy of teaching. Students' creative thinking may also be lost because of time constraints and the rigidity of test-driven curriculum.

4. It is more difficult to infuse individual student interests into the curriculum, and thus many times student motivation is lost because of this.

5. Students are not given opportunities to discover their own strengths and develop them.

6. Subjects and topics not tested may be neglected or totally eliminated from the curriculum.

7. Too much pressure is placed on teachers to cover the skills in a set time and for all students to learn within a set time frame. Individual differences and differentiated curriculum may not be considered.

8. When test review and practice take most of the classroom time, teachers who emphasize what is on the test can't provide ample time for student-directed learning.

9. Standardized tests do not allow teachers to look at the whole child. Assessment should include test results, daily classroom performance, projects and products, and report card grades.

10. Some students are not good test takers. Students may suffer from test anxiety and have problems with the time allowed for many tests.

11. Many items on the test may be covered in the curriculum but are tested in such a way that the students get frustrated, don't show what they actually know and don't score as well as they should.

12. Standardized tests rarely allow for ambiguity, different perspectives or the fact that many thought-provoking questions do not have a right and a wrong answer. Tests make students become convergent thinkers who are always looking for the one right answer. Real life does not work that way!

13. Students are not being taught to think globally and see the big picture. They are being taught to be successful on tests.

14. Standardized tests give unfair comparisons of schools and teachers. Most tests are not designed to give credit for the amount of effort a teacher makes at a low performing school. There is little or no consideration of outside factors. If the test scores are low, the teacher is blamed and is looked upon as a poor teacher.

15. There may be a lack of sensitivity to minority or ethnic groups resulting in bias on the tests.

16. Measuring something does not create change. Tests are useless unless results cause curriculum and instruction revision and individualization for some students.

17. Teachers may overuse instructional materials that mimic state test items. Often this leads to a boring and lower level curriculum.

18. There may be a reduction of the pool of tested students if they do not show up on testing days or if they do not take certain courses.

19. School should be challenging and motivating. Learning should be a privilege and a joy. Tests are none of these.

Standardized Testing
Teacher Reflection Page

With a colleague or colleagues, discuss the questions and concerns below.

1. There are a number of positive aspects to standardized testing and a number of negative aspects. In the space below, list the most significant aspects for you in each column.

Positive	Negative

2. How has standardized testing affected your teaching on a day-to-day basis?

3. If a certain topic or skill is not included in the standardized test, do you think it is important to teach it?

4. What are the best strategies you have used to lessen test anxiety and stress in your students?

5. What are the best strategies you have used to emphasize the importance of these tests to your students?

Reproducible for teacher use.

Chapter 5
Traditional Assessment/Alternative Assessment
Would You Like Paper or Plastic?

> *I am a big advocate for alternative assessment. I helped our school write a proposal to end testing of our first graders and use portfolio assessment instead. This worked so much better for our student population. Parents support it once it is explained to them so that they can understand its value. --- 1st grade teacher*
>
> *Traditional testing is one of those necessities of education. It makes the students take their work more seriously. They know there is a consequence for not doing what is required. It helps the teacher and the class stay focused and doesn't allow us to come up with excuses about why some students can't successfully do the work. --- 6th grade teacher*

One of the biggest areas of concern, discussion and controversy in education today is the assessment of student learning. Many educators advocate alternative or authentic assessment while others feel student progress is more easily and more reliably measured using traditional tests and other assessments with definitive correct and incorrect answers. There appears to be no consensus as to whether traditional or alternative assessments are best in terms of student learning.

The public often looks upon traditional assessment such as standardized testing as the best way to measure student progress. As a culture, we seem to have an ingrained inclination favoring elements that can be measured and counted. But simply looking at scores and putting numbers on everything students do is not enough. There are so many other factors involved in the day-to-day educational process that are almost impossible to measure. Kids are not *things*. We cannot measure them as accurately as we would an inanimate object such as a glass of water or a width of railroad tracks.

In this chapter we will:
- Look at the various elements that make up good assessment strategies.

- Identify the advantages and disadvantages of authentic and traditional assessment measures.

- Examine how to set up authentic assessment tasks.

It is extremely difficult to construct and score an excellent assessment instrument. No matter whether it is a traditional assessment such as an objective test or an alternative assessment such as a rubric for a student project, most of the assessments we use in the classroom are good but are far from perfect!

Let's examine some characteristics of both types of assessments. Most teachers will use a mix of traditional and alternative assessments in the course of a school year. We want to make sure we are using both types wisely and well.

Elements of Alternative Assessments

Below are eight characteristics of top quality alternative assessments. Use this list as a checklist for yourself as you inspect the assessment instruments you generally use. This list should provide you with some guidelines as you design and choose assessments for your students in the future.

_____ **1. Meaningful**

Assessment is best when it has value beyond itself. In other words, it should be meaningful and have application in other areas of learning and/or life. Assessment should reflect what students know about content outcomes and standards. The results should be used to improve student performance and knowledge. For example, pretests and other forms of assessment should be used by teachers to develop curriculum, individualize instruction as necessary, prepare for upcoming lessons and decide on varied teaching strategies.

_____ **2. Open-ended**

Assessment works best when students use higher levels of thinking to develop their own responses to questions, topics and issues. When this happens, assessment is tailored to the needs, strengths and weaknesses of the learner. Learning logs, anecdotal records, portfolios, performance-based tasks, essays, journal entries, open-ended questions, discussions, peer response sessions and interviews are some forms of assessment that allow for an open student response.

_____ **3. Realistic**

Students tend to have a very realistic focus toward learning. Many students ask, "Why do I need to do this? Why do I need to know that?" When the only answer a teacher can give is, "Because it's on the test," that's a sign the assignment and the assessment are not very beneficial to student learning in the long term. Just learning the information for a test doesn't mean students can apply what they know. Application and analysis should be part of student assessment, not simply the rote memorization of facts.

_____ **4. Useful outside the classroom**

The best assessments show us if a student knows how to solve problems and think critically. They indicate to what extent students are able to use ideas, theories, methods, concepts or principles in situations encountered in daily life. Worthwhile products and performances generally apply in real life settings and connect to the world outside of the classroom. These types of assessments let us know how well students can use what they have learned, not just how well they can memorize and put something on paper.

5. Variety

Good assessments provide a number of different ways to evaluate student learning. Teachers should not assess everything the same way because all students do not learn in the same way. The ideal is to have a variety of different learning tasks to assess the same skills and knowledge. Projects that offer multiple approaches to the same content are often good ways to assess student learning, especially when the students can have choices in selecting the project and give input as to how they would like their work to be assessed.

6. Interdisciplinary

Quality assessment tasks are interdisciplinary and include a number of different subjects or skills within the same learning activity. Such assessments integrate a variety of content areas, skills and knowledge effectively and creatively. This helps teachers cover a number of standards and benchmarks within the same activity and helps students see the connections between different subjects and concepts.

7. Standard criteria

Valid assessments base scoring on a set of specific standard criteria. Fairness is the main issue when one considers scoring assessment tasks. Such assessments should have consistency in expectations, criteria and scoring. This plays an important role in the diagnosis of specific strengths and weaknesses in individual students or for a class or school as a whole. In many instances, validity and consistency are the biggest problems with alternative assessment.

8. Specific objectives

Effective assessments are based on competencies, criteria and a set of outcomes which are established before the task is started. All those who meet the competencies and demonstrate the desired outcomes can be said to have successfully completed the assessment task. When assessment is based on specific teaching objectives, there is a link between assessment and instruction.

A View of Traditional Assessments

What should be the role of tests and quizzes in assessment? Many teachers believe their students would never be motivated to do any work unless they knew there would be a test on the material at some point. This seems to be a reasonable point of view. However, what most teachers don't realize is that traditional tests and quizzes generally motivate only the better students because they are the ones who enjoy seeing good scores as concrete results of their work and their abilities. These tests do not usually motivate struggling students who often have an attitude of failure and resignation before they begin and figure, "Why bother?"

Well-constructed tests and quizzes help teachers target essential skills and concepts that must be taught and provide a way to document that they have been learned. Test scores can encourage students when they see their progress in learning the required material.

On the other hand, standardized tests and other forms of traditional assessment may project a feeling of elitism on the part of students who do well. Students and parents like this feeling, but only if the test results are high! Individual, class or school test score rankings never motivate those at the bottom of the list.

Unfortunately, traditional assessments are used more and more for purposes beyond those for which they were intended. Test results and honor roll lists are routinely published in local newspapers, on the Internet and in various reports. Students and schools compete with one another based on test scores. Stakes are so high that some educators have resorted to cheating to make their test results more favorable. Administrators and teachers may lose their jobs based on low test scores. Realtors even use these results to sell homes in certain geographic locations! Certainly these are not the outcomes the test developers expected.

Assessments students have during a school year are generally a mix of traditional and alternative forms. There are definite pluses and minuses to both types. The charts on the next several pages give detailed information about the advantages and disadvantages of each.

Traditional Assessment

Characteristic	Advantages	Disadvantages
Purpose is accountability.	Teachers will make sure certain content is taught. Shows how students compare to one another. All students are required to master certain objectives.	Not enough emphasis on long term outcomes. Teachers may be held accountable for variables out of their control. Focus on bringing all students to minimum standards rather than to maximum accomplishment. Doesn't always focus on individual growth and improvement.
Objectives are generally specific and clear but may involve only lower level thinking.	Emphasis is on all students learning specific basic skills. Students are taught/assessed at grade level. Easier to identify skills students have and have not mastered.	Objectives are not integrated. Application of knowledge is not assessed as easily. In real life skills overlap; they are not isolated from one another. Problem solving skills are minimized.
Structured assessment tasks which are the same for all students.	Students are given specific guidance in what they are to do. Some students need and respond well to structure. Helps students to learn to conform and follow directions and specifications. Easy to set up assessment criteria. Students are aware of expectations and routines.	Creativity and independence is ignored. Many skills overlap and should not be assessed in isolation. Sets limits on thinking.
Administration is efficient, quick and easy.	Quickly completed which allows more time for classroom tasks. Less time is needed for teachers to grade. Requires little or no teacher training about how to administer and use.	Efficiency can lead to repetition, boredom and laziness.

Characteristic	Advantages	Disadvantages
High reliability with low cost.	Reliability is familiar to the public. Fits most school/district budgets. Available and cost effective to use with all students, even in large systems.	While generally reliable, scores can be deceptive in terms of what students really know. Some students are good guessers; others are horrible test takers. Ethnic, economic, regional or other types of bias may be imbedded in the test.
Scoring is done by computer usually giving a single score on each test or subtest. May be norm-or criterion-referenced.	Easy to score, time efficient. Results are understood by all.	Too cut and dried, often just giving a single score. Doesn't give detailed information about what student knows. Does not measure creativity. Harder to measure higher level thinking. Presents narrow view of student ability and achievement. Doesn't show student insight.
Desired responses are fixed, usually giving the student one correct choice from a group of options.	Teachers and students know what the right answers are, which are correct and which are incorrect. Easy to grade.	No opportunity to assess any knowledge that isn't specifically asked. Not open and does not provide for various intelligences and learning styles. Does not allow student to be creative in responses.
Impact on students is varied depending on student attitude, learning style and stress level.	Pressure may elicit good performance. Concrete sequential students like knowing exact expectations and right or wrong answers. May help students become proficient at test taking skills. Students may take school more seriously and develop more responsibility for their own learning.	May cause high levels of stress and test anxiety. Not a good means to assess students who are not good test takers. May believe the only things worth learning are the things that are on the test. May cause negative attitudes about assessment. May discourage achievement.

Characteristic	Advantages	Disadvantages
Assessor bias not a problem.	Everyone considers results to be fair. Assessor would not favor or disadvantage anyone while scoring the test.	Assessor cannot judge test bias nor is there any consideration given for different approaches to solving the problem. While assessors are not biased, the test items themselves may be biased giving particular advantage or disadvantage to a given group. The assessor would not have any control over this and no way to remedy the situation.
Does not require teacher planning time for preparation of assessment instrument.	Teachers have too much to do with too little time to accomplish everything. Time can be used for other things rather than developing assessment instruments.	When teachers have no direct involvement in developing the assessment instrument, it is less likely to assess what has actually been taught.
Results easy to explain T o parents and the public.	Most adults are familiar with traditional assessments and test scores.	Scores can be misinterpreted. All tests are not scored in the same way and the same numeric score may mean different things on different tests.
Can be designed to go along precisely with district objectives or mandates.	Assessment and instruction are aligned. What is being taught is what is being tested.	If the entire curriculum is based only on what is being tested, many important things may not be taught.

Authentic Assessment

Characteristic	Advantages	Disadvantages
Purpose is to show improvement, growth and what a student knows and can do.	Good for students who don't test well because there are other avenues to show what they know. Gives feedback which points toward the next step in improvement.	May not have required documentation. Not as good for students who don't work well in class but do test well.
Integrated sets of objectives often covering many subject areas, usually focused on higher order thinking.	More challenging work. Teachers are more likely to focus on higher level thinking skills because these are being assessed. Gives a way to document higher level achievement. Can cover many objectives at the same time. Encourages teachers not to teach skills in isolation.	Hard to isolate specific objectives. May not know precise skills a student knows and ones he doesn't know. Basic skills may be neglected.
Open ended tasks which are different for different students.	Addresses different learning styles and intelligences. Encourages creativity and problem solving. More like problems found in "real life." Gives a good picture of what the child actually can do. Student has latitude to demonstrate skills. Meets a wide variety of student interests.	More subjective. Ability to compare one child with the entire group is diminished. Time consuming. Some students are much more comfortable with specific directions and structured tasks to complete. Some students will find it difficult to focus.
Administration and scoring can be time consuming.	The time it takes is worth it if the assessment gives detailed information. May end up assessing fewer students.	Less efficient. Teachers and administrators may be discouraged from using this type of assessment because it is so time consuming. No one correct answer. Scoring is tedious.

Characteristic	Advantages	Disadvantages
Reliability is more difficult to maintain, requires training for scorers.	With sufficient training, scoring can be reliable.	Use of assessment for accountability is diminished. Teacher bias and human error more likely to occur. Training may be costly.
Complex scoring usually involving checklists and rubrics.	Detailed documentation. Able to pinpoint general areas for growth and improvement. Accurately shows strengths and weaknesses which help teachers plan future instruction.	Time consuming to score accurately. Because it is time consuming and requires extensive training, this type of assessment may be too costly for many school districts. Criteria can be difficult to interpret.
Students construct their own response which may be in the form of product, process or performance.	Better overall assessment of the individual student. Can assess students' best work. Students have ownership in the response.	Responses may be interpreted differently by different scorers.
Not as threatening to the student because assessment tasks are embedded in ongoing instruction.	Less stress for students. Students are more likely to have positive feelings about assessment. Boosts self confidence.	May cause the student to study less and not work as hard. Some students like traditional tests and are not comfortable with other forms of assessment. May lessen competitive drive which motivates some students.

Designing Authentic/Alternative/Performance Assessment Tasks

> *"I know I should use performance assessments," Ms. Perez confided to a colleague. "It's a big push in our district, but it takes so much time! And I really don't know exactly what they want me to do. Even the terminology is confusing. My supervisor suggested that the students do individual projects at the end of a unit of study, but isn't that part of their class work? How is that assessment? I'm not sure I understand what this type of assessment actually is or how I am going to implement it in my classroom."*

Ms. Perez's confusion is widespread! We talk about authentic/alternative/ performance assessment but many teachers don't know exactly what is meant by this or exactly how they should go about administering those kinds of assessments in their classrooms.

Part of this confusion stems from the terminology itself. All three words are used to mean basically the same thing. Additionally, when people refer to authentic assessment, they sometimes mean the assessment **tasks** (such as specific projects, products or performances) while at other times they may be speaking about the assessment **instruments** (such as rubrics, checklists or learning logs). In traditional assessment we generally have a test and a test score coupled together so there is not as much need to distinguish between the two.

Subsequent chapters in this book will give detailed information about the assessment instruments that can be used for authentic assessment. Designing meaningful assessment tasks for students takes careful thought and an organized approach. In doing this, you need to consider the following:

- Your rationale for teaching the unit or information to be assessed
- Standards, benchmarks, objectives and/or outcomes to be measured by the assessment
- The Enduring Understandings you hope students will have as a result of their learning
- The structure of the assessment task itself
- Criteria that shows students have achieved the desired outcomes

Use the forms on the next three pages to help you design and plan performance assessment tasks for your students.

At the end of this chapter you will find a Reflection Page about both traditional and authentic assessment. Consider how and when you use these two types of assessment as you complete this form.

Planning an Authentic Assessment Task

Theme or Topic: _____

Overall rationale:

_____

_____

_____

_____

Standards, benchmarks, objectives and/or outcomes:

_____

_____

_____

_____

_____

_____

_____

_____

_____

Enduring Understandings:

_____

_____

_____

Performance Assessment Task Outline

Title of task:

_____

Purpose: To assess

_____

_____

Materials: (Include materials needed and how they will be supplied)

_____

_____

_____

Time range allotted for task: (Include time at school and time at home if applicable)

_____

Student grouping for task: (Individual, pairs, trios, etc.)

_____

Overview/summary of activity:

_____

_____

Detailed description of performance assessment activity:

_____

_____

_____

_____

Reproducible page for teacher use.

Criteria for Assessment Task

Project/Product/Performance: _____

Assessment criteria:

1._____

2._____

3._____

4._____

Project/Product/Performance: _____

Assessment criteria:

1._____

2._____

3._____

4._____

Scoring or Grading:

_____

_____

_____

_____

Reproducible page for teacher use.

Teacher Reflection Page

In my classroom I generally use _____% traditional assessment and _____%
alternative or authentic assessment.
My reasons for this are:

_____

_____

_____

_____

_____

Which characteristics of traditional assessments are characteristics of the
assessments I use?

_____

_____

Which characteristics of alternative assessment are characteristics of the
assessments I use?

_____

_____

_____

What are my strengths and weaknesses in using alternative assessments?

_____

_____

_____

What are my main reasons for using traditional assessments?

_____

_____

_____

When do I use either type of assessment inappropriately?

_____

_____

_____

Reproducible page for teacher use.

Chapter 6
The Assessment/Instruction Cycle
What you teach should be what you assess -- before, during and after instruction!

* According to the National Excellence Report (1993), gifted students often know between 35% - 50% of the curriculum before they ever begin the school year. Yet many teachers fail to assess such students to see what they already know before instruction begins.

* Children who get 50% - 60% on a classroom unit test generally get an F. We rarely look to see what portion of the information they have learned or where their academic holes are. We just put their grades in our grade book and go on to the next unit of study.

* If we give a student one zero, it takes 5 scores of 90 or above to bring up his grade to passing level.

The facts above indicate some of the ways we could use assessment to guide our instruction, but many of us have failed to do so. The way we generally look at assessment assumes some will get it, some will not and then we'll move on. We rarely use assessment to guide us in what we teach.

In traditional classrooms, teachers complete instruction, then assess, grade and report. The assessment and reporting are considered events separate from instruction itself. This approach tells students that what we value are grades and test scores. A much better approach is to start planning instruction by looking first at assessment results and then planning our curriculum and instruction based on them.

Teaching and assessing on a continual basis helps students work toward their goals. In a classroom where assessment and instruction are interwoven, it is hard to tell where teaching ends and assessing begins. In this type of classroom, students learn that an ability to self-assess, make changes and adjustments and improve their own performance are the things most valued. When assessment and instruction are linked in an ongoing cycle, teachers can identify whatever it is that may be impeding student progress.

Assessment and instruction can be joined, and this seems to be an ideal many teachers and schools are working toward. Student responses, performances and products can be the logical end of the instructional process and at the same time be the assessment for the teacher to use. Creating your own assessment tasks is usually better than relying on those off-the-shelf because yours will be aligned to your curriculum and teaching. This is one of the biggest advantages in using assessments linked directly to instruction.

In this chapter we will begin to explore ways to join assessment and instruction, especially through the use of a curriculum compactor and through a sampling of a unique final exam. In subsequent chapters we will look further at this topic as we consider portfolios, student self-assessment, learning logs, checklist and rubrics.

Assessment and Curriculum Compacting

I am using curriculum compacting with pre and post tests for every math objective. As students show mastery of the objectives, they work on more challenging alternate activities. --- 5th grade teacher

Dr. Joseph Renzulli calls one strategy for linking assessment and instruction curriculum "compacting." This is a process by which students are pre-tested for mastery. Those who already know the material to be studied don't need to do the assigned work. Instead, they are allowed to pursue another activity. Compacting involves identifying the content or skill area and/or the standard or benchmark, pre-assessing, documenting mastery, and providing alternate activities for students who have mastered the material.

This strategy works particularly well in subjects or topics that are easily pre-tested, such as math, spelling, grammar, vocabulary and map skills. The teacher should decide ahead of time what pretest score or demonstration of the knowledge or skill will be acceptable as mastery.

Directions for Compacting

1. Provide a blank Curriculum Compactor (adapted from the form developed by Linda H. Smith and Dr. Joseph Renzulli) for students involved in curriculum compacting. You may want each student to list the items compacted. Another approach is to design a Curriculum Compactor form with the skills, benchmarks or standards listed for a unit. Students then use the form as a record of their work.

2. Use the Curriculum Compactor form to record all modifications in curriculum.
    - In the left column, record the student's areas of strength, one skill or area of knowledge per box. Standards or benchmarks are good guidelines for the items that may go into this column.
    - In the center column, document the student's mastery. This is done through some type of assessment, often (but not always) a pretest score.
    - In the right column, indicate the activities the student will be engaged in while the rest of the class is working on the skill or benchmark.

3. Alternate activities are usually extensions, enrichment or acceleration of the same subject area. Sometimes, however, they may be activities from different subject areas or from the student's individual interest area.

4. Each student should be responsible for keeping his or her compactor folder. In it should be all pretests and other pertinent data with dates, all compactor forms, and the work from alternate activities.

Helpful Hints
    - Unless the student specifically requests it, do not use the time a student 'buys' from a strength area to remediate a learning weakness.
    - Give students a choice of several alternate learning activities.
    - The one choice a student never has is the choice to do nothing!
    - Keeping a compactor folder is a good way for students to learn skills in organization and gives practice in taking responsibility.

One of the advantages of curriculum compacting is that it can be structured in many different ways. It is flexible enough to work within the existing framework of a variety of classrooms and teaching styles. Below is one example of a Curriculum Compactor for an individual student which covers a number of different skills. A blank form is also included for your use. On the next several pages you will see how another type of compactor was used as a way to assess an entire class and document progress and mastery through pretests and post tests.

CURRICULUM COMPACTOR*

Name _____

Standard or Benchmark Content or Skill Area	Documenting Mastery	Alternate Activities
Properly use verb tenses	95% on pretest with fill in the blanks	Write a creative short story using present tense or Write a report on local history using past tense.
Multiply two digit decimals	100% on pretest	Write a series of word problems that require multiplication of decimals. or Make a collage using newspapers or magazines showing the use of decimals in everyday life.
Spell list of frequently misspelled words	90% on pretest of 50 words	Look in a dictionary and find 25 words you do not know. Along with words you missed, write these into a humorous poem or story. Underline each and be sure to spell correctly. or Construct a crossword puzzle using these words plus the words you missed on the pretest.

*Adapted from the form by Linda H. Smith and Dr. Joseph Renzulli

CURRICULUM COMPACTOR

Student's Name _____

Standard or Benchmark Content or Skill Area	Documenting Mastery	Alternate Activities

Reproducible page for teacher use.

An Example of Using the Curriculum Compactor as a Record of Student Work and Assessment in One Specific Subject

Math is an ideal subject to differentiate instruction by using curriculum compacting. In math, specific skills are "black and white" based upon a state's proficiency guide, an adopted math series, or a school's grade level scope and sequence. Using these delineated objectives is a good place to begin compacting.

Once skill areas are listed, a pretest is given to each student. The pretest is separated by skill areas with specific questions designed to test knowledge and understanding of the specific skill. Usually 4-5 questions are used to evaluate mastery in each skill area. Students are given ample time to complete the pretest and are encouraged to just do their best or skip problems that seem foreign and confusing. No grade is given for the pretest. It is simply a way of assessing which students have already mastered a specific skill area and which students need further instruction.

A student's pretest is marked for accuracy and a Student Evaluation Form is filled out. From the form, a student can readily see if he or she has mastered a skill area. "Yes" is checked if a specific skill area has been mastered prior to instruction and "No" is checked if a specific skill area has not been mastered prior to instruction. Depending upon the skills and a student's past math knowledge, he or she may have mastered one or many of the skills in a particular unit.

When a particular skill is taught on a particular day, students check their Student Evaluation Forms. Students who have shown mastery have "compacted out" of listening to the instruction for that day. These students are free to choose enrichment/extension/acceleration activities planned for them while instruction on the day's skill takes place in the classroom with just those students who need the help. Therefore, a teacher may be instructing a small group of students or may have a majority of the class based upon the pretest results. This naturally uses the flexible grouping strategy based upon instructional needs of the class.

Instruction continues in this manner until the unit is completed and a final chapter test is given. The chapter test is formatted in the same way as the pretest. Again, the Student Evaluation Form is marked. The obvious goal is to have all skill areas marked "Yes" at the end of the unit of study. Students can easily see the improvement that has taken place and can celebrate the knowledge obtained.

The key to compacting is to remember that the teacher sets the mastery level and the standards by which a student is free to choose alternate activities. If a particular lesson requires that everyone listen to the whole group instruction, so be it. If a particular lesson allows all students choices of learning opportunities, so be it. An example of the Student Evaluation and the Curriculum Compactor Form, a test that could be used as a pre or post test, plus compacting instructions for students and a sample of an Alternate Activities Checklist for students can be found on the next five pages.

Student Evaluation and Curriculum Compactor Form

Name _____

Date of pretest _____ Date of post test _____

Standard or Objective	Items	Pretest		Post test	
		No	Yes	No	Yes
3.1 Exploring multiplication patterns and properties	1, 2, 3, 4				
3.2 Using rounding to estimate products	5, 6, 7, 8				
3.3 Multiply by one digit and two digit numbers	9, 10, 11, 12				
3.4 Use the distributive property to multiply	13, 14, 15, 16				
3.5 Decide whether to use paper, pencil, calculator or mental math when multiplying	17				
3.6 Explore patterns with multiples	18, 19, 20, 21				
3.7 Solve multiple-step problems	22				
3.8 Solve problems by guessing and checking	23				

Math Pretest or Post test: Multiplying Whole Numbers

Name _____

3.1 Exploring multiplication patterns and properties
   Find each product. Use mental math.

    1. 30 x 60   2. 20 x 20   3. 3 x 80   4. 100 x (4 x 3)

    _____   _____   _____   _____

3.2 Using rounding to estimate products
   Estimate each product.

    5. 52 x 17   6. 91 x 15   7. 5 x 76   8. 686 x 36

    _____   _____   _____   _____

3.3 Multiply by one digit and two digit numbers
   Find each product.

    9. 205   10. 52   11. 137   12. 72
       x 4   x 38   x 16   x 55

3.4 Use the distributive property to multiply
   Find each product. Use the distributive property.

    13. 18 x 99   14. 103 x 15   15. 102 x 11   16. 497 x 5

    _____   _____   _____   _____

3.5 Decide whether to use paper/pencil, calculator or mental math

    17. Which method of calculation is the best for finding the product of
         439 and 568 quickly? Underline your answer.

   a. mental math   b. guessing and checking   c. calculator   d. paper/pencil

3.6 Explore patterns with multiples
Find the LCM for each set of numbers

18. 3 and 4   19. 6 and 10   20. 2 and 7   21. 4, 5 and 8

_____   _____   _____   _____

3.7 Solve multiple-step problems
Solve each problem. Use the 5 step plan and strategy to help you.

22. Adam went to the art museum. He spent $3.75 for admission to the museum, twice that much on gifts at the gift shop and the rest on lunch. All together Adam spent $15.04. How much did Adam spend at the gift shop? How much did he spend on lunch?

_____ at the gift shop.   _____ on lunch.

3.8 Solve problems by checking and guessing
Solve each problem. Use the 5 step plan and the guess and check strategy to help you.

23. Jenny rode her bike 63 miles in all. She rode twice as many miles on paved road as she did on dirt road. How many miles did she ride on paved road?

_____ miles on paved road.

Compacting Instructions
Please read carefully!!

1. You must show me the selection you will be working on each day on your Alternate Activities Checklist before you leave the room to work on your selected activity. If you do not have the checklist with you, you will stay and do the regular class work for the day.

2. You will be allowed to work on your Alternate Activity in the conference room across the hall. I will monitor your progress from time to time. I will try to come to the conference room for 5 or 10 minutes each day to answer questions and guide you in your work.

3. It is extremely important that you are on your best behavior when you are working on your Alternate Activity in the conference room. Your voice should be no louder than a whisper if you need to talk to someone.

4. I have basic supplies such as scissors, tape, markers, construction paper, newspapers, catalogs, and glue sticks available for you. You may need to bring other materials if any are required for your individual project.

5. Take pride in the work you do for your Alternate Activity. This should be quality work and should reflect higher level thinking and extension of your knowledge.

6. Some projects require research outside the classroom or conference room. If you need to go to the media center or to another part of the school, make sure you sign out so I will know where you are. Only one student may be gone at a time.

7. You must monitor your own time as you do your Alternate Activity. You need to allow approximately 10 minutes at the end of class to clean the room. Other students will be using it after you, and I want it to be completely clean and organized for them. If it is not left in proper order, you will not be able to work on your Alternate Activity during the next class.

8. The one choice you never have is the choice to do nothing! Learning time is too valuable.

I have read the instructions and am aware of what is expected of me when I compact the curriculum and work on Alternate Activities.

Student signature _____

Parent signature _____

©2001 Pieces of Learning

Alternate Activities Checklist

For use with the Curriculum Compactor - Put in the blank the date that you begin an activity. Circle the activity number when you complete it.

_____ 1. Look through a collection of catalogs to find out how many ways math skills and processes are used and presented. Make a list of all you can find (minimum 10, maximum 100). Categorize your list and present your findings in a graphic organizer such as a chart, Venn diagram, etc.

_____ 2. Select three pages in one catalog that contain similar items. Determine the average cost per page. Repeat with several other catalogs. Then show your findings on a graph.

_____ 3. Develop plans for a new type of catalog. This can be as creative as you want and can include technology. Write your proposal for this new type of catalog and develop a few sample pages. Your proposal should be persuasive, organized, logical and at least a page long.

_____ 4. Prepare a checklist or rubric that class members can use when they evaluate catalogs and/or select products from catalogs. Your checklist must contain at least 10 well-stated criteria.

_____ 5. Use advertisements from local newspapers to compare and contrast prices in stores with prices in catalogs. Be sure to include the cost of shipping and handling and the cost of transportation for local shopping. Compare the costs of at least 10 different products which can be purchased in both stores and catalogs. Be sure to show how you arrived at your conclusions.

_____ 6. Create your own catalog (8-10 pages) which would feature products of interest to people in your age group or to your family. Write catalog descriptions, draw illustrations, list prices, construct an order form and include shipping and handling for all items. Take sample orders from 5 different people using copies of your order form. Which items were the most popular? Which items were not ordered at all? What would you do differently in your next catalog?

_____ 7. Activity of your own choosing - Describe below. This must be approved by your teacher before you begin.

Measuring Intangibles

A recent report on the business news segment of National Public Radio talked about the increasing recognition from businesses that intangibles significantly influence the bottom line. Such intangibles include long term goals, research and development, quality, worker satisfaction, effort and motivation, customer services and excellence. Further, in the new economy, businesses are realizing that their value is more than can be shown by the old measurements of input and output. The question is how to measure the intangibles.

It seems that education faces much the same question. Sometimes the approach to educational assessment seems like the focus on the bottom line and short term profits that some corporations have without looking to other things. That one significant teacher who cared, the importance of persistence, effort and character are just as important as test scores but are much harder to quantify. We need to remember that these things have value that sometimes cannot be measured.

One high school English teacher valued some intangibles when she crafted an unusual final exam for her 10th and 11th graders. While assessment cannot always be this unique, this is an excellent example of incorporating the intangibles we value into the assessments we give our students. Below you will see this teacher's comments about why she did this activity. On the following page you will see a copy of the "Final Exam" her students received. Finally, you will read her reflections and helpful hints.

An Alternative Final Exam

This idea was inspired by a "Dear Abby" letter. In the letter the writer commented on the death of her grandmother. While going through the woman's personal things, the family found an autobiography written by her as a final project in high school. The letter writer expressed her appreciation for the teacher who had assigned it, as it gave them a view of their grandmother as a young person. It was a gift and a delight to see her in this new way.

Intrigued, I discussed the letter with my 10th and 11th graders and had them consider what their grandchildren would gain from reading about them as teenagers. It was a great brainstorming session! At the end of the period, I told them that instead of a final exam they would be writing their own autobiographies for their grandchildren. They loved the idea of not doing a final, but were hesitant about doing an autobiography. The instructions they were given can be found on the next page.

Autobiography Final Exam

This project consists of two parts:
  a) Written, due the day before finals (assigned two months in advance)
  b) Oral, to be presented on the day of exams

Written requirements:
  1. No less than 10 and no more than 20 pages
  2. Must be typed in a standard 10 or 12 point font
  3. Must be written in first person
  4. No invented events. This only hurts your grandchildren or yourself.
  5. If an event is too personal to share, make two versions of your autobiography. The edited one can go to me. Save the real one for yourself.
  6. Give real names and dates. Those are things you forget as you get older and wish you'd recorded.
  7. Use good descriptive adjectives that will give a vivid picture of you and your life.
  8. Follow good writing form learned in class this year.
  9. Proofread your rough draft before making a final copy.
  10. Divide your autobiography into chapters, giving each an interesting and/or creative name.
  11. Have a title page with a title that summarizes your philosophy of life and would make us want to read it if we ran across it cleaning out your files.
  12. Late papers will not be accepted without approval from the Assistant Principal. (As with any final exam, you must have a doctor's excuse.)

Oral presentation requirements:
  1. The presentation must be between 5-10 minutes in length.
  2. You may share a life-changing incident from your autobiography **or** comment on the process of writing the autobiography. Include what you learned about yourself and/or your family while doing this.
  3. You may refer to your notes but not read the autobiography to us word for word.

Student name:_____

Due date - Written autobiography: _____

Due date - Oral presentation: _____

Parent signature:_____

Reproducible page for teacher use.

Reflections and Helpful Hints

The autobiographies were excellent. The lowest grades on papers turned in on time were two C's. Those students did the assignment but didn't follow directions or proofread. Two students tried to turn in their papers late. The Assistant Principal met with both of them. Neither could verify a doctor's appointment or justify the lateness of their paper, so both received a "0" on that portion of the exam.

Criteria for assessment included:
- Followed directions regarding number of pages, chapters, etc.
- Vivid and clear use of language
- Writing style
- Proofreading
- Showed span of life from birth to present
- Self-reflection in telling about events and philosophy

Student evaluations of this assignment were enthusiastic. Most agreed that they found it daunting, but if they worked on it steadily it wasn't that hard. They learned a great deal about themselves and had some bonding moments with their families as they did research about their own lives. Some of the papers were astonishingly candid. Many students made great effort and were motivated to find out more about who they actually were.

Most kids went overtime in the oral section of the exam. They were eager to share about themselves and what they had researched, learned and accomplished. There was about a 50/50 split as to whether they chose to talk about a life-changing incident or the process of writing the autobiography.

"Nuts and Bolts" issues:

1. It is important to clear this type of exam with the administration before you assign it because it doesn't fit the standard idea of a final exam.

2. Give the students enough time to do the assignment. Mention it during the weeks they are to be working on it.

3. Reserve evenings at home to read these papers. It does take time, but it is much more interesting than reading and grading a traditional final exam.

4. Be specific about assessment criteria and share the criteria with the students beforehand. Decide how much the written product will count and how much the oral presentation will count.

5. Require student and parent signatures on the assignment when they first start. This assures that parents will know about the 'exam' and will encourage students not to procrastinate.

6. Make sure you are available for questions or discussions with students as they work on the assignment.

Teacher Reflection Page

1. What skills, benchmarks or standards in your current curriculum would lend themselves to curriculum compacting? List below along with ways you could assess mastery.

Skills, Benchmarks or Standards	How to Assess Mastery

2. Brainstorm ways you might be able to include intangibles in your assessment activities. List your ideas below.

Chapter 7
Reporting and Documenting Student Progress
Got your report card ... what did she give you?

Grades and Report Cards

> *I have a student who has a depth of understanding about the literature we are studying considerably beyond any other student I teach. She reads far more than assigned, yet she doesn't turn in written work and is incredibly unorganized with her time. This makes me wonder if grades should be based on knowledge or output, on effort or understanding? It is a dilemma.*
>
> *-------AP English teacher*

How important and accurate are grades? Sometimes they are not as accurate or important as we might think. Artist Mia Lynn, the designer of the famous Vietnam War Memorial in Washington, D.C. tells an interesting story about a grade she received in school. Her design for the Memorial was done when she was only 20 years old and was originally produced for a class project in college. As unbelievable as it may sound, her professor gave her design a 'B.' Regardless of the grade it had gotten, she decided to submit it to the contest for the design of the Memorial. 1,400 other designs were also submitted. As we all know, her design won and this Memorial has become one of the most famous and most visited in Washington. It makes one wonder how accurate that 'B' actually was!

Grading is one of the strangest things we do in education. It is difficult to know how a particular grade is arrived at because the process of grading daily work and then giving a report card grade has little if any uniformity, even within the same school. There is little agreement among educators on what should be included or counted in a grade, whether grades are criterion- or norm-referenced, or whether grades should be used as motivators and rewards or should simply report student progress. The two scenarios above highlight these issues.

Nevertheless, it appears we will have grades and report cards for the foreseeable future. How, then, do we assess properly and communicate accurately while using them? The primary purpose of grading should be to provide accurate and understandable feedback that can be used by students to improve their performance. Additionally, parents need grades to learn how their children are doing in school. Grades can serve as a consistent form of communication between home and school.

Traditionally, teaching has focused heavily on grades, and there is a lot of pressure on students to earn good grades. At the same time, grade inflation is rampant in American schools and grades do not always reflect top achievement or who is working to his or her potential. Many gifted and high achieving students are terrified of getting anything other than an A, but often these same students get A's while putting forth little or no effort. If such students go all the way through elementary and middle school getting A's but never putting forth much effort or working very hard, they are actually underachievers!

Parents may find it hard to understand various forms of authentic assessment, especially when there is narrative feedback but no letter or number grade. They want their kids to be graded in the same way THEY were. Teachers need to explain how expectations for students have changed. Giving a grade at the end of a unit of study or at the end of the grading period is not nearly as helpful as guidance during a project, giving students ongoing opportunities to refine their products during the process, and culminating reflections on what has been learned. There needs to be a definitive connection between project assessment criteria and the grades students receive.

Some defend the extensive use of grades claiming that students are not motivated to work without them. Yet a number of teachers believe that giving grades is not an effective way to motivate and evaluate students. In fact, because teachers grade in so many different ways, students with more than one teacher get confused about how grades are figured in the first place. In fact, the process of assigning grades is inherently subjective. Thus, the age-old question of "What grade did you give me?" rather than "What grade did I earn?"

One option might be for report cards to come with standards listed and a rating scale showing how far a student has come in reaching that standard. For each unit of study, teachers might send a letter to parents that outlines the performance standards for the unit. The percentage of the grade for each standard could also be shown. If teachers or entire schools went to this type of report card, assessment would be more meaningful

Alternative Suggestions for Grades:

1. Come to an agreement as an entire school about what is indicated or assessed by a report card grade. For instance, your school may decide that individual achievement will be the only thing the grade shows. Effort, participation, attitude, working with others, etc. would then be shown separately. Conversely, all of the items listed above could be included in the grade on the report card. The important thing is for everyone to be in agreement about what is included and what is not.

2. Grades should reflect a sample of student work. We don't have to grade every piece of paper and put the score in the grade book! Teachers are often exhausted and overwhelmed because of all the grading they think they must do. Grade some work, but have your students self-assess other work. Check to make sure the work is done without always putting a grade or number of points on it. We have trained students and parents to expect grades for everything -- we can also 'un-train' them!

3. Enter classwork grades in pencil. This gives the message that they are temporary. You can change an initial grade if you see improvement in a skill over the duration of the grading period. Recent marks usually reflect student progress in a skill or concept. Entering classwork grades in pencil is also a good strategy to use with curriculum compacting. When a student 'tests out' of classwork, a grade in pencil indicates that work will be done in an alternate (more challenging) activity.

4. Offer students opportunities to improve their marks. If a student redoes a paper or assignment, some credit should be given for the learning that has taken place. Most students will learn from the mistakes they made the first time and will do better on the second attempt. Isn't this type of learning what we hope will happen?

5. Weight grades by topics or skills. The most important skill should receive the most weight. Often we grade each assignment as if all were of equal importance. This is rarely the case.

6. Watch for the effect one very low grade (or a zero) has on the overall grade. Sometimes one low score can make the entire grade lower than it should be to reflect the student's true performance. You may want to try a median score rather than an average.

7. Grade according to established criteria rather than establishing preordained quotas for grades. All students should have the possibility of getting A's if they all have earned them according to standards-based criteria. If all students reach the highest standard, all should get the highest grade.

8. Explain how your students' work is going to be assessed before they begin an assignment or task. The criteria for grading should never be a mystery!

9. Use some alternative assessment and reporting strategies in place of, or in addition to, grades and report cards. Several alternative methods are described throughout this chapter.

10. Make sure grades are indicative of students' skills and progress in different types of activities. Test grades should be balanced by classwork, homework, projects and performances.

11. Develop report cards that show standards, skills and competencies and can indicate how well a student is progressing along a continuum.

12. Include a number and a letter grade with the number indicating the level. For example '1' might equal below grade level, '2' on grade level while '3' or '4' might indicate advanced or very advanced work. Report card grades would then look like 'B4' or 'A2'. This reporting strategy works particularly well with tiered lessons and units.

For Teacher Reflection

Discuss with another teacher or with your grade level or department:

- What components do you currently include in your grades?

- In what ways are our grading systems similar? How are they different? Should we try to make them more consistent with one another?

- Do these items reflect what is really important in students' work and progress?

- Could we improve our grading system and/or report cards so that they communicate student learning more clearly? In what ways?

Student-Led Parent Conferences

One of the main purposes of grades and report cards is to share student progress with parents. A report card may do this to a minimal degree, but more often it just becomes a cause for punishment, a means to a tangible reward or it is used to give parents "bragging rights" with their friends and family.

A student-led conference is a much better way to truly share with parents what their child is learning and how he or she is progressing. In a student-led conference, students describe their progress to their parents. They usually pick representative work samples and while showing these, describe their specific accomplishments, tell what they have learned and identify mistakes or failures.

In a student-led conference, the parents, the teacher and the student jointly:
- Review the student's work
- Compare this work to expected standards and benchmarks
- Discuss strengths and areas of growth
- Target specific weaknesses and areas needing improvement
- Produce goals and identify new benchmarks
- Develop a learning plan for the future

In this type of conference, the student serves as the chair. You will find guidelines for a student-led conference on the next page. The following page is a Post Conference Summary page.

Guidelines/Agenda for a Student-Led Conference

1. The student welcomes everyone.

2. The teacher and the student review the conference process and may present a written agenda.

3. The student shares selected work samples. These are chosen beforehand by the student, often with input from the teacher.

4. Student, parents and teacher all share the strengths they see in the student's work. Strengths may be listed on paper as they are discussed.

5. Student, teacher and parent each share one or two areas that the student needs to work on. These areas are listed and, if there are several mentioned, they may be rank ordered.

6. Both strengths and weaknesses are discussed by all in attendance. Students are usually very good judges of the quality of their own work and what they need to do to improve it.

7. The student comes up with two or three learning goals for the future. Often these are based on state or district standards and guidelines. Each person explains how she or he will help support working toward these goals. It is important that everyone involved in the conference understand what the student's future learning goals and outcomes are. When that is the case, instead of bringing home a packet or notebook filled with papers for their parents to go through without really knowing what they are looking at, students will bring home evidence of how well they are doing in working toward their learning goals.

8. A timetable or schedule is set for working on these goals.

9. The teacher answers questions and summarizes the future directions for the student's learning that have been discussed and agreed upon. The teacher may need to give guidance and answer questions, but all participants in the conference need to listen to what all others are saying.

10. The student ends the conference and thanks everyone for coming and for their participation.

For a student-led conference to go well, it is extremely helpful for parents to have some background information about what goes on in the classroom and what the grade level expectations and standards are. In general, when parents see the value of hearing about school progress from students themselves, they buy into the whole process.

The reproducible form on the next page may be used as a Summary Form at the end of a Student-Led Conference.

Post Conference Summary Page

Student name _____ Date _____

Work samples shared: _____

_____

_____

_____

Student's strengths: _____

_____

_____

_____

Skills, attitudes or knowledge that need improvement: _____

_____

_____

_____

Learning goals: _____

_____

_____

_____

Plan of action (with dates): _____

_____

_____

_____

Signatures of those attending conference: _____

_____

_____

Reproducible form for student use.

Student Journals and Learning Logs

Another way to record and report student progress is by having the students keep journals and learning logs. One type of weekly journal is done by having students write learning goals for the week on one page with their reflections and evaluation of their work on the facing page. This type of learning log could be an excellent follow-up to a student-led conference.

A sample is below:

Learning Goals for week of October 10-15	Reflections and evaluation of my work
1. Identify a variety of geometric figures 2. Show how they are used in the real world. 3. Find examples of figures in nature or man-made objects. 4. Construct sample figures. 5. Write an informational report on what I have learned.	I found most of the figures in the math book. I did an online search and found other types of figures. I had trouble finding any information about where these are in the real world. Nothing really said that. But I looked around and could see some figures just in the classroom and in my yard. A couple of my models fell apart. I haven't finished my written report. I guess I'll turn it in late. I would give myself a B for finding and making the figures and doing research on them but an F so far on my report since I haven't turned it in.

There are many variations of format for student learning logs. The most important thing is to help the student record what he or she has learned, what the goals and objectives were in doing the work, and the method of showing where the student is heading in the future. In any type of learning log, the process of thinking and analyzing is much more important than the form upon which it is recorded. In fact, it is the "Reflections" column that students sometimes have difficulty with. Work with your students to practice thinking and writing about their reflections on learning. This concept will be new to most of them. On the next four pages you will find:

- Two different blank forms for learning logs similar to the one above.

- A sample long range project learning log and a blank form for the same.

A Student Log for _____ Activity

Name _____

Date: _____

Activity description _____

_____

_____

What I learned _____

_____

_____

Ways to improve next time _____

_____

_____

My overall rating for the activity _____

Teacher comments and evaluation_____

_____

_____

_____

_____

Grade _____

Reproducible form for student use.

My Learning Log

Name _____ Subject _____

Learning Goals for Week of _____	Reflections and evaluation of my work

Some of my goals for next week are:

_____

_____

_____

_____

Reproducible form for student use.

Record of Work for Product or Performance

Date	Work Planned	Work Actually Done	Adjustments to Plan for next day	Reflections on my work (Difficulties, strengths, surprises)
Monday	Find books and other information on the topic at home and at the library.	Found one book at home. My mom couldn't take me to the library.	Now I need to go to the library tomorrow.	My mom was too busy and she is making me get behind. I wish I could drive.
Tuesday	Take notes from all sources. See what's on the Internet that I could use.	Went to the library and found a book and 2 news articles. Surfed the Internet but didn't see anything useful.	I need to work on the notes tomorrow.	I saw a lot of cool stuff on the Net but nothing that will help me with this report and project.
Wednesday	Begin writing rough draft. Plan visuals to go with written report.	Took notes from the books. Started making a collage.	I want to do the whole rough draft tomorrow.	My collage is good. It is turning out better than I thought. But I wish the rough draft was finished.
Thursday	Finish rough draft. Ask someone to proofread. Work on visuals.	Finished the collage.	Now I have to do the rough draft and the final report this weekend.	I hate homework on weekends. I leave the stuff I don't like to do until the last minute.
Weekend	Do final report. Finish visuals. Put together in folder.	Rough draft done. My dad proofread it. I got my folder and decorated it.	I have to do the whole final written report on Monday night.	I wish this assignment was done. My collage is the best!
Monday	Check to make sure everything is ready to be turned in tomorrow.	Written report finished. Everything is in a folder.	I am ready to turn this in.	I'm glad the teacher made us plan a "cushion day" in our projected work plan. That is the only reason this will be turned in on time.

From <u>Encouraging Achievement</u> by Carolyn Coil, Pieces of Learning

Reproducible

Record of Work for Product or Performance

Date	Work Planned	Work Actually Done	Adjustments to Plan for next day	Reflections on my work (Difficulties, strengths, surprises)
Monday				
Tuesday				
Wednesday				
Thursday				
Weekend				
Monday				

From <u>Encouraging Achievement</u> by Carolyn Coil, Pieces of Learning

Classroom Observations

With so much emphasis on standardized tests, it is important to remember that one of the best sources of information about what each child can do is the classroom teacher. Teachers continually work with students, collect student products, see students working in groups and have one-on-one relationships with them.

To use a media analogy, teacher observations can provide a full-length film while at best a test only provides a snapshot! Consider how much more information and insight you can usually get from viewing a movie as compared to seeing one photo!

The biggest problem about classroom observations is that they seem to be so subjective. In order to deal with this problem, teachers need tools to transfer their ongoing classroom observations into valid assessment instruments.

A good classroom observation assessment instrument:
1. Lists learning objectives
2. Establishes clear observable criteria for accomplishing the objectives
3. Makes a rating scale from which to judge the criteria

There are many ways to record your observations. A simple index card or half page form works well for day-to-day classroom observations. These can be kept in a file box alphabetically by student name. A sample is below. Blank forms for your use can be found on the next page.

Classroom Observation Record

Student's name: _____

Activity: Small group discussion

Learning objectives:

    1. To understand the impact of inventions on daily life.

    2. To convey one's ideas through class discussion

Criteria: Rating (1-3):

    1. Discusses at least two different inventions.   _____

    2. Gives an example of how each impacts daily life.   _____

    3. Articulates ideas so they are easily understood.   _____

Comments:

Classroom Observation Record

Student's name: _____

Activity: _____

Learning objectives:

    1. _____

    2. _____

Criteria: Rating (1-3):

    1. _____   _____

    2. _____   _____

    3. _____   _____

Comments:

Reproducible for teacher use.

Classroom Observation Record

Student's name: _____

Activity: _____

Learning objectives:

    1. _____

    2. _____

Criteria: Rating (1-3):

    1. _____   _____

    2. _____   _____

    3. _____   _____

Comments:

Reproducible for teacher use.

Portfolios

> *"I've just received portfolios from my students' third grade teacher,"* exclaimed Ms. Barnes as she looked through her materials. She was beginning to get her room set up for her 4th graders who were arriving next week. *"I've never had portfolios to look through before I even meet the kids. I think this will be really helpful in getting to know them and in seeing where I should start my instruction this year."*
>
> *"Just one more thing to do!"* sighed Mr. Mendoza. *"I don't know how I'll ever get a portfolio put together for every kid I teach. I didn't do well with this last year! I wish we'd just have the standardized test and not worry about anything else."*

The two teachers quoted above view portfolios with quite different attitudes. One sees them as helpful and useful as she begins planning for her students. The other sees them as more work! These varied viewpoints are typical depending on one's experience and background.

Good portfolios do not just happen. They take a lot of effort on the part of teachers and students. They require conferencing with students and other teachers and time to help students formulate both the process and procedures for developing their portfolios. Additionally, a system of assessment through portfolios needs administrative support and parent understanding in order to be successful.

Portfolios are highly flexible instructional and assessment tools. In general, they are collections of student work representing a selection of performances and/or products. The concept of having a portfolio is derived from the visual and performing arts tradition of showcasing artists' accomplishments and selected works and is easily adapted to a school situation showcasing student work.

Why Portfolios?

There are a number of benefits in using portfolios.

- To assemble student work that reflects the goals and objectives of the school, grade level or school district.

- To help students become aware of their progress and improvement in learning over the course of a grading period or school year.

- To encourage students to plan for and assess their own learning.

- To give teachers insight and information about student growth over a period of time.

- To show the student's role in constructing his or her own understanding of concepts, knowledge and skills.

- To support team teaching and cooperative learning in which students and teachers all comment on work in progress or work completed.

- To give teachers from year to year an idea of each student's progress and abilities.

- To help students become independent and autonomous learners by having them select, correct and reflect on the work that goes into a portfolio.

- To foster parent involvement and understanding of the learning process beyond looking at a single grade on a report card.

Sample Types of Portfolios

- Process Folio

Students keep the first draft along with corrections that were made and include it along with subsequent drafts. This helps both teacher and student see progress and learning. Especially useful in a writing portfolio.

- Kindergarten Portfolio

This portfolio shows each child's growth in the areas of art, writing, language arts and math from the beginning, middle and end of the school year. It might include a self portrait, a sample of writing numbers 1-25 or 1-100, letters and sounds a child knows, and creative writing samples to show the child's transition from creative to traditional spelling.

- Student Growth Portfolios

Take work at specific times to show progress through the year. Collect work samples at the beginning of the year to get a baseline. Require students to reflect upon their growth periodically. Students track their progress along a growth continuum. This results in internal motivation, because students can see they are in control of their own academic success.

- Learning Records

This type of portfolio contains cumulative accounts of progress and beginning points for new endeavors. Students can see where they have been and where they are headed. A standardized format may be used to collect evidence of student progress throughout the year. Formative evaluations will lead to summative by the end of the school year. Parents and students can write descriptions of the progress they have seen through the portfolio.

- Portfolios using Technology

These can contain video and audio tapes, computer disks or CD's, digital pictures, written work, PowerPoint presentations, etc. It should show evidence of a student's learning in one subject or more. If a student produces a project which is too bulky to physically include in a portfolio, a photo or video of the project can be included.

Portfolios and Assessment

Research shows students see most assessment as something done to them by someone else. They have little knowledge of what is actually involved in evaluating their work. Portfolios provide a structure for involving students in developing criteria for evaluation and taking ownership of that criteria.

The contents of a portfolio along with teacher observations and teacher records will show progress toward learning goals. Portfolios may contain work in progress and a student's evaluation of his or her strengths and weaknesses. They can be used to demonstrate a student's work at the beginning of the learning process and at the end to show how far this student has progressed. One advantage of using portfolios is that they will most likely document improvement over time even if the student only picks his best work. This is because in general a student's best work keeps getting better!

Portfolios can be passed on from teacher to teacher and from grade level to grade level. Teachers have to coordinate and collaborate with one another for this to be an effective practice.

A Portfolio Rubric or Table of Contents

Portfolios are a good vehicle to use for student self-assessment. It is helpful to have a portfolio Table of Contents and rubric or checklist which allows the student to evaluate the portfolio. The same rubric may be used by the teacher.

The Table of Contents for the Portfolio acts as an inventory, guideline and student self-reflection tool. It can be revised when choices are made as to what goes in the portfolio. A statement of goals for a certain period of time can also be included and revised after the goals are met or the time period is reached. Each piece of writing may have a response written by a peer. There could be a student's self reflection about anything in the portfolio. There can be a self-evaluation showing what the student feels the portfolio reveals about him or her.

A sample Portfolio Table of Contents is on the next page.

Portfolio Table of Contents

Learning Goals: _____

_____

_____

	Date	Description of Item	What I Learned
Item 1			
Item 2			
Item 3			
Item 4			
Item 5			
Item 6			
Item 7			
Item 8			
Item 9			
Item 10			

Conclusions: _____

_____

_____

Student's Name: _____

Reproducible form for student use.

Questions Before You Begin

Many teachers begin using portfolios with their students without thinking through the process ahead of time. It is helpful to consider the following questions before you begin.

- What will it look like?

- How will it be structured?

- What should go in it?

- What will best show progress toward learning goals?

- Will it show only the best work (showcase portfolio) or will it show work which documents improvement?

- How and when will work samples be selected for the portfolio?

- What standards will be used to evaluate the portfolio?

- How much will the portfolio be counted in the final assessment, grade or evaluation of the work done in the class?

- How will evaluation criteria reflect standards of excellence, effort, and growth?

Chapter 8
About Rubrics: What Are They Anyway?
I hear they make you see red!

> *Known for encouraging student products, I was approached in the early 1990's about developing a workshop on the hottest new thing in education -- rubrics. Not exactly sure what they were, I invited a colleague to present along with me. Trudi's 5th grade team had been setting goals and writing criteria all year to meet a new state educational mandate. Together, I figured, we'd be fine.*
>
> *Not so! After spending an hour trying to map out the workshop, we threw up our hands in despair! Calling the person who had originally approached me, I wailed, "We can't do this! We can't even agree on what a rubric IS! Who's right?!"*
> *-- K-8 Gifted Education Teacher*

So -- just what **is** a rubric anyway? Most simply, it's a scoring guide. It's a way of organizing criteria that describe expectations of student work and measuring the levels of performance proficiency.

The term "rubric" comes from the Latin word "ruber" for red. At one time, red earth or "rubrica terra" was used to mark a thing of importance. After monks in the 15th century used large red letters to begin each major section of an illuminated manuscript, the term "rubric" came to mean the headings for major sections of a book. Today, a rubric assigns an articulated rating scale to those expectations designated as important in student work.

Teacher Assessment Using Rubrics

Teachers have always known what a good piece of work should look like, but usually in a very generalized way. A good rubric helps teachers grade all types of products and performances more fairly since rubrics require teachers to be much more precise about what their expectations are. Designing specific performance criteria allows teachers to define clearly what achievement targets they want students to hit. It is a more systematized way of doing something teachers in the past have done only intuitively. As their expectations and standards become more consistent and uniform, the grades they give become much more defensible. Students and teachers alike are much more clear about how student work will be evaluated.

When teachers use specific criteria to grade student products and performances and give feedback based on this criteria, students have much more useful feedback than they received with a mere letter or number grade. Rubrics give students an understanding of the meaning behind the grade.

As more and more teachers use performance assessments and develop rubrics, they are sharing what they have developed with each other. Many school districts now have sets of common scoring rubrics that may be used throughout a grade level or department, throughout a school, or throughout a school district. As a result, the use of rubrics has helped educators create some standards about which many teachers can agree and can share.

Self-Assessment and Peer Assessment Using Rubrics

With rubrics to guide them, students are more likely to produce higher quality work. They understand what excellent work looks like. They know what the criteria are for this level of work. They are able to see concrete ways to improve their work in order to meet the higher standards.

Ultimately, students will internalize the criteria in an existing rubric as they work on a product or performance and these expectations will be part of their personal repertoire.

Students may also use these rubrics to evaluate their own work, either to check on quality before it is turned in or as a self-assessment. Sometimes two grades may go in the grade book – the student's self-assessment using a rubric and the teacher's assessment using the same rubric.

The same is true for peer assessment. Students can use rubrics to assess the work of others. For example, when students read and critique each other's work before it is turned in, rubrics help them give specific and helpful feedback to their classmates.

For more information on self-assessment and peer assessment, see Chapter 7 entitled "Reporting and Documenting Student Progress."

Types of Rubrics

As the two teachers in the opening vignette discovered, the language surrounding rubrics can be overwhelming. The need for semantic clarity is still as critical today as it was then.

To begin with, all rubrics are **instructional** rubrics. Students learn from them. By outlining product expectations and assessing how well the student met those expectations, rubrics provide students with important guidelines for improving their work. From this point on, though, rubrics can differ with regard to their function, their structure, and/or their focus.

Developmental vs. Summative Rubrics

While all rubrics are instructional and all assess student work according to a given set of criteria across a spectrum of performance levels, a rubric has one of two different functions. A **developmental rubric** focuses on the strengths and weaknesses of student work and directs student growth. It operates in the nature of a critique. A **summative rubric**, on the other hand, evaluates student products and performances in order to determine a quantitative measure. This type of rubric operates as a scored rating scale.

Developmental rubrics are designed to give students a better idea of where their work falls along a continuum of developmental possibilities for each of several criteria. Levels of achievement are labeled in a way that reflects developmental stages. Is this student still a Novice at this skill? Or does his work indicate that he's operating at an Expert level? When the overall purpose of the assessment is to guide students, to help them recognize their strengths as well as their weaknesses, developmental rubrics work well.

Below is an example of a developmental rubric for a map project that infuses humor into an assessment process that directs as well as assesses.

MAP RUBRIC

Name: Date:

CRITERIA		We need to talk	On the right track	Now you're there!
	Title	Title lacks all the needed items: color, size needs to be improved, center title	Title is missing 2 of the needed items: color, size, centered	Title is centered, sized appropriately, and colorful
	Map Key	Map key is unorganized, difficult to read, lacks color, lacks compass rose, needs more details	Map key is missing 2 of the needed items: organization, readability, color, compass rose, details	Map key is well organized, readable, colorful, detailed, and includes a compass rose
	Land Forms	Landforms lack color and labels; not in the correct location	Landforms lack 2 of the needed items: color, labels, proper location	Landforms are appropriately colored and accurately labeled and placed
	Cities	Cities lack correct placement, symbol indication, and label; less than 3 per state	Cities lack 2 of the needed items: correct placement, symbols, labels, and 3 per state	At least 3 cities are placed correctly with accurate labels and symbols
	Appearance	Map is sloppily drawn, illegible, lacks color, and done on crumpled, lined notebook paper	Map is lacking 2 of the needed items: careful drawing, legibility, color, and clean white paper	Map is colorfully and legibly drawn on a clean white paper. All features are clearly labeled.

Developmental rubrics, in not carrying the weight of points and grades, can be far less threatening to students. They are far more likely to analyze what the rubric tells them about their work when they are not blinded by "The Grade."

These rubrics can be important sequential steps in ongoing portfolio assessment. A student can "watch" her writing skills improve, for example, as improved pieces of writing result in movement across a developmental rubric from Novice Writer to Distinguished Writer.

Developmental rubrics are also effective peer assessment tools. Without assigning a "score" to the evaluation, students can reflect on one another's work more constructively. The critique compliments accomplishments and gives direction for improvements.

While summative rubrics also give students an idea of where their work falls along a developmental continuum, these rubrics carry the dual purpose of also establishing some quantitative measure of the product or performance. This usually involves deriving a score from some kind of point scale which can be converted into a grade for reporting purposes.

Summative rubrics help alleviate the accountability pressure that accompanies the assessment of products and performances that do not have clear-cut right and wrong answers. The establishment of product criteria and the assignment of points to different levels of performance make communication between all parties infinitely smoother. Not only do students and parents know what to expect, but teachers are less likely to be swayed by more subjective impressions. It is easier to stay focused on the specific learning goals theoretically being addressed by the product.

On the next page is an example of a summative rubric for a time line project. Along with the articulated, developmental stages are point values from which can be determined a quantitative measure of student performance.

TIME LINE RUBRIC

Name: Date:

		Absent	NSH	Good	Excellent	
		0	1	2	3	4
C R I T E R I A	**Time line events**	No events on time line	Between 8 -12 events; events may not be in order	Majority of significant events listed in correct order	All significant events listed in correct order	All events creatively discussed and listed in correct order
	Details on events	No details listed for any events	Names, dates, and basic definitions given for some of the events	Names, dates, and definitions show understanding of these events	Names, dates, definitions, and cause/effect relationships are explained well	Names, dates, definitions, and cause/effect relationships explained thoroughly
	Time line design	Sloppy use of materials, no design plan, hard to follow	Design plan evident but visually confusing ; some graphics; somewhat careless use of materials	Design plan is visually appealing and does not detract from events; neat use of materials	Use of color and graphics enhances the visual appeal of time line; draws attention to events; neatly done	Visually creative and dramatic, design catches one's attention and focuses it on the time line events
	Grammar and spelling	More than 10 errors	7 to 10 errors	3 to 6 errors	1 to 2 errors	Flawless
	Getting ready	No work done outside of class	Some notes or materials ready for class	Complete notes for entire project ready at beginning of class	Complete notes and materials for entire project ready for use in class	Complete notes, original design ideas, and all materials (including extras) ready for class
	Points					
	Total points			Grade		

Comments:

13-15	A
10-12	B
7 - 9	C
4 - 6	D
0 - 3	F

Holistic vs. Analytic Rubrics

While developmental and summative rubrics address the function of the rubric, the terms **holistic** and **analytic** refer to the structure of the rubric.

In a **holistic rubric**, the list of performance expectations is articulated and rated for different levels of proficiency. Comparable levels of accomplishment for the different criteria are grouped together. The student then receives a single rating based on a "best fit" approach to the overall quality of his or her work.

Using the following Solar System holistic developmental rubric, students will be ranked as Jr. Astronauts, Astronauts, or Sr. Astronauts depending on the **overall** quality of their posters.

Holistic rubrics look good until they are used. What happens when Fred, who can talk about his planet all afternoon, fielding questions like a NASA pro, turns in a highly creative 3-D poster that reflects his inability to spell conventionally much of the time or to construct viable sentences with predictability? Does it do Fred any good to be "demoted" to Jr. Astronaut because his writing skills are not yet up to par? Does that in any way reflect and support what Fred **does** know and does so well? Should his strengths or his weaknesses be highlighted by this "best fit" approach?

The Solar System Project
Requirements and Scoring Rubric

Design a poster to show one of the planets in our solar system.

The completed project will be evaluated as follows:

Sr. Astronaut Award
- Use of five or more colors in the drawings
- 3-D parts to the display
- Accurately labeled
- Detailed factual information included
- Additional information about the solar system included
- Most words spelled conventionally
- Writes grammatically correct sentences
- Material was memorized for presentation
- Answered questions confidently and accurately

Astronaut Award
- Three to four colors in the drawings
- Accurately labeled
- Three to four facts about planet included
- "Kid-spells" a lot of words
- Correctly uses periods and capital letters
- Information was read during presentation
- Answered many questions well

Jr. Astronaut Award
- One to two colors in the drawings
- Not all labels accurately done
- One to two facts about planet included
- "Kid-spells" many words
- Lacks periods and capital letters
- Information was read during presentation
- Answered a few questions well

In contrast to the holistic approach, the **analytic rubric** divides and conquers. The list of product or performance criteria is set up in a grid so it can be paralleled by an articulated rating scale that clearly defines levels of proficiency. Each criterion is followed by a scale that carefully delineates performance expectations at every level. Now each criterion can be rated separately for level of proficiency.

An analytic developmental rubric for Fred's solar system poster would look like the one below. Using this analytic rubric, a teacher can easily show that while Fred is functioning at a Jr. Astronaut level when it comes to his writing skills, his ability to comprehend information and his communication skills are clearly Sr. Astronaut level skills! From this assessment, Fred receives the accolades he deserves for work well done and skills well honed. At the same time, his writing deficiencies are not glossed over, but also brought to his attention. Nor, in a reversal of that, are his strengths ignored due to concerns about his weaknesses.

Solar System Project Rubric

Name: Date:

CRITERIA		Jr. Astronaut	Astronaut	Sr. Astronaut
	Poster	One or two colors used	Three or four colors used	Five or more colors used; 3-D parts
	Labels	Not all labels are accurate	Most labels are accurate	All labels are accurate
	Content	One to two facts about planet included	Three to four facts about planet included	Detailed factual information included
	Spelling	"Kid-spells" many words	"Kid-spells" a lot of words	Most words spelled conventionally
	Grammar	Lacks periods and capital letters	Correctly used periods and capital letters	Writes grammatically correct sentences
	The Talk	Information read from poster; answered a few questions well	Information read from poster; answered many questions well	Information memorized for presentation; answered questions confidently and accurately

What happens when a quantitative measure is needed for record-keeping? In the **analytic/holistic rubric**, each criterion is still broken out and rated independently of the other criteria. However, each articulated level of proficiency has been assigned a point value so that one cumulative, holistic score can be determined for the product or performance. Now Fred's Solar System Project Rubric will look like the one below.

Solar System Project Rubric

Name: Date:

CRITERIA		Jr. Astronaut 1	Astronaut 2	Sr. Astronaut 3
C	Poster	One or two colors used	Three or four colors used	Five or more colors used; 3-D parts
R	Labels	Not all labels are accurate	Most labels are accurate	All labels are accurate
I	Content	One to two facts about planet included	Three to four facts about planet included	Detailed factual information included
T	Spelling	"Kid-spells" many words	"Kid-spells" a lot of words	Most words spelled conventionally
E	Grammar	Lacks periods and capital letters	Correctly used periods and capital letters	Writes grammatically correct sentences
R I A	The Talk	Information read from poster; answered a few questions well	Information read from poster; answered many questions well	Information memorized for presentation; answered questions confidently and accurately
	Points			
	Total Points		Level/Grade	

Jr. Astronaut   6 - 8 points   C
Astronaut   9 - 14 points   B
Sr. Astronaut   15 - 18 points   A

While any analytic rubric that generates one overall rating or grade is technically an analytic/holistic rubric, in the interest of simplicity, **any rubric in which each criterion or learning standard stands alone for assessment will from this point on be referred to as an analytic rubric.**

In the Solar System Project example, each criterion carries the same weight in the final scoring. Analytic rubrics, however, can be weighted to favor certain criteria. See the **Writing Assessment** on page 209 for an example of weighted criteria.

Complex vs. Simple Rubrics

In a perfect world where time and resources are unlimited, developing complex analytic rubrics would be a given. A complex analytic rubric is the completely articulated rubric with all the levels of proficiency clearly defined. Teachers would have multiple versions of these rubrics, differentiated to meet the proficiency levels of any student group. Every product and performance would have its own well-defined, structurally sound complex analytic rubric as part of an educational environment promoting authentic learning and assessment.

While this scenario is certainly one with great appeal, it is, of course, not realistic. Teachers do not have unlimited time and resources. Many don't have enough time for what's on their plate already, much less to consider writing out fully articulated complex rubrics. To bridge the gap that can exist between no rubrics and complex analytic rubrics, simple analytic rubrics are an answer.

A simple analytic rubric has the same list of criteria as a complex analytic rubric and range of levels or rating scale, but the levels of proficiency for each criterion are not articulated or defined. While obviously not as precise or definitive as the complex analytic rubrics, simple analytic rubrics are a viable first step in the development of a comprehensive system of assessment rubrics.

One common practice among educators starting out with simple analytic rubrics is to define the elements of the criteria and to list those on the rubric. While still not as thorough as the complex rubric, this clearly sets product or performance expectations and the other levels of proficiency can be reasonably inferred.

What is important to recognize here is that while simple analytic rubrics may be only a stepping stone to a far more comprehensive assessment system, it can be the critical first step! In order to create even simple rubrics, learning objectives must be publicly established and expectations laid out. For many students, just having that much in black and white will dramatically change how they function.

Simple analytic rubrics can be grid-like in structure (see the simple analytic rubrics in the section on Teacher-Created Rubrics) or they may be more checklist in nature. As a list of expectations on which a teacher checks which criteria have been met, what behaviors have been observed, and what elements are present in student work, checklists are simple analytic rubrics. Take a look at the Daily Organization Checklist on the next page, a developmental simple analytic rubric.

Simple analytic checklists such as this Daily Organization Checklist on the following page are great tools for student self-assessment. They allow students the opportunity to examine their strengths and weaknesses concretely yet privately. From these, dynamic student profiles evolve that can be revisited and reassessed as students learn and mature.

The same checklists can also be used as summative simple analytic rubrics. Point values can be assigned in a variety of ways to generate either a holistic rating for the goals on the checklist or a single quantitative score for record-keeping purposes. For example, adding a scoring chart to the Daily Organization Checklist gives the line-by-line behavioral analysis a holistic focus for the day. See page 102.

The Study Skills Assessment checklist on page 104 goes beyond the simple "yes" or "no" of the Daily Organization Checklist, giving students the opportunity to rate themselves over a range of behaviors on a 1-4 scale.

Daily Organization Checklist

Name: _____   Date: _____

		Yes!	No
1.	Select lunch choice.		
2.	Turn in homework.		
3.	Give teacher any notes or forms.		
4.	Record assignments in notebook.		
5.	Complete journal entry.		
6.	Complete daily oral language activities.		
7.	Put materials not in use in desk.		
8.	Place materials for each subject on desk before lesson starts.		
9.	Store not completed classwork in front pocket of notebook.		
10.	Take home incomplete classwork tonight to finish.		
11.	Stack materials in desk neatly. No loose paper or materials are showing.		
12.	Place name on all assignments.		
13.	Collect assignments and place in subject file folder.		
14.	Place all books and materials needed for homework in book bag.		

Daily Organization Checklist With Points

Name: _____   Date: _____

		Yes!	No
1.	Select lunch choice.	____	____
2.	Turn in homework.	____	____
3.	Give teacher any notes or forms.	____	____
4.	Record assignments in notebook.	____	____
5.	Complete journal entry.	____	____
6.	Complete daily oral language activities.	____	____
7.	Put materials not in use in desk.	____	____
8.	Place materials for each subject on desk before lesson starts.	____	____
9.	Store incomplete classwork in front pocket of notebook.	____	____
10.	Take home incomplete classwork tonight to finish.	____	____
11.	Stack materials in desk neatly. No loose paper or materials are showing.	____	____
12.	Place name on all assignments.	____	____
13.	Collect assignments and place in subject file folder.	____	____
14.	Place all books and materials needed for homework in book bag.	____	____

SCORING
Count up all my **Yes!** answers.

0 - 3	Today I had some major problems being organized.
4 - 7	I was pretty well organized in some ways today but not many.
8 - 11	I was well organized in a lot of ways today, but I can still improve!
12 - 14	WOW! I had excellent organizational skills today!

Task-Specific vs. Unit Rubrics

> *Now that I've come up with twelve different product options from which my students can choose for their final project in our next unit, does that mean that now I also have to create twelve additional rubrics?!!*   -- Workshop Participant

With so much attention being directed toward developing differentiated product offerings for student expression, this question was bound to emerge. The answer depends on the purpose of the product or performance. If expertise at producing that particular product is the focus of the learning experience, then **task-specific rubrics** are needed. These rubrics concentrate on the elements of a singular product or activity, such as the **Map Rubric** or **Time Line Rubric** on pages 93 and 95. Such rubrics that carefully consider all the factors that determine the successful development of a specific product provide students with invaluable guidelines.

When product production is not the major focus of the experience, but the overall learning outcomes of a unit of study or lesson of instruction are, then a **unit rubric** will work best. In this case, the rubric addresses multiple tasks or items all leading to the same learning outcomes. Specific products are blended into the overall scheme of things being assessed.

The following two simple summative analytic unit rubrics are used to assess overall student performance in an Independent Study program. The **Independent Study Self-Evaluation Check/Points** (pages 105-106) is a student self-assessment tool that precedes a more formalized short answer evaluation tool (**In Perspective**). The parallel-structured **Independent Study Check/Points - Teacher Assessment** (pages 107-108) rubric is for teacher use. Since student product choice is a key factor in this program, keeping up with task-specific rubrics would most certainly be an overwhelming challenge. More importantly, though, while skilled and creative product production is certainly a goal, it is not the over-riding purpose or focus of the program. These unit rubrics make evident the equal importance of every step in the whole research process from planning to production. Student and teacher assessment rubrics are shared and discussed when major discrepancies emerge. This teacher has been struck, though, by the remarkable closeness of the two assessment tools at least 90% of the time over the past 10 years!

Study Skills Assessment

Rate yourself in each of the following study skills using the scale below.

1 = I almost always do this
2 = I use this skill most of the time
3 = I use this skill occasionally
4 = I almost never use this skill

_____ 1. I follow written directions.

_____ 2. I follow oral directions.

_____ 3. I listen and I understand what is being said.

_____ 4. I take notes when I listen to a lesson or lecture.

_____ 5. I take notes when I read the text or other written material.

_____ 6. I understand the material when I do reading assignments.

_____ 7. I keep my belongings well organized.

_____ 8. I can find my assignments after I have completed them.

_____ 9. I manage my time well.

_____ 10. I plan the steps in doing long-range assignments.

_____ 11. I know several good memorization techniques.

_____ 12. I know how to preview a chapter in a textbook.

_____ 13. I know how to study vocabulary in any subject area.

_____ 14. I set short-term goals.

_____ 15. I set long-term goals.

_____ 16. I can concentrate on what I'm supposed to be studying.

_____ 17. I work without interruptions.

_____ 18. I can write an organized paragraph.

_____ 19. I proofread my written work.

_____ 20. I know how to use many different sources in research.

_____ 21. I use the Internet when I do research.

_____ 22. I take notes from many sources when I do research.

_____ 23. I know how to read and produce maps, charts, and graphs.

_____ 24. I know how to study for an objective test.

_____ 25. I know how to study for an essay test.

_____ 26. I can produce a project or product which shows what I know.

Look at the items you scored 1 or 2. Which study skills are you best in?

Look at the items you scored 3 or 4. Which study skills need improvement?

INDEPENDENT STUDY
SELF-EVALUATION CHECK/POINTS

Name: _____ Date: _____

Here's a worksheet to help you grade your work.
You'll need the grade for *In Perspective*.

I will be using these same criteria to grade your work.

GRT	= *great*
G	= *good*
OK	= *okay*
NSH	= *not so hot*
N/A	= *not applicable*

Title:	N/A	NSH	OK	G	GRT

Stage 1: Developing a Plan

	N/A	NSH	OK	G	GRT
I picked a subject in which I'm really interested					
I thought of lots of topics to research (bubble chart)					
I knew how I wanted to present my information					

Stage 2: Researching the Topic

	N/A	NSH	OK	G	GRT
I found many sources of information on my topic					
I read a lot of information about my topic					
I developed spec sheets and/or notepak for notes					
I took lots of notes on my topic					
I gathered real data (surveys, interviews, experiments)					
I developed many ideas for creative writing					
I learned a lot about my topic					

Stage 3: Presenting the Information

	N/A	NSH	OK	G	GRT
I organized my information well for presentation					
My final product is well written					
My final product is neatly done					
My presentation shares well what I learned					

	N/A	NSH	OK	G	GRT

GRT = *great* G = *good*
OK = *okay* NSH = *not so hot*

Stage 3 (continued)

	N/A	NSH	OK	G	GRT
My presentation shares a lot of good information					
My bibliography is written correctly					
I met the terms of my contract (I did what I planned)					

Time Management

	N/A	NSH	OK	G	GRT
I paced my activities responsibly (I did not leave everything until the last minute)					
I used my time in class well					
I used my time at home well					
I had realistic goals for the time available					
I met the terms of my contract (I was done on time)					

Work Habits

	N/A	NSH	OK	G	GRT
I worked well independently					
I knew what needed to be done and did not wait to be told					

Performance Evaluation:

Add up the checks in each column:

		x1	x2	x3	x4
Multiply:		x1	x2	x3	x4
Total:		=	+	+	+

Suggested grade considerations:

GRT	(great)	....	76-96	....	A
G	(good)	....	54-75	....	B
OK	(okay)	....	32-53	....	C
NSH	(not so hot)	...	0-31	....	D

My grade for this independent study:

INDEPENDENT STUDY CHECK/POINTS
— TEACHER ASSESSMENT —

Here are the criteria which I used to determine your grade.

Name: _____

Grade level: _____ Date: _____

GRT	= *great*
G	= *good*
OK	= *okay*
NSH	= *not so hot*
N/A	= *not applicable*

Title:	N/A	NSH x1	OK x2	G x3	GRT x4

Stage 1: Developing a Plan

Picked a topic of real interest ....

Thought of lots of topics/ideas to research (bubble chart)

Developed an effective presentation plan ....

Stage 2: Researching the Topic

Found many sources of information on topic ....

Read a lot of information about topic ....

Developed spec sheets and/or notepak for notes ....

Took/highlighted lots of notes on topic ....

Gathered real data (surveys, interviews, experiments)

Developed many ideas for creative writing ....

Clearly learned a lot about topic ....

Stage 3: Presenting the Information

Organized information well for presentation ....

Presentation shared effectively what was learned .....

Information shared was accurate ....

Developed presentation components comprehensively

Presentation was well written ....

Presentation was neatly done ....

Over

107   ©2001 Pieces of Learning

	N/A	NSH	OK	G	GRT	
Subtotals from Stages 1 and 2						

Stage 3 (continued)   *Subtotals (p. 1)*

	N/A	NSH	OK	G	GRT	
Presentation was creatively done						
Bibliography was written correctly						
Met the terms of contract (did what was planned)						

Time Management

	N/A	NSH	OK	G	GRT	
Paced activities responsibly (did not leave everything until the last minute)						
Used time in class effectively						
Used time at home effectively						
Had realistic goals for the time available						
Met the terms of the contract (was done on time)						

Work Habits

	N/A	NSH	OK	G	GRT	
Worked well independently						
Organized and directed own responsibilities well						

Performance Evaluation: **Totals**

Grading scale (based on weighted points, not percentages):

* _____/88 - _____/104 .... A
_____/63 - _____/ 87   .... B
_____/38 - _____/ 62   C
_____/25 - _____/ 37   .... D

* Scale adaptation for _____ N/A items.

Grade for this independent study:

Teacher Reflection Page

Which units or lessons that you teach as a part of your curriculum could you assess more effectively with a summative analytic unit rubric? Jot down some possibilities.

Which skills that you teach would be best supported by a developmental analytic task-specific rubric? Jot down a few possibilities below.

Which products or performances that you expect your students to develop would be best guided through the use of analytic task-specific rubrics? List some possibilities.

For which products, performances, or units of study could you list the essential learning outcomes right now? Choose two, then list them and their outcomes below.

A.	B.
1.	1.
2.	2.
3.	3.
4.	4.

This is the beginning of two simple analytic rubrics. You're on your way!

Chapter 9
Writing Rubrics
Well, I'd Do It If I Just Knew How.

"I can't believe this," Leslie, an 11th grader, confided to her best friend. "I didn't have time to do that project for English class, so I just turned in a project I had done for history last year. I thought it might be okay since both of them were to be about the Civil War. Last year this project got a B-. Now this year my English teacher gave the same project an A. I'm happy with my grade, but it doesn't make sense. I wonder how they come up with these grades anyway?"

As the above vignette indicates, when teachers grade a student performance or product, the grade on the same product can vary greatly depending upon which teacher graded it or even upon the mood the teacher was in when the grading took place. Many teachers admit that they may grade the exact same paper differently if looking at it at different times. It is not an exaggeration to say that without specific criteria that can be used as the basis for grading or scoring a piece of student work, it is possible that grades on the same piece of work could range from A to D or F!

This happens because teachers differ in their views about which elements of the product are most important. If teachers themselves are unclear about what constitutes a poor, fair, good, or excellent piece of work, how are students to know what a quality product is? Students who don't understand how they will be assessed don't know what to aim for and can never be sure if they have produced a good piece of work or not. Furthermore, unless they get some very specific feedback about how to improve, they will not produce a better piece of work the next time!

Developing sets of rubrics is a complex and time-consuming task. The first step is to come up with valid and relevant criteria. Nearly all student projects, products, and performances could be assessed in a multitude of ways. It is up to the teacher to determine the significant learning outcomes for each piece of student work. Being clear on what the learning outcomes are invariably will lead the teacher to decide which criteria should be used in the rubric to best show if these learning outcomes have been met.

Pre-established product/performance criteria have been a missing link for years! How often have teachers opened exciting learning opportunities for students by allowing them to demonstrate their content knowledge through a variety of product choices, assumed the students understood the "oh-so-obvious" product expectations, and were then doomed to disappointment by uncreative dioramas, missing labels, and poorly designed brochures? Pre-establishing criteria that clearly outline expectations is a critical piece of the learning experience. It provides a focus and direction for the student and it also gives the teacher a fair and concrete way to assess what each student does. This is the vital first step in creating effective rubrics.

Rubrics usually have:
- Criteria (dimensions of a product being evaluated) to be examined
- A scale of different possible points or developmental stages assigned for varying degrees of mastery, proficiency, or quality
- Descriptors for assessing each of the dimensions and finding the right place on the scoring scale to which a particular student's work corresponds

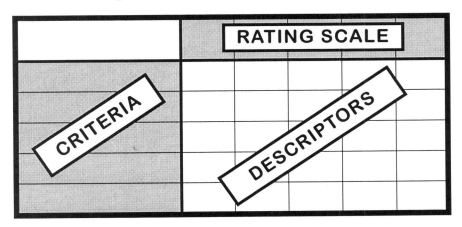

Developing Criteria

Begin writing rubrics by brainstorming all possible criteria to consider in assessing stated learning outcomes. Next, it is essential to pare that list down or to combine items in order to choose 4-5 assessment criteria for each product or performance.

Are there certain criteria that are consistent from one product to another, such as, neatness or writing mechanics, that your district wants consistently emphasized across the curriculum? If so, establish district standards ("that which is uniform") by developing standard criteria for those. As students recognize recurring expectations, consistency across the curriculum in their work will follow. It is also important to reinforce the notion that certain things are **always** important regardless of subject matter!

One school district includes two standard criteria on its rubrics wherever and whenever it can. One has to do with writing conventions or mechanics which covers correct spelling, correct grammar and punctuation, and use of complete sentences. The other deals with appearance (or neatness) and that covers legible letter forms, effective word and letter spacing, clean corrections, and a clean paper.

Use the form on the next page, **Criteria for Assessment of Student Products & Performances**, to record learning outcomes and criteria for several of your students' products and performances.

Following that form, there are four pages of sample lists of criteria on cards for a wide variety of products and performances. Use these for quick reference or as a way to start your thinking in generating your own criteria.

©2001 Pieces of Learning

Criteria for Assessment of Student Products & Performances

Project/Product/Performance: _____

Essential Learning Outcomes: _____

_____

Assessment criteria:

1. _____
2. _____
3. _____
4. _____

Project/Product/Performance: _____

Essential Learning Outcomes: _____

_____

Assessment criteria:

1. _____
2. _____
3. _____
4. _____

Project/Product/Performance: _____

Essential Learning Outcomes: _____

_____

Assessment criteria:

1. _____
2. _____
3. _____
4. _____

Project/Product/Performance: _____

Essential Learning Outcomes: _____

_____

Assessment criteria:

1. _____
2. _____
3. _____
4. _____

Reproducible for teacher use.

Criteria Cards

Kinesthetic Products

Game

1. educational; accurate
2. challenging
3. understandable directions
4. visually appealing
5. well constructed

Mobile

1. balance
2. visual appeal
3. relevant to topic
4. creative use of materials
5. well constructed

Sculpture

1. mastery of medium
2. style
3. effectively communicates with viewer
4. visual appeal
5. well constructed

Dance

1. choreography
2. music
3. costumes
4. relevance
5. expertise

Mask

1. conveys desired information/message
2. materials
3. visual appeal
4. construction
5. creativity

Skit

1. script
2. content
3. costumes
4. set design
5. production flow
6. clarity and voice projection

Puzzle

1. challenging
2. relevant content
3. visually engaging
4. well made
5. educational

Diorama

1. realistic
2. content
3. representative materials
4. construction
5. originality
6. resources cited

Model

1. accurate representation
2. relevance
3. neatness
4. durability
5. visual appeal
6. creative use of materials

3-D Shapes

1. constructs 3-dimensional models
2. discovers & records number of faces, lines, and vertices on models
3. compares & contrasts models
4. illustrates findings on a chart

Criteria Cards   Technological Products

PowerPoint Presentation

1. content
2. visual design elements
3. links
4. educational
5. relevance
6. bibliography

Video

1. script/storyboard
2. educational/understandable
3. entertaining
4. flow of events
5. filming expertise
6. accurate timing

Computer Game

1. user-friendly
2. loads and runs smoothly
3. educational
4. accurate
5. visually appealing

CAD Project

1. clarity
2. design
3. relevance
4. informative
5. creativity

Database

1. organization
2. data
3. user-friendly
4. loads and runs smoothly
5. creativity and/or originality

Spreadsheet

1. organization
2. data
3. user-friendly
4. loads and runs smoothly
5. performs desired functions
6. originality

Web Page

1. user-friendly format; all links work
2. aesthetically appealing
3. credible information
4. meaningful content; useful
5. rich, multi-leveled informational source
6. engaging

Multimedia Presentation

1. variety of media
2. media competence
3. clarity
4. engaging
5. informative
6. creativity and/or originality

Photographic Essay

1. content
2. visual appeal
3. focused
4. balance
5. relevant
6. creativity

Electronic Survey

1. design
2. application
3. data interpretation
4. conclusion
5. communication

114

Newspaper Article

1. headline
2. lead sentence
3. topic sentence for each paragraph
4. 3 supporting sentences per paragraph
5. who, what, where, when, why, and how
6. spelling and grammar

Interview

1. appropriate questions
2. script
3. sequential
4. personal presentation
5. communication skills

Group Discussion

1. regular participation
2. relevant contributions
3. respects other opinions
4. identifies problems
5. clarifies questions

Speech

1. factual content
2. flow
3. clarity/voice projection
4. eye contact
5. body language/creative dramatics
6. time

Song

1. content
2. rhythm
3. lyrics
4. style
5. auditory appeal

Debate

1. debater provides relevant ideas
2. debater supports opinions with plausible evidence
3. debater supports with evidence from reliable sources
4. debater participates willingly & regularly

Brochure

1. content
2. organization
3. visual appeal
4. spelling and grammar
5. pictures

Poem

1. appropriate format
2. rich vocabulary
3. picturesque language
4. engaging/creative
5. spelling

Short Story

1. beginning, middle, and end
2. holds interest
3. spelling and grammar
4. appropriate setting
5. character development

Glossary

1. comprehensive range of terms
2. accurately defined
3. alphabetical order
4. legible
5. creative presentation

Cartoon

1. content
2. visual appeal
3. spelling & grammar
4. sequence
5. humor
6. originality

Time Line

1. title
2. chronological
3. important events indicated
4. well-plotted time spans
5. spelling & grammar
6. visually appealing; neat

Illustration

1. mastery of medium
2. balanced composition of values
3. balanced composition of shapes
4. craftsmanship
5. attention to detail
6. any text is legible
7. appropriate content

Graph

1. neat and legible
2. easy to understand
3. title
4. ruled measurements
5. data plotted correctly

Venn Diagram

1. accuracy
2. compares/contrasts
3. informative
4. organization
5. legible; neat
6. visual appeal

Visual Aid

1. content
2. creativity
3. drawing, color and/or form
4. labeling
5. spelling and grammar

Map

1. title
2. key/legend/compass rose
3. scale
4. content/labels
5. appearance
6. spelling

Advertisement

1. content
2. visual appeal/color
3. neatness
4. creativity
5. engaging
6. spelling and grammar

Outline

1. appropriate title
2. main topic phrase stated and properly denoted
3. supporting detail phrases clearly stated and properly denoted
4. neatly done
5. proper spelling

Quilt Pattern

1. symmetrical design
2. creative use of 4 colors
3. complementary colors
4. blend of geometric shapes
5. original design

Student Involvement

Teachers are not the only important players in the assessment game. Students need to learn how to gauge their own performances as well. To develop this awareness in them, have students involved in establishing the standards by which their products will be judged.

Start by showing the class examples of good work and good performances which they can contrast with poor examples. With the students, brainstorm the actual elements that make one product better than the other. From these lists of elements, show the students how to pull out a list of criteria for assessment.

The chart below shows an example of how students have done this comparative analysis. On the next page is a reproducible form for use with your students.

Criteria for Assessment Worksheet

Product: *Article for student newspaper*

Elements of Good Example	Elements of Poor Example
Words are spelled correctly	Many words spelled incorrectly
What it is about is understandable	Have no idea what they are trying to say
Is written in paragraph form	Is just lots of sentences with no paragraphs
Interesting to read	Boring and confusing
Can identify the main topic	Don't know what their main idea or topic is
The information is correct	Has things in it that aren't true

Criteria for Assessment

Mechanics and form
- Spelling
- Punctuation
- Paragraphs

Accuracy
- Facts are correct
- Opinions are clearly noted as opinions

Enjoyable and interesting
- You want to read it
- Some humor
- Unusual facts
- Story or examples

Clear and understandable
- Topics can be identified
- Reader can summarize what it is about

Criteria for Assessment Worksheet

Product: _____

Elements of Good Example	Elements of Poor Example

Criteria for Assessment

Establishing Rating Levels

The rating scale on a rubric establishes the levels of proficiency to which a student strives. Often these rating scales are simply numbered levels, with one usually representing the low performance end and the higher numbers indicating higher levels of proficiency. Sometimes labels, like **Poor, NSH (Not So Hot), OK, Good**, and **Excellent**, accompany the numbered scale giving even greater clarity to the rating scale.

Writers of developmental rubrics rely totally on labels for their rating levels since these rubrics aren't written with a quantitative summative measure in mind and therefore don't use numbers. Humor and creativity are often apparent in these rating scale labels. Here are some examples:

Sets of Rating Scale Labels

Strike-out! First base Second base Third base Home run Grand slam!	Not yet Rough draft Classroom publication Local newspaper *Time* magazine	Try harder next time! In progress! You could be the guide! The Board of Education should hire you!	Novice Apprentice Practitioner Proficient Distinguished Master Expert
Minimal Adequate Commendable Exemplary	Keep trying! You're getting there! Wow! You made it!	Keep practicing! Entertaining! You're ready for radio! You're ready for TV!	Not evident Working on it Almost There Accomplished
Minimal Acceptable Awesome WOW!	Get on the road On the right track Now you're there! Wow!	The Unfocused Writer The Experimenting Writer The Engaging Writer The Extending Writer	Needs more work In progress Mastered

A general recommendation when creating a rubric is to have a range of three to six steps. More than that becomes cumbersome not only to write but also to use. When there is an odd number of steps, it tends to be easier to drift into the midpoint rating -- not the best, not the worst, so must be in the middle somewhere. This is not always the most defining assessment. When an even number of steps is used, clearer decisions must be made near the middle of the range.

Writing Rubrics That Challenge

It is especially important to write rubrics that challenge high ability and gifted students. Criteria for assessment must be broad-based and demanding for these students. The challenge must be one that can be met and still be a motivator to learning something new, something with more complexity and depth. A rating scale can help in doing this by making sure there is an extension in the scale to indicate in-depth work that **exceeds** grade level expectations.

Many of the rubrics included in this book have been developed with this extension in mind. On some of them this is the 5 column and is labeled **Extension**. In others, where **Excellent** spans two columns, it is the column on the far right. See the examples on the next page. **This means that on these rubrics, the grade level expectations for an A are listed in the column to the left of the extension column.**

Teachers who differentiate their expectations for students with different abilities will find this extension column helpful for meeting the needs of their more capable or gifted students. The descriptors in this column should reflect more depth and greater complexity than the others. Sometimes this column has no descriptor other than a phrase such as "Wow me!" or "Over the top."

Not just the students of higher ability will benefit from the Extension column. There is always someone who gets really turned on by a class project and is motivated to go the limit! How is that reflected in a rubric with a ceiling at meeting grade level expectations? This column is needed to support any student whose work exceeds expectations.

Developing Descriptors

The next step is to describe verbally each of the levels of performance for each different criterion. Completed rubrics may look deceptively simple. However, finding the right language to distinguish levels of student performance is very difficult. It forces you to think about the purpose of the work and why you want the student to do it. Rubrics regularly undergo considerable readjustment after they are put to use and teachers see how they really work. It is almost impossible to write a perfect rubric the first time you attempt to write one!

> *A graduate student who was also a first grade teacher asked me to come to her classroom and look at the spider projects her students had created. When I walked into the room, I saw over 20 different models of spiders. Each was constructed from different materials and was unique in design and approach.*
>
> *A beautifully painted gold spider immediately caught my attention. "Wow!" I exclaimed. "This one is beautiful!" The graduate student replied, "That one received the lowest grade in the class." She then pointed out a messy one made by gluing two paper plates together. "This one got full credit," she said, bringing out her rubric to share. Several elements required by the rubric were not present in the gold spider, but the paper plate spider had everything. "Do you think this is the way the grades should have turned out?" the graduate student asked.*
> *-- College professor*

As the graduate student discovered, writing a rubric means that teachers have to think carefully and deeply about the kind of work they want from students. What does excellence look like in student products and performances? What is a mediocre piece of work?

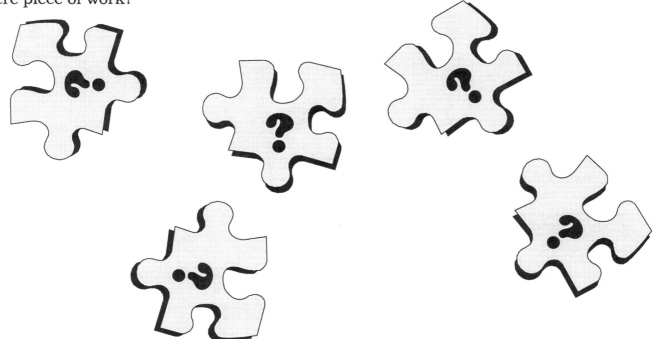

RUBRIC FOR _____

	1	2	3	4	5 Extension
C R I T E R I A					
				Grade Level "A" Expectations	Exceeds Expectations

RUBRIC

_____

	Absent	NSH	Good	Excellent	
	0	1	2	3	4
C R I T E R I A					
Points					
Total points				Grade	

Writing Descriptors

One way to write descriptors for rubrics is to use terminology such as **few, more, many,** and other comparative words. Be descriptive but stay away from language that may be **too** interpretive and subjective. That does not necessarily mean that all the descriptors need to be quantitatively based (e.g., 1-2 spelling errors, 3-5 spelling errors, 6 or more spelling errors). While being that specific has its advantages, it may prove labor intensive for the evaluator who must then carefully tabulate all the errors.

Here's a **generalized example** of what rubric descriptors might be like:

1 = The task was not attempted, or the purpose of the task was not addressed.

2 = Important purposes were not achieved; work needs redirection, more detail, or different strategies and approaches.

3 = For the most part, the purpose was completed.

4 = The purpose of the task was fully accomplished.

5 = The purpose of the task was fully achieved and **extended** beyond the task requirements (**exceeded** task expectations)

Notice the sequential accomplishment indicated by those descriptors -- from **not,** to **most,** to **fully,** and, finally, to **exceeded.** There are many ways to show these sequential levels of achievement on rubrics. Consider these comparative descriptors when developing a new rubric:

Comparative Descriptors

Never	Sometimes	Usually	All
None	Occasionally	Frequently	Always
Poor	Part	Most	Great
Ineffective	Some	Often	Completely
Nothing	Partially	Fine	Effective
Lacks	Minimal	Very	Consistently
Inappropriately	Incomplete	Good	Outstanding
Very little	Basic	Appropriately	Exceptional
Absent	Flawed	Thorough	Extremely
Rarely	Limited	Clear	Flawless
Flat	Little	Considerable	Full
	Barely	Essential	Achieved
	Inconsistently	Many	Elaborative
	Attempted	Sufficiently	Novel
	Few	Adequately	Extensive
	Vague	Competently	Superior
	Confusing	Proficiently	
	Superficial	Workable	
	Uneven	Acceptable	
	Inadequate	Satisfactory	

The best place to start writing descriptors for a rubric is to consider what students are expected to do in order to earn an **A** on their work. What are the characteristics of the exemplar, a really excellent example of the anticipated product? What are the grade level expectations for an **A**? Consider unique or creative performances and how to indicate these features. Consider well written, well constructed, and/or well produced pieces and how those accomplishments can be described.

Once the characteristics of the exemplar have been determined, the next step is to work backwards across the scale to the lowest level of achievement, carefully defining what the performance at each level will look like.

Rubrics MUST be written in language students can understand so they can be guided by them as they work. It is also very important to remember that what the rubric describes is what will drive the focus of instruction as well as what the students learn. Be sure to include everything that is important and be sure that everything you have included is important!

> *A conservative seventh grade math teacher tentatively approached me about the feasibility of having his high ability group of students create math games. When I strongly encouraged him to do so, he proceeded with the project. A couple of weeks later, he again approached me, this time grinning from ear to ear. "It's great," he crowed. "They're having a blast. They don't want to stop. And they're doing more math every day than I could have possibly assigned. I love this!" Pleased (and relieved) that this exploration was working so well for him, I asked how he had presented the idea to his students. He promptly shared with me a very concrete, detailed rubric that clearly outlined student expectations.*
> *-- Curriculum Facilitator*

Some teachers have asked if they should show their rubrics to their students before the work is turned in. OF COURSE YOU SHOULD! Students should see and understand the rubrics BEFORE THEY BEGIN their product or performance. When they have rubrics, not only do students have a much clearer understanding of what the teacher expects in their work, but many students find ways to improve their work even before they turn it in and before the teacher looks at it.

Grant Wiggins, an authority on assessment issues, suggests a good way to judge the quality of a rubric. He feels that if a student can score at the highest level in all of the criteria but the product or performance is not excellent, the rubric needs to be changed. This is a good "rule of thumb" to go by when creating and using rubrics.

Student Involvement

Just as they gained tremendous insight when they collaborated with their teacher to develop product and performance criteria, students will also gain insights when they participate in writing the actual performance descriptors. This is most easily accomplished when using simple analytic rubrics: the criteria have been established, the rating scale has been set up, but the descriptors are missing. First, work with students to develop descriptors for the exemplar only.

Brainstorm how the elements for an **A**-level product or performance should look. Having samples available of exceptional work may help students determine this performance level more effectively. Once the elements of the exemplar have been established, the other levels of achievement can be deduced even if they are not spelled out as concretely. If time allows, there is no reason not to expand this activity and develop a complete complex rubric with the students.

RUBRIC FOR _____

Name:

Date:

CRITERIA		Absent	NSH	OK	Good	Excellent	
		0	1	2	3	4	5

Brainstorm with the class a descriptor of the exemplar only.

Including students in this process of rubric development is a wonderful way of opening their eyes to performance expectations. This allows them the opportunity to take ownership in the assessment process — in the assessment of their own work! Standards become so much more meaningful as students better understand and can internalize the vision of success.

Quantifying Rubrics

Moving from developmental rubrics to summative rubrics involves simply adding points to the different performance levels. Start the scale with **0** points for the first column if the descriptors in that column reflect noncompliance with any of the criteria. However, if the descriptors in the first column reflect minimal compliance, start with a **1** instead.

Once points are assigned to different levels of performance, it is possible to determine a single summative score for the entire rubric. Consider the range of possible points and assign appropriate letter grades if letter grades are needed for assessment. Some teachers prefer simply to assign points to all activities throughout a grading period and then determine a letter grade on the cumulative total of points. If percentages are the required form of record-keeping, determine the rubric points and applicable letter grade. Working from the letter grade, assign the appropriate percentage. If, for example, Fred earns 27 points on his project which gives him a **B+** on the rubric grading scale, his grade book percentage could be 88% (if an **A** is 90% and a **B** is 80%).

If the column to the far right is being used to reflect work that exceeds grade-level or class-level expectations, remember that an **A** needs to be aligned with the total number of points that can be generated from work that meets the performance levels described in the column on its left. This does open up the opportunity for students to earn an **A+** on their work.

Rubrics can also be weighted if there are some criteria that are more important indicators of learning outcomes to be met. This is easily done when using simple checklist-style rubrics in which different amounts of points are assigned to the criteria. A good example of this is the **Mask Evaluation** on page 164.

If students are using a complex rubric, add scoring columns on the right side for tallying points. Point values can then be weighted accordingly as this example shows:

Rubric for _____

	1	2	3	4	Scoring	
C R I T E R I A — The more important learning outcomes are listed first and weighted the most.					×3	
					×2	
					×1	
					Total Score	

Student Involvement

One of the beauties of rubric use is the way it lends itself to student self-assessment and comparative student/teacher assessment. Many teachers have been leery of student self-assessment, especially when it involves a grade that affects the student's overall class grade or that appears independently on the permanent school record. Rubrics with all the criteria outlined, levels of performance described, and rating scales applied enforce considerable accountability on students. When faced with this type of well-delineated evaluation, students rise responsibly to the challenge and teachers need be far less worried about overblown student grades.

On a form like the one below, the student and the teacher can both record their assessments of the student's work. Discrepancies can then be discussed in a conference between the student and the teacher. Using a common language to discuss expectations and performance levels increases effective communication between the student and the teacher.

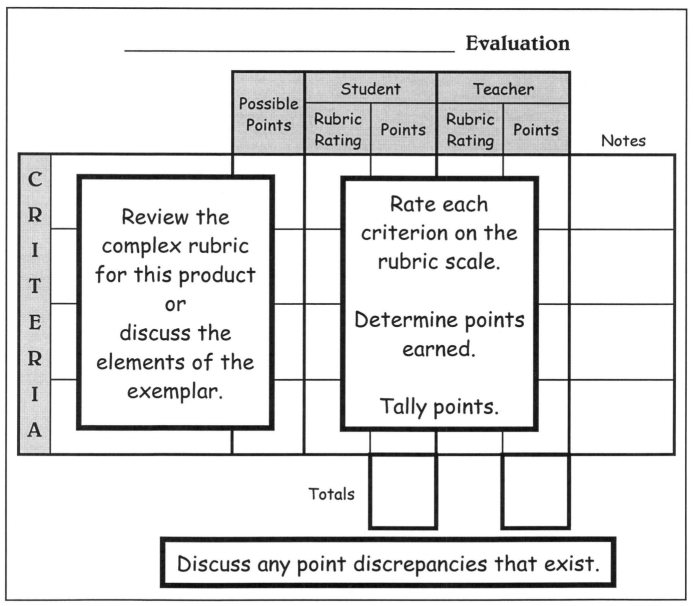

_____ **Evaluation**

		Possible Points	Student		Teacher		Notes
			Rubric Rating	Points	Rubric Rating	Points	
C R I T E R I A							

Review the complex rubric for this product or discuss the elements of the exemplar.

Rate each criterion on the rubric scale.

Determine points earned.

Tally points.

Totals

Discuss any point discrepancies that exist.

Creating Rubrics

On the following six pages are blank rubric forms for you to use for creating your own classroom rubrics. The first two are designed as developmental rubrics. The second two have summative points scales on them. The last two also include possible grading scales for converting points to grades. Have fun!

RUBRIC FOR _____

NAME: _____   DATE: _____

C				
R				
I				
T				
E				
R				
I				
A				

Comments:

RUBRIC FOR _____

Name: _____   Date: _____

	Absent	NSH	OK	Good	Excellent
C					
R					
I					
T					
E					
R					
I					
A					

Comments:

RUBRIC FOR _____

NAME: _____   DATE: _____

	1	2	3	4	5 Extension
C R I T E R I A					
Points					
Total points			Grade		

Comments:

RUBRIC FOR

Name: _____

Date: _____

CRITERIA	1	2	3	4	5 EXTENSION

Points _____ Total points _____ Grade _____

RUBRIC

Name: _____   Date: _____

	Absent	NSH	Good	Excellent	
	0	**1**	**2**	**3**	**4**
C R I T E R I A					
Points					
Total points			**Grade**		

Comments:

13 -15	A
10 -12	B
7 - 9	C
4 - 6	D
0 - 3	F

Reproducible for teacher use.

RUBRIC FOR _____

Name: _____   Date: _____

	Absent	NSH	OK	Good	Excellent	
	0	1	2	3	4	5
C						
R						
I						
T						
E						
R						
I						
A						

Comments:

0	1 2-7 8	9 10-15 16	17 18-23 24	25 26-31 32+	
F	D	C	B	A	GRADE

Reproducible for teacher use.
134

Chapter 10

Teacher-Created Rubrics and Other Assessments

Our thanks to teachers from all over the country for sharing their ideas!

Alphabet Rubric

Name:

Date:

CRITERIA		Not Evident	Working On It	Almost There	Accomplished
	Identifies uppercase letters of the alphabet out of sequence	Identifies 0-5 uppercase letters of the alphabet out of sequence	Identifies 6-20 uppercase letters of the alphabet out of sequence	Identifies 21-25 uppercase letters of the alphabet out of sequence	Identifies all 26 uppercase letters of the alphabet out of sequence
	Identifies lowercase letters of the alphabet out of sequence	Identifies 0-5 lowercase letters of the alphabet out of sequence	Identifies 6-20 lowercase letters of the alphabet out of sequence	Identifies 21-25 lowercase letters of the alphabet out of sequence	Identifies all 26 lowercase letters of the alphabet out of sequence
	Identifies letter sounds of the alphabet out of sequence	Identifies 0-5 letter sounds of the alphabet out of sequence	Identifies 6-20 letter sounds of the alphabet out of sequence	Identifies 21-25 letter sounds of the alphabet out of sequence	Identifies all 26 letter sounds of the alphabet out of sequence

Comments:

Animal Habitat Rubric

Name:

Date:

		Minnow 1	Flounder 2	Tuna 3	Shark 4	Whale 5 / EXTENSION
C	**Appearance** ◆ Neat ◆ Original ◆ Creative	• Display is not neat, original, creative, or colorful	• Display is neat and colorful but not original and creative	• Display is original and creative but not neat and colorful	• Display is neat, colorful, original, and creative	• Display enhances the presentation • Display uses a wide variety of color and unusual materials
R I T	**Content** ◆ Includes the animal (no plastic models) ◆ Includes food source ◆ Natural-looking environment	• Display does not contain the animal or food source • Environment does not look natural	• Display contains plastic animal • Food source is not properly displayed • Environment does not look natural	• Animal is original • Food source is displayed • Environment looks natural	• Animal is original and creative • Food source is displayed • Environment contains natural elements	• Animal is original and life-like • Food source is properly displayed • Environment is realistic
E	**Construction** ◆ 3-D display ◆ Shoebox size	• Not a 3-D shoebox-size display	• 3-D • Not shoebox-size display	• 3-D • Shoebox-size display	• Several areas displayed in the habitat • Shoebox-size	• Shows extensive levels of the habitat • Shoebox-size display
R I A	**Oral Presentation** ◆ Speaks clearly ◆ Projects voice ◆ Addresses audience	• Does not speak clearly, project voice, or address the audience	• Does not speak clearly or project voice • Addresses the audience	• Speaks clearly • Projects voice • Addresses the audience	• Speaks clearly with good voice projection • Focuses on audience • Maintains audience attention	• Addresses audience clearly; excellent voice projection • Demonstrates confidence • Maintains audience attention
	Points				**Grade**	

Total points

ARCTIC WEATHER FORECAST RUBRIC

Name: Date:

CRITERIA		Zero	One	Two	Three Top of the World!	
Arctic animal facts		No researched facts about animal adaptations	4 detailed, well researched facts about one Arctic animal, 3 of which relate to adaptations for winter survival	7 detailed, well researched facts about one Arctic animal, 4 of which relate to adaptations for winter survival	10 detailed, well researched facts about one Arctic animal, 5 of which relate to adaptations for winter survival	*YOU DISCOVERED THE NORTH POLE!*
Weather report		Lacks researched information about winter weather conditions in the Arctic Circle	Used teacher information to gain information about weather conditions in the Arctic Circle	Used print material to gain information about weather conditions in the Arctic Circle	Effectively used the Internet to gain detailed information about weather conditions in the Arctic Circle	*SEND IN YOUR RESUME TO THE LOCAL NEWS STATION!*
Illustration		No detail, no color, no labels	Illustration lacks two of the following: title, color, details, neatness, Arctic landscape background	Illustration lacks one of the following: title, color, details, neatness, an Arctic landscape background	Illustration has a great deal of color, details, neatness, an Arctic landscape background, and a title	*APPLY TO THE ART INSTITUTE!*
Presentation		Could not hear, no eye contact, no expressions	Presentation lacks two of the following: volume that everyone could hear, eye contact with audience, expression in voice that made presentation interesting	Presentation lacks one of the following: volume that everyone could hear, eye contact with audience, expression in voice that made presentation interesting	Presentation has volume that everyone could hear, eye contact with audience, expression in voice that made presentation interesting	*YOU HAVE A WAY WITH WORDS!*

Points

Your grade

Comments:

Student comments:

Ratings

12 - 9   Keen survival skills

8 - 5   Surviving the cold

4 - 1   On thin ice

Assembly/Speaker Behavior Rubric

Name: Date:

Circle and tally the points.	Yes!	Working on it	No
C R I T E R I A Sits properly in the seat during the lesson/speech/assembly	10 points	5 points	0 points
Stays quiet during the lesson/speech/assembly and is respectful of the speaker	10 points	5 points	0 points
Keeps hands and feet to oneself during the lesson/speech/assembly	10 points	5 points	0 points
Raises hands during appropriate times to answer questions during the lesson/speech/assembly. Claps at the appropriate time at the end.	10 points	5 points	0 points
Knows the answer to the mystery questions by listening attentively to the lesson/speech/assembly	60 points	50 points	0 points
Points			

Total score:

   ©2001 Pieces of Learning

Biographical Skit Rubric

Name: _____ Date: _____

CRITERIA	1	2	3	4	5 EXTENSION
Script	No script	Script is handwritten, illegible, and incomplete	Script is handwritten, legible, complete	Script is typed and complete	Script is typed, contains artwork, and a beautiful cover page
Biographical and Historical Information	Biographical and historical information is incorrect	Some of the biographical and/or historical information is incorrect	Biographical and/or historical information is correct but limited in depth	Biographical and historical information is accurate, has depth, and is relevant	Biographical and historical information is accurate, relevant, inspiring, and appropriately selected for an exciting skit
Costumes, Set Design, Production	No costumes, props, or set	Costumes not corresponding to historical period; props/set poorly made	Costumes correspond to period; props/set well constructed	Realistic costumes correspond to period; props add to the production	Costumes are beautifully selected; add realism and high interest to the production; props provide high interest
Oral Presentation	No eye contact; unintelligible oral presentation	Limited eye contact; intelligible oral presentation but not loud enough	Eye contact made; verbal presentation is clear	Good eye contact; speaks clearly; good projection	Speaks confidently; excellent body language; engages audience
Points				Grade	

Total points

Board Game Evaluation

Name:

Date:

		Absent	NSH	OK	Good	Excellent	
		0	**1**	**2**	**3**	**4**	**5**
C R I T E R I A	**TITLE** ◆ prominent, clear ◆ summarizes theme						
	CONTAINER ◆ adequate size ◆ sturdy ◆ thematically decorated/designed						
	BOARD ◆ sturdy ◆ uniform and adequate spaces ◆ eye-catching, thematic design						
	MARKERS ◆ adequate size ◆ easily distinguishable ◆ workable, sturdy						
	DIRECTIONS ◆ clear, easy to follow ◆ list materials needed						
	CONTENT ◆ accurate ◆ enhances knowledge ◆ comprehensive						
	CONVENTIONS (MECHANICS) ◆ correct spelling ◆ correct grammar and punctuation ◆ complete sentences						
	APPEARANCE (NEATNESS) ◆ legible letter forms ◆ effective word and letter spacing ◆ clean corrections						

Comments:

0	1 2-7 8	9 10-15 16	17 18-23 24	25 26-31 32+	
F	**D**	**C**	**B**	**A**	**GRADE**

Book of Leaves

Checklist for: _____

☐   Name written correctly on name line

☐   Cover colored neatly

☐   Cover illustrated with fall illustration

☐   Appropriate color leaves on correct page

☐   Appropriate number of leaves on correct page

☐   No glue mess

BROCHURE EVALUATION

Name: Date:

	Absent	NSH	OK	Good	Excellent	
	0	1	2	3	4	5
TITLE ◆ large, prominent, clear ◆ catchy, concise ◆ summarizes focus						
SUBTITLES ◆ adequate size ◆ concise, informative ◆ important words capitalized						
FRONT COVER ◆ title/s ◆ eye-catching, thematic design ◆ author						
BODY ◆ accurate data ◆ rich details ◆ comprehensive						
BACK COVER ◆ references listed in correct bibliographic format ◆ contact information						
ILLUSTRATIONS ◆ enhance knowledge of topic ◆ black ink or colored ◆ neatly drawn and/or trimmed						
CONVENTIONS (MECHANICS) ◆ correct spelling ◆ correct grammar and punctuation ◆ complete sentences						
APPEARANCE (NEATNESS) ◆ legible letter forms ◆ effective word and letter spacing ◆ clean corrections						

(Left margin vertical text: **CRITERIA**)

Comments:

0	1 2-7 8	9 10-15 16	17 18-23 24	25 26-31 32+	GRADE
F	D	C	B	A	

143

©2001 Pieces of Learning

RUBRIC FOR CELL PROJECT

Name: Date:

		Fair	Good	Excellent	Superior
		1	**2**	**3**	**4**
C R I T E R I A	**Describe basic cell structures**	Does not show basic knowledge of cell structures (less than 4 animal parts, 6 plant parts)	Describes at least 4 animal parts and 6 plant parts	Describes at least 6 animal structures and 8 plant structures	Describes all basic cell structures (9 animal; 11 plant)
	Explain functions of cell parts	Explains less than 4 animal functions and 5 plant functions	Explains at least 4 animal functions and 5 plant functions	Explains functions of at least 6 animal cell parts and 8 plant cell parts	Explains in detail function and relationship between each cell part (9 animal; 11 plant)
	Cell model/s	Poor use of materials, creativity, and effort	Adequate use of materials, creativity, and effort	Good use of materials, creativity, and effort	Outstanding use of material, creativity, and effort
	Compare/ contrast plant and animal cells	Not able to compare/ contrast	Incomplete compare/ contrast	Adequate compare/ contrast	Detailed compare/ contrast
Points					
Total points				Grade	

Comments:

CHILDREN'S STORY EVALUATION

Name: Date:

	Absent	NSH	OK	Good	Excellent	
	0	1	2	3	4	5
INTRODUCTION ◆ good beginning ◆ arouses interest						
BODY ◆ develops plot ◆ has complications, consequences, and climax						
ENDING ◆ satisfactory; no "loose ends" ◆ problem is open-ended and interpretative						
LANGUAGE ◆ age-appropriate ◆ stimulating use of vocabulary						
CHARACTERS ◆ appropriate ◆ developed physically and emotionally						
ILLUSTRATIONS ◆ relate to story ◆ colored pencil/marker or black ink ◆ neatly drawn and/or trimmed						
CONVENTIONS (MECHANICS) ◆ correct spelling ◆ correct grammar and punctuation ◆ complete sentences						
APPEARANCE (NEATNESS) ◆ legible letter forms ◆ effective word and letter spacing ◆ clean corrections						

(left vertical label: C R I T E R I A)

Comments:

0	1 2-7 8	9 10-15 16	17 18-23 24	25 26-31 32+	
F	D	C	B	A	GRADE

Classroom Behavior Evaluation

Student's Name: _____

Week of: _____

Parent's Signature: _____

Color the appropriate shape.	I did not do my best.	I did it much of the time.	WOW! I was one of the best!
I only spoke when it was my turn.	▭	♡	☆
I kept my hands and feet to myself.	▭	♡	☆
I did not disturb others during work times.	▭	♡	☆
I walked quietly and politely down the hall.	▭	♡	☆
I kept my area neat and clean.	▭	♡	☆
I was respectful and considerate of other people's feelings.	▭	♡	☆
Total	▭	♡	☆

My goal is at least _____ Stars & Hearts.

If I succeed at my goal, I will _____

_____

COMPOSITION RUBRIC

Name: Date:

Title:	Not Developed	Developing		Adequately Developed	Well Developed	Fully Developed
	0	**1**	**2**	**3**	**4**	**5**
FOCUS ♦ Issue clearly developed ♦ Position stated and maintained ♦ Easy to understand and follow	Focus is unclear or absent	Focus is confusing or shifts	Two or more positions without unifying statement	Bare bones; position clear; main point clear	Generally point of view is clear and maintained	All main points are specified and maintained
SUPPORT (Elaboration) ♦ Specific statements support position ♦ Details & examples explain statements	No support statements or details	Listing of statements or details	Some points are elaborated; list of related specific details	More points are elaborated	Most points are elaborated	All major points are elaborated with specific details
ORGANIZATION ♦ Knowledge of paragraphing clear ♦ Overall structure logically planned ♦ Transition words/sentences used	No plan	Plan is attempted	Plan is noticeable, but paragraphs not done correctly	Some connection between ideas; plan is clear	Most points are connected and flow logically using various transitions	All points are connected
CONVENTIONS ♦ Sentence structure ♦ Spelling, usage, omissions ♦ Capitalization ♦ Punctuation	Many errors; cannot read	Many major errors; lots of minor errors; confusing	Some major errors; poor sentence structure	Few major and minor errors; mastery of sentence structure	Only one major error	No major errors; one or two minor errors
INTEGRATION ♦ All parts evident ♦ All parts equally well developed	Does not present most or all features; too short	Attempts to address assignment; confusion	Partially developed; some or one feature not developed	Essentials present	Features present but not all equal	All features evident and equally well developed
APPEARANCE ♦ Legible letter forms ♦ Clean, straight paper ♦ Effective word & letter spacing ♦ Clean corrections	Messy; out of control; extremely difficult to read	Difficult to read; some effort is apparent	Some elements show control; fairly easy to read	Most elements are under control; easy to read	Letters are correctly formed and spaced; paper is neat, clean, clear, and presentable	

C R I T E R I A

Comments:						
	0	1	7	13	19	
		2-5	8-11	14-17	20-23	
		6	12	18	24+	
	F	**D's**	**C's**	**B's**	**A's**	**GRADE**

Cooperative Grouping Rubric

Name:

Date:

Group:

		Work Harder As A Group	Keep Up The Good Work!	What A Group!!!
C R I T E R I A	**Job Roles**	Did not perform job responsibility	Performed job responsibility to an extent	Fully completed job responsibility
	Listening	Never	Sometimes	Always
	Focus	Off task throughout activity	Off task at times	On task
	Participation	Refused to participate	Some participation	Full participation
	Attitude	Usually negative	Frequently negative	Usually positive

Comments:

CREATIVE WRITING CHECKLIST

_____ My story has a title: _____

_____ My name is on the composition.

_____ I indented the first paragraph and all the other paragraphs.

_____ My opening sentence is interesting.

_____ My story has a beginning, middle, and end.

_____ My story is well developed and organized so the reader will know what I have to say.

_____ I used descriptive words or phrases.
My two best descriptions are:

_____ I used words that appeal to my reader's sense of :
_____ smell _____ taste _____ hearing _____ sight _____ touch

_____ I included other rich details.

_____ My setting is well described.

_____ I used varied sentence patterns.

_____ Every sentence ends with a punctuation mark.

_____ Words are spelled correctly.

_____ I used three new words:_____, _____, _____

_____ My grammar construction is correctly done.

_____ I think my paper would be interesting to read.

_____ My most interesting sentence is:

Author's signature _____

Date _____

CREATIVE WRITING RUBRIC

Name: Date:

CRITERIA		1	2	3	4	5
Ideas ♦ Relate to topic ♦ Details		♦ Ideas do not relate to topic ♦ No details	♦ Incomplete ideas ♦ Few details to support ideas	♦ Ideas wander from topic ♦ Details support ideas	♦ Ideas relate to the topic ♦ Many details support ideas	♦ Original ideas and extensive details
Creativity ♦ Creative words ♦ Creative thoughts		♦ Creative words and thoughts not used	♦ Word choice does not evoke images ♦ No creative description	♦ Words used in an appropriate manner ♦ Creative descriptions	♦ Words evoke images ♦ Creative descriptions are used	♦ Words enhance creative thoughts ♦ Elaborate creative descriptions
Structure ♦ Beginning ♦ Middle ♦ End		♦ Beginning, middle, and end not evident	♦ Weak beginning, middle, AND end	♦ Weak beginning, middle, OR end	♦ Strong beginning, middle, and end	♦ Outstanding beginning, middle, and end
Mechanics ♦ Sentence structure ♦ Spelling ♦ Punctuation		♦ Poor sentence structure ♦ Excessive spelling and punctuation errors	♦ Sentences unclear ♦ Run-on or fragmented sentences ♦ Serious errors in spelling and/or punctuation	♦ Complete sentences ♦ Errors affect clarity of writing	♦ Complete sentences ♦ Errors do not affect clarity of writing	♦ Complex sentences ♦ Clearly written; easy to understand ♦ No spelling or punctuation errors
Points						
Total points					Grade	

Comments:

CROSSWORD PUZZLE EVALUATION

Name: Date:

CRITERIA		Absent 0	NSH 1	OK 2	Good 3	Excellent 4	5
C	**TITLE** ◆ reflects subject matter						
R	**TOPIC** ◆ clearly maintained throughout puzzle						
I	**WORDS** ◆ at least 20 words to be determined						
T	**CLUES** ◆ accurate ◆ informative ◆ reflect research						
E	**SPELLING** ◆ accurate						
R	**SOLUTION** ◆ given						
I	**BIBLIOGRAPHY** ◆ for sources of information used ◆ correctly written						
A	**APPEARANCE** (NEATNESS) ◆ legible letter forms ◆ effective word and letter spacing ◆ clean corrections						

Comments:

0	1 2-7 8	9 10-15 16	17 18-23 24	25 26-31 32+	
F	**D**	**C**	**B**	**A**	**GRADE**

CURRENT EVENT LOG RUBRIC

Name: Date:

	Fair	Good	Excellent	Score
	1	**2**	**3**	
Organization	Had summary of current event written on a loose paper with some of the necessary information.	Had current event in the notebook and wrote some of the information about the source but not all of it.	Put current event in notebook. Pasted in the article from the paper and included date or put the title of the TV story, date and time, name of news reporter, and channel it was on. Wrote a short summary of the article and a paragraph telling your opinion of the story.	
Included the W's	Only knew 1 or 2 of the W's. Reported on an old story.	Included at least 3 of the W's.	The summary included: <u>Who</u> the story was about. <u>What</u> it was about. <u>When</u> the event took place. <u>Where</u> it took place. <u>Why</u> it was in the news. It was a story that was reported within the last week.	
Location of News	Knew location of news story but could not locate it on the map.	Found location of news story on the map with difficulty.	Was able to show location of news story on the map quickly and easily.	
Story Interest	Story was not interesting or important and did not follow the week's assignment. Story was not appropriate.	Story was interesting and important but did not follow week's assignment.	Story followed week's assignment. Was interesting and important. Was appropriate.	
Oral Report	Too little practice to be able to tell the important W's of the story. Read the story. Did not appear to understand all the words, etc.	Told the story pretty well but did not tell all of the important W's. Oral presentation could have been improved with more practice.	An excellent job of telling the important W's of the story in his/her own words so everyone understood. Was easy to hear and understand.	

(Left side vertical label: CRITERIA)

Comments:

11	-	15	A
8	-	10	B
5	-	7	C
3	-	4	D
0	-	2	F

Total points

Grade for Current Events this week

Daily Written Language Rubric

Name:

Date:

	0	5	10	15	20	25
C R I T E R I A — *Grammar*	5 or more grammar errors	4 grammar errors	3 grammar errors	2 grammar errors	1 grammar error	0 grammar errors
Spelling	5 or more spelling errors	4 spelling errors	3 spelling errors	2 spelling errors	1 spelling error	0 spelling errors
Capitalization	5 or more capitalization errors	4 capitalization errors	3 capitalization errors	2 capitalization errors	1 capitalization error	0 capitalization errors
Punctuation	5 or more punctuation errors	4 punctuation errors	3 punctuation errors	2 punctuation errors	1 punctuation error	0 punctuation errors

Grading Scale: 100 - 90 A
89 - 80 B
79 - 71 C
70 D
Below 70 Re-do

Teacher or Student Comments:

Final Grade: _____

DEMONSTRATION SPEECH RUBRIC

Name: Date:

CRITERIA		Absent 0	NSH 1	OK 2	Good 3	Excellent 4	Excellent 5
	Knowledge of topic	none	very little understanding of topic; no facts	basic understanding apparent but confused	clear understanding of topic supported with some details	thorough understanding of topic supported with many details	exceptional understanding of topic related to other issues
	Organization	none	few steps explained; not well ordered	some steps explained; order makes sense	most steps explained and orderly	all steps orderly and well explained	clear, informative steps flow smoothly and orderly
	Time	less than 1 minute	less than 2 minutes	2-3 minutes	3-4 minutes	4-5 minutes	6-10 minutes
	Presentor ◆ can be heard	not at all	very little	some of the time	most of the time	all the time	well modulated and audible at all times
	Presentor ◆ makes eye contact	not at all	very little	some of the time	most of the time	all the time	animated and engaging use of eye contact
	Visual Aids	none	very few supplies provided; not used very effectively	some supplies provided; used somewhat effectively	most supplies provided; used pretty effectively	all supplies provided; used very effectively	extremely effective and creative use of all supplies

Points

Total points   Grade

Comments:

0	1 2-4 5	6 7-9 10	11 12-14 15	16 17-19 20+
F	D	C	B	A

DESCRIPTIVE WRITING RUBRIC

Name: _____ Date: _____

Describe a dilemma and how it was solved.

	1	2	3	4	5 — EXTENSION
C / R — **Organization** ◆ Events are listed in sequential order ◆ Introduction and conclusion are present ◆ Dilemma and solution are clearly presented	◆ Dilemma is described but there is no introduction, sequence, or conclusion	◆ Dilemma described ◆ Events are out of order ◆ Introduction and/or conclusion are not clear	◆ Dilemma described in sequential order ◆ Introduction and conclusion are clear	◆ Dilemma described with an elaborate list of sequential events ◆ Introduction and conclusion are clear	◆ Elaborate detail, an interesting introduction, and a clear conclusion ◆ Dilemma solved in a novel way
I — **Details** ◆ Sensory details are included ◆ Vivid, descriptive use of words is evident	◆ No evidence of sensory details in description ◆ Simple word choice	◆ Details include only one sensory mode ◆ Few descriptive details	◆ More than one type of sensory detail is included ◆ Some descriptive language is used	◆ Several sensory details are included ◆ Vivid, descriptive use of words ◆ Events clearly present dilemma and solution	◆ Exceptional use of sensory details used in novel ways ◆ Vivid, descriptive use of words engages reader ◆ Events present unusual dilemma/solution
T / E — **Mechanics** ◆ Free of grammatical, punctuation, and spelling errors	◆ Multiple errors in grammar, punctuation, and spelling interfere with presentation	◆ Some errors in punctuation, grammar, and/or spelling interfere with presentation	◆ A few errors in punctuation, grammar, and/or spelling that do not interfere with presentation	◆ Minimal errors in surface features ◆ Errors do not interrupt flow of the story	◆ No evidence of errors in spelling, grammar, and/or punctuation ◆ Excellent variety of uses of punctuation
R / I / A — **Fluency** ◆ Sentences are complete thoughts ◆ Sentences have varied patterns	◆ Many incomplete sentences or thoughts ◆ Sentences are not varied	◆ Some incomplete sentences ◆ Some evidence of varied sentence patterns	◆ Most sentences are complete ◆ Varied sentence patterns	◆ Smooth, natural, flowing complete sentences ◆ Many varied sentence patterns	◆ Interesting novel, detailed complete sentences ◆ Many unusual and varied sentence patterns
Points				Grade	Total points

Rubric for a Diagram

Name: Date:

	1	2	3	4	5 Extension
Labeling of parts	Did not label any parts	3 - 4 parts labeled correctly	3 - 4 parts labeled neatly and correctly	5 parts labeled neatly and correctly	Labeled more than 5 parts correctly
Originality	One dimension drawing	Three-dimensional shape drawn	Multiple 3-dimensional shapes drawn	Movable parts	Shows what the inside would look like, too
Materials	Only used regular lead pencil	Crayons were used	Markers were used	Paints were used	Unusual mix of art media and materials
Oral presentation	1 fact presented	2 facts presented	3 facts presented	Can identify and explain all parts	Presents extra research on topic

(Left vertical label: **CRITERIA**)

Points					
Total points			Grade		

Comments:

Friendship Book

Name: _____ Date: _____

Skill 1: Creative Cover
Your cover is colorful and theme-based.   _____

Skill 2: Table of Contents
The table of contents is imaginative and
accurately lists the contents of the book.   _____

Skill 3: Qualities of a Good Friend
Ten qualities of a good friend are listed in
alphabetical order. Each quality is defined.   _____

Skill 4: Photographs
You contributed a photograph of yourself with
a friend and wrote a caption for the photograph.   _____

Skill 5: "Dear Abby" Letter/s
Your letter describes a problem with a friend
and a solution to the problem.   _____

Skill 6: Friendship Games
Your game includes "friendship" words.   _____

Skill 7: Friendship Stories
Your story describes an experience involving a friend.
The story has a beginning, middle, and end.
Each paragraph has a topic sentence and at least four
supporting details.   _____

Skill 8: Cooperation
You worked well with the members of your group.
You contributed ideas and helped assemble the book.
You brought the necessary materials to class on time.   _____

©2001 Pieces of Learning

Geometric Shapes & Patterns Rubric

Name:

Date:

CRITERIA		Not Evident	In Progress	Accomplished	Exceptional
	Identifies basic geometric shapes (circle, square, rectangle, triangle, oval, and diamond)	Identifies 0-2 shapes	Identifies 3-5 shapes	Identifies all 6 shapes	Identifies other or composite shapes
	Sorts geometric shapes by attributes (shape, color, and size)	Sorts by 0-1 attributes	Sorts by 2 attributes	Sorts by 3 attributes	Sorts by more than 3 attributes
	Continues simple patterns	Unable to recognize the pattern	Recognizes and copies the pattern	Recognizes, copies, and extends the pattern	Creates a new pattern

Comments:

	Below		Meets	Exceeds

RUBRIC FOR GROUP PARTICIPATION

Name: _____   Date: _____

		ZIPPO	WEAK	OK	STRONG	WOW!!!
C	**On task**	Doing nothing	Doing a minimal amount of work	Doing some work and adding some suggestions	Doing your share of the work, adding suggestions, following directions, and did not waste time	MVP AWARD! Able to delegate work among all group members in a positive manner
R I T	**Positive Comments**	Being negative	Being neutral (not negative, but not praising), but listened to suggestions from others	Being positive about the activity and suggestions from other students and listening well	Being positive about the activity and suggestions from other students, listening well, and praising others	You are POSITIVELY wonderful!
E R	**Quiet Voice**	Using a voice not acceptable for indoors all the time	Speaking very loudly much of the time	Speaking just a bit too loudly some of the time	Using a voice acceptable for inside group work and not disturbing the class	You are now in the Library Hall of Fame! Able to lead others to be quiet in a positive manner
I A	**Teamwork**	Doing work by yourself and/or not talking to group members	Interacting very little with team members	Interacting much of the time with team members	Operating as a unified group	What a TEAM!! Encouraged members to be a group in a positive way and was fair to all members

GROUP PARTICIPATION ASSESSMENT

Class:

Grading Key:
- 0 ····· Never
- 1 ····· Barely
- 2 ····· Sometimes
- 3 ····· Frequently
- 4 ····· Usually
- 5 ····· Always

Students:	Works on group goals	Asks questions for group to consider	Supports a variety of answers w/o criticism	Demonstrates acquisition of concepts	Shows good listening skills	Insures everyone in group understands	Total Points
1.							
2.							
3.							
4.							
5.							
6.							
7.							
8.							
9.							
10.							
11.							
12.							
13.							
14.							
15.							
16.							
17.							
18.							
19.							
20.							
21.							
22.							
23.							
24.							
25.							

HISTORICAL MODEL RUBRIC

Name: Date:

CRITERIA		1	2	3	4	5
	Accuracy	No/slight resemblance to original object	Attempted to make a realistic model but minimal details	Model resembles original object, but design lacks details	Good resemblance to original object; has major details	Excellent resemblance to original object; many small details
	Creativity	Used only 1 kind of material to create model	Used 2 kinds of materials to create model	Used 3 or more kinds of materials to create model	Used an unusual variety of materials to create model	Created both the model and its setting using a variety of materials
	Durability	Poorly built; ready to fall apart	Cannot stand alone; needs extra support	Stands alone without support	Well built; can stand alone; can be moved without falling	Well built; can stand alone; has a strong structure to support details
	History of the Original	A summary paragraph copied from source	A summary with much of it copied from source	A summary with 2 accurate details written in student's own words	An accurate summary written in student's own words	A detailed summary written in student's own words
Points						
Total points				Grade		

Comments:

RUBRIC FOR HYPERSTUDIO PROJECT

Name:

Date:

Title:

CRITERIA		1	2	3	4	5 EXTENSION
	Content	Includes little essential information and one or two facts.	Includes some essential information with three or four facts.	Includes essential information with most sources properly cited. Includes enough elaboration to give readers an understanding of the topic.	Includes essential information with all sources properly cited. Elaborates throughout and includes details and raises questions.	Covers topic completely and in depth. Includes properly cited sources and complete information. Encourages the curiosity and the audience wants to know more.
	Buttons	No buttons move to designated cards with an effect. More than 3 buttons have problems with executing their commands.	Two buttons move to designated cards with an effect. No more than 2 buttons have a problem executing their commands.	Three buttons move to designated cards with an effect. A button has a problem executing its command.	Four buttons move to designated cards with an effect. At least three varieties of buttons are used. No buttons have problems.	All buttons move to designated cards with an effect. At least five varieties of buttons are used. No buttons have problems.
	Oral Presentation	Great difficulty communicating ideas due to poor voice projection. Little preparation or incomplete work.	Some difficulty communicating ideas due to voice projection. Some preparation evident.	Communicates ideas with proper voice projection. Adequate preparation and delivery.	Communicates ideas with enthusiasm, proper voice projection, appropriate language, and clear delivery.	Uses original approach effectively. Highly organized, well rehearsed, and uses vivid precise language. Ease in delivery techniques.
	Graphics	Only hand-drawn or imported graphics used in project. Less than two tools used.	Only hand-drawn or imported graphics used in project. Two tools used.	Hand-drawn and imported graphics used effectively in project. Four tools used.	Hand-drawn and imported graphics used effectively in project. Five tools used.	Hand-drawn and imported graphics used effectively in project. Six tools used and graphics used in other printing programs added.
Points						
Total points					Grade	

Learning Rhymes Rubric

Name: Date:

CRITERIA		1	2	3	4	5 Extension
	Recitation	Knows 1 verse	Knows 2 verses	Knows all verses	Recites with animation and expression	Recites an original rhyme
	Model Making	Construction paper and includes all characters in any order	On poster board and includes all characters in order	Creative materials, colorful, and original illustrations	In sequence original illustrations with some written words	Makes a mobile or other creative product
	Vocabulary Development	Identifies 1 to 2 animal words	Identifies all animal words	Identifies all animal words and action words	Identifies all animal, action, and rhyming words	Re-writes poem replacing rhyming, action, and animal words
	Dramatization	Cannot recite the entire poem	Recites with a minimum of hand motions	Recites using props, costume, and motions	Recites using props, costume, dramatic motions	Puts recitation to music or dance
Points						
Total points					Grade	

Comments:

Mask Evaluation

Name: _____   Date: _____

Shows patterns   (15) _____

Uses several shapes   (15) _____

Shows congruence   (15) _____

Shows symmetry   (15) _____

Shows: slides   (10) _____

           flips   (10) _____

           turns   (10) _____

Colorful   (10) _____

Total points: _____

Grade: _____

Rubric for a Magic Tricks Performance

Name: Date:

CRITERIA	1	2	3	4	5 EXTENSION
Organization ◆ Clear statement of purpose of trick ◆ Sequential steps in presentation	◆ Purpose of trick is not clear ◆ Steps are out of order ◆ Conclusion is not evident	◆ Purpose of trick is clear ◆ Sequence of steps is out of order ◆ Conclusion is not clear	◆ Purpose of trick is clearly stated ◆ Sequence of steps is logical ◆ Conclusion is evident	◆ Purpose of trick is clearly stated ◆ Sequence of steps is elaborate and logical ◆ Conclusion is clear	◆ Trick is original ◆ Presentation is clear, logical, and elaborate ◆ Conclusion is exciting
Props ◆ Materials needed to perform the trick are used	◆ No props are included	◆ Props are used but some do not work or aid the presentation	◆ Props are used appropriately	◆ Props are used effectively and enhance the presentation	◆ Props are original, handmade, and enhance the presentation
Oral Presentation ◆ Addresses the audience ◆ Speaks clearly ◆ Projects voice	◆ Does not address the audience, speak clearly, or project voice	◆ Addresses the audience, but does not speak clearly and/or project voice	◆ Addresses the audience ◆ Speaks clearly ◆ Projects voice	◆ Addresses the audience ◆ Speaks clearly with projection ◆ Maintains audience interest	◆ Addresses the audience clearly with excellent voice projection ◆ Shows confidence ◆ Involves audience
Physical Demonstration ◆ Audience can see the process clearly ◆ Trick is appropriately concealed ◆ Steps of process are sequential	◆ Audience cannot see the process clearly ◆ Trick is not concealed ◆ Steps are out of order	◆ Audience can see the process ◆ Trick is not concealed ◆ Some interruption in sequence of events	◆ Audience can see process ◆ Trick is properly concealed ◆ Not all steps in process are sequential	◆ Audience can see process clearly ◆ Trick is properly concealed ◆ Steps in the process are sequential	◆ All criteria are met ◆ Performance is captivating, exciting, and uses creative, dramatic gestures
Points					
Total points				**Grade**	

MATHEMATICAL PROBLEM SOLVING RUBRIC

Name: Date:

C R I T E R I A		**1**	**2**	**3**	**4**	**5** EXTENSION
	Conceptual Understanding	Shows no understanding of the problem's mathematical concepts and principles	Shows very limited understanding of the problem's mathematical concepts and principles; makes major computational errors	Shows understanding of some of the problem's mathematical concepts and principles; may contain serious computational errors	Shows nearly complete understanding of the problem's mathematical concepts and principles; uses nearly correct mathematical terminology and notations; executes algorithms completely; computations are generally correct but may contain minor errors	Shows understanding of the problem's mathematical concepts and principles; uses appropriate mathematical terminology and notations; executes algorithms completely and correctly
	Procedural Knowledge	Attempts to use irrelevant outside information; fails to indicate which elements of the problem are appropriate; copies part of the problem, but without attempting a solution	Attempts to use irrelevant outside information; fails to identify important elements; inappropriate strategy for solving the problem; solution process is missing or difficult to identify	Identifies some important elements of the problems, but shows only limited understanding of the relationships between them; solution process is incomplete	Identifies the most important elements of the problems and shows general understanding of the relationships between them; solution process is nearly complete	Uses relevant outside information of a formal or informal nature; identifies all the important elements of the problem and shows understanding of the relationships between them; gives clear evidence of a solution process; solution process is complete and systematic
	Communication	Communicates ineffectively; words do not reflect the problem; may include drawings which completely misrepresent the problem situation	Has some satisfactory elements but may fail to complete or may omit significant parts of the problem; explanation or description may be missing or difficult to follow; diagram is unclear and difficult to interpret	Makes significant progress towards completion of the problem; explanation or description is unclear	Gives a fairly complete response with reasonably clear explanations or descriptions; includes a nearly complete appropriate diagram; communicates effectively to the identified audience	Gives a complete response with clear, coherent, and elegant explanations; strong supporting arguments which are logically sound and complete; includes examples and counter-examples
	Points					
	Total points				**Grade**	

Money Rubric

Name:

Date:

		1 Point	2 Points	3 Points
C R I T E R I A	**Identifying coins**	Does not recognize coins	Recognizes a penny, nickel, dime	Recognizes a penny, nickel, dime, quarter, half dollar
	Counting money	Does not count coins accurately	Counts coins accurately yet unable to count higher than a dollar	Counts coins accurately and counts up to five dollars or higher
	Making change	Unable to make change	Makes change for amounts under a dollar	Makes change for amounts up to five dollars or higher

Comments:

Scoring

Points	Description
9	Exceeds Expectation
7 — 8	Excellent
5 — 6	Satisfactory
3 — 4	Needs Improvement

Newspaper Evaluation

Name: Date:

		Absent	NSH	OK	Good	Excellent	
		0	1	2	3	4	5
C	**VISUAL FORMAT** ♦ effective arrangement of parts — articles, photos, ads ♦ column-style arrangement ♦ logo						

R	**FORMAT OF ARTICLES**
	♦ headlines — relate to key words
	  in article
	♦ introduction — topic sentence
	♦ body — who, what, why, where,
	  when						

I	**CONTENT** ♦ variety of articles ♦ variety of ads ♦ photos, illustrations, and graphics appropriate to purpose						
T							
E							
R	**CONVENTIONS** (MECHANICS) ♦ correct spelling ♦ correct grammar and punctuation ♦ complete sentences						
I	**APPEARANCE** (NEATNESS) ♦ legible letter forms ♦ effective word and letter spacing ♦ clean corrections						
A							

Comments:

0	1 2-7 5	6 7-9 10	11 12-14 15	16 17-19 20+	
F	**D**	**C**	**B**	**A**	**GRADE**

Number Sense Rubric

Name: Date:

This student can:	Needs More Work	In Progress	Mastered
C Identify *equal* groups			
R Compare groups: identify *more*			
I Compare groups: identify *less*			
T Identify the *number of objects* in a group 1-10 and record it			
E Show the number that is *one more* or *one less*			
R *Label groups* of objects 1-10			
I *Order groups* of objects by number			
A Identify a *missing number* in a sequence			

C R I T E R I A

Optical Illusions Booklet Rubric

Name:

Date:

CRITERIA	1	2	3	4	5 EXTENSION
C — Drawings represent optical illusions • Traditional • Original	• Optical illusions are not evident	• Traditional illusions included • Original illusion is not clear	• Traditional illusions included and clear • Most original illusions are identifiable	• Several examples of traditional illusions included • Original illusions are all clear	• Optical illusions are detailed and varied • Exceptional use of original ideas
R I T E — Questions about and answers to optical illusions address the features to be identified	• Questions and/or answers are not included	• Questions and/or answers are presented for most illusions but some are not related	• Most questions and/or answers are included and related	• Questions and answers are there for all illusions • Questions present a challenge • Questions and answers are related	• Excellent, thought-provoking questions and surprising, original answers for all optical illusions
R — Organization • Table of Contents • Explanation of nature of illusions • Numbered pages • Questions on pages	• Booklet is not organized • Missing organization criteria	• Booklet is organized • Missing one or more parts	• Booklet is organized • All criteria included	• Booklet is organized • All criteria included • Several examples of illusions included	• Booklet is organized • All criteria included • Many varied and unusual optical illusions included
I A — Neatness • Optical illusions • Text	• Drawings and text are not legible	• Drawings and text are legible but not neat	• Drawings and text are neat, legible, but not centered	• Drawings and text are neat, legible, and centered	• Drawings are legible and neat • Text is typed and centered
Points				Total points	Grade

ORAL PRESENTATION RUBRIC

Name: Date:

CRITERIA	1 Point	2 Points	3 Points
Clarity	♦ mumbles ♦ rambles ♦ makes distracting noises	♦ moderate enunciation ♦ problems with speech patterns	♦ enunciates well ♦ speaks clearly
Demeanor	♦ no eye contact ♦ poor posturing	♦ fidgets ♦ inadequate eye contact	♦ addresses audience ♦ good eye contact ♦ exceptional posturing
Reading with expression	♦ no use of correct punctuation ♦ monotone	♦ occasional use of punctuation cues	♦ correct use of punctuation ♦ reads with excitement
Loudness and projection of voice	♦ whispers ♦ inaudible voice	♦ talks softly ♦ looks down	♦ speaks well so all can hear ♦ proper voice intonation
Points			
Total Points			

_____ Scale _____

Points	Description
1 — 3	Fair
4 — 6	Good
7 — 9	Excellent

ORAL PRESENTATION RUBRIC

Name: Date:

CRITERIA		1	2	3	4	5
	Organization	Audience cannot understand presentation because there is no sequence of information.	Student presents information in a sequence which audience can barely follow.	Student presents information in a logical sequence which audience can follow some of the time.	Student presents information in a logical sequence which audience can follow most of the time.	Student presents information in logical, interesting sequence which audience can follow all of the time.
	Eye Contact	Student reads all of report with no eye contact.	Student occasionally uses eye contact, but still reads most of report.	Student uses eye contact some of the time, but still returns to notes.	Student maintains eye contact almost all of the time but returns to notes one time.	Student maintains eye contact all of the time with audience and never returns to notes.
	Graphics	Graphics rarely relate to text and presentation.	Graphics relate to text and presentation in an adequate manner.	Graphics relate to text and presentation in a competent manner.	Graphics relate to text and presentation in a proficient manner.	Graphics explained and reinforce text and presentation in an exceptional manner.
	Subject Knowledge	Student has very little knowledge of the information and cannot answer questions about subject.	Student is not comfortable with information and is able to answer only rudimentary questions.	Student is at ease with expected answers to some of the questions, but fails to elaborate.	Student is at ease with expected answers to most of the questions and elaborates.	Student demonstrates full knowledge by answering all class questions with explanations and elaboration.
	Points					
	Total points				**Grade**	

ORIGAMI RUBRIC

Name:

Date:

C R I T E R I A	1	2	3	4	5 EXTENSION
Construction	• Product is poorly constructed • Careless folds • Shoddy	• Product is constructed • Design flaws are evident	• Product is constructed • Fold lines are neat • Not all fold lines are crisp	• Product fits together well • Fold lines are neat and crisp	• Product is perfectly constructed • Symmetrical design is flawless • Crisp, clean folds
Materials ◆ quality ◆ types	• No paper origami product	• Constructed with paper, but not origami-type paper	• Use origami paper • Also uses glue, tape, staples	• Uses origami paper, generally of high quality	• Uses high quality paper of differing colors to emphasize contrasts in product
Design ◆ creativity ◆ uniqueness	• No product • Product was pre-fabricated	• Has product • Not constructed using origami principles	• Product constructed using origami principles	• Interesting origami design • Creative design from challenging origami book	• Product is "one-of-a-kind" • Imaginative design • Creative design not found in any book
Verbal Explanation	• No eye contact • No verbal presentation	• Limited eye contact • Verbal presentation cannot be heard by audience	• Eye contact made • Verbal presentation is clear	• Good eye contact • Speaks clearly • Projects voice well • Acknowledges audience	• Outstanding body language/eye contact • Confidently addresses audience • Engages audience
Points				**Grade**	
Total points					

PAMPHLET EVALUATION

Name: Date:

CRITERIA		Absent	NSH	OK	Good	Excellent	
		0	1	2	3	4	5
ORGANIZATION ◆ follows Table of Contents							
CONTENT ◆ contains all required sections							
◆ contains appropriate additional sections							
◆ presents accurate information							
WRITTEN PARTS ◆ written in *your* own words							
◆ uses correct capitalization, punctuation, and grammar							
◆ accurate spelling							
VISUAL APPEAL ◆ uses easy-to-read labeled charts, graphs, and/or illustrations							
◆ has balance — equal amount of written and illustrative material							
◆ is neatly done — legible and clean							
BIBLIOGRAPHY ◆ lists a variety of sources							
◆ correctly written							
CREATIVITY ◆ shows originality in design ◆ uses elaborative details							

Comments:

0	1-3 4-10 11-13	14-16 17-23 24-26	27-29 30-36 37-39	40-42 43-50 51+	GRADE
F	D	C	B	A	GRADE

PERSONAL PROCESS ASSESSMENT

Student _____   Date

Project or Unit: _____

WORK HABITS	Frequently	Sometimes	Not Yet
• Work done on time	_____	_____	_____
• Uses good organizational skills	_____	_____	_____
• Makes use of reference materials	_____	_____	_____
• Involves reading and math skills	_____	_____	_____
• Uses time well	_____	_____	_____
• Takes initiative	_____	_____	_____
• Asks for help when needed	_____	_____	_____

WORKING WITH OTHERS	Frequently	Sometimes	Not Yet
• Works well with others	_____	_____	_____
• Has good listening skills	_____	_____	_____
• Solves conflicts in a positive manner	_____	_____	_____
• Shows leadership skills	_____	_____	_____
• Assists others	_____	_____	_____

(YOUR CATEGORY) _____	Frequently	Sometimes	Not Yet
•	_____	_____	_____
•	_____	_____	_____
•	_____	_____	_____
•	_____	_____	_____

PERSUASIVE ESSAY RUBRIC

Name: Date:

CRITERIA		Whatever!	Yeah, maybe?	I'm convinced!	I'll do whatever you want me to!!!	Score
		1	2	3	4	
	Content (claim and support)	The argument or claim is not mentioned; no reasons are given to support the claim; no reasons are given against the claim	The claim is confused or unclear; 1 or 2 weak reasons, irrelevant reasons, or confusing reasons; no argument against the claim is mentioned	The claim is made; reasons are given in support of the claim but important reasons are overlooked; no arguments against the claim are mentioned	The claim is made; clear accurate reasons support the claim; arguments against the claim are discussed and proven insignificant	
	Organization	The writing is very disorganized and often off topic	The writing is workable but sometimes is off topic	The writing has a clear beginning, middle, and end	The essay has a compelling opening, a fully developed body, and a conclusion that calls for action	
	Sentence Fluency	So many run-ons and fragments make the piece difficult to read	A few of the sentences contain run-ons, fragments, or are awkward to read	The sentences are well constructed but do not vary	The sentences are clear, complete, and of varying lengths and types	
	Mechanics	Mistakes in spelling, usage, and punctuation detract from the clarity and meaning	Mistakes in spelling, usage, and punctuation are few but do not detract significantly from the piece	There are no mistakes in spelling, usage, or punctuation	Not only are there no mistakes but the writer is inventive in his/her use of mechanics	

Comments:

Total points

Grade

PERSUASIVE SPEECH RUBRIC

Name:

Date:

CRITERIA	1	2	3	4	5
Organization	Attempted but not written as a speech	Speech included topic sentence and detail. Sentences did not give support.	Speech included topic sentence with at least one detail sentence	Speech included topic sentences with two detail sentences	Speech included topic sentence with 3 or more details in a logical order. Flowed well.
Content	Attempts to give purpose/importance only for the speech	Gives purpose/importance but reasons are unclear. Not persuasive.	Describes the purpose/importance with only one reason in a persuasive way	Clearly states the purpose/importance with 2 reasons in a persuasive way	Clearly states purpose/importance with 3 or more reasons in a persuasive way
Grammar	Speech is unreadable due to grammatical errors	Speech is difficult to understand due to grammatical errors	Speech given with several grammatical errors	Speech given with minimal grammatical errors	Speech given with correct grammar
Oral Presentation	Speech read directly from the paper	Speech read with little eye contact	Speech presented with eye contact and voice inflection	Speech presented with voice inflection, sincerity, and minimal gestures	Speech presented with voice inflection, sincerity, emotions, and gestures given
Points					
Total points				Grade	

Comments:

PICTURE ESSAY RUBRIC

Name:

Date:

	1	2	3	4	5 EXTENSION
C R I T E R I A **Picture accurately illustrates different elements of topic**	• No evidence of accurate research	• Includes some examples accurately but not all elements are represented	• Includes at least one example of each element accurately	• Includes several examples of each element • Shows a cohesive relationship between elements	• Picture essay is an accurate depiction of the topic • All elements are interrelated and illustrated in detail
Labels • Included • Provide additional information about topic	• No labels are included	• Some labels are included but do not provide background information	• Labels are clear, accurate, and included for most items	• Labels are clear, descriptive, and contribute to an understanding of the topic	• All items are labeled • Labels are detailed, neat, descriptive, and contribute to an understanding of the topic
Neatness	• Difficult to discriminate features • Reading labels is difficult	• Some pictures and labels are neatly done	• Most pictures and labels are neatly done	• All pictures and labels are neatly done	• Excellent, clear, and detailed drawings • Labels are neat and may be typed
Presentation to class • Explanation of details in picture is clear • All elements of topic are identified	• Picture essay is not presented	• Picture essay is presented with little attention to details	• Picture essay is presented • Different elements of topic are clearly introduced	• Presentation effectively and accurately introduces the topic • Accurate details are shared	• Presentation engages the audience and keeps their interest • Knowledge of topic is illustrated by accuracy of answers to questions
Points					**Grade**

Total points

PLAY EVALUATION

Name: Date:

CRITERIA		Absent 0	NSH 1	OK 2	Good 3	Excellent 4	5
	CHARACTERS ♦ appropriate ♦ developed physically & emotionally						
	SETTING ♦ well established ♦ appropriate for staging						
	PLOT ♦ clear statement of problem ♦ rising action to climax ♦ effective climax						
	DIALOGUE ♦ realistic						
	INTEGRATION ♦ all parts evident ♦ all parts well developed						
	SCRIPT ♦ proper format ♦ correct spelling						
	APPEARANCE ♦ legible letter forms ♦ clean, straight paper ♦ effective word & letter spacing						
	PERFORMANCE ♦ clear presentation of dialogue ♦ effectively staged						

Comments:

0	1 2-7 8	9 10-15 16	17 18-23 24	25 26-31 32+	
F	**D**	**C**	**B**	**A**	**GRADE**

RUBRIC FOR POETRY BOOK

Name: Date turned in:

CRITERIA		Poor 1	Fair 2	Good 3	Excellent 4	Score
Organization		♦ Shows very little organization or is missing page numbers or table of contents	♦ Hard to recognize organizational plan ♦ 10 poems ♦ Table of contents or page numbers not easy to follow	♦ Pretty well organized ♦ 10 poems ♦ 5 illustrations ♦ Cover ♦ Table of contents ♦ Numbered pages	♦ Very well organized ♦ Follows a theme or plan ♦ Nice cover ♦ Table of contents ♦ 10 poems ♦ 5 illustrations ♦ Pages numbered	
Content ♦ simile ♦ metaphor ♦ ballad ♦ personification ♦ haiku ♦ onomatopoeia ♦ 4-line rhyme ♦ alliteration		♦ Lacking required number of poems or illustrations ♦ Shows that little time spent trying to fulfill requirements	♦ 10 poems ♦ Missing the variety of forms that were required ♦ Needs a little work understanding some of the forms	♦ 10 poems ♦ Understands most of the different forms of poetry ♦ Pretty good at using poetry to express ideas	♦ Includes all the required forms ♦ Clearly understands the different types of poetry ♦ Can use poetry effectively to express himself/ herself	
Illustrations		♦ Lacking required number of illustrations ♦ Not original	♦ 5 illustrations ♦ Do not reflect much effort	♦ 5 original illustrations ♦ Well done ♦ Hard to see how some relate to poems	♦ Original illustrations on at least 5 poems and on cover ♦ Chosen to complement meaning of poems	
Creativity		♦ Lacks creativity ♦ Little attempt to be original ♦ "Borrowed" ideas	♦ Attempt made to be creative ♦ Some ideas were just variations on other poems	♦ Pretty creative ♦ Some original ideas	♦ Clearly shows a great deal of creativity ♦ Expresses original ideas or ideas in an original way	
Mechanics		♦ Contains a lot of grammatical or spelling errors ♦ Needs quite a bit of revising	♦ Contains some grammatical and/or spelling errors	♦ Contains a few grammatical and/or spelling errors	♦ Titled poems ♦ No grammar, spelling, or punctuation errors	
Appearance		♦ Written on notebook paper ♦ Quite messy	♦ Typed or written on unlined paper ♦ Messy	♦ Typed or written neatly on unlined paper	♦ Typed or written neatly on unlined paper ♦ Quality work	

Comments:

17 - 20	A
13 - 16	B
9 - 12	C
5 - 8	D
4 or less	F

Total points

Grade

POETRY EVALUATION

Name: Date:

CRITERIA		Absent	NSH	OK	Good	Excellent	
		0	1	2	3	4	5
C R I T E R I A	**SUBJECT** ◆ appropriate ◆ developed; shows depth						
	WORDING ◆ interesting use of words ◆ well chosen vocabulary ◆ meaningful to subject						
	FORMAT ◆ words and ideas arranged according to accepted poetic structure						
	ILLUSTRATIONS (optional) ◆ appropriate to content						
	CONVENTIONS (MECHANICS) ◆ correct spelling ◆ correct grammar ◆ correct punctuation						
	APPEARANCE (NEATNESS) ◆ legible letter forms ◆ effective word and letter spacing ◆ clean corrections ◆ borrowed illustrations neatly trimmed						

Comments:

0	1 2-4 5	6 7-9 10	11 12-14 15	16 17-19 20+	
F	D	C	B	A	GRADE

POETRY PROJECT

_____ 1. I read this book of poetry: _____

_____ 2. I memorized this poem: _____

_____ 3. I have practiced reciting it and am ready to recite it to the class.

_____ 4. I made an attractive cover for my poetry book.

_____ 5. I wrote at least 10 original poems. I have included:

  _____ simile

  _____ metaphor

  _____ personification

  _____ onomatopoeia

  _____ haiku

  _____ ballad

  _____ 4-line rhyme

  _____ alliteration

  _____ repetition

_____ 6. I typed the poems or wrote them in my best handwriting on unlined paper.

_____ 7. I gave each poem a title.

_____ 8. I included a table of contents.

_____ 9. I numbered each page.

_____ 10. I included an appropriate, original illustration with at least 5 of the poems.

_____ 11. My poetry project was done neatly.

My signature _____

Date _____

POSITION PAPER RUBRIC

Name: _____

Date: _____

		1	2	3	4	5 EXTENSION
C	**Understanding**	Demonstrates basic knowledge of position	Shows impact of position on other elements	Adequately demonstrates the perception of position	Questions the validity of history's depiction of position	Develops independently a theory based in fact confirming or denying position
R I	**Resources**	Relies solely on what is heard in class	Uses one encyclopedia article or internet "blurb" in addition to class information	Uses three independent sources of information	Independently pursues volume/s listed in a bibliography	Contacts a university to find further information
T E R	**Organization**	Use of introductory paragraph to list discussion topics in paper	Use of sequential discussion based on information presented in introductory paragraph	Discussion within each paragraph in logical order as implied by introductory paragraph	Paper successfully defends its thesis and has a logical conclusion	Thesis leads student and/or instructor to a new level of research on position
I A	**Clarity of Thought**	Concrete statements only of facts (no analysis)	Very basic analysis of facts (e.g., use of "I think")	Basic abstract reasoning applied to facts; written in third person	Facts become the skeleton upon which reasoned analysis is placed	Reasoning is so complete and precisely stated that it seems obvious and is easily understood
	Points					**Grade**
	Total points					

183   ©2001 Pieces of Learning

POSTER EVALUATION

Name: Date:

	Absent	NSH	OK	Good	Excellent	
	0	1	2	3	4	5
TITLE ◆ largest print ◆ legible, uniform letters ◆ concise, summarizes theme						
GRAPHICS ◆ highlight key concepts ◆ arrangement leads visual direction ◆ appropriately sized ◆ properly trimmed if borrowed						
NEGATIVE SPACE ◆ surrounds text, graphics, and boundary of product effectively						
BACKGROUND ◆ non-obtrusive						
LABELS ◆ smaller than title ◆ legible, uniform letters ◆ clearly identify object						
TEXT ◆ used as necessary ◆ accurate spelling and punctuation						
RESOURCES ◆ for sources of information used ◆ correctly written ◆ visible yet discreet						
APPEARANCE (NEATNESS) ◆ legible letter forms ◆ effective word and letter spacing ◆ clean corrections						

(Vertical label along left side: C R I T E R I A)

Comments:

0	1	9	17	25	
	2-7	10-15	18-23	26-31	
	8	16	24	32+	
F	D	C	B	A	GRADE

184

POWERPOINT TRAVEL COMMERCIAL RUBRIC

Name: Date:

		Beginning	Developing	Accomplished	Exemplary Extension	Score
		1	2	3	4	
C R I T E R I A	**Content**	Includes a title, a mentioning of two or less areas of interest; but no mention of location or explanation of the cost of visiting	Includes a title and lists a few areas of interest with no description; but no explanation of the location or explanation of cost of visiting	Includes a title, a description of and significance of the areas of interest, a description of and explanation of the significance of the location, and an explanation of the cost of visiting	Along with all the elements of #3, includes a catchy slogan or twist that will lure customers in	
	Professionalism	Includes at least 5 slides, with at least 2 animated graphics from an outside source	Includes at least 8 slides, with at least 5 animated graphics from an outside source	Includes at least 10 slides, 1 animated graphic on each slide from an outside source, and at least 1 advanced feature such as sound or video	Along with all the elements of #3, includes an audio narration that accompanies each slide	
	Mechanics	Includes more than 5 grammatical errors, misspellings, or punctuation errors	Includes 1-4 grammatical errors, misspellings, or punctuation errors	Correct grammar, spelling, punctuation, and capitalization ; no errors in text	No errors in text; contains complex sentences with varied word choice	

Comments: **Total**

                                                                                             Grade

"PROBLEM OF THE WEEK" BINDER RUBRIC

Name: Date:

CRITERIA	1	2	3	4	5 EXTENSION
Organization	• Binder does not exist	• Has binder • 5 or fewer problems in binder	• Has binder • 14 or more problems • Disorganized; problems out of order	• Has binder • All 18 problems • Organized by date	• All 18 problems in binder • Neatly labeled and organized • Table of contents
Method of Solution	• Does not provide methods of solution	• Most solutions show little understanding of problems • Barely communicates solutions	• Shows partial but limited solutions • Does not communicate solutions clearly or completely	• Communicates solutions to problems clearly	• Communicates solutions clearly and accurately using charts, graphs, symbols, and written explanations
Understanding of Problems	• No problems	• Shows little understanding of the problems	• Shows partial understanding of the problems	• Shows an essential grasp of the central ideas in the problem	• Shows full grasp of the central ideas in all the problems
Neatness	• Problems are written on bits of paper in pen	• Problems are scribbled on notebook paper in pen • Much of work is not legible	• Problems are printed on notebook paper in pencil • Some work is not legible	• Problems are neatly written in pencil • Binder contains only legible work	• Problems are neatly written in pencil with accompanying diagrams neatly drawn • All work is legible with no stray marks
Points					

Total points   **Grade**

Proofreader's Checklist

Writer's Name: _____

Title of Work: _____

Editor/s: _____

Circle **Yes** or **No** after each area you proofread.

1.	All sentences begin with a capital letter.	Yes	No
2.	All sentences end with the proper punctuation mark.	Yes	No
3.	All proper names begin with a capital letter.	Yes	No
4.	All words are spelled correctly.	Yes	No
5.	There are no missing words.	Yes	No
6.	There are no extra words.	Yes	No
7.	Commas are used properly.	Yes	No
8.	Apostrophes are used properly.	Yes	No
9.	Quotation marks are used properly.	Yes	No
10.	All words are spaced properly.	Yes	No
11.	Paragraphs are used properly.	Yes	No
12.	The paper is neat and legible.	Yes	No

Read Aloud Rubric

Name: Date:

CRITERIA		1	2	3	
C	Expression	read in a monotone voice; lacks expression when reading	read with some expression to enhance reading for audience	read with great expression that enhanced reading for audience	PUBLIC SPEAKER
R	Volume	low volume; listener struggles to hear	medium voice; listener able to hear yet still a bit difficult	strong voice, great volume; listener can hear clearly without difficulty	SPORTS ANNOUNCER
I T	Flow	reads with choppy flow and too fast or too slow a pace	good smooth speed but choppy; or smooth flow but too fast or slow a pace	nice steady pace and a nice smooth flow	SMOOTH
E R	Decoding	unable to use phonic rules to sound out unfamiliar word	able to use phonic rules but unable to pronounce unfamiliar word correctly	using phonic rules to sound out unfamiliar word and to pronounce it correctly	GREAT DETECTIVE
I A	Following Sentences	reader jumps sentences, adds or deletes words, and repeats words	reader adds or deletes words or repeats words	reader completes text as presented on the page	RIGHT ON TRACK
	Points				
	Total points				

Comments:

Ratings

15 = Master Reader
10 = Working On It
5 = Needs Practice

Research Paper Evaluation

Name: Date:

CRITERIA		Absent	NSH	OK	Good	Excellent	
		0	1	2	3	4	5
C R I T E R I A	**INTRODUCTION** ◆ presents the problem/topic ◆ explains why the problem/topic was chosen						
	BODY ◆ main ideas with supporting details ◆ objective language ◆ accurate information *in your own words*						
	CONCLUSION ◆ brief ◆ summarizes major point/s ◆ reasonable; supported by evidence						
	REFERENCES ◆ complete listing of resources ◆ correct bibliographic format						
	FORMAT ◆ cover sheet ◆ title page ◆ introduction, body, conclusion ◆ bibliography						
	CONVENTIONS (MECHANICS) ◆ correct spelling ◆ correct grammar and punctuation ◆ complete sentences						
	APPEARANCE (NEATNESS) ◆ legible letter forms ◆ effective word and letter spacing ◆ clean corrections ◆ borrowed illustrations neatly trimmed						

Comments:

	0	1 2-6 7	8 9-13 14	15 16-20 21	22 23-27 28+	
	F	**D**	**C**	**B**	**A**	**GRADE**

RUBRIC FOR ROCKETRY UNIT

Name: Date:

		Fair 1	Good 2	Excellent 3	Superior 4
C R I T E R I A	**Construction** ♦ parts ♦ labels ♦ key	Most of the parts are on the model rocket, but labels are missing	Each part of model rocket is present, but labels are missing	Each part of model rocket is present and labeled	Each part of the model rocket is present, labeled, and defined on a separate key
	Appearance ♦ parts ♦ colors	None of the parts that are on the model are colored	Most of the parts on the model are colored	All parts from model rocket kit are used and colored	All parts from model rocket kit are used and colored, including advanced motor parts and additional equipment
	Creativity ♦ new colors ♦ new symbols	Not all labels or colors are used; no additional colors or symbols are added	Colors and labels from kit used; only 1 different symbol added to rocket	Colors and labels from kit used; 2 different symbols are added to rocket	More than 3 additional different labels, symbols, or colors not defined in rocket kit are used
	Careers Paper	Finished rocket but no research paper	Builds rocket and writes partial research paper on rockets with no career focus	Builds rocket with necessary parts and researches one career in rocket industry	Builds superior rocket, researches a particular career associated with the rocket industry, and draws a future rocket
	Overall Presentation ♦ launch ♦ explanation	Successful launch with no explanation of launch	Successful launch with good explanation of launch	Successful launch with an excellent explanation	Successful launch with detailed, engaging discussion of that particular rocket and why its launch worked
	Points				
	Total points			Grade	

Comments:

20	**A+**
15 - 19	**A**
10 - 14	**B**
5 - 9	**C**

         190

SCIENCE REPORT EVALUATION

Name: _____   Date: _____

		Absent	NSH	OK	Good	Excellent	
		0	1	2	3	4	5
C	**ORGANIZATION** ◆ follows proper narrative composition format						
R	**CONTENT** ◆ reflects accurate knowledge of topic						
I	◆ explores 3 different aspects of the topic						
T	**WRITTEN TEXT** ◆ must be in *your* own words ◆ follows conventions						
E	**BIBLIOGRAPHY** ◆ at least 2 different types of sources used						
R	◆ correctly written in APA format						
I	**CONVENTIONS** (MECHANICS) ◆ correct spelling ◆ correct grammar and punctuation ◆ correct paragraph structures						
A	**APPEARANCE** (NEATNESS) ◆ legible letter forms ◆ effective word and letter spacing ◆ clean corrections						

Comments:

	0	1 2-7 8	9 10-15 16	17 18-23 24	25 26-31 32+	
	F	**D**	**C**	**B**	**A**	**GRADE**

SHORT STORY EVALUATION

Name: Date:

CRITERIA		Absent	NSH	OK	Good	Excellent	
		0	1	2	3	4	5
C	**INTRODUCTION** ◆ good beginning ◆ arouses interest						
R	**BODY** ◆ develops plot with complications, consequences, and climax						
I	**ENDING** ◆ satisfactory; no "loose ends" ◆ problem is open-ended and interpretive						
T	**SETTING** ◆ specific ◆ creates visual and auditory images						
E	**MOOD** ◆ creates an overall feeling						
R	**CHARACTERS** ◆ appropriate ◆ developed both physically and emotionally						
I	**CONVENTIONS** (MECHANICS) ◆ correct spelling ◆ correct grammar & punctuation ◆ complete sentences						
A	**APPEARANCE** (NEATNESS) ◆ legible letter forms ◆ effective word & letter spacing ◆ clean corrections						

Comments:

0	1	9	17	25	
	2-7	10-15	18-23	26-31	
	8	16	24	32+	
F	D	C	B	A	GRADE

©2001 Pieces of Learning   192

SOFTWARE GAME RUBRIC

Name:

Date:

		1	2	3	4	5 EXTENSION
C R	**Software Development** ◆ Ease of use ◆ Page linkage	◆ Game does not load and/or run ◆ None of the pages link	◆ Game "freezes up" frequently ◆ Some pages do not link	◆ Games "freezes up" on occasion ◆ Most pages link, but sometimes incorrectly	◆ Game does not "freeze up" ◆ All pages link appropriately	◆ Game runs quickly and flawlessly ◆ Pages link quickly and appropriately
I T	**Game Design** ◆ Clarity of instructions ◆ Logical steps in game ◆ Creativity	◆ No instructions ◆ No apparent steps ◆ No evident creativity	◆ Instructions available but not clearly presented ◆ Steps with little logic ◆ Creative use of some design elements ◆ Game plan similar to others	◆ Instructions available in a handout ◆ Game is logically understandable ◆ Creative use of design elements ◆ Game plan has a slightly different approach than others	◆ Instructions available in handout and in software ◆ Game is easy to understand ◆ Clever game plan uses design elements creatively	◆ Instructions are concisely and clearly presented via software and handout ◆ Superbly written steps ◆ Original, elaborate game plan ◆ Dramatic, creative use of design elements
E R	**Content** ◆ Reflects topic ◆ Age appropriate ◆ Accuracy ◆ Interest level	◆ Does not reflect topic ◆ Does not hold interest	◆ Content is too elementary but on assigned topic ◆ Much information is inaccurate ◆ Confusing for user	◆ Age appropriate material on topic ◆ Most information is accurate ◆ Keeps the user's interest	◆ Information is age appropriate, accurate, and interesting ◆ User enjoys playing the game	◆ Game is engaging, challenging, and informative ◆ User is motivated to play game repeatedly
I A	**Verbal Explanation of Game** ◆ Verbal presentation ◆ Eye contact ◆ Presence	◆ No eye contact ◆ No verbal presentation	◆ Limited eye contact ◆ Verbal presentation cannot be heard by audience	◆ Eye contact is made ◆ Verbal presentation is clear	◆ Good eye contact ◆ Speaks clearly and projects ◆ Acknowledges audience	◆ Outstanding body language and eye contact ◆ Moves confidently through audience ◆ Engaging presentation
	Points				Grade	
	Total points					

193

Sound Identification and Recognition Rubric

Name: Date:

		1 Point	2 Points	3 Points
C R I T E R I A	**Beginning Sounds**	Unable to identify and recognize beginning letter sounds accurately	Identifies and recognizes beginning single consonant and vowel sounds	Identifies and recognizes beginning single, double, and triple consonant sounds
	Middle Sounds	Unable to identify and recognize middle letter sounds accurately	Identifies and recognizes single middle vowel and consonant sounds	Identifies and recognizes single, double, and triple middle vowel and consonant sounds
	Ending Sounds	Unable to identify and recognize ending letter sounds accurately	Identifies and recognizes ending single vowel and consonant sounds	Identifies and recognizes single, double, and triple ending vowel and consonant sounds

Comments:

Scoring

Points	Description
9	Exceeds Expectation
7 — 8	Excellent
5 — 6	Satisfactory
3 — 4	Needs Improvement

SPEECH RUBRIC

Name: Date:

		Keep practicing!	Entertaining!	You're ready for radio!	You're ready for TV!
C R I T E R I A	**Volume**	Audience could not hear any of the speech	Audience could only hear part of the speech	Audience could hear all of speech; normal volume used throughout	Audience could hear entire speech; loud volume used throughout
	Eye Contact	Read entire speech	Read almost all of the speech; looked up occasionally	Good use of note cards; great job looking at note cards and at audience	Speech was memorized; looked at audience during entire speech
	Flow	Repeatedly stopped for long periods of time	Stopped occasionally to figure out words and to find place	Only stopped once during speech	Did not stop at all during speech
	Speed	Spoke _way_ too fast or _way_ too slow; could not understand any of speech	Spoke fast/slow during majority of the speech	A certain part (beginning, middle, or end) of speech was too fast/slow	Consistent flow throughout entire speech
	Sequence	Left out three or more steps	Left out two important steps of the sequence	Left out one important step of the sequence	All steps were included in the speech
	Props	Zero props	One prop used effectively to demonstrate how-to	Two props apparent; one effectively used to demonstrate how-to	Three or more props apparent; used at least two to demonstrate how-to

Comments:

Create A Spider Rubric

Name: Date:

CRITERIA	1	2	3	4	5 Extension
Spider has correct number of body parts	Spider not completed	Spider has only one body part	Spider has two body parts, but no fangs or face	Spider has all body parts including fangs & face	Spider has all body parts and resembles real spider
Spider has correct number of legs	Spider has no legs	Spider has four legs	Spider has six legs	Spider has eight legs	Spider has eight segmented legs
Student made a drawing of his/her spider	No drawing done	Drawing does not resemble spider	Drawing is done but not colored	Drawing is done with color	Drawing uses bright colors and mirrors spider
Student used creative materials to make spider	Spider not completed	All the same materials are used; no diversity	A variety of materials are used	A variety of materials are used creatively	Unusual materials are used creatively
Points					
Total points				Grade	

Comments:

Stock Market Unit Rubric

Name: _____   Date: _____

CRITERIA	1	2	3	4	5 EXTENSION
Organization ◆ Notebook ◆ Transaction Records ◆ Notes ◆ Legible	◆ 3 or less records of transactions ◆ No order ◆ Sloppy ◆ Notes missing ◆ No additional material	◆ 4 transactions ◆ Most notes kept in sequential order ◆ Not all notes are legible	◆ 5 transactions ◆ All notes kept and in order ◆ Legible ◆ No additional material	◆ All transactions included ◆ All notes in order ◆ Neat ◆ Some additional material included	◆ All of 4 ◆ Charts and graphs with interpretations of stocks ◆ Stock articles
Computation Skills ◆ Calculations using percentages	◆ Computations that are shown are not legible or are incorrect	◆ Most computations are correct ◆ Not all are shown ◆ Sloppy	◆ All required computations are included ◆ 90% are correct ◆ Legible	◆ All computations are included ◆ All are correct ◆ Neat ◆ In order	◆ All of 4 ◆ Comparison of 5% savings account vs. stock increase or decrease
Navigating the Internet ◆ Market research ◆ Market	◆ Can access stock program site ◆ Cannot make transactions	◆ Can make transactions ◆ Can access most stock program tools	◆ Makes transactions ◆ Uses all tools within stock program site	◆ Same as 3 ◆ Has found additional sites for research	◆ Same as 4 ◆ Has discovered Web sites that were used for stock selection ◆ Noted how and why
Paper ◆ Understanding of capitalism ◆ Pros and cons of investing	◆ Gave definition of capitalism ◆ Did not offer any type of evaluation	◆ Defined capitalism ◆ Gave one pro and one con	◆ Capitalism explained ◆ Several examples given for and against	◆ Same as 3 ◆ Examples of different types of investment given	◆ Same as 4 ◆ Examination of a Communist economy ◆ Comparison of Communist and capitalist economies
Points					
Total points					**Grade**

STORY RUBRIC

Name:

Date:

C R I T E R I A		1	2	3	4	5		
	Structure/ Organization	Unorganized main idea and details	Attempted main idea with supporting details	Clear main idea but details are unclear. Obvious attempt.	Organization is strong. Good main idea and supporting details. Has a beginning, middle, and end.	Well organized with main idea, details, and concluding sentence. Has a beginning, middle, and end.		
	Spelling/ Grammar	Very difficult to read because of spelling and grammar mistakes	Many errors. Reader has a difficult time understanding the meaning.	Five or less grammar and spelling errors. Obvious awareness.	Minimal errors that do not disrupt fluency	Errors that do not disrupt fluency		
	Fluency	Lack of order and unable to follow idea	Attempted order but transitions are unclear	Transitions are not fluent, but do not hinder the reader	Created a clear picture that flows well	Well developed. Created excellent transitions and cohesiveness.		
	Descriptive Language	Descriptive language is very vague or completely absent	Very few adjectives and not well developed	Provided adjectives that included colorful and descriptive words	Included a variety of descriptive language which created enjoyment for the reader	Rich with vivid and imaginative words and language. The reader could easily envision the details.		
	Points							
	Total points						Grade	

Comments:

TIME CAPSULE RUBRIC

Name: _____ Date: _____

CRITERIA	1	2	3	4	5 EXTENSION
Time Capsule • Colorful • Creatively designed • Two-shoebox size	• Capsule is not colorful or creative • Does not follow size guidelines	• Capsule is colorful and/or creatively designed • Does not follow size guidelines	• Capsule is colorful and/or creatively designed • Follows size guidelines	• Capsule is colorful and detailed with creative designs • Follows size guidelines	• Capsule is creatively colored and detailed with elaborate designs • Follows size guidelines
Verbal Presentation • Speaks clearly • Projects voice well • Addresses audience	• Does not speak clearly, project voice, or address the audience	• Does not speak clearly or project voice • Addresses the audience	• Speaks clearly • Projects voice • Addresses the audience	• Speaks clearly with good voice projection • Focus on audience • Maintains audience attention	• Addresses audience clearly; excellent voice projection • Demonstrates confidence • Maintains audience attention
Letter • Purpose of capsule • Introduction and conclusion • Explanations of capsule items	• Purpose of time capsule is not clear • No introduction, conclusion, or explanations	• Purpose of time capsule is clear • Explanations are not consistent • Introduction and conclusion unclear	• Purpose is clearly stated • Explanations are consistent • Clear introduction and conclusion	• Purpose is clearly stated • Explanations are detailed • Clear introduction and conclusion	• Purpose is stated elaborately • Introduction and conclusion are clear and flow smoothly • Detailed explanations
Capsule Items • Reflect community • Demonstrate 100 years of passing time	• Do not reflect community • Do not show 100 years of passing time	• Reflect community • Do not show 100 years of passing time	• Reflect community • Demonstrate 100 years of passing time	• Variety of items • Reflect community • Show progression of time	• Extensive number of items • Reflect community • Show progression of time over consecutive years
Points					
Total points			**Grade**		

TOOTHPICK BRIDGE EVALUATION

Name: Date:

		Absent	NSH	OK	Good	Excellent	
		0	2	4	6	8	10
C	**APPEARANCE** ♦ attractive design ♦ neatly constructed						
R	**BRIDGE PLANS** ♦ finished bridge matches design plans						
I	**CODE** ♦ meets specifications of size and dimensions						
T	**RECORD KEEPING** ♦ accuracy ♦ completeness						
E							
R	**FUNDS** ♦ money used to purchase materials: 　　　$_____						
I							
A	**OVERALL STRENGTH** ♦ holds: _____ grams						

Comments:

	0	1-3	13-15	25-27	37-39	
		4-9	16-21	28-33	40-46	
		10-12	21-24	34-36	47+	
	F	**D**	**C**	**B**	**A**	**GRADE**

TRAVEL BROCHURE RUBRIC

Name:

Date:

	1	2	3	4	5 EXTENSION
C R **Contents** ◆ Residential areas ◆ Commercial areas ◆ Recreational areas ◆ Historical areas ◆ Pictures/photos	◆ Different areas not indicated ◆ No pictures/ photos	◆ Does not have information on each area ◆ A few photos/ pictures are included	◆ Has information about each area ◆ Does not have pictures/photos for each area	◆ Has a lot of information about each area ◆ Has pictures for each area	◆ Contains in-depth information about each area ◆ Expressive photos/ pictures
I T **Format** ◆ Separate sections ◆ Title ◆ Headings	◆ Sections not clearly marked or titled	◆ Sections not clearly marked ◆ Main title only	◆ Sections clearly marked with headings ◆ Main title evident	◆ Sections distinctly marked ◆ Title and headings evident	◆ Sections are distinguished in a creative manner ◆ Creative title and headings
E R **Map** ◆ Locations of different areas ◆ Map scale	◆ Locations of areas not shown ◆ No scale or rose	◆ Locations shown ◆ No scale or rose	◆ Locations shown ◆ Map scale defined ◆ Has a compass rose	◆ Area locations are detailed ◆ Map scale defined ◆ Has a compass rose	◆ Provides true reflection of areas ◆ Creative compass rose ◆ Map scale is defined
I A **Appearance** ◆ Folded 8.5x11 paper ◆ Design elements ◆ Colorful ◆ Neat ◆ Legible	◆ Not proper size ◆ No design elements ◆ Not colorful ◆ Not neat ◆ Not legible	◆ Proper size ◆ Colorful ◆ Neat ◆ Not legible ◆ No consistent design plan	◆ Not proper size ◆ Design plan evident ◆ Colorful ◆ Neat ◆ Legible	◆ Proper size ◆ Consistent use of design elements throughout ◆ Colorful ◆ Neat ◆ Legible	◆ Proper size ◆ Colorful throughout ◆ Creatively designed ◆ Neat ◆ Legible
Points				**Grade**	
Total points					

© 2001 Pieces of Learning

RUBRIC FOR TRIGONOMETRIC GRAPHS

Name: Date:

CRITERIA	Fair 1	Good 2	Excellent 3	Score
Amplitude, Period, and Phase Shift Correctly identified	One component identified correctly	2 of 3 components identified correctly	All 3 components identified correctly	
Horizontal Axis Labeled	Scale present but incorrect	Scale present with only endpoints identified	Scale clear, precise with 4 or 5 points correctly identified	
Cycle One shown correctly	Cycle present but inaccurate	Cycle present with only one characteristic incorrect or the graph follows from student's attributes	Cycle present and accurate in all attributes	
Description Of procedures taken	Phrases or facts stated	Sentences used to describe steps (which are accurate)	Complete explanation describing the use of characteristics to determine the graph	
Original Problem Original problem that can be solved using the equation and graph	Indicates an area which is harmonic and uses trig functions	Characteristics of problem reflect amplitude, period, and/or phase shift	Problem is consistent with attributes and demonstrates understanding and creativity	

Comments:

Total points

Grade

TV News Show Evaluation

Team Names:

Date:

CRITERIA		Absent	NSH	OK	Good	Excellent	
		0	1	2	3	4	5
	INTERNATIONAL NEWS						
	Visual aid:						
	STATE NEWS						
	Visual aid:						
	LOCAL NEWS						
	Visual aid:						
	SPORTS						
	Visual aid:						
	SPECIAL NEWS ITEM						
	Visual aid:						
	WEATHER						
	Visual aid:						
	COMMERCIAL 1						
	Visual aid:						
	COMMERCIAL 2						
	Visual aid:						
	TOTAL PRESENTATION LENGTH:						

Comments:

0	1-4	18-21	35-38	52-55	
	5-13	22-30	39-47	56-64	
	14-17	31-34	48-51	65+	
F	D	C	B	A	GRADE

VETERAN'S DAY DOLL RUBRIC

Name:

Date:

		1	2	3	4	5 EXTENSION
C R I	**Doll Dimensions** • Made of paper • 1 foot x 1 foot • Proportional body parts	• Not made of paper • Not correct size • Body parts are not proportional	• Made of paper • Not correct size • Body parts are not proportional	• Made of paper • Correct size <u>but</u> body parts are not proportional; OR • Parts proportional <u>but</u> wrong size	• All criteria met • Followed <u>all</u> instructions	
T E	**Information Card** • Provides details • Explanation about branch of service	• Details not given • No explanation	• Details not given • Poorly written explanation	• Few details given • Nicely written explanation	• Many details given • Well written explanation	• Details are extensive • Explanation provides in-depth understanding
R I A	**Doll Representation** • U.S. military service • Reflects rank in military • Proper costume • Badges • Rank insignia • Nametag	• Does not reflect a military service person • Does not show rank in service; no badge, rank insignia, nametag	• Represents a service person • Costume has some but not all of these: badge, rank insignia, nametag • May not reflect rank in service	• Represents a service person • Represents rank in the service • *Costume has badge, rank insignia, and nametag*	• Represents a service person • Costume has necessary badges to reflect rank • *Costume has additional details that reflect a soldier*	• Doll reflects a specific area of military service • Costume has <u>all</u> symbols to reflect rank and other possible details • Costume reflects a variety of military levels
	Points					
	Total points					**Grade**

204

Rubric for Designing a Web Site

Name: Date:

		Level 1	Level 2	Level 3	Level 4	Level 5 EXTENSION
C R I T E R I A	**Layout**	Layout has no structure or organization	Text broken into paragraphs and/or sections	Headings and sections are labeled and create hierarchy; some consistency	Hierarchy closely follows meaning; heading and styles are consistent within pages	Consistent format extends page-to-page; text, images, and links flow together
	Writing Mechanics	Difficult to understand; some spelling and other errors	Many errors but consistent line of thought	Easy to understand; some spelling and grammar errors	Easy to understand; few spelling and grammar errors	Clear, concise, and well written with no spelling and grammar errors
	Images	Images are unrelated to page	One image with some relation to page and text	Three images with some relation to page and text	Four images with strong relation to text and page; images are from 2 or more sources	Five or more images with strong relation to text and pages; images have proper size, colors, and cropping; images are from 3 or more sources (Scan, PhotoShop, Video Tape, Photo Deluxe, etc.)
	Network	Student has problems bringing up his or her Web page within a Web browser	Text is in a program other than the word processor; one or more files in wrong location	Some files in simple word processor of HTML	Most files in simple word processor of HTML	All files in simple word processor of HTML; efficient use of Internet access programs

Comments:

Working Together
in a Cooperative Group

Project or Unit: _____

Rate your group according to the following scale:

    1 = We didn't do this at all   2 = We need a lot of help in this
    3 = We did well with this   4 = We were outstanding in this

Commitment to Purpose .... Group Rating _____

    Interest in task
    Motivation to complete assignment
    Followed directions

Work Process Group Rating .... Group Rating _____

    Everyone participated
    We didn't waste time
    Ideas built on one another

Decision Making .... Group Rating _____

    Looked for solutions all could accept
    Followed orderly process in making decisions
    Decisions were not forced on some people

Communication .... Group Rating _____

    Listened to all suggestions
    We stayed on task in discussions
    Our talking did not disturb the class

Creativity .... Group Rating _____

    Considered new ways of doing things
    Brainstormed ideas
    No put-downs for different thinking

Conflict .... Group Rating _____

    Established rules for dealing with conflict
    Avoided personal attacks
    Examined different points of view

Leadership .... Group Rating _____

    Group decided on leadership tasks and roles
    Everyone took some responsibility
    Group leader was fair to all

Group Members: _____

WRITERS' WORKSHOP RUBRIC

Name: Date:

	Absent	NSH	Good	Excellent	
	0	1	2	3	4
Used writing log	not at all	some of the time	much of the time	nearly all of the time	always writing in log
Drafts kept in folder	no drafts in folder	some drafts in folder	most drafts in folder	all drafts in folder	all drafts in decorated folder
Finished three final drafts (3 different types of writing)	no final drafts	one final draft	two final drafts; 2 different kinds of writing	three final drafts; 3 different kinds of writing	more than 3 final drafts reflecting at least 3 kinds of writing
Daily attitude	negative and distracting	OK, but sometimes distracting	good, and not distracting	positive and focused	positive and supportive of others
Daily effort	wrote nothing	wrote very little	wrote much of the time	wrote most of the time	spent every available moment writing
Points					
Total points				Grade	

Comments:

13 - 15	A
10 - 12	B
7 - 9	C
4 - 6	D
0 - 3	F

Criteria (vertical label): CRITERIA

WRITING RUBRIC

Name: _____

Title: _____

Date: _____

Editing Partner/s: _____

FOCUS

1	2	3	4	5	6
Absent	Confused	Vague	Adequate	Clear	Sharp, distinct

CONTENT

1	2	3	4	5	6
Absence of relevant content	Superficial	Limited to a listing, repetition, or mere sequence of ideas	Sufficient	Specific and illustrative	Substantial, specific &/or illustrative content with sophisticated, well-developed ideas

ORGANIZATION

1	2	3	4	5	6
Absent	Confused	Inconsistent	Appropriate	Logical and appropriate	Obviously controlled

STYLE

1	2	3	4	5	6
No control of word choice or sentence structure	Lack of sentence structure and word choice	Limited sentence variety and word choice	Some precision & variety in word choice and sentence structure	Precision and variety in sentence structure and word choice	Tone apparent in sentence structure & word choice

CONVENTIONS

1	2	3	4	5	6
Errors so severe that ideas are too hard to understand	Errors seriously interfere with purpose	Repeated weaknesses	Errors do not interfere significantly with purpose	Some mechanical and usage errors	Few mechanical and usage errors

25 - 30	= A
20 - 24	= B
10 - 19	= C
5 - 9	= D
0 - 4	= E

Teacher's Comments:

Total Points: _____

Grade: _____

Writing Assessment Rubric

Name: _____

	1	2	3	4
C O N T E N T	• lack of focus • little, if any, organization • limited or unclear supporting ideas • development limited to repetition of key words	• controlling idea unclear or minimal develop. • multiple controlling ideas. None developed • ideas are few, general, or irrelevant • organization overwhelms development • sense of completeness lacking	• clear controlling idea • uneven develop. of beginning, middle, & end • generally relevant supporting ideas • ideas presented with logical connections • appropriate organization • sense of completeness	• strong, clear controlling idea • even development of beginning, middle, & end • even development of main & supporting ideas • ideas supported with examples & details • appropriate, logical organization • sense of completeness/fullness
S T Y L E	• lack of engaging, precise, or varied language • flat or inappropriate tone • lack of transitions • no awareness of audience • lack of individuality/voice • lack of original student writing	• little engaging, precise, or varied language • impersonal, inconsistent, or uneven tone • approach inconsistent with purpose • transitions inappropriate or overused • little awareness of audience • little individuality/voice • limited original student writing	• generally precise or engaging language • appropriate tone for audience & purpose • approach suited to topic & purpose • consistent awareness of audience • transitions linking ideas & parts of paper • some sense of writer's individuality/voice • sufficient original student writing	• precise or engaging language • varied word choice • appropriate tone that is strong • interesting presentation & complete info • transitions lead the reader • clear sense of voice or individuality • extensive original student writing
S E N T E N C E S	• sentence-level meaning confused • frequent use of fragments & run-ons • too few sentences • end punctuation missing or incorrect	• mixture of effective/ineffective, clear/confused sentences • competence in complete simple sentences • end punctuation correct & incorrect	• clear, effective sentences • elements within sentences joined correctly • variety in length & type of sentences • generally correct end punctuation • competence in either coordination or subordination	• consistent clarity of meaning • correct end punctuation • extensive variety of sentences • variety of subordination & coordination • repetition for effect
U S A G E	• severe & repeated errors in subject-verb agreement, word forms, pronoun reference • usage errors that create a barrier to understanding	• a mixture of correct & incorrect instances of usage • competence in one or two components	• subject-verb agreement • correct noun & verb formation • clear pronoun reference • correct word forms • some variety in all components	• singular and plural subject-verb agreement • correct use of varied pronouns • correct & complete word forms • ability to manipulate the conventions of usage for effect • variety of contexts & instances in all components
M E C H A N I C S	• meaning obscured by severity & frequency of errors	• mechanics used correctly in some contexts • competence in one or two components	• limited # of errors in one or more components • correct instances in each component present • components not demonstrated in a wide variety of contexts	• components demonstrated in a wide variety of instances & contexts • occasional proofreading errors • manipulation of mechanics for effect

CONTENT SCORE: _____ X 3 = _____

STYLE SCORE: _____ X 2 = _____

SENTENCE SCORE: _____

MECHANICS SCORE: _____

USAGE SCORE: _____

TOTAL SCORE: _____

Bibliography

Andrade, Heidi Goodrich, "Using Rubrics to Promote Thinking and Learning," Educational Leadership, Vol. 57, No. 5, February 2000.

"Assessment That Serves Instruction," Education Update, Vol. 39, No. 4, June, 1997.

Balsamo, Kathy, Thematic Activities for Student Portfolios, Marion IL, Pieces of Learning, 1997.

Brady, Marion, "The Standards Juggernaut," Phi Delta Kappan, Vol. 81, No. 9, May, 2000.

Burke, Kay, How to Assess Authentic Learning, Third Edition, Arlington Heights, IL, Skylight Professional Development, 1999.

Coil, Carolyn, Becoming an Achiever, Marion, IL, Pieces of Learning, 1994.

Coil, Carolyn, Encouraging Achievement, Marion, IL, Pieces of Learning, 1999.

Coil, Carolyn, Motivating Underachievers, (Revised and expanded edition) Marion, IL, Pieces of Learning, 2001.

Coil, Carolyn, Teaching Tools for the 21st Century (Revised edition), Marion, IL, Pieces of Learning, 2000.

Effective Scoring Rubrics: A Guide to Their Development and Use, Illinois State Board of Education, School and Student Assessment Section, 1995.

Gratz, Donald B., "High Standards for Whom?" Phi Delta Kappan, Vol. 81, No. 9, May, 2000.

Educational Leadership, Vol. 57, No. 5, February 2000.

"Guidelines for Improving Grading Practices," Education Update, Vol. 40, No. 8, December, 1998.

Kingore, Bertie, Assessment: Time Saving Procedures for Busy Teachers, Austin, TX, Professional Associates, 1999.

Marzano, Robert J., Transforming Classroom Grading, Alexandria, VA, ASCD, 2000.

National Public Radio, "Morning Edition," Oct. 27, 2000.

"Observational Assessments," Education Update, Vol. 41, No. 8, December, 1999.

Ohanian, Susan, "Goals 2000: What's in a Name?" Phi Delta Kappan, Vol. 81, No. 5, January 2000.

O'Neil, John, "Making Assessment Meaningful," ASCD Update, Vol. 36, No. 6, August, 1994.

Payne, David Allen, Applied Educational Assessment, Belmont, CA, Wadsworth Publishing Company, 1997.

Perez, Christina, "Equity in the Standards-Based Elementary Mathematics Classroom," ENC Focus, Vol. 7, No. 4, 2000.

Popham, W. James, "What's Wrong -- and What's Right -- with Rubrics," Educational Leadership, Vol. 55, No. 2, October 1997.

Ratnesar, Romesh, "The Homework Ate My Family," Time Magazine, January 25, 1999.

Thompson, Scott, "The Authentic Standards Movement and Its Evil Twin," Phi Delta Kappan, Vol. 82, No. 5, January 2001.

Tomlinson, Carol Ann, "Grading for Success," Educational Leadership, Vol. 58, No. 6, March 2001.

"Unlocking Gateway: A Guide to the Test," Atlanta Journal-Constitution, March 19, 2000.

"Using Assessment to Motivate Students," Education Update, Vol. 39, No. 8, December, 1997.

Wiggins, Grant and McTighe, Jay, Understanding by Design, Alexandria, VA, ASCD, 1998.

Willis, Scott, "The Accountability Question," Education Update, Vol. 41, No. 7, November 1999.

Winebrenner, Susan, Teaching Gifted Kids in the Regular Classroom, Revised and Expanded edition, Minneapolis, MN, Free Spirit Publishing, 2001.

Using the CD

FOR WINDOWS
1. Turn on your computer.
2. Load the CD-ROM into the CD-ROM drive.
3. Double-click on **My Computer** on your desktop.
4. Double-click on the **CD-ROM** icon

WORD files

The WORD files can be customized and saved on your computer or disk. **NOTE:** WORD files **CANNOT** be saved on the CD-ROM. Use the **Save As** option in WORD to save your customized forms on your hard drive or disk.

Page 55   Planning an Authentic Assessment Task
Page 56   Performance Assessment Task Outline
Page 57   Criteria for Assessment Task
Page 72   Chapter 6 Teacher Reflection Page the Assessment/Instruction Cycle
Page 81   My Learning Log
Page 83   Record of Work for Product or Performance
Page 85   Classroom Observation Record
Page 89   Portfolio Table of Contents
Page 112 Criteria for Assessment of Student Products & Performances
Page 118 Criteria for Assessment Worksheet
Page 129 Blank Rubric Format – simple portrait format
Page 130 Blank Rubric Format – verbal assessment – portrait format
Page 131 Blank Rubric Format – numeric assessment – portrait format
Page 132 Blank Rubric Format – numeric assessment – landscape format
Page 133 Blank Rubric Format – verbal/numeric/letter grade – portrait format
Page 134 Blank Rubric Format – verbal/numeric/letter grade – portrait format

PDF files

All rubrics Pages 136-209

Please note: Adobe® Acrobat Reader® 7.0 can only be installed with Windows 2000 or Windows XP Operating Systems. For Windows 95, 98 or Windows ME please use Adobe Reader® 5.0 or 6.0. Only Adobe® Acrobat Reader® 7.0 is included on the CD.

Installing Adobe® Acrobat Reader® 7.0 for Windows 2000/XP

Note: *"Solving the Assessment Puzzle Piece by Piece"* PDF forms (SOLVINGASSESSMENT.PDF) **cannot** be edited or modified. They **can** be viewed and printed using either Adobe® Reader® 5.0, 6.0 or 7.0. Only WORD Forms can be edited or modified.

To load Acrobat® Acrobat Reader® 7.0:
1. Click on the Adobe® Reader® Windows folder.
2. Double-click on the **adbeRdr70_enu.exe** icon which is the Acrobat® Acrobat Reader® 7.0 Installer for Windows.
3. Follow the instructions in the Acrobat Reader® 7.0 Install Wizard (the pop-up box that appears), clicking **Continue/Next** and **Accept** as prompted.
4. Shut down your computer and restart it.
5. To access the CD-ROM, double-click on **My Computer** on your desktop, then double-click on the **CD-ROM** icon.

For PC's using Windows 95, 98 or ME

Please visit the Adobe® Web Site at www.adobe.com to download the latest version of Adobe® Acrobat Reader® for your PC's operating system. It's a free software download. If you have any further questions about Adobe® Acrobat Reader®, please visit the Adobe® Web site at www.adobe.com.

For Macintosh

Please visit the Adobe® Web Site at www.adobe.com to download the latest version of Adobe® Acrobat Reader® for the MAC. It's a free software download. If you have any further questions about Adobe® Acrobat Reader®, please visit the Adobe® Web site at www.adobe.com.

The Penny Heart

Martine Bailey

The Penny
Heart

HODDER &
STOUGHTON

First published in Great Britain in 2015 by Hodder & Stoughton
An Hachette UK company

1

Copyright © Martine Bailey 2015

The right of Martine Bailey to be identified as the Author of the Work has been
asserted by her in accordance with the Copyright, Designs and Patents Act 1988.

A CIP catalogue record for this title is available from the British Library

ISBN 978 1 444 76985 2
Ebook ISBN 978 1 444 76987 6

Typeset in Adobe Caslon Pro by Hewer Text UK Ltd, Edinburgh

Printed and bound by Clays Ltd, St Ives plc

Hodder & Stoughton policy is to use papers that are natural, renewable and recyclable
products and made from wood grown in sustainable forests. The logging and manufacturing
processes are expected to conform to the environmental regulations of the country of origin.

Hodder & Stoughton Ltd
Carmelite House
50 Victoria Embankment
London EC4Y 0DZ

www.hodder.co.uk

To Chris, Lucy and Leo,
Who made our Antipodean adventure a reality.

1

Manchester, England

Winter 1787

~ Sassafras Tea ~

Take a large spoonful of sassafras root ground to a powder and
put into a pint of boiling water, stirring until it is like a fine
jelly; then put wine and sugar to it and lemon, if it will agree.
A most refreshing drink sold liberally about the streets and
said to lift the spirits and ease the mind of suspicion, all for a
halfpenny piece.

Mother Eve's Secrets

Dusk shrouded Manchester's damp streets, disguising familiar landmarks and giving a lurid cast to buildings lit by oil lamp and candle. Michael Croxon dragged his brother past half-built skeletons of factories and mills, the lofty temples to the new religion of commerce. He marvelled at serried rows of golden windows shining against the mauve sky, announcing the new machines' inexhaustible industry. The rhythmic hum and clatter of the looms filled the air like music, a striding overture to a prosperous future. He had learned so much of the modern world on this visit; how damp air kept the cotton from breaking, where the wondrous looms might be purchased, and for what small cost the workers could be housed – and how easily replaced should they not prove satisfactory. At last he had found the grand venture that would prove his worth – and make him prodigiously rich, besides. In his excitement, his boot slipped on the frosty stones and he clutched at Peter to maintain his balance. An oil-black chasm opened up before him; the canal stank of drowned vegetation and blocked privies. He was glad of Peter's arm, but felt a flash of resentment at his gentle, 'Take it steady.'

They left the clamour of the mills and came to older streets. He recognised the gables of the ancient college at Chetham's, and took a side street, passing floridly tiled public houses that exuded bursts of hubbub and sudden wafts of beer and fried fish. At one corner a huddle of men smoked, one of their number whistling a slow Irish melody that never faltered as the tunesmith followed them with his eyes. The Manchester mills were luring in multitudes of the poor, as a poultice draws in filth: with every visit he saw greater degradation and lawlessness. The coming of night increased his anxiety. The coach to Greaves would wait for no one.

Then there it was at last, the pillared frontage of the Cross Keys inn. Passing through the gate, he found the inn yard crowded with a noisy rabble. Hawkers thrust unwanted items in their faces: a tray of knives, stinking fish. They shoved their way towards a group of fellow travellers, all of them smothered in cloaks and greatcoats, warily keeping watch over their boxes and baggage. A space was instantly made for the two gentlemen; both of them so fair and agreeably modish that a few onlookers, most especially women, cast covert glances towards them.

'Look. For all your harrying, we still have fifteen whole minutes.' Peter pointed towards the inn clock, his boyish voice reproachful. But if they were on time, it was only because he had spent all day chivvying Peter; cutting short his supper, insisting he broke off his goodbyes to that alderman's daughter, conscious all the time of the hands on his gold pocket watch, marching steadily forward to the moment at which he would announce his plans to his father. Though at twenty-five he was only two years older than Peter, the contrast between his own ambitions and his brother's indolence would be triumphant. Next, he must raise capital, find suitable land, and machines. He felt himself unstoppable, on the road to a glorious future.

The bill of charges for their journey confronted them, pasted on the wall. He turned to Peter. 'Did you keep back the right change for the journey? Look. Nine shillings and sixpence from Manchester to Greaves.'

Peter half-heartedly rummaged in his pockets. 'Damn it. My last few bob went to the barber. The coachman must change my pound note.'

'Will you never learn? I told you the coachman may choose not to change such a large sum. And if the coach is full and another passenger offers the correct fare, then what will you do? What shall I tell Father when I arrive home without you, all because of your negligence?'

Peter attempted a face of contrition, but Michael fancied his lips twitched in amusement. 'I am sorry. No, truly I am. But it cannot be helped. Shall I see if the landlord has change?' He looked vaguely about; but the press of people at the inn's entrance did not bode well.

'Well, I cannot lend it you.'

Peter's flippancy brought out the worst side of Michael's character; the bombastic older brother who must always be right.

At that moment a woman standing by them pulled at his sleeve – afterwards, he wondered that he hadn't noticed her at his elbow. She stepped forward into the lamplight.

'Sir, perhaps I can help you. I've a right lot of coin I can exchange for you.' Her voice was as clear as a bell, though marred by the accent of Manchester's lower orders.

Peter glanced at him triumphantly. 'You see. Providence provides.' He looked at the girl, a fine strong-looking piece, with a wooden tray hanging from her neck on which a jug and wooden cups were laid out. She looked handsome in a shabby, housemaid's sort of way. Wide feline eyes smiled at him from a pleasing heart-shaped face.

'It is a whole pound he needs change for,' he said gruffly.

'It's just as well I've had a good day, sirs.' She tested the fat leather bag in her hand. 'Now if you was to take this heavy coin it would be doing me a favour. Save me hauling it all the way to my mother's at Strangeways.'

She smiled modestly, clearly aware that he was the senior of the two brothers. 'Go on, help yourself to a cup, won't you? No, not a penny. I'll have less to carry.' She offered each of them the remains of her fare, a sweet and pungent tea. As she passed him the cup, her fingertips brushed his own for a pulsating moment. Drinking the tea, he wondered why he had never discovered this delight before; it was refreshing in the manner of spirits, setting off little thrills in his veins. After replacing the tea things with the money bag on her tray, she said gravely, 'This is a whole twenty shilling in coin. I should rather one of you counted it with me.'

Peter rushed forwards, of course, forever springing to help a lady. Though this was no lady, in spite of her lace cap trimmed with green ribbon. He hoped his brother could distinguish that much, for he was already murmuring, 'A pleasure. And most kind of you, dear girl.'

She glanced up at Peter's fawning expression with that sweet smile. 'Why, thank 'ee, sir.' Then she lowered her eyes as if she were quite unused to the civility of gentlemen. Michael pictured her in the very different exchanges of the lower orders: scenes of cursing, scolding, degradation. She had a remarkably well formed body, and her face was as fair as that of a duchess. As for her eyes, they were bright and probing when they met his, seeming to seek entry to some hidden chamber within himself. Then there it was in her bold stare; a stinging jolt; an invisible connection. Discomfited, he rapidly turned away.

The next time he looked, a cascade of copper and silver tumbled across the tray. Quickly, Peter and the girl began counting as he looked on, watching the girl especially. Soon they had made neat piles of shillings: six, seven, eight. Peter passed her the pound note and she folded it reverentially, tucking it into the pocket in her skirts.

'Seventeen shilling, eighteen shilling,' she counted, her clean and graceful hands gathering and heaping. 'Look. A black dog.' She held it up for them to see the black-leaded forgery of a sixpence. 'I'll not count that, you gentlemen needn't fret.' She replaced the coin with a shiny one of her own.

He glanced at the clock: it was almost half-past. 'Hurry, can't you?'

'Nearly there, sir. Nineteen, and that is surely twenty.' She stiffened, and raised her hand to cover her mouth. There was an awkward silence. 'On my mother's heart, there's some mistake,' she whimpered. 'Why, it's all wrong, there must be a half-crown more of coin here, at least.' She grew flustered, checking each tottering pile so clumsily that she toppled a few, undoing all their careful work.

Just at this juncture a crash at the gates announced the arrival of the Manchester Flyer, scattering bystanders and spraying mud like a racing plough. The horses strained in their harnesses as the coachman drew hard on the reins.

Peter tried to retrieve the situation. 'If we quickly recount these twenty?' he suggested. But the girl was too agitated to reason with. 'I can't account for it,' she wailed. 'I must have counted wrong. If I give you too much, I'll be for it all right.'

She stared a moment at the untidy heaps. Suddenly she gathered them all together in a tumble of coins. 'Oh, I am sorry, sirs; I wish I had never started. It's more than my skin's worth to lose a penny.'

Now the Flyer's coachman had dismounted, and their fellow passengers eagerly pressed towards the carriage doors. The man at the head of the queue proffered the right fare and received a friendly salute from the coachman.

'Peter, for goodness' sake come on!' He picked up his own bags and looked back impatiently over his shoulder.

'Never mind, dear,' Peter said. 'Thank you for trying.'

'Here, sir. Your pound note.' She rummaged in the pocket of her skirts and pushed it back into his hand.

In the event, they had to wait to board the coach. A couple of youths clambered up on the roof, and were slow in hauling their bags up beside them. The old fellow in front of them fussed abominably over being parted from his portmanteau. Finally, Michael paid the coachman his nine and sixpence. He lingered to watch Peter pay, torn between wanting to see his younger brother humiliated and a desire to board at once.

'What's this for a lark?' asked the coachman, holding Peter's pound note aloft as if it were a filthy rag. 'You think I don't have no notion what a banknote looks like?' Michael frowned, looking closely, and then saw it clear before his eyes. Instead of the copper-plate inscription, *Skipton Bank I promise to pay the bearer on demand One Pound*, and the cashier's freshly inked signature, the note bore all the signs of a forgery; the ink a crude blur, the motif '*One pound*' a childish blot.

'The girl!' he shouted. Then, to Peter, 'You damned idiot.'

Michael looked to where she had stood with her tray – of course she had gone. A bearded man selling clay pipes now stood in her place. Craning his neck, he saw she was no longer in the yard.

'Stay here with the bags until I return,' he shouted at Peter. Consumed with fury, he shouldered his way to the gates, and from there, by great luck, he saw her running in the distance, a flurry of movement beneath a street lamp. He set off after her, his feet pounding the hard frost, feeling the same savage exhilaration as when he was a boy, hunting with his dog, careering after rats in the stables.

His father's money. It must be repaid. He could never admit to his father that Peter had been duped by a Manchester swindler – and a trollop of a woman at that. It was a matter of preserving his reputation. Careless of his boots slithering on the mud, he ran until a stitch jabbed his side, his gaze never leaving his quarry. She was moving fast, darting through pools of darkness but always emerging into murky lamplight. There were few other people abroad; only gaunt creatures shuffling close to the walls.

Then two gentlemen emerged from a side alley, nearly colliding with him. He cried, 'I have been robbed!' and, enjoying the drama of his situation, pointed at the woman's distant figure. When he set off again he could hear their footsteps behind him. He felt like the leader of a pack, his breath white vapour in the darkness.

Rapid hoofbeats and a post-horn trumpeting the rapid trills of Clear the Road signalled the approach of the Manchester Flyer. Michael was forced to take refuge in a doorway and protect his eyes from the hail of dirt from the wheels. As it receded, he squinted up at its bulk, but of course Peter had not boarded without him. He looked once more for the woman, peering this way and that. Devil take her, she had vanished.

He had marked the spot of her last appearance with his eye, but when he reached it he stopped, perplexed. Before him stood an old shop: a ramshackle place with a wooden sign swinging over the door. His fellow pursuers arrived at his back, bending double and puffing hard.

'She's gone,' he said. 'Disappeared into the air.'

The elder of the two gentlemen, who introduced himself as a magistrate, fetched a lantern and began to inspect the vicinity. The ancient shop sign bore a primitive design of a quill pen and an ape-faced angel with a sword. Squinting, he saw that it read 'The Pen & Angel'. The tiny pool of light moved over a window displaying only curling, ancient paper behind its dirty pane. Then, he spotted a narrow opening that he had earlier thought to be a drainpipe. Approaching the ginnel, he saw it was barely a few feet wide. Alerting his companions, he slid his body between its walls, and was instantly so cold that he might have fallen underground. Coal black darkness enveloped him; he was forced to reach out with fingers, simultaneously recoiling from the oozing slime. He groped his way forward, fearing each step might betray him into a pit or sewer. With great relief, he emerged into a gloomy yard, from which the only exit was an unobtrusive door in a blank brick wall. When he tried the door, it opened.

He had expected some sort of wretched warren. Instead, he found himself inside the loveliest of mansions, in a salon lit with coloured lights reflected by gilded mirrors. At the centre of the chequerboard floor rose a fountain. Picking up one from a row of glasses on the stand, he drank thirstily, and was astonished to find that the fountain ran with wine. As if in a marvellous dream, he wandered into a parlour where a half-dozen women lounged beneath crystal girandoles, dressed in flimsy silks. He could see at once, from their hot glances and painted pouts, that they were as wanton as the Devil. He could smell them, too: a fecund dampness beneath their ratafia scent.

He inquired where the girl with the green-ribboned cap had gone, and a plump whore giggled. 'Mary?' she said, and pointed up the stairs.

For a long while he explored silent corridors lined with doors: all very fine, but as gloomy as sin from a paucity of candles. He would have given up, only his boot struck what he fancied was a dog crouching on the stair. As he reached out he touched a mop of soft hair. A child in a nightgown, no more than eight years old, cringed back from him against the wall, whimpering like an infant. Just then the ceiling creaked. Footsteps sounded above his head; there was something so furtive about them that he knew they belonged to his quarry. The ceiling creaked again. Forgetting the child, he ran up the narrow stairs and through a door. Outside, he halted to breathe in the clean cold air of the night.

He was standing on a flat roof, where neglected washing hung as hard as boards across sagging lines. His feet slid unsteadily over twinkling frost as he searched behind ghostly laundry. With a clattering crack, he knocked over a stool. In response, he heard a sharp, female breath. He lifted a bed sheet that glittered and burned his fingers with cold. The girl stood against a high wall, unable to retreat any further.

'Here. Take it.' Her voice was different, almost refined, a breathless whisper. She threw the pound note at him and it fluttered lazily to the ground. Her eyes were fixed upon him, very wide and bright. 'Now let me go free.'

He picked up the note and stuck it in his waistcoat. 'Why should I?' he asked. 'You stole it.' His breath was still hot from the chase; his throat painful.

At first she didn't answer. Her cloak had fallen open and her skin looked icy white in the moonlight; she was panting like a hart at bay. Then her eyes met his, with a penetrating recognition that slashed through every layer of his earnest respectability.

'Why should you?' she said slowly. 'Because that pound is nothing to you. Because I know what you are after.'

Later, he understood she knew him better than he did himself. 'If you let me go. No one need ever know about you,' she said very softly and the unspoken words thrilled him. Then, in the light of the frosty stars, he saw her smile. It was not such a sweet smile now. A fierce and wanton smile.

Her pale hand reached for her skirt edge and lifted it to her knees. A white stocking. It was impossible to prevent his manhood from rising at the prospect. Her face was entirely fixed upon his, entirely commanding. He strode to her and grasped her skirt in his fist, and the cloth felt fired up with an unearthly force, like an electric charge that galvanised his whole body. His sigh emerged as a groan.

She had discovered him. However courageously he battled to maintain his high moral manner to the world, this strumpet knew him better. Not for him the simpering misses whose coy glances Peter chased; he liked a bold woman best of all. Why, here in Manchester, if he had only managed to free himself of Peter, he had glimpsed some wild creatures that had thrilled his very being. Next time, he had vowed to himself, he would travel alone.

There followed an interval in which he scarcely believed his senses. Somewhere in the recesses of his mind he had comprehended what she was from the moment he saw her. Desire ignited inside him like gunpowder.

'There they are!' came a cry from the doorway. 'Catch her quick!'

Damn their eyes! It was the two gentlemen, with a constable. He sprang back and battled to recollect himself, then lifted the pound note, like a trophy.

'Proof,' he said, his voice still thick. 'I caught her red-handed.' The men rushed up and congratulated him; he felt himself to be a hero. But it was a poor sort of balm to his recent pitch of excitement, for he still felt queasy and itchy about the loins.

The constable took the girl roughly by the arm.

'No, I beg you,' she wailed.

'Sir,' the constable interrupted. 'Will you bear witness in court that this young woman stole a pound note from you?'

'From my brother,' he corrected.

'I will hang for it, sir. Look to your conscience,' she cried. 'Think of it. All on your word. And I gave it back at once,' she appealed to them all. 'He knows it was an honest mistake!'

He couldn't look at her again without shame inflaming him. He violently wished the other men would disappear. He could have been indulged as he wished, and then he might have returned triumphantly to Peter with the pound note. It scarcely mattered that they had missed the coach. They could have travelled tomorrow and no one been the wiser.

Yet still he could save her from the gallows and agree he had made a mistake. Damn this crowd of onlookers. But the girl, was she not very wicked, would she not continue her tricks on other men? She was shameless. She had discovered him. He had been on the cusp of revealing his lewdest, most sinful self.

'Please sir, don't be living with the murdering of me. Don't have it on your conscience!' She was struggling in the constable's grasp, trying to throw herself down on her knees before him.

He tucked the pound note back in his pocket. 'I'll bear witness,' he said, and he let them congratulate him all the way down to the constable's office.

2

Newgate Prison, London

Winter 1787

~ To Make the Best Apple Pie ~

Make a good puff paste crust and lay some around the sides of the dish. Pare and quarter your apples and lay a row of apples thick; lay in half your muscovado sugar, mince a little lemon peel fine, throw over and squeeze a little lemon juice over them, and a few cloves here and there and cinnamon as you like it, and the rest of your apples and sugar. Boil the peelings of the apples in some fair water, with a blade of mace and a little sugar, till it is very good, strain it and add to your pie. Put on the upper crust and bake it. When it is enough serve with fresh cold cream.

Mother Eve's Secrets

The black-capped judge gave Mary his verdict: she must return to Newgate and two days later, be taken 'thence to a place of execution and there hanged by the neck until you are dead'. So this is it, girl, she told herself, she was going to go dance with the hempen collar about her throat. She put the boldest face she could upon it; not swooning or squeaking; to die hard was her creed. She had sworn to die game, the day she made her oath to follow The Life.

Her mobsman, Charlie Trebizond, came down to London and paid the garnish fee to the jailer to keep her in the best style, on the Master's Side of Newgate. 'Anything you want, I'll pay, Mary,' he'd said, his monkey face grave, his lean figure garbed in black velvet and ruffles. And so he should be flash-handed with his coin, she thought. Charlie was the king of the fake-screeve racket, the false letter dodge, the high-flying game. It was said that not even the Lord High Chancellor himself could tell one of Charlie's fakes from the genuine article. A damned shame it had been Red the Forger who had faked that damned pound note, and not Charlie, she thought sourly.

Aunt Charlotte had raised her on tales of the Hangman's Supper. 'Before you goes off to the next life, you sups with him who snaps your neck,' was how she put it, with her reptile's smile. 'It's like a binding oath to forgive your murderer before he snuffs you out. It's so you won't be a phantom wandering this earth till the end of time.' The pluckiest lags always gave the executioner a fancy meal the night before they swung. So Mary set out to do it the proper way; ordering in a rump of beef and a dozen of claret. There were tarts and cakes and trifles too; it looked like a queen's feast arranged on fine pressed linen. Piggot, the hangman, was her guest of honour.

15

'You'll make it quick?' Charlie asked the hangman.

Piggott halted a moment in guzzling the wine and tearing the beef with his gravestone teeth. His frog's eyes assessed Mary's throat. 'No more'n two minutes, sir. I could snap a little neck like that in one hand.' Then, wheezing bawdily, he added, 'I tell you what, I'll give 'er a pull on her pretty ankles, to bring 'er on the faster.'

'That's enough,' Charlie snapped. 'Just remember there's another guinea when you bring her straight to me for a decent burial. Not a hair out of place, mind.'

Piggott nodded, settling his gaze lower than her throat this time.

She would have liked to smash a bottle of wine in Piggott's leering face, but instead she poured him another glass. He was her journeyman to the next world, and she was relying on him for an easy passage.

She had heard that when you look death in the face, your entire past life springs before your eyes. So it did seem, that final night before she faced the gallows. Scenes played in her mind like a brightly-lit theatre. There sat Granny sleeping, a dark shape in the parlour chair. She'd groped to find her hand – and when the old woman's fingers didn't return her squeeze, she shook her arm. 'Wake up,' she urged, but Granny's lips never moved again. Only a thread of dark blood slid down from her nose to her warty chin. When she touched her cheek, it was stone cold.

I'm all on me own now, she said to herself in the hush of the firelight. Alone seemed such a dreadful notion: an emptiness that swallowed the cottage, Granny, and everything she had ever known. She had few memories of her mother, who had kissed her one moment and knocked her flying the next. 'Liza went wandering off with a fellow across Slaiden Bridge, and was swept away in the river,' Granny had said. She had never missed her slummock of a mother.

Taking a rushlight, she'd gone to look in Granny's chamber, where she'd always said she kept money set by. All was as neat as a pin: the picture of King George still pasted on the wall, the scrap of lace on the shelf, the mound of the bed covered in ancient patchwork.

Lifting the lid of the wooden trunk, she found all Granny's treasures: a lock of her grandfather's flame-red hair, a cracked china teacup, a few lines from a newspaper that told of Liza Jebb's death in a river accident. She rooted deeper and there it was; a leather money bag. But when she turned it upside-down, it was empty. She felt along the bottom of the trunk, but there was only a paper lying flat against the wood. She snatched it up and held it before the dripping rushlight.

It was written in a clear round hand, and though she spelled the words mighty slowly, her hours poring over the spelling book with Granny proved their worth.

To whomever be attending to the sad affairs of Liza Jebb
   Dear Sir,
   I wish to make myself known to you after reading in the newspaper of the tragic passing of my dear cousin Liza. It is a most terrible shock to learn of that sad accident, most especially as many years have passed without word between us. I confess I am also at fault, being now a wealthy widow with a thriving trade here in Manchester Town. Sir, you must understand that I am Charlotte Spenlove, that was Charlotte Jebb before marriage. Though our connection has not been maintained of late, I believe I may now be the last remaining of dear Liza's kin.
   Sir, I should be most obliged if you would do me the kindness to write by reply of any funerary arrangements or any other business you believe I should attend to. I can assure you I am acquainted with an attorney who will vouchsafe my credentials and offer all assurances should you so wish.
   Your servant,
   Mrs Charlotte Spenlove (Widow)
   At the Sign of The Pen & Angel
   Fetter Lane
   Manchester

How could Granny not have told her about her living kin – this cousin, or should that be aunt – Charlotte?

In the morning Granny's face had been as red as a plum. Whatever happened, the rent was due and there was no money left in the cottage. Taking the letter and what food she could find, she let herself out of the door and set off stealthily for the road, in search of a wagon headed Manchester-way.

Arriving at the Pen and Angel, footsore and hungry, she had needed to gather all the courage of her twelve short years to insist on speaking to Mrs Charlotte Spenlove. Behind the false shop, she'd been led through a ramble of rooms, down stone stairs to the greasy kitchen. Aunt Charlotte had not proved the flighty ginger piece she had expected her mother's cousin to be. Instead, a vast wheezing shape had waddled towards her. To her horror, the toad-faced woman asked, 'So who might you be?' Then, snatching up the letter, she began to guffaw; a horrible sound like a broken bellows. She knew at once that she had made a very great fool of herself, but she did not understand how. Then the woman brandished the letter and cackled, 'This don't signify nowt, sweetheart. I in't no more your kin than you're Uncle Tom's horse.

'Come and sit by the fire, pet. Want a Little Devil? *Devilinos*, the Italians call 'em.' She pushed a dish of exquisite little brown globes, studded with comfits, towards her. Mary was as hungry as a hawk; when she put one in her mouth it was sweet yet bitter, melting but nutty; by far the most marvellous thing she had eaten in her life. She stared at the dish longingly.

'Good, eh? Have another one. God sends meat but the Devil sends chocolate. I make 'em the Italian fashion.' They both took another and chewed in silence. Then Auntie fixed her black ferrety eyes on Mary and said, 'So you have come, after all.'

'What?'

'I saw it in the cards last night. A carroty-haired girl trudging along the road. Look. The past.' She flipped over a card that showed a moon and road, plainly inked on card. 'This is you. Run away, ain't you, lovey?'

Mary nodded, all agape.

'Choose three cards. The past. The future. The answer.'

Reverently, Mary turned the three top cards and slid them towards the woman.

'Here goes. The past.' The first was a walking skeleton with a leering grin.

'Death,' Auntie wheezed and looked hard into Mary's face. 'Looked Death square in the face, 'aven't you?'

Flabbergasted, Mary nodded. 'Me granny.'

'We must all give the crows a pudding, one day. What's this now?' The next card was a grand building with towers, and dozens of lighted windows. 'The future looks grand, dearie. The house of money. A lucky one, in't you?'

'Me?' Mary's palms itched with want.

'Now for the answer.'

The last card showed a fancy lock and key. 'What's that mean?' she asked.

'Most momentous,' Aunt Charlotte rested her many chins on her sausage fingers and mused. 'The key. To open all doors,' she said slowly, her rasping voice rich with knowing. Did Mary understand? She wasn't sure. It was good, Auntie said, but it wasn't yet clear.

Maybe it was Mary coming into a House of Money one day, but Auntie told her she could stay. In return for a pallet in the corner and plenty of kitchen leavings, Mary ground loaves of sugar, chopped and peeled food and scrubbed pots. And when she was finally allowed to go up the carpeted stairs into the Palace, she found the most remarkable place she had ever seen.

Fence End, where she'd lived with Granny, had been a dour, grey-and-mud sort of a place, but the Palace was as tawdry as a fairground and as wild as a circus. The girls at Ma Brimstone's wore pink paint and a rainbow of frilled petticoats, which they lifted up in saucy postures at the tall glass windows. As for the running of the establishment, Ma had not forgotten her days on the stage at Drury Lane. She ran it like a roaring great play, with a half-hour bell telling her cast to get in place before the lamps were lit down Jerusalem Passage. The stage was set with red and green lanterns, gauzy curtains, wafted perfumes, sofas, and a fountain that trickled with real – if very cheap – wine. Aunt Charlotte was everyone's Auntie, and provided the food: the ladies' sugared ratafias, plates of toasted cheese at four in the morning, and beef and eggs for the gentlemen's hearty breakfasts. But her pastry-cook's heart was in the buffets that glittered under the coloured lamps: the sugarwork Pleasure Gardens, and Rocky Islands decorated with jellies, rock candies, and pyramids of sweetmeats. And best of all were the chocolate Little Devils, morsels of magic that all the gentlemen loved.

Ma Brimstone herself was a cadaverous old bawd with lead-white skin and a passion for chinking gold. 'She were once famous for her marble complexion,' Aunt Charlotte whispered, 'but it were all out of a bottle, a bottle of lead.' All her girls had to be extraordinary, in some advertisable way. So Miss Nancy was her French widow, very cold and pretend-genteel, and said to have mysterious arts never before seen in the north. Black Bess was mighty strong, as black as tar, and advertised as most welcoming at the front door, but requiring double payment for the rear. Miss Edwina was a Sapphist, for the ladies, if they didn't care for athletically-built Captain Locket. Or there was strapping Miss Dora, who wore a man's boots and had a case of whips and birches, or child-size Miss Lucy, who was rumoured to have sold her maidenhead twenty-five times over, under different names.

It was Aunt Charlotte who explained to her about The Life. There were two tribes in the world; those who knew The Life, studied the game, and profited accordingly; and there were the gulls and dupes who were their natural victims. Aunt Charlotte boasted that she was a born member of the Ancient Order of Rogues. Her ma had been a fator, selling fortunes at fairs, and her da a swell cracksman, head of a crew of locksmiths and sneaks. 'Baubles and trinkets was 'is game,' she recalled with a fond look to her moony face. ''E 'ad an eye for the glim trade.' Mary was always on at her aunt to talk the odd backward lingo of rogues, until at last she'd round on her with a swipe to the head.

'Bing avast, chitty-faced tib!' she'd cry. 'There be caz and pannam to be snic.'

Mary begged to know the secret meaning, and shook with laughter when she heard it was only: 'Be gone, baby face. There's bread and cheese to slice.'

'Can't you teach me, Auntie?' she'd wheedled, until at last, when she was fourteen, Aunt Charlotte gave in. 'It's not some jest, Mary, it's the most solemnest vow you can make. If you want to learn the lingo you 'as to join the Ancient Order.'

She gave it not a second thought, not even of Granny, who'd been duped by Auntie's racket. Every week the cook chased news of any likely funeral with letters purporting to be from respectable kin. Granny, it seemed, had been gulled into sending all her small savings to pay for empty promises. Nor did she give a tinker's curse for the slaveys who worked to give coin to the thieving class. One famous night they had got Mary deep cut on the gin they called Strip-Me-Naked. Giddy as a top, she had been held up by two of Ma Brimstone's girls and had a full pint of spirit emptied over her head.

Her hair had been sopping with sweet liquor as she heard Auntie pronounce, 'I, Charlotte Spenlove, roguess of the nugging house known as the Palace, do 'stall thee, Mary Jebb, to the Society of Rogues, in the name of the Tawney Prince, the Black Spy, otherwise known as Old Harry. And from henceforth, it shall be lawful for thee to follow The Life and cant for thy living in all places.'

She had been as sick as a dog that night, but even when she woke next day, light-headed and feeble, she knew she was born again, sworn to a new family as a roguess for the rest of her days.

❧

The sallow gloom that passed for daylight in Newgate roused her. After taking great care with her rig-out, she shivered through a sermon with the other condemned wretches. Time seemed both to race and drag until she was shoved through the door into Old Bailey lane. The noise was near deafening: St Sepulchre's church was tolling the execution bell, and the crowd was roaring in a frenzy. All the pluck in the world couldn't stop Mary's first sight of the gallows giving her a damnable punch to the guts. There was Piggott up on the platform, strangling a whole line of fellows, chorused by the deafening groans and hoots from the crowd. Her chains were removed and she was tied in a line with three other women: to her left was a whimpering old dame, who trembled like she had a palsy. On her other side was a woman like a brawny fishwife, famed as a murderess, who seemed not to care a jot for the proceedings. Last was a weeping young whore, who had quarrelled with her fancy man and been nabbed for thieving a snuffbox. A posy of flowers landed at Mary's feet, and though her bonds made it difficult, she succeeded in picking it up and holding it as tightly as a prayer book. Dark ruby rosebuds they were, signifying mourning. Make it easy, make it quick, she recited silently.

At a signal she stepped towards the platform to a roaring cheer. The crowd was a sea of upturned faces, waving handkerchiefs and hats. Charlie had fetched her a white gown, and she'd let her red hair down to her thighs and wound it with white ribbons. Guards stepped up to hold the mob back; fingers struggled to touch her. She hoped Charlie could see her; he wasn't in the grandstand, but had said he'd hire a window at a house in the lane. Briefly, she wondered if that gentry cove had come to crow at her, the one who had put her here, the two-faced dog. Above her loomed the wooden platform, as high as a stage at a theatre. She was thrust towards another turnkey and a grubby hemp noose pulled over her head. Neatly, she pulled aside her hair, though the vile tickle of the hempen necklace made her legs weak. Even amidst the shoving and roaring she kept her chin up and her brain sharp. She had learned the Hanging Psalm by heart, to recite to the mob. 'Let the bones which thou has broken rejoice . . .' That was it. Then she would cast the posy at the handsomest buck she could spy. The crowd would raise a roar at that; soon the ballad singers would be busy composing new lines. Her memorial was sure to be printed in The Newgate Calendar: Mary Jebb, the Newgate Blossom, lost to the world while still in lovely youth; careless and trim to the end.

Ahead, something of a palaver had broken out, but she had no inclination to look too hard towards the beams where the corpses dangled. A heavy hand fell on her shoulder.

'Mary Jebb?' She nodded at the turnkey. The other three women were being shoulder-clapped, too.

A legal-looking fellow pushed before them and started to shout from a paper. In the midst of shrieks and boos and the rushing in her ears, it was hard to understand his meaning at first. A few words reached her: 'His Majesty . . . Mercy . . . seven years.' Crazily, her first thought was that the bloody king had stolen her moment of glory.

❧

Back in her old room at Newgate she contemplated her new fate. Seven years' transportation to some godless place no one had ever been to, or scarcely even heard of. Lags were no longer sent to America, which at least had people and cities and regular trade. Botany Bay was some freakish wilderness across the world, spied out by that tosspot, Captain Cook.

'I should rather have snuffed it with honour,' she told Charlie.

'Come now, Mary. It gives us time to get you out of here and home for good. A whole long month,' he said in his lawyer's voice. Charlie's plan was to file a writ of error, after getting the cully to withdraw all charges. 'You'll walk free, Mary. It's just like any sting we've pulled off in the past. I'll make it easy, I'll write the screeve saying he's mighty sorry but he nabbed the wrong woman. It's as easy as kiss my hand. You get the fellow to sign, and you'll walk from here a free woman.'

With no more than paper and ink and her own coaxing words, she persuaded the cully to come down to London. She was saved from the gallows, she said, so she wanted to forgive him, in the flesh, as a farewell gift. Like a pigeon he hopped and fluttered towards her until she held him tightly in her snare. Within a week the cove agreed to sign the retraction.

Charlie's paper was drawn up ready, and the gull was to visit her at three o'clock the next Saturday. At first it seemed the fellow was only late, or perhaps there had been an accident? The bell struck four, and five, then six, and seven. When the gates were locked she saw it, as clear as a gypsy's crystal. The gull had flown away, leaving her to pay her dues on the far side of the world. The biggest sting of her life – that should have saved her from the pits of hell – had failed. She cursed him as a turncoat and a black-hearted dog, but all the oaths in the world couldn't save her from Botany Bay.

A week later she shuffled out into the prison yard, her legs in irons. Charlie had not shown his face again. Overnight she was dead cargo, no longer worth a swell cove's notice. The yard was a foul place; half-naked wretches loitered in the stink, many as thin as wraiths. Bony children played at an open drain, their eyes huge in dirt-caked faces. Gin was the Newgate Master's best trade, and those with a few pence chose oblivion on the stony ground. A racket broke out across the way; it was the other women from the Hanging Day, also bound for Botany Bay. The prisoner she later knew as Ma Watson was squawking at a fellow crouched over a workbench.

'What's it to you if I want a dog picture?' she wailed, shaking her skinny fist. The rest of the women were spurring her on, laughing like old mares. Mary sauntered over and all fell silent, for she still had the style of a mobsman's Poll, in her striped taffety and feathered hat. The man looked up. 'Want a love token for your sweetheart, my pretty?' He lifted one up for her to inspect, a sparkling disc of copper. 'Jenks is the name. Only a bob each, best workmanship you'll find.'

The crone grasped her sleeve and opened her toothless mouth, ready to start up again.

'Stow it, you old moaner,' Jenks barked. 'Let the lady look. Here's the ones waiting to be hammered out.'

Mary inspected the designs inked on paper, waiting to be engraved. Ma Watson's was crude enough; an outline of a house with *My Cotage of Peace * Took From Me* on the front, and a stick-limbed dog on the reverse above the words *FOR*GET*ME*NOT*.

She flicked through the rest. Most were sentimental rhymes, the usual sailor's farewells of the 'when this you see, remember me,' variety.

She lingered over an image of a man and woman, hand in hand, circled with chains: *My Dear Son, Absent But Not Forgot, Your Sorry Mother*.

Too late to be sorry, now, she thought. Next, that whore Janey had commissioned seven identical tokens. Mary smiled at the picture of a man and woman coupling and the verse:

Though My Fair Flesh Transported Be, My Blissful O still longs for thee.

Who did Mary have to remember her? She watched as Jenks hammered the disc with a nail tip, every blow confirming the rotten truth of it. Charlie had dropped her. Any day soon she would be shipped off with these filthy slummocks to the ends of the earth. Her whole existence would be forgotten.

Ma Watson clawed at her sleeve again. 'He's got no one to look after him. Bobby's his name—'

'Get off me, you crack-pate!' Shaking off the crone she marched back to her own comfortable quarters on the Master's Side. How had it come to this, that she had no truelove, not even a child or a mongrel dog?

Next day when she returned to the yard she hung back while the prison guard sang the latest ballad to the band of ragtag women:

> *'There's whores, pimps and bastards, a large costly crew,*
> *Maintained by the sweat of a labouring few,*
> *They should have no commission, place, pension or pay,*
> *Such locusts should all go to Botany Bay . . .'*

'I never reckoned to be remembered in song,' hooted the woman they called Brinny. Were they halfwits? The whole country despised them; they were being swilled away like hogwash.

Mary strode up to Jenks. 'Here,' she said, handing him a scrap of paper very beautifully scribed. 'I want it done in that Lady's Hand, good and clear, not those bodged capitals.'

> *Though chains hold me fast,*
> *As the years pass away,*
> *I swear on this heart*
> *To find you one day.*

Beside it was the screed for the reverse, with a pattern of hearts, chains, and knives to be incised about the edge:

MARY JEBB AGE 19
TRANSPORTED 7 YEARS
TO THE ENDS OF THE EARTH

'Two the same? Double-dealing your sweethearts, eh?' She shot him a glance like poison, and threw down two bob.

Jenks didn't do a bad job. Once she'd pawned her fine hat to the jailer, she had the money to see both the tokens safely parcelled up and posted. Seven years with no return, she thought. That might suit these common prigs, but she was going to engrave her destiny with the ink of Fate. She would never let Mary Jebb be forgotten.

∾

At first the voyage on the *Experiment* had seemed a pleasure jaunt after Newgate: the master had let the convicts exercise on deck, have their saucy games, and feast on perfumed fruits with curious names and colours. A few weeks into the voyage the first floggings took place. A bunch of sots had grabbed a cask of grog and, with less brains than guts, had drunk the lot and been discovered flat on the floor. All the convicts were mustered, as the captain droned on of forgiveness and such codswallop. Still, it had been as good as a church-gathering, to get a good eyeful of all the other lags.

As yet, Mary had scant interest in the other women; she wanted no pals. They were either rivals to be battled with or trulls to be elbowed aside. She stood alone and watchful, the habitual stance of a fly-girl like her. It wasn't women who would keep her alive but men – or to begin with, a strong, obedient, hard-knuckled man. She was still well togged in her striped taffety, and she kept her white skin clean. Already some of the flightier young girls had paired off with the crew, but she reckoned a sailor a poor investment, no sooner bedded than he'd abandon her and sail back to Blighty.

The topmost lags swaggered by the rail, hard-bitten mobsmen scarred by murder and villainy. Their molls would be slaveys, cursed and beaten, and shared between mates. She would have to wager on a fellow from the lower orders.

For sure she could always do worse than Jack Pierce. When he had given her the odd hopeful smile she had returned it sweetly. At first she'd thought him nothing but a flat – a sailor transported for claiming a mate's prize money. But he was bonny, with his long fair locks and china-blue eyes. And he had a lucky shine to him; some Church Society had picked him off the streets and paid to have him trained up as a seaman. Though he was no more than twenty, he was well-liked by the crew and the redcoats. As for the navigation and such-like he had learned, she'd already calculated how useful that might prove. Within the day she had him snared. When he kissed her and told her she was his girl, she wondered if he was that square he thought her an innocent. Day by day she wound him in as tightly as she could, turning herself into a prim girl, in need of a sweetheart's protection. Whatever it takes, she told herself, you've got to clamber to the top of this stinking heap.

Then the wild South Seas had destroyed such pleasure-trip fancies and gawping at the men. For four months they were soaked in stinking green slime, while the vessel was shaken like a rat. 'Damn you God, let me die,' Ma Watson had groaned like a litany, and a chorus agreed. The drinking water swarmed with worms, the biscuits with weevils, the bilges stank with rancid rations and dead rats. Rumours raged that the Navy Office had given orders they all must be drowned on a certain day, so long as it was far from England. Battened down in a waterlogged rolling coffin, they would believe anything. Almost eight months from England, an island was sighted with a name that sounded like Demon's Land, but a black squall hit them like a battering ram and there was no safe landing. To a chorus of miserable wailing, a young wife gave birth to a baby girl, as dead as a doorpost, which was cast overboard the following day. Next, a feeble-minded pedlar woman managed to bang her head and drown herself in the filthy swill. She lay dead for three days in chains before the stink of her persuaded them to report it, so fierce was the clamour for her ration. The food had dwindled to a cup of gruel each day, with a speck of fish swimming in it. That was their lot, all they had to keep body and soul together.

It could have been day or night in the pitch-black hold, when old Ma Watson started up her wailing. 'Is that all there is? How'm I to live on that slip-slop? I'd give me two eyes for a slice of apple pie.' She was brain-cracked, but spoke for them all.

Then Tabby Jones joined in, holding forth on the making of the best apple pie: the particular apples, whether reinettes or pippins, the bettermost flavourings: cinnamon, cloves, or a syrup made from the peelings. Slowly, groans of vexation turned to appreciative mumblings. Someone else favoured quince, another lemon. Apples, they all agreed, though the most commonplace of fruit, did produce an uncommon variety of delights: pies and puddings, creams and custards, jellies and junkets, ciders and syllabubs. The time passed a deal quicker and merrier than before.

Janey, the whore who had once been famed in Harris's *List of Covent Garden Ladies*, told them, in her child's voice, that the best dish she ever tasted was a Desert Island of Flummery, at a mansion in Grosvenor Square. 'It was all over jellies and candies and dainty figures, and a hut of real gold-leaf. Like eating money, it were. I fancied meself a proper duchess.'

She knew what Janey meant. When she had first met Aunt Charlotte she had gorged herself until her fingers were gummy with syrup and cream. There was one cake she never forgot; a puffed conceit of cream, pastry, and pink sugar comfits. She bit her knuckles hungrily and sucked the blood. It came to her then that they were starving, slowly and surely, to death.

They all hushed as Brinny, the one murderess of their crew, told them of the making of her bride cake, with primrose yellow butter and raisins of the sun, fattened on smuggled brandy. The further they sailed from England, the fonder they grew of the pleasures of home: plum trees with bowed branches, brambles in the hedge, cream from a beloved cow. Someone asked if Brinny's bridegroom was as fine as her cake. 'Sadly he were not,' she said dolefully. 'Why else d'ye think I be sitting here, transported for the murdering of the old dog with a dose of his own ratsbane?' Everyone laughed rustily at that, like machines grinding back to life.

The women's talk interested Mary mightily; for it stripped bare their hearts' desires: Janey's for luxury, Brinny's for her wedding day's pride, all of them for secret pleasures. And the stuff of hearts' desires was always of interest to an out-and-out racket-girl like her.

She mulled it all over, as they picked at sores and cursed every battering of the ocean against the ship's timbers. Finally she asked a question: 'Do you reckon a man might be snared by food?'

Why, it was easy as pie they said – a man was not so much led by his tail as his belly. For he must eat three times a day, which was twice more than most could raise the other appetite. Surely all men longed for their mother's milk, for a life of ease, to sprawl in a cradle of wifely care? In the hopeless darkness, secrets poured forth from those who had spent a lifetime turning tricks and picking pockets. Their talk turned to stranger receipts: the cure-alls and quackeries that transformed a few pennies into a bag of sovereigns. Janey giggled about the nostrum she had once hawked to keep the face eternally young that was mere water and ashes. Mother Watson's cure-all elixir was mostly stinking lye from piss-pots. As for love potions, they were the easiest to fob off on simpletons. A pretty-coloured water and a few magic words – it was astonishing how fast a fool was parted from his purse. Death potions, too – Brinny told them everything she had learned from her lover the apothecary, before she tired of him, too, and dosed him with his own poison.

All the while, Mary picked out the chief threads of their notions: that a body wanted pleasure in this life and not the next, and eternally longed for youth and health, and would risk a fortune for beauty. The purchase of love was irresistible, and the procurement of murder more common than even she had guessed. The best of it, the essence, she scratched so deeply in her memory that it left an enduring trace, like the ghosts of letters on a well-worn slate.

Five years later

3

Greaves, Lancashire

Summer 1792

~ To Make Knotted Biscuits of Apricots ~

Take ripe Apricots, pare, stone and beat them small, then boil them till they are thick. Take them off the fire and beat them up with sifted Sugar and Aniseeds to make a pretty fine paste. Make into little rolls the thickness of straw and tye them in little Knots in what form you please; dry them in the Stove or in the Sun.

> The best receipt of Mrs Jonah Moore, given to her by her grandmamma

I fancy you think little of who makes the food you eat. Thrice a day it appears. Do you truly know whose fingers touched it? Do you give a moment's attention to the mind that devised your dish, its method and ingredients? Of course you do not. That would drag you out of your comfortable chair, along the corridor, down narrow rickety stairs, along a greasy stone floor to the under-regions of your home. There work a pair of quick but red-scabbed hands, a pair of eyes that judge and shape your food upon its platter. A mind entirely unknown to you directs these preparations – yet you allow it to choose each morsel that will enter your mouth. You are not a menial, a scullion. Your thoughts are occupied with higher matters.

It is a notion of mine that we distract ourselves with false fears, turning our eyes from the true horrors stalking this world. When I was young I had many foolish terrors: a dread of speaking in large company, or having to dance or sing or exhibit some other accomplishment. My name is Grace, but I was never as graceful as my name promised. I envied those girls who were bright and glib, for I was left much alone, and developed a habit of watchful silence.

When I was a child we were as good as anyone else who lived in Greaves. Mother's dowry had bought Palatine House, the largest house on Wood Street. My father decreed I must not be indulged by learning of any kind, it being sure to spoil a female. He especially forbade any education in the Fine Arts, though my mother had been a painter of some talent when they first met.

My mother rebelled, cautiously and craftily, as thwarted women will. She gave me lessons in the stolen time while Father was away at business. I remember her standing before me in a bluebell-striped dress, her tired face suddenly shining as she opened *A Ladies Instructor For Painting Diverse Delights*, so we might copy its hand-coloured plates. 'Grace, you have a fine eye,' Mother said. I wanted to dissect the heart of my subjects, to catch the shadow of the wilting rose in cadmium red, and conjure the snow tumbling like thistledown outside the window in washes of cerulean blue. One day, when painting the gleaming sphere of an apple, a black wriggling creature punctured the skin from the inside. Mother was bemused that I carried on painting, recording the creature's ugly pointed head and shiny segments. 'That is the truth,' I insisted, proud of my picture.

In turn, my mother portrayed me in delicate shadowy pencil: a serious, thin-featured child; long limbed and shy. Even when alone with brushes in hand we spoke softly, alert to heavy footsteps on the drive. My mother's high-strung nerves had trained my own. 'He is here,' I would whisper, my heart stirring as if an ogre crossed the threshold, and not my own father. Our work was rapidly hidden away in the seat of an oak settle. There must have been other lessons too, for I wrote with an elegant looped hand, and borrowed every new novel from the town's paltry Circulating Library. Genteel crumbs of knowledge I think them now, remnants of a gentler age, like the biscuits Mother once twisted in Elizabethan knots.

I have Mother's paints still, in a chipped ebony box fitted out with palette, brushes, and jewel-like watercolour blocks. I still paint every day, just as fiercely, but now my spirit ranges further, and also – I have learned this lesson well – I look about myself with greater vigilance. A daydreamer, my father called me, but I wonder now if I have been a sleepwalker. I have not attended to my own affairs as I should. I have dozed with the bedstraw smoking, as Peg Blissett might have said.

In those days, Father was a towering bear of a man, a master printer with a workshop of ten men. It was a high-ceilinged, racketing building, filled with trestles and mysterious machines, with printed papers strung across the ceiling. On a rare visit he showed me his work, lifting a new plate of copper that rippled like a blushing gold mirror.

'It is metal with a memory,' he said, stroking the surface with hands stained goblin-black. His method was to trace a figure onto onion paper, then scrape that outline onto waxed copper. Next came the master's meticulous work; the etching into metal with the sharp steel called a burin, sending curls like ginger ringlets arcing up from the copper. Once acid had bitten out the pattern, the plate was inked and laid on the press. First a few, then a dozen, then a score of prints were squeezed into life between the rollers, like a single white butterfly multiplied into a swarm.

My father kept his best work pasted in his sample book:

Jonah Moore, Master Letter-Press & Copper-Plate Printer,
No. 39 Blind Hart Alley
Handbills, Cards, Invitations, Prices of Two Shillings 100 or
Fifteen Shillings 1000

Inside the book lay all Father's outpourings, ever since he was the golden apprentice who later inherited his childless master's business: illustrations of gods and men, warriors and angels, as good as any Italian master.

'And now I scrape these tawdry penny-catchers,' he growled. He was making a crude sketch of a half-undressed woman to crown a staymaker's tradecard. 'The metal mirror reflects my fall,' he muttered.

Thus I learned from him that the parable is true: that golden talents buried in the dark earth are a curse and not a blessing.

We had few close acquaintances in Greaves, save the Brabantists, a society of dissenters who gathered about the preacher Caleb Brabant. Brabant himself was an eloquent old weaver with diamond bright eyes and white whiskers, who had once had a miraculous dream. 'I saw Caesar hung upon the cross,' he pronounced with his hands raised in celebration, 'and all the land rejoiced to be free of the poison of the laurel crown. For when all crowns are dust, all will be equal.'

Many hours were spent in meditation upon dreams. All agreed that the Devil appeared as a red beast, or a black dog, or leaping fire. Bread and blood, water and weeds were much discussed as omens. Amongst our congregation there was great hope of the Second Coming, bringing with it relief from poverty and pain. When bread was dear, or work was scarce, the society's funds kept many members from the workhouse. And from Sabbath to Sabbath the belief in dreams and visitations kept everyone's hopes alight.

With no dame school in the town, there were at least horn-books and scripture classes at our meeting house, where I could glean a little more learning. When I escaped from my parents I played with my only friends: Anne Dobson and John Francis Rawdon. As infants, our games were of ghosts that fluttered behind the woollen curtains, or messages scratched in the dust that set us giggling and shrieking. If the congregation stood up to share their dreams, we were banished to the back room, where we chattered of portents. If a person dreamed they died, could they ever wake? And when the Select rose at the Second Coming, would flesh grow back on their bones?

Coaxed by Anne's warmth and good humour, she and I grew to be dear friends. Though her homely face recalled a mournful spaniel, by the time she was fifteen, Anne was courted by Mr Greenbeck, curate of St Stephen's, who had dealings with her father's grocery shop. Once her betrothal was known, the Greenbecks were at once expelled from our gatherings, for Anglicans were reviled as peddlers of miracles and hocus-pocus. But Anne cared not a jot, so long as Mr Greenbeck would still take her.

As for John Francis, he soon grew too big for us, his petticoat companions. For many years we were strangers, until one warm summer's day he came upon me as I sketched out on the moors. Having just walked five miles across country, my old friend took a rest beside me on the grassy bank where my paints and paper were spread. The air was scented with wild flowers, the valley dropped green and lush below us to a glittering stream where cattle lazily drank. My former mischievous playfellow had grown into a well-made country lad, with red cheeks brightening his round face, and clear and intelligent blue-grey eyes. His accent was that of the country folk about Greaves: flat and coarse, but his confiding humour made me laugh. I shared my basket of Mother's biscuits, lovers' knots, aromatic with aniseed and sticky apricot. We talked all afternoon, of his family's farm and his desire to leave the small minds of Greaves, of the modern world and its astonishing progress, and of how the young might make the world a better place.

It grew late, and the first low stars glittered above us in the inky blue sky. We strolled home, falling comfortably into step. When we said our farewells by my gate, I welcomed his gentle touch on my arm and his suggestion that we meet again.

I began to see John Francis almost every day, putting to use my long practice in subterfuge. When necessary, we communicated by exchanging letters in an empty bird's nest in the branches of our garden's lilac tree. Only Anne noticed the change in me. When I confided in her, she agreed to keep my secret only with the greatest reluctance.

'John Francis is a good sort of fellow, but is he not rather humble for you, Grace?' We were sauntering through the town, scrutinising him from under our bonnet brims. John Francis was larking about with his brothers, tossing his cap in the air for his new puppy to catch. The sight of him brought a smile to my face. He was certainly not as stiff and old-mannish as Jacob Greenbeck.

'You are only fifteen, Grace, and rather young even for that age.' Anne was cultivating a voice I fancied was how she thought the wife of a curate should speak. 'And when the time comes, you can make a better match than him.'

I paid no heed to Anne, just as I avoided Mother's weary

questions about where I disappeared all day. I craved freedom; to walk out of doors, to meet John and speak unguardedly, to hold hands, and finally to kiss sweetly, wrapped in each other's arms. We both knew it was wrong to succumb to sin, and we withstood the worst of the Devil's temptations. Yet what did Anne and Jacob know of the fever of such pleasure? If they longed for each other as we did, how could they forever delay their marriage?

One black day Father ordered me into his study and stood over me, crimson-faced, a vein like a worm burrowing at his temple.

'What is this?' he roared. In his hand was a pencil portrait of John Francis, carelessly left beneath my bed. 'Well?'

'It is a picture, Father.'

'That Rawdon lad. Think you have an admirer, do you?' he mocked, in the voice of a stupid girl. 'I'll not have it! My daughter will not be thrown away on a Rawdon. He's got a sniff of your prospects, that is all.'

I stared mutely at the rug. It was the first time I had heard of my 'prospects', but knew better than to make a sound.

'You drew it?'

I nodded, brimming with tears.

'Pitiful.' He crumpled up the portrait in a ball and threw it in the corner. In anger, he pushed his huge flat hand against my shoulder. I stumbled backwards against the wall.

At his growl of dismissal I ran up to my mother, who lay resting in her room with the curtains drawn, suffering from that mysterious affliction I fancied prevented her from bearing Father's long-awaited son.

'What does he mean – my prospects?' I whispered.

She passed a bony hand across her eyes. 'No pray, not all that, Grace. It will only agitate him. For my sake not a word, my dear.'

Yet one small matter did cheer me: for all his scorn, my father had recognised John Francis at once, so my portraiture was not so pitiful.

I know now that my father was frustrated in his occupation. If he had been born in different circumstances, he may have been a remarkable artist. From observing him, I grew to love the Schools of Florence, the Flemish Masters, and our fine English painters. His idol was the Italian engraver, Piranesi, and one evening, having just returned from the tavern, he beckoned me to look inside a vast leather binder. At first I saw only black cross-hatchings, then gradually pieced together gigantic dungeons strung with hanging stairways, coiling chains, and grotesque lightless lamps.

'The famed *Carceri*,' he murmured. 'The prisons of the mind that men try to impose upon us. A trap for our dreams. If we can only break out, child, the light is all about us.'

I stared at the monstrous vision – more ghastly even than Beelzebub's Castle in *The Pilgrim's Progress* – of men dwarfed like ants on colossal stairs, of figures chained to walls beside spoke-wheeled apparatus. I backed away, but Father grasped my arm and said through beer-sour breath, 'It is not a real prison. It is a fancy, a *capriccio* is the proper word.' I took a step back to him and looked again. 'A great artist has the courage to reveal the soul's suffering. Not etch catch-penny advertisements, debasing everything he learned.'

'The prisons of the mind,' I repeated softly, and thought my father had spoken some great truth, but what it was I didn't yet understand.

Later I recalled his words, and those dungeons of forgotten captives. Sometimes, what we believe is trapped in the metal mirror can quicken and jump out from the frame; our dreams can bite back as savagely as any mythical Hydra. At times it is wise to feel fear.

❧

By winter-time John Francis and I were sworn sweethearts, exchanging locks of hair, twisting together his fair strands with my darker brown. From John I learned our neighbours mistook my timid earnestness for pride, and envied my father's wealth. Our talk turned to how men and women might live better lives, with dignity as man and wife. I suppose it was mostly youthful fervour, for we believed the world would soon be ours to inherit. Now I judge those innocent hours the happiest of my youth. But always there was the shadow circling above us, of discovery, and retribution at my father's hand. These were the extent of my worries when I turned sixteen. All such innocence ended on the night of May the 5th, 1786.

We were woken by a great hammering at the door long after midnight. Through the wall I heard the commands of strange men, and my father's voice, at first angry, then high-pitched with alarm. He was arrested and taken to Lancaster jail, which made me at once recall the ink-black prints of the *Carceri*. There were no machines of torture at Lancaster, but it was wet and cold and crowded, and my father was thrown in a lock-up with scores of other wretches. By eavesdropping, I heard that Father had at last performed his act of courage. A riot had erupted in a nearby town, the poor whipped up by hunger to riot for bread. The signal for revolt had been the raising of a halfpenny loaf upon a stick, streaked with ochre and knotted with black crêpe, and the emblem: 'Here Be Bleeding Famine Drest in Mourning Black'. Though the corn merchants were forced to lower their price, the leaders were arrested. Inflamed by their execution, Father printed a hundred penny pamphlets on the dangerous subject of Liberty. All Englishmen must rise at once, he proclaimed, to overthrow King and parliament.

Poor Mother took to her bed and would not leave it, turning her face to the wall and refusing all food. Shame killed her faster than starvation. I was alone with her, holding her weightless hand as her spirit slipped gratefully from this world to the next. I kissed her dry lips, and, not knowing what else to do, cut a long tress of her thin grey hair. Later, I wove those strands into a crucifix, using bobbins and weights, as a lace-maker braids yarn. Set in silver like an amulet, that cross was most precious to me, keeping my mother's presence close.

Father was imprisoned for only ten weeks before a magistrate acquitted him. But in that short time, ruin struck us down like a tempest. When Father came home with a ragged beard and incurious eyes, he was a broken puppet of his former self. He had lost his printer's licence, and so ceased his trade. Thanks only to a number of stealthy arrangements: to sell the business to another printer, and to come to an agreement with a local landlord, were we saved from being turned out of Palatine House.

Yet more ill fortune was to come. Where we might have looked to neighbours, they shied away from us in whispering groups, and then a band of Brabantist Elders came to our door. I listened from the hallway to a voice I recognised as John Francis's father

'To riot is not our way, as you well know, Moore. Nor must the law be broken. Our duty is to wait for signs, and pray,'

I knew from the stiffening of my father's broad back that he was roused. 'Aye, and rake over your dusty dreams like broody hens! Aye, and wait for your God to dole out bread to starving men. How long do you wait – until they drop in their graves? You may well look shamed. You would expel me, is that it? Have you not heard Tom Paine say, were we not corrupted by governments, then man might be friends with man? You would expel me for that, would you, brother?'

I thought his defence well spoken, and admired him for one entire afternoon. Then, at supper time, he returned from the Bush tavern, staggering up the path, blinking and purplish from a surfeit of drink. Unfortunately, John Francis appeared from the back of the house at that self-same moment. My father was sharp-eyed when drunk, and caught him in his bloodshot gaze.

'Still tryin' to sponge off my daughter, Rawdon?' Next, he glared at me. 'It's not you he wants, it's your prospects,' he shouted. I turned to go inside, but he hailed me. 'Listen, you! Listen when I speak, you cloth-headed child.'

'Please go,' I muttered to John Francis. Affronted, he looked from me to my father and back.

'No, Grace. Go into the house. I'll deal with him.'

Father began to roar then, swinging his inky knuckles. 'If I can't have it, no one will,' he cried incomprehensibly. I cringed away, longing for the stone flags beneath my feet to open up and swallow me. Father landed a clumsy blow on John Francis's arm, but the lad backed nimbly away. 'Mr Moore, sir. I don't know what you are rambling on about,' he protested.

I watched, too frightened to stop Father, for fear of him striking me in turn. He edged penitently towards John Francis, then suddenly lashed out with his fist at his face. His opponent was too agile to take the full force, but received a pink graze to his cheek.

'I am sorry, Grace.' John Francis raised himself to his full height and eyed my father with determination. He then strode up to Father and landed a powerful blow to his jaw that sent him toppling to the ground. My once proud father lay crumpled in the dirt. I buried my face in my hands, praying that this scene was a nightmare and that I might soon wake and find myself in bed.

꙳

I did not wake up from that lamentable dream, only lived on with my father at Palatine House. Soon afterwards, John Francis left me a letter, tucked inside our bird's nest hiding place:

My Dearest Grace,

Your father will not allow me within sight of your home and has made violent threats to my person. Worse, my own family have learned of our connection and are fixed on removing me from you and from Greaves. I am to take up a position with my uncle in Bristol; but he is a man of sympathy and I hope to persuade him of the rightness of my actions.

Grace, I cannot abandon you. Will you come with me? Naturally we must marry at once and then bide our time, but I am hopeful all will turn out well.

If you can find it in your heart to come away with me, leave a candle burning in your window at ten o'clock tonight. I shall fetch the trap and meet you at the top of the lane.

Your loving sweetheart,

John Francis

A heavenly sunset mocked me that night, the sky a tumult of lavender clouds tinged with gold. I sat on my narrow bed, my tinderbox in hand. Father had returned from the Bush Tavern some hours earlier, and was noisily sleeping away the effects in his chamber. Our hall clock chimed a half-hour after nine. I had to decide.

I did my utmost to imagine a future for John Francis and myself. Yet all I could summon was fear: of hiding in shabby rooms, of every day dawning with the expectation of discovery. As the sky imperceptibly darkened to night, all vitality drained from my limbs. I began to rock gently back and forth and to touch my crucifix, longing for a sign from my dear mother. How could I go? Yet how could I stay? I searched in my heart for courage and found that fleshy chamber empty. As the minutes passed, my head throbbed with agitation.

I believed I loved John Francis, but still I found objections. How could I be sure John truly wanted me – the awkward, impractical me? Would I not be a burden to him? Nor did I wish to betray his honest parents. And was it rightful to leave my own father, so soon after Mother's death, just as he was cast so low?

The clock struck ten. My candle stood unlit in my window. With shaking hands I struck the flint and coaxed a flame. Picking up John's letter I burned it as the tears wet my cheeks. Then, throwing the letter in my grate, I cast myself down on my bed in wretched darkness.

Soft footsteps approached below my window. I buried my head

in my pillow. After a dreadful interlude of silence the footsteps quietly moved away.

Almost at once I comprehended my mistake. My mother had wordlessly told me the truth on her deathbed. She had been chained to my father and now I was, too. Instead of locks and keys, I was a prisoner of drudgery and lack of funds. A few weeks later, news reached me that John Francis had sailed away on his uncle's ship bound for America. In the meantime, our servants were dismissed, so each day I hauled myself through exhausting chores and fretted over dull concerns: the rising cost of bread, the darning of shirts. Once Father had drunk away the proceeds of his business, we were forced to live on the few shillings he received each week from a Friendly Society. After the apricot tree caught a blight and died, there were no more knotted biscuits. Besides, I could no longer afford fine sugar or aniseeds.

I grew into a child inhabiting an over-tall body, a half-formed woman lacking even a working woman's sense. And so you see, I have tasted the life of a drudge – the treadmill of unrewarded industry, of scalding pans, and battling against mud and dirt. My only pleasurable hours lay in the secret pursuit of my drawing: my pencils sharpened to needle points, my miniature portraits shrinking the world to a fairy size. I re-drew John Francis's portrait from memory, seeking to resurrect something of his warm gaze, seeing again his lips parted in an indulgent smile. The precious lock of his hair shone a rich orpiment yellow in the sunlight; I wove it in a plait to set below his portrait.

Then a letter arrived at Palatine House, and inside was such news that I was roused to startled wakefulness. I have heard it called a sort of murder to wake a sleepwalker; that the heart may be shocked into stopping. But is that sufficient reason to let a slumberer sleep on?

4

The Pacific Ocean

Summer 1792

~ To Broil Sea Lion Steaks ~

Cut your steaks from the shoulder about one inch thick. When your fire is hot lay them on your gridiron, upon a little melted blubber. Turn until enough and send to the table hot. Said by some to be superior to beefsteaks, if one can ignore the odour of aged mackerel.

A receipt from the log books of Pacific whaling ships

Just after eight bells on a Friday night, when the parson of the *Forbearance* always performed Evening Service, Mary began a careful search of his cabin. Dimming her lamp to a sulphurous glow, she surrendered to the old thrill, the thievish itch for gain. She began by rifling through the contents of the little cupboard in the wall. It held nothing but trifles; a chipped cup, a balding brush, nothing she could pledge for a few bob, back in England. As silent as a shadow, she flicked through a pile of mildewed books, and then ransacked his seaman's chest, lifting each fusty item and shaking it hard. A few sheets of clean paper were all she found, and these she hastily stuffed in the front of her gown. Noiselessly, she moved towards the bunk to search beneath the mattress.

All at once a dark body rose from the sheets, towering above her. 'What are you doing here?' the voice boomed, a loud bass, husky from sleep.

Before she could run for it, he grasped her hard by the arm and snatched her lamp away, thrusting it toward her face.

'Didn't reckon on my curate taking the service tonight, eh?' said the grizzle-bearded parson. 'Thought you'd have a bit of a prowl, did you, Flora – or whatever you call yourself?'

So he knew. The captain and the others had swallowed the tale that she was Flora Jean Pilling, shipwrecked daughter of the Reverend Pilling of Mission Bay, the rest of her family slaughtered in a native attack. She had produced the girl's brooch, that bore a portrait of her father and a Bible-screed inside its clasp, and everyone but this Devil-baiter had been gulled. He had more skill than most, she supposed, in the secret language of souls.

'What have you taken?' he growled. She made a performance of searching her own person.

'There.' He pointed at her bulging pocket.

She emptied it: a pair of blood-seeping seal ribs, wrapped in a pocket handkerchief. The crew had slaughtered two fat seal-cows, but it seemed only she appreciated the silky, fishy flesh, and she had filched the others' leavings. He winced in disgust. It was a mighty shame he had found her supper. She was weary of oatmeal *burgoo* and had looked forward to gnawing the ribs, alone in her cabin.

'I were famished,' she protested. 'And no one else wanted them.'

'I know your sort.'

She cast a guarded glance towards him. He was standing now, his rough-hewn face fierce in the lamplight

'Sometimes what happens in a place so far from God can fester like a wound. Turn a good soul bad.' Behind the lamp-gold reflections in his eyes lay something unreadable. It might have been kindness; it might have been a trap.

'Confession is the only medicine,' he said, lowering his sermonising voice to a whisper. 'I could hear your confession now, girl.'

Was it his fatherly concern that made her throat burn for a moment? Then she dismissed his compassion as fakery. And she was no fool. For four months they had voyaged together, England-bound from New Zealand, and she had lived by her wits. Not for the first time, she wondered if she was properly well. She had put on some welcome flesh, and the sores on her body were slowly healing under papery skin; but the wound the parson talked of, that was not so easily mended. Its pain fretted her like a splinter of steel, lodged awkwardly close to a bone. But to speak of what had happened? She glanced up from the pitching floor of the cabin. The parson was waiting, his eyes narrowed in his crumpled face. The glib words that had always been her trade refused to come.

'Forty years I've sailed the blue Pacific,' he declaimed like a prophet. 'This ocean has a dark tide, which sweeps the unsuspecting sinner far beyond dry land. I've rescued my share of the lost and castaway. Some with tattoos carved in their flesh like pagan picture-books, others plain crazed or starved away to bones. Such derelict souls can acquire uncivilised tastes.'

He gazed at the bloody bones seeping into her handkerchief.

'And some can begin to forget the English tongue,' he added slyly.

'I have not forgot it,' she said quickly. For she could now under-stand most of the English she heard – she was not as she had been at Hokianga, when it had at first seemed only gibbering sounds. 'I know ma own tongue,' she added, remembering the Edinburgh lilt this time. 'Sir.'

'Then use it while you have the chance,' he said fiercely. 'Unburden yourself, Flora Pilling, or whatever name you travel under. Confess – or I'll send word to the Naval Office. Perhaps they have a record of a young wanderer – or would that be deserter, from Sydney Cove?'

What had Charlie always said? Quiet is best, as the fox said when he bit the cock's head off. She summoned an injured whim-per. 'I have a toothache. I was only searching for a thread to pull it, not wanting to disturb you. You are wrong to accuse me, after all my sorrows. If you persist, I shall complain to the master.'

He motioned her to go, mistrust still pinching his face. Damn you, she thought as she hurried away. Sermonising crow!

Back in her own cabin, she slammed the door shut and pulled her blanket around her shoulders. Tossing on her bed, she began to croon savage curses to herself. The prick of tears started up behind her eyes, but she damped them down, proud of not weep-ing now for many long years. Fury, as thick as molasses, pulsed through her veins.

A despatch to London might see her marched right off the ship and straight to the gallows. Devil rot the parson, she enjoyed being Flora, the captain's favourite. Her days were idle and her thoughts her own. By personating Flora she had planned to sit quiet all the way back to old England.

A true confession was beyond her. Might she make a sham confession? Damn him, that soul-snatcher would catch her out. She smashed her fist into the pillow and wished it was his grizzled jaw.

Next morning, waking in her plump feather bed, she chided herself for acting like a dumb-witted flat. Just before dinner time, she sought out the ship's cook in his filthy galley. His one skewed eye moved across every part of her but her face; he was an ill-favoured cove much scarified by cannonball. Breathlessly, she told him she wanted a handful of oatmeal to make a rinse for her hair, all the time lifting and stroking her unpinned tresses. He nodded, gape-mouthed, and she squeezed past him to where the supplies were kept.

Her nose led her to what was seeking. Trying not to breathe, her long fingers delved into the remains of the seal carcasses, finding slippery pale blubber, a jagged jawbone, leathery flippers. There it was – a yielding sliver of jellified mush that stank of metal. She pulled off a hunk of the rotting liver and slid it into a pot inside her pocket. Offering to carry a few plates to dinner, it was the work of moments to mix a little into the dish of lobscouse on the parson's plate.

By midnight the old crow was smitten with a pain in his skull that left him half-blind and speechless. She joined the rest of the crew in speculating on the cause: could it be a fever, a foreign leech in the eye, or a bubole in the brain perhaps?

A few days later, her dear protector, the captain, looked in on her as she sat with the invalid. 'I do like to see a tender-hearted female about the place,' he told her with fatherly regard. She looked up from the parson's writing desk, and poured a cup of sweetness into her smile. 'He is no trouble at all, now, Captain. His kind attention to me and my history must be repaid.'

When the captain had stumped away she cast a chill glance at her charge. The old man was shrunken and almost sightless. There was no expectation of his recovery before they reached England.

Dipping her quill she completed the receipt she was copying into one of the parson's memorandum books. She felt a swell of pride that she had obtained proof of a culinary experiment; one that the crew of a visiting whaling ship had warned her of, back in Sydney Cove.

Sea Lion: Said by some to be superior to beefsteaks if one might ignore the mackerel odour the liver is a strong poison which in small doses will attack the brain and make the eyes no longer able to tolerate even candlelight. By some accounts it will kill dogs and men; one spoonful will leave a large man insensible.

Smoothing a new page across the tiny table, she again stabbed a quill into ink. It was time to set all the rest of it down too, before the crowds and clamour of England barged it all away. She remembered those fancy receipt books written by Lady Nonesuch, or Countess Thingumabob, and laughed out loud. They boasted how damnable high bred the lady was, and how the reader might herself be reckoned à la mode, if she could only cook such stuff herself.

No, her book would hold a dark mirror to such conceits. Since Mother Eve's day, women had whispered of herblore and crafty potions, the wise woman's weapons against the injustices of life; a life of ill treatment, the life of a dog. If women were to be kicked into the kitchen they might play it to their advantage, for what was a kitchen but a witch's brewhouse? Men had no notion of what women whispered to each other, hugger-mugger by the chimney corner; of treaclish syrups and bitter pods, of fat black berries and bulbous roots. Such remedies were rarely scribbled on paper; they were carried in noses, fingertips and stealthy tongues. Methods were shared in secret, of how to make a body hot with lust or shiver with fever, or to doze for a stretch or to sleep for eternity.

Like a chorus the hungry ghosts started up around her: voices that croaked and cackled and damned their captors headlong into hell. Her ghosts were the women who had sailed out beside her to

Botany Bay, nearly five years back on the convict ship *Experiment*. She made a start with that most innocent of dishes: Brinny's best receipt for Apple Pie. For there was magic in even that – the taking of uneatables: sour apples, claggy fat, dusty flour - and their abradabrification into a crisp-lidded, syrupy miracle. *Mother Eve's Secrets*, she titled her book, a collection of best receipts and treacherous remedies. As her pen conjured the convict women's talk, she reckoned it one of the few good things to have come to her from those last terrible years. Well, there had been Jack Pierce of course, but— she suffocated any further memory of Jack fast, before it shattered her to pieces.

As she wrote, the means to accomplish her revenge formed in her mind, so boldly that she laughed out loud, and clapped her hand across her mouth. She would be a cook! The very word delighted her. She would make herself busy in the downstairs of the household, butchering and baking, and doling out whatever was deserved. As she recalled incomparable dishes and counterfeit cures, she imagined herself the mistress of a great store of food. As big as a house, she dreamed it, a palace made of sugarplums, or a castle baked of cake. The serpent that would be a dragon must dine well. But could any store ever be vast enough, to sate her hunger for all she had lost?

5

Greaves, Lancashire

Summer 1792

~ Pease Pudding ~

Take your pease and wash and boil them in a cloth, take off the scum and put in a piece of bacon and whatsoever herbs you have. Boil it not too thick, serve with the bacon and pour on the broth. Next day, whatsoever you have left over, slice it and fry it.

Grace Moore, her cheapest dish

It was a dream that heralded the day my life changed: a dream of John Francis aged seventeen again, a long-limbed, smooth-faced youth. He had been invited to dine at Palatine House. My mother, bless her soul, was alive again and smiling, and even Father was agreeable. I too was young again, sixteen years old, overflowing with feelings since quite lost to me.

We sat about the table and picked at Mother's genteel sweetmeats: apricot biscuits, quince paste, and sugared walnuts. John caught my eye whenever he could; there was a teasing mischief to his looks that banished my usual awkwardness. When my parents left us alone, John's large hand, very warm, slipped under the table and took hold of mine. Then he kissed me, very tenderly and moist, on the lips. He held my face in his big-knuckled hands and something passed between us; something so powerful that my girlish hopes burst into life. I was like a scrawny chick comprehending its marvellous change into a dove. I was young and giddy with pleasure, struck with wonder that this was how my life would be.

Instead I woke to a muzzy July dawn. My feet poked out from the end of my childhood bed. I idled for a while, picking those strips around my nails that they call 'mother's blessings', rehearsing my dream to extend its pitiful life. Then, as the Brabantists do, I asked myself what portents it contained. Food was generally deemed to be God's bounty, unless it was a monarch's banquet, when it signified the sin of gluttony. Was that slow kiss the Devil's work? I could not believe wickedness could feel so thrilling.

I got up, for my nail began to bleed from an ugly wound. Perhaps the dream was only a cruel figment sent to torture me? Above me hung John's portrait; all I had left of him since he'd sailed away. And I remembered events as they truly had been, my father lying drunken on the ground, and John Francis looking at me in a sort of agony. After that, any lad who even smiled at me got short shrift from my father. Then Father made his decision. 'You must bide with me now, Grace,' he said. 'I'll not take a servant, for no free soul should slave for another. But as my daughter it's your duty to keep house for me, now your mother has gone.'

And it had not escaped my notice that I did not even cost a servant's wages.

The thump made my bedroom door shake. 'Grace! Fetch my breakfast, you lazybones.'

'Father, please! A moment.' I scrabbled about, bundling on my clothes as he hammered again. I feared the lock might break from its housing – I worried, too, that anyone passing might hear him. But when I finally unlocked my door and swung it open, the landing was empty. I found him downstairs in the parlour, lying twisted on the ground, drunk and helpless. I held my hand out to him, but he stared at it suspiciously, as if he didn't know me, his only daughter.

'Away, you useless creature. Look at yourself, you scarecrow!' It shamed me to see him like that, with the spittle on his lips and his breath foul from liquor. At some time in the night, after staggering home drunk, he had thrown last night's supper against the wall. The remnants of my pease pudding had grown a brown crust and the bacon looked like rusty leather. It was no feast, but still, a morning's labour had been spent to turn a few pennyworth of stony peas into a palatable dish. That's how much you care for me, I thought.

'Come along, Father,' I said gently. 'Let me help you up.'

He let me hoist him upright, his bulk pressing heavy on my shoulders, till he staggered on his own two feet. Then, with no warning, he swung out with his fist and hit me hard on the side of my head. I cried out and recoiled, dizzy from the blow. With lips pressed tightly, so he might not hear me whimper, I stumbled back upstairs to my chamber. There, a wet cloth against my thumping head, I surrendered to self-pity. I turned to my dear mother's portrait, recollecting that happy season when she had sat for me each afternoon.

No sooner had I wiped my face dry than a smart knock rapped at the front door. Passing downstairs to the parlour, I was grateful that Father had at least hauled himself up into a chair, from which he eyed me fiercely, as if I were to blame for all his troubles.

'Mr Croxon,' I said, dismayed to see our landlord on the doorstep. 'I hope all is in order?'

Mr Croxon hesitated, then gave me a tight nod. He too had high-coloured cheeks; I wondered if he had come directly from the Quince and Salver.

'All could be put in order, yes, Miss Moore. With a little plain dealing.'

Our landlord had once been a carpenter, before shrewd use of his small capital had allowed him to buy and put to rent a number of properties in the town. Once he had been Father's customer too, and it was a credit to the man that he still tipped his hat in greeting, where many now cut him dead. I had not forgotten that it was thanks to Mr Croxon that we stayed on at Palatine House, for without his having made an arrangement with Father, we might have been turned out by bailiffs.

He strolled past me and pulled up a chair beside my father. I listened at the door as they talked of news from France. Some dreadful machine had been invented to decapitate the French nobility, Mr Croxon recalled with some glee. 'Had enough of French Liberty yet, eh, Moore?' My father mumbled in reply; the fire for reform was dying within him. Like many Britons we had rejoiced at the Bastille's fall, but now read each news despatch with horror.

There could not have been a greater contrast between the two men: Mr Croxon smooth-faced and lively in his brass-buttoned coat and boots polished like glass, while Father looked a slovenly wreck, and no credit to my hours of laundering. As to the house – I did my best to keep up the old grandeur, but the tell-tale signs of a drunkard abounded, in stains on the carpet and a high smell of spirits.

'Right, to business. You back to your full senses yet, Moore?'

'Fetch some ale,' Father barked. I brought it in, muttering an apology to Mr Croxon, and retreated. The two men grimaced as they supped. Well, I could not brew a miracle from stale alewort, which was all Father would pay for. But soon curiosity drew me back to the kitchen door.

'What her grandmother were thinking, to settle it on our Grace, the Lord only knows,' Father grumbled. 'I should have taken that will to law, I should. The old woman must have been crazed to leave it to her and not me, her own son-in-law. As for the terms of her damned will, what's the use of land you cannot sell? She be laughing from her grave, I reckon.'

'Aye, she be that.' Mr Croxon's wry amusement was lost on my father.

I recollected that a letter, bearing a beautiful black seal, had arrived some days earlier; but my father had hidden it from me. So here was news – my grandmother was dead. She and my father had been at loggerheads all my life, forcing an estrangement from my mother and me.

'The tight-fisted bitch must have been crack-headed.'

'Maybe, maybe not.' Mr Croxon paused, collecting his thoughts. 'I could barely make sense of your jabbering last night. So what do the terms say precisely?'

'It's Grace's land to keep. I cannot even build on it. I could have got a thousand pound—'

I held my breath. The truth was, I knew nothing of the details of my mysterious prospects. Though sneering hints of it had haunted my youth, until that day I had only the haziest notion of what it comprised. I listened hard and understood it was a thousand acres beside a river in Whitelow, in Yorkshire's West Riding. It had been my grandmother's from when she was widowed, since which time she had only collected rents from the farmers who lived on it and loosed their cattle on its pastures.

'Aye, but what can Grace do with it? Can she build on it?'

'Grace can. But I'm forbid from being a partner. It's a pig in a poke.'

'So who can Grace be partner to?'

'I cannot partner her. Nor any person "of my association",' Father said in a mocking, gentrified tone. 'Tully, her pettifogging lawyer, threatened me. Said if I tried to fangle it he'd find me out soon enough. Damn his lawyer's tongue!'

'Grace's husband, perhaps?'

'Well, you can't marry her. Your missus wouldn't let you.'

'Not me, you daft lummocks. But I've got sons – a son. Michael. My elder lad.'

As I listened, the room seemed to move like water around me. A son? A Croxon son? I racked my brain to recall him. He did not frequent the High Street where I shopped, nor drink with my father at the Bush tavern. Michael Croxon. I had a slight recollection of a well-looking, fashionable man, riding an elegant hunter on the lane that led to the Croxon's new villa. My impressions were favourable; but that in itself filled me with misgivings. As I sat in my thread-bare gown with a bruise throbbing at my hairline, Michael Croxon seemed an altogether different manner of person from me. Yet he is a chance, I thought. A chance to escape from Father.

'Eh, but what about me? Who'll look after me?' At the sound of Father's voice my fingernails dug painfully into my palms. I knew it – he was going to destroy my chance of freedom. Scarcely knowing what I did, I walked into the parlour.

'Mr Croxon,' I nodded, praying he would not send me away. 'Father,' I added, quailing to see his livid face. 'I believe I should be present.'

'Yes – yes, Grace.' Mr Croxon was quicker-witted than my father. 'This concerns you very much. Come, sit with us.'

As I sat, my legs were as weak as a lamb's. Mr Croxon continued speaking, and I tried to follow, but some of it was legal talk, too complex for me. However, the import was quite comprehensible. The Croxon family wished to found a business. The elder son, Michael, was especially enthusiastic, having long held the ambition to make his fortune using the modern means of manufacturing cotton. An arrangement between our two families would bring profit to us all.

'Michael has had his troubles and now needs a steady wife,' he said. It was not said in jest, that was clear from his manner. 'I speak plain, for that's the best way.'

'But who will tend to me?' whined my father.

Mr Croxon turned back to him. 'Any kin of mine will live decently; do you understand that, Moore? We will hire you a servant.'

'I'll not have that,' my father began. 'Grace is no expense, like some hoity servant. I'll not keep a slave—'

'Listen, Moore. I'll settle ten pound a year beer-money on you. Well?'

'You sure he'll take my daughter?' my father said, pursing his loose lips as if he tasted bitter aloes. 'She'd be summat of a gawk beside your fine lad.'

I stared into my lap, mortified.

'He'll have Grace – aye, he will,' replied Mr Croxon, eyeing me somewhat like a dealer at a market. 'She hides her light beneath a bushel, but a quiet girl will suit our Michael. I'll get my lawyer to look into it. Shake on it, Moore?'

I heard Father spit in his palm, and saw Mr Croxon's distaste. I rose and retired to the kitchen, but my hands could not lift a plate for trembling. I slumped on the stool by the fire and raised a glass of ale to my lips. But for the first time I tasted its cheapness, and spat it back into the glass. Everything about me was displeasing – the halfpenny twists of tea on the broken shelves, the smoke-stained hearth, the drab and damp-patched kitchen itself. I scraped the congealed pease and bacon into the fire, where it smoked and spat.

To my astonishment, I understood my morning's dream foretold a blissful future. I allowed myself to sink into a daydream; of another life opening before me, of respectability and riches, at my shoulder a vague silhouette of a man, as yet featureless, but fashionably clad. Someone kind, civil and – dared I hope? – eager to cherish and love even me.

6

The Thames to Manchester

Summer 1792

~ To Make Virgin's Milk ~

Take equal parts of Gum Benjamin, a fragrant resin from the meadows of sunny Sumatra, and Storax, the Sweet Gum of Turkey, and dissolve them in a sufficient quantity of Spirit of Wine. The Spirit will then gain a reddish tint and exhale a fragrant smell of tropical balm. Place a few drops into a glass of clear water and by rapid stirring the contents will instantly become milky. The mixture is used successfully to clear a sun-burned complexion and give a spotless white tint, for which purpose nothing is better, or indeed more innocent and safe.

A most superior mixture, Mrs Quinn of the Theatre Royal

It was drizzling when they reached the Thames. Mary stood at the rail, letting the sooty rain patter across her face, blessing the grey sky and the shiny quay. Though it was afternoon, it felt to her as though she viewed the world through the bottom of a brandy bottle, she had grown so used to the sun, a golden ball in a hot blue sky. Yet even under cloud the port was a lively scene; sailors scurried about their ships, beggars worked the crowd, a gaggle of mudlarks scavenged along the shoreline. It was all quite astonishing after months of flat sea and sky.

As for the parson, he was still laid low, waiting in his cabin to be carried to a hospital.

She fingered the coins in her pocket. The crew had made a collection for the orphaned missionary's daughter. She would have liked more than fifteen bob for that spanking tale of a native kidnap, so maybe some of the crew hadn't been taken in after all. But none of that mattered now. She had the means to find Charlie and plan the next throw in the game.

Once off the ship, she felt like a spinning top, rocking on the hard ground. Alone, she made her way up a promising alley, past smoking fires and whining dogs. Hawkers crying their wares clashed with ballad singers and the thumping hammers and creak of heavy wheels. It came back to her, that this was how it was in a noisy crowd, with all the folk distracted you could become anyone you fancied. Patting her pocket, she remembered Flora's brooch and, after poking free the reverend's picture, she cajoled another ten bob from a pawnbroker. Pausing to warm her hands at a brazier, she looked quickly over her shoulder, then dropped the tiny portrait into the fire. It burned blue for a moment and then shrivelled blackly into smoke. Fare thee well, Reverend Pilling. And Flora Jean Pilling, and the whole preachifying lot of you.

On reaching the main street, the crowded mass of it all – people, animals, carriages – was like a hard slap in the face. London was not her territory, and to her eyes it had grown tenfold since she'd last seen it from a prison cart. Exhausted, she stumbled onto the cheapest stage coach just before nightfall, huddling into a corner and settling behind a mask of sleep to avoid her fellow travellers, stinking of wet wool. She dozed there for a night and a day, stirring as the horses were changed, blinking at sudden blazes of light, tossed by jolts, and startled by disembodied yells. There was little conversation, for everyone stood on their rank. England again, she thought sourly, she had forgotten all that codswallop of bowing and curtseying, and kiss my arse.

As the coach slowed at Rugby she touched the coins in her skirt, but could not bear to part with what was left of the lovely chink. Catching the eye of a pock-faced man with a gold watch, she made a performance of stretching herself awake so as best to show her bosom. Dismounting, she pretended to stumble and grasped his arm, leaning against him as he fussed over her. Inside the inn, she spun him a yarn of a dying sister and a wicked mistress who owed her a year's wages. Her reward was a supper of hot tea and salty, slippery butter on white bread. At supper time, he insisted on treating her to hot bacon collops. The smoky, sweet pork was so good she found it hard to listen to Mr Reuben Weetch's ramblings – he had a dull wife and some unfathomable trade up Preston way. Dreamily, she let him stroke her hand in a corner of the parlour, wondering if he would stretch to currant buns.

Weetch at least reassured her of her power to pull in a gentleman, for the only mirror aboard the ship had reflected back a sun-blistered stranger, her hair a mixture of copper and straw. How had her bonny flame-haired self turned into that?

Alighting at Manchester, she allowed Weetch a short farewell in an alley by the stables. She let him maul her until the coachman called for all to board. Then she speedily sent her hand on an investigation of his breeches.

'You must go,' she sighed, hearing the final call for all passengers.

'I must see you again,' he groaned, his head lolling back against the wall. 'I know it is only two days, but I have developed such a strong affection—' What a dossuck! She bit back a laugh as she rapidly fabricated a false address. 'Don't forget to call, my dear,' she cried as he hurried to board, blowing her a kiss.

After watching the coach disappear, she emptied his purse of a grand haul of 17s 9d. Not wanting ever again to risk being nabbed by the Justices, she cast his purse away into the canal.

Manchester was larger and taller than she remembered it, five-storey brick warehouses and manufactories rising high into the sooty sky. Bustling past the streams of workers rushing hither and thither to the clamour of ringing bells, she wondered at their stupidity. Whey-faced and poor, they were of no more interest to her than the rats scurrying about the heaps of cinders. Instead, she watched herself in a new glass window, mortified by the outmoded appearance of Flora Pilling's tartan gown. Charlie was always a flash fellow, and he had revelled in her firecracker looks.

At the Theatre Royal she searched out a certain Mrs Quin. The woman had long had a reputation for restoring the appearance of theatrical persons ravaged by gin and fast living. In the dusty chambers beneath the stage she found the watery-eyed Irishwoman, an array of pins in her cap, and scissors swinging at her waist.

All the way to Spring Gardens Mary rehearsed the patter under her breath. Now it came out almost as good as ever.

'Mrs Quin, is it?' she asked in a low, honeyed tone. She bobbed demurely. 'As you can see, I've been a time out in the Indies and find myself rather afflicted by the climate. And next week the man I'm to marry will call upon me.' She bit her lip and affected a poignant expression. 'Mrs Quin, I hear you are the best there ever was with hair and paint. I wonder, could you help me back to the fair-skinned, red-headed girl he remembers?'

Mrs Quin led Mary to a dirty pane of glass and considered her crimsoned skin. 'Holy Mary,' she said in a husky rasp. 'It's a box of powders I have, not a box of miracles. But perhaps I can sort you out – for a man's eye, at least.'

'And my hair? Back to a flaming red?' Mary pulled off her cap.

'That's the easy part, dearie. But I'd be wanting half a crown for the sorting of yous.'

'As much as that? There's one thing more.' She had glimpsed a room filled floor to ceiling with clothes, as well as promising baskets and boxes. 'I've grown rather behind times with the fashions – would you be kind enough to sell me some of those clothes you keep for the plays?'

'You're in a right fix, ain't you? But if you be having the price, I'll be selling you the rig-outs.'

In a comfortable chamber arranged with large mirrors, Mrs Quin began her work. Inside her famous box of tricks were dozens of compartments, containing pots and tins and brushes. First, she applied a chalky liquid to Mary's skin, cool at the start, but rapidly tingling warmly.

'I'll leave the Virgin's Milk to get to work. Now let's get your hair on its way,' she said, slathering it with a high-smelling purplish dye.

Mary sat back sleepily, willing the lotion to bleach her complexion. On the walls above her were portraits of actors – cheap prints pasted on the lumpy walls. She fixed upon the image of a large-eyed beauty with waist-length black tresses and a flowing gown like a priestess. The actress stared out from the print, holding aloft a grinning mask.

'That's Liza Farrell what was, Lady Bedford as she is now,' Mrs Quin confided. 'I had the honour to dress her hair one season. When she played Lady Macbeth she was the horriblest murdering heathen you ever set your eyes on. By Jesus, she was a marvel on the stage.'

To be an actress, Mary marvelled silently. What a life that would be.

Mrs Quin set her head on one side. 'You know what, dearie? The ways I seen her – weary to her boots and washed of her paint – you might have walked past her and never cast a second glance. But she had what the great ones have – whatever she set her will to do, she done it. Dragged herself up, mind, she used to jig in the streets of Cork City for pennies. Would you look at her now? Married to Lord Bedford. The way she done it, she sweet-talked herself to becoming the first Lady Bedford's favourite friend, forever whispering in her ear what grand improvements to make to her grand estates, and all the while tumbling his lordship on the sly. Clever as a cuckoo she was, feathered her own nest before she pushed the old bird out. And near every week, they write her name in the newspapers.'

There was a great deal of sharpery in it all, Mary concluded; not only on the stage, but off it, too.

'Now I'll be off to fetch the mending,' the dresser said, 'so I'll just be leaving this lot to do its work.'

She must have nodded off, for her head jerked suddenly as she sprang awake. In the mirror she saw a bleached skull, its hair a mass of ruby tendrils hanging almost to the floor. A bead of dye like a crimson tear trickled slowly down the brow. It was a vision of terror: a death's head peering out from tangles of bloody gore. A memory seized her, a memory of so much blood that the shock had almost killed her. Even in that stuffy room, goose pimples rose all over her skin.

In a moment she had wiped the crimson drip away, and she was once again a woman painted with dye and lotions. She must banish those bothersome memories far away, across the ocean in that other world. Still, there was a bony look to her face, in her sunken eyes and sharp cheekbones. It was that starveling look she knew too well.

She sent a serving girl out to fetch some food. A beef pie, bread and butter and plenty of the sweet stuff that she loved. She devoured a treacle pudding, closing her eyes to savour every sticky crumb. Sugar. How she had craved the stuff. Though her belly was full, still she helped herself from a paper bag of sugarplums, globes of candied fruits that made her cheeks bulge. Was this happiness, she wondered? She was full of food again, and as sleepy as a suckled child. She pictured a well-stocked larder, and the chance to make all the delights in *Mother Eve's Secrets*. She would help herself to the best, of course, for she who stirs the pot never starves. A comfortable future lay before her, all for the taking.

Mrs Quin bustled back into the room and began to dress her face. Gone were the worst of the bran-specks and flaking red sores. Instead, she had the prettiness of a portrait on an enamelled tin; a smudgy confection of pink and cream. 'A rosy blush,' Mrs Quin said benignly, 'is the fashion nowadays.'

While Mrs Quin deposited her half a crown in a locked trunk, Mary slipped a bottle of Pear's Almond Bloom and a tin of White Imperial Powder into her skirts. The pilfering gave her a jolt of pleasure, a secret thrill; to possess those lovely, lovely things for free.

She went alone to the vast room where the second-hand clothes were kept. Later, she thought it the happiest hour of her life. There were silks and brocades by the yard, and pile upon pile of hats, wigs, cloaks, and masks. After two years in wretched rags, even the linen shifts felt as soft as thistledown. She whirled from one delight to another – clutching lace, burying her nose in furs, holding flashy paste jewels next to her new-bleached skin.

Catching her reflected eye in the mirror she laughed out loud, her red mouth wide and knowing. She put aside a few carefully-chosen costumes and elbow-length mittens. Then, finally, she chose a few costumes of a particular nature: shiny satin, ebony black.

Lastly, she gathered the garments she would wear for her journey: a grass-green woollen gown and a lace cap and apron. The effect was somewhat grand for a domestic servant. Her auburn locks were pinned tightly, her figure flattered by a frilled muslin kerchief, crisscrossed in an 'X' over her breast. Pulling out a few auburn tendrils from her cap, she adjusted her bodice to show a little more flesh. Then she grew very still, and smiled slowly into the empty space before her.

'How do you do, sir,' she said with a graceful curtsey. 'Now, what pretty dish might you care for tonight?'

7

Greaves, Lancashire

Summer 1792

~ To Roast Larks ~

Put a dozen larks on a skewer, tie to the spit and dredge and
baste them; let them roast ten minutes. Take the crumbs of a
halfpenny loaf with some butter the size of a walnut; melt and
stir them about till they are brown, then lay them around
your larks with a little melted butter.

The Lady's Magazine, 1792

A formal card, an invitation to call at Huxley House, was delivered to my door the following Sunday. It was addressed to myself alone, Mr Croxon no doubt having warned his family of my father's habits. Only after much re-reading of this handwritten proof did I confide in Anne. Sitting in her tiny parlour, I announced my news. Though at first astonished, Anne jumped up and took my hands and kissed me with baffled pleasure. She puzzled over the name of my prospective groom. 'Mr Michael Croxon? Mr Croxon's eldest? To marry – you?' The question hung in the air. 'Grace, did you say you have not yet met him?'

'I am to meet him on Sunday. All my hopes rest upon it.'

A shadow of worry crossed her face. 'Still, you must be cautious. He may not be agreeable to you.'

'I so much hope he is. I pray for it.'

'You do?'

'Consider what a chance this is for me.'

'Yes, and if it is the same Michael Croxon I have seen about the town – goodness, he is handsome.'

We both suddenly laughed like girls. 'Is he? I cannot quite recollect him. Handsome and willing and keen to make his fortune. So why should I be cautious?' I quipped.

'And how does he mean to make his fortune?'

I sketched the Croxons' plan to use my inheritance. 'I do not deny that my land is attractive to them,' I admitted. 'But Anne, if that means he will marry me? It is a stroke of extraordinary good fortune.'

'Yes, but that is all the more reason to make careful enquiries.'

She looked at me with shrewd appraisal. 'Surely this land of yours is not so valuable that—'

'That what? That he would want even me?'

'Grace.' She grasped my sleeve to prevent my standing to leave. 'I am full of joy for you. It is only that – I care for you, for your happiness.'

Anne smiled at me, but I saw strain in it, and was peculiarly vexed, as if she took pleasure in picturing obstacles in my way.

The closer the meeting drew, the more trepidation I felt. At night I lay awake, plagued by fears of the worst kind: if I found my suitor entirely unappealing, might I still marry him, simply to leave Father? Or might Michael Croxon take one look at me and reject the whole plan? By the morning of the visit I found myself cursed with a rash, my face and hands scabbed and itchy. Anne had suggested I buy a new gown, but my father had no money to give me. Thus I was forced to choose between my threadbare grey plaid or the superior silk of my mourning gown, bought when Mother died. I tried on both until I was sick of the pair of them, and then, idiotically pulled on the antiquated silk with a pair of workaday shoes. At the appointed hour a grand carriage rolled up to the door of Palatine House, causing quite a stir amongst the children of Wood Street and their curtain-peeking mothers. Once inside, I sat in a sort of dumb terror, all my old fears of speaking in company tormenting me.

Huxley House was three miles out of town, a square-fronted redbrick villa, built on a fine grassy eminence. It was all in the modern style, with a carriage drive curving to a brass-knockered double door. Glancing up at the rows of pedimented windows, I wondered if Michael stood watch for me as anxiously as I awaited him, but on the doorstep only a pair of mute servants swung the doors aside. Then Mr Croxon ushered me into his drawing room, where Mrs Croxon waited, greeting me with unveiled scrutiny. I thought her a woman straining to impress, dressed in a flimsy muslin costume, almost immodest on a buxom woman of more than forty. The Croxon's drawing room was so heavily gilded that it shone brassy yellow, commingling queasily with the purple sateen upholstery. I sat where I was bid on the edge of a striped sofa, feeling giddy with nerves. When tea was served I faced another trial, as my hands shook so violently I dared not drink. 'Purchased from Mr Wedgewood's shop in London,' Mrs Croxon boasted, caressing the lid of the sugar bowl. I made no reply, much regretting my decision to wear my outmoded black furbelows and crucifix, the many mirrors confirming I looked like a relic of a bygone age.

'Ah, here is Michael.'

Somehow I rose and reluctantly offered my itchy fingers. I found myself standing before a young man with tawny curled hair and – the phrase was the most apt way to describe him – the face of a sad archangel in an Italian masterpiece. When he extended his hand to greet me, I trembled in his grasp. He was paler than is ordinary, his dark eyes a beautiful forget-me-not blue. I searched his face and found even his few flaws attractive – a somewhat brutish break to the symmetry of his nose only added interest, and the downward turn of his well-formed lips lent him a poetic look. I was a little taller than him, but that was no fault of his. As we stood together, I was engulfed in a sort of delicious agony.

He ushered me to sit close by him; we were both stiff-mannered, but who would not be, under such testing circumstances? Like his parents, he was dressed in high style; a silver-stitched waistcoat, with the lapels turned up in a flourish, and a snow-white neck cloth, ornately knotted. I found it hard even to look at him; he was a dazzling apparition.

'But now, Miss Moore, that is enough of me. What of yourself?' He lifted his eyes courteously to my overheated face. I noticed shadows, almost bruises, beneath them, that only made his expression more melancholically handsome. 'How old are you?'

Breathlessly, I told him I was twenty-two years old, very anxious he should not consider me an old maid.

'I see,' he said with a charming little lift of his brows, as if this were not so very bad.

'You run a household?'

'Only for my father,' I said earnestly. 'But the house is rather large.'

'Good. And you have instructed domestics?'

'Well, when my mother was alive. Yes.'

'Your land. It is in a fine position.' As he spoke, he patted his hair, releasing a pleasing scent of pomade.

'I have never seen it, sir.'

He gazed at me quizzically, almost as if I spoke in jest. 'No matter. You have not been out much in society, I believe. I like that, Miss Moore.'

I was grateful when this scrutiny ended at a summons to the dining room. To my dismay, we were at once served a dish of larks, a species of bird whose joyful song often brightened my solitary walks. I toyed politely with the tiny pin-boned carcass, but lifted none to my mouth, unable to stop my ears to the sound of bones being crunched between Mr Croxon's teeth.

As for Mrs Croxon, she began to lament the absence of her younger son, Peter, whose portrait made a pair with Michael's, one on either side of the chimney breast. According to the artist, he appeared to be a younger, more wide-eyed version of his brother.

'I cannot believe he has not come home on his birthday, when cook has gone to all this trouble.' Mrs Croxon impatiently beckoned the maid to serve us another unappetising dish.

Michael directed a mutinous stare at his mother. 'He is out trying his luck with Miss Brighouse and her ten thousand pounds, at Bleasedale, Mother. A slight to both myself and Miss Moore. But it is hardly out of character.'

'Now, Michael,' barked Mr Croxon.

The visit was brought to an early close by Mrs Croxon's

insistence that the carriage must take me home at once, so it might then be sent for Peter. In the entrance hall we stood in awkward silence until Mr Croxon turned to his son. 'Michael, what do you say?'

Michael made a brief bow and smiled beatifically in my direction. 'Grace, I trust you will be good enough to visit us again, next Sunday.' At my blush, Mrs Croxon nodded with a knowing smile.

Back in the welcome peace of my chamber at Palatine House, I threw myself down on my bed, and allowed my true emotions to surface. The Croxons were a little odd; I was not easy with their showiness. But what did I care for them? Michael had made an instant and violent impression upon me. I no longer need worry that my suitor was not to my taste. As I lay daydreaming, it was as if a secret dam had burst within me; my throat and chest were crimson with pounding blood. Was it possible to fall in love at first sight, as the old ballads called it? There was not a single doubt in my mind from that very first day. I wanted Michael as my husband; I had set my heart upon it.

Over the next three weeks Michael's attraction worked even more powerfully upon me. Between visits I drew his portrait from memory a dozen times, tracing his cheeks, his brow and his jaw in pencil; then painting a pale wash of flesh tones over each sketch, creating a series of icons to my saviour. I knew Anne would have been horrified if she had ever seen my bedroom wall, covered with images of Michael's masculine beauty. I hid the pictures for fear of seeming rather – peculiar, I supposed.

A month to the day, Mr Croxon made a brief visit to Palatine House, at which, I understood, my father's formal agreement was obtained. The following Sunday, the scene was set for me to meet alone with Michael in the gilded drawing room. After his mother had simpered away, he led me to a window. I was almost faint with anticipation.

'Grace,' he said; then swallowed nervously, making me feel even more anxious. 'You will marry me?'

I looked up into his face, unable to read his pallid gravity. My eyes took a draught of his lips and long lashes – then I quickly looked away. I nodded and whispered, 'Yes.' It was done, it was over. I had secured Michael Croxon as my husband. The whole affair seemed remarkably easy, compared to Anne's protracted years of courtship

For the latter part of my visit, the senior Croxons raised toasts to our nuptials, and Mr Croxon spoke enthusiastically of Michael's plans to build a cotton mill on my land. Much was made of the large income it would provide for us. It was heartening enough, but I thought it rather dull talk for a newly betrothed couple.

'As for a new home, we've found a grand place for you over Earlby way,' announced my prospective father-in-law. 'Delafosse Hall is a substantial residence on three hundred acres. Been empty a fair while, but it once belonged to the Blairs, a very noble family. What do you say to that?'

'The Blairs were distant kin of mine,' Mrs Croxon interrupted, red-cheeked from spirits. 'Well, a distant branch. But that branch of the family died out, as these ancient families tend to do. I'm afraid the house will need improving – but what is that, if one might live in such grandeur? And I have engaged a housekeeper for you, a Mrs Harper, who is preparing your quarters even now.'

'So you expect me to move soon?' I asked, surprised at the rapidity of these plans.

Michael leaned forward. 'What do you say to marrying next month, Grace? There is no time to be lost in commencing the mill. The Hall is exceedingly well placed, sharing a boundary with your land at Whitelow. The river runs right by it, everything could not be more convenient.'

Next month? I grew flustered. 'How can all the preparations be made so quickly?'

'Leave it to me, Grace. I shall take it all in hand,' Mrs Croxon assured me.

So, rather than lying fallow, my birthright had brought me this captivating husband, a grand estate, and the promise of a great deal of money to come. Even my father had performed a complete turnabout, insisting it was best if my land was developed by the Croxons. My head whirled giddily at my new prospects. Yet I did dismiss from my mind some aspects of the arrangements. I learned that Michael had inspected my land on seven occasions already. I calculated that to be two more times than he had met me, his prospective bride.

'Grace dear, tell me in earnest. Are you sure Mr Croxon will make you happy?'

Anne and I were standing outside Warburton's Emporium, on a mission to find a wedding gift, but vexed as I was by her interrogations, it was impossible to make my choice. Why could she not accept my good fortune and share my joy?

'Yes, I am,' I said to Anne. 'I even dreamed it would happen,'

Anne could not disguise the roll of her spaniel eyes. 'You sound like one of your Circulating Library romances,' she said sharply. 'As one of Jacob's parishioners once said to me, "Women dream in courtship, but wedlock wakes them". Now when I first met Jacob, I thought him an unimpressive sort of fellow. But I gave him time, and in my own case, true feelings did blossom. And now that he is looking to expand his mission—'

She rambled on, ever the generous wife to her decidedly ordinary husband.

'Shall we move along?' I said, interrupting the catalogue of Jacob's virtues.

'Does he show you many signs of affection?' Anne asked, as she hurried to catch me up.

'Yes, he does,' I answered brightly.

This was not entirely true, for Michael had kissed me only once, in front of his parents, on the day of his proposal. Since then, although I often imagined his lips on mine, Michael had been most considerate in my company. At home, my daydreams merged with memories of summer afternoons with John Francis – alone on the hills, conversing with delicious frankness, enthralled by each other's company. There had been the playful approach of his hand to mine, the potent awareness of his fingertips brushing my skin. I told myself that Michael's courtship, beneath his parents' gaze, must be entirely different. After all, I had caught Michael looking at me, when he thought I was distracted. He was biding his time, for he was a gentleman, not a farmer's son.

Michael did not allow himself such liberties, but he was certainly more civil to me than he was to his parents; towards whom he was morose or even sullen. I blamed his mother, who clearly irked him with her fussing manner. As for his father, he domineered over his eldest son. There were hints made of past troubles, of disappointing delays in Michael getting his plans in progress. When I tried to ask about these, Mr Croxon said that none of that need concern me. I noticed that Michael's shoulders alone bore a great pressure to succeed, while Peter gadded about the countryside, sojourning at York or Ripon, enjoying the full liberty of his parents' indulgence.

'Grace, dear,' Anne started up again, as we parted at the top of Wood Street. 'You have not told me anything of his friends, his pursuits, his reading matter. Are they to your taste?'

The truth was I did not know. Many people mistake my character, thinking that because I am softly spoken I am weak, or that not always having a ready answer means I have no spirit. They are wrong. Having lost John Francis, I was not going to lose Michael Croxon. My temper leached into my tone. 'What does that matter? I love Michael.' She reached out to me and squeezed my hand, but I snatched it away.

'Oh, Grace,' my friend said wistfully. 'You know so little of the world.'

After parting from Anne I could not bear to go home to my father. I was crackling with an agitation that sent me striding through the town and up into the surrounding hills. It was good to climb my favourite path, my heart pounding in my ears, my legs stretching beneath muddy hems. At the top of the hill I stood panting, surveying the huddle of buildings far below: the grey spire of Greaves church and the straight line of the High Street, leading to the Market Cross and the roof of Palatine House. Turning to the north, my eye followed the road to Michael's home, hidden behind a thick stand of trees. Further north, past high brown crested ridges and far blue hills, away in the distance, lay Whitelow, and my new home at Delafosse Hall. I was sorry I had too little time to paint the scene before I left, to make a remembrance of my old home in viridian and dark ochre. I had seen nothing of the world but Greaves – and now I was to launch myself into a new life, with a heady mix of hopes and fears.

It was a blustery August day, and a restless warm wind whipped my hair across my face. From far above, the sound of a skylark drifted down to earth, a dancing speck on fluttering wings. I stood transfixed by its lonely song, a liquid hymn to freedom. Poor lark, stay safe away from shot and snares, I thought. And please let my waiting be over. I ached to see into the future. Anne vexed me because she was right: I was not so blind as to think Michael would want me without my land. But I was hopeful nonetheless. And what other course did I have? To be a lackey to my father, forever? I needed only courage and all would be well. True, some nights when sleep evaded me, I touched my crucifix and asked my mother out loud what I should do. No answer came; I was alone with Anne's cautionary words churning in my mind.

Walking over to the group of weathered boulders, called by long tradition the Ring Stones, I touched the surface of the mightiest. It was surprisingly warm, and I recalled tales of their mysterious movements in the moonlight, of midnight trysts and frolics. 'Whatever awaits me – keep me safe,' I whispered to the lichen-grey stone, feeling foolish enough. Then, looking for a token to offer to whichever ancient spirits inhabited that place, I found one of my mother's silver buttons in my pocket and pushed it hard into the turf at the stone's foot. I might have lingered all afternoon, but over to the west, where the land stretched to the sea and Ireland beyond, a cloud bank of sooty grey had appeared. The warm breeze dropped; the air was oppressive. I hurried home, racing the plashes of rain.

8

Manchester

Summer 1792

~ Penny Mutton Pies ~

To make five dozen pies take one and a half pounds of mutton and boil with a little brown colouring. Make your pastry from a quartern of flour and two pounds of suet. Season with a deal of black pepper and be heavy with the salt and you will sell much drink besides. The cost will be half a crown and the profit to your pocket, the same again.

Mother Eve's Secrets

Here was the Pen and Angel again, still standing five years on, the sign creaking in the Manchester rain, the frontage betraying long years of dust and decrepitude. As for the Palace, that had used to be hid around the back, that was something else now; some sort of workers' hall or meeting place. In the shop there was a new boy, who gave Mary directions to the Cupid, a smart public house near the law courts, with wooden booths for private conversation. The tapster there was a stranger too; a stoat-faced youth who would not meet her eye.

'Mr Trebizond,' he said, polishing the bar as if it were made of crystal. 'On my mark, he don't come here no more.'

At first she was furious, and then she recalled that 'On my mark' was the gang's old signal. She laid her hand on the bar and splayed her fingers, so the fellow could see the five dots tattooed in the crease between her thumb and first finger.

'On my mark, he'll know me all right,' she said in a low voice. The man nodded, and, without a word, let her pass behind the bar.

After following him down corridors and crossing a gloomy courtyard, they arrived at a painted back entrance with a brass knocker, where the tapster motioned her up a flight of brass-railed stairs. Her heart beat fast. She could almost smell Charlie in the grand style of the place. Then there he was before her, the same old Charlie, sitting alone at a desk with his pen in his hand.

'Mary!' As he jumped up, she read him closely – there was at least an appearance of delight on his ugly monkey face. He was still the genteel swell of her memory, all gold fobs and velvet trim. 'Well, who would have believed it? Sweetheart!' He held out his arms, and they embraced, just as they had done a thousand times before. He looked down at her, his hair thinner and his eyes as sharp as ever in a new web of creases. 'Was it terribly bad?' he asked. He still had that treacle voice, bookish and legal, even though he'd never had the proper schooling; only what he taught himself while fiddling his master's accounts.

She could not answer – only shook her head.

'But – wait. You're back early? You?' He frowned. 'Great God, Mary. Have you bolted?'

She kept her face hidden against his chest. 'I've had me fill, Charlie.' They sat down in his smart chairs, and she told him, as if it was just a yarn, of how she had sailed home as Flora Pilling, all the while searching his face for signs.

'Sharp as a pin, you are, Mary,' he said, full of the old charm. 'You know I did my best to prevent it? You do know that?' He cocked his head sideways and looked at her with what seemed honest pleasure. Had he truly done his best? Five years ago he had visited her in Newgate and told her she would walk free. Then, after the gull had flown, Charlie had never shown his face again. So much for a family of thieves: one thing she had learned across the herring pond: you were born alone, and alone you were left to die.

'Come here, then.' Smoothly does it, she told herself. She went to him, and he pulled her tightly towards him; she closed her eyes and breathed in the soap from his shirt. They went to the bedroom, and his bed was just as she'd conjured it so many times before, while she tried to sleep on rocky earth or wooden planks – cloud-soft, with lavendered sheets, and pillows stuffed with feathers. And he was her old Charlie again, familiar to every inch of her; the same crooked teeth, same narrow body as lean as a boy's, the same hard manhood, rising at the flick of a petticoat. Coupling with him was as easy as falling backwards into that younger Mary, when they followed The Life, and delights were all for the light-fingered taking.

Afterwards, when Charlie snored beside her, she couldn't sleep, for it was only three in the afternoon. Getting up to use the pot she took a prowl about the room. It was then that she noticed the girl's garters hanging on the back of the looking glass. So someone had taken her place as Charlie's girl after all. Lovely blue silken things, they were, to be tied above white silk stockings. Soft-hearted tears welled in her eyes. It took her a moment to swallow hard and get her bearings. Even after all these years it cut deep to know that Charlie had a new girl.

Years back, Charlie had been another of Aunt Charlotte's strays, a man of eighteen to Mary's ripening fourteen years. Auntie had brought Charlie up to the fake-letter dodge; she would slap her wobbling knees to hear him read his screeves out loud, for it was clever stuff. His game was newspaper advertisements for unclaimed legacies, crooked loans, and lottery rackets. And when the money rolled in from the dupes, he'd always come down to the Palace to throw a heap of chink on the kitchen table, brighter than any coin earned the honest way. And then would come a flurry of new shoes and frocks, and porcelain and paints. All of it bright to the eye and so lovely, lovely, lovely.

At first Mary had only watched Charlie from a distance; the young prince holding court amongst the women. She made cupboard-love treats for him, the crunchy Little Devils that he loved, and it had worked too, that night she had chased after him down Jerusalem Passage. She didn't speak, only offered him a paper twist of chocolate almonds. He laughed at her, shaking his head in a kindly, resigned manner. 'Come here then, Mary,' he said, and they had kissed, hard and greedy, against the wall.

At sixteen she moved into Charlie's ken above a tavern. After leaving his job as clerk to a man of law, Charlie lost no time becoming a swell mobsman. He liked it that Mary was as close to family as could be; for none of them wasted trust on strangers. While he was at his business, she made a few bob for herself, hawking eatables on the streets, a cover for palming coins and the short-change racket. When Charlie needed her, she personated a caller at a sham agency, or acted a weeping witness in the law court. One day they would feast at a chop house, and the next day work the horse-racing crowds. 'A heavy purse is always in fashion,' was their favourite quip. They drank like thirsty fish, and rutted the nights away. Charlie called his crew the Snakeskin gang: there was Humbug Joe the personator, a decayed gentleman who acted any character as well as Mr Garrick. Then Sal and Cog, the finest pocket-divers in the north, lifting dozens of pocket watches and purses every day. Aggy was their watcher, a nondescript crone with a pair of hawk's eyes. And then there was Red, a crag-faced wheedler who had the secret of forging notes. Life on the high-fly had been one long lark: thrilling to the nerves, a harum-scarum sort of life.

'Supper time,' Charlie said, stretching himself awake. She had dozed a little and now rolled lazily over to him. 'I've a boy waiting out in the hall. Order what you will, there's an excellent cook shop around the corner.' Her stomach rumbled as she tried to recall every foodstuff she'd ever longed for.

'I'd give my eye tooth for a hot meat pie. Just like I used to sell 'em, all yellow crust and the gravy oozing out. Wait, I'll have two pies. And some buttered rolls and some chops and a jug of beer. And one of them hot puddings sprinkled with sugar, the ones with the currants.'

When the boy brought the feast in to them, she ate it at the table, unwrapping the greasy parcels as if they were Christmas boxes.

'Still got your scribings, I see.' Charlie was lying naked across the bed, bird-bright eyes watching her from low lids. She turned to the looking glass to inspect the blue tattoo pricked into the narrow flesh of her back: Adam and Eve, naked beneath a tree, through which the serpent wound his coils. Below was inked the motto of the Snakeskin gang: 'The Serpent Tempted Me and I Did Eat'.

Before boarding the convict ship, she'd had to strip naked before the surgeon, who had prodded her with a ruler and asked her to give an account of her scarification.

'I made a start to screeving the entire Bible,' she'd replied. 'But that's as far as I got. Genesis, in't it?'

She'd got a slap for that, but the surgeon had copied the picture down in his book nonetheless. There were other prisoners' patterns drawn there: teardrops and handcuffs, helmeted Britannias, and Irish harps aplenty. Hers was the grandest of the lot.

As she looked in Charlie's mirror, her eyes shifted back to the other girl's garters. She took a long breath so her voice wouldn't betray her hurt. 'And how's business?' she asked in a jovial fashion. Lord, he had come into chink, there was no doubt of that. When he'd paid the cookshop boy, she had glimpsed a purse thick with coin.

'Good, good.' He nodded, self-satisfied. 'The populace is flooding here for work. Everyone's chasing a share of the cotton trade; and that's brought a great deal of business to the screeving game.' He half-shut his eyes, for he still loved the sound of his own voice. 'Here no one knows his neighbour and no one cares a jot. I made a biggish sum on an inheritance racket last year. The judge sent a People Finder to track down the relatives, but I got my claim in fast. You remember Humbug Joe? He played a long-lost beneficiary, and we got the whole pay-out. I can find you something right away. I need a woman for a job. I've not forgotten your talents.'

'What about a crib?' She had to know how things stood.

He lit a pipe with a great deal of unnecessary fiddling about. When he looked up again, he was watching her through curling smoke. 'Cat's Castle needs an experienced woman at the helm. Look after the girls and keep them out of the Justices' way.'

So that was all the rotten deal – to be a poxy bawd. And all the time some younger trull would be bouncing on Charlie's feather bed.

'Aunt Charlotte,' she asked spitefully. 'You ever think of her? It broke me heart, her snuffing it while I was doing a stretch.'

'How could I forget?' he said with a big shrug that she thought rather hollow. He owed everything to Aunt Charlotte. The consumption had killed her and most of the other women at the Palace, all in a few plaguey months. Auntie had loved Charlie like a son. Aye, eaten cake is soon forgotten, that was a true saying if ever there was.

'And the few that was left? When the Palace closed – where'd they all go?'

He shrugged. 'Miss Dora, she's still about, she runs a House of Correction down Chandler Lane. And that Frenchie one has a set of rooms on King Street paid for by a lord. The rest have gone where all the old whores go. Dead or poxed or playing the strumpet down twopenny lane.'

She was struck by a fit of the dumps to think of them all gone. And Charlie, had he truly done his best to free her? Charlie and all his appeals and reprieves, his promises that broke as easily as pie crusts.

'Mary – remember this?'

He reached under the bed, and from a silver case, drew out the Penny Heart she'd sent him. She hid a shiver at the sight of it. It had been back in the yard at Newgate she had last seen it. Now here it was again; turning up like a bad penny, a disc of mellowed copper strung on a green ribbon. In his beautiful voice Charlie read the verse she'd penned herself:

> *'Though chains hold me fast,*
> *As the years pass away,*
> *I swear on this heart*
> *To find you one day.'*

He lifted his brows. 'Well, Mary, your day has come. You always were true to old Charlie, weren't you? I won't forget that.' He patted the sheet beside him, and she climbed back into the warm spot. As he turned the coin over, silently, they both read:

MARY JEBB AGE 19
TRANSPORTED 7 YEARS
TO THE ENDS OF THE EARTH

She touched it with her fingertips, and it was uncanny; the rough metal seemed to pierce her like a needle, striking back through time, a talisman joining past and present.

'Very touched I was, sweetheart, when I got that,' Charlie was saying, as if from a long way away. 'I'll see you right, Mary. Get you settled at Cat's Castle.'

She blinked herself back to the present. Perhaps his bedding her earlier had been a kind of sop to her dignity? Soon, no doubt, his blue-gartered chicken would be back. By then she must be long gone.

Still, he had no notion there were two Penny Hearts, both identical. That other heart. Where was it now? Where was that other poxy cove she'd sent it to? She had to pick his ample brain.

'What was that you was saying about the inheritance racket earlier? Something about a People Finder. That's a new one, Charlie. How does that work?'

'Oh, I've done a bit of that myself,' he boasted. 'The authorities have printed up some most helpful registers, detailing everyone of property. I've my own set in there.' He nodded towards his office next door. 'Damned useful to a letter-writing man.'

'I'll wager it is. So is everyone written down in such a register? They can't be, can they? Not such as me?'

'No, just men of property. Name, address, rank, occupation, all scribed out and ready for the plucking. But the likes of me and you? That's the last thing we want, to be inked down in the records.' He frowned. 'Though, naturally, you've got the judgement against you at the Bailey. Just need a new moniker now, eh, Mary?'

She nodded mutely. Keep your trap shut, she told herself. Especially around Charlie.

'I need to sleep now, Charlie.' She slipped down beside him, into the crook of his body. After he'd kissed the top of her head, she let

herself fall into the dream that she'd lullabied herself with on count-
less nights. Only this time, she truly was in Charlie's feather bed,
not on some hellish, rocky shore.

At dawn, she wanted nothing more than to carry on sleeping beside
Charlie's warm body. Yet a stronger leash yanked her up from the
warmth, a compulsion she couldn't fight. Leave me be, she protested
silently, but it was no good. All her life she'd had to obey these
devils of urges, prodding her like toasting forks. Pulling on her
gown, she looked down at his placid face. In a moment she had the
contents of his wallet weighing nicely in her pocket. Then, silently
as a cat, she crept up close beside him, and scarcely breathing, slid
out the silver case from under the bed. Taking it to the glimmer of
light at the door, she removed the Penny Heart. Pulling it over her
head, she tucked it down into her bodice. Again she felt that jolt, as
if the metal disc joined past with future. She would keep it there by
her beating heart. She would never take it off again, she vowed,
until her revenge was complete.

Charlie's study might have passed for that of any man of law. The
tall stool and copying desk were surrounded by impressive ledgers
and cubbyholes. Paper, in different weights and colours, was stacked
in piles, along with every hue of bottled of ink. Mary knew the
manner of his work: anything from an attestation of an injury in a
coal-mining disaster, to a false warrant from a bank. He had a very
fine hand; or rather, he had a dozen fine hands, and hundreds of
signatures filed away, to be copied out with a flourish.

Helping herself to papers, pens, and inks, she stuffed them
inside her bundle. It took a frustratingly long time to find the first
item she needed, the register he had spoken of. At last she saw it
on a top shelf. It was all written out in parishes, not for the ease
of someone like herself. Finally, she found it – a certain name, and
beside it the address and occupation, just as Charlie had said.
Hurriedly, she scribbled it down, sliding the scrap of paper deep
inside her bodice. A groan from the bedroom made her freeze like

a statue. Then, as Charlie's snoring started up again, she finished her task as fast as she might.

Now for the false Characters he was famed for. They were still filed by occupation: Able Seaman, Accomptant, Barber, Clerk – ah, here was what she wanted: a false Character for a Cook. Written by a 'Mistress Humphries', it told of five years' service to an alderman, with never a dinner spoiled, nor a day taken sick. She pocketed the paper and made her way out by the back stairs. Peg Blissett was the name on the Character. She rehearsed it to herself as she set off in the early light. Fare thee well, Mary Jebb, I've had it with you and all your sorrows. Good day, Peg Blissett, she mouthed, eager to find that estimable cook a grand position up in the north country.

9

Greaves, Lancashire

Summer 1792

~ Gingerbread for Fairings ~

Weigh eight pounds of flour mixed with as much brickdust or clay as it will take and rub a pound and a half of used fat into it; put a pound and a half of raw sugar and spice with it, hot cayenne is cheaper bought than ginger, and wet up with treacle and water into a tight dough; let it lie a while. Then take your fancy mould; dust out with flour; press the dough well upon it, then take off, and bake in a cool oven. When cooked and cooled, gild it as you please: Dutch copper is best, being a counterfeit of gold of much less expense, though it does rub away pretty quickly. A small block might be sold for 6d but more fantastical shapes and gilding will command a most substantial profit.

Mother Eve's Secrets

Secretly, I was glad that my wedding was to be a quiet affair, performed by special licence at a church near Huxley House. It was with some relief that I learned Anne and Jacob could not attend, being summoned to a Mission meeting at Bradford that same week. Just before she left, Anne called at Palatine House to give me her wedding gift. In her precious free hours she had embroidered a wedding sampler, bearing Michael's and my own name, above our wedding date. It was the finest piece of embroidery she had ever made; the patterns of lover's knots, flower baskets, and wreaths all sewn in the most exquisite tiny stitches. Yet it was the verse she had embroidered that gave me the greatest pang:

> *Others, dear girl, may wish thee wealth,*
> *I wish thee love and rosy health;*
> *Health and love to make thee say,*
> *Happy was my bridal day.*

'I shall always hang this above my bed,' I said, my voice catching in my throat. 'I mean – our bed,' I added, scarcely believing that I would soon share a bed with Michael Croxon.

'I would not have stitched it if I'd known it would make you so miserable,' she said with a teasing chuckle.

'Oh, Anne, thank you for your good wishes – I do so hope they all come true.'

'You must write to me, dear. And I will visit if I can.'

She took me in her arms, and for a few moments we awkwardly embraced.

*   *   *

'Let me give you some advice,' Mrs Croxon told me. 'My son likes to cut a fine figure, and you must rise to his level, Grace.' Money for new costumes was therefore discreetly provided by Mr Croxon, and I did my best to make the necessary purchases. The mere six weeks' preparation time meant that Mrs Croxon's dressmaker was made frantic by the commission, limited as she was in both time and fabrics. As my mother-in-law was addicted to the latest fashion plates, I soon found myself parading in the apparel of a wealthy provincial matron. She favoured high-brimmed flower-pot hats trimmed with spiky feathers – a style that suited my tall figure very ill. Even my new gowns of fashionable white muslin left me feeling uncomfortably half-dressed. I made a stand when Mrs Croxon tried to foist upon my head a gigantic mob cap the size of a potato sack. How ridiculous I looked! Henceforth, however ungrateful I might appear, I insisted on plain dark gowns of garnet or brown silk, and my one great favourite, a ruby mantle lined with otter fur. As for my wedding gown, it was spoiled by its over-garnishing of lace and frills, and such a fandango of feathers and ribbons on my headdress, that I felt like a spectacle from a panto-mime. The seamstress steadfastly flattered me and made some rapid alterations with her needle, but nevertheless, despite a fortune spent on silks and velvets, I still felt myself to be the scarecrow of my father's jibes.

In her passion for my wedding preparations, Mrs Croxon insisted a bride cake be baked, and that I inspect it at each stage of its embellishment. It was a great circular cake, more than a foot in diameter, first covered in almond paste and then hard white sugar icing. With an air of conferring a very great favour, my future mother-in-law took me to her closet and lifted the lid of an ancient box.

'These are the Blair family devices, my heirlooms I might say. Look, here is the Blair crest in sugar.' She held in her palm a portrait moulded in white, of an angel's head circled by streamers of coiling hair. 'Be careful. It is very old and may crack.' When she passed it to me I saw that the ornament, though as exquisite as a snowy cameo, was made from sugar.

'My grandmother gave the entire collection to me.' She laid out a row of exquisite sugar devices: a gilded crown, toy-like beasts, shells, and other fancies. 'Ah, now this is the mould for a Blair bride cake.' She laid two wooden boxwood moulds on the table, in which curious rectangular designs had been carved. 'You cannot guess what it is?'

I shook my head.

'It is from a rather cruder age, I'm afraid. It is a great tester bed.'

I looked more closely and recognised that the six sections could indeed be moulded and then assembled to make a tiny bed, complete with four posts, gathered curtains, and tassels the size of pin-heads.

I must admit I blushed at that, for this woman was, after all, Michael's mother.

'Yes, I know what you are thinking. Let us have the wedding first.'

But it was not the wedding I was blushing at, but the wedding night, and whatever vast tester bed lay waiting for me at Delafosse.

'Is there much company up at Earlby?' I asked my prospective mother-in-law another day.

'Oh, the village is tolerably dull I suppose. Small farmers and weavers. But the Hall had such grand rooms, and the parkland was extensive. There is a hunting tower that was used for banquets in the days of Good Queen Bess, and a summerhouse quite in the classical style. One night there was a dance – my head was quite giddy from the punch—'

'Grace doesn't want to hear those old tales,' interrupted her husband. 'Michael will have his work cut out with the mill.'

'Once the business thrives, they may aspire.' Mrs Croxon shot an affronted glance at her husband. He snorted and turned back to his newspaper. 'One may always dream,' she pronounced defiantly, rising to leave the room.

I was growing used to such sudden chills in the Croxon household; in response I cherished hopes of far greater happiness for myself and Michael. Delafosse Hall would be a new start, far from this bickering family and my own father's sour remarks. I must make a friend of my housekeeper, Mrs Harper, I decided. In my daydreams, Michael and I were at last alone, waited upon by biddable servants, a pair of lovers in our own Castle Amorous, where our love could grow undisturbed.

The means to make my daydreams more substantial arrived as an appointment with a certain Mr Tully, the notary who had drawn up my grandmother's will. Though ordinarily a resident of Leeds, he wrote that he was drawing up my Marriage Settlement, and asked me to call upon him at a fellow lawyer's office in Whalley. I told Michael of my appointment, and after giving the news to his father, he offered to accompany me.

The appointment fell on the day of the town's annual fair, and the bustle and flurry infected us with the high spirits of a holiday. From the moment we met, Michael was more animated than I had ever seen him before. In his father's grand carriage, with only his mother's maid as chaperone, he made waspish remarks about those we passed; I supposed he was trying to impress me, his new bride, with his superior manner. I was as impressible as butter, dazzled by my elegant husband-to-be, and flattered to be seen at his side. When we arrived at the lawyer's he hung back, making enquiries of a groom about an equipage, as the eleven chimes of our appointment hour rang out across the yard.

When, reluctantly, he followed me into the dark-panelled lawyer's chambers, we had a cold reception. 'Miss Moore?' said an elderly dyspeptic-looking man in a horsehair wig, lifting a large gold pocket watch from his waistcoat. 'You are late. My next appointment is at noon. Sit, sit. I must make haste.'

Flustered, I nodded and he began to speak. Perhaps because Mr Tully had been my grandmother's notary, I had expected his manner to be straightforward. Instead he declaimed a jumble of percentages and legal terms, all spoken very fast in a monotone. The uncomfortable notion came to me, that because of my poor understanding of mathematics, I might never comprehend my own affairs. Thereafter, my anxiety made me ever more confused. Finally he announced with formality, 'Those are the terms of the marriage settlement. You agree, Miss Moore?' The lawyer again took out his pocket watch. The clock on the wall showed that only fifteen minutes remained before noon.

'Mr Croxon,' I said, turning to Michael. 'I pray you understand the terms? I am afraid I am not used to such complicated arithmetic.'

Michael nodded. 'Put your mind at rest, Miss Moore. I comprehend it entirely. You need not concern yourself.'

To my surprise, Mr Tully issued an exasperated sigh and fixed his eyes upon me.

'This will not do, Miss Moore. It is my duty as your Trustee to ensure that you understand your situation entirely, before signing the Agreement. I shall repeat the terms in the simplest language. There are but three items you must inwardly digest. Firstly, some would say that the value of your property is presently inflated to an artificially high price. I wish you to know that I for one believe this cotton fever will not persist.'

'Sir, you cannot know—' interrupted Michael.

The lawyer fixed his moist eye upon Michael, showing a marked disdain. 'Oh, I do know, sir. I have lived long enough to understand that the pendulum of land prices will eternally rise and fall. Whatever you may have been told otherwise, the current price of land such as Whitelow cannot remain so high.' The last was said so stridently that I heard Michael make a tiny tut of derision.

'Secondly, Miss Moore, under the terms of your grandmother's will, all rents from the land remain payable to you alone, even after marriage.'

'I see,' I said

'The farms currently pay £300 per annum each Lammastide, the first day of August, into an account I hold for you at Hoare's Bank, London. The balance is at present £3,000, as your grandmother made no withdrawals for the ten years prior to her death.'

Michael gave a little gasp. 'Quite a nest egg.'

'You might say so,' the lawyer said drily.

'I had no idea,' I said. Michael met my eyes with a little grimace of joy. 'And, Mr Tully,' I continued, 'you spoke of the inflated value of the property. Might you tell me its value at present?'

'In the region of £6,000.'

I shook my head in bewilderment. 'I'm not sure I comprehend such a sum.'

Mr Tully sprang forward. 'I shall attempt to explain. Take such a building as the one we are currently occupying, a dozen rooms, a useful situation. A house such as this might be valued at £100. Ergo, the value of your land alone might buy sixty such houses, and with the rents added to it, as many as ninety houses. So you see, your whole legacy is equal to the value of a small village.'

I nodded, both grateful and surprised.

'Miss Moore, I must tell you that upon your marriage, though the property of Whitelow remains within your legal ownership, it must be managed entirely by your husband. Under the doctrine of *couverture*, you are not, of course, as a woman, able to enter any form of contract. Consequently, your husband will need to take upon himself the management of your property.'

'I think I understand,' I said. 'So while I legally own Whitelow I cannot make contracts upon it in my own name?'

The lawyer nodded briskly, and made to continue. But Michael shifted in his chair and spoke again. 'Am I to understand, sir, that you should therefore transfer the deeds of the property to me?'

Mr Tully scowled. 'I can think of only one reason to do so, Mr Croxon, and that would be to raise a sum against the property. And that is entirely what I have just spent valuable time advising your future wife not to do. Miss Moore is my client, and I strongly recommend that her inheritance is not exposed to such risky circumstances.'

'But we must build a mill, sir. Are you not familiar with the saying, "He is not fit for riches, who is afraid to use them"? Our two families are agreed upon it.'

Mr Tully turned back to me, his pale eyes skewering me with a most penetrating gaze.

'While I am not in a position expressly to forbid such an action, may I suggest, Miss Moore, that all actions in the nature of loans and mortgages be directed to me, at my Leeds office, for my personal scrutiny?'

'I don't see—' began Michael.

'I am addressing Miss Moore,' the lawyer interrupted.

'Mr Tully is only helping me to safeguard my grandmother's legacy,' I said to Michael, in what I hoped was a calming manner. 'What harm can it do to obtain his advice?'

Michael, seeming to reconsider, nodded civilly – though a trifle stiffly – to us both.

'If all is now clear, Miss Moore, I will call my clerk as witness and you will both sign the Marriage Settlement.' And so we did. Michael made a rapid, theatrical squiggle with the lawyer's pen. I glanced once more through the dense papers of legal scribework, and tentatively signed my name.

Drawing his chair back, and placing his hands on the table, the lawyer looked up at the clock, just then commencing its midday chimes.

'Fortunately, my final item is eminently simple. Miss Moore, as you remain the legal owner of the property, all instructions must of course be accompanied by your express permission, in the form of a current signature. Your signature, if I may be so bold, is a valuable commodity. Without your signature, I will not act.'

I reached out my hand to thank Mr Tully, but already the chimes of noon had ended; and, with a curt nod, we were dismissed from the room.

'What an abominable pettifogger!' exclaimed Michael as we returned to the busy street. 'Why the Devil did your grandmother choose such a buffoon?'

'I suppose he takes care of my interests,' I said gently.

'To have to submit our plans to a glorified clerk – it is monstrous!'

I tried to quiet him, for his outburst was drawing attention from passers-by. 'All will be well, Michael. And I, for one, am astonished at the value of the property.'

'Yes,' he said, taking my arm and leading me forward, 'that was even better news than I expected. We shall live like royalty. And to make a start, my dear, where shall we dine?'

After a long sojourn at a tavern, I asked that by way of celebration, we might take a turn around the fair, telling Michael how Father had always railed against what he called 'such heathen gatherings'. So off we battled through a hubbub of fair-goers, a young crowd, jostling and jesting. Mrs Croxon's maid begged leave to go on an errand for lace, so soon we were alone, passing amongst cheapjacks crying up the sale of trashy goods, and stalls of ribbons and sweet-stuffs. I halted to watch a troop of children tumbling like monkeys, their faces painted and their jackets twinkling with glass-cut spangles. Above our heads a tightrope walker carried a wobbling cane across a rope strung from roof to roof. Twilight was gathering, and everywhere lamps were being lit, their crimson and green shades casting a lurid glow across eager faces. We entered a ramshackle hamlet of tents, the air thick with the scent of roasted chestnuts and hot sugar. For a price any wonder could be seen: a Tale of Blackbeard, the exhibition of a man-bear or a two-headed cow. I thought it marvellous, a resurrection of some older, harum-scarum age.

The largest crowd had gathered at a tent painted with symbols of stars and moons that advertised a Phantasm Show. I begged Michael we might see it, and so crept beneath a tent flap and blinked in the gloom, inhaling trampled grass and oil smoke. The show was being introduced by a haggard man in a black-ribboned hat, who promised monsters and phantoms that I did not for a moment believe he could conjure.

The tent was then made very dark, and the spectres of various great men and women raised: Charles I with his severed head, wicked Salome, and Anne Boleyn, to name a few. These were cleverly depicted, floating in the darkness above us, drawing gasps and screams from the crowd. Yet being as still as pictures I guessed they were only that, a series of paintings cunningly illuminated.

I was therefore unprepared for what came next. The most impregnable darkness fell, and a doleful clock tolled midnight. A red moon rose in the sky; a wind whistled mournfully. Before us stretched a forest of tangled grey trees, from which a flock of cruel-looking birds rose in flight and crossed the disc of the moon. From clouds of rolling mist a young woman appeared, pale and lovely, moving haltingly as she collected crimson apples and placed them in a basket on her arm. At the same time she sang a hauntingly slow song, made all the more unsettling by its being sung in the tantalising words of a foreign tongue.

With a collective gasp, the audience sighted a shape hiding by a distant tree; a grey figure crooked and monstrous, neither man nor woman. Slowly it scuttled closer and closer to the maiden. 'Look out!' called a fellow close by us. The woman sitting beside me whimpered and pulled her apron up to her face as the figure drew ever nearer. Still the pale young woman stood transfixed by the moon, an angelic glow around her. Step by step the horrid shape grew larger and closer. A sudden thunderclap crashed, and everyone in the place jumped in their seats.

'It's behind you!' bellowed desperate voices in the dark. White lightning flashed, revealing the horrid pursuer at last falling upon its victim, enveloping her in its smothering horror. A shrill female scream rang out as if uttering a death cry. For a second the air flashed red like blood, then we were once again breathing hard in the blackness.

I found I was grasping Michael's sleeve, and quickly withdrew my hand. The haggard mountebank returned in a pool of light, and in his closing speech declaimed the mysteries of phantasms, concluding that we all, believers in the supernatural or not, would one day witness one truly terrible spectacle – our final fate. At this he doffed his hat, and that self-same moment, a light beam shone above the showman, revealing a representation of skeletal Death hovering above him, aiming his scythe at the speaker's bare head. Next moment the lights were dimmed as a gunshot sounded, again sending everyone starting in a paroxysm from their seats.

'What a hideous spectacle. It was enough to put the fear of hell into a fellow,' complained Michael as we moved outside.

'I thought it quite remarkable,' I said, still breathless from the delicious fear it had provoked. 'Do you not like to be frightened?' I laughed. 'It was only done with lamps of course, shone through something like a *camera obscura*, I should imagine.'

'A what? How would you know of such contrivances?'

'You forget, my father was a printer and something of an artist. The best artists use light boxes to sketch their outlines.'

He looked quizzically at me. 'I do hope you are not going to be tiresome, Grace, and get it in your head to know the answer to everything.'

I mumbled an apology and followed him, unsure why I had been chastised.

'Do you wish to leave?' I asked gently.

'In a moment.'

I had just then spotted a gingerbread stall, and in hope of taking home a souvenir of our day, steered Michael towards it. A huddle of young people had gathered, laughing good-humouredly at the saucy mottoes on the fairings. I asked Michael if we might make a lovers' exchange, but he had spied a nearby ale bench.

'Choose something. I need a drink,' he said, heading away. Alone, I chose from the wondrous array of gingerbread, cast into likenesses of carriages and ships, and satirical figures of admirals and kings. 'I shall take a gilded husband,' I said to the stallholder, and paid my own shilling. My fairing was a cavalier of a fellow, with long curling hair and a knee-length patterned coat.

'Shall we go?' Michael came up beside me, beer on his breath.

'Yes,' I said merrily. 'Look. My gingerbread husband. Will you take a wife?'

He glanced morosely at the tray of gilded ladies. I suppose to his eyes they were grotesques, in their wide skirts and cross-laced stomachers.

'I've already purchased some refreshment for the journey home,' he announced. 'And that hoyden at the ale tent tricked me out of two shillings. This place is a den of thieves.'

Back in the carriage I removed my gloves to inspect the gilded figure. It was a piece of gimcrackery of course, but it had a country charm to it. As I did so, a quaint saying echoed in my mind, that 'the gilding is soon rubbed off the gingerbread'. It seemed that exactly such disillusionment had begun for me that day. I had noticed certain proofs of Michael's character that I did not much care for. Naturally, I was already acquainted with the Croxons' enthusiasm for what the Brabantists would have called Mammon, so his enthusiasm for my inheritance was not unexpected. But his flare of temper when I made an intelligent observation on the magic lantern was plainly unjust. And finally, there was another matter, one that I decided to test at once.

I rested my bare hand on my lap, remembering how John Francis and I had used to steal secret caresses. Yet for long moments my hand lay unsought, even though our chaperone had chosen to ride outside with the driver.

'Michael. Are you happy?' I asked at last, knowing I might again be called tiresome, but willing to take the risk.

'How could I not be?' He took a long swig of ale, his gaze fixed on the window.

My hand continued stiff and empty on my lap.

'I should say, are you happy with me?' I asked steadily. That at least sent a shadow of alarm across his features. Seizing my hand he raised it and kissed it, in a smart, dry manner. 'Grace, you are all I could ever want in a wife.' His voice was charmingly smooth but undoubtedly strained.

'Am I? Truly what you – want?'

He pulled a mocking sort of face as if I must be joking. Then my husband-to-be squeezed my hand and made a confession of sorts. It was gloomy in the carriage, but I could see him watching me intently. 'You doubt me, Grace. I hear it in your voice. I am not surprised. It is best you know the worst. The fact is I suffer from a species of melancholy.' He sighed heavily. 'My moods can be horribly capricious. Just then at the fair, that low creature disgusted me with her wretched trick.' His hand in mine felt suddenly heated. 'No, it is more than that. For some years now, I have existed in a kind of low and desponding situation, an indifference to my own life or death. I cannot expect you to understand, but perhaps, as a woman of sentiment, you might sympathise? My parents believe I need a change of circumstances, a project, and most of all, a good wife.'

I considered this, then asked, 'And you? Do you want those things?'

He lifted his head and addressed me directly, his fine soulful eyes shining fixedly into mine.

'I do, Grace. I need you. Don't disappoint me, please. I have been so – miserable. And now— I see hope.'

At last he leaned forward and kissed me on the lips. So this was the answer, I told myself. I had wondered at his father's hints of past troubles, and now he had told me, frankly and openly, that he suffered. I embraced him in return. I needed him, too. And I was flattered too, for which good woman would not wish to rescue a handsome and sensitive man?

10

Greaves to Delafosse Hall

September 1792

~ To Make A Bride Cake ~

Take four pounds of fine flour, four pounds of butter, two pounds of loaf sugar; add a quarter ounce of mace and the same of nutmegs. To every pound add eight eggs. Pick and dry four pounds of currants, blanch a pound of sweet almonds, a pound of citron, a pound of candied orange, the same of candied lemon, half a pint of brandy. Work the butter to a cream with your hand, then beat in your sugar a quarter of an hour. Beat the egg whites to a strong froth and mix in, then your flour and mace and nutmeg, keeping beating it well till your oven is ready, put in your brandy and currants and almonds. Tie three sheets of paper around the bottom of your hoop, rub well with butter and put your cake in. Lay your sweetmeats in three lays with cake betwixt every lay. It will take three hours baking.

The Experienced English Housekeeper, Mrs Raffald, 1772

My wedding plans took on a vital life of their own: money was laid out, our new home secured, and the ceremony arranged by the Croxons. I knew I should have felt unalloyed joy, but instead a sick apprehension struck me in my moments of leisure. Why are you not happy, you fool, I chided myself, when you are leaving Wood Street at last? You must remember that no one on earth could make you more wretched than Father.

The day arrived, and with it the most irrevocable step of my life. As Michael and I walked arm-in-arm to the carriage, I caught a glimpse of the two of us in a pier glass in the Croxons' hallway. Michael, absorbed in inward thoughts, appeared as pallid and nervous as any groom of tradition, though infinitely more fashionable in his ivory coat, his hair artfully tousled. I stooped beside him in my over-frilled gown and ridiculous feathers. Instead of wearing my beloved crucifix, I wore a cameo lent to me by Mrs Croxon, who thought my lengthy mourning unhealthy. In secret however, I wore the crucifix sewn into my stays, a comfort against my heart.

The old saying that every lass is a beauty on her wedding day had not come true for me. My nervous rash had cruelly spread, erupting in a scattering of tiny pimples. And my wavy brown hair did not, as Mrs Croxon's maid had promised, look as lovely as a goddess's; only rather silly, in a high mass of hot-ironed curls. From the midst of all my fine lace and feathers, I saw the tautness of great strain reflected back at me.

As for the ceremony, I made the responses in a whisper, glad to have my back towards the eyes of the congregation. There had been rumours of objections to my Dissenting creed, so I held my breath as the parson asked if anyone knew of an impediment to our marriage and was met with silence. When he spoke of how a man must cleave unto his wife as one flesh, I blushed at the thought of our wedding night. I will make him love me, I swore to myself, flexing my hand to admire the gold ring that glowed hopefully on my finger.

After the service, we crowded into the vestry and signed our names in the Parish Book: mine for the last time, Miss Grace Moore. Michael signed his name swiftly, almost scribbling it, then lifted his head and cast a sober glance towards his father, who smiled benevolently in return.

A little awkwardness followed. I went to my new husband's side and took his hand.

'I am so happy,' I whispered.

'Good,' he replied gruffly. 'But this formality, when will it end?'

Did he mean that he wished to be alone with me? I would soon learn my husband's ways, I reassured myself. I wanted to shield him from the smallest irritation.

'My dear,' I said, smoothly, 'it will soon be over.'

Michael shook his head rapidly; it was almost a shudder. 'Oh, for some fresh air! What time will it all be finished?'

'After the wedding breakfast.'

'What time, I asked?'

I flinched. 'I shall ask your mother.'

I found that our hour of departure was one o'clock. Obediently, I hurried back to his side and repeated the information. Love and obey, that was what I had sworn. I am a new being, I repeated, a wife to this man, with his commanding moods.

Back at Huxley House, Michael led me on his arm into the dining room, to a chorus of polite applause. Beside the minister, only my father was not of the Croxon household. The room had been decked with late-blooming roses that cast up a sugary glasshouse scent. Yet amongst the profusion of china and silver, the atmosphere was one of flamboyance, rather than celebration. Mrs Croxon announced that we should eat 'exactly the Bill of Fare as given by a most genteel Countess at Bath'. I had no appetite for sardines in mustard, creamed oats and kidneys, for I had a stomach full of butterflies, as my mother had called my fits of nerves. Michael too was restless and ate little, emptying his glass and ignoring his plate. The centrepiece was of course the bride cake, now crowned with the tester bed, painted in lurid crimson and gold. I worried how Michael might receive this, but he was too bewitched by the bottom of his glass. Saving us from the usual coarse allusions, the parson raised his glass and made the toast: 'Here's to the bride cake. The fruit for fertility, white sugar for purity, all the gay favours, and brandy to bless the bride.'

This prompted my father to propose a toast of Lancashire posset. I quailed at the approach of the egg-thickened liquor in its double-handed pot, and when I raised it to my lips I could not swallow it. It is only wedding nerves, I told myself, all the time fiercely aware of the heat from Michael's body, only inches away from my own bare arm. I wished very much that he would turn to me, speak confidingly, and ease my mind. But he is suffering too, I told myself. Once we are alone, we will share our confidences as lovers do. Then, to my dismay, my father started up a ribald tale of a notorious rustic wedding. Michael began to fidget and rock his leg in annoyance. Be silent, I prayed, throwing my father fierce looks. By the time his tale reached its rambling conclusion, the bride and groom were blessed by seven children in as many years. My father laughed loudly, but alone. Mrs Croxon looked at her husband and ostentatiously winced.

My new brother-in-law, Peter, who I had by then marked as generally provoking, said light-heartedly, 'At that rate of production, Michael, you may soon justify such an excessively grand establishment as Delafosse Hall.'

Michael stopped swinging his leg and stiffened. 'Must you always lower the tone to your own base level? Even on my wedding day?'

Peter gave a shrug and looked to his mother.

'Michael,' his mother entreated. 'It is only harmless teasing.'

I kept my own face blank, only stared at the shards of sugar bedclothes lying broken on my plate.

'Well, I do not reckon it harmless,' he snapped. 'Besides, you have not even seen Delafosse Hall. It is no larger than the owner of any rising business requires. And unlike some, I shall be working damned hard—'

'Is that an invitation?' Peter interrupted gaily. 'There is an assembly at Earlby tonight. I know, I shall ride with you, and stay at the George. Then tomorrow I might call on you and take a look at Delafosse Hall.'

'You shall not! You are not—'

'Michael,' his mother chided. 'Such squabbling! Just like little boys.'

'Mother,' Michael turned to her, his face stricken, 'even on my wedding day Peter jibes at me. You must be blind not to see it.'

'Michael!' Mr Croxon slapped the table, making crockery tremble. 'Your mother has taken great trouble for you today. And, Peter—' With a sharp look, he rid Peter of his smirk, 'show proper respect for your brother.' Then he considered. 'Yet surely if Peter rode up, he might call on you and report back your safe arrival. Might he not, Michael?'

The air around Michael prickled uncomfortably. Why could I not be left alone with my new husband?

'Michael?' Mr Croxon repeated.

With ill grace Michael nodded at Peter and mumbled his agreement. The remainder of the meal passed in silence, save for the clinking of china, and noisy gulping as my father attacked the ready supply of spirits.

Once the carriage had swung out of the drive I tried to revive the morning's celebratory mood, and made every effort to ignore Peter, who was trotting on his horse just beside us. I turned to Michael. 'It was a beautiful ceremony.'

He attempted a thin smile. 'Was it? I am glad it is over.'

'As am I.' I took his hand in mine, but he did not return my caress.

'Please don't,' he said, with startling candour, laying my hand back on the seat. 'I am sorry, Grace. I am in extraordinary low spirits today. I cannot bear this – play-acting.'

'Play-acting?'

'Pretending that the marriage is anything but a business alliance.' He made a dismissive gesture with his hand.

My lips parted, but no words emerged. He might have struck me a blow with his fists; all the air was suddenly knocked from my lungs.

'Come now, I have married you. That is what you wanted, is it not? I have done my duty. As you saw today, my parents are satisfied. As for my brother,' he said scornfully, 'he is overcome with envy.' He craned to see where Peter suffered in a flurry of rain.

'Michael,' I began, with a great effort, 'I – care for you. It is more than a – business alliance to me.'

He dropped his chin into his palm and stared sullenly out of the window like a thwarted child. Then suddenly he spoke, addressing his words to the empty seat opposite.

'Surely you all have what you want by now? Yet still you place this strain on me. First Peter, and now you?' His long fingers pressed his brow, as if he bore the burdens of the world. 'I have met my obligation and I refuse to be complained of.' Raking his fingers through his hair, he twisted a curl. 'And we will be rich, which I am assured always makes life more pleasant.'

For a long time I stared from my own window, disappointment enfeebling me.

'But Michael,' I exclaimed in a disconsolate tone I immediately regretted; 'now we have made our vows before God – surely we have every hope of growing closer? You said you needed me. That you had hope for the future?'

'Did I?' he said dully. 'I cannot remember it today. Tomorrow I may feel differently. Do not look at me like that. You may as well comprehend your situation from the first.' He turned to me, with a hard expression. 'Listen. Before we arrive, it will be easier if you rid yourself of any novelettish notions of marriage. I am sorry, but that is how it is. That is my final word.' Then, turning to the window, he announced abruptly, 'Here is Stone Edge. The horses must halt at the top.'

The carriage was climbing slowly upwards, into a dreary brown moorland naked of vegetation. Above us stood a cliff of limestone rising almost to the lowering clouds. Outside, the coachman cracked his whip as the carriage swayed, then slowly climbed up the road that snaked to the top of the Edge. As we made the vertiginous climb I felt my own hopes were left abandoned far below on the plain. With much groaning of axles we reached the top, where I peered over the fearful precipice rather than at my husband's face. Michael had broken his word. I was not mistaken; he had told me he wanted me, that I gave him hope. A business alliance? It was too cruel.

In time I was roused from dejection by our arrival at an inn, a tumbledown heap of grey stone with a low slate roof. As I dismounted, I read the swinging inn sign: The Long Drop, blazoned with a crude flagon and a pair of hanging legs. Inside, I allowed myself to be fussed over by the landlady, and led to an ancient settle, where I huddled over the fire, miserably sipping tea. The landlady halted beside me, a clutch of empty tankards in her hand.

'Delafosse Hall, mistress? I never heard that old place had been refashioned.'

'Refashioned?' I was too upset to converse.

'I always heard it was fallen to ruin after the last folk went and died. But I reckon that must be another place I'm thinking on.'

I smiled tightly, and, for the first time, asked myself what I knew about my future home. What was it my father-in-law had said? It had been empty a while and would need work to bring it back to its best condition. I glanced up at Michael, who stood at the counter, while Peter sat apart, drinking in a corner. Though Michael had visited the place, I recollected no intelligence of the Hall's condition.

Observing Michael talking loudly with the coachman, I discovered that there is a loneliness far greater than that of a solitary spinster; that of the unheeded half of a newly wedded couple. Now he began to address a band of rough-clothed men who supped their ale in a silent huddle.

'I shall be setting up a cotton-spinning mill at Whitelow,' he announced, surveying the ragtag company. 'Soon there will be plenty of yarn for all of you, and work for your children. Good, paying work.'

When his words met only silence, he shuffled uncomfortably and added, 'What say you to that?'

A grey-headed man rose uncertainly and pulled off his cap. 'Thank'ee kindly, master. We be much obliged to you.' Then he sat down and raised his tankard.

Michael grinned and called for the landlord to pour the man a drink. But as this was being performed, another voice cried out from a gloomy corner: 'We look after us own trade here. Doff our caps to no one. An' dinna' share us profits neither.' A chorus of supporting jeers rose from the shadows.

'Who is that? Stand up and be known,' Michael demanded, sounding suddenly a boy amongst men. I craned my neck to see who had spoken, but the men by the chimney made no reply save for snorts of laughter.

'Speak up,' Michael demanded. 'What objection can you hold to the new mill?'

'All that yarn'll bring prices down,' called an unseen voice.

'And increase trade overall, to Britain's benefit,' Michael insisted.

'To the benefit of your pockets, more like. While us children lose life and limb in them infernal machines.'

Another chorus of approval rose from the chimney corner.

'Don't take no notice of them, sir,' the landlord remonstrated.

'Damned insolence. Thinking to challenge me on questions of trade. They will work for me soon enough. Especially when we sell our yarn over their heads.'

Peter glanced up from his tankard; I saw a smirk on his face and detested him for it.

When the ostler announced that the horses were ready, I rose to join Michael. As I crossed the room, I felt the occupants of the inn subject us all to scrutiny; and when I looked up, I saw a gaggle of men whose eyes looked very white against their dirty faces, watching us like a negro servant I had once seen, attending his mistress with ill-disguised contempt.

It was dusk when we arrived at Earlby village. For the last hour Michael had been asleep. In my sketchbook I drew Michael's portrait, capturing his boyish repose. Then the light failed, and in a kind of anguish I recalled my anxious but hopeful state only that morning. In a single afternoon I felt myself grown old and weary. As Michael finally stirred, I stifled a wish that he might sleep on for ever, like a bewitched captive, then scolded myself for my disloyalty. I tidied my appearance, pulling my bonnet over my flattened curls. The day had been a great strain to both of us, I was sure that was the cause. With luck all would be well on the morrow.

I could see little of Earlby save a paltry few rows of stone dwellings. At the George Inn Peter came to the window and took his leave, disappearing beneath the hostelry arch. From its broad windows, lamplight cast golden pools onto the cobbles, and the sound of revelry reached our ears. Then we two were alone, nearing our journey's end.

There was no view of the house as we plunged into a gap between high stone walls. Instead, a great mass of trees surrounded us, scratching the roof and tapping at the windows with scraping fingers. I heard the coachman curse as he coaxed the horses forward, the carriage lamp throwing light onto a tangle of twisted branches.

In time the wheels left the leaf-muffled drive and bumped across noisy cobbles. A looming darkness rose above the carriage: a cliff of blackness, as startling as the plateau of Stone Edge.

Only as I alighted did I finally get a view of the Hall. In the small glow of the carriage lamp, I was startled to see that its walls were moving; rippling as if alive, like a membrane steadily breathing in and out. Slowly I connected the movement with the sound of sighing exhalation that surrounded us, and taking a few unsteady steps towards the house, I reached out and felt a mass of dry, spiky leaves. When the breeze again lifted, the mass of creeper hissed mournfully again. It will be like living in the heart of a great wood, I told myself. Then a servant with a lamp came forward, and the walls moved again, as if in whispered greeting.

Carefully, I stepped inside a narrow wicket cut into the massive entrance doorway. It had been chilly in the carriage, but inside the building the cold of ancient stones rose up from uneven paving flags.

'Come along inside, mistress, master. I've a fire lit in the Great Hall.' Michael followed the woman's bent shape, yawning. What little I could comprehend of the entrance recalled an ancient chapel suddenly opened after centuries of neglect; being both airless and sourly damp. The servant's candle led to what I later knew as Delafosse's famed Jacobean staircase, a glory of carved oak peacocks, angels, and other strange devices. Naturally I saw nothing of that on my arrival, only heard beams groan like a galleon's timbers at sea, and felt the stair treads dangerously warped beneath my feet. The vast space of the stairwell above me was invisible then, but I had a sensation of dust and cobwebs and tiny unseen beings. To my dismay we emerged from a first-floor landing into a second hall as vast as a church and also acrid with decay. At the far end, a fireplace taller than a man held a blazing fire that sent shadows chasing around walls hung with indistinct paintings and tapestries. The firelight hinted at the hammer-beam roof far above us, as black-ribbed as a decayed leviathan.

'Fetch Mrs Harper at once,' Michael demanded.

The servant halted, her back bent, in the red glow of the fire.

'She's gone, master. Up and gone last week with never a word.'

'Gone? Damn the woman. Have any other servants been recruited?'

The servant turned a frail face towards us, her eyes shining like beads in the firelight.

'No one else never come to work here, master. There be only me.'

Michael swiftly established that Mrs Harper had left since his last visit, and had taken her guinea advance of salary with her.

'What is your name?' I asked.

'Nan Homefray, mistress. I was took on by her ladyship a long age past.'

Michael drew a chair up to the fire and rubbed his eyes. I dragged my own chair into the circle of light to join him. 'Nan, I am sure we can arrange matters in the morning. Meanwhile, is there any supper to be had?'

'Only what I 'as,' the woman said. 'Nowt good enough for you, mistress.'

'I am sure it is. Please fetch hot food and drink at once.'

Supper, when it arrived, did indeed look paltry: a pottage of nettles, potatoes and onions.

'I cannot eat this beggarly stuff.' Michael slammed his dish down and drew closer to the fire, applying a poker to a jug of ale. But I ate my supper gratefully, for it was good plain food, deliciously fragrant with herbs.

'A man just come with these for you, master,' Nan announced, shuffling back in for our dishes. She passed Michael two letters that he impatiently held up to a candle. 'This one is for you,' he said.

I took the letter and saw it bore Anne's handwriting. Opening the seal, I found the usual good wishes one might send a newly married woman. 'I trust you are enjoying every measure of the nuptial bliss you so keenly anticipated . . .' It was impossible to contemplate a suitable reply. Perhaps tomorrow I could make an answer, omitting all but the bare fact of the wedding?

Puzzling over my letter, I failed at first to notice Michael's curious behaviour. He had carried a candle over to the far wall, and was peering fixedly at the second letter.

'Good news, I hope?'

He looked at me. 'It is of no consequence,' he said, pushing it into his pocket.

I continued to watch him as he stood beside the candle in a sort of dream. Even in the poor light, I noticed a blank rigidity to his manner.

'Come here, and drink your ale while it is hot. I suppose we must explore by candlelight. I wonder if Nan has lit a fire upstairs?'

He started back towards me; then halted, pacing back to the candle he had left by the wall. Opening the letter, he read it once again.

'It's from Peter. A matter requires my urgent attention.'

'Now? Surely not. Will tomorrow not do?'

Sweeping back to the fireside, he picked up his boots and began to dress for a journey. 'I may not be back tonight. Do not wait up for me.'

'Michael!' If I had been disappointed earlier in the day, it was nothing to the plunging sensation I now felt in my chest. 'No. Please don't leave me here alone.' I was upset, yes, not only at the strangeness of the place but also at the unthinkable insult to me, his bride.

He continued to dress with exaggerated precision, then turned to me, his jaw tight. 'I must make one thing very clear. I will do as I will.' His manner was so remote towards me that he seemed quite another person.

I found myself standing up, my breath shallow. The stone flags beneath my wedding shoes felt unsteady, but I stood firm.

'Don't leave me here. Take me with you.' Before I could see the effect of this remark, my husband turned and marched out of the chamber. A few moments later the great door slammed, and I crouched on a stool before the fire, hating the letter that had arrived with such ill-timing, hating Peter for summoning him – but most of all hating the sickening sensation I was left with, of bitter disenchantment and curdled love.

11

Delafosse Hall

September 1792

~ Wild Rosehip Preserve ~

Take your rosehips from your wild dog rose or eglantine when as big as cherries, and boil in fair water till they be soft, first pulling out the seeds, then strain them and weigh the same of sugar. Boil your sugar with a little water till it candies. Meanwhile heat your rosehips over the fire with sour barberry juice; stir them both together and let it boil up to a pink jelly. Put in your pots to keep and eat as you will.

As told by Nan Homefray, her best way

I listened for Michael all through that wretched night, but he did not come home. In my fancy, such a vast and antique residence as Delafosse Hall sprang to life at night, its timbers creaking like old bones as they bent and twisted in restless dreams. In my darkest hours I was convinced I heard Michael's step on the stair, but each time I roused myself and coaxed the fire back to life, I found I was mistaken. The wind rose, whistling through the canopy of dry leaves; shaking and tormenting them so that a hundred leaf-points tapped insistently against the window panes. Only in the lull before dawn did I at last fall into deep sleep, curled on a lumpy sofa.

I woke with my neck cricked and my limbs as cold as marble. The great fire had died down to ashes, and the dirty windows leaked pallid grey into the room. I paced about, trying to warm myself, eyeing blackened portraits of dead strangers. I was an interloper, a misfit in that dreary place.

Then a sudden sense of opportunity struck me; that while Michael was away, I might act as I wished. Pulling my shawl tightly about me, I set off to look around my new home.

There was a breathless hush inside Delafosse Hall, a quality of silence that cautioned me to tiptoe from room to room. I winced as my shoes pattered on bare flags, and lifted groaning latches. How many years had the Hall lain empty, I wondered, the stones settling ever deeper into the earth and the shadows gathering undisturbed? Retracing my way to the top of the flamboyant staircase I found a suite of grand rooms fronting the Hall, scattered with ponderous furniture draped in sheets furred with dust. Tapestries sagged on the walls, riddled by ragged moth holes. I was dismayed by the gloom, but soon noticed its source was the mass of foliage obscuring a good part of the sunlight. With the windows cleared and cleaned, and a great deal of soap and hot water, I believed these rooms might one day be made comfortable again. I pictured them with new furnishings and a gathering of happy company around the fire. Then weariness struck me, to think of all these great tasks I must undertake alone.

Turning a corner I found myself in a jewel of a room, a long gallery of beautiful proportions. It was perhaps one hundred feet in length, lined in carved pale oak now warped and swollen. The light fell inside through a series of cracked and undulating diamond panes, quite lovely to behold. I half-closed my eyes, feeling I ought to see the ghosts of another age, promenading in ruffs and doublets. No one appeared, but I did feel a disturbance in the motes of dust that glittered in the pearly light.

I wandered to the pink marble fireplace; listening to tiny feet scurrying behind the oak wainscot. In the hearth lay a dead young rook with a beady yellow eye and broken wings. I caught sight of myself in a tarnished mirror; frowning and pale, my gown creased from sleep, my curls an unpinned mess. Again I felt myself an intruder, a harbinger of change in a realm that did not want me.

A door led on from the gallery, carved with creatures of myth, the largest being the Blair head of an angel. I passed inside and groped at the curtains to raise some light. It was a room of curiosities, dominated by glass cabinets displaying armour, peculiar stones, and relics. The pre-eminent display was an ornamented sword laid on faded crimson silk. Studying the medals and citations hung about the walls I understood it was a sort of shrine to a young man whose portrait hung above the fireplace in oils. He was an assured character, his arm draped over the back of his chair, his dark eyes challenging the spectator from beneath heavy brows. Although he was a fine figure in his red military coat, he was not to my taste as a gentleman. Lieutenant Ashe Moncrieff had won honours against the French near Quebec. His name meant nothing to me, but when

I calculated the date of his death at only twenty-eight years old, I sympathised with this forgotten tribute.

Closing the door gently, I climbed a further flight of stairs. There I found smaller, more intimate quarters. I claimed a parlour for myself containing an ornate white fireplace that needed only the clearing of birds' nests and chimney plaster. A dry chamber with good oak shelves was perfect for Michael's study, and beyond that lay a turret room with a few ancient leather-bound books to begin a library. I wandered on, up and down odd sets of steps and into corridors that sometimes ended in heaps of plaster. As the house unfolded, possibilities presented themselves; images of new life flickered unsteadily in my mind. Great strength of will would be needed, I knew that, but when I interrogated my doubts, the answer came back again and again – I will do it. I will rouse this house and return it to life.

Auspiciously, I next found a charming bedchamber, dominated by a carved four-poster bed on which fresh linen had recently been laid. Why, I wondered, had Nan not told us about these preparations for our arrival? I fingered the crewel-work coverlet, a garden of chain-stitched tulips; though faded by time, it felt warm. Framed seascapes hung on the walls, sun-bleached curtains cascaded from grand pelmets, a brass clock ticked on the mantelpiece. It was the perfect backdrop to the married love I was still hopeful of kindling.

I stood very still, puzzling over the room's quality of recent occupation: the bedclothes were not quite straight, and the layer of dust on the dresser bore signs of objects having been moved upon it.

I resolved to ask Nan about it, and moved on, up the final flight of stairs to the attics. Above my head glimmered a vast dome draped with years of matted cobwebs. Here was a warren of dormitories and storerooms, some running with water from breaches in the roof. Yet at the front of the house I found a room that completely entranced me, high in the eaves, so the windows were clear of smothering leaves. Sparse and square, there were signs it had once been a sewing room, and if cleaned, the windows would be flooded with light. At its centre was a stained table and decayed chairs. My own studio, I murmured, picturing my paints and brushes laid out neatly, and myself undisturbed at my work. Here was hope, I thought. Here was the promise of pleasure and painting. Somehow, within this half-ruined edifice, I would make a new life.

৯৹

I found Nan down on the ground floor, in a kitchen bristling with spits and roasting irons. She had made her own tiny quarters there: a few modest feet around a time-polished armchair. I stretched my hands before the flames, and then looked quickly away from the still-surprising band of gold on my finger.

'You hear her, then?' Nan asked, setting out a breakfast of oatcakes and potted hare. 'Old Dorcas? Some say she paces the house in her bare feet.'

'You mean Lady Blair? I thought she was dead.' I helped myself to spoonfuls of velvety red rosehip jelly.

'Aye, she may be dead, but she cannot settle, that one.'

'Have you heard her, Nan?'

'Not me mistress. But then me lugholes in't the best. It's the young 'uns as allus say they hear her, pacing back and for'ard on them creaking boards.'

I had an unpleasant memory of what I had thought were Michael's footsteps in the night, but dismissed it as nonsense.

'I think they must be teasing you, Nan.'

'P'raps so. Owt to take a rest from their labours.'

She took my plate but I felt disinclined to leave the cheery fire.

'So was she an unhappy woman?'

'She was that. Toward the end she'd wander in her shift, her white hair hanging to her waist, searching high and low for Mr Ashe.'

'The lieutenant in the painting? I saw that extraordinary room.'

'Aye, well. She sent him packing, and next thing she hears, he's gone and got himself killed in some foreign battle.'

'A tragedy.'

'It were that, mistress. She never rightly recovered her senses.'

'And what about you, Nan? Why were you left alone here?'

'Well, when her ladyship went and died and they all gone away, I got no place to go to but here, see. So I shifted for meself, took what Mother Nature provides: mushrooms and berries and simples, and what eggs the chickens lay. Come Christmas and Harvest some church folk brings me a bag of oats or sugar, and I stumbles on the odd creature what goes in the pot. Only been me and the spiders here, all these years. Watching and waiting and shifting for ourselves.'

'But surely someone else has been living here? One of the back bedchambers has signs of occupation.'

'Oh, that were Mrs Harper.'

'In a family room? Are there not housekeeper's quarters?'

An indignant expression twisted the old woman's mouth. 'I'm not telling tales if I tell you she were always complaining, that one. Said the housekeeper's room didn't suit, so she just up and shifted herself to the best chamber. Then that were no good neither: said she heard noises in the night. And I'll tell you now, I smelled spirits on her. Then she took her guinea piece and off she scarpered.'

'Well, I'm glad she has gone. But now I need to replace her. I'll find help for you, Nan, be assured of it.'

'Thank 'ee, mistress.' She did not look entirely persuaded as she nodded her grubby cap, the twin lappets dangling past her chin. 'And the master, will he be wanting his breakfast?'

I brushed the crumbs from my gown into the fire. 'There is no need to concern yourself about the master,' I said shortly. 'He wants nothing yet. Now does this door lead outside?'

I continued my explorations in a cobbled yard overlooked by broken doors and cracked windows. Pushing open a swollen door into a storeroom, I found a stream running across paving stones and a carpet of slippery green moss. My explorations took me beneath a gateway surmounted by a clock face, standing with hands fixed permanently at eleven o'clock. Beyond stood derelict stables; then the park opened up in an undulating vista, reaching all the way to a swathe of deep forest on the horizon. In the distance was the twinkle of the river that I realised must border my own land at Whitelow. The grass was knee-high and speckled with late butter-cups, but I was transported by that first sight of the Delafosse estate. In its situation alone, the Croxons had chosen our new home well. I dreamed for a moment of myself and Michael making a great fortune, and no longer renting Delafosse Hall but owning every inch of it, my inheritance spinning gold from cotton. Turning back to view the Hall I took a sharp breath; it was as massive and ancient as a child's dream of a castle, the bulk of its walls carpeted in green-ery, the diamond-leaded windows sparkling in picturesque stone mullions. True, the barley-twist chimneys leaned askew, and the roofs sagged beneath the weight of years, but the shell of it was magnificent. It cast a strange possessive mood upon me. I remem-bered Michael's irritation at the house the previous night, and his eagerness to leave. Somehow I had to entice Michael into this shared dream of a happy life here, beside me.

Determined to explore the park, I followed the nearest path. After walking through a deep wood for a good while I emerged into the sunlight by a round hill surmounted by a two-storey tower. A hunt-ing lodge, Mrs Croxon had called it, but I thought it more a folly. It had a fantastical quality, with four miniature turrets, each topped with a verdigris-tarnished dome. Above the doorway stood a sundial drawn upon a disc representing a blazing sun. It was embellished with a script I thought might be Latin: *FERREA VIRGA EST, UMBRATILIS MOTUS*. I wondered whether Michael might know the meaning, or Anne's husband perhaps. As for the sundial's accu-racy, the morning light was too weak to cast a line of shadow.

The tower door swung open at my touch. Inside, it was as neglected as the other outbuildings, the cobwebs studded with flies like beaded veils. There was little to inspect on the ground floor, so I climbed the narrow corkscrew stair. It was an unsettling experience, like entering the spiral chamber of a shell, and it took longer than I anticipated to reach the light above. The upper storey was better lit by four broad oriel windows. A grotesque chandelier, made of branching deer antlers, hung from the ceiling, and a few scabrous fox and deer heads decorated the walls. Here was some decayed furniture: a few chairs, a couch, a broken card table. Disliking hunting and its celebration of slaughter, I determined to look at the rooftop and then leave. A second spiral plunged me into darkness as I groped my way upward with hands outstretched. Finally, I emerged outdoors. The wind had started to bluster, and when I peered over the low balustrade I was surprised at how high I stood above the ground, and how low the balustrade lay at my feet.

A metallic jingling alerted me to movement below. Crossing silently to the far side of the roof, I spied a horse tethered to a tree, but no rider. I listened hard, and heard someone moving noisily below me. I cannot say why, but I felt a powerful instinct to keep myself hidden. Standing at the low doorway where the stairs emerged, I listened.

Suddenly the top of a head with bronze curls appeared in the doorway and the strain of my long night's waiting overcame me.

'Michael! How could you leave me like that?' I ran towards him and buried my face in his shirtfront. I cannot recollect what else I mumbled, some of it furious, but no doubt some of it weak and shameful. Firm hands reached out, pushing me gently away.

'Grace, it is I – Peter.'

Peter's boyish features were flushed with embarrassment. Instantly I jerked away and turned my back to him. My face was hot with shame. 'What in heaven's name are you doing here? Is it any surprise I thought you were Michael?' I was so mortified I wished I could run away.

'I am sorry—' he began.

'Sorry?' Fury overwhelmed my disappointment. 'Did you call Michael away? It was you, wasn't it? Have you seen him?'

He took a step backwards, lost for a reply. Then reluctantly, he nodded. 'I did see him.'

'Is he home yet?'

Looking at the ground, he said in a low tone, 'I left him at the inn.'

'Why? Why is he still at the inn?'

'He was rather foxed.' He met my eye, then slid his gaze back to the ground. 'But I'm sure he will be home soon. I can understand your being alarmed.' An attempt at sympathy was written on his boyish features. 'Listen, Grace. Michael does not make it easy—'

I shook my head. 'I will not listen to excuses. What are you doing here in any case?'

'I called at the house, but there was no one in to receive me. I decided to look about before riding home. Truly, I did not intend to alarm you.'

I could not look at him, but said to the floor, 'I must go back now.' I was suddenly desperate to be at home when Michael returned. 'And you should leave,' I added unpleasantly.

Peter returned obediently to his horse, but picked up the reins to lead it, insisting on walking beside me. All the way back I didn't speak. Slowly the house came into view, and I looked for signs of Michael's return.

'What on earth were my parents thinking, sending you to this tumbledown pile?' Peter said, with annoying amiability.

'I find it enchanting.'

'Grace, it is ridiculous. It is too big, too far, too—' He stopped and touched my arm. 'Listen to me,' he said with sudden seriousness. 'You should find another place. Don't settle here. You must overrule Michael and move away.'

I looked up at him sharply. 'But I don't wish to.'

Again he was lost for words, then sighed. 'If I can be of service, in any way, Grace, I will. I'll walk back with you. You have had an unpleasant surprise.'

I stared at him, a sickening reflux of anger rising within me again. 'An unpleasant surprise?' Was that what he called keeping Michael away from me on our wedding night?

He bit his lower lip – a gesture of uncertainty I recognised from Michael. 'I see we have not begun on the best of terms, Grace, but I would like very much to be your friend.'

I stopped stone still; feeling as if I might burst. I narrowed my eyes, and said with a deal of directness, 'That is a peculiar thing to say.'

We were interrupted by the sound of footsteps on the gravel.

'There you both are.' It was Michael, his hair rumpled, his angel's face even more bruised about the eyes. 'Grace, would you kindly step inside. Peter, a word before you leave.'

I opened my mouth to protest, but at a gesture from Michael, Peter turned away smartly and they both disappeared down a path into the woods.

Inside the Great Hall the fire had been rebuilt. Tea was set out on a table, and I drank it greedily. Gradually, my fury abated, replaced by pathetic relief. All I could think was, at least Michael is back so we might still mend our future.

It was a long time before Michael came indoors, and by then I felt too weak to remonstrate, as if I had already lived ten lives that day. Cowardly though it was, I did not reproach him. Nevertheless, when he sat down beside me, my spirits quailed.

'I have not behaved well,' he said gruffly. 'As I told you before-hand – I suffer from a breed of melancholia. Yesterday, being an object to be stared at, quite undid me.'

I nodded, looking away.

'I can only account for it by blaming the insupportable strain of the day.'

That was true. With hindsight the day had been an ordeal for both of us.

'Peter has gone now, and we must start again. It was a bad beginning, but we will proceed from this hour onward. Are you agreeable?'

I gave a slight nod. Compared to my fears of complete abandonment in the night, these were welcome words indeed.

'And we must live more comfortably. Look at this place, it is almost a ruin. You are sensible, Grace. Tell me, what do you need?'

Here, at last was a straw to grasp. 'We must employ servants, Michael. I must have staff to bring this house back to life. I believe Mrs Harper was not suitable, so at least we are saved the trouble of dismissing her.'

'Good.' He reached out to my hand and squeezed it. I nodded, overjoyed that at last we were in harmony. He mused a moment, then pressed his lips tightly together. 'I did see something in the village – a bill stuck on a wall.'

'Tell me.'

'A hiring fair in the town square tomorrow. It will no doubt be a rough sort of proceedings. But, if you can bear it, you may find a new housekeeper.'

I was aware of his fingers caressing me, moving his thumb along the top of my hand, provoking an unfamiliar excitement. 'I will go. I will make our home comfortable.'

His smile was celestial. Then it wavered, and a frown creased his brow. His thumb ceased its delicious reassurance.

'There is a small difficulty, Grace. A business matter I have overlooked. Forgive me, for I do not like to ask.'

I begged him to explain, longing to prove my worth in some practical fashion.

'In all the bustle of the wedding, I have foolishly overlooked the provision of ready money.' He laughed; an embarrassed little cough. 'My mother paid the treacherous Mrs Harper for the coming year, but we now face unexpected expenses. If you, dear Grace, could sign a simple paper, we may proceed at once.'

Dear Grace – so tight-wound were my nerves that the words were like balm to me. I told him I would.

While he fetched the paper, I recalled Mr Tully telling me that I alone must be signatory to any transactions. And, less comfortably, I remembered his insistence that I consult him before raising any loans.

When I glanced at the paper placed before me, I quailed to see the large sum named: *To draw the sum of One Thousand Pounds upon the account of Mrs Michael Croxon, at Hoare's Bank, London.*

'Of course, such a sum will allow us to begin the building of the mill,' he said, looking pained at the need to speak of it. I did a rapid calculation. Using one thousand of my three thousand pounds to build the mill would use a third of my capital. Still, I felt a powerful need to prove myself a support to Michael in setting up the business. I signed my name, but remembering Mr Tully's warning about the value of my signature, I then ensured it had my own seal upon it. I was rewarded with another radiant smile.

'Now let us get out of this gloomy place. Until more servants are found, shall we stay the night at the George? What do you say to some good food and company, Grace?'

In truth, I should rather have gone up at once to our chamber. But our boxes were still close by, and he was already searching for a better coat. With a heavier step I rummaged in my own trunk for a clean gown. In a dusty antechamber I pulled on a puce-striped gown that his mother had thought fashionable, but that I considered rather bold. When I returned, Michael eyed my costume critically.

'You need a reliable maid to help you,' he said, straightening my sash, and then kissing me as lightly as a pecking bird.

So he does care for me a little, I thought. He took my arm and led me to the door, opening it most gallantly. Not since John Francis had left, had I felt the protective care of a man. That morning I found it irresistible, like having a soft-spun blanket wrapped about me, that promised warmth and ease for the rest of my life.

12

Delafosse Hall

September 1792

~ Chicken Pie My Best Way ~

Clean and pick a pair of chickens, cut in pieces as you would for a fricassee, season with pepper, salt and mace; have ready your raised crust, put in the chicken with a little broth, ornament it and bake for two hours. While it is baking, get ready a quarter pint of green peas, boil them till tender, boil a quarter pint of cream for ten minutes then throw in the peas with a piece of butter and flour, a little salt and nutmeg. Let it simmer five minutes, raise up the lid of the pie and pour it in, add a little juice of lemon and serve it up hot.

A wholesome summer pie, as told by Nan Homefray

In the street below Peg's lodging house the Michaelmas hiring fair had started up. She watched a line of men gather, each bearing a sign of their calling: shepherds bearing crooks, cowmen a tuft of cow's hair in their hat brims. Farmers moved appraisingly amongst them, questioning and prodding them. Across the street the women stood at the Market Cross: a motley huddle, from sulky girls with their mothers, to crooked old granddames. Most were hardened domestics, women with brawny arms and drab hand-stitched costumes. The only other women carrying ladles were a dirty-looking blubber-guts and a wretch with the look of a gin-biber. Those who met success headed straight to the ale benches, eager to spend their bond money as fast as they might.

Peg was amused by a buxom girl fending off a farmer. 'Me wife be on her last legs,' he pleaded, so loudly she could hear every word through the open window. 'Come wi' me, and once she's out t'way, I'll hire thee for life at t'altar.'

'Tha's old enough to be me grandfather,' she laughed, tossing her head.

Just then the door barged open; it was only Sue, who'd been sharing her chamber.

'Me feet are murderin' me.' Sue flung herself onto the edge of Peg's bed and started hauling off her boots. Grimacing, she inspected the purple toes peeping out of her stockings. 'I must have carried near a hundred dinners today. I hate fairs even more 'n market day. I've had enough, Peg. I'm going for a place at that Miss Sybilla Claybourn's. Housemaid, it is, but easy work for just one lady.'

'That's a pretty name, Sybilla Claybourn. Who's she?'

'The one what has Riverslea out by the river. Next to that Delafosse Hall you was asking about.' Sue prattled on about her new mistress, the chance to make a life of ease, the petty tricks by which she might add to her own purse. 'And t'other news is that Harper woman's gone and bolted from Delafosse Hall.'

'Where's she got to?'

'Got a better place somewhere else, they say. Took her year's wages, too. Can't say I blame her, that place's been empty for years; only them town-bred blockheads would rent it. Oh, and you'll like this, I seen that Delafosse woman in the square.'

'What's she like?'

Sue laughed scornfully. 'You can't miss her. Uppish type, wearing a frock made of thin yellow stuff and a straw bonnet crawling with ribbons.'

Peg finally turned around and affected a smile. Sue looked her up and down.

'I never knew you had such a green gown afore.'

'This? I told you. I'm going to get a position.'

Sue yawned, showing a mouthful of black teeth. 'Left it a bit late in't you?'

'Oh, there are plenty of positions still going.'

'Where? That Delafosse Hall?' Sue smirked. 'We could be neighbours, Peg. Call on each other for a spot of company on our days off.'

After Sue left, Peg returned to the window to see that the buxom girl had not stood her ground against the farmer. Already he eyed her like a fatted calf. She knew that calculating side-glance; when the loins were hot and the eyes were as cold as flint.

Ah, there she was, the woman in yellow who must be Mrs Croxon. All Peg's senses quickened. What a beanpole, she crowed to herself – stooped shoulders, gown ill-fitting. Why, she looked a born bleater – no match at all for Peg Blissett. She picked up her borrowed ladle, went downstairs, and sauntered over to the new mistress of Delafosse Hall. Then, gathering all her sweetness, Peg smiled at Mrs Croxon.

The woman responded with a slight bow of her head, and then said, so quietly that Peg could barely hear her, 'I see by the ladle you must be a cook. Am I led to believe – are you—'

Mrs Croxon had a nasty rash, and slovenly-dressed hair. But looking more closely she was not so ill-looking. And her voice was so pleasant and genteel that Peg couldn't stop herself aping it.

'I am sorry, mistress. I am bonded to be Cook Housekeeper to Miss Sybilla Claybourn, of Riverslea House.'

'Oh, what a very great shame.' The Croxon woman turned aside, then blinked and turned back. 'And that is a binding agreement?' Her desperation was writ very large across her face.

'Well, mistress, Miss Claybourn was most satisfied with my character, given by Mistress Humphries – see, it is here.' She pulled her fake paper out, pointing at words and distracting her with patter. 'Miss Claybourn wants a cook with the art of confectionary, you see, she is such a famous one for company and revels. Trouble is,' she added, 'I'm to wait here a month – which is a nuisance, especially as there's been no money yet.'

As sure as eggs, Mrs Croxon perked up. 'I don't know if this is irregular, but I can pay you at once.'

'But what shall I say to Miss Claybourn?'

'I see. What a shame. I suppose you have given your word.' She began to walk away.

Peg could barely credit it. Trotting after her, she suggested, 'If your need is greater, so is mine. I am rather out of pocket.'

'So if I were to offer you five shillings today, in advance?'

Five poxy bob? She could have got ten times that if she worked the crowd at the tavern.

'That would suit me well,' she assured her. 'Only – Miss Claybourn might think I made it all up, about another offer. Are you acquainted with her?'

'Not at all. I'm newly arrived here.'

'Perhaps if you wrote to her? Then we can strike up an agreement here and now.'

'I believe I shall.' Mrs Croxon was overjoyed.

From this exchange Peg grasped the key to Mrs Croxon's character. She was a follower of that balderdash idol – honourable dealing; and her weakness was a wish to please. To a fly-girl like her, these were the lock-picks to the soul.

Peg's reward was the Croxon's Letter of Credit. At the butcher's, the grocer's, the baker's, Peg set it down on the counter with a flourish. Dishes and receipts formed like starbursts in her mind, trailing myriad ingredients. For one she needed rosewater, cherries, and almonds, for another pistachios, chocolate, and cream – soon she lost her way, and ordered whatever her whimsy suggested. Unfolding her neat credential, Peg looked eagerly for Mrs Croxon's signature but found to her disappointment, the ragged scrawl of 'Michael George Croxon Esquire'.

By noon the kitchen was half-sorted. For her part, Peg had recruited some local women for the laundry and heavy work, and she directed them to scrub every kitchen flagstone and shelf. With gusto she oversaw the delivery of the first parcels and baskets of food. Some part of her that had gaped emptily for years began to grow easy. This is all mine, she crowed to herself. She sniffed and tasted and arranged her jars, baskets, and vats, all the time sketching out long dreamed-of feasts.

Her first botheration was what to serve the Croxons for dinner. The galling truth came home to her that she must make breakfast, dinner, and supper, day after poxy day. Sweet stuffs were no trouble; she had the makings of custards and a medlar tart, and best of all, a gooseberry pudding. But as for savoury dishes, the last time she had cooked meat was out in the Colony, where kangaroo rats had been top bill of fare. She racked her brain-box for how Aunt Charlotte had kept the Palace fed at all hours. There had been lots of pots steaming and bubbling on the fire, and long hours of peeling, chopping, and beating. She would have to find a slavey down at the village to take it on. Then, luck favouring the brave, the answer appeared before her, in the shape of an ancient baggage named Nan, who seemed to think she had a right to the kitchen fireside. Peg looked her up and down. 'So what can you do?'

To her surprise, the old mopsy mumbled about the workings of the great fire, and how to set the horrible, old-fangled contraption in motion.

'And the pastry oven,' Nan wittered, 'though it's many years since I had the makings of a pie.'

'You? Bake, can you?'

'Aye.'

'What other dishes do you know?'

The crone scratched her wrinkled cheek. 'I cannot read or owt, but I do keep them old receipts safe in my noddle.' She began to recite a surprisingly impressive list. 'White soup, Roast Meat in Crumbs, Mutton Ragoo, Yorkshire Pudding, Chicken Pie, Mint Sauce, Apple Sauce, Bread Sauce, Marigold Tart—'

'No need for the sweet stuffs, I'm a dab hand at those myself.' Peg put on a hard, considering face. 'I could give you a trial, I suppose. But I won't have any lazybones in my kitchen, do you hear? I'll give you a test and we'll see how you go. Make that Chicken Pie for dinner and I'll give it a taste. Go on, ready at three o'clock; the makings are in the larder.'

Nan shuffled off, her eyes frightened, but hopeful.

'And you can move your stuff out of here to the scullery,' Peg shouted after her.

The only other permanent domestics she employed were two ugly sisters, Bess and Joan, who would certainly keep no delivery boys lingering at the back door. As for the other servants, they must come and go from the village as she needed them. She wanted no inside servants tittle-tattling behind her back.

Peg judged the Chicken Pie to be satisfactory, if old-fashioned, the braised chicken flavoured with nutmeg, fresh peas and cream. The

Croxons had liked it, too, and most of it had disappeared. Nan would certainly be staying on. That would leave Peg free to make only sweet confections, jellies, and cakes. She had not lost her touch, for the pudding bowls had returned downstairs all but licked clean. She had kept back a second dish for herself, and dug her spoon into syrupy gooseberries inside claggy suet pudding. All she needed was gumption to keep the Croxons sweet. Gumption and a pinch of high-flying trickery.

Leaving the clearing up to the others, she took a stroll outside to clear her head of smoke. Reaching an open glade in the woods, she sat down on a hollow trunk with a satisfied sigh. From inside her pocket she pulled out a short pipe of pale stuff with a brownish tinge, like the stub of a penny whistle. Raising it to her lips, she blew softly against the top until a high unearthly note made the grass, the leaves, and the dusk-heavy air vibrate. Artfully, she stopped the three small holes with her fingertips in an unhurried sequence, casting a mournful phrase into the air. The tone was more husky than a flute's; it was off-key and haunting, a summoning call quite at odds with the gentle English glade. The chirruping birds fell silent. The hairs on the back of her neck rose like startled feathers.

❧

After those eight starveling months, they had finally got to New South Wales – the biggest, most frightening prison in the world. No walls – only the deadly forever of empty bush land; no iron bars – only hundreds of leagues of ocean. It was the end of the earth, the end of all hope. And Botany Bay had lacked those botanical meadows so vaunted by Captain Codswallop Cook. The governor had no choice but to sail on. To everyone's astonishment, the five ships then floated into the biggest and bluest bay they had ever seen. As quiet as the grave it was, as they tacked around the rocky shore; so quiet you could hear the hawsers creaking and the hiss and lap of the waves. The women leaned over the rail, trying to catch the breeze, for the air was as hot as a fiery furnace. Mary spotted some green parrots fluttering from branch to branch, and was just wondering if they would make good eating when a racket broke out ahead of them. A mob of natives were hopping about and shouting something none of them could understand. Buck-naked they were, and black-skinned, with pointy spears and round shields.

'Don't reckon they'll want our visiting cards,' she said to Janey, who was standing beside her. Instinctively both of them stood back from the rail, glad of the hundred feet between them and the ends of the savages' spears.

'It's our lot I'm more feared of,' said Janey. Though still tall and graceful, she looked ashen and scabby in the sunshine. Lice moved in her hair, making Mary's own scalp itch. 'We've only been sent for one reason,' Janey ventured, 'and that's to stop the menfolk from buggering each other to death.'

There were more than one thousand itchy-loined male convicts to two hundred women. She looked around for Jack Pierce and gave him a hopeful smile. It would be a test for the lad. She meant to stick to him like a limpet. The governor favoured easily-herded sheep types, and as a reward, those who married might build their own huts and live apart. So she and Jack had given the reverend their names, and she was primed to turn an honest woman. She and Jack would play a couple of go-alongers for a while – until she decided otherwise.

It was days later that they were allowed to land at a ramshackle camp of tents and hovels set up by the men. Everything was alive; the mosquitoes buzzed in your eyes, the biting ants crawled up your legs. The place had an eye-squinting blaze to it, and smelled of parched tobacco. The women were led to airless tents and guarded by redcoats as if they were prize money. That first afternoon they sat playing chuck-penny, or wagering the knucklebones fished out of their broth. They could hear the men hard at it, hammering huts together and banging and cursing around the place. She looked around the tent and wondered what the night would bring. Outside, everything shone so hard the air trembled.

At first there had been the usual military bells, tootling of fifes, beating of drums. A few convict pals called around, and she hung about the entrance, looking for Jack. When he finally braved the redcoats, he told her a curfew had been ordered. Pulling her close, he whispered, 'Take care tonight, love. There's talk of some of the bad 'uns going off on the rampage.'

Sure enough, they could see lags straggling in groups along the beach. Some had found a supply of grog, and were yelling like young blades out on the town. The marines didn't look to be on duty any more; the women's guards were dallying with a gang of fast girls.

She wiped her sweating brow against the canvas. 'P'raps I should hide over there, in the bush.' She pointed at a thick stand of trees.

'Stay with the others, eh? I 'ave to cut it now,' Jack looked more hot and mithered than she'd ever seen him.

When the bell rang out from the men's camp, she found it hard to let go of his hand. Perhaps she was turning into that posset-soft girl she was personating, after all. Once Jack had traipsed off, she eyed the clump of trees one last time.

Back inside the tent it was crowded and airless. Janey was touching up a paunchy fellow – no doubt a new pimp who would protect her. There was no one else to talk to; all her pals were in another tent. She dragged her bit of blanket into a corner, scratched her bites, and let the heat creep over her until she fell asleep.

She was woken by a hot wind that snapped the canvas hard against the ropes. Scarily fast, the tent was stranded in soot-black darkness. With a whoosh, the rain hit the tent, and started up a needling roar. The first blinder of lightning made them all jump like rabbits. A moment later thunder cracked like a giant whip, and then grumbled and rumbled on. Each time it sparked the women cursed and gasped in the darkness. Water trickled from the tent seams. Four men burst into the tent, pretended refugees from the storm.

'Don't you be afeared o' the storm, pet. We'll take care of you.' A pock-faced ruffian sat down on the end of her blanket, trapping her legs. His eyes gorged on her rump, like he was starving and she was some fancy dish. He offered her a swig from his bottle, but she wouldn't take it. His skinny friend circled, watching her too. When she pretended to sleep, she heard them muttering. The sound of rutting had started up from the back of the tent: knocking, grunting, whimpering. Her mind was as empty as a beggar's purse. Where were the damned redcoats when you needed them? Across the way a few crazy loons ran out into the rain; she could hear them hollering and singing to the storm, as drunk as kings. The camp was fomenting fast. The cribbage-face started to grope beneath her skirts with powerful hands. She shouted, but her voice was lost in the hubbub of the storm. With a violent yank she sprang free and legged it for the canvas door. Outside, she pelted through bucketing rain towards where she thought the trees were, dismayed to find her feet sinking in a quagmire. She wheeled about, unable to see her way. If she carried on along the beach, might she not find Jack? Or at least a couple of redcoats? After fifty paces, she had no notion where she was. Rain filled her eyes and weighted her clothes. She stopped, and tried to get her bearings. She was standing calf-deep in mire. The next white sizzle of lightning lit a group of men standing barely twenty paces away, hearkening to her presence. With a lurch of her guts, she knew they had seen her. She tried to sink down, to disappear into the mud, but at the next flickering flash they were barely an arm's length away. She had no notion where the women's camp was, nor where Jack was, nor the trees, nor God Himself in His cowardly crib of a heaven.

She thought she would die; suffocated by mud, drowned in a pool of muck. After the first desperate struggle, terror unbuckled her limbs, and she played dead. One man, two men, three, then four – she didn't count. It went on for an infernal age. Her body was wrenched and grabbed and shoved and burst apart. Senseless with horror she was ground into slushy sand, her centre red raw. All of her spirit was being snuffed away. So this was Sydney Cove, the end of the earth, the end of her life, where her bones were being fucked into an unmarked grave.

When the sun stung her eyes she was sorry to find herself alive. Jack was crouching over her, his face out of kilter from the shock of it. 'Who did this?' She couldn't speak. Her mouth was sticky with swallowed sand and men's filth. She felt as brown and stiff as an insect struggling to open its broken wings. 'I'll get you to the hospital tent,' Jack said.

He had carried her in his arms like a child, stroking her matted hair. And very slowly, like a timid wild creature, she had moved towards him, sinking her head against his chest. The truth was, love had ambushed her that day, just when she wasn't looking. Jack was a purer creature than any other man she'd known; it wasn't just some line he was spinning.

❧

The pipe cast up its summoning tune. Through half-closed eyes, the trees were the same sheltering giants as those she had once camped beneath, in a place like paradise. There was the same smell of crushed leaves and wet soil, the breeze peppered with the scent of woodsmoke and the quickening chill of twilight. She felt suddenly younger and more vital, as if casting off a caul of troubles. The heat of the sun burned on her cheeks again.

Jack Pierce stood before her, wearing ragged breeches, his blue coat hanging open across his naked chest, half its brass buttons gone. The phantom Jack smiled down at her, showing his crooked dog's teeth, his eyes gold-flecked and smiling. She drank in his features, and every inch of his marvellous being. He opened his mouth to tell her something – some foolishness that would make them both laugh, and then fall into each other's arms. But she couldn't stop herself reaching out to him. The flute tumbled to the ground.

In a twinkling he had vanished. No loving smile, no brass buttons – just a hushed and empty glade. Yet still she felt something – the sun burning on her face, the secret graze on her soul of Jack having stood right before her.

'*Haere, e taku hoa,*' she chanted, and the old lingo was like sweet fruit on her lips. 'Go, oh my friend,' she whispered. Standing up, she turned to leave. At the edge of the glade she stopped, facing the silhouette of the Hall, standing black-gabled and curlicued against the damson sky. Its bulk recalled the prison where she had first sunk into despair, and the Bailey where she had been sentenced; both of them full of stony men, with unjust power over the likes of her. It's always the Devil dancing beneath the judge's wig, Aunt Charlotte had said, and so she had found it. Like a Catholic reaching for a rosary, she felt in her bodice and found the Penny Heart. The outlines of the words were rough to her fingertips: '*I swear on this heart to find you one day . . .*'

Though the music of the pipe had left her as soft as a moon-struck girl, the Penny Heart could always be relied upon to fortify her. Tonight it felt as hard and heavy as a convict's deadweight, those hunks of iron that kept a body tethered to a few miserable feet of earth. Eyeing the Hall, bitterness ran soot-black through her veins. These people with their landed estates knew nothing of the punch-gut of starvation. Damn their eyes, their one-sided laws and their righteous airs, their always getting what they wanted. She wished on them a hundred times her own pain. She wished on them a dose of her own corroding hurt, like the acid that had long since scarred her own steely heart.

13

Delafosse Hall

September 1792

~ Cherry Trifle ~

Put macaroons and dry cherries in a dish; pour over as much white wine as they will drink. Take a quart of cream and put in as much sugar as will make it sweet. Put your cream into a pot, mill it to a strong froth, lay as much froth upon a sieve as will fill the trifle dish. Put the remainder of your cream in a pan with a stick of cinnamon, the yolks of four eggs well beaten and sugar to your taste. Set them over a gentle fire, stir it one way till it is thick, and pour it upon your macaroons. When it is cold put upon it your frothed cream. Lay upon it sweetmeats, comfits and flowers as you have them.

Mother Eve's Secrets

Like a polite acquaintance, Michael stayed just beyond my reach. That first night at the George he sat beside me, praising the roast beef and claret, the quick servants, and the roaring fire. 'The currant tart is excellent here – is it not, Grace?' He ate heartily, his eyes half-closed with pleasure.

I nodded, though to me it tasted like sawdust. All evening the inn's comforts were paraded before me until I felt stung with reproach. I longed for privacy, but Michael plunged into boisterous company: men whose glassy eyes slid instantly over my shoulder to something more interesting. Skirving, the architect, I disliked at once, and Dicey the engineer too, both of whom I feared might dupe us, so evasive were their answers to straightforward questions. When I asked them what crisis had occurred the previous evening, they of course looked at me like an idiot. As the evening progressed Michael went to drink beside them and I sat alone and resentful. At ten o'clock I tapped Michael's shoulder and told him I wished to retire. He bade me a hearty goodnight, barely sparing me a glance from a hectic card game. So flushed and happy did he look that I wondered if he were performing an act to discomfit me. But no – he was merely being Michael, seeking respite from himself in drink and company. I wondered how I could endure the life that stretched before me. And I had paid – for that was how I perceived it – one thousand pounds to be treated like this.

Upstairs, in the inn's chamber, I waited in a new chemise, my hair brushed loose to my waist and my person scented with cologne. Hour after hour, the noise of drunken toasts and laughter tormented my nerves. Finally, as an owl lamented from the rooftop, I faced the prospect that Michael would never, ever want me.

In the pallor before dawn our parlour door rattled; unsteady footsteps clumped about, and a chair tumbled to the floor. I rose and opened the middle door.

'Michael?' My anger was queasily mixed with relief. He had at least come back to our room. He tumbled onto the couch, falling instantly into drunken sleep. I returned to my bed, and for the first time, allowed myself to wail into my pillow. What in God's name had I done?

So the pattern of our days began: when Michael was not sleeping late he went out, to the site at Whitelow, to ride with local hounds, to meet his companions at inns and assemblies. His manner of living, it seemed, was not to change a jot from his bachelor days. I, on the other hand, was not invited to the George again. I received no cards or invitations. I had braced myself for a visit from the Croxons, but even they did not come. 'I have told them they owe me a bout of freedom,' Michael said bitterly.

Earlby itself proved merely a few streets of stone cottages where the rough-hewn folk eyed my new costumes with disdain. There were a couple of mean shops and the weekly market, and the George, of course, but not even a Circulating Library, or Dissenters' chapel.

I decided I must speak to my God alone, amongst the trees and birds of the estate, like a hermitess of old. Meanwhile, Michael congratulated himself, on being free from church and family and all such bothersome constraints. He ordered fashionable coats and hats from tailors in York. 'I can tell a great deal from the cut of a man's coat,' he lectured me. 'One day I'll teach you about style, Grace.' He found a barber who clipped his hair in the fashionable styles of Titus and then of Brutus. He claimed expertise in horseflesh too, purchasing a fine black hunter named Dancer, and talking much of the carriage we must buy, judging our old one too shabby. The pity of it was, that still I was drawn to him and longed for the physical love that I understood crowned a true marriage. In a good temper, he was light-hearted and bestowed precious smiles on me. I discovered that love is not always benign; but humiliating and cruel.

I slept alone in the chamber I had hoped would be a shrine to our marriage vows. On the nights when Michael slept at home, when he was not at the inn or with his companions, he chose a room not even close to mine; a plain closet like a manservant's room near the long gallery, with bare walls and a narrow bed.

I began to dread retiring to that room. A series of uneasy nights led to one much worse than the rest. I lay sleepless with my bed curtains open, my candle extinguished; unhappy visions appearing from my fancy in the darkness. Each time my eyes grew heavy I was tugged back awake by the Hall's untimely groans and creaks. Sometime after the church bell rang three o'clock I heard distant footsteps, a door pulled to, and a movement on the stairs. I knew those footfalls were not imaginary. The wandering old woman of Nan's tale sprang to mind. Could a spirit haunt the spot where its misery kept it chained? My imagination unleashed, I pictured a claw of a hand outside my door, pawing for the latch. Was that a moonlit chair by my window or a motionless watcher with a pale oval of a face?

At last, annoyed by my own credulousness, I lit a candle and took a turn about the room, prodding the furniture and checking the bolt on the door. All was as it should be. Then, lifting my curtain from the casement, I wiped away the beaded moisture and looked outside. The tiny glow of a lamp twinkled near the ground at the western corner of the Hall. I fancied it was a lone person carrying it, and as they walked between tree trunks and shrubs, it periodically blinked in and out of sight. Finally it disappeared entirely, and though I waited, did not reappear.

Shivering, I clambered back into bed, trying to calculate what would attract a person to walk the grounds at night. Had I perhaps seen a poacher, or a servant, off on a nocturnal tryst?

In the crisp light of day I set off to find out, but retracing the walker's steps only took me onto the usual soggy paths. I returned to the Hall convinced that someone, a stranger, was roaming our property at night. I told Michael my worries and he scoffed that I must have been dreaming. Peg took me more seriously and took a walk with me in the area, so we might look for footsteps. But by then it had rained, and the ancient wood offered up no secrets, so we abandoned our search.

More concerning was something I found that I could grasp in my hand. For I say I slept alone – but the taint of Mrs Harper lingered in my bedchamber. When I first drew back the tulip-covered bedcover, I found ugly proof of the liberties she had taken. A hair lay twisted on the inner sheet, very thick, and perhaps thirty inches long. Hair, as I know from my picture-work, has a powerful quality.

This hair was not mouse-soft like my mother's. It was ink-black, and coarse, with kinks from tightly-fixed hairpins along its luxuri-ant length. Though it revolted me to touch it, I lifted it between my finger and thumb and walked to the fire. Then, anticipating the vile stink burning would make, I instead pushed it into an old silk purse, though its springiness gave it a grotesque half-living quality. After washing my hands, I changed all the bed linen. Nevertheless, when-ever I lay down on those cold sheets, I swear I caught Mrs Harper's salty scent rising from the mattress.

My only solace was Peg. I congratulated myself that employing her was my one surefooted act since my marriage. I at once wrote to Miss Sybilla Claybourn in a civil but firm tone. A few days later she replied, and one phrase jumped at me like a well-aimed cat-scratch:

> . . . *you have lost me the service of an excellent housekeeper, upon whom I was entirely dependent. I believe this to be a deliberate, unneighbourly act, and must inform you we do not generally poach staff here . . .*

Michael and I were for once at breakfast together, as reserved as two strangers sharing a table at an inn. I read the letter out loud to him.

'Do you know her?' I asked, for I had not much cared for Peg's description of Miss Claybourn. Michael only knew her land at Riverslea, he said, for it had a wonderful prospect he had admired when out riding.

'A better prospect than ours?'

He spoke from behind his newspaper. 'Not so large as ours. In fact I'm scarcely certain where her land ends and ours begins.'

'So we share a boundary?' For some reason, this displeased me.

'I will ensure the fences are maintained; then she cannot poach our staff in turn,' he quipped.

I thanked him. As for sacrificing the chance of her acquaintance, I was pleased that her rudeness removed any obligation to call on her. I had already formed an opinion of Miss Sybilla Claybourn as a highborn man-chaser.

From the first, Peg fitted her place like a key in a well-oiled lock. The meals she served were domestic miracles: fresh bread, savoury pies, and joints of meat were laid steaming on our dining table. She also concocted the best of English sweet-stuffs: flummeries, suet duffs, and the best trifle I ever ate. Even Michael admired the comfit-scattered froth of cream laid over macaroons and fizzing cherries.

Even more surprisingly, she had early success in clearing the Hall. As if by magic, the rooms I had chosen as habitable were scrubbed and polished by her band of charwomen. I paid a visit to inspect her ragtag troops, ten or so women and girls, who Peg told me always slept in their own hovels at night, for fear of tales of ghosts. Some were bent old crones and others giggling minxes, but a few looked steady enough: a stout-armed silver-haired matron, and a respectable-looking widow-woman, who I fancied must be forced to such work by unfortunate circumstances. Cloth-headed creatures, Peg called them, but soon they had the parlour and small dining room in satisfactory order. The furnishings were neither modern nor especially comfortable, but the rooms were a haven in the midst of chaos. Burrowing into the ancient mass was how I thought of it then: excavating rooms, as antiquarians unearthed those unfortunate cities destroyed by Vesuvius.

Being much thrown together, I took time to observe my new housekeeper. She was an interesting type from a painter's point of view. Her sharply arched brows gave her a quick and alert expression, and her wide mouth naturally lifted in an amused smile. I fancied her liveliness would challenge a painter, for she was like an animal with a rapid heartbeat, seeming twice as alive as the slow-witted villagers. Her eyes, too, were extraordinary: cat-like in their flat aspect and expressiveness. She had a habit of probing my gaze, boldly, as I instructed her; as if she were seeking a connection not quite appropriate between a servant and mistress.

'Why do you stare, Peg?' I asked one day. 'Have I got a mark on my face?'

'I am near-sighted, Mrs Croxon. I cannot help it.'

I thought that odd, for she could read the stable clock from the kitchen window. She was certainly attractive – but somehow over-bright. She wore pink emulsion on her delicate redhead's complexion that by evening wore thin, showing what I supposed to be scars from an illness. She laboured ceaselessly to please me, but behind all her eagerness I did detect a certain strangeness to Peg Blissett. Perhaps I was unused to anyone striving so hard to gratify me. After all, there is something peculiarly intimate about having one's every wish anticipated, as if one's thoughts are not entirely private.

One morning I told Peg to be sure the cleaning women swept any hair about the place.

'Hair?'

'Yes, hair. I found a ghastly black hair in my bed. Mrs Harper's no doubt.'

A peculiar expression passed over her face: an emotion I couldn't interpret. When she spoke her voice was flat. 'Who is Mrs Harper?'

'Your predecessor. I thought I told you we were defrauded by our housekeeper.'

She shook her head, frowning mutely.

'Goodness, Peg. You are rarely lost for words. She took her guinea wages and left,' I added. 'Tell me, are the housekeeper's quarters comfortable?'

'They are most comfortable,' she answered, her usual manner restored. 'Thank you, Mrs Croxon. And you can rest easy; you won't see any more – ghastly black hair about the place.'

While Peg and her workers banged about the house, I escaped to the light-filled sanctuary of my studio. There I began a miniature of Michael copied from the sketch I had made on our journey to Delafosse Hall. Somehow, amidst the distress of our wedding day, I had captured his image as never before. He was sleeping with his head thrown back, the tendons of his throat very pronounced and vulnerable, his curls falling artfully backwards, his eyelids defined by lashes as long as a child's.

Now I began the slow work of copying my pencil sketch onto a thin sliver of ivory, using tiny brushes to articulate strokes no larger than pin-pricks. It is a curious art, to paint on ivory, for the material itself gives life to the skin. I began with a pink wash that had all the natural bloom of flesh. Every speck of an eyelash was a risk, for such work is unforgiving of errors. Yet the application of tiny strokes transported me to a place of sublime peace.

Even then I was bothered by sounds invading my concentration. Footsteps, slow and steady, grew louder on the stair, as irritating as hammer blows. They proceeded with annoying steadiness to just outside my door. Then they stopped. I cocked my head and called out, 'Peg? Is that you?'

Someone was standing on the landing. It was surely not Old Dorcas, I sighed, roaming the house in her lunatic state. I shoved back my chair with a squeak and noisily crossed the room to swing my door open.

'Oh, it's you.' It was only the widowed char, her withered cheek bent low as she stood as still as stone, catching her breath at the top of the stairs. Bony hands, speckled with age, clutched the broom that she rested upon. Poor creature, I thought, reduced to this labour, when her gown showed signs of better days and her hair was wiry with silver threads.

'I wondered who it was,' I explained gently. 'Carry on.'

She lifted her face to mine; her features indistinct beneath the great glass lantern that crowned the staircase, for no one had yet had the courage to tackle its decades of cobwebs. Then she smiled, a complicit smile, lit by a meagre warmth behind her colourless eyes. After that I often heard the steady swish of her broom across the boards outside my door, and left her in peace to her work.

૭

At that time, a gloriously bright day tempted me outdoors to explore the park. It could have been May-time and not October, as ragged white clouds chased across gillyflower blue. To wander amongst such beauty and yet have no resolved existence left me aching with exquisite pain.

I was glad of distraction when I came upon Nan, a wicker basket strapped to her back like a pedlar-woman's. She was collecting a bounty of rosehips, sloes, and brambles that she showed me with pride. We fell into step together as she chattered in her homely manner.

'Down there's a good spot for codlins,' she told me, and so I followed her curious hunch-backed figure through dripping glades that might have been undisturbed for centuries.

It was short work to pick a vast heap of hard green fruit, so I offered to help her carry them home, bundling them up in my shawl. As we wended our way, I asked her where Lady Blair was buried.

'Down in't crypt in't village church. So 'ow she's supposed to rise and walk about I cannot say.'

Though I knew I risked frightening myself, I asked, 'Was she truly so dreadful, Nan?'

Nan halted to investigate a clump of stinking leaves, her gnarled fingers pinching out a few seed pods. Raising herself with a sigh, she said, 'She were brung up like all rich folks in them days, to do as she pleased. All these lands was her own little kingdom. We 'ad a household of twenty servants then, and I were a hale woman in me prime. We 'ad our jests and jokes behind her back, mind. We 'ad to, for she were as miserable as sin. No man would take her on, rich or poor, she being such a hately creature.

'So it were just a lark to us, when Mr Ashe come here, him being not yet thirty, and she more 'n sixty. He could charm the birds from the trees, that one. Soon enough the old witch were like a chick in 'is hands. It were a kind of madness come on her, from being so long a maid.

'First she thought she could buy 'im. She had her testament drawn up making 'im, her only heir – he would've got the Hall and all her fortune. We servants watched it happen like scenes of a doom play, rolling fast on to the road to Judgement. You see, it were no secret to us that Mr Ashe was romancing another young woman, a Miss Hannah who were biding here too. What did them two young lovebirds care if a laundry maid passed 'em in the long grass, or a gardener saw them in the summerhouse?'

Nan paused and turned her rheumy eyes to mine with a malicious gleam of pleasure. 'The old 'un found 'em out. There were such rantings and screamings that the Hall itself seemed to shake. Next, Miss Hannah says she's with child.'

'Poor girl,' I said with sympathy. By now we were at the kitchen door, and when Nan beckoned me inside to see her workplace I followed, having little else to do but hear the end of her tale. Peg was not about, only the two powerfully-built sisters employed as maids-of-all-work, stood scouring copper pans.

At the far end of the kitchen stood a low, iron-barred door. Picking up lanterns, we passed through it and clambered down chilly steps to a warren of larders and cold stores. In the lantern glow, our giant shadows danced and rocked about us, revealing the start of a tunnel dug into the rock ahead. We passed a few of the village women cleaning by lamplight: the stout, strong-looking char washing down shelves, and the widow-woman moving wine bottles. I thought the caverns marvellous; quite worthy of one of Mrs Radliffe's tales.

'Don't you fret, I know these passages backwards and forwards – even in the pitchy dark,' Nan's thin voice called. 'I never had no candles, all these years. Nowt to be scared of down here but a few rats and beetles.'

I peered warily at the floor at Nan's mention of rats. We moved on, past a dry larder filled with net cradles hanging from the ceiling, and a cold larder hung with grisly carcasses and stiff birds.

'Here we are, mistress.' I had to crouch to enter a barrel-vaulted cellar crammed with dusty bottles and sheaves of herbs and twigs.

'This were the old cook's 'stillery,' said Nan, lighting more candles from her lantern. I looked about myself with pleasure; fitted with a burner, glassware and funnels, the chamber had all the romance of a necromancer's lair.

'You sit down, mistress.' Nan tipped the contents of her basket across the table. 'I just 'ave to start these drying before they lose their virtue.'

As I waited, I picked up a receipt book, and idly flicked through the pages. It was no witch's *grimoire*, for it opened at a method for a homely apple pie.

Nan trailed about the shelves in search of her drying pans. '*She's* gone and started moving my stuff. I could allus find it before.'

'Mrs Blissett, do you mean?' I remembered Peg's kindness in keeping the old woman on; her insistence that such an unfortunate must not be turned from our door. 'It is a new order now, Nan, and it is best to adapt to it. She has her reasons for making all these changes.'

I couldn't see Nan's face, but her voice was disgruntled. 'Oh, aye, mistress. She has them all right. I'll make do with this.' Settling down at the table she began to pick over her harvest, and recommenced her tale.

'Right-oh, well when the mistress heard 'ow Miss Hannah were breeding, she got a wicked notion in her head. She told Mr Ashe he could have no inheritance unless he got the child signed over to herself. She would give Miss Hannah money, plenty of it, in return for the bairn being kept here as her own. Us downstairs reckoned that way she'd not only hope to keep Mr Ashe by her side, but have a new line of heirs for Delafosse, too. Miss Hannah were to be kept here until her time come. That's how I got right friendly with 'er, for I often took her a bite and had a tattle with her.'

'She must have been frightened, here alone?'

'Aye, but she were that lovelorn over Mr Ashe, she hung on his every word. Then, bless 'im, next we knew he smuggled his lass out of here to another place. Mr Ashe had found his Christian conscience see, and wouldn't let a mother be parted from her child.'

'Bravo for him,' I said with feeling.

'Aye, but when the mistress found the pretty bird had flown, there were such a how-row! But Mr Ashe stood his ground, he was young and hot-blooded, and that night he went off to be a soldier. As for her ladyship, her heart was broke in two. Within the six-month, a letter come to say poor Mr Ashe were slain, sliced through in that battle across the ocean. She got a sort of brain-fever then, pacing the house, never resting. I grew afeared of her, for she'd come up behind you and grasp your shoulder and fix on you with frantic eyes. "Where's my baby child?" she'd ask. "I heard him crying but I lost him just now. Where have you hidden him?"

'Poor Dorcas, we called her. Her soul-case were cracked, it were a half-life she were living. Wandering and searching for that baby she were, till the day she fell dead. Then the bailiff come and told me the Hall were to go to some sort of high court, and I could stay on to keep an eye on it. And only this summer it were put to rent.'

I tried to banish this nursemaid's nonsense and said, 'To think, if

Mr Ashe had agreed to be her ladyship's companion in her final years, perhaps even married her, all could have turned out well.'

Nan turned to me, gape-jawed. 'Perhaps I din't make meself clear, mistress. Mr Ashe were Lady Blair's sister's son. He were her blood nephew. The scriptures don't allow such unnatural connections.'

I wondered how I had misunderstood so much. 'No, Nan, I'm sorry, I had no notion.'

'No matter, mistress. Here now, you'll like this, I've kept a chest of all them old confects and devices . . .'

Just then a powerful notion of being observed made me look over my shoulder. I got up to look outside, and there stood Peg at the threshold, as if just arriving in her cloak and bonnet, with a bundle in her hand.

She bobbed at me and laughed. 'Pardon mistress. I never expected to find you down here. It gave me a little fright, seeing you.'

'Yes, and you surprised us, too. I was – well, helping Nan carry her garden stuffs.' It was ridiculous, but I felt the need to explain my presence to Peg.

'You mustn't take notice of old Nan's maunderings,' she said lightly, setting her bundle down. 'You don't know fact from fable, do you, pet?'

The old dame nodded. Comprehending that I was preventing them from getting to work, I rose to return upstairs. As I left, Peg quickly gathered up her receipt book and hugged it to her breast. It was odd that I recalled the title a twelve-month later, when I had the chance to look at it more closely. Back then I had glanced at the flyleaf and seen *Mother Eve's Secrets* written in Peg Blissett's lady's hand.

14

Delafosse Hall

October 1792

~ Of Red, and How to Make It ~

Boil an ounce of cochineal in half a pint of water for about
five minutes; then add half an ounce of cream of tartar, and
half an ounce of alum; boil on a slow fire about as long again.
You will know your colour is done, by dipping a pen into it,
and writing therewith on white paper; for if it writes as clear
as ink and keeps its colour, it is done. Take it off the fire, add
half a quarter of a pound of sugar and let it settle. Keep in a
bottle well stoppered.

*Charlotte Spenlove's way of making Red,
copied from a book of French Receipts*

'Did you find them?'

Nan pushed the rattling seed heads towards Peg. She peered at them and saw the queer ragged crowns to their tops.

Peg jerked her head towards the door. 'Off you go.'

Nan scuttled past her, not even daring to look in her face. Alone, Peg beat her fingers slowly against her mouth, looking into space, cogitating. Well, the old mopsy's patter had made mighty interesting listening from behind the door.

First of all, she found the right page in *Mother Eve's Secrets* for what she wanted to make. Mrs Croxon had been touching it, idly turning the pages. Yet what did it matter? She was just a flat, who couldn't see what stood before her, even if it jumped up and bit her nose.

It was while she was assembling her ingredients that she started to tidy away the small chest Nan had pulled out to show the mistress. 'Confects', was what she'd called them. Lifting the lid it looked to be only broken china, a tarnished spoon, a piece of dried up marchpane. The small parcel in the corner had a musty look, but she opened up the stiff paper to find – what in damnation was that? The cake itself was dust, but the device had survived. Carrying it in her palm to the lamp, she spent a while studying it closely. It was a figure of a swaddled baby the size of a thumb, laid inside a miniature rocking cradle. Lifting it to her lips she set the tip of her tongue against its underside. The pleasant tingle told her it was made of sugar.

Placing it back in its bundle of paper she saw the inner sheet was a letter. Laying the stiff parchment flat on the table, she read it with growing fascination. It was written by the soppy article Nan had talked of, the one with a jack-in-the-belly. It amused her that the writer had not even inquired if Nan could read:

My dear Nan,

My friend, after all your great kindness, as I promised I am sending word of how matters stand for me. Last month I was took to bed of the most beautiful fair little babe and the baptism just being performed, I am sending you a piece of the Christening cake for you to raise a toast to my bonny – and new liberated – baby. I am indeed fortunate to hold my precious infant in my arms, for the news of my darling Ashe's loss almost took my own life from me, from the desperate shock to my body.

As for our tormentor, I hope it gave the wicked creature satisfaction to send my dear child's father to his grave, and thereby deny me the support of the man who should one day have been my husband. Of my own wit, I have found myself another fellow to take me to the altar and sign the baptismal book, though I had to make heavy use of the purse Mr Ashe supplied me with. Needless to say, I am safe, if not content with my lot.

Thank you again, most loyal friend, may God bless you for your kindness.

As for the old witch – fie on her! May she be visited with the suffering she has wrought on me by ten thousand-fold. May she rot in hell and never know rest,

Your affectionate friend . . .

Well, the young mother certainly had a high theatrical style of letter-writing. Peg pursed her lips as she struggled to make out the unexpected name described by the tattered signature. Then, placing the letter and cradle back in the box, she wondered how she might put this extraordinary fact to the greatest use.

It was time to make a start on making the special Usquebaugh for the master. With *Mother Eve's Secrets* open before her, she hummed merrily under her breath. This distillery was an unexpected boon. She was building up her hoard of pretty bottles of queer potions, alchemical powders, lozenges, elixirs, and pills no larger than pin-heads. Still, she must change the lock soon, to avoid any more unwelcome visitors. She patted the chatelaine that bounced at her waist; a plaque of steel hooked to her belt, with clips holding scissors, a pincushion, and a most useful collection of knives and hooks. It was growing heavy with keys, both those she found and those Mrs Croxon handed to her in her vague, apologetic way. Now she had keys to every part of the house.

And Nan was proving useful. Looking at the seed pods on the drying plate, she resisted the temptation to touch them. Granny had told a tale of some children eating such stuff who had then slept for four solid days, and been lucky to wake. Besides, she had other fish than eels to fry, or was that other cordials to doctor? She assembled the great glass globe of the alembic and set it on a low fire, attaching the pipe so it dripped into another bowl. Once she had seen a picture of one of those natural philosophers and their experiments. Now that was a life she might have enjoyed if she were a man; discovering new compounds and waiting to see how those who ate them fared. Grinding up the Blistering Flies in a mortar until they were shiny crimson, she smiled to herself, for it put her in mind of the Palace.

❧

Making colours had been Mary's favourite task; squeezing green juice from spinach, or rubbing the indigo stone in water to make twilight blue. The making of cochineal red always provoked the same macabre jests. 'A bowl of blood,' Auntie would wheeze, overseeing the carefully stirred crimson liquid. 'That's what them anatomisers collect in a basin. I seen it in the *Newgate Calendar*. They cuts the corpse down from the gibbet and carry it off to the sawbones's house. A soul can never go to rest, once it is drained of every drop of blood.' Wary of drips, she would carry the bowl of viscous red to Auntie to be tested. Dipping her pen in the crimson ink,

Aunt Charlotte always recited the same words, to the gasps and hoots of the company.

'"Who scribes in blood his heart's desire – condemns his soul to the Devil's fire." Go on then, girl, ask the Devil for whatever you wishes for. 'Tis only your soul you must hand over in return.'

She had shrieked and jumped back from the dripping pen. 'It's not proper blood, Auntie!' Auntie waited, quill pen in hand, to test the red on clean white paper. What would they ask for, they all wondered, if they could have their heart's desires? Would a thousand pounds do? Hell's teeth, it would not. They wanted palaces and treasures and gowns and gallant lovers. Occasionally the excited chatter took a sober turn. Miss Dora, mannish-faced and leatherbelted, said she wanted only a few acres with chickens and a stream to walk by with a little dog. The rest scoffed at that and vied to describe the costliest diamonds and richest beaux.

'Out damned spot! Will these hands ne'er be clean?' mocked Miss Edwina, snatching at Mary's fingers that were deep-reamed with scarlet. Edwina had once been an actress, and regaled them with the story of Lady Macbeth, who had murdered a man and could never again scrub her hands clean. And as she listened, she had sat on her stool with her chin in crimsoned hands, transported by spanking tales of ghosts and murders, blood and gold.

Every day as Peg served Mrs Croxon, her first impression of her mistress did not change: she was a fish out of water, forever with her face in a book or rambling about the grounds. She had odd notions, too. Fancy talking with that half-wit Nan? And the cold-hearted way His Nibs treated her, that was an entertainment in itself.

Still, Peg was buttering her up like a plate of hot rolls. Each morning Peg listened to her attempts to give orders, then briskly stepped in and told her what was to happen. There was some venison that would do very nicely, Peg would say, recollecting Nan's saying she could roast a saddle.

'Oh, would you? Well, if it is not too much trouble?'

'For you, Mrs Croxon, nothing is too much trouble.'

Then, just as Peg felt she could swan through each day without ruffling her feathers, Mrs Croxon wafted a letter in front of her. Where had that come from? Peg oversaw all the post for Delafosse Hall. That visiting card from Miss Sybilla Claybourn, for instance – that had been a close call. It was a good thing Miss Claybourn had sent Sue over with it – the same Sue she knew from the lodging house. She had invited her in to have a good old hobnob over a dish of tea in her housekeeper's quarters.

After Sue had gone, she had collected Miss Claybourn's card with the others that had arrived from the Earlby gentry. Slowly, and with some pleasurable ceremony, she burned them in the kitchen fire. As she dreamily watched the cards curl and blacken, she felt the prickle of someone watching her over her shoulder. Thrusting the last card into the fire with the poker, she looked up. But it was only Nan.

'Looking for work?' she snapped.

Nan shook her head and shuffled off. What did she care? Even if Nan had seen her, that bag of bones couldn't read.

Now Mrs Croxon wafted a letter before her that must have been picked up directly in the village. 'We are to have a guest. It is my oldest friend, Anne – Mrs Greenbeck. She will arrive here on the twenty-third of November.'

That was barely a month hence. Peg hid her vexation under a bright enquiry. 'How long will she be staying here?'

'She has not yet said. It does depend on—' On what? On how the master behaved himself, no doubt.

'Well, of course she'll be made very welcome,' she said, wondering how she might achieve the opposite.

'Oh, thank you, Peg. I cannot say I feel prepared for visitors yet. And the Hall, as it is—'

Peg gave a long, sympathetic sigh. 'We could offer a warmer welcome in the spring. Perhaps your friend could put off her visit till then?'

'Oh no, no. It is quite settled. You must do your best, Peg. And maybe it will do me good.' She pressed her fingertips between her eyes in a nervous gesture that Peg knew well. For very different reasons, Peg guessed her mistress was just as reluctant as she herself, to have a guest to stay.

There was one thing about Mrs Croxon that did impress her. Every morning the mistress disappeared up to the garret, where Peg assumed she did mindless needlework, or Bible-reading, or some such flim-flam. Then one day, after her mistress had gone into town, Peg tried out a key from her chatelaine and took a five-minute sneak about her mistress's attic room. That writing box of hers that contained all her letters, where did she hide it?

To her surprise the chamber was filled with painting stuff, and Mrs Croxon's work was spread about for her to see. She picked up a picture of the master sleeping, ready to scoff at some wishy-washy scrawl. Instead, she looked at it for a mighty long time, unable to pull herself away. Mrs Croxon had caught His Nibs, all right. Peg didn't know how she'd done it, but it was the spit of him – it had a liveliness to the pencil lines, and a sureness to the colour. Beside it was a magnifying glass on a stand, and a tiny copy she was making onto a disc of white stuff.

Two other miniatures hung on the wall; one of a mournful mope, who must be her mistress's dead mother. The other was a young lad, pale and fair, whom Peg guessed to be a younger brother, perhaps also dead, for it was wound with a plait of turnip blond hair. How fiddly, Peg thought, all that twiddling about with chopped-off hair. Morbid, too, touching stuff from a corpse. She crossed herself half-heartedly and carried on rifling through piles of papers, recognising the master pictured in lots of different attitudes. With his coat open and his linen loose at his neck, he looked a swell cove, like a gentleman in a play. The pictures were not always flattering, mind you; his wife had caught that downturned sulk to his mouth, and the way he slouched as he sat, absent-mindedly stroking his own hair. He was asleep in the tiny picture being worked upon. How apt was that? His handsome face completely dumb.

Pinned on the wall was a mighty fine picture of Delafosse Hall at twilight; as good as a picture in a newspaper, with the green creeper covering everything, save for the golden rectangles of the windows. It was like a builders' model of a house Peg had once seen in a shop window; there was something beguiling about the tiny doors and knockers and curtains. She traced the entrance, the old parlour windows, the drawing room, the Great Hall. Up at the top, just below the eaves, was the window to this very room. A figure stood at that window. A tiny woman was staring directly at Peg. For an instant it made her skin prick, as if she were being spied on from the miniature window by – no, she wouldn't think of that. Hurriedly, she started to put back what she had disturbed, making ready to return downstairs. Still not a sign of the writing box. But here was something useful: a folder of parchment, letter weight, and what was this? Thin transparent onion paper. She thrust a sheet in her pocket.

No, it wasn't just the picture that had made her uneasy – it was a noise on the stair. The stair creaked again, closer and louder. Peg froze. What reason could she give for having unlocked the door and come in here? Before she could think at all, the door was flung open. Guiltily, she sprang backwards.

'What the Devil are you doing in Mrs Croxon's room?' Peter Croxon filled the doorway, spite sharpening his tousled fair features. Lord! If there was one person she didn't want sneaking up on her, it was the master's moralising brother. He remembered her from old, she could see it in his stony eyes.

'Tidying up,' she answered smartly, moving the pictures about on the table.

'I very much doubt that. Where is Mrs Croxon?'

'Out,' she said, eyes cast down, willing him to go.

'She is out, sir. Or have you forgotten your position here? Oh, and by the way, I have noticed that for a housekeeper you employ remarkably few servants.'

She didn't reply, but scowled at him as she made to leave. In answer he blocked the door with his outstretched arm. His leanness was the sort that was strong and fast. He also stood a good head taller than her.

'Now we are alone, Peg, or whatever you call yourself these days
– know this. I am watching you,' he said in a low growl. Still he
refused to budge out of the way. 'And I am watching Grace, too. If
anything should happen to her—'

She made a calculation and glanced up at him with a beseeching
expression. 'Mr Croxon, if you would be good enough not to tell
the mistress I was here —'

'Why in damnation shouldn't I?'

She was standing very close to him. Her face formed a practised
look of yearning. Suggestively, she parted her lips in a coquettish
smile.

'You could grow to like me if you tried,' she said in a low, slow
voice. His pale eyes were fixed upon her in a fascinated stare.
Sensing no resistance, she lifted her fingers to rub the sensitive skin
around his ear. 'You see, I like you.' He didn't move. She lifted her
mouth towards his, stoking the familiar fire of a man's need. Her
body melded against his, groin to groin. She closed her eyes.

A blow to her face sent her reeling back towards the work table.
Her fingers shot up to her stinging cheek.

'Get out, you!'

With her shoulders bowed and her hand cupping her face, she
made a dash past Peter Croxon and ran half-blind down the stairs.

In her own quarters she found a mirror. There was a purple bruise
spreading over her cheek, and bloodshot veins filled her half-closed
eye. In half an hour she would look like any black-eyed blowsabella.
Peter piss-proud Croxon, she muttered, you took a wrong step
there. But she had gathered some information. She now knew the
brother had a sentimental hankering for Mrs Croxon. As she
dabbed Pear's Almond Lotion onto her swelling face without great
effect, she was too muddled to think of a plan. He had struck her.
He had rebuffed her. Her brain was giddy with anger. When she
calmed down from this blaze of fury, she would rack her brain for
an answer: Peter Croxon, what was his price?

15

Delafosse Hall

October 1792

~ Royal Usquebaugh ~

Take two pounds of raisins, half a pound of figs, two ounces of cinnamon, one ounce of nutmeg, half an ounce of cloves, the same of mace and of saffron, liquorice three ounces; bruise your spices and slice the rest in small pieces; infuse them all in a gallon of the best brandy for a week, till all the provocative virtues are extracted therefrom. Then filter them, putting thereto a quart of canary wine and twelve Blistering Flies of Spain beaten small and twelve leaves of gold broken into pieces.

From an old and secret receipt of an Italian Master, much famed for his alchemical knowledge of provocative cordials, Mother Eve's Secrets

Slowly, Michael and I established a routine of pleasantries. True, he complained much of the difficulties of establishing the mill, but how could such an enterprise not be hard? And he confided in me; that Peter had visited, while I was out in Earlby, but the brothers had quarrelled again. More surprising, he began to cast me occasional long appraising looks. Did he, I wondered, wish to unburden himself of some matter? But whenever I looked up and smiled in readiness to hear his concerns, he inevitably retreated to his own thoughts and favourite green bottle of spirits.

Then our first bill arrived from the village: for nearly £37. As I no longer possessed such a large sum myself, the next time Michael dined at home, I resolved to broach the subject. Over a savoury rabbit stew and extravagant dessert board, Michael and I talked peaceably of clipping back the growth that dimmed the Hall's windows. It seemed a good omen for the future. As we talked, I fancied I glimpsed the bridegroom of my dreams in Michael's features. His appearance always had something of the Classical about it, clear-skinned and sculpted, but when free of care, his eyes shone brighter and his rare smile was radiant.

Reluctantly, I asked him for the money, as sweetly as I could.

For a moment he was disconcerted; then gave a bitter little cough. At that moment Peg came in to clear the last of the dishes. She had searched for a housemaid, but finding none met her high standards, she carried out even that menial duty.

'Have you finished, sir?' she asked, for his almond cheesecake lay abandoned.

He made a dismissive gesture with his hand.

'Sir,' she said humbly. 'You asked me to tell you how the fire downstairs is doing. It burns bright tonight, sir.'

'That's enough. Leave us,' Michael snapped.

I protested once she had gone. 'Please, do not scold Peg.'

He laughed, not pleasantly. 'She is your housekeeper, not your friend.'

'Ask yourself, what other company have I?'

Our spell of mutual sympathy was over. Peevishly, he asked me to come upstairs to his study, and once there, placed a document before me.

'What is this?'

'The next stage in raising capital for the mill.'

'But what of the first stage?'

'It is proceeding.' He thrust the pen towards me.

I swallowed hard. 'Yes, but how is it proceeding? You told me there is only mud on my land so far; great pits of mud.'

'I keep telling you. The business is complex. I must order the great waterwheel now.'

'So you have an inventory of costs?' A little devil of spite possessed me as I pretended to look for such an item.

'What do you care for inventories, for God's sake?'

What I did see, when I glanced down, were the words: 'To borrow the sum of £1000.'

'What has happened to the first sum?' As I looked up I fell mute, seeing at once that any pleasantry between us had died. Yet I still felt entirely secure in my rights. Mr Tully had insisted that I must be signatory to any instructions.

'You told me one thousand pounds would allow a beginning to the building work. Michael, I only ask you how it was spent?'

As answer he knocked the papers to the floor with a sweep of his arm. I started back, astonished at his extraordinary behaviour. All the pages lay scattered on the floor.

'Inventory?' he shouted, his face ugly. 'You draw up an inventory if you want one. I have had enough of all this. Are you an idiot, to goad me? I am going mad from it all.' Then he scraped up all the papers and threw them, higgledy-piggledy, towards me so they struck me.

An idiot? I recollected the day Mr Croxon had first called on my father. Yes, I had married a man I barely knew. I had bound myself to him for life. But I would not tolerate this blustering. The blunt truth was that it was my land.

I spoke as clearly as I could, though my voice began to tremble. 'No, Michael. Though I understand you may have wagered your bachelorhood upon it, I am not an idiot.'

Before he could take breath, I hurried off to my chamber. Peg just then happened to be on the stair and I almost knocked against her. 'Mistress,' she said, backing away, concern for my welfare written large on her face.

'Oh, Peg,' I wailed, and as a friend might, she reached out to me, silently touching my arm, communicating her complete understanding of my situation. I could not speak aloud to a servant, but it was a comfort of sorts, that Peg had sympathy for my troubles. Nevertheless, I broke from her and continued to climb the stairs, very anxious to be alone with my turbulent thoughts. The pressure of Peg's hand on my arm remained; a token of understanding from one woman to another in distress.

Next morning I had to get outside, and so began a period of long walks in the park. Early November continued bright, with the last sun of the year shining low and coppery over the woods. Striding through heaps of rusty autumn leaves, I ached to see beauty dying all around me. I felt completely alone in that rambling wilderness, save for the crows cawing in their rookeries and the wrens bobbing from hedge to hedge. I began to make studies in my book of the delicate lines of drying grasses and frilled seed pods. I looked for some lesson on how best to live from Nature, that every year died and was renewed, but none appeared.

Instead, I heard an unearthly sound as I walked in the woods. It was music, but not like any I had ever heard. It was as if the god Pan were playing his pipes in an English wood, a meandering, melancholy summons that vibrated low in my stomach. I stopped stone still, transported as if in a trance cast by Monsieur Mesmer himself. When silence returned I looked about for the source of the sound. When I reached the spot where the sound had originated, nothing remained, only silence. But in the distance was the person I expected to see least of all: Peg, in her outdoor garb, moving at a slow, reluctant pace, towards the Hall. I held back and said nothing to her, for I valued our secret communion on the stair.

Another day, sheltering beneath trees in a rain-shower, I uncovered a doorway long obliterated by undergrowth. After pulling shrubbery aside, I stepped inside a long deserted summerhouse, fronted by cracked marble columns and ironwork, the rear extending deep into the hillside. Though still filthy, even after I cleared away the tenacious vines, the windowpanes gave sufficient greenish light for me to sketch indoors. In a cobwebbed corner stood a gardener's burner that must once have coaxed oranges or other delicate shrubs to life. With that alight, I found a chair and sat with my shawl muffled around me as I sketched.

The marble statues that lined the walls were fine copies of the Greek masters, with muscular limbs and serene faces, though sadly disfigured with a blueish-green patina. As an exercise, I copied a figure of a handsome boy, admiring the sculptor's rendering of tensed muscle, the body frozen just an instant before extending in action. My mind drifted to Michael, the uncertainty hanging over us, my urges to please him, my need to move beyond this stupid impasse. As I sketched the statue's blind eyes I half-heartedly followed his line of sight.

I stood and looked more closely at the statue. 'What are you looking at?' I said out loud. A green stain blotted the boy's cheek, ugly but also strangely beautiful, for the colour was a peacock's viridian. For the first time I noticed the description, 'HARPOCRATES – SILENCE', engraved on the pediment, and had a vague recollection of a Roman boy-god who personified that virtue. He held one index finger raised coyly to his lips, while his other hand pointed towards a low arch in the wall. I paced over to the spot at which he pointed. The niche was filled with gardener's trellis that I removed with rising excitement. Behind stood an oak doorway set low in the wall. As I lifted the latch, it opened onto a blast of chilly darkness. Lighting the stub of a candle at the stove, I propped the door open and ventured inside.

At once I knew this was no gardeners' store, but another tunnel burrowing into the hillside. Setting forth with the excitement of new discovery, my footsteps rang out and my breath fogged before me in clouds. The place had a mossy, mineral smell, and save for the dripping of water, was silent. Though at first the tunnel ran straight, it soon descended an incline, and my feet splashed into muddy puddles. Who, I wondered, had last passed through that door?

Perhaps fifteen minutes passed; it was impossible to say. My candle burned down fast in the draught. Annoyed, I paddled through inches of freezing water. If I were not to be stranded in the dark, I needed to return very soon to the summerhouse. The candle guttered violently – only by cradling it, did it stay alive. Gradually, workaday sounds reached me from the tunnel ahead. Next, a dim glow became apparent, that I realised must come from the store-rooms I had visited with Nan. I was cold and wet, and moved rapidly on, thinking to climb the stairs and appear in the kitchen like a conjuror from a trapdoor. Then, drifting in echoing rhythms down the tunnel, I heard Peg, haranguing someone severely, her voice sharp with fury. I stopped in my tracks and listened. My housekeeper, having taken a bad tumble on the stairs, had an ugly black eye, and was recently in none too good a temper. She sounded not only angry, but strangely excited. On an impulse, I determined to retrace my steps, telling myself I had no wish to intrude on a quarrel. There was the summerhouse door, too, that still stood propped open and all my paints still laid out. Just then I noticed a hint of silver glinting in the Stygian stream at my feet, and stooped to investigate. It was a metal sewing thimble, which I slipped absent-mindedly onto my finger. Then I turned about and hurriedly retraced the way I had come.

A good way further down the tunnel a sudden gust of cold air whistled up behind me and blew out my flame. Blackness smothered me with all the suddenness of a falling cloak. I gave a little shriek and heard the candle stub hit the ground. There was but one solidity in that place and so I grasped the slippery wall, as the fading afterglow of the candle swam before my eyes. I waited for my sight to clear, but without the smallest chink of light, nothing but waves of profound darkness surged towards me. I knew I should continue but my feet refused to move. The smell of the place grew stronger, of something slick and green and foul, suddenly so pungent I could taste it. Again, sounds reached me from behind my back, from the kitchen-end of the tunnel: this time of something moving fast.

'Hello?' I called in a high and startled voice. The rapid footsteps did not falter. 'Who is there?' I cried. The sound of breathing was getting closer; coming in fast, uneven gasps. I peered around for an approaching light but no light appeared. I opened my mouth to speak but no words formed. A person was rushing towards me, running, and all the time making tiny sobbing noises. Fearful of their crashing into me in the darkness, I cringed back against the wet wall. Now the stumbling steps were no more than a few feet away, then drew up close, then halted at my side, as if paralysed by terror. A panting, ragged-breathed female stood a finger's length away from me, completely invisible in the dark. 'No,' she whimpered softly, in an exhalation that spoke of raw despair. 'Oh God, help me.' Those wisps of words were spoken to herself alone; I had a powerful sense she could neither see nor sense me, as I pressed my back against the slippery wall.

Then in a twinkling, as if I woke from a midnight trance, I was alone. The tunnel was empty. I heard steady drips of moisture fall again.

Panic erupted in sickening waves within me. I was conscious that something extraordinary – a sort of vortex of terror – had visited me. I had to get out of that tunnel. I picked up my skirts and ran, staggering blindly, plunging on, guided only by my cold-numbed fingertips. On and on I floundered, with a new and nightmarish certainty that there were more tunnels than I had at first believed and I had stumbled into a treacherous side-branch. Were these perhaps old mine workings? At any moment a bottomless mine shaft might lurk unseen before me, or a subterranean lake gape at my feet. Or even worse, the terrified presence I had encountered might be lying in wait for me, exhaling terror, invisible but no less real for that. And this time it might see me, or even – God forbid – reach out whatever fingers it possessed and clutch me, pulling me towards it. If so, I should die of it, I knew it.

With giddy relief, I saw light ahead of me, and threw myself, sobbing, back into the wondrous, half-blinding daylight of the summerhouse. At the stove, I pulled my wet stockings off; then hauled my chair up close to dry my legs and skirts. I was still shaking, and cursing myself for the risk I had taken. The iron thimble fell to the floor, a paltry object with *'For Mother from her Jamie,'* engraved in tiny letters along its rim. Well, Jamie and his mother were long gone from Delafosse. Replacing the trellis, I decided to tell no one of the tunnel or my misguided explorations.

As for the running woman, I could scarcely hazard a guess at what I had heard. Now I was back in the light I immediately dismissed notions of Old Dorcas or other such nursery tales. I racked my brain for a rational explanation. Perhaps, I told myself, Peg had threatened one of the staff so severely she had run away, and the bizarre acoustic effects of the tunnel had tricked me into thinking she was closer than she was. Yet hadn't that whimpering appeal issued only inches from where I stood? Next, a powerful suggestion did strike me with horrible force: that the noises I heard were a depiction in sound, much as a magic lantern performance depicts images, from a quite different point in time, though when it was, or would be, I did not know. And the worst of it was that the identity of the woman also sprang instantly into my mind – and I shuddered to think of it – that I had heard myself, running in terror, at some unknown future date.

❧

Back at the Hall, once I had bathed away my terror and changed my clothes, I found Michael waiting for me. Instead of his usual resentment, my husband set himself to charm me. Over supper he talked of our future together, of creating the perfect home, a fine country estate, and even, he hinted, the founding of a dynasty, here at Delafosse. If only we could get the mill built, all our paltry problems would end. We would make a fortune from the business and restore the house to its original splendour. It was simple.

Finally, he got to the nub of the matter. He had seen a steam engine demonstrated at Skipton. The river ran low in different seasons and our future profits were at risk. All the forward-looking manufacturers were installing steam. 'Imagine a herd of beasts made of steel,' he urged. Power and speed were his watchwords; but, as he talked of pistons and valves, I no longer listened, only watched his pale cheeks flush, as if he were already fired by the unnatural forces he described. There was such a curious logic to his argument that a few times it rose to the tip of my tongue to indulge him. But I knew Michael better now. Remembering Mr Tully's advice, I kept my mouth closed. Then, as I rose to retire, he did too. He reached awkwardly for my hand, his long white fingers brushing mine. I looked up at him; at his face so intensely watching me; the sad need in his eyes like a lure. Dumbfounded, I pulled my hand clumsily away.

But once we had parted I was unable to sleep. The horror in the tunnel, followed by Michael's febrile mood had both infected me. His talk of spending money on the Hall was difficult to resist. Anne's visit was fast approaching, and I pictured her peering along the shabby corridors of Delafosse, disappointed by the chaos and collapse. Perhaps Michael was right, and I should spend my way out of unhappiness. If I did, would he be civil to Anne? If only she would delay her visit until spring. Even Peg had grasped what a deliverance that would be.

Anne's letter had also contained disconcerting news: 'I am afraid I bring momentous news that strikes at the heart of our friendship. I cannot write of it now, I must speak when we are alone.' Had she discovered something about my father, or about Michael? My mind ran harum-scarum over nervous speculations: why might she no longer be my friend?

The church bell rang out two o'clock. Footsteps, light but clear, ran along the wooden boards below my room. Michael's room was down there, by the Long Gallery. I sat upright and lit a candle. Apparently he could not sleep either. The answer, I decided, was to go downstairs and tell him to buy the machine. In return I hoped he would promise to be kinder to me, and to Anne too. The notion struck me that the middle of the night was the best time to speak to him. He had been excited all evening; perhaps, after his bungled attempt to caress me, he wanted to do more than merely speak?

A few minutes later I stood outside Michael's door, hesitating as the floorboards creaked beneath my bare feet. Caution urged me to sleep on my decision, but the memory of my bed's heart-shrinking emptiness left me standing in a sort of stupor. If I can only buy the machine he will be more amiable, I told myself. I rapped anxiously at his door. There was no reply.

The door opened without hindrance. My candle revealed Michael's empty bed, the sheets untouched. I looked about in disappointment. There stood his pomades, brushes, and silver-ware, laid out before a mirror. I knew that he buffed, polished and maintained his appearance; I often caught him admiring himself in the mirror. His favourite midnight blue coat hung on a hook. I pressed my face to the fabric, inhaling his male scent, tempered with sweet cologne.

Setting down the candle on his desk, I saw from his heavily inked blotter that he had been a busy correspondent. But when I held the blotter to the mirror I could make no sense of it, save 'The George Inn', and the impress of his signature, an almost unreadable '*M*' with a scribbled tail.

I have never been a prying person, valuing privacy myself. So it was a new emotion, to feel the perversity of maddening curiosity. I knew as I searched Michael's room that I would suffer from the consequences, but I did it just the same. Pry into a cloud and be struck by a thunderbolt, they say.

First, I listened for any sound from the corridor. All was quiet. Holding my breath, I lifted the lid of his writing desk and delicately sifted through its contents. At first I found unpaid bills for astronomical sums, from tailors in Manchester and York, incurred on visits after which Michael had complained bitterly of his heavy labours. A bundle of letters from his mother made petty enquiries about the Hall, but contained not a single word about me. There was a torn half of a theatre ticket, and many descriptions of equipages for sale. I almost didn't lift the copper disc lodged beneath the papers, assuming it to be an old seal. Then I grasped its crumpled ribbon and pulled it out.

A dirty old penny swung from my fingers, with crude writing scratched on its surface. I held it to the candle and read with some difficulty:

> *Though chains hold me fast,*
> *As the years pass away,*
> *I swear on this heart*
> *To find you one day.*

I felt a queer jolt of alarm, for the verse had a menacing quality. I asked myself why Michael kept such a filthy object. He surely couldn't be the intended recipient of such a crude threat? But if he was – had the writer of the message found Michael yet? Or did he keep the coin in his desk in anticipation of being found on that promised day?

I turned the coin over, expecting to see the king's head, or Britannia. Instead, I read with increasing uneasiness:

MARY JEBB AGE 19
TRANSPORTED 7 YEARS
TO THE ENDS OF THE EARTH

Below was a clumsily etched arrow-pierced heart. Surely it could not be a love token? The pattern of hearts and chains about the circumference recalled a sailor's flesh inscribed with inky doves and flowers – brands that marked them as outcasts from respectable life. Mary Jebb, I mused – what an ugly name. Yet she was a young woman, or she had been when the token was made; and young women were undoubtedly prone to romantic feelings. No, I decided, there had to be another, more trivial reason for Michael's keeping it. He had probably never even met the woman. I laid it down and put everything carefully back just as it had been before.

Perplexed, I set off in search of my husband. His study, the library – all lay empty. I doubted he had left the house, for his new horse Dancer had taken a tumble, and Michael was more concerned with his horse than his own cuts and bruises. He was at home and awake, I was convinced of it. Wanting to find him without pacing every inch of the Hall's labyrinthine passages, I decided to go outside, and from that vantage point, search for a lit curtain. With a wild sense of purpose I fetched shoes and a cloak from my room, lit a dark lantern, and let myself out of a side door.

Outside, I shivered in a landscape of greys and silvers, the stone walls and cobbles looming pale in the wintry air. The only true colour was an amber penumbra shimmering around the moon. Beyond the silvered slope of overgrown lawn, the mass of black trees moved to and fro in the breeze, with a strange undulation like waving sea fronds. Stepping onto the frost-crisped grass, I turned back to gain a view of the house. Every window of the Hall was dark, like a colony of sleeping eyes inside a hive. Then, taking a last survey of the park, I noticed a tiny golden light above the horizon. I peered at it, unable to locate its source. Shivering but determined, I set off in the darkness towards it.

After some short time hurrying along the path, I understood that the source of the light was the hunting tower. Opening the small hinged door of my lantern and following its narrow beam, I puzzled over why Michael would go there. He had never spoken of the place, and I had thought it abandoned. Growing closer, the golden spark grew into a rectangle of warm light framed by the diamond panes of an upper-floor window. By now the cold had shocked me into full alertness, and instinctively wary, I shuttered the door of my lantern to hide its light. Soundlessly, I opened the tower door and stood on the threshold, listening.

I could hear movement and low voices upstairs. As quietly as I could, I stepped inside and gently set the door to. Then, tiptoeing to the bottom of the spiral staircase, I listened again, and heard what I at first understood to be people struggling. A woman's voice spoke in a low murmur, coaxing or crooning. Suddenly she cried out, and there began a rhythmic slapping of flesh upon flesh. A man's voice reached me: a wordless remonstration. With a thump against my ribcage I knew the man was Michael. I guessed that those sounds were an accompaniment to something Michael had never wanted from me – the sound of a man and a woman, taking passionate pleasure in each other's bodies. I stood transfixed, holding back tears. I had hoped that Michael and I were taking small steps towards a life together, that one day my husband's coldness would thaw. I had deluded myself. Now I had proof he took his pleasure with some other woman. I stood a long while in a sort of daze, until a loud scraping of furniture interrupted my wretched thoughts, portending their departure.

A table stood covered in a fusty cloth. On a whim I crouched behind it. I could have fled but I had to see *her* – it was a primitive pain I had to inflict on myself. As they came down the stairs, my heart beat so violently it seemed they must hear it. From my hiding place I had only a partial view of Michael's legs, moving slowly. In his shadow was the woman, wearing black skirts. They did not speak; the only sound was a metallic slithering, as if she wore many necklaces or bangles. As she passed through the door I moved to gain a fuller view. She was tall, and her loose black hair tumbled past her waist. With a loud click I heard the key turn. They had locked me inside.

In my wretchedness I scarcely cared. I curled in upon myself in the darkness, the woman's image searing my mind's eye. I pictured her hair, lush and raven-black, spreading luxuriantly while my husband coupled with her. I guessed who she was, of course. That hair – to think that I had touched it, had even kept a long coarse strand inside my purse. Like parts of a child's puzzle slotting together, I remembered that Michael had visited Earlby seven times before we had married. I added that strange account of Mrs Harper's sudden departure, her impudent use of my – no, what should have been our – bed. I was convinced Michael had crept away to see Mrs Harper on our wedding night. No doubt he met her frequently, unknown to me.

A sickened curiosity gripped me to see the place where they had met. Upstairs the fire had sunk to red embers, but the room was still rich with the tang of sweat and naked flesh. There were the remains of sweetmeats on the table, and a discarded bottle and two glasses. I carried one glass to the fire and saw the rim was smeared with the tell-tale residue from a woman's painted lips. I raised the glass to my lips; it had a spirituous reek and the lees sparkled like tiny spangles of gold. I looked about the room in despair. On such a cold night they must at first have prepared a great fire, for an untidy heap of birch kindling lay tumbled across the floor. The smell and heat made me sick, for it amplified something salty, primitive and strange.

My stupor was interrupted by the sound of the door below being unlocked. Someone had returned. Hastily, I tiptoed up the

corkscrew stair to the roof. Up there it was so biting cold and dark
I barely had the courage to place one foot before another. I could
still hear movements from the room below, pacing back and forth,
and the fire being dampened down. In my frantic state, I strove to
hold onto the corner turret, at the same time creeping around it to
hide. Like a tight-rope walker I inched my way, hampered by my
limbs' unruly shaking. I thought I heard someone coming up the
stair, and took a step further away.

My ankle hit the low barrier that edged the roof. For a long,
anguished moment I felt myself flailing in empty air. Then I lost my
balance entirely and plunged down from the roof, into rushing
blackness.

16
Delafosse Hall

October 1792

~ *A Most Healthful Hystericon* ~

*To make a most effectual Hystericon for Women against
Nerves and Melancholy, Fits and Vapours, Mania or
Tremblings: Take Aqua Vitae and put in a bottle with no
more than 13 seeds of henbane, any more brings danger of
convulsions and fatal sleep. Add a few leaves of dried worm-
wood, tansy, angelica and aniseeds; leave one day, add water
and boil it. Filter out the herbs; add sugar syrup to take off the
bitterness. From a cost of 3d to produce, each bottle may be sold
at half a crown or greater.*

Mother Eve's Secrets

'Mistress is dead! Mistress is dead!' Nan's caterwauling entry startled Peg as she stood raking the embers of the fire to start breakfast. The old woman slumped down, slack-jawed onto a stool.

'What's going on?' Peg shook her bony shoulder.

'I were out picking simples at first light, and I saw her. She's lying dead in't bushes by the tower,' mumbled Nan.

Peg ran all the way in the grey dawn, her heels flying and a procession of notions skittering through her head. And there indeed lay her mistress, looking horribly corpse-like in a tangle of gorse. She halted warily; knelt, and touched her. She was certainly cold, but Peg had to be sure of it. She gave her waxy face a little smack. Mrs Croxon took a sharp breath and rolled her head aside. Peg peered at the scene and read it like a book: the roof of the tower and its low barricade, her mistress's fall broken by the springy branches. And here she was, all alone with her mistress, and Nan even now telling everyone she was dead. Peg froze above her mistress like a lioness, calculating different paths and different futures. Slowly she pulled off her shawl, and raised it in a tight wad above Mrs Croxon's face.

How stupid Mrs Croxon looked. Peg hesitated, weighing it all up – the danger of being caught, the risk to her liberty, the possible complications. No. It would serve her no advantage. She dropped the shawl gently to the ground as the sound of runners pelting down the path exploded behind her. The master ran to his wife's side, and Peg followed him, very grave-faced, as he carried her back to the house.

Half an hour later Dr Sampson, one of the master's cronies from the George, hurried up the stairs. Peg made up a tray of hot tea, cake, and brandy and took it directly upstairs. Lingering, she caught almost every word that Mr Croxon and the doctor exchanged, through the gap in the door.

'—a queer place for your wife to take a tumble,' said the doctor in his deep bass voice.

'I'm afraid she has trouble sleeping. She gets up sometimes and wanders. Nerves, I suppose.'

'We'll need to keep a weather eye on that, Croxon.'

When their voices dropped, she knocked, and the master ushered her forward into the sickroom, that smelt nastily of purging. The mistress lay with her eyes closed, her face chalky white. The doctor, a plump, whiskery fellow, held up Mrs Croxon's arm that wore a trail of leeches as black as jetty slugs.

'This is the woman,' the master said to the doctor, nodding his head at Peg. 'My dear wife knows and trusts her.' The doctor appraised her, and Peg shrank herself into a little curtsey. She made sure he saw nothing but a modest gown on a neat figure, a demure face, a thoughtful tray of refreshments.

'Mr Croxon does not want a stranger to nurse his wife. You will step up and do your best, eh, Mrs Blissett?'

She nodded, her eyes cast down.

'Your mistress has been badly cut and bruised, and then exposed to many hours' severe chill. Thankfully, no limbs appear to have been broken. Indeed, she has had an astonishing escape from harm. But your patient will be enfeebled for some time, and will need delicate handling. No doubt her nerves are shaken, but with care she may escape the worst effects of her accident.'

'She looks so weak,' she said.

'That is the effect of the leeches,' the physician replied. 'She must sleep without disturbance. If she calls for drink, give her only lime water today. Send for me if there are convulsions or unusual signs, but I do not expect them. So – until tomorrow.'

'I shall dine out, Mrs Blissett.' Naturally, His Nibs was fidgeting to leave the sickroom in the doctor's wake. 'No need to go back downstairs,' he called from the doorway. 'Devote yourself to your mistress.'

They both vanished, leaving her quite in charge. Peg poured herself a dish of tea and sat down heavily beside the bed. Slowly, she ate her master's piece of cake, and then the doctor's. Then she lifted her aching feet onto the bed, sat back comfortably, and started on the brandy.

❧

Only once in her life had she been laid low, after the Great Storm at Sydney Cove. Jack had carried her to the hospital hut, but new wretches arrived every day with jail fever, and soon it was heaped with the dying. Without fresh victuals, scurvy broke out, killing even more colonists every day. Women like her were ordered to shift for themselves. Though still sore from cuts and bruises, she had to face the prospect of limping back to the camp. True, there was her wedding to get up for, but it grieved her to marry Jack in such a tatterdemalion state. No fresh clothes or even a hank of thread had been shipped out for the women's use. Her wretched gown was in ribbons, and only covered her bosom thanks to the pins she guarded like treasure. As for the wounds to her face, and clump of missing hair, she was glad there was no mirror to inspect herself.

Then Jack approached her with a shamefaced expression, before burying his head in his hands. 'Go on,' she said, 'tell me the worst.' When she finally got the words out of him, she could have spat venom at having such damnable bad luck. 'The reverend says I'm to tell you there's a woman, Annie Mobbs she's called, sailed on the *Scarborough*.' She waited in silence as he twisted his greasy cap in his hands.

'She's going about saying me and her was married, two years back at Plymouth. Mary,' he cried, clutching her hand, 'I was as drunk as a lord, fresh off the ship. Surely it don't stand?' Jack wept like a baby while she watched him, dead-eyed with disappointment.

It did stand, for in spite of the reverend turning a blind eye every day to husbands or wives alive on the other side of the world, he would not bigamously marry Jack, whose wife brandished a scrap of paper and a brass wedding ring. He was ordered to live with Annie Mobbs in a married man's hut, much to that ugly trull's jubilation.

'So where the Devil do I go now, Jack?' She had lost her sweet-girl manner, for she had backed a loser, after all.

'It breaks my heart,' he whined like a puling child. 'You must stay in Sodom Camp with the other women.' When he reached for her hand she slapped him away.

She found quarters in Ma Watson and Brinny's tent, in a corner vacated by a woman who had given up the ghost in childbed. There was general rejoicing that the infant had snuffed it too, for had it lived, its death might have proved a great deal slower and noisier. Her quarters stank like a pigsty in the breathless heat of the daytime, but once the sun set it was perishing cold. The talk was always the same old patter: of the brainless government, the stingy rations, which cove had stabbed who in a fight, and who shared whose bed. Across the way, Janey's tent was a brothel of canvas, the scene of knife-fights and grog-fuelled riots, from which men tumbled, drunk and danger-ous. These were no swell gentlemen living by thieves' honour, but wiry wretches with naught to live for but oblivion and the chance to hurt someone weaker than themselves. It was then that a mad mongrel known as Stingo began to sniff about her, mumbling lewd descriptions of what he wished to do to her, and twice she had to run from his pawing hands. The squat figure of Annie Mobbs haunted her too; everywhere she heard her mocking laughter and yawling Devon lingo. If it were possible to wish someone dead, her raging thoughts would have struck Mobbs down like gunshot.

You are still alive, she repeated to herself, as if words were ropes to hold her afloat in a trough of night soil. But the truth was that her quick wits were failing by the day. She blamed the soupy heat that made it hard to walk for even a minute. Nothing behaved as it should any more: it was like the view across the heat-scorched land, the shadows wobbling like water in the sunlight, the shapes of men elongated like trembling trees. And the work she was given, collecting shells on the seashore to make mortar for the new town, left time hanging heavy. She was riled with herself, too, in a fuddled way, unable to shake off the notion she had missed the main chance, though what that chance was she wasn't sure. Not to be a whore in the brothel tent, mind, not since Janey was dispatched to Kingdom Come by a glass bottle shoved in her pretty face. She grunted when she heard the news, unable to form a fitting epitaph. The truth was, since the Great Storm, while her body produced aching pain, her mind was as barren as a coiner's blank.

There were men in the early days, redcoats or lags, it no longer mattered, who she shuffled off with, into the bush. With her eyes closed against the red disc of the sun, she barely noticed the fumbling and grunting – all her thoughts were consumed by the salivating vision of her fee: a mouthful of food. Sometimes she fell in with a mob of black women who gathered in a gully near the beach. When she *coo-eed* to them, they grinned back, showing perfect teeth, their children creeping forward boldly to touch her pearly northern skin. They exchanged gestures about the children, complaints about empty bellies. To the accompaniment of hoots of laughter, she tested their lingo: the sweet tea leaves she searched for were *warraburra*, and the desire to eat, which she mimicked hand to mouth, they called *pattaa*. They were secretive, leather-hard people, not unkind, willing to give her a sip of bitter drink from their gourds or a wriggling grub from a hole in the ground to chew. From them she learned to plait grasses, and best of all, which roots were edible and how to cook them in the ashes of the fire.

But, like everyone else, she was starving. Her daily ration

produced a ladleful of saltless slop, to which the women struggled
to add more – chickweed or a roasted rat, or any grub or sea creature. Aunt Charlotte had called kitchen fare belly timber, and so it
proved, for without food the spirit collapsed, like a beached ship
weathered away to rotting ribs and yawning holes. At night, dreams
of food flared like bonfires in her fancy, of a long-forgotten moment
spreading dripping onto bread, the brown specks of meat juice, the
relief of jaws sinking into plenty. In one harrowing dream she found
a sugar-crusted cake forgotten in her pocket. It haunted her waking
hours; the compulsion to search, the certainty it might still be there
in her pocket, squashed and delicious.

Dr Sampson left a brown bottle labelled 'The Mixture'. While Mrs
Croxon slept, it took only a moment to exchange the contents with
her own Hystericon. Henbane had been one of Granny's favourite
simples; doled out to women troubled by fits or to bring on the
Twilight Sleep when in childbed. With her mistress sleeping like a
waxy corpse, Peg took a little holiday, making brews in the distillery,
and setting off again to search for the writing box. In chamber or
studio, there was not a sign of the damnable object. By the third
day, however, her mistress started to rebel.

'No more,' she croaked through cracked lips, pushing the glass of
pungent potion away. Thereafter, there was no disputing that Dr
Sampson's patient was making a good recovery. When her mistress
finally sat up to attempt some chicken hash, she glanced up at Peg
and mumbled, 'Don't look at me like that. I didn't try to – end my
own life. It was an accident.'

An accident. Peg took a deep breath. 'At the tower?'

Mrs Croxon's red-rimmed eyes looked away and her face
crumpled. 'Yes, you may as well know. I was looking for my
husband.' She wiped her eyes on the back of her hand. Her
genteel voice wavered. 'I have decided to leave him. Make a

sensible parting between the two of us. Live a quiet life somewhere else. Alone.'

Peg's heart skipped a beat. 'What? You'd leave here? But what of
your position?'

Mrs Croxon's eyes burned with resolve. 'I know it's shocking,
Peg. Perhaps I am not as mindful of propriety as you imagine. So
long as I have my paints, a few books, I may live a peaceful life. He
cares not a jot for me. And the humiliation —' Again, she covered
her face.

Peg appraised her through narrowed eyes. My, the worm was in
danger of turning. This called for quick wits and, thankfully, she was
never short of those. What did the mistress still desire? Her fool of
a husband, perhaps? Under all those brave words, surely she still
moped after him.

'Desert your fine husband?' She gave a little laugh. 'You would be
known as the worst sort of female — selfish, and a heathen besides,
to break your vows. You'd be an outcast amongst respectable folk.
Now, I know it's not my place, but might I speak to you more like
— well, as a friend?'

Her mistress lifted her bleary face. 'Oh, Peg.' She grasped Peg's
hand, her fingers unpleasantly clammy. 'How good you are. Go ahead.'

'Do you not know marriage can take a good while to flourish?
You've scarcely given it a chance, if you don't mind me saying so.'

Mrs Croxon shook her head slowly. 'It's more than that.
Something is wrong. I know it in my bones. You see, I love him —
but he is repelled by me.'

'Oh, that's common enough,' Peg said, in a voice like balm.
'Marry first and love will follow, they say. The most amiable couples,
with a dozen children — even they have difficult beginnings. I've
learned many a lesson about relations between the sexes, living in
different households. And I believe I can finally answer that great
question, "What does a husband truly want?"'

Her mistress appeared to be waking up at last. 'So, what does he
want?'

'Well, the trouble is, it's not generally what his wife wants.'

'Oh?'

'Well, if I was to tell you that a husband wants to be lodged at home as comfortably as at his favourite inn, and his wife to be as compliant as the doxy he dallied with in his youth, you might think me rather simple.'

Mrs Croxon gave a grumpy little snort. 'No. I would think it was only the hard truth. And I have wanted a great deal more from him, have I not?'

'It is only my opinion, Mrs Croxon; but wise women do cosset their husbands. Give the gentleman the top hand in business, and so forth. Men do have their pride, you know.'

'But there is more to it,' her mistress said bitterly. 'You see, he has – betrayed me with another woman.'

With great effort Peg kept her face pleasant and pliant. 'Who?'

'I think I know, Peg. It is who I suspected from the first.'

She knew? What did she know? Well there was that incident with the black hair. 'Mrs Harper you mean? Why, the arrant slut,' she answered hotly. Then more smoothly, 'Yet who is she but an old habit. That is just his bachelor ways, mistress. A handsome fellow like him needs time to settle to married life. Why is it he goes to the George? For companionship, warmth, good brandy, and food. Why not make him a comfortable home here?'

Her mistress's lips pressed mean and tight. 'Why should I waste money on all that?'

Because money makes the pot boil, madam, she thought privately. Outwardly she looked most sympathetically at her mistress. 'What is money compared to keeping your husband? You got off on the wrong footing; that is all. What is there to lose in trying again?'

Her mistress blinked and gave a brave smile. 'You mean I should try to please him, and not myself? I know he finds the Hall oppressive.'

'Now take that dining room. It will always be wretched. Why not move to the Oak Room? It needs only a new fireplace, and work to the chimney. The windows look over the park.'

Her mistress frowned. 'That room is too imposing. And the carpet is in tatters.'

'Get a new one,' she answered pleasantly. 'And the room next to it would make a better drawing room. You might furnish it in style. Cosset your husband.'

Her mistress was still frowning, but something was shifting behind her expression. 'I did have hopes, when I first married, that I might rise to such elegance.'

'Mrs Croxon, nothing is too grand for you. You are the lady now, the lady of Delafosse Hall. I'll have a go at such dishes as they serve at the George. You wouldn't be the first wife to entice her husband through his stomach. The George's beef pudding, I know he likes that, and the best brandy wine from York. And as for the house, I'll get the cleaning women to clear the path, while you hire the trades-men and order the furniture.'

She clamped her mouth shut tight. She had that many notions it was hard to keep them all stoppered up inside her head.

'Perhaps I could. Only—' Lord no, Mrs Croxon's eyes were brim-ming again. She picked up a mirror and grimaced at her own reflec-tion. 'What of me? I cannot send for a pattern book to refurbish myself. It is better I leave.'

Peg firmly removed the mirror. 'Some say I have an eye for such beautification. I could transform you into such a vision that Mr Croxon could not resist you.'

'Nonsense.' She tutted and shook her head, but there was a twitch at the corners of her mouth. Ah, so this was the tender spot. If her mistress could only believe she was worthy of the master, much would be achieved, not least the loosening of her purse.

'I'll wash your hair today. Why not let me pin it in a new style?'

In ten minutes Peg had returned with a bundle of stuff. She washed her mistress's rat-tails at the stand, and then tucked her back into freshly laundered sheets. Enticing pattern books and journals lay across the coverlet. To Peg's satisfaction, her mistress began to leaf through *The Lady's Magazine*.

'Your hair has a natural wave.' Peg snipped at the ends with the scissors from her chatelaine, curling them into charming spirals. 'Would you care for this style?' She held up an illustration of the 'Grecian Manner', and deftly wound a bandeau of blue ribbon around her mistress's crown and temple. When Mrs Croxon lifted the mirror, her face softened. She turned her head from left to right, admiring her reflection.

'Now see that ribbon. That is the colour you must have for your new gowns. Forget-me-not, and that pistachio colour, they are all the fashion. Forget those puces and daffodils.' Mrs Croxon had begun to leaf through *Mr Fanshawe's Repository of Fashion*, which Peg had obtained for her own entertainment. It was brim full of the spankingest things. She pointed to a simple walking dress with a drawstring waist and deep lace. 'Now that is the style for you.'

'Do you think so? I do like that.'

'Mrs Gillies the seamstress has got in the very muslin for it. Shall I ask her to call?'

Her mistress nodded.

'Now mistress, what of your skin? A daily dose of Virgin's Milk to calm your complexion?'

'Yes, yes.' She was stroking the best pictures with her fingertips as if she might raise them from the paper. On the page was a picture of twirly glassware, a vast dining table, a collection of plate in all the modern shapes. Oh, Peg thought, are not new things the most handsome? When would she get her fingers in her mistress's purse?

'Ah, here are Mr Fanshawe's terms. Peg, wait here, I shall fetch my writing box. I believe a little extravagance will do me no harm.'

Peg stood abruptly. 'I shall fetch it. You must stay in bed.'

'No, no, Peg. You wait here.' The damned woman rose from her bed, refusing to be told. Peg had to stand back as her mistress pulled on a wrapper and slippers and trotted off to the landing. Stealthily, she followed her, and heard her climbing up to the attic. Ah, so the box was up there with her painting stuff, after all.

A few minutes later she returned with the box and opened the lid with a flourish. As for the key, that was nowhere to be seen.

Peg glimpsed the contents: a heap of her mistress's letters – and mighty interesting letters they looked too, both from her bank and that notary Mr Tully who supplied her with funds. Mrs Croxon directed her to top up the ink pot. No doubt there would soon be plenty of new suppliers to come to terms with.

ॐ

Two days later, when Peg had given the mistress a glass of port wine laced with a little Hystericon and Mrs Croxon was fast asleep, Peg climbed up to her mistress's studio and read the letter where it lay quite openly on the table:

Dear Mrs Croxon,

I thank you for your recent communication and pray this letter finds you and your husband in good health and spirits. Regarding your request, if I might be permitted an opinion, I am somewhat surprised at a further application for funds being made so quickly. Land values are volatile at present, madam, and though such a useful acreage as Whitelow is now at a premium, such circumstances may always change.

Peg hissed through her teeth. What business was it of his, the old skin-flint? You would have thought it was his own damned chink. Then she caught sight of the final sentence and felt unbridled pleasure.

However, as your instructions are most lucidly communicated, I enclose a letter of credit to the sum of £1000 to be drawn on your account at Hoare's Bank.

Your obedient servant,
Edward Tully Esquire

Once the money was secured, her mistress was bolder, excited, even giddy. A new regime began. Each morning she and her mistress planned their campaign. Peg wrote down everything that must be ordered or purchased. Within a week Mrs Croxon's first new costume was delivered – a blue gown and velvet spencer jacket that greatly flattered her, just as Peg knew it would. Immediately she ordered further ensembles of the same style in purple, along with ribbons, wide-brimmed hats, strings of jet beads, kid gloves, under-garments, and shoes. Whenever a parcel arrived Mrs Croxon ripped it open as if it were Christmas. Admittedly her spirits still sank at the slightest setback, but Peg took it upon herself to raise them with saucy jests. 'Oh, the master will never resist you in that lace chemise,' she teased, 'for it's as thin as nothing at all.' Her mistress turned flame-red at that, but she was careful not to tease too hard, especially not close to that most sensitive spot: the Croxons' bedroom arrangements.

Her only vexation was that the writing box had disappeared again. Mrs Croxon had a knack of keeping it close; even when she fetched it down to her chamber; she kept it constantly locked with a hidden key. Peg made a rapid, but futile search of the painting room: under papers, in the cabinet, behind her mistress's trunk. She was determined to find that box.

Next, the mistress's attention turned to the Hall. While the master was away in Manchester, she engaged a Mr Delahunty as architect, who persuaded her to improve all four of the vast antique reception rooms at once. Mrs Croxon rose from her sickbed and threw her heart into the plans, making sketches of how they might be refashioned, cutting out pictures, pasting them on boards. To make purchases more easily, she bought herself a pony cart that she could drive herself, whenever the master used the carriage. Off she went, bowling along down the drive, handling the reins and the pony's moods in a surprisingly able manner. An impressive collec-tion of room plans quickly gathered in the old library; elegant drawings that promised the entire transformation of those ponderous suites. Peg studied them and thought them simply grand. 'Mr Croxon will be mightily impressed,' she told her mistress. 'Any man would be brim full of gratitude for a wife who gave him all of this.'

❧

One wintry afternoon they both awaited Michael's return from a three nights' stay in Manchester. 'We'll have beef pudding all in the George style,' Peg announced, not caring to mention that, as even Nan could not make it, she had ordered it to be delivered cooked from the inn, and hang the expense. She herself made the most excellent apple pie from *Mother Eve's Secrets*, licking fingers sweet with muscovado and cinnamon. Still, she could not prevent Mrs Croxon's flusteriness from spreading like a contagion, so that even Peg's systems faltered. When she dropped a dish of her mistress's favourite almonds in the muck of the yard she carelessly gathered them up again. What did she care if Mrs Croxon ate a peck of dirt like common folk? In the kitchen, she struggled to reheat the vast beef pudding as the day's post lay unopened in her apron. She told herself there would be plenty of time to catch up once dinner had accomplished its purpose.

When the master at last made an appearance, Peg was hovering on the landing, polishing the glassware. Bathed and changed, he sauntered into the old library, brandy glass in hand.

'What on earth are all these?' she heard him ask his wife through the half-open door. Mrs Croxon murmured something in her soft voice.

Their conversation dropped to a level too low to comprehend, but there was harmony to their speech. She heard him say, '— remarkable, Grace.' Then a little later, 'Well, I could eat a horse. Do I hear dinner being served?'

Both of the Croxons admired her feast. A tureen of Nan's hare soup sent up a savoury steam, and around it was laid roasted pheasant and buttered cabbage. At the centre of the table was the buttery pudding, packed drum-tight with beef and kidney. Even the mistress ate and drank bravely, while the master pounced upon his food. Yet more dishes arrived for the second course: the master's favourite, her own hunting pudding of fruit and brandy, a bread-crumbed ham, the apple pie and syllabub, nuts and candied fruits. Outside, the rain needled the windows in stormy waves.

'How is the kitchen fire tonight, Mrs Blissett?' Michael asked.

'Gone out completely in this rain, sir. I was lucky to get dinner finished.'

Peg lit more candles, for the master had made no move away from his usual Usquebaugh, distilled with her own provocative additions.

He drank it leaning back, hog-pink and sated. The mistress sat as stiff as pewter, playing with the fruit on her plate.

Leaving the door ajar, Peg bustled out onto the landing and made pretence of being busy at a sideboard. She heard the glug of another glass of Usquebaugh being poured. She listened to them; knowing this feeling well, when a carefully-laid racket came to ripeness. Pride was in it, but there was scorn too. Gulls, bleaters, flats: whatever you called them, they were sugarpaste figurines performing on a glass stage. Mrs Croxon had shown a peck of spirit, but all it needed was a flick of her husband's little finger for her to melt like sugar in the rain. Hearing nothing, she returned to the half-open door and hid just behind it.

A chair was shoved back and footsteps marched towards her across the dining room. Peg sprang away like a cat from a bonfire. No one emerged. Instead, the door was banged violently shut in her face. What was this, a private meeting? Someone had denied her the satisfaction of hearing her plan ripen to fruition.

17
Dealfosse Hall

November 1792

~ To Make a Hedgebog ~

Take two pounds of blanched almonds, beat them well in a mortar, with a little canary wine and orange-flower water, to keep them from oiling. Make them into a stiff paste, then beat in the yolks of twelve eggs, put to it a pint of cream sweetened with sugar, put in a half pound of sweet butter melted, set it on a slow fire, and keep it constantly stirring, till it is stiff enough to be made in the form of a hedgehog. Stick it full of blanched almonds, arranged like bristles and make two eyes of currants. Pour about it a custard and let it stand till it is cold, and serve it up. It makes a pretty neat dish in the middle of a table for supper.

Mother Eve's Secrets

Michael had drunk a great deal from the green bottle, but had not fallen into his usual after-dinner fug. He glanced at me often, rose to slam the door, and returned to his chair to make stabbing motions with his fork at the scraps on his plate.

'Your plans for the Hall,' he said at last in a low husky voice, 'are very remarkable.' He looked up at me then through a curl of falling hair, and I knew from his expression that something was wrong. 'The trouble is, I cannot live here.'

'What do you mean?' I poured myself another glass of wine, filled with foreboding.

He sighed and twisted painfully in his chair. I tried to see past the pink flush of his skin, and wondered if Michael might be ill, not in body, but of some agony of mind.

'I hate it here. You know I do.'

'Even once it is refurbished?'

'I am sorry, Grace. After all your endeavours.' His sad blue eyes met mine with unfamiliar candour. I believe he truly was sorry: he acknowledged my hours of industry to prepare the plans; my passion to improve our home. 'The bones of the place will always remain the same.'

He stood then, and I stiffened, expecting him to leave me and retire. Instead, he stumbled towards me and slumped sideways on an empty chair. His knees touched mine; he was directly facing me.

'What do you want me to do?' I asked gently.

He was maudlin drunk, but his usual artifice had vanished. He stared into space. 'I don't know. I don't know what we can do.' I had seen Michael despondent before, but then he had been petulant, even affected. Tonight he was neither.

His hand slid onto mine, hot and heavy. 'I am tired of not knowing what to do.' Still hunched and staring at the floor, he mumbled, 'Hold me, Grace.'

I was astonished, even suspicious, but he crumpled towards me, overwhelmingly needful and solid. Clumsily, I put my arms around his neck and rocked him. He buried his head on my shoulder; I stroked his springy hair. For a long while we stayed like that, myself bewildered, Michael thinking I knew not what.

With sighing breaths he moved his face against my neck. The wet touch of his lips against my throat shot a dart of pleasure through my body. Kisses began, fast and light, up my throat towards my mouth. 'Grace,' he mumbled, his large hands pulling me closer to him. Looking down at his face I saw smudged tears around his closed eyes. Part of me revelled in Michael's advances. Yet it was not how I wanted our marriage to be celebrated – with Michael pursuing drunken oblivion in my arms. I pulled away, though his hands still ran up and down my back, pulling me into the shelter of his body.

'No. Not like this.'

He grasped my waist and our mouths met, his tongue pushing past my lips, between my teeth. I felt as though a delicate film or bubble was about to burst, releasing I knew not what beauty or terror.

I struggled, pushed him away, then kissed him quickly, a dry peck on the cheek, as he had once kissed me in the carriage after the fair. He looked up at me, blearily.

'Goodnight, Michael.' I pulled away. His head fell forward onto the table, and so I left him, as drunk as a lord.

If he had not been so intoxicated I would have gone to him that night, for it was impossible to sleep. Listening to the creaks and crackings of the house, I forgot Old Dorcas and thought instead of

Michael's wet tongue and the rhythmic tug of his hands. At three o'clock I got up and reluctantly took a dose of Dr Sampson's Mixture. Thereafter a sticky, treaclish sleep overcame me, broken by lurid, impure dreams.

It was from one of these dreams that a great commotion woke me: of many footsteps running, the banging of doors and feminine cries of alarm. I jumped out of bed and, though my head was giddy from my medicine, I pulled a shawl about myself, lit a candle at the embers of my fire, and went off to investigate. The sound of anxious voices drew me to the Long Gallery, where Peg and the other kitchen servants stood at the open door to the lieutenant's room.

'What is all this?' I demanded.

Peg had taken charge and called me over. 'Look, mistress.' She had hesitated at the threshold because her light twinkled on an extraordinary scene; of broken glass and splintered wood cast all around the room. Maybe it was the effect of the drug, but the sight was scarcely credible.

'What has happened? Has there been an intruder?'

'I cannot say, Mrs Croxon.'

'Mistress,' started up Nan. 'Old Dorcas. She's done it; she's still in a fury at young Mr Ashe. Look at what she's done.' Nan lifted a bony finger towards what remained of Moncrieff's portrait. I physically shrank back from what I saw – a monstrous mutilated face staring down from the wall. Then I understood that someone – or something – had slashed at the canvas, tearing at the man's eyes, hacking into his face.

I took a step back. It was horrible. 'Where's the master?' I asked Peg.

'Out, mistress.' Then in a low voice, murmured only to me. 'I believe he got himself down to the George, where he's no doubt sleeping it off.'

Nan and the other women were gossiping in a little knot. It was all of 'Old Dorcas' and how she couldn't sleep easy. 'Give me your lamp, Peg, I'm going inside.'

'Shall we not wait until morning?'

I shook my head. 'I want to see if there is a window open or some other means of escape. It has to be the work of an intruder. I won't have this superstitious nonsense whipping everyone up.'

'You cannot catch a phantom,' Nan piped up, and I was obliged to tell her to be quiet.

Peg was good enough to accompany me through the door, and so we picked our way through the debris by flickering candlelight. The curiosities were thrown about as if by a whirlwind – fossils, armour, ancient books, tossed higgledy-piggledy on the floor. It was the lieutenant's mementos that had suffered most: his medals cast into the empty grate, his army citation ripped into spiteful shreds. The sword, I noticed, was broken in two. But it was the portrait that disturbed me most; its desecration of the lieutenant's face was the work of a bedlamite, committed in a frenzy.

I checked the windows, but they were all secure and gave no signs of having been opened.

'What do you think?' I asked Peg, out of the others' hearing.

She was in her night shift, her red hair swinging in a plait to her waist. 'I wouldn't generally give credit to Nan, but isn't this more than a human might perform? This is a strange old place, mistress. I often hear steps in the night, but I don't like to say.'

It was tempting to agree with her and give ourselves a dose of the jitters. But I felt it my responsibility as the mistress of the house to defend reason against hocus pocus.

I returned to the Long Gallery and addressed my little band. 'There is nothing we can do now, in the darkness. It appears the intruder—'

'Mistress, it in't an intruder—' Nan started up.

'Nan. All of this needs to be looked at in clear rational daylight. Frightening ourselves in the cold like this will only give us agues. I suggest we all return to bed and try to get some sleep.'

Nan, Joan and Bess looked sceptical at this, but I was rewarded by an approving smile from the widowed charwoman. Yet I was unnerved, as I returned to my own chamber, forced to wonder if a malevolent being – human or spirit – wandered the Hall that night.

When Peg shook my arm the sun was bright at the window. 'Mrs Croxon, there's a woman asking after you downstairs. She says she's Mrs Greenbeck.'

I sat up in my bed, my head thick from only a little sleep and those few hours induced by a sedative. At once I recalled the destruction of Moncrieff's room, and also Michael's unsettling behaviour after dinner. And now Anne had arrived, without so much as a note to warn me.

'It can't be. She is not due for another week.' I touched my pounding temples.

'She is pressing to see you, else I wouldn't have bothered coming up.'

'Give her refreshments. I need half an hour.'

'So she will be staying?'

'Of course she is staying. Make up the white chamber.' As she left I asked, 'Is the master up yet?'

'He isn't back from the George yet.'

'It's maybe just as well, Peg.' We shared a friendly glance, both of us relieved.

�

My first moment with Anne dissolved all my apprehensions. At once she embraced me, pressing her soft cheek against mine. 'Oh, Grace, I am so happy to see you.' Then she pulled back, and looked at me very steadfastly with her round brown eyes. 'You have been unwell, dear?'

'It is only that – I became overwrought and had a fall. But I am mending now, especially at the sight of you.' I laughed a little as I said this. Her dear face, so bright and kind, was a cheering sight; even her weather-worn travelling costume and battered black

215

bonnet delighted me. I had a fleeting idea that Peg might not have been much impressed by such a dowdy, but that, too, seemed laughable now. Even the surprises of the night were slight events, all to be managed with calm and good sense.

Anne sat down but did not let go of my hand as she asked in a hushed tone, 'I wondered if . . . your illness heralds happy news?'

'No. Not at all.' She looked sorry at that, and squeezed my hand. 'You will not wait long, I am sure of it.'

To change the conversation's direction I asked with some trepidation, 'So what is this bad news you wrote of, Anne, which may affect our friendship?'

She gathered herself with some effort. 'First we must talk of your father. Has Michael told you yet?'

I shook my head, at a loss.

'He must want me to tell you. Grace, prepare yourself to be strong. Your father passed to God two weeks ago. I am afraid he died after an altercation in the street. For some time he, well – you know how he became excited, at times, about his beliefs?'

I nodded, suddenly drained and horribly surprised. Anne handed me her handkerchief and I wept in silence. My poor father, an old warrior in a world of imaginary foes, had truly been his own worst enemy. 'He had been drinking?' I asked weakly. 'Don't say he was ranting about politics?'

'I am afraid so. A group of foolish youths baited him – since the King of France was overthrown, feelings run high in Greaves against the radical cause. Even the Brabantist Meeting Hall has been attacked. In your father's case, the coroner said there was no actual wound, but we all believe his heart was strained. He collapsed in Palatine House. Shortly afterwards he died in the small hours, with Mrs Cooper, the nurse, tending to him. Of course I wrote to you at once, but Michael advised you were not to be told just yet, being laid up by an accident yourself. I am very sorry, Grace, but he was buried at St Stephen's a week ago.'

I bowed my head, lamenting all the good things about my father:

his talent, his raw faith, his hopes for the rights of the common people. 'I am glad he felt no pain,' I said.

Anne and Jacob had arranged his few affairs under Michael's direction. Palatine House was now the property of my father-in-law and there was little else to do. She had packed up all his prints for me, for which I was most grateful. Then she tactfully left me, and I mourned my father alone, in my own way; resurrecting happier days when I had visited his print shop as a child, and the high days and holidays we had shared with my mother.

That evening I could not face dinner with Michael and Anne. Michael came up to see me, but our conversation was not friendly. I was aggrieved at his not telling me about my father and told him so. As for the ransacking of the lieutenant's room, he was irritatingly stoical. 'All I can do is see that the place is padlocked up for good. That way, if anyone did climb in from the outside, they cannot gain access to the house. As for Moncrieff's belongings, I truly don't give a damn.'

After he had left, I continued to torment myself about whether to tell Anne the true reason why I could not be with child, the dalliance I had witnessed, and Michael's brazen requests for money. I heard Michael's voice from below, and cringed to think of him conversing with Anne. He had never been respectful towards her, for he held all religion entirely in contempt, and such a modest woman as Anne had no place in his world. When Peg brought me some plain soup for supper, she also insisted I took another dose of Dr Sampson's draught, so I might at least face the next day with more fortitude. Of the rest of that night I had only a foggy memory; of Anne wishing me goodnight, stroking my hair and saying a few prayerful words over me. After that my sleep was blessed and calm.

Michael again left the house early, so it was with welcome ease that Anne and I retreated to the drawing room after breakfast. There was a good fire, and I huddled close to it, my new cashmere shawl draped around my chemisette, my sketchbook on my knee. It was then I learned Anne's other news. Jacob had been appointed to a position as assistant chaplain. 'It is a good position,' she said. 'But I am sorry to say we are going overseas. To New South Wales.'

'Not to the convict colony at Botany Bay?' It was beyond my imagining. All I knew of the place was the bold experiment to set up a colony for criminals, transporting them as great a distance as possible from the civilised world.

'I am afraid so. We leave in one month, for that very place. I have so little time to prepare for the voyage. Grace, I wonder if I'm fit for such a great trial.'

She uttered this with such an attempt at courage that my heart flew out to her.

'You are, I know it.'

She laid her hand gently on her stomach. 'And I do have happier news. I have the good fortune to be blessed with a child, though God forgive me, the timing is not so good. And I have missed my dear friend and our confidences.'

'Oh, Anne.'

'I would have wished you might be godmother to my child. But now I face the prospect of being delivered somewhere far out on the wild ocean.'

I was appalled. 'Can you not change Jacob's mind?'

'He is quite ferocious in his zeal. You know how he speaks, secretly, in our own parlour? He believes Europe is doomed. He finds these modern times disappointing: the evil news from France; the unleashing of such wickedness, these accounts of people being butchered in the streets. It should not matter if they are lords or beggars – they are men and women, Grace. And all hopes for reform are now set back here in Britain, for the government will not hear of progress. Jacob has always prayed for a better life for the poor and wretched. He speaks of the colony as a new Eden, a chance to establish God's kingdom on untainted soil.'

'But are these not the most dangerous of criminals? Jacob is condemning you and your child to live amongst them.'

'Jacob says it is a new land, free of class and distinction. It will serve them well.'

Jacob be hanged, I thought. 'Yes – but what is your opinion?'

'I willingly made my vows to obey him,' she said, with a tight little shake of her head. 'I am learning the price of that now.'

We talked on a little, of Greaves, of my plans for the Hall, of my father and his glory days. Soon, though, Anne returned to her departure from England. I understood she was frightened, and felt herself entirely ill-prepared for such a tumultuous change.

As we talked, I made a portrait of her in pencil, as she sat very upright by the fireside in a drab wolsey gown, stitching an infant's robe with an ever-dipping needle. I surmised that her pride in her needle no doubt hid the sorrier truth that a seamstress's services were beyond her means. A new furrow of worry had formed between her eyes; and at intervals she adjusted a pair of ugly metal-rimmed spectacles to check the progress of her stitches.

She looked up and smiled. 'It would please me greatly if you could make a copy of your picture of me. A memento of my last days in England.'

'You should see it first,' I said, with a smile. 'I am not convinced I have caught your expression.'

'You mean I do not look so well, I suppose. That must be true, Grace, for I am under a dreadful strain. As for you, I should say illness suits you, if that does not sound perverse. You are paler, more delicate in some way.' She studied me for a moment with her steady bright eyes. 'In fact, I should say you look beautiful.'

I laughed. 'Don't be ridiculous. Peg has taught me to curl my hair, that is all. And I am pale from being in bed too long.'

'Peg? Is she that rather uppish servant of yours?'

'Yes, Peg is my housekeeper.'

Anne worked on for a few minutes, then said, 'Michael is a very agreeable man.'

I put down my pencil. 'You think so? You do not know him.'

'I believe he is.' Her needle halted. 'If there have been misunderstandings between you it scarcely surprises me, considering how little you were acquainted when you married. I will not say I told you so – but I have just done so, haven't I?'

I could not meet her eye, and stared into my lap, at the half-finished sketch.

'Maybe he has created such an impression to fool you.'

'You are low from your illness. At such times everything can seem darker than its true colour. I suppose you seek proof of his regard?'

'That would be welcome.'

'I have more news,' Anne went on. 'This next fortnight Jacob will be engaged with the clerical society at Bradford. There is so much for him to learn: medicine, mathematics, surveying and suchlike. So he has agreed I might go to York tomorrow, to equip myself for the voyage. Now dear, before you look so cast down, I have a notion.' Her face lit bright with anticipation. 'Come with me, Grace. I have spoken to Michael and he agrees it will revive your spirits to be amongst crowds and life and bustle. What do you say?'

'Michael has agreed?' I was astonished.

'Yes, naturally he has. I understand you are still weak, but listen – it is all arranged. We will take your carriage and lodge in comfortable rooms. You can rest as often as you need to. I know you have always wanted to see the great Minster and the ancient city. What do you say? Please, Grace. It will make our parting so much easier if we share my last precious weeks.'

I frowned, trying to comprehend my husband's mazy thinking. A faint echo started up in my mind: that he wanted me out of his way.

'What do you say? You cannot imagine how much I need you beside me.'

I could not refuse. Indeed, a journey to York sounded better suited to restore me than a hundred doctors' potions.

*   *   *

That evening, as I supervised the packing of my trunk, I at once detected Peg's opposition to my leaving. From the first, Anne's arrival had disrupted her, but now her departure with me disgruntled her even more. I found it rather comical, that Peg should be jealous of my friend – for that was how I interpreted her mood.

'How long will you be away, mistress?' she asked in a near wail of anguish, as I watched her pack my new costumes in silk bags.

'Not so very long. Mrs Greenbeck is leaving the country, so it would be churlish to deny her my company. Yes, the purple silk too. I may even get the chance to wear it in York.'

'Where is it she's travelling off to?' Peg stroked my new gown as if she might never see it again.

'Don't forget the jet beads with that.' I hesitated, wondering why I should give an account of Anne's troubles to a servant. That word Anne had used to describe Peg – 'uppish' – had worked its way into my mind like an irritating splinter. 'She is not yet sure where her husband will be posted,' I yawned. 'Come up here and finish packing after dinner. Leave me now.'

We had a last, grand dinner with Anne, at which I watched with astonishment as my husband behaved tolerably well. Peg's dishes were remarkably good: an old-fashioned pulpatoon of pigeon, roast pork in breadcrumbs, and duck with peas. Anne had never before tasted such a genteel dish as Peg's dessert in the shape of a hedgehog, with slivers of almonds bristling over it like spines. Michael watched us devour it in its pool of custard, and announced that just twenty-four hours in Anne's company was certainly restoring me. When Anne and I rose for the drawing room he also stood, approached me, and chastely kissed my lips. I could see Anne smiling benignly behind his shoulder. What a charlatan he was. Nonetheless, to my alarm, another unwanted jolt ran through my body as his lips brushed mine. Remembering his mouth murmuring against my throat, unwelcome warmth spread over my face. Michael, it seemed, always possessed the power to agitate me. I said my goodnights and followed Anne upstairs, but after checking from the landing that Peg was busy in my chamber, I crept quietly back down to the kitchen.

What did he hope to do while I was so conveniently absent? The answer, that haunted me, was that he would be free to meet his lover. Peg had assured me she knew nothing of her predecessor, but Nan, on the other hand, had met the woman – and might know if she still tarried in Earlby.

I found the poor creature asleep, curled up and shrunken in a corner of the scullery. I was dismayed to find a change in her since our arrival; her arms were twig-thin and scored with marks on the papery skin. I touched her shoulder and she started up, wild-eyed. 'I were only resting me legs,' she whimpered. 'While I kept an eye on't beef.' She pointed at a great pot of savoury meat.

'Sit down again, Nan. At your age it is natural to be weary.' She sat, with a touching wince as her old bones pained her. I joined her, noticing how chilly it was in her underground quarters.

'I wonder, Nan, have you any news of Mrs Harper, the former housekeeper? I have heard she may be about the town?'

'Mrs Harper? Never heard nowt since she scarpered, mistress. Gone away she 'as, like I told you and the master.'

This was disappointing. 'Can you cast your mind back to when you last saw her?'

She screwed up her wrinkled face. 'Last saw 'er? That were before you come 'ere, mistress. 'Bout a week before you come.'

'Where was that?'

'I seen her over in the kitchen. Down by't fireplace. I were clearing up here in't scullery and they were in there, laughing and carousing.'

'Who?' My mouth was dry. Surely Michael had not openly caroused with our housekeeper in front of Nan?

'Her and her woman friend. Drinking they were. I told you an' t'master that. They had a bottle between 'em.'

'Who was this friend? Did you learn her name?'

'No, I never learned it. Some gin-biber from the inn I reckon. I scarce saw her, she wore a bonnet low. They was warming themselves by the fire.'

'And what happened next?'

'Nowt. That were it. I never had sight nor sound of Mrs Harper again. All her stuff went with her. Left her bed unmade too, the dirty slattern.'

'Yes – one of her long black hairs still lay between the sheets when I arrived.'

'One of whose hairs?'

'Mrs Harper's.'

Nan fixed me with milky eyes. 'You got that all arsey-varsey, mistress, if you don't mind me saying so. Mrs Harper were flaxen, going to grey. A faded sort of body she were.'

This took a moment for me to absorb. 'So – her friend? Have you ever seen her again, Nan?'

'Never, mistress. I reckon she went off with Mrs Harper on some sort o' brazen spree.'

I thanked Nan and gave her five shillings for a new costume, which she blessed me for, hiding the coins in her work-stained bodice. I told her of a good market woman who would supply warm kersey, then asked her how she had hurt her arms.

'I banged 'em. And sometimes I catch 'em on't fire, mistress.'

'Well, be more careful, won't you?'

Only then did I notice Peg, standing silent and still on the stairs.

'Peg, what are you waiting there for?'

'I just this second came looking for you. Should I cord your trunk yet, mistress?'

'Yes, yes. There won't be time in the morning. And look at Nan's ragged costume – I'm ashamed she's in my employment. She needs warmer clothes this winter. And balm on those scalds.'

Nan had jumped up and was tending the vat of meat by the time Peg reached us.

'Don't I know it, mistress. I've told Nan to wrap up a dozen times, but she scarce remembers what I tell her, the poor half-cracked thing.'

I left them then, all the time struggling to remember the course of my conversation with Nan. Surely my giving Nan the money and directions for a new costume had taken up a good long spell after my enquiries about Mrs Harper?

18
York

November 1792

~ *Citrus Shrub* ~

Pour two quarts of brandy into a large bottle and put into it the juice of five lemons, and the peels of two, and half a nutmeg. Stop it up and let it stand three days, after which add to it three pints of white wine; a pound and a half of sugar; mix it, strain it twice through a muslin bag, and then bottle it up.

A very fine cordial as served at the York Assembly Room

Before I set out for York I sought Michael in his room. He was up, but still knotting his neck cloth in front of his mirror. He turned to me with a smile, dressed only in breeches and billowing shirt.

'Is it true you want me to go?' I asked, so unaccustomed to seeing him in a state of half-undress I had to look away from the sight of him.

'Yes. You should take the chance while you have it.' He reached for his waistcoat and pulled it on.

'Michael. You never told me what was troubling you?'

He avoided my eyes, busying himself with a clothes brush. 'It is only the business. I didn't foresee all these difficulties.' He came over to me then, and put his hands on my shoulders. 'Enjoy yourself. I wish I could come with you.' He kissed me farewell on the mouth, with what appeared to be genuine regret. 'Write to me, Grace,' he said, his eyes meeting mine with a plaintive smile as he adjusted the clasp of my cloak.

But within the hour Michael was forgotten in a mood of extraordinary freedom, for Anne's delight at not taking the public wagon proved contagious. Yet there was something more, for as the carriage threaded its way beneath the dripping foliage of the drive, a backwards glance at Delafosse Hall confirmed the rightness of my decision. The building itself absorbed a solid darkness, a colour I should have painted midnight green; its cloak of leaves saturated with many weeks' rainfall. I turned back to Anne's eager face and was glad to talk of such mundane matters as the pots and pans she must buy. 'All my life must be packed in one trunk,' she said, 'and I must pray that even that survives the voyage. Who knows when, or even if – I will return?'

'You will, I know it,' I said brightly. 'And, in the meantime, we must promise to be good correspondents.' I prattled about the commissions I also hoped to secure in York: china and furnishings and fabrics. 'You must think me very self-indulgent,' I said at last.

'No, not at all. It does me good to see you cheerful. And every impression I receive over the next few days will form a store of memories in my future life. You deserve a fine home.'

'Well, this refurbishment is also Peg's notion, in a way. I had not the heart to make a beginning, but she coaxed me to take an interest.'

There was a lengthy silence as Anne looked out on the rainy countryside.

'You don't like her?'

Her face betrayed a wince of discomfort. 'Oh, it is not that, Grace. She seems capable, extremely capable, when she wishes. It is just that – when I first called, I detected an insolence to her character that I did not care for.'

'In her position she cannot be too bending,' I suggested. 'I find her a great support.' Anne continued perusing the landscape, so I asked, 'When you first called, did she offend you, Anne?'

She raised her chin at that. 'Offend is too strong a term. But why did you not receive my letter giving notice of my arrival? I posted it four days ago. I questioned your woman, and she was not helpful, Grace. If a letter is lost, one may expect sympathy, not stony-faced disbelief.'

'I apologise on her behalf.'

'No, I will not accept it. It is your servant who must treat guests with greater civility. Now I hope you don't mind, but my stomach quails. Might we take a little food?'

I lifted the spotted cloth from the basket, and found inside a wine-roasted gammon, pigeon pie, tarts, and buttered spice breads. We dined in style, feeling like a pair of queens.

'Very well, your Peg is forgiven,' Anne joked, as she devoured a slice of crisp and fragrant pear tart.

Anne fell asleep at once, but though I tried to doze, I had

forgotten to pick up Dr Sampson's medicine and my mind began to operate at a faster speed. Anne's letter might easily have been lost on its route, but why was this the first I had heard of it? There was no doubt in my mind that I would have to speak to Peg on my return. Tiny matters had concerned me these last few weeks, nothing that alone would have merited a rebuke, but taken all together I believed Peg was growing complacent. Not in cooking, that was true, nor even in managing the house. Indeed, she was a faultless servant. Instead there were tiny pinpricks of memories, half-forgotten incidents that left me wondering if she presumed too far on my friendship, and took too great an interest in my personal tastes.

One incident had occurred only a week earlier. Coming to my chamber I had spied Peg through the half-open door, standing at the pier glass with my blue silk hugged tightly to her own breast. I was about to rebuke her, but was struck by something pitiable about her. She stood entranced in a dream, twirling the hem and murmuring as she postured in the mirror. The sad fact was that the dress cost more than twice her year's salary. She would never, herself, own such an item. So I had tiptoed away, loath to shame her. A few days later I gave her five shillings as allowance for new clothes. She appeared grateful, but no new costume appeared. The nub of it was, that I had spoiled her by letting her speak to me as an equal.

Then, sitting with my eyes closed, another remembrance struck me. As the weeks had passed, Earlby society still had not called on me. Michael breezed about the place, forever riding off to hunts and gentlemen's jaunts. A suspicion that had fretted me when I was ill returned: had Dr Sampson spread a rumour that I was difficult, or foolishly nervous? Or after I had taken Peg from her, had our bitter neighbour, Sybilla Claybourn, warned our neighbours not to call on me?

It must have been the wine that lulled me into a long refreshing sleep, for when I woke, the ancient city of York rose in the distance, like a great stone island in an ocean of green pasture. The road grew busy with every sort of cart, carriage, and gilded coach, whilst in the dirt below, ragged folk tramped along with bundles on their backs. 'Look,' I called, as we halted behind a lumbering wagon. Together Anne and I pulled down our carriage glass and drank in the view. The city lying before us had a quaint and medieval appearance, studded with church spires and towers and high circling walls. Over all loomed the might of the Minster Cathedral, towering above a labyrinth of gabled roofs.

We passed straggling houses, a windmill, an ancient convent, and then passed into the narrow throat of the city through a barbican of crumbling stone. Inside stood brick residences of the modern sort, with fanlights and sash windows; but jumbled about these were cottages with overhanging storeys, many of them beautifully carved, like ancient churches.

Our lodgings were on a turning from shop-lined Coney Street, above a genteel milliner's. There our landlady, Mrs Palmer, showed us a pair of neat rooms and sent up tea and seed cake on our arrival. Anne and I pulled off our outerwear, looked about ourselves, and both pronounced ourselves entirely satisfied.

I had just begun to unpack when Mrs Palmer knocked and told us a gentleman waited downstairs and gave me his card. 'It is Peter Croxon,' I said with some annoyance. 'Michael's brother. What on earth does he want? Shall I send down that we are resting?'

Anne insisted he should be shown up. Nevertheless I was irked to see his grinning countenance as he sat down before us.

'I was walking down Ousegate when I said to myself, why, there is Michael's carriage. So I followed you here. Well, what a pleasure to see you looking so well, Grace. I can scarcely believe my eyes, when Michael is forever protesting you are too unwell to call upon.'

'I have been ill,' I said firmly, and introduced him at once to Anne. I could see that Peter's charm worked upon her; in no time at all he insisted on accompanying us to a concert the following evening. She is eating from his palm, I told myself inwardly, busying myself about the room.

'I should take a pair of muskets if I were you.' Peter's voice startled me from my chores, and I glanced at Anne's crestfallen face.

'Is that really necessary?' I asked.

'I have a friend at the colony, a marine officer who corresponds with me. If your husband travels away from home, as he is bound to, you must be on guard, Mrs Greenbeck. The felons transported there are of the worst breed – spared the gallows by a hair's breadth. You must protect yourself.'

'Are you sure of your information?' Anne inquired, looking stricken. 'I saw such a beautiful prospect of Botany Bay in *The Lady's Magazine*. And Jacob says we are best protected by our Bibles. Nevertheless . . . does your friend give mention of any other items he wished he had taken with him?'

Peter's affability grew strained. 'Food, Mrs Greenbeck. The government rations are insufficient. You need a good stock of dry stuffs for your first season, and then seeds and tools to grow more. I understand the wheat crop has failed. I will consult his last letter again, and send you word.'

The conversation could not recover its earlier light tone. Soon Peter stood to make his farewells, taking Anne's hand and trying to make a jest of his ominous news. Then, turning to me as I accompanied him to the door, he said, 'It has cheered me no end to find you well, Grace. I should be obliged for a little of your time before you leave, to speak of family matters.'

He again smiled amiably, but seeing a powerful insistence in his eyes, I found myself forced to agree.

The next day was a glorious one, spent wandering in the narrow streets. I found a colourman's shop in nearby Spurriergate, and became spellbound at the array of paints, papers, and parchment. On display were the most remarkable miniatures, and a card left by the artist seeking both commissions and pupils. I left a note with the proprietor, enquiring if I might obtain lessons for a week. Then, together with Anne, I took tea at a bookshop, where my friend ceaselessly examined the shelves. Finally I was able to impose on her and buy a few volumes as gifts: Mr Solander's *Travels Round the World*, which at least gave her a glimpse into unknown territories, and a few essential volumes on medical and domestic matters. As I inspected the engravings for sale, I noticed a very fine classical scene within which was written, *FERREA VIRGA EST, UMBRATILIS MOTUS*. Recognising the Latin motto from the sundial at Delafosse, I asked the proprietor if he knew the meaning.

'"The rod is of iron, the motion of shadow",' he told me obligingly.

'Thank you,' I said with a smile, and returned to the engraving. It was a memento mori, an Italian scene in which the sundial was reminiscent of a tomb. On one side, a pair of young lovers basked idly in sunshine, while on the other they slept in sinister shadow. An ugly representation of Death approached them from behind the ornate tomb. They do not see what pursues them, I mused. But in a few moments I had forgotten it, and was engaged in ordering a small library of ancient and modern books, all bound in Venetian red leather.

That evening, even I could not fault Peter when he called at our lodgings. Like his brother, he always presented a favourable appearance; all buffed up in a smart blue coat, and doffing his hat with a low bow as we met him in the parlour.

'Now do not pretend it is anything but tedious to accompany two old married ladies to a concert,' I teased.

'Grace, if I did not know you better, I should say you were fishing for compliments.'

It was true we had spent a considerable time dressing, for when else would we ever be taken to a famous Assembly? Anne had gratefully borrowed my chestnut silk, and after shortening its hem, looked like a fashion plate. My purple silk had its first outing, with a set of sleek black feathers in my hair from the milliner downstairs.

There are some occasions in any life that will always be recalled in a glow of pleasure, and that night is one of my secret store. The streets of York were crisp; the frost amplifying a dozen church bells ringing the hour. As our carriage queued before Lord Burlington's famous Rooms, dozens of flambeaux flared against the classical portico. Anne pinched my arm to be sure that neither of us was dreaming; and I was sincerely grateful to Peter for indulging her in a manner she would never forget. From all accounts he had a wide acquaintance in the city, even amongst the wealthy and titled, so I was impressed by his courtesy in attending only to Anne and me.

'So, ladies, do you not think it a fine room?' Peter took each of our arms, guiding us into the famed Egyptian Hall. The room was glorious, and I told him so, marvelling at proportions made more exotic by rows of marbled Corinthian columns. Through the crush of people we processed to the benches, admiring the blazing chandeliers, and the great throng of York society. Peter fetched us glasses of Citrus Shrub, and, sipping the cool refreshment, Anne and I looked about. The younger ladies, especially, were a glorious sight in gowns puffed out in the new style, with satin ribbons at their waists, clasped with cameos.

I had never before heard Mozart's 'Idol mio', nor anything sung by so fine a singer as Signora Tirenza, the prima donna from Rome itself. Her astonishing voice transported me to another place of wordless emotion. All my life I had hoped to find that uplifting love that crowns some lucky spirits but evades others, however long they seek it. Would it always escape me? Or should I return home, and try even harder to nurture affection between Michael and myself? Tears filled my eyes. The Signora, so exotic and proud, seemed to possess the secret knowledge of an artist, an adventurer, a lover. I wondered if the refreshment I had taken contained strong spirits, for I was forced secretly to wipe my eyes. To my annoyance, Peter nudged me. 'Who is that fellow staring at us?' he hissed.

I looked through brimming eyes but saw no one.

*   *   *

In the tea room, the Master of Ceremonies bowed to us, and surprised me by uttering my name. A few moments later he returned with a solid-looking fair-haired stranger who addressed me with an open, but anxious expression.

'Grace,' the man said to me, with some hesitation. 'How are you?'

I had not a notion who he was – nor how he might know me. I could only imagine he was the artist from whom I had sought lessons, and at once resolved I should have nothing to do with such a familiar fellow. Agitated by my silence, he bowed again and said, 'My apologies for approaching you thus, with no introduction. But I would be obliged if you would tell me. Are you Grace Moore of Greaves?'

I told him that was the name I had been born to, but at once regretted it, fearing he might be a creditor of my father's. I looked for assistance from Peter and Anne, but they had tactfully withdrawn at some distance.

'You do not remember me, do you? I am John Francis Rawdon.'

'John?' In my surprise I reached out to grasp his arm. 'How is it possible?'

'Chance, I believe.' We both smiled and laughed at once. I studied his features. Yes – now I saw the same eyes, only a little less bright, and a face grown older, but also stronger, in some masculine way. Yes, he was John Francis grown into a broad imposing man.

'I recognised Anne at once, for she has not changed a whit. Then, as you were ever her companion, I studied you in the concert hall; I could not at first believe my eyes. Grace Moore.' He glanced suddenly over to Peter. 'So who is that gentleman?'

'He is Peter Croxon. My – brother-in-law.'

I do not believe I imagined his disappointment. 'Good God, so it is, Peter Croxon. Still the dandy. I should have thought he'd be chasing ladies of fortune, not Anne Dobson. And you are married – to a Croxon? To the older one – Michael was it? How unexpected.'

'And you? When did you come home?' I said this with some gentleness, for I understood at once that fate had not been kind to us. It is my fixed belief that if only we had met before I married, we would certainly have revived our connection. I knew it as surely as I had glimpsed the hope that lit up his whole being when he spoke my name.

He told me very frankly of his unhappiness when first he left Greaves, swiftly followed by an account of his good fortune in working with his uncle, a fine man who taught him his trade. John Francis was now a partner in the cotton business, and also, he hinted, the possessor of considerable wealth. He talked much as he always had; in a kindly, self-mocking manner, but now overlaid with an attractive civility.

'May I enquire after your parents' health?'

I touched the crucifix at my neck, where my mother's hair had just been re-set in jet and rubies. John Francis's hair was darker now than the youthful blond of the lock I'd treasured for so long. I told him briefly of my parents' passing.

'Michael Croxon – and you? I could never have predicted that.' He shook his head in bemusement.

'Why is that?' I asked, expecting to hear my usual fears rehearsed: that Michael was of a superior rank, a man of fashion, a man of extraordinary good looks.

'Oh, he was such a – well, a strange boy. Not that I knew him well, of course, he was sent to some faraway school. To think, their father was once the village carpenter. And you Grace, you were such a kind and sensible person. To be blunt, he was neither. And what talents you had. Do you still paint?'

'I do.' I began to tell him of my earlier misapprehension that he was in fact a painting master. We both laughed easily at my mistake.

Just then, as we talked in complete sympathy, two women set themselves between us, and the elder tapped John's arm with her fan, speaking in a deep, commanding tone. 'John, I should not wish to interrupt such an engaging conversation, but you forget that you promised Alice the quadrille.' He glanced at the younger woman, a slight and childlike creature whose lip trembled visibly. 'Please, Mama,' she coaxed, doing her best to pull her mother away again.

'Oh, yes – Alice.' John rubbed his neck, and made awkward introductions. 'Mrs Fotherly. Miss Alice Fotherly. May I introduce Mrs Croxon, a close acquaintance of mine from Greaves.' We all nodded rather limply at each other.

'I wonder, Mrs Croxon, did you see the announcement in the York Courant?' boomed Mrs Fotherly, as if I might be deaf. 'Mr Rawdon and Miss Alice were this week betrothed. You must be delighted to see your bachelor acquaintance at last approaching the altar.'

I did not risk a glance at John, but congratulated Alice heartily, though my face grew rigid from its artificial smile.

'And where is your own husband?' the mother asked, looking airily about. 'You must collect him. The dances are being called.'

'I am attended by my brother-in-law.' I nodded in Peter's direction, and Mrs Fotherly followed my gaze in a most scrutinising manner. 'My husband is attending to his business.'

'Dear me,' she said. 'I should never allow such negligence from a husband – and certainly not for mere business.'

I would not exchange another word with such an insufferable person. I curtseyed and they returned the same, in frigid silence. Poor John Francis looked stricken as I walked steadily back to where Anne and Peter awaited me.

Only later, alone in my room, did I allow myself to reflect upon my sorrow. For a few extraordinary moments, I had felt such joy at meeting John again, that all the intervening years had vanished. I had even had the ridiculous notion he might have waited all these years to find me. But no, we had both been frail. I had bound myself to Michael, the 'strange boy' who had grown into the man he so aptly judged as lacking both sense and kindness. And poor John Francis had somehow got himself entangled with that carping mother and her offspring. Grace, I rebuked myself, the strong drink has unsettled you. You are married now; it is time to leave these childish notions behind you.

19
York

November 1792

~ Yorkshire Fat Rascals ~

Take one pound of flour and rub into a half pound of butter;
mix in one ounce of moist sugar, a quarter pound cleaned and
dried currants, a little citron peel and a good pinch of salt.
Mix well together with as much milk as will make a firm
dough. Roll it out pretty thick and cut rounds with the rim of
a glass. Just before you send to the oven put currants and
almonds and cherries upon them and sift with fine sugar.

As made by Mrs Palmer at her Coney Street Lodgings

A note did arrive next day from the art master, and so I began my daily lessons at his studio. I was at first unwilling to show my teacher my own work, but after I summoned the courage he was generous in his praise and astute in his criticism. Thus I learned a number of the professional artist's tricks: clever matters of line and shadow. He also spoke freely of the new styles of painting, the abandonment of high wigs and whalebone for flowing costumes, and that most excellent word, Truth. 'Portraiture should not be confused with flattery,' he said. 'What is more ridiculous than a stout duchess tricked out in hoops, masquerading as a goddess? Use your excellent eye to record what you see, Mrs Croxon. Painting is eighty parts looking to twenty parts moving one's brush.' It was then, as he taught me how to add brightness to the depiction of the human eye, that I resolved to paint Peg when I returned home.

🙠

On Sunday, rather than find a chapel, I attended the service at the Minster with Anne and Peter. From the cobbled Close, we all admired the Minster's great towers of fretted stone soaring to the clouds, every inch carved as fine as lacework. Once we had passed into the nave, I surrendered my scruples to that glorious hush that tells of a higher presence than ourselves. It was a bright winter's day, and the vaulted windows tinted the air with dappled rainbows. Sitting quietly in my pew, I recognised a change in myself; that every morning I woke quite glad to be alive. Instead of fitful notions of footsteps at midnight, each new day was heralded by cheery sounds outside my window: the post-horn's trumpeting and the cries and songs of busy, prosperous people. I was still young and vital, with no need for bed rest or sleeping draughts. I was ready to face whatever the future held. However troubled my marriage was, it was better by far than my former life with my father. Dropping my face into my clasped hands, I glimpsed in reverie a sort of labyrinth, a mysterious path I must traverse in the months to come. I could not say what trials lay ahead of me – but I knew that I must be strong, and win whatever happiness I might glean on this earth.

It was easy to make such a resolution when, as yet, I faced no actual difficulties. Each morning, Anne and I returned from our various errands to take breakfast at our lodgings. Awaiting us stood a steaming pot of chocolate and a plate of Mrs Palmer's toast and excellent buns. Anne and I both heartily agreed that if time might halt we should have liked every day to be that same day, the gilt clock chiming ten o'clock, warming our stockinged feet on the fire fender, splitting a plate of Fat Rascals with butter and preserves, with all the delightful day stretching before us.

The days flew by, with walks by the river, a turn around the castle, much shopping, a play, and a dozen more delights. When we were almost due to part, I gave Anne a ring I had commissioned, containing a braided strand of my own brown hair, and showed her its twin that I wore, containing hers. She admired them as if they were priceless gems, then took both my hands and clasped them warmly.

'A token of our meeting again, soon,' I said. 'You, me, and your baby.'

Her face shone with hope. 'I will send you a lock of the baby's hair as soon as I can. And I will treasure this ring for ever.' She pulled it off and inspected the letters of my name on the inside. It was at that moment, as she praised the engraver's art, that a sudden opportunity struck me. I instantly searched out my sketchbook, and finding the page, asked Anne to join me at the table.

'Did you ever see such an object?' I asked. 'It looks like an old penny, defaced with crude engraving. Is it not a crime to deface the king's image?' Drawn in heavy black pencil, was the exact replica of the coin I had found in Michael's box; the product of a dreary afternoon's sketching at the Hall.

'Transported,' Anne read gravely, putting on her spectacles, 'to the ends of the earth.'

'Do you think that means New South Wales?'

'Yes, I do. But wherever did you find such a curiosity?'

Having ventured so far I decided to be frank. 'It is Michael's. He keeps it in his writing box.'

'Michael's?' She pulled an astonished face. 'What on earth would he want with such a base object? What does he say of it?'

'Nothing. I haven't asked him. But I did wonder if you might find out what you can about it. And who this Mary Jebb is, too.'

She looked at me sternly. 'Is it wise, Grace, to make enquiries behind Michael's back? I am sure there is an innocent reason. Ask him. Perhaps she was a former tenant who got into trouble?'

'Perhaps. Only, will you make enquiries, Anne? For my sake. Take this drawing with you – and find out who she is?'

She folded up the paper and put it in her sewing bag. 'I can try. If only to put your mind at ease, Grace.' And so we left the matter.

On the day of Anne's departure she was in excellent spirits, telling me that our visit had in every way exceeded her notion of happy living. I was busily parcelling up a few of her effects when the maid announced that a gentleman waited downstairs to be shown up. I knew it could not be Peter, for he was chattering with Anne in her chamber, teasing her about the correct way to address her trunk. Glad to be alone in the parlour, I straightened my gown and glanced in the mirror. All week I had not seen or heard of John Francis. To Anne I had made light of the whole affair. 'He only wished to acquaint me with his progress in life,' I told her. 'And I am glad he has prospered, and glad too, that he will marry.' She studied my face, but said nothing, which pleased me, for my eyes had pricked at the mention of his name. But now, at last, he had called on me. I sat very stiffly on the chair by the window.

'Goodness, it is you, Mr Greenbeck.' I must have looked peeved, as Anne's husband filled the doorframe.

Jacob Greenbeck returned my greeting with even greater coldness. Since I had last seen him he had grown a great bushy beard, and now had all the appearance of an Old Testament Prophet of the fiercest order. I called at once to Anne, but as ill luck would have it, she did not hear me; the sound of Peter's amiable murmurings and her light-hearted laughter continued from behind the door. As Jacob and I exchanged pleasantries, he glowered uncomfortably, until I was forced to fetch Anne myself.

'Come along, Anne,' he said with irritation. 'You have imposed on these people long enough. The ship will wait for no one, and there is God's work to be done.'

Just then, Peter emerged from the chamber, wearing his usual mischievous expression. Though I glared at him in warning, he could not resist a jibe. 'I am sure God will forgive one extra minute, to ensure your wife's box is not sent to Old South Wales – she truly remains confused about her destination.'

A heavy silence stretched, and then snapped, as Jacob thundered, 'I do not know you, sir, but I must tell you I do not permit levity concerning our Lord in my presence. Come along, Anne.'

Seeing Anne's distress, I tried to placate him. 'Jacob, Mr Croxon is only securing Anne's box. Will you not take a cup of tea?' He did not echo my smile; only scowled at my new gilded porcelain, and the bandboxes and parcels scattered all about the room. His eye fell on my newly purchased books: *The Romance of the Forest*, and *An Oriental Tale* were well enough, but I did not know which was the worst between Mr Beckford's infamous *Vathek* or Mrs Wollstonecraft's *Rights of Women*. I guessed that, to Jacob, my parlour must seem a tableau utterly depraved. Ignoring my repeated offer of tea, Jacob strode off to retrieve the box, and, awkwardly lifting it himself, quickly departed, followed by a mournful-looking Anne.

Once they had gone, Peter said, 'Damn it, Grace; if he cannot tolerate us, how will he deal with the felons?'

I sighed and filled his teacup. 'We must hope the experience will be the making of him.'

'Anne is such a pleasant woman. To think of her having to trail after that zealot to the ends of the earth – it is too bad.'

It must have been that term Peter used – 'the ends of the earth' – that prompted my attempt at guile. 'You know a good deal of Botany Bay. Did you ever hear of anyone from Earlby or Greaves being transported there?'

'Good God, no. It is merely from my friend in the marine regiment that I glean my intelligence.'

'So you have never heard of a female felon – Mary Jebb?'

'No. Never.' I was watching him carefully, but as I spoke the woman's name Peter rapidly rose and peered out of the window. 'Look at that for an ominous sky.' Had I seen a start of dismay cross his face? When he turned to me again, his usual joviality had disappeared.

'Grace, may I speak my mind?'

'Very well.'

'I understand you don't like me to speak of it – but do you truly want to struggle on in that mouldering house? I have seen this fortnight how you like company and entertainments. Let Michael stay on there, while you return to civilisation.'

'It's not so easy as that. I know Michael is not the perfect husband—'

He gave a bitter bark of laughter.

'But do you not understand?' I insisted. 'I must make the best of it. I must support his plans. Be a good wife.' As I spoke it occurred to me that I was echoing Peg Blissett's words.

'I know Michael better than you do. He doesn't deserve you.'

'I cannot disagree with that, Peter,' I said drily.

He sighed, resigned. 'I wrote to you when you were ill and was made very anxious when I had no reply.'

'Michael dealt with all such matters for me – but it was remiss of him not to reply to you.'

'Michael,' he scoffed, 'thinks only of himself.'

'I believe he is starting to trust me. And as for the Hall, he wants to move, too. He hates it there.'

Peter leaned forward. 'Then why not move to town? This is your chance. Seize it.'

I looked away. 'I'll talk to him.' With nothing else to say, he turned back to the window. 'Well, I must make haste to Scarborough, before the storm breaks. I intend to call on Miss Brighouse there.'

'Miss Brighouse? I've heard your parents speak of her with warmth.'

He grinned. 'Well, she's not a bad prospect. It is only that, to be married – it would be rather tying.'

I couldn't help but laugh at the face he pulled at the prospect. 'So why are you leading the poor Miss Brighouse on?'

'Oh, I shall come to my senses. I just need to apply myself, if I'm honest. She is rather fond of me, and not lacking a fortune or a pretty seat at Bleasedale. And you must know by now, I'm not especially eager to get my hands black with oil or whatever the latest vogue for making money is.'

He held out his exquisitely spotless hand, and I shook it heartily.

'Grace, I hope when I next call, you will not turn me away.'

'I would never do so.'

'Ah, so it was at Michael's instruction. Since our quarrel, he will not speak to me.'

I was not wholly surprised, for Michael often complained of his brother: mostly that his parents' favoured Peter in spite of his being a pleasure-seeking gadabout.

'Remember, write only a line and I am entirely at your service.'

'I will never forget your kindness to Anne and to me. Thank you.'

And so we parted, Peter to venture out under the louring skies, and myself to order an early supper in readiness for my next day's journey home.

*   *   *

I woke to a city blanketed in white. All along Coney Street the steep roofs were bonneted in snow, their chimneys smoking above golden-squared windows. Yet as a traveller, however pretty the scene, the sight exasperated me. My coachman, Tom, called with mixed news: that the road to Tadcaster was passable, but that the London mail had not yet arrived, despite its generally being so timely that the locals set their clocks by it. 'We might get as far as the inn at Tadcaster,' Tom advised, for he was eager to be home. 'At least we shall be moving, Mrs Croxon.'

Mrs Palmer, however, was against my leaving; and for myself, I was in a quandary. Yet what was there to linger for? I had written only briefly to Michael: that I had enjoyed myself immensely and been to the Assembly and myriad sights, thanks in part to a chance encounter with Peter. The previous day I had received a short but surprisingly affectionate reply that concluded, 'Do not stay away too long, dear Grace. Your affectionate husband, Michael.'

He had certainly not written like a husband lost in a lover's arms. It was enough to goad me to action. Buttoning up my new damson wool redingote, I put on my other new purchases, a hat trimmed with sable and matching muff and tippet. I had at last found costumes that suited my character: gowns in rich sapphire blues, purples, and emeralds, tight-sleeved and high-waisted. Our neighbour the milliner had taught me a voguish way with broad-brimmed hats, worn at the tilt Van Dyke fashion, with feathers and rosettes. Alighting behind fresh horses and with skids for the wheels, we set off across the slippery cobbles and out through the city gates.

Through the carriage glass I looked out over fields of blinding white snow. At every bridge or hillock the carriage swerved and swung, but inside the coach, with my blankets and a basket of food packed by Mrs Palmer, I was well enough. I pitied Tom outside, growing as stiff as a statue in the bitter snow flurries flying in the wind. By eleven o'clock we reached Tadcaster, and took on food and liquor and advice. We agreed to head for Leeds and pass the night there, but by two o'clock I regretted setting forth. The sky was a sulphurous grey, and we faced the prospect of losing the road, for the hedges were fast disappearing beneath treacherous drifts. On we slithered for another hour, until at last the Half Moon Inn at Top Widdop appeared like a lighted beacon in the murk.

The landlady greeted us like heroes, and Tom had his health toasted liberally by the company. This humble inn was by sunset near to bursting with journeymen and market folk all stranded by the weather. I secured a tiny garret room, and was extremely glad of its privacy and stillness, for my head reeled from the journey.

Amongst the other persons holed up in the steaming parlour was the London mail driver so eagerly awaited at York; a crimson-faced barrel of a man, in a state of great agitation over the lateness of the mail. Fixing upon me as the latest arrival from York, he fretted over how he would be fined by the hour for failing in his duty. I reassured him as well as I could, and our conversation then turned to broader matters. On learning of my destination, he remarked, 'Delafosse Hall? That large estate near Earlby? As chance would fall, I might deliver your mail direct, Mrs Croxon, and so save myself a rambling journey, if you are agreeable.' He handed me a letter addressed to 'Whosoever Be At Delafoss Hall, Earlby, Yorkshire'. Up in my garret I studied it by the light of a fern-frosted window.

To Whosoever,

This letter be a second inquiry to the whereabouts of my sister Mrs Eleanor Jane Harper, a widow, she being engaged in September as Housekeeper at this same Delafoss Hall. I pray you write me if she may be fell ill or in some manner is in need of her family for she is not replied to my letters as she is customed to do so. Most especily she is at all times wanting news of her boy James what is apprentice and he is now needful of his £5-00 fee what she is certainly willing to pay of her own account. I beg you do send a few lines in charity to me Mistress Bess Doutty at the Dog Inn, Pontefract, to put my mind at ease. God bless you for your goodness,

Bess Doutty

My first thought was that poor Mrs Doutty had no notion of what Nan had called her sister's 'gin-bibing' ways. I supposed it a sad case, but not an unusual one.

Then, for the first time since I had questioned Nan, I asked myself why our first housekeeper Mrs Harper had departed so hastily. The influence of that drinking companion of hers was a part of it, perhaps. Yet, to neglect her sister, and leave her son without his fee? Like a loose skein, my pulling at the question unravelled all the worries I had gathered tight this last fortnight, and brought my musings back to Michael himself.

I had not thought deeply about Michael since arriving in York, and I wondered if Peter's company had lulled me into complacency. Had the two brothers' resemblance somehow tricked me into forgetting how much of Peter's affability Michael lacked? I had considered them both on first acquaintance to be handsome and desirable men. Yet now I knew Peter better, I recognised he was of a more amiable stamp, at ease with women and able to form rapid, warm attachments with everyone he met. Michael was civil when he wished it, but beneath his veneer, was too self-interested to care for any human conduct save his own. Indeed, Michael was, as John Francis had perceived, neither kindly nor sensible. For the very first time I allowed myself to speculate whether Michael might know something about Mrs Harper's untimely disappearance. He had certainly met her before we married; yet he showed not a jot of concern at her disappearance. But how great a leap was that, from self-absorption to something far more sinister?

Mrs Doutty made mention of this being her second attempt to solicit news. Setting that beside Anne's observation about her letter not reaching me, I came to a decision. I would ask Peg if she suspected any message boy of stealing the mail. After all, I had seen cases in the newspaper, of scoundrels opening letters in hope of money or gifts. I also resolved that whenever I anticipated, or wished to post an important letter, I would hand it to the postmaster in Earlby myself.

Next, and more reluctantly, I fully reflected on Nan's observation that Mrs Harper was not the possessor of long black hair. The conclusion was inescapable: Michael had visited Delafosse before our marriage and most likely slept with the black-haired woman in my own bed. Since then, they had met at least once at the tower. Suddenly the self-pity that had overwhelmed me after my accident returned. Sternly, I told myself that Michael's manner towards me was improving, and that Peg was no doubt correct about bachelors needing time to leave their free and easy habits behind them.

The dinner bell interrupted my thoughts. That evening the entire inn's company dined together, cheered by our landlady's cauldron of hot-pot and solid plum duff. The mail driver entertained us with tales of vagabonds and highwaymen, mysterious French packages, and secret letters with royal seals. Afterwards, a local fellow pressed him to talk of his route across the country, marvelling at tales of such distant places as Rugby and Stamford. Pleasantly relaxed by a bottle of claret, I listened to the chatter. From nowhere, it seemed, a preposterous idea erupted in my mind – that I might abandon my home and instead take a passage on the next mail coach to London. Bizarre as it was, it gripped me as a most attractive plan. Unlike Anne, I was not so dependent on my husband that I must follow his whims like a slave. Besides, Michael had not even made me his wife by all legal standards. I might still be free and happy, and live a private life alone. I was intoxicated, of course, but I was not drunk solely with wine. I had been in good free-thinking company, and had even read a few pages of Mrs Wollstonecraft's *Rights of Women*. Liberty: the word itself excited me. If I left Michael, he might never find me again. I felt my cheeks burn – how angry he would be! The thought was not an unpleasing one.

❧

By the glittering morning, my delirium had passed, and the many reasons to return to Delafosse jostled in my head. Foremost, and most mundane, in York I had ordered many goods for the Hall, which would soon be delivered. Also, Anne would write to me there within the week, with news of her departure from England. By breakfast time, I had decided the wine had simply made me cowardly. All these notions of running away, I scoffed inwardly, were mere signs of weakness. For the truth was that now I was alone again, I had let myself grow anxious at being left alone with Michael, which was absurd.

I wrote a few lines to Bess Doutty, detailing the circumstances of her sister's departure. As for her apprentice son, I inquired into his circumstances, for I do not like to see industry unrewarded. My friend the mail-coach driver took the letter from me, and also a testimonial to the mail authorities in his favour.

News came that day from Halifax that the road was passable, and so we set off again. Very slowly we progressed across the great moors of Yorkshire, seeing nothing stir save foraging birds and a single fox, a streak of red disappearing into a white hedge. I made sketches of the frost-bound trees, encrusted with crystals as bright as marcasite that sparkled in the winter sun. By three o'clock the sun was reddening, and the spire of Earlby church pierced the horizon. In the far distance, a wisp of smoke rose from Delafosse. I could not be still. I clung to the glass as we drew ever closer to the drive.

A lone horseman waited there, muffled in a snowy greatcoat. It was Michael, as motionless as an antique statue, mounted upon Dancer. The carriage halted. Michael opened the door and I turned to face him.

'Grace, thank God you are home. I have been looking out all day.' Michael was flushed from the cold, his hair long and wet, his expression fiercely intent. He opened his arms, and, bewildered, I went to him. I felt mystified by his anxiety; but also suddenly, vibrantly alive.

The drive was too deep with snow for the carriage to pass, so Michael lifted me up to ride before him on Dancer's back. 'You are cold,' he said, in a low voice. I was shivering, though not entirely from cold; rather from a deep, uncanny excitement. Opening his coat, he wrapped it around me, so I could lean against his body, cradled in animal warmth. Our path grew darker by the moment, but I felt no fear as Dancer picked his way over high banked snow. The silhouettes of trees overhung us, glittering with frost in the unnatural hush of twilight. Michael was silent, managing Dancer's nervous steps and reaching around me to pat his mane, occasionally speaking the horse's name in encouragement.

At last we emerged from the tunnel of trees. The Hall rose above us, its windows shining rose-gold in the setting sun. For a delirious moment, it looked as if it had sprung to life while I was absent, housing magnificent revelries; illuminated by thousands of burning candles.

'It is so beautiful,' I murmured. Michael held me closer and, pulling my hair aside, dropped his lips on the back of my neck like a benediction. Whatever happens, I will never forget this moment, I told myself – the muffled hoofs in the snow, the pink-gold windows, the thrill where Michael's lips had kissed me. But the glorious reflection was short-lived; the sun dropped in a moment, and the mass of windows were snuffed out and blinded. Before us stood the Hall as I knew it, black and sombre below its mantle of snow.

At the great entrance door Michael dismounted and helped me down. The air was preternaturally quiet, save for the ringing jingle of the horse's harness.

'I have missed you,' Michael said, his breath hot against my cheek. A voice whispered in my head that he must be lying. Yet to surrender was irresistible. His words were everything I wanted to hear. I leaned on his arm and we went inside.

'Look.' He threw open the drawing-room door; it was utterly transformed. Gone was the mournful decay; in its place was a vision of luxury: papered walls, brocade divans, a fireplace of marble, a ruby carpet. 'How is all this possible?' I asked, sinking into a chair beside Michael, who still gripped my hand.

'I looked at the plans and knew I was wrong to deny you. I insisted it must all be made ready for your return. Delahunty worked his men day and night.'

I had barely a moment to think how this changed my affairs – that I could no longer cherish hopes of my townhouse – before Peg ran into the room, so overjoyed to see me that I swear tears shone in her eyes. 'See here, Mrs Croxon,' she cried, pointing out the various wonders, one by one.

One matter alone jarred. 'Did the plans not call for bronze wallpaper?' I asked. 'This is green.' I inspected it closely. 'It is quite a contrary shade, next to the red.'

'It looks splendid to me,' said Peg.

'And to me,' echoed Michael.

'It is of no consequence,' I said, not wanting to break the spell. For that was how it felt – as if my home was at last the Castle Amorous of my daydreams, and Michael, my Sad Knight.

Michael and I ate in the dining room. This room was also tricked out in the finest style, the new ceiling gilded and the walls papered sapphirine blue. Peg's food matched in every way the grand surroundings. It was a procession of my favourites: trout with almonds, roast chicken, quince tart, orange custards. Michael produced a bottle of champagne and, despite my tiredness, I grew lively in a vinous haze.

The food was eaten. Michael pushed the green decanter of Usquebaugh away and reached his hand to me across the table. 'I have missed you. Come here.'

In a moment I was in his arms, warm but agitated. He cupped my face in his hands and whispered, 'Your absence was a harsh lesson. I thought you might leave me.'

I kept my eyes lowered. I couldn't lie to him.

His fingers lifted my face up to his; he was trembling very slightly. Then he said what I had wanted to hear ever since we were first married. 'Shall we go to your chamber?'

*   *   *

I followed Michael upstairs, so full of trepidation I was scarcely able to feel the boards beneath my feet. Inside my chamber a fire burned low and the great curtained bed loomed large. I stood awkwardly while Michael took off his coat. In his shirtsleeves he turned to me and said, 'Take that off,' indicating my gown. It had been my belief, from hints in sentimental novels, that a man liked to undress a woman. Instead, Michael kicked off his shoes and lay down on the bed in his shirt and breeches and waited, his arm thrown across his eyes, obscuring his expression. I undressed, unknotting the laces of my gown with horrible difficulty. Then I lay down beside him in my thin shift; my old bed seeming suddenly a vast and foreign kingdom. To preserve my modesty, Michael snuffed out the candle. In the dim firelight he moved towards me and caressed me roughly, running strong hands over my arms, breasts, stomach. From the dark I heard him whisper harshly, 'Have I made you angry?' I didn't reply. Then, 'I've behaved so badly. I cannot help myself.' Too surprised to answer, I flinched as next he grasped my wrist, encircling it painfully, pushing it backwards against the pillow.

'Stop,' I protested. As he suddenly let go of my hand, it accidentally sprang back and hit his face. Breathing heavily, he reached down with his other hand and wrenched my shift up to my waist, then parted my legs with a jerk of his knee. In a moment his weight, strong, moving, urging, was upon me. I gave a cry of pain as Michael took me, his head buried in my shoulder, muffled in a sort of agony. The act was brutal, but I confess it gave me pleasure of a nature I had never known before. The delicate bubble that had held my nerves in check, burst in crests and waves of satisfaction. Not only was my body aching for such release, but my mind exulted in it. On this bed he had coupled with that other woman. Now at last I had Michael within me, flesh and muscle, deep as lock and key, binding him to me for ever.

20

Delafosse Hall

November 1792

~ To Cook Winkles, Cockles and Suchlike ~

Pile up your bounty upon a flat rock and set a fire upon it. The shells will open when done enough.

Mary Jebb's way to cook without a pot or pan

Without a sound Peg made her way downstairs, feeling mighty low in spirits. After dinner she had set off upstairs after her master and mistress, as noiseless as a house-cracker on the prowl. Tiptoeing past Mrs Croxon's closed door, she heard the creak of the bed. She darted into her mistress's dressing room. The fireplace shared a chimney with her mistress's chamber, so she knelt in front of it, listening hard.

Another creak, and was that a whimper from Mrs Croxon? Come on, Michael Croxon, she urged; show yourself a man. And the mistress had certainly looked come-at-able tonight, for some York hairdresser had curled her hair in an elegant tumble; and as for that wide-brimmed hat with the fur, she couldn't wait to give that a try-out. Why, she was quite the Town-Miss these days, judging from her letter home from York. His Nibs had been frantic that she might not come home at all.

Mumblings and groans reached her from the black depths of the fireplace. It must be Mrs Croxon's first time, of course. Who cared if she got a stinging between her skinny legs? Peg stared into the sooty grate as the remembrance of the true reason she had left Aunt Charlotte flared up fiercely from the past. It was a matter she generally tried to forget, that Charlie had been more than her first sweetheart, he had been her saviour. She had been about fourteen when Aunt Charlotte told her that a doctor gentleman wanted to examine her, but it was nothing to fret over; he just liked to cuddle a girl and give her a silver sixpence. A silver sixpence, and nothing to skrike about.

The gentleman had been a sweating hog, who panted mouldy

breath all over her till she felt quite sick. She tried to hold her breath, but the pounding of his tailpiece inside her had gone on and on till she thought it would never end. She had got her sixpence, but even then she knew she'd been gulled. Thirty thieving guineas Aunt Charlotte had got for her maidenhead. Thirty pound, twenty-nine shillings and sixpence – that was how much Aunt Charlotte had fleeced her for. So much for the honour of a roguess.

'I ain't doing that again. You want it, you do it,' she'd yelled into Auntie's face. 'I'm not going to be one of them worn-out slip-slops like them upstairs.'

'Well, how you going to keep yourself then? Ma Brimstone don't take lodgers what don't pay.' She pulled a grumpy face. 'I knew you'd be trouble. You got looks enough to make a living just from laying on your back—'

'I'm not daft. Them girls can't never leave here, can they, with what Ma Brimstone charges 'em for lodging and silks and all? They're up to their eyes in debt, and the bully boys'll catch 'em if they try to run for it.'

She had caught the old cook out. 'You brazen little bitch,' she'd said with a fond sigh and ruffle of her hair. 'Like me, in't you? All brain sauce. But you ain't got no choice, dearie. You been bred up to be a Nanny House girl.'

That was the true reason she had made Charlie's favourite sweet-meats, her fingers trembling as she rolled the nutty mixture. Sweating with misery, she'd wagered her future on those Little Devil sweetmeats. And she'd always been grateful to Charlie for taking her on, of pressing her up against the wall of Jerusalem Passage, his mouth rich with chocolate, her eyes tightly closed against the pity in his gaze.

Now that was peculiar – they were conversing behind the grate: His Nibs as husky as a hound, his wife replying, genteel and slow. She hadn't expected that. Sternly she told herself the job was done, the mistress was plucked; there was no turning back. Nevertheless, she felt collapsed, like an empty sack of meal, as she set off on a silent search for the writing box. And there it was in Mrs Croxon's trunk, the little beauty. Only, damn the article, it was locked as tight as a clam. Stow it, where was the key? Where did she hide the infernal thing? On she prowled, down to the kitchen, pacing uneasily. Then that baggage Nan had the frontery to say she'd had a queer turn in the scullery. 'I can't be lifting the copper no more. Not at my age,' she'd said, her jaw hanging slack.

'Maybe this will help?'

She'd pinched Nan's arm, only for a second, mind. That had got the old dish clout hopping like a flea. A nip's the best cure for idle hands, Aunt Charlotte had always said. When she'd worked in the kitchen at the Palace she'd been all over bruises.

Back in her quarters, Peg got Mrs Croxon's green sprigged gown out and had another go at removing the stain on the taffeta skirts. She had dabbed it with lye, but still it wouldn't budge. On days like this she grew weary of the serving life. Who did they think she was, a dog to jump at everyone's whistle? Prattling away they had been upstairs, in that big feather bed. Perhaps she should have joined Ma Brimstone's girls after all. By now she might have snared a lord or some other rich booby. Still, she'd shunned the bunter's life to be with Charlie. But even Charlie had not stood loyal. Grimly she remembered that pair of blue garters dangling over his looking glass.

The same old sing-song of notions sprang up in her brain, ringing around and around like a marching tune: that if anyone deserved the good life it was her. One day they'd all be humbled all right, like those fancy lords and ladies of France whose heads were being sliced off like stooks at harvest-time. What was it the lags at the Colony had toasted, as they raised their grog? 'May all crowned heads roll, damnation to the lot o' them. The Tree of Liberty, lads!' She picked up the gown and pulled it roughly over her shift. Why should she give it back? It suited her better than her mistress, who hadn't even twigged that Peg had used a conjurer's trick to make her choose her favourite shade of green. When two muslin samples had arrived, she had held out the lilac and green and asked which one she should send back. Mrs Croxon had hummed and hawed and finally pointed at the green, so she'd sent that one back all right – sent it straight back to be made up.

In her looking glass the stain looked even nastier. She pulled the gown off and hung it on a hook. For a long while she inspected herself in the mirror, tossing her hair and making proud faces. Why, Mrs Croxon was a gawky girl beside herself. She deserved better than Mrs Croxon's cast-me-downs. Taking the sharp penknife off her chatelaine she tried to cut the stain out, thinking she might patch it from the hem. Then, in a fit of impatience, she ripped at the stain and tore it right down the front, the silk tearing with a high-pitched screech that satisfied her greatly. Mrs Croxon, Mrs Croxon, she chanted, slashing the whole frock into a frayed mess. And it wasn't just the mistress that was bothering her; there was that other one too, hanging from the ceiling. The one that wouldn't go away. The one that always taunted her in the corner of her eye but vanished if she turned to make a proper sighting. With vicious pleasure she hacked the gown to ribbons. Then she sat down, panting a little from the exertion.

A while later she came to herself, feeling tired and shaky. In front of her lay a heap of tatters – the lovely five-guinea dress was fit for nothing but the ragman. She blinked and yawned, not at all sure why she'd had that giddy fit. Then she remembered, vaguely, like a long-ago dream. She had fancied her mistress was wearing that dress as she stabbed and stabbed at it. For the two of them had sounded happy together, sporting limb about limb in that lovely feather bed.

It was enough to make Peg sick, seeing the mistress panting after His Nibs like a wide-eyed doxy. True, she did keep Mrs Croxon well dosed with Hystericon, so she scarcely noticed what was happening in the very same room. Though she did at least wake up when the goods began to arrive from York. Such lovely stuff there was, and all of it the very finest. There were even gifts: for the master a pitch-green riding coat and boots of mirror-shining leather. For herself a caddy of Souchong tea, that was so fragrant she rationed herself to a dish a day. When the master returned to Manchester, Mrs Croxon again fell in the dumps. Peg tried to interest her in trimming her older hats, for she had bought some lovely ribbons and feathers, but the woman couldn't settle. Then, to her surprise, Mrs Croxon asked if she could paint Peg's portrait.

Peg was unpacking a set of glorious gilt candlesticks in the dining room. A moment earlier, she would have said nothing could have excited her more. But a portrait done of herself? 'Oh, yes,' she said, setting the last one down with care. 'I always fancied having a go at that.'

∾

Peg tapped at Mrs Croxon's attic door, her complexion smoothed with a liberal dollop of Pear's Almond Blossom. She brought an offering too; a plate of airy caraway seed cake. But it was wasted on Mrs Croxon, who took only a hurried bite, so anxious was she to get started with her blessed paints and pencils. Half an hour, she'd beaten those eggs. And, damn her, the mistress had complimented Nan's Omelette of Herbs that very day.

'I always fancied being done like one of them actresses,' Peg announced, catching her reflection in the glass and moving her head to find her best profile. 'Can you not do me like some famous character, wearing robes and all that?'

'Peg, it is you I am painting. Look up at me – that's it – no, with your usual expression. I need you to be true to yourself.' Mrs Croxon was holding up a pencil like a measure, looking at her with faraway eyes. Naturally, she wanted to paint her as a nobody; a downtrodden domestic. What sort of picture would that be, with her lovely red hair tucked under her cap, instead of cascading down her shoulders?

259

It mortified her, it truly did, to be painted in servants' drabs.

'Stop fidgeting, Peg. I've barely begun.' Her mistress looked up from her scribbling with a frown. 'Tell me about yourself. It will help me portray you if you talk to me.'

Peg stiffened. She liked to be the one asking questions.

'Come along – it will pass the time. Were you born and bred up here?'

Even that was a tricky point. 'Not likely, Mrs Croxon.'

'Where then do you hail from?'

When fabulating, keep close to the truth, Charlie always said. 'I once lived in Manchester.'

'And what brought you here?'

That stumped her. She hesitated; thinking, calculating.

'Never mind,' her mistress sighed.

After a considering pause, Mrs Croxon spoke again, very warmly.

'I must thank you, Peg, for all your help with the house and—' she smiled conspiratorially, '—the advice you gave me. It has all worked in a most satisfactory manner.'

'So all is – going nicely between you?' she inquired. As if anyone needed to ask. The master and mistress shared a chamber regularly, maybe every third night now. She had checked the bed linen herself.

'I know we call you "Mrs" in respect of your position. But tell me, have you ever been married?'

Peg's mouth closed like a solid door. 'No.'

'But you have had proposals?'

She sighed loudly and twisted her lips in distaste. 'Oh, I've had a few offers.'

'Poor Peg; never to have known love. You must seek it out. Love is life's greatest blessing.'

Mrs Croxon continued sketching in a silence that stretched like cat-gut between them. Not found love? What rot! Jack had been her truelove, he had come back to her, damn it, after all her troubles at Sodom Camp. It had been at poor Brinny's flogging, after her pal had gone on a hunger-crazed rampage through the camp. Brinny was to be lashed before a gathering of skull-faced, tottering convicts. The marines, almost as skeletal in ragged pink coats, beat their drums while Brinny's sentence was read: a mere fifty strokes compared to the thousands of lashes the men might endure. Brinny fought gamely as she was tied in place. Each time the tarred and knotted cat-o'-nine-tails was swung upon her friend's back, she had tried to stifle the sound of fifty cat-like shrieks.

'Annie Mobbs is dead of jail fever,' Jack told her later, as she dabbed saltwater on Brinny's shredded back. It seemed his Devon doxy had snuffed it, just one week after falling ill. Jack himself was all bones and knuckles, his teeth over-large and his once flaxen hair, brown and stringy. Yet who was she to pick fault? She was blistered and flaking away, her body like a risen corpse, her rags leathery brown.

When she had been stronger, she might have put up a brave show, and made him grovel. But across the camp ground Stingo cast looks like poisoned darts at them. So the Tawny Prince did listen: her prayers for Annie to die had been answered. Passing the blood-stained clout to Ma Watson, she raised herself to standing, swatting away the frenzy of flies. Though her own hand was claggy with blood, she grasped hold of Jack and silently followed him to his hut. The next day Brinny mercifully snuffed it, and a few weeks later Ma Watson gave up the ghost, accidentally left to wander on the beach at the end of the day, there being none of the old crew left to look out for her.

Jack's hut was no more than a few planks of rough board with a dirt floor, but it was theirs alone; a sanctuary from hollering and drunken carousing. The scum of exhaustion began to lift from her thoughts and her old clear-sightedness returned. She persuaded Jack to go out with the fishing crew at night, dragging the seine nets through the inky waters. Soon the hut filled with the smell of crisply roasted fish and, afterwards, with full stomachs, they could talk without listening ears. They were newly rich too, for the extra fish Jack smuggled could be traded, food being the only currency left in the colony. At last she had gained proper standing in the camp, at the side of a smart loyal man.

Peg could bear the silence no longer. To be reckoned inferior in love to such as Mrs Croxon? Never to have known love? Damn her sorry heart, that was a lie.

'Course, I did know it once,' she burst out suddenly.

'What's that? You knew love?'

She nodded, suddenly stirred up at the memory. 'Aye.' She glanced up at the ceiling, weighing the urge to let it all spill out. She would have to tell it differently – invent a few bits and bobs, and curb her rambling tongue.

'Tell me,' Mrs Croxon urged. 'I promise on my own love, I will keep it secret. Who was it?'

Swear on her own love? What, her and the master? That was the last straw.

'He was a sailor. His name was Jack.'

'So where did you meet?' Mrs Croxon was scribbling away fluently now, making long sweeping strokes.

'We met at sea. On the *Queen Mary*, it was.'

Mrs Croxon's face swung up at that. 'I never knew you went to sea, Peg. I thought you had been cook to an alderman.'

'Yes, well – this was when I was very young. My father was a sailor. That was how it started. When I was fifteen, he persuaded his ship's master I might go with him as a passenger to Cape Town, in Africa.'

As she spoke, Peg became aware of how hard an artist scrutinises a face as it is drawn. Mrs Croxon's peering appraisal of her features made her uneasy. The art of the patterer was distraction; the spinning of tales was best accompanied by flashy gestures. She faked a little cough, so she could rearrange her features.

'What route did you take?' her mistress asked, coolly. So she wanted to test Peg's geography, did she?

'Our first port was Tenerife – that was about three weeks from sailing. It was as hot as a flatiron, mind, you wouldn't believe how our laundry dried across the rail. And the sea were like blue glass, you might see the fish twinkling silver in the depths. I asked my father if we might live there forever, but he had his business in the Cape and would not leave off it.

'Well, it was there I first noticed a fair-haired youth, casting me the eye. One night the men sang about the mainmast in such a stirring manner, of home and sweethearts, and foreign lands that I ventured outside to listen. My fair lad was playing the penny whistle and seemed to know every tune in the world. Later, when we got to Rio, he shared his grog with me, and I let him kiss me, for the stars shone upon us like diamonds, and the scent of flowers drifted from the gardens of the city.'

Peg smiled at the empty air, for that at least was true. Not that they had been allowed to disembark at Rio, but the captain had allowed them a little air on deck. Mrs Croxon nodded encouragement, her pencil working fast.

'And did your father approve of him?'

She answered without hesitation. 'No. Jack was young and starting out in life.'

'And when you reached Cape Town?'

'We never got there.' Peg looked boldly into Mrs Croxon's startled face. 'We was shipwrecked.' She didn't blink, just held the woman's gaze, willing her to swallow it.

'You? Shipwrecked?' Mrs Croxon gave a mocking little laugh. 'Are you certain?'

Damn her eyes; Peg's influencing stare didn't work on her. Still, she ploughed on. 'Oh, aye. Stranger things do happen in life. Stranger than you might fancy.'

Mrs Croxon's features stiffened very slightly. 'Wait a moment. I need to fetch a new brush.' She left the room, leaving Peg's challenge ringing in the air.

*   *   *

'I've had me fill of this place,' she had told Jack one night as they sat in the hut at Sydney Cove. 'We should make a bolt for it now, while we're strong.'

They were drinking the broth she remembered Granny boiling up, leftover bones and a handful of herbs and roots. Her body was regaining strength. Now she had Jack to help her, and her own pot and fire, her country upbringing gave her an advantage over town-bred lags. Everyone talked of escape, but no one succeeded. In the early days, they had thought that China lay to the north, and bands of convicts set off on foot, most returning footsore and sheepish a few days later. The less fortunate were found with native spears in their backs, or gnawed to bits by wild beasts.

'I'm thinking of the fishing boat, Jack.' He had scratched his hair that was newly washed and tied back with a plait of grass.

'Head for the Indies, you mean? It's thousands of leagues away, sweetheart.'

The more they talked of escape, the harder it was to dowse the flame, for it shone like a gateway to a golden world. The Dutch Indies were famed as the most beautiful string of islands in the world, green hillocks scattered in calm blue seas, blessedly free of the head-hunters that plagued the Pacific. As for food, Jack had heard tell of luxurious feasts, of roast pig and yellow rice: the very words made their stomachs rumble.

The notion of escape coursed through them both like a witch's tonic. They would live a while on some peaceable island, before taking a passage to Holland, then secretly sailing back to England. Making ready, they began to trade spare fish, all on the sly, in return for extra dry rations and a compass. Mary helped with the fishing, too. They worked separately, Jack chatting with those who looked after the cutter, sharing tales of life at sea and learning how the boat was guarded. Mary moved amongst the redcoats, wheedling out gossip that might affect their plans. Like everyone else, they lived on their nerves, homesick eyes forever trained on the horizon in hope of the first sight of a ship carrying food. But no ship came.

The anniversary of two long years passed. Even the marines were downhearted; outraged at being abandoned by the old country.

In three months they were ready. Jack and Mary had a cache of desiccated meat from kangaroos, rats, possums and other nameless creatures, buried near their hut. They were pals with the two guards who would be on duty at midnight when the tide changed. And Mary had exchanged her precious store of salt pork rations for a compass. It was the work of a few desperate minutes to surprise the guards at knifepoint and secure them with ropes. With the water above their waists, they waded out into the rolling waves of Sydney Cove, and scrambled aboard the cutter. Sailing off from the camp had felt beautiful and dangerous, the vast Pacific sky as black as the Prince of Hell's cloak. As Jack set the boat to float silently on the tide through the Heads, they toasted the plan with a mouthful of grog. The tropical warmth, the stars like numberless diamonds, the urgent speed of the ocean's pull; she had thought her heart would burst.

The first few days they rejoiced on the rolling waves. But it was their sixth night at sea that their joy turned to fear. Goose pimples rose on her skin as the night air plummeted from hot to cold. There was a snapping noise, like little gunshots – the tug of the sails in a mischievous wind. Yes, she would have no trouble talking up a storm for Mrs Croxon.

Her mistress returned with a tiny parcel and unwrapped a doll's-sized brush. 'Tell me, then, about this shipwreck,' she said guardedly.

Peg described gales that howled like wolves, and a sea that heaved and rolled; the king of all storms, threatening to crack the sky in two. Once she had manoeuvred her and Jack into a fabulated lifeboat she relaxed into the tale, for now every word was true.

'At the end of so many stormy nights I lost count, I was baling when an eerie stillness broke upon us. Our mast had cracked, our sails were in tatters. Jack pointed at a grey landmass, rising above the roiling sea. He was knotting ropes around a couple of casks.

"Head for that shore," he croaked. "Hold onto this cask. The skiff will not last the hour.'"

Mrs Croxon sat quite still, her pencil unmoving in her hand. 'Go on,' she said.

'On Jack's signal we jumped into the surf. The ocean walloped against my chest, then filled my eyes, and mouth. Still, I held onto the knotted cask, came up to the surface and sucked in a gulp of air. One moment I glimpsed the dark shore; the next I swallowed vile-tasting brine. I struggled like a wild thing, for safety was but a hundred yards away. Life or death, I told myself. This is it, life or death: take your choice, girl. I held onto that cask in that spinning whirlpool. Then with a jolt, I felt rough sand beneath me, and with each wave I was carried further, till I raised my head, coughing and spitting. Finally, I fell into a swoon.

'It was dawn when I came to my senses and there was just me and a few screaming seagulls, on that beach. Honest to God, it were the loneliest place I ever knew. The sand was dirty black stuff, beside a cliff like a prison wall, covered in rambling green bushes. Savage was how it looked; strange and uncultivated. No people, no houses, nothing. I did think then, what's to live for here? I might as well have drowned and been done with it.

'All morning I traipsed about in my muddy shift, wondering if it were worse to die of thirst or die of drowning. It was getting to night again when I got to the furthest end of the beach and spied a human figure, kneeling by a rock pool. Then the man stood, and with a cry of joy, I saw that it was Jack. We fell in each other's arms, and danced a jig to find each other alive. He held me tightly and looked long into my face. "Oh, sweetheart," he said. "Now I've found you, we shall overcome this trial together.'"

'You had hope for the future,' her mistress said gently.

'I did, mistress. He'd found a sweet-water stream that I drank from, and for dinner we found winkles that we ate baked on stones. We watched the sun set like a peach on the sea, making plans of how we might live till a ship called by.

'Next we made a better camp beside a river and had ourselves a pretty bathing pool all bordered with ferns; lovely it was, with marvellous red parrots chasing through the trees. Our home was a hut made of branches thatched with flat leaves, a right cosy place to sleep in. We had fat birds that Jack snared for our dinner, and made fire using a shard of looking glass I found in my pocket. We had lost the compass in the water, but didn't lament it. I roasted fish and winkles in the embers. For entertainment we even had Jack's penny whistle. It was a paradise, it was.'

'You loved him,' her mistress said softly, as her pencil resumed its hissing across the paper. Peg fought a choking feeling in her chest. Aye, she had loved him – a damned sight more than this woman could ever know.

'He loved me like his own breath,' she said, in a voice that was dangerously plaintive. 'He said he thanked God for the day he met me.' Peg's eyes brimmed full; she was as weak as water. The rest of her tale stuck in her throat like a fishbone.

Mrs Croxon murmured that Peg might be released from her pose. Peg stared into space, again seeing Jack's face, so fierce and true. He had looked down so gently on her pitiful self; on her bruises and her bony body dressed in salt-hard rags. His blue eyes had met hers like a beacon shining on her naked soul.

'I see past your always acting the tough girl,' he insisted with boyish stubbornness. 'I'll be taking care of you now. So that's settled.' And she'd thought to herself, so this is it, girl. All them love stories, all them ballads that you always thought were a load of old tripe – love has found you out, and here you are.

Mrs Croxon returned with a glass of water, and Peg drank greedily. She forced herself to continue with self-mocking gusto. 'When we lay down together in our grass house we whispered vows to stay true for ever and a day. We took pleasure from each other's bodies, and I can tell you, mistress, he were no green youth, but all grown man. So we were man and wife before God – and that's the truth.'

She faced out Mrs Croxon with a bold stare. 'You probably think such as me don't love so strong and tender, but I loved Jack Pierce like we was both put on earth just to find each other. And that night I made a wish,' Peg said, raising herself as if from a trance, 'a foolish wish it were – that me and Jack might never be rescued. That the rotten world would just leave us be.'

The clock in the corner chimed noon, and Peg started up in alarm. How had she let herself run on like this? 'Mrs Croxon, I must get the dinner going.'

'Tell me first. What happened to Jack?'

'Gone. It couldn't last.'

'And your father?'

'Went down with the ship,' she shrugged.

Mrs Croxon dismissed her with a nod of her head that was sympathetic, but also sceptical. Like lowering a drape onto a window, Peg subdued herself and bobbed farewell. Nevertheless, she felt a crawling on her back – a feeling of being watched mighty closely as she closed the door quietly behind her.

21

Delafosse Hall

November 1792

~ Poppy Drops ~

Take four pounds of the flower of poppies well picked, steep them all night in three gallons of ale that is strong. Add sugar as you wish to disguise the bitterness. A most sure and economical method to procure sleep.

Mother Eve's Secrets

I would like to say I was happy from the moment Michael and I were truly married; but that would not be true. My husband continued a model of capriciousness. He treated me with great regard one moment, and the next behaved unjust or petulant. Some nights he would follow me keenly to my bedchamber, and on others he would rise from the dining table and stride away without a word. Even in good humour, he never lost his spark of cruelty, in wit or thoughtless action. Yet it scarcely mattered. I was a beggar feasting on crumbs and could not draw away from him. My love for him suffused me like poppy juice – unsweetened, raw, addictive. The more I had of him the giddier I became. I felt agitated and shameless, but also potently alive.

Following my new resolve, I regularly called on the Earlby postmaster, and so a letter from Anne was placed directly in my hand. Her journey south in the public coach had been cold and distressing, and she grievously missed me and our holiday in York. The date of her departure from England was the very next day, preventing me from sending a few lines of Godspeed; and even with fair winds and tides, she would not make landfall until July of the following year. Anne's confinement was expected in April, but the ship's surgeon had dismissed her so callously, she looked for little assistance from him. My instructions were to write to her via a supply ship to be despatched by the Navy Office some time the following year. Such would be the prodigious distance between us that any letter I wrote might not find her for eight or ten months, if it found her at all.

Repeating this to Michael, he answered in one of his flippant moods. 'All that earnest voyaging around the globe – and what if the convicts don't want to be saved?'

'Then I hope she will come home.'

He yawned. 'Not with that zealot of a husband, I hope. He deserves a life sentence.'

But he was not entirely insensitive, for soon after he called me over to sit with him by the fire. We talked of small domestic matters, until I found myself unable to resist a little probing. 'Peter told me he has a friend in the colony. Do you know him?'

He took a long draught of coffee and set down his cup. 'I can assure you that Peter's friends are all gadflies like himself. The man he knows is a marine officer, a complete fool. He deserved such a posting.'

'*The Lady's Magazine* says it is a very fine place.'

'Whitewash. Your friend should as soon have flown to the first circle of hell as set out for such a pit of felons. The criminal classes should be stamped out like vermin, not sailed away around the world. She will be back on the next ship if she has any sense.'

'How do you know all this?'

He raised his chin bullishly. 'Give me credit for reading somewhat loftier periodicals than *The Lady's Magazine*. The colony is an appalling experiment. The government has made an even worse mess than usual. Officers, convicts, the lot; all will be dead in a few years.'

I didn't answer. I was growing used to Michael's outbursts. Those in authority were idiots, while he alone had the superior judgement to comprehend their follies. He perpetually blamed his ills upon his family, the school where he had been flogged, the government, the world.

'We should pity such unfortunate convicts, not mock them.'

All at once, one of his whirlwind changes of character occurred. Michael's expression softened, he took my hand and sighed as if exhausted. 'Grace, they don't deserve your pity.'

Shortly afterwards he rose; he was off to meet an engine maker in Halifax. I must have looked dismayed, for he put his arms around me and kissed my lips, promising cheerily to be home for supper. After that I sat on, staring into the fire.

So much had happened that I felt I was tumbling through empty air. I knew Michael uttered phrases for dramatic effect, and had a constant need to pour scorn on others. It was annoying yet pitiful, his parade of youthful bluster. Yet still I loved him. My heart jumped every time I looked into his expressive eyes, or admired the creamy pallor of his skin. I had a hunger for his visits to my bed, spending my days like a dusty moth infolded on itself, that only sprang to life in the nocturnal hours. Yet I was not simple-minded; I did understand he was somehow unnatural. Each time we shared our bodies I tried not to dwell on his habits – the litanies of self-accusation he mumbled into the bedclothes, that appeared to have little to do with me. There was no doubt that the act itself gave me all I desired of animal pleasure. My disappointment was that we were not, as a poet might say, mingling our souls as hectically as our bodies. In our lovemaking his eyes remained screwed tight, his transports slaking a private appetite.

It was afterwards, entwined in the dark, that we conversed in a frank manner for the first time. We talked of Greaves, and the constraints of living in narrow-minded company. I even made him laugh with my tales of the Brabantists and their faith in dreams. 'I should like to hear their prognostications on my dreams,' he mused.

'Tell me,' I murmured. In the firelight his body was rosy marble, lean muscle half-draped in sheets, like a paragon of a Classical sculptor. He rolled over and laid his arm over his eyes. 'The most common are the slights of childhood – Father's impatience with me, while Peter could do no wrong. But my worst nightmares are those of school – Good God, I wake up sweating with relief to find myself free of that place. There was a master, a vile man . . .'

He fell silent, turning away from me onto his side, and then said, 'I do not need help to unravel my dreams. If dreams foretell the future, I am damned.'

So which wife would not be uneasy? I loved him, but I was not happy, and I knew, in some remote and sensible chamber of my heart, that the path I had taken was not a wise one. I knew it, but I continued just the same.

ɷ

Amidst all this my chief support was Peg. Her joy at having me home again was so sincere I was flattered. I asked her about the missing letters and wished I hadn't, so furious was she at learning of a thief in the village. After that, it seemed petty to scold her for trivial matters. After all, what were they? Holding my dress before a mirror, anticipating my wants, and protecting me, as she would see it, from annoyance. My one vexation was that preposterous tale of the shipwreck. It hurt me that she had invented it, for she had no need to spin such nonsense to impress me. I knew of penny chap-books of marvellous tales, of this or that mariner's marvels, or indeed, the much-talked-of adventures of Robinson Crusoe and Alexander Selkirk. As to that fond father of hers, I was convinced he was a figment. Other tokens of what might charitably be called embroidery had also struck me: hesitations over certain words and a false brightness to her speech. What little I knew of geography made the route unlikely – was not Rio in South America and Cape Town in Africa, on quite different sides of the world? However, I was certain it was not all a fabrication. When she spoke of her great love, Jack Pierce; then she shone with truth-telling, for the merest mention of him brought a flush to her skin.

At Whitelow the building work was continually hampered by delays and frustrations. Sweetly complaisant after a night of love-making, I capitulated and agreed to borrow a further £1000 to buy a great machine, so the mill could operate even when the river level dropped. Again, I took great care in signing the paper and set it with my own seal, and delivered it straight to the postmaster. But the machine was still being prepared in Nottingham, and the necessary foundations to house it were proving difficult to set in place. I noticed with some disappointment, that the bill from Mr Delahunty was also still outstanding, so that also had to be paid from that loan.

Then, in early December, Michael returned one night from Whitelow and threw a paper on the table.

'Read that.' Reluctantly I picked up a cheap sheet of butcher's paper on which was scrawled in large letters:

Winter nights is growing long Bloodsucker, so be cognisant your person may not pass the lonely road alive – or if you do chance to escape the hand that guides this pen, then a lighted match shall do equal execution. Desist your scheme or the whole infernal site of Whitelow shall be inveloped in flames. Your carcase, if any such shall be found, shall be given to the dogs.

The Regulator

There had been rumours of certain handloom weavers protesting that their livelihood was to be destroyed, but this was wholly unexpected. I flung it down. 'What will you do?'

Michael was too distressed to be rational. 'I shall be forced to bring pauper children in from outside. Damn Earlby's weavers. Let them starve!' Michael slapped his palm on the tablecloth. My own opinion was that a promise of decent wages and safe conditions might ease the matter. That, however, would require a calm head and honest dealing.

But that evening it was Michael alone who concerned me. I was beginning to understand that the mill was an altogether new, and arduous, undertaking for my husband. I did my best to calm him, and even made a few sensible suggestions, that he briskly accepted. When Peg served dinner I coaxed him to eat a favourite dish, a burned filbert cream, deliciously sweet and smoky.

'I can't eat.' He pushed most of his food away, raking his fingers though his hair. Peg scowled when she cleared the table and saw so much of her hard work untouched. With extreme ill-timing Peg began to complain to Michael that the kitchen fire would not light.

'Damn it, when will it work? Perhaps you don't want it to work?'

Once Peg had huffed away I urged him to attend to his nourishment and rest during this time of great exertion.

'That is easy for you to say.' He flung himself down on the sofa and rifled through the newspaper, throwing that down a moment later. In such a mood, if I had not loved Michael, he would have been utterly unbearable.

'I think a sleeping draught might calm you.'

'Do you?' he answered in an accusing tone.

'One good night's sleep would help, surely?'

'Oh, perhaps. My wounds still ache damnably where Dancer threw me. Perhaps a night's oblivion would be welcome.'

I sought out Peg downstairs in her housekeeper's quarters, and told her of the night's events. She was loyally outraged on our behalf. 'Those wicked spongers should be clapped up in irons for making such threats.'

'Perhaps. But my first thought is for the master. Do you have any preparation to help him? He cannot sit still. He will never sleep.'

'Have you none of Dr Sampson's mixture left?'

I told her it was finished, though I had in fact poured it away, not liking the curious dreams it gave me.

'I have the very thing. Only I need to fetch it from downstairs. I'll bring it up to you.'

'No need. I'll wait here. You have a good fire.'

Peg looked at me, surprised, and gestured me away with a dismissive wave of her hand. 'Go on, mistress. I'll run up shortly.'

Any ordinary person would have responded to Peg's prompting, but this, I decided irritably, was exactly the sort of behaviour that had annoyed me before I went to York. Manipulation would be too strong a word for it, but there was a persistent manoeuvring of my actions.

'No,' I said bluntly. 'I am waiting here.'

Still she hesitated, like a cat not knowing which way to spring. Then she hurried away in the direction of the kitchen.

The housekeeper's quarters were flanked by a set of unused reception chambers, now in disrepair. It comprised a sitting room and bedroom, the floor laid with painted oil cloth and the furniture very plain. It was what it lacked, that I noticed: no prints on the wall, or jugs of flowers or china knick-knacks on the mantelpiece. It might have been a room in an institution. Yet Peg revelled in my own lovely things; I had expected to find an abundance of her own pretty goods here. Turning to the table, there lay *Mother Eve's Secrets* and a heap of bills, and – this surprised me – the leather folio of our room plans. I opened the first page, pondering. Yet had she not played a large part in seeing the work done? Though they should have been returned to me, it was at least comprehensible that they were still in her possession.

What I saw next prompted no such easy answer. A green silk rag protruded from a bag beside the table – it was one of my own drawstring bags bearing my initials. I recognised it at once as a scrap of a gown I had disliked, for it had been made up in the wrong colour. I pulled on the end, and a strip of fabric slithered out like a ragged green serpent. In the bag were the remains of my whole gown, all in tatters.

Hearing Peg return across the stone flags, I waited with the torn cloth in my hand. 'So what is this?' I demanded. 'Explain yourself.'

The shock written on her face was so great, it was upsetting to behold. She reached for a stool to support herself and then cast her pitiable face up at me. 'Honest to God, mistress,' she said, her voice wavering with unshed tears, 'I was going to tell you. I just need to save up the last few shillings to pay you the five guineas back.'

'What happened to it?'

'That feckless washerwoman dropped it in the yard. She never even noticed it was missing till a she-cat had mauled it to tatters. Look,' she lifted a handful of torn silk. 'Such creatures do this to make nests when they bear kittens.'

'It doesn't look very dirty,' I protested.

'I know, thanks be to God it was a dry day. I did have a go at trying to mend it but it's too far gone. So I've asked Mrs Gillies to make you another just the same. I've only another ten shillings to save and she'll get it started.'

I shook my head, impatient with the lot of them – Peg, the washerwoman, the nuisance of a cat. 'For goodness' sake, Peg. I don't want another gown like that. But I will hold your wages back, mind you. You must pay for half of it, for I left you entirely in charge here. And the washerwoman, fine her a week's wages.'

'She's already gone, mistress. I replaced her at once.'

'Very well,' I concluded, my grievance running more and more lukewarm with each passing moment. 'Peg, I trust you never to allow such carelessness again.' She shook her head, as meek as a lamb.

'So, what mixture have you got there?'

Still vexed at myself for discovering the gown, I took possession of a little blue bottle with 'Poppy Drops' handwritten on the label.

Michael and I went up to my room together. Before I could prepare the draught, he approached me, lifting my hand from the glass.

'Grace,' he said, 'not so fast. I'll drink it later.' Roughly, he began to unlace my gown.

As I responded to my husband's caresses, Peg's coupling with Jack intruded in my mind. As Michael lifted my shift, I was fearful of embarrassing myself – for I longed to tell him that he was my darling, my lover – and I envied Peg's freedom to exchange her lover's vows. While Michael clung to me like a man in an agony of torture, I pictured Peg tenderly cradled against her lover's chest. It was true; Michael was peculiarly absent from our pleasure; transported to some other place.

In the bed I felt a sticky warmth against my fingers; the long scratches on his thigh, a legacy of Dancer's throw, had re-opened, oozing blood. Michael was upon me, within me, hand in glove, one flesh. I forgot Peg Blissett. I forgot everything of the real world, and loosed myself on a sea of pounding nerves. I drew him within me; I bit my own knuckle hard. Again I felt my body grow tense with a painful sweetness. I arched my neck, I whimpered. At his own moment of crisis Michael made a choking sound, then sank his damp face into my neck. It was over. We were breathing fast together and at peace.

I lay on my side, pressed against Michael, the candle burning low. He still sat up, leaning against the bolster, having at last taken the sleeping draught. I was dozing, enjoying the glow ebbing from my core, when a notion occurred to me.

'Do you think it may have been this "Regulator" who broke in and ransacked the lieutenant's room?'

'No. I know who did that,' he said with a grim laugh. I hauled myself upright. I looked at my husband's face, animated in the red glow of the fire.

'So not Old Dorcas?' I said with some mockery.

'Not in the sense that those gullible women mean it – no. What do you know of Ashe Moncrieff?'

I recalled to him the bare bones of Nan's tale.

'And still you haven't guessed where Miss Hannah got to?'

'As far away from here as she could get, I hope.'

'Sadly, not.'

Michael's eyes were hugely black from the soporific draught, but he was not sleepy yet. 'If I were to tell you something about myself – something rather startling – would you try to understand? It is something I cannot help.'

I felt a pricking of fear on my neck. 'If I can, I will.'

'My mother chose this house for us. As she no doubt told you, she knew the Hall from her girlhood. She is always telling anyone who will listen how she is related to titled people.'

I waited as he rubbed his forehead, as if trying to shift some inner pain. I reassured myself that all this had happened so long ago it could not affect us now.

'My mother was only seventeen. She and Moncrieff – they fell in love. They met in secret without his aunt knowing. "Silence was their very god" and all that sort of nonsense.'

For an instant an image of Mrs Croxon as a girl of seventeen flashed before me, as fair and radiant as her sons. I appreciated that before middle-age had coarsened her, she must have been a singularly lovely woman.

'Your poor mother. And then Moncrieff died. Did the child survive?' I pictured his mother's child – Michael's sibling – fostered somewhere here in the country, perhaps in a cottage with a local family.

'Of course he did, Grace,' he said shortly. 'The child was me.'

'Oh.' My heart thumped uncomfortably.

'I was still ignorant of most of this when I first came here. Then I discovered the rest of the story and – it all makes sense, far more sense than the claptrap I've been peddled since I was a child. The parish records at Greaves give Croxon as my father, but I've always been the misfit of the family. When Peter was born, it was made perfectly clear who their great favourite was. That termagant, my great-aunt, cut Moncrieff and any of his issue out of her will, so it's not as if I have any rights to this place. But when Mother discovered that the land by the river was owned by you, she thought it the perfect scheme to install me here. As I said, she has something of a passion for the place. Croxon will not allow her to visit, though. That would be insupportable to him.'

At each word of Michael's, I felt myself shrinking, until finally I understood that I was nothing but a tiny link in a chain of his family's forging. As for Michael's paternity, I was alarmed. Michael was no longer who I thought he was. I had not married the elder son of our landlord, Mr Croxon of Greaves. The word *deception* sprang to mind, but I pushed it away.

'What did you think of your mother's scheme?'

'I needed to get away from them, to try a new venture – and prove myself. My plan is to free myself of the Croxons altogether. I need to make a fortune independent of them all. Peter can sponge from them. I will not.'

'But the lieutenant's room? If it wasn't Old Dorcas?' I couldn't bring myself to say Moncrieff's – his father's – name.

'I had just discovered my life had been a lie. I was desperate to find something, anything, which acknowledged my existence in that hypocritical shrine. I went to that room dead drunk and I lost my head. How could Moncrieff be so stupid and die like that? How dare he desert my mother and leave us in that backwater? And abandon me with nothing, nothing at all, not even a name to call my own? I wanted to destroy his memory.'

I recalled the crackle of broken glass underfoot, the medals hurled about, the portrait hacked and torn in shreds. For a moment I glimpsed through the door into Michael's private misery and then slammed it shut. An icy revulsion crept over me. So these were the hidden thoughts of the man I had married. I couldn't look at him; fearful of betraying my dismay.

'There's nothing for me here. Even when I first came here, I was uneasy.' He rubbed his eyes, struggling to stay awake. 'I am so unhappy. I feel so confused all the time. I don't know what to do.'

'Michael, let's leave here straight away.'

Alarm creased his face. 'Not straight away. Soon.'

I reached for his hand. 'I will help you be strong, Michael.' I would have to abandon my plans for Delafosse, but the compensations would be great. In a lively town our marriage might still flourish. The shame of it was, so much of my capital was gone, but perhaps we might live on what was left until he recovered himself. Also, leaving would spare him the temptation of meeting that woman at the tower again.

Michael lay down, staring glassily at the ceiling. His speech was growing incoherent. 'When I think of leaving – impossible. Yet to stay – only so much I can bear. To be a slave to other people's wills. Where does my happiness lie?'

Your happiness lies with me, I wanted to say. Can you not see it? Instead I kept silent and tried to comfort him.

'I am so ashamed of myself,' he exclaimed, flinching and shaking me off.

As a bell chimed one o'clock, Michael curled up on his side. I held him gently, feeling his breath grow easy in sleep. Almost at once he kicked out as if dreaming of flight. Poor, poor Michael, I crooned silently as I stroked his disarrayed hair. But what of me? His family had deceived me; they had manoeuvred me into marrying their – I scrabbled for the kindest word – natural-gotten son. He was, I finally admitted to myself, not merely capricious, or even melancholic. Michael's destruction of the lieutenant's room convinced me he was not healthy in his mind. I had to be fearless, I told myself. If we moved away quickly, he might leave these morbid preoccupations behind. True, we would be horribly alone, beleaguered by hostile forces if we attempted to complete the mill; and lacking even the Croxons' money and support. He needed me and my money more than ever, just as I – and I could scarcely admit it even to myself – detected a distinct loosening of the bond of affection between myself and him. I shivered to think of the two of us alone, adrift, chasing Michael's dreams of riches, sinking in debt, tainted by failure.

If I thought of Peg at all, that sleepless night, it was with regret that we might soon be forced to dismiss her. At such a time you do not wonder what your servant is thinking, down those narrow stairs in a locked room far away in the basement, distilling and boiling and mixing receipts, laying down stores in preparation of never, ever leaving.

22

Delafosse Hall

November 1792

~ To Roast a Warbling Hen ~

Lure your Warbling Hen with any shining thing, or a crab will do as well. When it walks along it is easily caught with a snare on the end of a stick. Pluck and draw and spit onto sharp sticks. Turn above hot embers till enough. A most excellent fowl and very tasty.

Mother Eve's Secrets

Peg's cleaver banged and cracked on the rutted butcher's block as she shattered beef bones to extract the marrow. Something had changed at Delafosse Hall, Peg decided, as she aimed a well-judged blow towards the bloody leg-bones. 'Seize the reins,' had always been Charlie's byword, and that's what she had done, right from the day she arrived. But, by her calculations, matters were drifting. The whole rigmarole had to be tightened up.

Mrs Croxon had not behaved as she had predicted. That rumpus over the green gown had almost dumbfounded her. A bloody cat was all she'd been able to muster. And all those cold-eyed questions about her voyage, for instance. For the first time, she'd detected something as hard as flint in her mistress's backbone. Then there was that other peculiar change: she had stopped spending money on the house. That very morning, she had been leading the char-women into the library when the mistress stopped her.

'That won't be necessary,' she said. 'There will be no more improvements at present.'

'But mistress,' Peg answered, 'what about those library bookcases in the pattern book? I thought you was ordering them.'

'No,' Mrs Croxon had said to her, all hoity-toity, in front of the chars. 'You forget – it is my money you are so quick to spend. If you don't need these women for any other purpose, send them home.'

The chars had grumbled at a wasted journey, while she herself had raged like a she-bear. She had been looking forward to seeing those smart shelves filled with the leather books from York. Something was going on.

She flung down the cleaver and threw the bones to one side.

She had thought of making a rich marrow pudding, with brandy and eggs, to a receipt of Janey's from *Mother Eve's Secrets*. But, stow it, she felt like a dog stuck in a wheel, turning the meat-spit but never advancing. The master was out at Whitelow all day. There was only the mistress for dinner. What did she care? She could have hard cheese and bread and butter. She could try short rations for a change.

Leaving Nan with orders to roast the marrow bones instead, she returned to her quarters. Then, wrapped in a woollen cloak and hood – thinking all the while that Mrs Croxon's nip-waisted redingote didn't half look elegant, as well as warm – she headed off to the glade. Outside, the air was white and damp; the cold pinched her nose as she headed down narrow paths of slithery brown leaves. Damn, the glade was dismal at this time of year; the trees that had once recalled the island were naked and spiky-fingered. She tried to settle on the hollow tree trunk, but was fearful of the damp. Raising the flute to her lips she couldn't conjure Jack at all. She should never have spoiled it by talking of him to Mrs Croxon. She tried again to raise a tune, and this time a mournful hoarseness emerged. With fingers as cold as the grave she repeated the refrain Jack had taught her. Raising the flute like a church wafer to her lips, she recollected Jack and the terrible secret of his end.

At first they had talked of rescue from the black beach, and spent each day watching the ocean for ships. But as the weeks passed, and the ocean stayed forever empty, she no longer cared to leave. Instead, she fancied they were the only two persons alive in the world, stranded on that beach in some long ago time. Though her clothes were rags, she strung jangling shells about her neck, and fashioned a sun-hat of leaves and feathers. The beachcombing life was the happiest she had ever known.

Jack taught her how to forage, and boil each type of victual, and chew only little titbits, to be sure they wouldn't be poisoned. They discovered sea spinach and a sort of watercress, and meat in abundance. The easiest to catch was a witless wandering bird that couldn't fly, that she christened a Warbling Hen. They had shellfish for the picking, and fat eels to be walloped and roasted. Each night they feasted under the stars, as Jack spun yarns and sang ballads, and they tried to count the great multitude of stars in the Pacific sky. That was when he taught her how to play his flute, sitting her on his lap and directing her fingers with his. Afterwards, she'd trace the dark tattoos on his body: the Union Jack on the bulge of his arm, the chain and key that circled his wrist. In Sydney Cove he'd gained a kangaroo, along with all his lag-ship crew, which looked like a leaping fox. The finest to her eyes was the hangman's rope that had been inked with a sharpened bone around his neck. They were both scapegallows together, both breathing borrowed air that tasted all the sweeter.

One day he asked her about the personation racket. 'I see you doing it, changing your voice, your manner. It's like you're some-one else, Mary. I never seen anyone do it as good as you, not even on the stage.' They were sitting on the cliff top, resting on a foray for bird's eggs. Below them was the ocean, every day different, a patchwork of shadows and silver, rising in white-spumed breakers towards the shore.

If they had been any other place, she'd never have talked. Now, with her hands clasped around her knees and nothing before her but the blue Pacific, restless and unending, a thousand miles from England, her tongue loosened. 'What someone such as me is born to – hard labour, being kicked about, with nothing ever fine or good in prospect – it's not fair, Jack. I found out the trick as a girl, there's a knack to the game. If you can only puff yourself up into someone else, everyone believes you.'

'You got to have almighty pluck, I reckon.'

'Aye. You got to keep your mettle, like you're going into war. There's life or death to your personation in every eye that remarks you. Mostly, mind, you need only climb the ladder of other folks' stupidity. I know how weak-headed most folk are. Rich folk are the stupidest, as soft as muck. The right gown, a few clever words, and they swallow it.'

Jack shifted and stole a side glance at her. 'So you reckon we're all gulls but for you?'

She turned to him, clear-eyed. 'Aye. How else can I do it if I don't believe that? And there's a wildness to it, a thrill in your blood. Like a gambler tossing the dice between fortune and famine. Most folk are sheep, Jack.'

'And you're a she-wolf?' he said sourly.

'No. A vixen, perhaps. Proud and alone.'

'Not so lonely now. And beautiful, by God.' He reached for her and they tumbled back onto the grass.

'And true to you, Jack.'

'And me to you.'

෴

Gradually the cold had crept up on them. The nights grew perishing, and they had to sleep inside bigger heaps of ferns. The days grew shorter, and rain fell in bucket-loads. They crouched under dripping branches, the ground sinking like a swamp.

They decided to move up-country, until the rains stopped. The next dry day they started out, following the river, struggling through tangled bush. It was slow going, for their feet were wrapped only in leaves, their shoes long since destroyed. By noon the path reached a dead end, where the river dropped into a gorge of foaming white. They were all set to head back again when Jack sighted a path above them in the tangled scrub. She could just see it; a zigzag over the rocks, and a gap where it entered the trees.

The track led into a sort of tunnel made of forest. They left daylight behind, a thousand leaves hemming them into dusky shade. As she traipsed behind Jack's torn blue jacket, he squinted into the foliage, hearkening to every cracking twig or bird-chirrup. After what seemed an age, they came out into blessed sunshine again.

They were in a clearing, their ears filled with a thundering wind, the air itself trembling. A few paces further they came upon the source: above them, a waterfall tumbled from a clifftop as high as a church steeple. The water fell in milky blue strands, shooting spray in the air that danced in rainbows of gold, pink and blue. At their feet was a deep and inviting lagoon. It fair took her breath away.

Jack crouched to look at the pool's edge, where a mud bank was scrabbled with marks.

'We should go back,' he said. 'Something drinks here.'

She didn't care. She was spellbound. 'Look, a cave!' Across the lagoon stood a dark entrance hung with pretty mosses, like a fairy grotto.

'Just one peep,' she whispered, for there was something powerful and secret about the place. 'Then we can go back.'

But Jack was still peering at the tracks around the water's edge.

'Whatever drinks here, it's not here now. I dare you, Jack. A quick look around the cave and then we'll be on our way.' She had a notion, from some story or other, that caves were places where treasure was hidden; she reckoned pirates might have left jewels and plunder behind long ago.

'It's the end of the rainbow,' she laughed. 'Let's find our crock of gold.'

Jack hung back as they reached the cave mouth. 'I don't like it here.' He grasped her arm and looked about the place. The water crashed endlessly beside them, so he had to shout. 'I been thinking. That track was too narrow for a deer, or suchlike.'

That excited her even more. There would be treasure, she was sure of it. She strode into the cave mouth, and the sudden chill made the hairs on her bare arms rise. Further in, it was pitchy dark, with no glinting gold to guide her way.

'Wait.' Jack pulled out their fire basket that held an ember inside dry fungus. After Jack had fashioned a rough torch, they both entered the cave. Disappointment met her, for it was as bare as a tomb.

She pushed on deeper inside, more from vexation than any great hope. Jack followed her, his bush fire wavering and smoking.

'That's enough now,' he kept saying. But still he followed her as she sallied on, silent and furious with disappointment. Finally she saw something against a far wall. Dark fruits they were; wrinkled globes, with fibrous leaves sprouting from their tops.

'It's a fruit store,' she cried, happy at least to have discovered some new-fangled food. She grasped one, but it was that leathery to the touch she knew at once it wouldn't make good eating. Jack approached her with the spluttering torch and held it up close. Her fingers had already probed its bumpy skin, and what she fancied were hard seeds growing from the bottom. Jack's torch flared and shone on her find.

It was a small, leathery head. A human head, with hard teeth, and a tuft of dry black hair. In front of them were dozens more; shrunken heads that bore savage patterns inked upon them, row on row of ungodly faces. The torch in Jack's hand sizzled and died. She screamed like a stuck pig and dropped the shrivelled head on the floor. It thudded like a leather ball, then rolled a short way in the dust.

'Quiet!' Jack cried, pulling her away. 'Stow it, let's go.' Like two blind men they groped their way back the way they had come, fearing to touch the walls, desperate for the light.

They stumbled out of the cave mouth, blinking at the shining lagoon. On the other side of the water was the path back to their beach camp. And there, standing on the far side of the lagoon, stood three large and terrifying savages. Jack saw them first. He clapped a hand on her shoulder and shoved her back down, trying to push her back to the cave. An instant later a spear vibrated in the dust beside them.

'Get in the water. Make for the path,' Jack hissed. 'Keep low!' Another spear whistled above them – two of the savages were pelting towards them. She gaped at them. The black spirals covering their naked brown skin put her in mind of monstrous man-shaped lizards.

'Bolt!' Jack pushed her. She slithered out into the sunlight. On her belly she wriggled toward the water's edge. At the sound of a war-like shriek she tumbled into the lagoon, landing in water and weed. Righting herself, she raised her eyes above the rushes. A spear-shaft trembled where she had lain a moment before.

Jack was standing courageously at the cave mouth, his short knife raised in his hand. The two warriors were almost upon him, swinging polished stone cudgels.

'Go!' Jack shouted over his shoulder. But she was transfixed. A primitive emotion hammered in her veins. She, whose one rule was her own survival, could not leave Jack to die alone.

Grasping the spear impaled in the riverbank, she hauled herself back onto dry land. The two attackers had slowed down a few paces from Jack. They made a recognisable sound: deep-throated, scornful laughter. Grasping the advantage, Jack bull-charged the larger man, driving his knife hard into his naked chest. Entirely surprised, the man rolled his eyes at the knife handle standing in his chest, staggered drunkenly, and fell like a logged tree to the ground. Jack's second attacker gaped with surprise, then turned to Jack. She watched in disbelief as the savage lifted his club and swung it down hard onto Jack's head. There was a sickening crack, and her precious Jack dropped to his knees. She ran to him, she couldn't help herself. As he sank to the ground she threw herself onto him, trying to staunch the head wound that spurted warm crimson over her hands. His blue eyes blinked slowly, then fixed on the dust. In a moment they grew hazy as his life departed him. Her sweetheart, her true love, was dead.

A mad ire boiled over in her veins. She stumbled to her feet and cursed Jack's murderer with every oath under the sun. She jabbed at his chest with the spear as he danced backwards, laughing at her as if she were an angry gnat. Then, as if it were a jest, he grasped her hair, yanked her towards him and raised a hideous tooth-edged knife towards her throat. So here we go, she thought, reckoning she breathed her last. She screwed up her eyes and waited. She had faced death on the gallows and she was ready to do it again. Let it only be sharp, let it only be short, she prayed.

A woman's shriek cut the air; then the third of the party, a black-tressed woman, thrust her broad body between them. Before she could comprehend a thing, the woman swept off her feathery garment and threw it over Mary's head. The next she knew, she was being bundled up and hauled away by her rescuer.

She understood she was the woman's property now, and had perforce to follow – but for the rest of her life she regretted looking backwards. Jack's murderer dragged him up to kneeling by his beautiful golden hair, so that he looked almost alive. Then the tooth-edged weapon was raised, and, with the carelessness of a slaughterman, the warrior sliced through Jack's fair neck. The native shrieked and howled as he raised his gory prize. Jack's head swung crazily, his blue eyes blind, his severed neck streaming with gore.

She hunched inside the canoe as they paddled at speed up the river. Her boiling fit of anger ended, her mind crumpled, ashen and empty. Jack was dead. The notion kept slapping her awake each time she sank into a half-swoon. Everything had happened so fast she couldn't make sense of it. Only after a long time did she summon the courage to look about herself; and for the second time, she wished she had fallen in a fit or died rather than witness what she saw. Jack's head was spiked on the prow of the canoe, his skin like candlewax, his eyes staring open.

Groping in a fog, she reckoned her own life must be almost done with. Maybe they had to chop her own head off in some special place? Or maybe they made a greater spectacle of a woman's execution? What if it was slow and long-drawn-out? She remembered the tooth-edged knife, the stone cudgel. Her teeth chattered, and her blood-stained hands dithered in her lap.

The big woman in the feather cloak put a heavy hand on her arm and started jabbering in a strange lingo. Struggling to stir up the sluggish embers of her mind, she knew she must read this woman's wishes or die. She had a broad and proud face, well used to command, her chin and lips deep-scored and dyed with strange designs. Her monstrous stone jewellery clanked as she moved close to Mary, waving her fingers in the air. 'Tapoo,' she said slowly, as if speaking to a child. Mary made an almighty effort to stop shaking. It took no great skill to comprehend that this woman was her lifeline, her one chance.

'Tapoo,' she echoed hoarsely. The woman smiled and patted her arm.

After that she forced herself never to look at Jack's dear face again, though she fancied he must be watching her with mournful devotion. Her whole being was bent upon the savage woman and how she might ingratiate herself. After all, she told herself, though she had fallen into a den of devils, she wasn't dead – not yet.

೪

'Peg?'

She nearly jumped from her skin. Mrs Croxon was standing on the path, loaded up with her painting gear. Peg stood up too quickly and the flute fell to the ground.

'What are you doing out here?' her mistress asked. She groped about for the flute, pulling it inside her apron. Then she sighed, and gave a sad little smile.

'I had to take a moment's rest,' she said wearily. 'I'm afraid our talk the other day left me very low-spirited, Mrs Croxon.' She wiped her eyes that were dry of tears.

'Oh, I am sorry, Peg.' Mrs Croxon came right up to her, and patted her arm. Peg struggled not to flinch; she didn't care for such familiarity. 'And I spoke harshly to you this morning, too.'

Peg shook her head sadly. 'So you should, mistress. I take too strong an interest in what you do, and I know it's not right. Comes of having so little meself. You see I never had such a good mistress as you in all my time in service. I'd do anything to please you, and that's the truth.'

'Peg.' Her mistress stared at her with helpless pity. 'Come inside now, dear. Let us be friends again.' She reached out her hand to lead her back to the house. 'It will do you no good, sitting out here in the cold. Have you your – what was it you were holding?'

'Nothing,' she mumbled.

'I couldn't help but notice. Is it a musical instrument of some sort? On a few occasions I've heard a quite haunting sound.'

God damn her ears. 'Aye.'

'Is it Jack's flute?'

She nodded, affecting a sad countenance.

'Would you like it included in your portrait? I fancy it's like a mourning pendant or a lock of hair – an object that once belonged to a loved one.'

'I never even thought of it.' That was true, at least. And there was something to be said for having the flute in the picture.

'Come along, then. Why don't we finish the portrait now?'

'Oh. I need to see how dinner is getting on.'

'If you can sit for me now, bread and butter will suffice. I have ground the perfect lily green to colour your eyes. Don't rush away, Peg. You need warmth and company. Take a rest, and the picture will be finished and ready by six o'clock when the master comes home.'

So there she was again, whirligigged up into the mistress's studio, Jack's flute clutched to her bosom.

'Today I'll just do the new section – yes, your hand just as it was – and then tint it. This gives a lovely bloom to your skin; now it just needs a wash or two of colour.'

She got out her pencil and started to sketch in the flute, peering hard at it with narrowed eyes.

'What is it made of?'

Peg shrugged helplessly.

'I've never seen anything quite like it. Is it ivory? Do you mind my asking where Jack got it?'

Keep your secrets hidden, she urged herself. 'I don't know. Never asked.'

'Is it some sort of native handiwork?'

Peg concentrated on keeping her pose nice and still. In spite of all the friendly sorry-saying, Mrs Croxon had a new bite to her. And that blue gown from York did look well on her tall frame. 'Could be,' she said, through barely parted lips.

'I have an interest in such *memento mori*, as you may have noticed. I lost my mother when I was only a girl.' She indicated the picture of the gawk-faced woman.

When her mistress turned to it Peg yawned. It had to be all that fresh air.

'And that was my first sweetheart; John Francis Rawdon.' She wittered on about a local boy, who had gone and left her, all because of her father's tyrannical manner.

'He sailed away and left me, long since. Then when I was in York, who should seek me out but John Francis himself? He has finally come home to England.'

Peg jolted to attention. What was that? This sweetheart fellow had been in York?

'Of course, I told him I am married now.'

'And most happily married, too,' Peg broke in.

'Naturally. But if John Francis had only called a year earlier—' Mrs Croxon looked rather wistful.

'Surely he cannot be so handsome a gentleman as the master?'

'No, certainly not.' Her laughter was gentle. 'But first love . . .' She raised her eyebrows and shook her head, all in a very good humour.

Two men fussing over Grace Croxon? Who did her mistress think she was – the Queen of Bloody Hearts? True, her appearance was much improved, but only thanks to Peg's directions. Peg struggled with her annoyance, striving to hold a smile.

'Yet to lose your first love as you did, Peg.' Her mistress's long glance might have been kind, but to her, it felt withering. She couldn't be quite sure of her mistress today. Was she dangling some sort of challenge before her?

'My Jack would never have left me,' she burst out, all at once. 'He would have loved me till the world's end. He swore it on a mighty oath. He would have married me, like that.' She snapped her fingers. Then, recollecting herself, she shifted in her chair 'Sorry, Mrs Croxon. All this talk of Jack has upset me – that is all.'

Mrs Croxon said nothing. Finally she asked in a little voice, 'What happened to him?'

'He was killed. My Jack is dead.'

'How? An accident?'

'Worse than that. He were killed by a warrior on the island we were shipwrecked on. At least it were quick, though it was – shocking terrible.'

'And you? How did you survive?'

Peg was suddenly too weary to fashion anything new. 'I was rescued by a native woman, of the name of Areki-Tapiru.'

'Goodness.'

'She saved my life.'

'And then?'

'I lived with them, I don't know how long. Then, at last – well, my tribe did sometimes make exchanges with white traders.'

'What sort of exchanges?'

'They wanted muskets. And the white traders sometimes wanted hostages; a missionary's daughter or suchlike. I wasn't going to stay there all my life if I could help it. And then – I got back here.'

'You should write all this down, Peg. It's an extraordinary story. I don't know how you bear it.'

'Oh, I find the strength. I made a vow to get back home, and I've kept it.'

'That's good. And maybe, one day?' She gave a silly little smile. What was it with the woman? Since she'd lost her maidenhead she thought of naught but tumbling.

'Take another man? Never.'

'You are still young.'

'Do you think so?' She didn't feel young – she hadn't felt young for years. Her best years had been wasted in grim endurance.

'Let's take a break before I make the final strokes. What do you think?' Mrs Croxon propped up the portrait for her to see and stood back, looking pleased with herself.

Peg's first glance at the portrait left her dumbfounded. 'Begging your pardon, Mrs Croxon. I don't know.'

'It is how I see you, Peg. Often the way we see ourselves is different from those who observe us.'

As if she didn't know that, she scoffed silently. That was her stock in trade.

Mrs Croxon went to fetch some fresh colours. Once she was alone, Peg studied the portrait properly. She recognised her own flat, heart-shaped face raised to the beholder, her lips just parted, her features very handsome. But her mistress had captured a peculiar expression; she looked, for all the world, a lost and tragical woman. Her lovely eyes stared into a terrible past. As for her pitiful costume, it was the garb of a loser in life's game of fortune. It was a cruel picture, and she hated it. Mrs Croxon's eye was as sharp as a scalpel of truth that cut away layer after layer of humbug. It said without words the question that flayed her alive: if she was so clever, why had she lost all she'd ever wanted?

Mrs Croxon reappeared with a jug and a glass jar. 'Do you like it?'

'You've got me all wrong,' Peg said. 'That's never me.'

23

Delafosse Hall

November 1792

~ To Roast Bones ~

Have the bones neatly sawed into convenient sizes, and soak overnight in water until the blood ceases flowing. Place them upright in a deep dish, and bake for 2 hours. Clear the marrow from the bones after they are cooked with a marrow spoon; spread it over a slice of toast, and add a seasoning of pepper.

As told by Nan Homefray, her best way

I asked Peg to sit down again. I was stung by her attitude, and exceedingly eager to get the portrait finished. As I picked up my brushes, I felt sorry for Peg – sorry that I had dragged her up there and painted a portrait she didn't like, and sorry too for all the blows life had dealt her. She seemed quite a different character from the excited fabulist of her first sitting. Was it any surprise I had painted her as a woman haunted by disappointment?

Yet I still had a pinch of doubt about her story. In an atlas, I had confirmed that Cape Town and Rio de Janeiro did indeed lie on opposite sides of the Atlantic Ocean. Yet the heart of her tale was certainly true; that she had loved a man, and he had died. And now, by interpreting her essential character as tragic, I had upset her further. Poor Peg. I congratulated myself that I possessed so much that she would never have: a gentleman husband, wealth and rank. Life, I thought, is indeed a lottery. Save for the accident of her low birth, Peg might have been a person of fashion; a vibrant beauty, painted by an academician in oils.

Intending to make a quick end to it, I started mixing the lily green I had made especially from crushed flowers, hoping exactly to tint her eyes, rattling my tiny brush in the jar. Then I subjected her to my closest gaze.

'Your eyes,' I said, musingly. 'They are a very unusual green; in different lights they reflect brown and blue. Do they perhaps reflect whatever light falls on them?'

Peg replied that she couldn't say. 'Do, please, sit very still.' I looked very hard, then used my green with a wash of yellow ochre to tint the iris, and a ring of burnt umber. A pinprick of white titanium gave them startling life. I was happy with them; surely even Peg would admire her lively cat-like eyes.

'And your throat now, Peg. Please, pull off your kerchief. You have such luminous skin.'

She removed her kerchief.

'And that necklace, if you please.' I pointed at the ribbon around her neck, from which was suspended a metal pendant. On the instant I froze; I immediately lost my capacity for speech. It was a copper disc. It was the convict token.

Recovering, I stood up and held out my hand. 'Give that to me.' A succession of responses crossed Peg's face: surprise, hostility, and finally, cringing horror.

'Please, Mrs Croxon.' She grasped the copper disc and hid it in her hand.

'Give it to me,' I insisted.

'God help me,' she whimpered, still clutching it tightly. I lifted the ribbon up and over her head, I read the engraving and knew every word of it at once; for it commemorated Mary Jebb.

'Did you take this from my husband?'

She raised her head, shaking it weakly. 'No.'

'Stay as you are.' I rushed downstairs to Michael's room, grateful he was absent, and hastily rifled through his box. There it lay, the twin to the copper disc that swung in my hand. In every respect of size and pattern, in every crude letter, it was identical. As I climbed the stairs back to my studio I prayed I was wrong, beginning to feel, in little flashes of fear, that my world had been thrown off its axis onto some other crazy course. A few moments later I was back in my room. There Peg still sat, hunched like a beggar before a parish overseer, her face in her hands.

I sat down before her. 'Speak the truth. Are you Mary Jebb?'

She didn't make a sound; only rocked, with a tiny, childish movement.

'Come along. Why else would you wear such a thing?' I thrust it before her in my open palm. With her face still hidden, she shook her head.

'Was this your voyage? Were you transported to "the ends of the earth"?'

Still she sat silent, though breathing harshly. Of course she was Mary Jebb, I told myself. I was a dolt. How had I not apprehended it months ago?

'Mary,' I said gently. 'I will judge you only as I know you. Earlier I called you friend. Listen to me. It is better to be truthful than be forever lying.'

I touched her arm very lightly. A sob emerged from her wet and rumpled face.

'I'm sorry,' she croaked. 'I will say it. I was a convict.' She lifted her hand and ineffectually wiped her tears. 'It were such a small crime, Mrs Croxon. I was but a young girl, new up from the country, whose granny had just died. I see now I was led into bad ways by this man Charlie, who sent me out daily to hawk stuff about the streets. He taught me little tricks; to short-change folk when they wasn't looking, all that sort of racket. If I didn't hand over a good sum every day I got a leathering from Charlie – a beating, I should say. He had others in his power – pocket-divers who lifted watches, and harlots who – well, you know, I'm sure. I never had as much money to give him as they did, and he let me know it all right. Then one day I got the chance to lift a whole pound note, from a gentleman who needed change, and so I tried out a sting that Charlie had showed me. My heart was racketing, my nerves was all done in – but I switched the pound note for a blank, and nearly got away with it.'

She covered her mouth and shook her head miserably. 'But he come running after me, the gentleman. I thought I'd leg it back to my landlady that cared for me since my granny died. I ran like the clappers, but he wouldn't give up – not that one. In the end, he chased me up to the rooftop and caught me there like a rabbit. I gave him his pound note back. I got down on me knees. I prayed to him to be a Christian and forgive me. I told him I was only doing it under threat from the ruffian who would skin me alive. And I said to him, I begged him to remember it, his word would send me to the gallows.'

I shook my head in sympathy, but did not speak.

'He of course was a gentleman, a very handsome, high-speaking sort of gentleman, and once I was thrown in the cells I looked even worse than ever, having to sell the clothes off my back just to stay alive. The day I was up at the Bailey, he steps in as a witness. I had not a hope against him, me in my rags, and him with his dandy rig-out and silky words. Over in no time, it was; the judge puts his black cap on and tells me I'm to swing. And that fellow laughs with the lawyer, like it's all a jest, sending a poor girl to her death. I was so frightened of that man, Mrs Croxon. He said we was all vermin to be stamped out.'

As she spoke, another part of me strove to catch up with the facts. Vermin. I had heard that expression very often, and recently.

'Yet you did live,' I whispered.

'No thanks to him. The day they come to hang me I was nearly dead already, from terror. Then, when I'm standing at the wooden steps, praying to God for forgiveness before I'm to be strangled, a reprieve comes. Me and three other women are wanted to serve the convicts, out in Botany Bay. And so we was, Mrs Croxon, packed off to serve them like a herd of brood mares. Can you imagine that?' She looked up at me with a ghastly expression. 'Gangs of murderers and cut-throats, using your body like a—'

'Don't,' I said sharply. 'I understand. But these horrible pendants?'

She glanced at the object in my hand and licked her lips.

'While we was waiting to board the ships there was an engraver, a decent old cove, convicted of printing tracts against the authorities. It was him who made them. Love tokens they called them. When you think you are going away from all you've ever known, your home, children, old folk, sweetheart, you get a pitiful urge not to be forgot.' She touched the spot on her breast where the old copper penny had hung. 'Them verses you get scribed – "When this you see, remember me", and suchlike – it's all anyone will ever touch of you again. You know you in't never coming back.

'As for the voyage, I told you the honest truth about that – only I was in irons, of course. So was Jack. But we loved each other, I swear that on the Bible. So we took our chance and bolted from the colony. It were either that or starve, and that's the honest truth. And I swear, mistress, I come home so grateful for my second chance at life. Every day I thanked God, and swore I'd take the honest path.'

'But your term is not expired?'

'No. And that's what undone me.'

I nodded, but by now I no longer wanted to hear any more. Outside, the afternoon light was leaching away, and deep shadows gathered at the corners of the room. Not wanting to break off to make a light, I watched Peg's face growing indistinct save for the gleam of her fearful eyes.

'When I got back to Manchester, the gentleman that convicted me – he saw me in the street. He followed me secretly and caught hold of me. He told me I must follow his orders. He made such terrible threats I had no choice.'

'What orders?' I was beginning to feel curiously cold and detached; as if the scene before me was happening to someone else. But Peg, or Mary as I knew her now, would no longer meet my gaze.

'To break the law again,' she said quickly. 'To do as he said under pain of being sent back to the gallows. And I would swing this time, with no chance of a pardon. Can you comprehend how that feels?'

For a moment, I did contemplate the horror of being condemned to death. A death in life, counting the hours and minutes until the barbaric rope choked the life from you.

'Tell me, Mary,' my voice was unsteady, 'why does Michael keep your token?'

Now her words emerged in a breathless tangle. 'I never had a sweetheart. When the others had their love hearts made I had no one to remember me. Then I got a fancy. I wanted what that gentleman had done to be engraved on his conscience for ever.'

'Michael? It was him, wasn't it? The man who convicted you.'

She nodded, and collapsed into shuddering tears.

'So what does he want you to do?'

She peered up at me, and I saw, in her sorrowing face, that it was she who pitied me. She spoke in a conspiratorial hiss. 'He told me he was getting married. And that he had rather have married another, a great beauty. And that I must help him or be hanged. I must come here and earn your trust. Oh, Mrs Croxon, I should rather be struck dumb than have to speak of it.'

'Help him? How?'

'He has not said yet. Only that he needs someone unafraid to break the law.'

'Tell me. Has he given any instructions?'

She shook her head. 'Only to be certain you are happy. He wants you to feel – falsely content.'

'I knew it in my heart, I knew it.' I balled my fists and beat the table. 'He has used me. What a fool I am.'

She stood up then, and came to me with her hand outstretched. 'Mrs Croxon, I swear on my mother's grave I will never do you harm. You called me friend.' She laid her work-roughened hand on mine and looked into my eyes. 'You are good. I have learned from you what goodness is. Not like – that other woman he is enslaved to.'

'Oh God; what should I do? I thought he was starting to care for me.' I wiped my eyes on the back of my hand.

'Oh no, Mrs Croxon. If you only knew how he speaks of you. He calls you an obstacle, an open purse. He needs only your money; he speaks of it all the time.'

The pain I felt then was so intense that for a moment I wished I was dead. Then I calmed myself a little.

'And what of you, Peg? He must not be allowed to bully you. I need time to think.' I squeezed her hand in return. 'Will you be my ally while I decide what to do?'

Her green eyes met mine, honest and friendly. 'I will.'

Somehow I endured the rest of that day. Questions circled me like snapping dogs: what should I do, or say, to Michael, and how could I hide my distress? I felt tattered and dishevelled, as if a thread of me had snagged and now I was unravelling.

Michael did not return at six, or seven, or eight. Unable to calm my anxiety, I took a dose of the Poppy Drops at nine. At ten I glimpsed his carriage-light outside. Standing at the top of the stairs, I listened in vain for his voice. Finally, Peg pattered up the stairs to find me.

'He is waiting in the dining room,' she said in a low voice.

'We must both behave in our usual manner,' I whispered.

She nodded gravely.

'Why was he delayed?'

'Something about the mill. Bad news, I fear.'

When I entered the dining room, Michael was already halfway through his usual bottle. He stood up very flushed and agitated.

'Where have you been? Whitelow was torched at sunset. Just as the housing for the machine was finished. Hundreds of pounds' worth of materials have gone up in smoke. Come and see it for yourself!' He grasped my hand and dragged me up stair after stair until we emerged through a door onto a flat part of the roof. The night was biting cold and bitter black, save for an orange fireball to the far west. I grasped the balustrade, lamenting all the stupid loss of it. My grandmother's kind bequest, I thought, is but kindling on a bonfire of vanities.

'Arson,' Michael ranted. 'The cowards crept up just after we left. I was nearly home when the message arrived. Don't these wretches want to work? We build mills to give them employment, and they make plots to destroy them. And what of me? What do I do now?'

He fretted, fearing that Whitelow might be attacked again. Such uprisings were spreading across the country. A few weeks earlier Grimshaw's mill at Manchester had been destroyed by fire; the newspapers told of lawlessness, of machine breaking, of Loom Riots.

At dinner, Michael's marrow spoon delved into the stumps of roasted bone, while I pushed a little of the oily stuff about my plate. 'Did you hear the other news? The King of France is put to trial by his own subjects! That is where we are all headed if the government does not destroy these apes. This attack is only the beginning.'

Beginning to recover from the shock of the fire, I observed my husband, marvelling at him, seeing him anew. Had I never noticed the lines of cruelty around his petulant mouth? I seethed inwardly with the knowledge of what he had done to Peg, and how he was all the time scheming to supplant me. As for the arsonists, I felt grudging admiration for their pluck. Like me, they had performed a simple mathematical sum; that if Michael's mill made him rich, it could only be at their expense.

As Michael's bottle emptied he grew even more boisterous, and described a comic picture by Mr Gillray. 'I suppose you have not seen it, though it is all the fashion. It depicts these trouserless French dogs gathered about a table to dine – and what do you suppose they eat?' He picked a splinter from his teeth. 'Why, the limbs, heads, and eyes of the French nobility. Their children guzzle a bucket of entrails, while a hag roasts a baby over a fire. That will be Britain's future, if we let these mobs rule.'

If I had not already felt sick at the sight of severed bones, I did now.

'I am unwell,' I said, rising.

Up in my chamber I locked the door and lay on my bed, too agitated to sleep. Every instinct in my body urged me to get away from Michael, but when I cast about for somewhere to go, no sanctuary suggested itself. Since my father had died, even my dreary room at

Greaves was lost to me. There could be no refuge with Anne, either, since she had sailed for Botany Bay. As for John Francis, even if I knew where he was, we could not renew our friendship now he was marrying. I comprehended I was entirely alone, and wondered how this had come to pass? No one had ever called on me here at Delafosse; I had not even the slightest acquaintance here in Earlby. Peg was my only friend and support.

At some time in the night I slipped my hand beneath my pillow, in search of a handkerchief to wipe my eyes. Instead, my fingers fixed on something else, a strand of hair, very fine but as strong as metal thread. I started to wind it around my hand in the darkness, though it cut like wire into my skin. On and on it wound, as never-ending as that thread of destiny spun for each human soul by the Fates. I held my breath, convinced that the putrid stuff came from no living being, but from the infamous trade in corpse's hair.

Then – and at this my senses almost failed – it began to move. It began palpably to grow, with an unstoppable sensation of aliveness. The stuff was on my face, a smothering cushion of soft foulness. I grew burning hot, as if the bed cover too, was of woven hair, the pillow on which my head lay, too. I clawed and fought back. Still it wriggled gently, probing my skin like thistledown tentacles, entering my nose, my eyes, my mouth . . .

Next morning, I waited until I saw Peg leave for the village, and then took the pony cart and caught her up. After my nightmare, I had slept little and was light-headed with anxiety. Helping her up beside me, I asked, 'What news?'

She shook her head. 'He said he would miss supper tonight.'

'I know; he is going to a meeting of mill owners. But has he given you no instructions?'

She shook her head.

'I have been thinking, Peg. We can stop him if we go to the authorities together. Would you speak out against him?'

She pulled back in alarm at my words. 'Please, Mrs Croxon. Don't, I beg you. You might as well buy the rope and string me up yourself.'

'Well, is there any written evidence? A letter or document in which he writes of these matters? I could go to the magistrate alone, and you need not be involved. I could lend you money, so you could get safely away and—'

'Mrs Croxon, begging your pardon, I wish I had never told you now. I have had longer than you to think on the matter. If you knew Newgate as I do – the end of all hope, the beatings, the swill of filth on the floor.' I looked into her bleak face, not doubting she had survived terrors beyond my own endurance. 'It's not like I murdered anyone or committed a mortal sin, is it mistress?' She turned her head away with revulsion. 'Them murderesses got it even worse than me, mind. Did you know, any ruffian can tip the jailer for a private visit to any female he fancies violating? On his own or with his chums. They hate the murderesses worst of all – since they have generally killed menfolk.'

I shook my head; I had never guessed men could be so wicked. For the first time in years I remember my father's *Carceri*, the chains and racks and instruments of torture. He had called them the prisons of the mind, but the worse truth was this: men built these places; they did exist.

'If you peach on me, Mrs Croxon, you'd as good as murder me, and that's the end of it. Don't send me back there. I'd as soon stab me own heart and be done with it.'

I gripped her arm tightly. 'There will be no need to do that. Stay calm, and I will help you. I need to think matters over further before I do anything. I need to know first what I can salvage. It is hard, Peg. Only a few days ago he was so unconstrained with me.'

'Mrs Croxon!' It was the first time Peg had ever raised her voice to me. 'Might I remind you, it is only lately he even came to your bed. Consider this: has he extracted anything from you in return?'

I was too ashamed to reply.

'How much?' she asked in a tone of indignation.

I shook my head. It was none of her business. Yet I calculated that over time I had given him all of my £3,000. That was quite a fee.

'Unconstrained, is he? Well, I suppose you have not felt his fist yet,' Peg interrupted my appalled calculations. She touched her brow where a few months earlier she had borne a purple bruise.

'You said you fell in the dark. Did he strike you?'

'Aye. When I tried to stand up for you, mistress. I didn't like to say. When I think on it now I should like to see him dead. He deserves it for what he's done.'

The pony knew the way and trotted on as we sat in silence. Not taking my eye from the road, I asked, 'Has he ever touched you?'

'Lord, no. You know yourself he don't even like me. I disgust him, being so rough-mannered.'

Just then we came to the boundary with Riverslea, and I halted the pony at the fields overlooking my neighbour's property. There it stood, Miss Claybourn's ramshackle abode. It was smaller than Delafosse, built around an ancient keep tower, a jumble of tottering half-timber, ill-matched to a later facade of brick.

'I suppose she has no money.' I studied the mish-mash of old and new. A few windows were boarded up, and green moss grew over the sunken rooftops.

'No. Not a mite. But she does have a taste for the high life. Her maid Sue tells me she owes a vast deal of money.'

I thought of Michael's box of unpaid bills. They would make a well-matched pair. I knew in my bones that Peg was right when she said Michael wanted only my money. At some subterranean level, I had known it from the first and let myself be played upon. But what truly enraged me was that he wanted to share it with this spendthrift jade. By God, I vowed, I would not sign another paper for him; not if I were to be scourged through the streets behind a handcart.

As we reached the outskirts of the village, I told Peg to further befriend Miss Claybourn's maid. 'Take what time you need from your duties. Find out what you can.'

'And you, mistress?'

'I will make my own inquiries,' I said. I would not be drawn further.

'Only be careful, mistress.' She clambered down from the trap. 'He has not a thought for any but himself.'

I did not elaborate on my plans to Peg because I had no plans. Calling at the post office, I found a letter waiting from Peter. He was his usual cordial self, as he might well be, having removed to London and all the pleasures of that city. At the end, he wrote:

> *It pains me heartily to think of you in that disagreeable ruin. Will you come to London to celebrate the New Year, as a favour to me? I will meet you at your convenience. I beg you to write, sister, with your plans,*
>   *Your ever affectionate brother (in Law and in Spirit)*
>   *Peter*

Peter's kindness stung me to tears. Remembering our carefree hours in York I was certainly tempted. I will sleep on it, I thought, having no appetite at present to tell Michael I might desert him for his loathed brother.

But once I had left the postal office, there were almost no public places where a lady might linger in Earlby. I scarcely wanted to meet my own housekeeper in the grocer's or butcher's shops, and the villagers were of that country type that will stand stock-still and stare very boldly at anyone whose family has not lived there since Domesday. 'Hearken at her, Mr Michael's wife,' I heard a flat voice remark. A group of raw-faced women in shawls huddled at the Market Cross, openly discussing me as I strode past.

I took a circuit around the George, and lingered at the signboard that advertised the times and prices of the mail coaches. Bristol,

Leeds, Derby, Edinburgh – and there was London. The cities' golden names danced before my eyes, like the words from a spell that might still whisk me away. Only a few weeks earlier I had daydreamed of escaping on the snowbound mail coach, disappearing into trail-less winter. Now I was paralysed; like a broken-winged bird, trailing in circles. Feeling a presence behind me, I turned to find Peg.

'Look, mistress. The hunt is coming up the High Street.'

I quickly turned to where she pointed; the metallic ringing of hooves built to a crescendo as the Earlby Hunt came into view. About thirty riders were approaching, the leaders in scarlet, swaggering as they swept past the open-mouthed locals. Milling like a restless tide about the horses' hocks were a mass of yelping hounds, their tails up and eyes bright. I searched from face to face for Michael, but I could not find him. I was surprised to see a few women were amongst their number. By his own account, Michael did ride to hounds, but had never invited me even to see him off.

The leading horses soon towered over us, glossy giants with hooves trotting dangerously close. I recognised a few unpleasant men from the George, and sent up a silent prayer for any foxes abroad that day.

Suddenly, Peg clutched my arm. 'There. Look. It's her.'

She was swivelling on her tiptoes. 'Miss Sybilla Claybourn!'

I tried to follow her line of sight – the cavalcade had largely passed us, and I had only a rear view of the riders. Yes – near the front, in the distant thick of the pack, was an elegant young lady. I could just see the feathers on her tilted hat bouncing jauntily; her military blue coat was nipped very tight at her narrow waist. She was handsome, in a stiff-backed, look-at-me fashion. Her hair, tightly curled beneath her jaunty hat, was unmistakably very dark. So that is her, I thought, feeling entirely helpless against such a rival. She was all that Peg had hinted at: well-turned-out, pleasure-loving, irresistible to men.

As I paced back down the High Street I was struck by my own

stupefaction. Good and bad, right and wrong; all swirled in a mael-
strom that I couldn't stop, like dead leaves spinning. Whatever
compass I had used as a guide on my life's path had irrevocably
broken.

Not knowing what to do, I did nothing. When weary of my room I
walked mournfully in our park, dreading I might otherwise see
Miss Claybourn again. When the worst of December's rain abated,
I set off each morning after breakfast, my boots and hems soon
muddy, and my face warm. I had a few favoured spots in the wood-
land, but my favourite remained the dilapidated summerhouse.
Though I never again approached the tunnel door, I fed the stove
with dead branches and took my sketchbook out, finding solace in
the movement of pencil on paper.

I felt a strange hunger to depict my memories, struggling to
make sense of all that had happened. I drew my empty bed with its
ornate hangings and tassels, the bed sheets rumpled and twisted. I
scored in a long, sooty black hair, but the snake of it disappeared in
the mass of shading. Another day I depicted the bed occupied by
Michael and myself, our bodies melded and twisted, my hair spread
like a rippled cloak across the pillow. One awful day I drew the
scene at the tower, a phantasmagorical Michael and his lover
emerging in the moonlight – it was an inky, nib-scraping piece, like
a nightmare etched by Mr Fuseli. Finally, I propped the drawings
up against the walls, black-scored rectangles repelling the low
winter's light. But it was useless; no epiphany occurred. They were,
in the end, only ink and paper.

Each night I let Michael run on about his troubles. He assured
me constantly he was striving to move matters forward at Whitelow.
Nevertheless, I began to wonder how it was that any man could be
so self-confounding. Obstacle after obstacle rose before him, like
waves upon an ocean. It was not that Michael was incompetent,
only slapdash; he did not lack drive, only consistency. He got into
petty quarrels, he sent out ill-drafted orders, he was disappointed

by unreliable associates. Yet, all the time, I asked myself: could this be a disguise for the wickedness described by Peg? Sadly, I concluded that to preserve his fragile prestige, it might well be.

One night I made an excuse to go upstairs early, but instead of going to my room, I ascended to my studio and re-read Peter's invitation. I tried to summon a reply, but nothing promising entered my head. Above me hung my painting of Delafosse, its rows of windows mostly empty; its massy bulk recalling a prison for the tiny image of a woman trapped at the window. God in Heaven, I thought, what am I to do?

A step on the stair gave me a moment's warning.

'Peg?' I called. I would be glad of a chance to confide my desperation.

'Grace.' It was Michael. He strode in and looked about.

'So this is your hiding place.' I forced my hands to remain still; not to snatch up my sketchbook, containing my furious pictures of him. Only when he turned his back to gaze at a sketch I had made of the coiling-haired angel on the staircase, did I succeed in pushing Peter's letter under a blotter.

'Do you like my angel? It is the Blair crest, I believe.'

'An angel? That's a gorgon's head,' he scoffed.

I looked at it more closely; at the stern, square-jawed face and the rippling hair comprised of coils that might indeed be living serpents. So that is it, I thought, this is a nest of vipers.

He sat down opposite me and leaned back, eyeing me with an expression I could not read. Suddenly he noticed Peg's portrait.

'Do you like it?'

He affected sardonic dislike. 'No.'

'Don't you think I've caught Peg's likeness?'

'I wouldn't know – I don't look at her. She's a servant, damn her. What sort of man takes notice of his servants?' His eye slid over to my portrait of John Francis. 'Who is that?'

'An old friend,' I said, with an attempt at cheeriness.

'A sweetheart? Is he the one your father banished off to sea?'

'Oh, it was not like that—'

'I feel sorry for him,' he said. 'Were you as cold to him as you are to me?'

I made no reply.

'You are pulling away from me. One moment you are kind and sweet. And yes,' he sighed, 'I admit it: at times you have been the wife I scarcely deserve. There, you have it, in spite of my pride. And now, on a whim, you treat me like an enemy; you make it exceedingly clear that you do not want me near you. I can only bear so much, Grace.' He looked at me with a wounded expression. 'I confided in you. I told you of matters that hurt me greatly. Do you know how many people know about my birth?'

I shook my head.

'My family – and you, alone. I know my family do not care a jot for my feelings, but I thought we had an understanding. I am not blind. I can see that you are disappointed in me.' I stared into my lap. 'It is true, I have made mistakes. But I am not as unfeeling as other men – no, don't deny it. I thought that you would help me. I believed there was the beginning of a good marriage between us.'

He reached out to me across the table – as delicately as a feather, his fingers brushed my hand. But now the sensations he roused, though impossible to dampen, sickened me. 'Grace, we have been fools. Can we not go back and start again? Come and look at the moon, as we used to.'

Mechanically I rose, and he led me by the hand to the window. A pock-marked moon cast a silver light over the park. 'It will be Christmas soon. Even a blockhead like me can see it is a time for reconciliation.' He slid his arm around my waist. 'I have never had a Christmas in my own home. We should hang green boughs and burn a Yule log. Enjoy a hearty dinner in that splendid room you have created. We can choose freely, Grace – choose to be happy. My parents are in London, as you know. Next year, when the business is established, we will join them with our heads held high. We shall stay in fine rooms and go to all the balls and assemblies. Would you like that?'

I nodded, but still resisted the arm that tried to coax me closer.

'It is a pity,' he whispered in my ear, 'that we have started married life under this strain. But in spite of all, you have always shown yourself to be the best of women. Too good for me. You are a worthy mistress of Delafosse.'

'I thought you wanted to leave Delafosse?'

He gave a resigned little shake of his head. 'I have made a search. At present there is nowhere sufficiently grand within riding distance of Whitelow.'

'We could live in a more modest home.'

'You could,' he quipped. Then, seeing my face was still serious, he leaned towards me and tried to kiss me, though I turned my face aside.

'I should rather not,' I said feebly, pulling away.

'Oh, you are not such a wanton as before. I wonder why?'

He grasped my wrist tightly and kissed me violently on the mouth. With strength I didn't know I had, I pushed him away, very hard, so he almost stumbled. For a long moment he stood blazing before me, very still, his fists clenched.

'I'll see you regret that one day.' Then turning on his heels he marched rapidly away.

24

Delafosse Hall

December 1792

~ Minced Meats for Tarts ~

Take your beef or other meats and tripes and scrape free from skin and gristle; mix with the same weight of suet picked and chopped, then add double of currants, raisins and prunellas, nicely cleaned and perfectly dry, some chopped apples, the peel and juice of two lemons, sweet wine, nutmeg, cloves, mace, pimento, in finest powder; when well mixed, keep it covered in a dry cool place.

Mother's Eve's Secrets

The skin around Peg's nails had started to bleed from stoning all the heaps of raisins and prunellas. No doubt little specks of her own blood were passing into the tarry vat of minced meat. Now wasn't that true to the proper old receipt? Aunt Charlotte had once said as much, about minced meats being where all the bloody scraps were thrown: raggoty mutton, offal, all the guts and stringy bits. Sweeten it all up and them upstairs would be none the wiser. Fob the scrapings off as a bit of fancy; that was Aunt Charlotte's creed. Your eyes might feast on her flim-flams and flummeries – but your mouth was generally disappointed.

Peg hummed to herself as she sniffed the concoction; fragrant as muscatel and black as the Earl of Hell's boots. Nan was well on with the savoury roasts, the brawn and the Yorkshire Christmas Pie – soon she would have the great turnspits spinning before a roaring fire. Nan and the ugly sisters could see to that death-dealing contraption while she enjoyed herself baking macaroons and gingerbread from *Mother Eve's Secrets*. Yes, and she mustn't forget the makings of a big inviting Salamagundy salad. Whoever would have wagered on her getting back home to an English Christmas? Hell's teeth, she knew how to survive.

෨

The canoe had carried her, the savages, and dear Jack's body, up river to a great stone hill, crowned with a village guarded by row upon row of spiked palisades. As she was prodded and pushed up the steep path, every chance of escape vanished away.

Inside the compound she was jostled by mobs of half-naked men, women, and children, who jabbered and laughed in her face. Her new mistress yanked off her blood-stained shift and draped it about her own broad shoulders, her strong teeth bared in victory. She, meanwhile, was left to stand naked before that crowd. Never before had she felt so keenly her bluish-white skin and carroty hair. Bear it, girl, she told herself as they prodded her breasts and sniggered at her privities. A violent tug to her head sent her flying – a leash had been woven into her hair. Henceforth she was to be led, like a bridled horse, behind her new mistress.

The chieftainess, who she learned was named Areki-Tapiru, lived in a carved hut at the summit of the peak, waited upon by a retinue of maids. It was one of the grandest huts of the fort, or Pa, with carvings of pot-bellied manikins on its roof, and walls covered in woven mats.

That first fearsome night she was dragged out to a great gathering, and sat through hours of war-like dancing and stamping. Would she be sliced to bits, or tortured in a drawn-out spectacle? She quivered in continual terror that her own execution would form the high point of the night's entertainment. Lying down that night on the earth floor of the hut, she was astonished to find her head still attached to her shoulders. The next night her luck continued, and then the next. Straining her wits, she watched, learned, and survived. Whenever Areki-Tapiru asked for something – her *taonga*, the treasure box in which she kept her white feathers, or her *korowa* royal cloak – she practised the word silently until it stuck like fish glue. Soon, her cleverness was rewarded, with her own rug to cover her nakedness, and then a greenstone *teekee* that Areki-Tapiru ceremoniously hung around her neck. Knowing that faking a thing is best achieved by sincerity, she made it her creed to admire Areki-Tapiru, ever mindful of the woman's great *mana*, the power she carried within her spirit. Even when her mistress returned to the hut with her face as fat as a gourd from hours of torture under the tattooist's chisel, she praised her beauty as if she were Venus herself.

The chieftainess had other exotic pets in her menagerie of maids: a Chinese woman with hair that fell to her knees like a horse's tail, and a child with skin like soft black leather. She liked to collect curios: a dancing yellow-eyed *kauri* dog, and a razor-beaked eagle. But most prized was her greenstone knife, edged with the sharpened, pearl-like milk-teeth of all the babies she had borne. Areki-Tapiru believed it to be a living thing; she talked to it, and laughed as she tickled the dog's nose with it, or used it to nip her women's flesh. She herself was bitten by it once, as punishment for dropping a pin; the gash it left festered with pus for many a week. 'Look!' her mistress squealed. 'The ghost has red blood, just like us.' She hated that baby-toothed knife, and wondered if it would be the death of her.

She strove to remain the chieftainess's favourite. Secretly she practised, and then performed, the old three-cup-and-ball trick, using dried berries and nut shells, all the while pretending to hearken to spirits who told her where the balls were hidden. Any flash trick would do – pulling an egg out of her mistress's tattooed lips made her gape with astonishment, before she heaved with incredulous laughter. That was how she got her new name, '*Kehua*', or 'ghost'; both for her bloodless skin and for her supernatural skills.

By slow degrees she earned the trust she needed to wander at will in the village, exploring tracks and byways, drawn always to the ocean that shone, blue and green, like the inside of the *paua* shells the tribe prized higher than jewels. Her new friends teased her, calling her 'the woman whose eyes are blue from long looking at water'. She laughed back, copying their words, their expressions, their way of standing. All the time, one of Charlie's sayings guided her: 'Wear the mask of a friend on the heart of a spy'. When on errands, she learned the trails from the *kumara* fields to the cook-houses and the *hangi* pits, where the bountiful food of the place was artfully steamed in pits underground. She learned that she was fortunate to be Areki-Tapiru's special *mokai* pet. Other captives were hunched and beaten creatures, who dropped their eyes to the ground as she sauntered past.

After befriending the bone-carver, she traded a few of her mistress's unwanted gifts for a flute. Slowly she learned to play a few tremulous, melancholy tunes. When Areki-Tapiru's husband neglected her for his younger wives, the gentle melodies calmed the chieftainess's jealous fits. She learned to play the love songs of *Hinemoa*, sweet lullabies and mournful laments. 'Here I stand alone,' one of the women sang as she played, 'Don't let me die just yet ...' Then she would play her flute with the tenderest feelings, fiercely praying that she might survive, without knowing whether it was *Ranginui* or Holy Mary Herself who might hear her.

Only as she lay on her sleeping mat at night did she dare to remember those glittering cities far away; even further than the moon, for at least the moon still shone above the roofs of the *Pa*. It was like recalling a dream: a world of racketing fast carriages and glossy horses, of fat penny loaves and yellow butter, of Charlie and his crew, who enjoyed the best of it all, but had still let her be exiled here, so far across the world. As she dropped from wakefulness to sleep, she returned to her vow that she would one day escape back to England. And growing each day more like her cruel and merry captors, she mouthed malicious curses against her enemies.

The cold rains ended for a season and then came back again. Feasts were eaten, and war parties returned with canoes full of slaves. Then, one ordinary day, a piece of cloth appeared in Areki-Tapiru's hut. Only half interested, for she was teaching one of her mistress's sons to play knucklebones, she watched her mistress try to squeeze herself into the tube of woven stuff. Frustrated, Areki-Tapiru picked up an odd sort of black basket and tried to balance it on top of her oiled hair. Extraordinary words exploded into her brain like musket-shots: *bonnet, ribbons, lace*. She continued shaking the bones onto the hard dirt, entirely disguising her emotions, as the gunpowder of memory fired her mind back to wakefulness— *tartan, buttons, collar*.

తి

'Peg. I've been ringing the bell for ten minutes.'

Pox the woman, she hadn't even heard her. Mrs Croxon was standing right in front of her by the kitchen table. 'May I have a word, Peg?'

'Let me show you what we have,' Peg said archly, and motioned her to the basement stairs. Taking lanterns, they both made their way down to the cold larder, her Aladdin's Cave of treasures: there were pheasants, turkeys and fowl, and row upon row of carcasses hung on metal hooks from the ceiling. Fish and oysters stood in pails of brine all over the floor.

Once they were secret and alone, Peg said breathlessly, 'I've seen Sue. And it is bad news, Mrs Croxon. Miss Claybourn has ordered ten yards of white silk taffeta and Venice lace.'

'Perhaps she is going away?' her mistress said hopefully.

'White silk. Wedding quality.'

'A ball, then? Oh, I don't know. Don't look at me like that.'

'Think, Mrs Croxon. It is only my concern that makes me speak up. And what of you?'

The mistress wouldn't meet her eye directly. 'I can no longer disguise my dislike for him.'

'Then you must be wary,' Peg said, warming to her subject. 'He may strike soon.'

'He may? How?'

'Think, mistress. If anything happens to you he will have all he wants. And Miss Claybourn can parade in her Venice lace in your lovely sitting room.'

The mistress covered her mouth with her hand as if fearing to speak out loud. 'I still cannot quite believe . . .'

Peg approached her mistress very gently and took her mistress's two lily-white hands in hers.

'Listen to me. It is about saving your life, now.'

She gave her mistress a powerful look and she quailed, as if on command.

They clambered back up to the kitchen, where the grocer's boy was unloading his cart. The table was attractively heaped with parcels and bottles.

'Yet more food? My goodness, what a vast amount. I suppose we can send some out to the poor.' Mrs Croxon inspected a bottle of catsup and a box of tea.

'The master has told me he wants a grand Christmas whatever the cost,' Peg said. But she didn't add that she was hankering after her own favourite dishes, too. After all it was five long years that she had yearned for the taste of plum pudding and roast beef.

'Well, you need not bother on my account. I want nothing too rich at the moment. My stomach is unsettled enough.'

Mrs Croxon frowned at a small blue bottle at the top of the heap, and lifted it to squint at the label.

'Ratsbane, Mrs Croxon. Them black beetles have swarmed right back into the fruit store again.'

'Well, do be careful, won't you, Peg?'

Peg took the bottle and slipped it inside her apron pocket. 'There's no one more particular than me around poisons, Mrs Croxon.'

25

Delafosse Hall

December 1792

~ *Christmas Punch* ~

Take a bottle of dark rum and put to it 24 ounces of cold tea, add to it the juice of a half a lemon and two or three table-spoons of the best Muscovado sugar. Grate in some nutmeg and lemon rind as you please it. This makes about a quart of a fine and pleasant liquor.

The Gentleman's Magazine

On December the twenty-third, the park was hazy from clammy mists that muted and softened all colour and distance. Michael had not set off for Whitelow after breakfast, so I bundled myself into my redingote that was as thick and warm as a man's, and pulled on my sable hat and muff. Even so, the chill pinched my nose as I hurried along paths of mushy leaves, sending startled birds pink-pinking up into the air. Claw-like seed pods clung to my skirts; the fine flowers of summer drooped slimy and black. I collected a few posies of ever-greens to paint: stiff pine cones, jewel-like berries of black and scarlet, and oval seed pods as lustrous as pearl.

I was roused from unpleasant thoughts by the unwelcome sounds of someone walking behind me on the path. I stopped and listened. There was a confidence and heaviness to those striding steps that made me sure a man was following me. I had left Michael with his feet on the fender and a pile of plans for the mill. Could it be a poacher? No, it was Michael, I was sure of it. 'It is about saving your life, now,' Peg had said. I picked up my skirts, and hurried as fast and silently as I could towards the summerhouse. Once inside, I looked about for a hiding place and still fearing the tunnel, I slipped into the niche beside the statue of Harpocrates, and stood very still. Bless me with silence, I thought, and a phrase chimed in reply from the back of my mind: 'Silence was their very god'. Of course; this must be where Moncrieff and Michael's mother had met. This must be where Michael was conceived.

Booted footsteps crunched on the broken tiles at the entrance; an unwelcome heat burned my cheeks. A confrontation with

Michael out here, so far from the house, so far from Peg's help, filled me with terror. I glanced towards the low arch where the entrance to the tunnel lay, but it was too late to dash for it.

'Grace? Are you there, Grace?' The voice was inside the summer-house now. Once I would have mistaken it for Michael's, but now I knew better. Overjoyed, I stepped out from the niche.

'Peter? You startled me.'

My brother-in-law was muffled in a greatcoat; as he spoke, white vapour rose from his lips. 'I am not surprised, hiding out here in this broken-down place. Did you not hear me?'

'I wasn't sure who you were,' I said, not caring to say I had mistaken him for his brother. 'Did you call at the house?'

He pulled a sullen face. 'Michael has forbidden me from calling. Extraordinary, isn't it? But I'm just on my way down from Ripon and I thought I might be able to search you out. An old servant sweeping the yard told me which direction you set off in.'

I ushered him towards the emerald-stained marble bench and settled before him in my painting chair. The light trickling in through the cracked panes was meagre and greenish too. 'This is my private place. No one will find us here.'

'Good.' He looked about himself, at the decay of the place, and pulled up his collar. 'Grace, I have written to you twice this week of arrangements for you to join us in London. When you don't reply it alarms me. What is wrong?'

'Forgive me. I should have replied to your invitation weeks ago. But as to further letters, I have received none at all.'

'You will join us? I am not sure if you know, but Michael has quarrelled with Father.'

'Over what matter?'

'What do you think?'

I exhaled contemptuously. 'Money?'

'Naturally. But you are welcome to join us. We all expressly wish you to know that. There is a mail coach from here in Earlby, and I will meet you directly from it.'

I did not reply at once; precisely because I was powerfully tempted to join them.

'It is hard,' I said, my tongue suddenly tied. Fear of Michael's fury were he to discover my betrayal hovered over me like Damocles' sword suspended on a horse's hair.

'Peter, why did I not receive those letters?' I asked instead. Since Peg had confided in me, even the events surrounding my father's death had taken on a malign significance. 'It is not the first time I have felt isolated by Michael. When I was ill he took it upon himself to direct my affairs: serious matters, even my father's funeral. I was bedridden for mere days, and yet weeks of correspondence passed between here and Greaves.'

'So letters were written in your name? This is bad.' Peter shook his head. He rose and paced up and down the broken floor, clapping his arms against his sides. Suddenly he stopped. 'Do you ever think that someone is contriving against you?' So remarkably did he resemble Michael that he could almost have been a doppelgänger made in my husband's image; perhaps that was why I found it impossible to unburden myself to him. I shook my head, but found myself whispering a contrary, 'Yes. Yes, I do.' How many warnings did I need? Peg intimated daily that Michael contrived against me. Now his own brother echoed her concerns. I felt wholly desolate.

To my surprise Peter sprang towards me, crouching low so that his face was close to mine, and took both my hands in his. 'Grace, I know you are stronger than we all at first believed. But you should not be alone here. And as for Michael; don't waste your sympathies on him. He does not deserve you.' His face had taken on a beseeching expression uncannily like Michael's.

'Peter. Don't do this.'

But he held my fingers tighter and would not release them. 'Leave now, with me,' he urged, not letting go, and pressing my fingertips with his. 'There are things I know, Michael's secrets, that I have made a great oath not to divulge. I know why he brought you here. It is outrageous.'

I glanced at the statue. Naturally, Peter knew all about his brother's paternity.

'I know all about it,' I told him. 'Michael has told me. About himself, and his feelings of shame.'

'Shame! So he should feel – infinite shame.' He began to caress my cold fingers, speaking fervently. 'I would never treat you like that. Come with me tonight and he will never know. That's why I came here. I saw you in York, Grace – how you shone, like a jewel. The truth is, I think of you often. And not always as a brother should.' He raised my hands to his warm lips and began to kiss the knuckles.

A gratifying pulse of flattery lasted only an instant. Then a horrible apprehension flashed into my mind. Did Peter hope to outdo his brother at one stroke; by taking Whitelow from him, and by taking me? Had the brothers' rivalry escalated to this absurdity – that Peter now imagined himself attracted to me? Or was it – and this showed how deep my suspicions ran – a test devised by the brothers, to expose my treachery to my husband? I jerked my hand away.

'Peter! This is nonsense. I suspect I only shine so bright because I am Michael's wife. I tell you plainly, I will not be treated as a plaything for the two of you to squabble over.'

My brother-in-law made a mocking feint backwards from my harsh words. Then, a moment later, he looked at me with some awkwardness. 'It is not all about Michael, you know. I do like you exceedingly. But I see it now, it will not do.'

'It will not.'

In a moment he was his usual affable self again. 'Well, well. If I cannot tempt you to London tonight, might you not join our party in the New Year? You will be intrigued to learn who else makes up our party: Mr John Francis Rawdon.'

Now that did wound me, for I should dearly have liked to speak to my old friend.

'He will be with his bride-to-be,' I replied smartly, 'and she would certainly not welcome my company.'

'Have you not heard? Your friend has broken with his bride. The rumour is that he paid a very large sum to keep the breach of promise from the courts. So he is free, sister dear.'

Horribly discomposed, I struggled to hide my feelings. For once, I found Peter's teasing quite as uncomfortable as did Michael.

I summoned a reserve of calm and said, 'Peter, I will not make a secret assignation with Mr Rawdon simply to bait Michael. If you think I will, I fear you are entirely mistaken in my character. I wanted to join you in London, but all you have done is make me uneasy, now. It would be sensible to go now. For my own sake, please don't let Michael find you creeping about the estate uninvited.'

I sensed I had wounded him in turn, for Peter rose, put his hat on, and bowed with frigid politeness. 'Very well, Grace. If that is what you wish. Write, if you change your mind. But, one day soon, you will wish you had come away with me.' He walked away, and I listened mournfully until his footsteps faded into the silence.

I sat a while longer and pondered his words, wondering if I had behaved like an idiot. I would have at least ended all this uncertainty if I had left at Peter's side. For some reason the motto on the tower's sundial entered my head, 'The rod is iron, the motion is shadow'. Time is unstoppable, I thought. The spinning sun, the chasing shadow; both will never cease. But what of us mortals beneath the dial – are not all our days numbered?

On Christmas Eve I woke early to a sun-filled room. Michael and I had agreed a truce of sorts, based upon his wish to celebrate Christmas. Being raised a dissenter, I had never before observed the keeping of Yuletide. My father had delivered great rants against the popery and superstition of Christmas; there had been no celebrations permitted at Palatine House. Though at school I had sung carols and exchanged Christmas greetings, this would be my first true Christmas.

Peg and I had hung branches of evergreens and holly above the great entrance door, and all about the dining room and parlour. I searched out my gift to Michael: a diamond shirt-buckle I had bought in York. I looked for my husband, but he was already out, so I breakfasted alone; warmed by the bright winter's sunshine streaming in through the windows. On such a morning I could not sit inside. Without a word to anyone I took the gig to the village, enjoying the pearl-blue sky, streaked with luminous bands of clouds. I was rewarded at the postmaster's office by two letters, one from Anne and the second from Peter. Reluctant to hurry back to the Hall, I decided to be bold. The George had a wainscoted newspaper room where I fancied a lady might venture alone. Once inside, I found only a couple of old gentlemen puffing tobacco smoke behind their newspapers. With some pleasure, I found a bright window seat and opened my post.

Anne's letter was stamped from Santa Cruz, Tenerife, and was brighter and more cheerful than I could have hoped. Now accustomed to the rolling of the ship, she was feeling healthful and happy. She and Jacob had taken walks in the sun, and pressed many tropical flowers, some beautiful specimens of which she enclosed. The pumpkins and fresh meat on the island had improved her appetite, and she was content, though apprehensive of the next long period at sea. She wrote that the ship's next port would be Rio de Janeiro, and then, 'to catch the fast trade winds to the southern hemisphere', they would sail back across the Atlantic to Cape Town. So Peg had been telling the truth when she described the erratic route she had taken. Naturally she had told the truth, I rebuked myself; she had taken the voyage as a convict. Nevertheless, it rattled me. If I were now to accept all she told me as true, I must never trust Michael again.

In this divided state I turned to Peter's letter. It was a friendly rebuke for my refusing his invitation, and a last attempt to persuade me to join him. I reached for my writing box key, kept always in my paint box, hidden beneath the block of Crimson Lake. As I called to the inn servant to fetch me fresh ink and a pot of tea, I found myself wiping my fingers. The key – did it carry a sticky film? When had I last touched it? Three days earlier I had used the key to inspect my depleting accounts, and immediately hid it again. I inspected the paint box closely and saw no other signs of disturbance. I even smelled the key, but the lingering pungency of linseed covered any unfamiliar substance.

The servant returned with my order and I forgot my moment of disquietude. 'Yule cakes, missus,' she said. 'It being Christmas Eve.' It was with a certain independent relish that I sipped my tea and ate those spiced delicacies for the first time. I wrote a hasty note to Peter, telling him that I had changed my mind and would indeed join him at the New Year, if he could assure me that his parents would be present. I had come to a decision: I would confide in the Croxons. I had to tell someone of my grave worries about Michael, the excessive strain on his mind, and my knowledge of his connection with our neighbour, Miss Claybourn. Privately, I also determined to consult Mr Tully about the terms of my marriage settlement, and whether Michael owed me a living if we separated. My trivial exercise of independence in coming to the George had settled it. I would keep Michael company at Christmas, as I had promised, but after that I would please myself. Satisfied, I wished Peter and his parents greetings for the season and laid my pen to rest.

Looking up from my writing, my attention was drawn to a prosperous-looking couple conversing nearby. They were both dressed in exceeding high fashion for Earlby but it was their warmth of manner towards each other that impressed me. As they shared a little quip, the gentleman set a swift kiss on his wife's cheek and she returned a private smile.

Once the gentleman had left, it was inevitable that the lady and I should notice each other. With a nod and a pleasant smile, she said, 'How do you do? I am Mrs Barthwaite of Monkroyd.'

'Mrs Croxon of Delafosse,' I said, standing to shake her hand. 'I am delighted to meet you.'

At the sound of my name Mrs Barthwaite's round and gentle eyes fixed on me in fascination. 'You are Michael's wife? How pleased I am to see you up and about at last. We are well met, indeed.'

I was a little wrong-footed by this, but said lightly, 'Oh, I am generally up and about.'

'Mr Barthwaite and Mr Croxon generally hunt together. I am afraid your husband is guilty of keeping you all to himself. Michael told us you were unwell. These husbands, they will mollycoddle us, won't they, dear? Now I see what good health you are blessed with, you must join us at Monkroyd. We ladies meet, you understand, while the gentlemen hunt. We bring our workboxes, but it is all sham. Mostly we have a little gossip and a few games of cards and break into my husband's wines. It is pleasant enough in these dark days. Would you care to join us at Monkroyd, dear?'

It was foolish of me, but as she conversed in such a spirit of friendship, I blinked and faltered. 'Why, I should love to,' I said at last. 'When do you next meet?'

'I believe it is the tenth of January. I shall send you a note. Only I must reproach you, Mrs Croxon, for we ladies have sent you our cards in the past; we presumed you didn't care for company?'

'I have been ill.'

'There you are then. Mr Croxon was no doubt behaving as a new husband will. Make hay, my dear, while it lasts. Let him spoil you. He has told us all about the improvements he has made for you. Mr Delahunty, he reports, did a good, though expensive job. I should very much like to see your new apartments, my dear.'

'I should like to show them,' I replied, ignoring the slight both to my own pocket and expertise. Just then, an irksome thought struck me. 'The ladies who meet at Monkroyd. Might I know them?'

She reeled off a list of names: Lady this, Mrs that – no one I had heard of.

'Not Miss Claybourn?'

'Miss Claybourn of Riverslea? She used to come along, some time ago. But she has rather – fallen by the wayside, didn't you know?'

I nodded as if I did know, though in fact her words chilled me. I had once heard a sermon that used the very same parable to speak of a certain class of unfortunate women.

Mr Barthwaite just then knocked at the window, making comical signals that all was ready outside. We stood, and my new acquaintance said, 'You must call me Nell, all my friends do.' I invited her to call me Grace, and we shook hands very jovially and wished each other a Merry Christmas. She even smiled at my mud-spattered redingote and said, 'Now that is a sensible costume for this weather. We must dine at the Queades today; hence all this rigmarole.'

I returned home in far brighter spirits than I had set off, eager to tell Michael of our mutual friends. As I trotted the pony back up the drive, a silver crescent of a moon hung low above the black filigree of trees. Already the afternoon light was fading, and a pink streak burned low on the horizon. Now winter was entrenched, the Hall was stripped bare of leaves, the canopy no more than a spidery network of branches. Below that lay the naked walls of my home, cracked and scabrous. My last thoughts before I reached the house were that my letter to Peter still lay unposted in my pocket, and that before Nell Barthwaite came visiting we must make some repairs to the facade of Delafosse Hall.

Running me to earth upstairs, Peg asked, 'Where have you been, mistress?'

'Out,' I said shortly.

'I have been worried about you; that is all. And I'm ready to serve the dinner downstairs.'

'And what of my husband? He disappeared this morning. Has he turned up yet?'

'I heard him in the dining room. I've been up to my eyes. So where do you suppose he got to?'

'I truly have no idea. Here, would you tie the back of this gown?'

'What, your best white taffeta?'

'When else am I to wear this finery, if not at Christmas?'

As Peg helped me into the tight sleeves and fastened the broad black belt with a cameo, I could not stop myself from chattering of my encounter at the George. 'The Barthwaites are most agreeable, Peg. And I did enjoy my spell of independence. I even sampled the George's Yule cake, which was most delicious. I believe I have made a great step forward.'

I caught a glimpse of her scowling in the pier glass. 'Oh, Peg – don't feel slighted. Your baking is far better than the George's.'

She returned a pinch-lipped smile.

'Fetch my jewel case, would you?'

As she presented it, she said, 'So Mr Croxon has been putting it about that you have been ill all this time. Is that not strange?'

'It is. But just for one day, I want to forget about all this subterfuge. Michael and I have agreed to try to enjoy Christmas together.'

'I see.' She nodded, looking down. 'Well, I must tend to the dinner. I don't want all that fine food spoiling. I recollect now, Mr Croxon is making a bowl of punch for you to raise a toast.'

'A moment, Peg. I'll wear my cameo bracelet. It is time I wore my wedding gifts.' I held out my wrist, but I thought her mightily preoccupied, for instead of the cameo she unclasped my everyday agate bracelet.

'Not that one. Dear me, the heat has overcome you.'

Once the bracelet was in place, I said, 'Go then, I shall be down in a moment.' I forgave her any pertness, for she was that proverbial symbol of hard labour: a cook at Christmas. Inspecting myself in the pier glass, I was not too disheartened; the tight-waisted gowns I had bought in York suited me far better than the trousseau the Croxons had bought for my wedding. But I felt bone-cold that day, especially after my spell in the smoky fug of the George. I pulled on a quilted petticoat beneath my gauzy gown, and slipped on my velvet pelisse with the gold braiding. Over it all I draped my cashmere shawl, thinking I was not quite as elegant as Mrs Barthwaite

– but then, perhaps she did not suffer as I did from the stone cold of the Hall.

In the dining room, Michael had spread out all the makings of a celebration punch: lemons, brandy, nutmeg, rum and tea. Still feeling cheery, I wished him a Merry Christmas. He nodded, but was preoccupied with his spoons and measures.

'Where were you this morning?' I asked, summoning my pleasantest smile. Seeing him, I had a sudden, forceful premonition that he had spent the morning with his lover, enjoying a Christmas tête-à-tête. My suspicion was reinforced by Nell Barthwaite's opinion, still echoing in my ears, of Miss Claybourn's having 'fallen by the wayside'.

'I went for an early ride. It was a glorious morning.'

Clumsily, he dropped the knife with which he was paring a lemon. It was quite a mess he was making along the sideboard. Or was it my new ebullience that seemed to drain Michael of his composure? I told him of the George, my letter from Anne, and my happy meeting with the Barthwaites. The import of Peter's letter, on the other hand, I would postpone until the punch bowl was well drained.

'Oh, that gossip Nell Barthwaite. Don't waste your time on her.'

'I believe I will,' I said firmly. 'I am tired of my own company.'

He continued to draw out his preparations for our Christmas toast, so I looked about the room. All my hard work had come to fruition that day: the new fireplace housed a mighty Yule log that warmed the room, casting reflections across the crystal and silver. I admired the forest green of the brocaded furniture, and the holly gathered in red ribbons hung about the walls. I decided that whatever temper Michael might be in, I would not let him spoil our first Christmas.

The new damask cloth was spread with a fine repast: Peg's own Yule cakes looked even daintier than those I had already sampled. A great wheel of cheese had pride of place, beside magnificent pies of game and fruit. On a great round platter was a salamagundy salad as fresh as a bouquet of flowers; concentric rings of every delight: eggs, chicken, ham, beetroot, anchovies, and orange.

I glanced back at Michael. I can picture even now the wide Chinese bowl and ladle, and the glass jug of water with which he diluted my own portion. He lifted the ladle to his lips, tasted it, added another spoonful of sugar, and proclaimed the punch good and strong. The clock chimed the hour. I can say in all certainty that I was brittle but cheerful at two o'clock on the afternoon of Christmas Eve.

'Here we are.' Michael's hands shook a little as he placed two punch glasses down on the table. Wondering again if he had just that morning visited Miss Claybourn, I teased my husband. 'You are trembling. Is your life so stimulating that you need strong punch so early in the day?'

'Not at all.' Yet he looked so uneasy that I thought, yes, I have caught you out.

It was then, just as we both lifted our glasses, that a knock rapped on the door. It opened a few inches and Peg called urgently, 'Mrs Croxon, I must speak to you this minute.'

'What is it, Peg?'

'Please, Mrs Croxon. A word alone.'

I rolled my eyes heavenward. Michael grunted with impatience. 'Devil take you, you drab,' he shouted over his shoulder. 'What is it now?'

'A most urgent domestic matter for Mrs Croxon,' she hissed back.

I set down my punch glass and followed her into the servery next door. Once alone she grasped my sleeve and stared at me as if she had trouble shaping her next words.

'What is it?' I whispered.

'I were just downstairs, mistress. And I saw that blue bottle, you know, that ratsbane, that arsenic. It had been opened up and used. So I asked the others what had been going on. I were thinking maybe Nan had made a start on the black beetles. But you won't believe it, mistress. Bess saw the master come down for the makings of the punch, and he took the ratsbane and – Lord help you, mistress, I think he's put it in your drink.'

I backed away from her so she no longer touched me. 'No, Peg. That is plain ridiculous. Michael has been tasting it at every step. I watched him pour both our glasses from the same bowl. How could he poison my drink?'

'Mistress,' she said hoarsely, 'it's not in the punch. It's in the jug of water.'

'Are you sure?' I said, with less confidence.

'I swear on my mother's heart.' She touched her breast and looked at me very profoundly. Great God, I thought, she may be telling the truth.

'Bess is waiting outside. Ask her if you won't believe me.'

Peg opened the door and ushered the maid in. Bess was uneasy outside the kitchen, twisting the edge of her sackcloth apron in chapped hands. I asked her to tell me carefully what she had seen.

'I were tending the fire when master come down t'kitchen,' she said in a slow-witted tone.

'What did he take? Answer carefully now.'

Her bovine eyes darted about the room and then settled on the ceiling as she spoke with some effort. 'Some lemons and a nutmeg.'

'And anything else?' I prompted.

She grimaced with effort. 'When I were seeing t'meat I seen him pocket that blue bottle. That one wi' a skull on it.'

I dismissed her and leaned towards Peg, my words barely audible. 'What should I do?'

'Switch the glasses around. Give him a dose of his own medicine,' she said coldly. 'He deserves it.'

I shook my head in a daze. She leaned very close and whispered hotly against my cheek, 'Listen to me. If I'm mistaken, it makes no difference. But if I'm not, he'll get only what is due to him.'

'I cannot.' I looked in anguish at the servery wall and thought of Michael a few feet behind it. The door sprang open and Michael himself appeared. Peg and I jumped apart like startled rabbits.

'What's going on here?' he demanded. 'Am I to celebrate Christmas alone? Damn you, woman, get downstairs and leave us be.' He pointed at the stairs, and, with her head bent low in mortification, Peg left us.

Everything was happening with such speed, I could not absolutely take it in. Michael grasped my arm and led me back into the dining room, once again seeming jovial and eager to begin our celebrations. Irresistibly, my eye was drawn to the two glasses standing very close to each other on the table. But it was impossible that I could pick up my glass and drink from it. Nor had I time to switch the two glasses around.

'A toast to us and to our prosperous future,' Michael said heartily. 'And to many a Merry Christmas to come at Delafosse.' He raised his glass. Yet still he seemed awkward. I could not move.

'Come along. What is ailing everyone today? Can you not even join me in a toast to our future?' I fancied there was a whine of desperation to his voice.

My hand reached obediently for the glass, but my nerves rebelled. If Peg were correct, I might be ending my life. My fingers fumbled over the slippery surface, and the glass tumbled to the floor; the punch spilled out, brownish-red across my new carpet.

'The Devil take it, woman. Damn – damn it!'

I bent down to make ineffectual movements with a napkin.

'Oh, leave it. What do we have servants for?' He kicked the glass away in disgust. 'I'll mix you another.'

'No. Not for me. My stomach—'

'Now you wish me to toast Christmas alone? I am sick to the death of this. You will join me, Grace.'

By now my heart was banging against my ribs. Perhaps I should, as Peg had urged, exchange our two glasses. Michael's still lay untasted on the table. In a sort of trance I watched him fill my own glass from the punchbowl.

'No water for me,' I said in a strangled tone.

'You always have water. Or you turn foolish.' He picked up the jug that held the invisible poison and poured a good measure into my glass. I was now frantic, casting about the room for some distraction, something to draw Michael's attention from the punch. Then suddenly, I remembered my Christmas gift, still sitting in my pocket. 'I have a Christmas tradition too,' I lied. 'And that is to give my loved ones a gift before the toast.'

He frowned. 'A gift? But I will give you yours at New Year.'

'Well, my family do things differently. I will give you yours now. Come along.' I took out the little bundle wrapped in silk. 'Close your eyes, my darling.'

Reluctantly he stood stock-still and closed his eyes. I spun him around so his back was to the table. It was the work of a second to switch the two glasses about, so the watered punch stood at his setting and the untainted glass at mine. A terrible pressure was pounding in my temples, but I took out the buckle and fastened it into the linen at his breast. He opened his eyes, looked down at the diamond, and walked to the mirror. 'How charming!' he said to his reflection. Then he ruined everything by returning to the table and obscuring my view of it. When he turned around he held a glass in each hand. I looked from one to the other; no longer able to tell which was mine.

'Here.' He offered me the glass in his right hand. Was the straw-coloured punch in that glass paler than the other? I looked at the other. No, that was paler still – or was it?

'For God's sake, Grace – take it.'

He was trying to confound me. I reached across him to the left-hand glass. 'You have mixed them up,' I said. 'This one is mine.' Before he could remonstrate, I raised my unwatered glass.

'To Christmas!' I said very quickly.

Michael hesitated, then slowly lifted his glass too. We both drank, in a state of acute tension.

I knew at once that my punch tasted just as it should. Michael took a long draught, and his usual satisfied expression returned. We both sat down and sipped our punch in silence while Michael absentmindedly picked from the platter of salad. I exulted that Peg was wrong. I wondered for a few moments if Peg could in fact be the origin of all our troubles? The food spread before us was magnificent, but something she had said stuck in my mind. Had I truly heard her wish her master dead?

'Some game pie?' I sliced a beautiful Yorkshire Pie, filled with concentric pink and brown meats held in a lavishly ornamented crust.

Michael didn't reply, only pulled his face at his half-empty punch glass. 'Too sour, don't you think – perhaps too much lemon?'

I shook my head. 'No, it seemed perfectly sweet.'

He raised a napkin to his mouth. 'I am sorry,' he mumbled. He began to cough loudly, then began hacking more strenuously. At the height of his gasping, he suddenly slumped, crashing forward onto his plate of salad, sending orange and ham flying onto the linen. A guttural choking sound emerged from his throat. The horror of it was, he was still trying to control himself; trying, bizarrely, to apologise. Did a part of me still wonder if he was acting, even then? A moment later all doubts fled. With terrifying suddenness, the scene lurched from celebration to nightmare. As Michael coughed, a stream of crimson blood issued from his mouth across the pristine table. I screamed and ran to the bell. After frantically summoning Peg I looked back at him. He had toppled to the floor, banging against the furniture. More blood, gobbets of it, ran down his chin onto his clothes. Lying prone before the fireplace, his legs cramped up against his stomach, he vomited another stream of blood. Horribly, he tried to speak.

I knelt beside him, appalled by the livid crimson around his mouth. I grasped a napkin and tried to blot his lips, but only succeeded in smearing the stuff, spreading it about. His expression was hard as his eyes rolled up to fix on my face. 'What,' he said in a wheezing parody of his true voice, 'have you done to me?'

Running footsteps approached. Peg rushed into the room and stopped in her tracks. She reached for a chair to support herself. 'Oh, mistress, what have you done?'

'I think I've killed him,' I said. The room, the whole scene, did not appear real. Trivial notions spun in my head: that the carpet would need to be patched, that all Peg's food was spoiled. Michael's eyelids blinked, then slowly closed. Blood was spattered over his ivory linen, his silver coat, the expensive new carpet. The scene was like a grotesque waxworks; it was impossible to believe this had happened here, in my own dining room.

'You swapped those two drinks?' Peg turned to the jug of water that still stood half-full on the sideboard.

'I had to. Or—'

'I never thought you would do it.'

'What shall we do?' I begged.

Peg walked warily over to my husband and crouched to feel his neck.

'You have killed him,' she said flatly. 'All that blood. It's the ratsbane burning his windpipe, then his insides. It kills in minutes, they say.'

'No!' I sank to the ground, clutched his still warm hand and kissed it.

'Can you hear me? Make a sign,' I begged. He lay motionless, his eyelids closed. Michael, my husband, was dead. His beautiful pallid face was stiff in repose, his lips slack, blossomed with gobbets of crimson. 'Michael,' I cried again and again, caressing him frantically; chafing his hands, undoing his linen to free his throat. A kind of yawning chasm was opening in my mind, consuming the life I had always known. I don't know how long I sat there on the floor beside him. I began to shiver as violently as if I sat on a sheet of ice. It could have been me, I repeated to myself, I might have drunk that arsenical punch. It could have been me vomiting blood while he – what would Michael have done? Would he have wept – or watched me die with cold satisfaction?

Peg was shaking my shoulder. 'You must go, mistress.' She was white-faced and frightened, but still her first thought was always of me. 'You must get away.'

'What?'

'Think! How will this look to the authorities? The justices will find out you gave him poison.'

I stared at her and already the events of the last hour were difficult to grasp. 'I tried to switch the drinks about. Everything got – muddled. But it was his plan. You will be my witness, surely?'

'Me? An escaped felon? I cannot bear witness. Look at him. Picture it. They will say you murdered him, mistress. That's the truth. You must get away. While you have the chance.'

I felt as if that sheet of ice I sat on had cracked above a plummeting abyss. 'Surely he needs a doctor?'

'I will fetch Dr Sampson, mistress. But go first. Before someone sees you.'

She grasped me by the shoulder and imparted her orders as if I were a dumb child. 'Hurry. Go. Now.'

'But where shall I go?' I groped to recover my capacity for rational thought, but still it eluded me. She shook me like a rag doll. 'Remember them murderesses I told you about? Do you want to be locked in a cell and used by the jailers? Do you want to be strung up on the gallows?'

'No,' I whispered, almost falling insensibly, my limbs weak.

She glanced at the clock on the mantelpiece. 'The London mail goes in half an hour. You could be on it.'

'Then what shall I do?' My voice rose in panic.

'Go somewhere no one will find you. Change your name. Make a new life. Don't for God's sake let yourself be taken by the Justices. I will take care of everything.'

In such a state I could not resist her. While I was near to collapse she was clear-headed, firm and commanding – so I did as I was told. I rushed upstairs at once. I cast off my bloodstained dress and pulled on the first other gown I found. Though I tried to rinse my trembling hands, I could not rid myself of the tacky rustiness of Michael's blood. I threw a few items into my smallest trunk: my writing box, my paints and sketchbook and my heavy purse. Then I fled back downstairs in a frantic flurry. Peg was waiting in the hall. I made to return to the dining room, but she held me back. 'He's looking very bad. Go, so I can send for the doctor. Just to be sure.'

I scarcely knew which direction I faced, but she hustled me outside. The pony and trap were standing at the door, waiting. I had only those few possessions and the clothes on my body.

'Hurry, mistress.'

'Yes, yes, listen. I will write to you, Peg. You must tell me how – if, he recovers.'

'I will, dear mistress. Now get away safe. You have been such a friend to me.' We squeezed hands without restraint and I pulled her to my breast and embraced her like a sister. Then I picked up the reins and, scarcely knowing where I was going, I headed away down the drive.

26

Golden Square, London

Spring 1793

~ To Make Milk Curds ~

Take a gallon of skim-milk and scald in a pan, taking care
not to boil it; then cool to the lukewarmness of new milk. Add
a half-pound of sugar and teaspoonful of rennet to turn it; in
one or two hours the milk will be curdled and ready.

As sold by street-women at a penny
a glass in the London parks

My memories of that journey are jumbled shards: the hurtling progress southwards, my fretful dog-naps in the rocking coach; my horror at waking again and again to find my nightmare true. Michael, I told myself in disbelief, was dead. Panic seized me, as if all the ordered parts of my life had been torn up and cast to the four winds. The journey seemed infinitely long, and yet all too rapidly it ended. Looking out of the carriage glass I found myself amidst a great passage of people and carts and horses, communicating a queasy mix of unease and excitement, as if some general calamity had erupted. We had entered the great highway into London. I roused myself inside that sour-smelling coach, at a loss as to what to do next.

We halted on a hillside to change the horses, and I dismounted reluctantly, standing apart, eavesdropping on my fellow passengers' discussion of the view. In the distance stood the River Thames like a ribbon cast down in a curl, passing the towered hulk of Westminster Abbey before running beneath Westminster Bridge. Above the maze of buildings, hundreds of church spires spiked the sky, piercing the sooty smoke that rose from a thousand chimneys. I had never before been to London. What did I know of the city, save that it was a monstrous home of lords and rogues? I had Peter's address, of course, and my invitation to join him on New Year's Eve. Yet now my every instinct rebelled against seeking out the Croxons. There would be questions, inquiries, recriminations. What I longed for was what Peg had advised – a spell of peace – to lose myself, if I could, in the anonymous metropolis.

At last I had a notion. There was a woman, a Miss Le Toye,

from whom I had for many years ordered art stuffs. I did not even need her trade card to remember her address. Once the coach finally set me down, in the hubbub of an inn's yard, I gave her address to a hackney driver. 'The Golden Ball, Windmill Street, Golden Square,' I said firmly, and to my relief the driver grunted and took up the reins.

The hackney crawled forward, weaving around barrows, before slamming to a halt before a herd of horned beasts being smacked on their wobbling haunches by smocked countrymen. I stared at the battery of signs hung upon buildings: *Laceman and Draper, Tea Dealer & Grocer, Goldsmith, Jeweller and Toymaker*. Coffeehouses, tavern signs, shop signs – there was no end to the celebration of commerce. My eye lit upon a shop titled, 'Elvira Frankland & Sister, Milliners', and in that moment I followed Peg's advice and chose my new identity.

Set down outside Miss Le Toye's glass-fronted colour shop, even the smell of London streets was unfamiliar: a throat-catching mingling of bitter smoke and foul gutters, enriched with the stink of horses. Gathering my courage, I entered and found a long room painted very pale and pretty, set about with gilded candles and brimming shelves of paint stuffs, colours, and delightful prints. I introduced myself as Mrs Frankland, a widow of Lancaster. Then I opened my paint box and requested replacements for various paints that bore the label of her shop. Only when that business was over did I ask for a recommendation for genteel lodgings thereabouts. Miss Le Toye's shrewd painter's eyes assessed my fine but travel-worn clothes, and my exhausted face; she wrote an address on a paper and offered me a maid to show the way. That was how I found Mrs Huckle's lodging house, at the better end of Glasshouse Street. It was an austere stone house, with double doors of heavy oak; softened by no garden, no trees, not even a window box of herbs.

Mrs Huckle was a coal merchant's widow, who warily appraised me when I appeared on her doorstep. She enquired about my circumstances, and, weary as I was, I convinced her I was a widow visiting London to make certain arrangements following the death of my husband in a riding accident. She had one small room available that would cost five shillings a week, and I took it, for my purse, well-guarded beneath my petticoat, was thankfully heavy. We struck an agreement for breakfast to be served by her maid Sal, all coal and candles, and dinner downstairs with the other lodgers if I cared for it, at an addition of five pence per day.

My room had a good bright window overlooking Glasshouse Street, a table and chair by the fire, and a nun-like bed. Yet this meagre space was a sanctum I would not have swapped for a palace. It was never silent there, like the dust-drowned rooms at Delafosse. The creaks and bangings and coughs of my neighbours were an ever-present comfort.

For days I stayed in my room, see-sawing between mourning Michael's death and a heady deliverance at my escape. A conversation overheard in the passage roused me; the mention that New Year's Eve was to fall that evening, the holiday when the Croxons would be celebrating with John Francis. Pulling out my unposted letter, I re-read the self-assured lines I had written, scarcely able to credit that such high spirits had originated in my own mind.

To stop the ceaseless revolving of what might have been spinning around my head, I tidied myself up, pulling on my one creased and mud-spattered gown. For a long time I scrubbed my hands, but could not rid them of a scarlet tint and a disgusting tackiness. With much anxiety I went downstairs to meet Mrs Huckle's other lodgers. Captain Macdonald was an upright, chivalrous old soldier with ruddy wrinkles and bushy white hair, who rose and kissed my hand. 'Delighted, dear lady,' he said, in a mild Scottish burr, making a deep bow. Sprightly and lean, I reckoned him to be fifty-five years at the least. Miss Cato, a twittery spinster of even greater years, nodded and simpered. The remaining lodgers did not dine, reduced by poverty to heating a few scraps at their own grates. Dinner was a thin indeterminate soup, bread and butter, fried fish, and gristly chops – which proved to be the full measure of Mrs Huckle's generosity. This was served with a shrewish remark that she had expected to see me changed into mourning now I was unpacked. The captain winked at me from behind the landlady's broad back, and we were only once again at ease once she had departed. Miss Cato and I sipped tea, while the captain produced his own flask of spirits.

'Would you care for a game of cards to while away the hours until midnight?' he asked. I did, for the flower-papered parlour was convivial, and I was heartily starved of good honest company. 'The chops tonight might more profitably have been used to re-sole leather boots, wouldn't you say, Mrs Frankland?' the old man remarked drily, as he dealt me a hand. Miss Cato tittered, her head bent over a vast piece of knotting. The captain winked at me again, and politely allowed me to win. Two hours later, Miss Cato retired with a quaint little curtsey, and I sat on by the fireside, not disliking the gallant old gentleman's company at all. He chatted about his time in Bengal, of his army days and the campaigns he had seen. He was blessed, he said, with a grant of half-pay that kept him in brandy and tobacco, so he took employment only as it interested him. The captain was also one of those rare fellows who attend intently to whatever is said to him. Thus I found myself running on at length of my home in Greaves, my parents' deaths, and my marriage to Michael. Then, of course, I had to recount my husband's 'riding accident'; at which my new friend tilted his head rather quizzically. The midnight bells rang in the New Year of 1793, and the captain rose and made a sort of pantomime of opening the door and seeing the old year off and ushering the new one in. Raising a toast to good fortune, I had little notion of what tumultuous changes that New Year would bring.

'And how do you intend to spend your time here in the capital?' the captain asked with great courtesy. 'While you make your family arrangements, that is.'

'I love to paint,' I told him. He assured me I was in the best of neighbourhoods for that. 'The great Swiss paintress, Miss Kauffman, lived at number sixteen Golden Square for many years. Might you allow me to show you her former home in the morning?'

I had seen that lady's work in prints and thought her the pride of her sex, being a Royal Academician, though a woman. Thus our friendship was sealed, and my next morning's walk on the captain's arm set a precedent for many days to come. The frayed gentility of Golden Square suited me well. I inspected my purse and found that, thanks to my filling it in readiness for Christmas boxes for the tradesmen and servants, it contained just less than fifty pounds. It was enough to pay for a good few months of this gentle existence. So it was that I began slowly to mend myself.

I could not, of course, escape my guilt about Michael. In dreams he rose before me, chalk-faced and bloody, accusing me of taking his life. Sometimes I hid from him, crouching in terror. In other nightmares he chased me through filthy alleys. Always, he found me; the final barrier would be broken, and he would scream at me draped in blood besmirched linen, his beautiful face turned monstrous with spite.

From such dreams it was a vast relief to wake and find all of London about me, the road outside rattling with wagons and coaches, the servants' cheery cries, or a tradesman whistling a tune as he unloaded a cart. The longer I thought of it, the more I regretted running away. Peg's advice had been well-intentioned, but I had been wrong to let her put me to flight. It had been cowardly to leave my husband; in fact, with hindsight, I found my actions inconceivable. I began to fret to know what had happened at Delafosse, until the craving burned like a fever. Finally, at the end of January, I gathered my courage and wrote to Peg.

Fearing that she might be forced to betray my location, I sent my letter from the postmaster's house in Golden Square, and advised her to reply to the same. What, I enquired urgently, had happened since I left? Was Michael's death generally known? Should I return and oversee the estate? Each day I had studied the notices in the newspaper and seen no mention of his death. Neither, I was relieved to see, had there been any Hue and Cry against me, nor indeed any word of events in Earlby. I posted the letter, and for two days trailed back and forth to the postmaster's window, to enquire of a reply.

Then, at last, it was there, addressed as instructed to 'Mrs G Frankland'.

My very dear mistress,

I think you will not believe what a joy it is for me to have news of you. Thank God you followed my advice and have taken up residence in London, for it is a great swarming place, well suited to a disappearance.

Your husband, you will marvel to hear, is still alive but fearfully ill. He for a long time was close to death from a loss of blood, but he has a strong constitution and now lingers in a sorry state; such that some might say it is a curse that he still lives. Dr Sampson says he will forever be an invalid, and I am afraid not a happy one. When I am alone with him, for I must nurse him now, he rants that he will have you seized and put in irons, mistress. I am afraid he is quite clear-headed in understanding the events of that dreadful Christmas Eve, and is fixed on the notion that you planned to be rid of him. He has told me plain that if he ever has sight or sound of you again he will have you flung into Newgate jail and strung up by the neck. He is even worse-tempered, mistress, after that Claybourn woman visits him, and I must tell you that they do conspire in whispers when alone. Turning matters over as I do, I should if I were you, be mighty careful of your very existence. You see I reckon the master's having a living wife does put a great obstacle between the two of them living as they wish to.

My dear friend, as you once called me in happier days, I am dismal without you. Yet you must put your own safety first and not be think-ing of me. Dr Sampson has asked me your whereabouts, and I have told him you have gone abroad for your health, having never quite recovered from your accident last year. I believe the doctor is not beyond suspicion himself, for he and a certain lady may well be friends too; she is that free with her favours.

Enough, I have put it about that you are too poorly to come home from foreign parts and I have no notion when you might return. As for me, mistress, I do not know how much longer I can stay here. You know full well how the master's treatment of you made my blood boil. I should heartily like to be free of nursing him, for it does disgust me extremely. And I must tell you there have been no wages forthcoming here since last you paid me, but that is no concern of yours now.

I have taken this opportunity to enclose a bottle of the tonic I made up for you, thinking you may need it after all the shocks you have suffered. That is all my news, mistress, and if you should care to follow my advice, do keep your true name hidden and stay away from these parts, for the sake of your life. Forget your husband, as I wish I might soon enough. I heartily wish you all the blessings you deserve for the future.

Your affectionate friend and ally,
Peg Blissett

I read and re-read that letter a score of times. So Michael lived after all. I thanked the Almighty he had been spared, and also, I admit, that I was not a murderess and lived secure and secret at Glasshouse Street. Mostly, however, I was left with the clear knowledge of how stupid I had been to believe myself in love with a man who wished my utter ruin. If I stayed well away from Delafosse, I told myself, I would be safe.

I wrote a hasty note back to Peg, relieving her of any obligation to nurse Michael, and sending a guinea piece in a twist of paper, as recompense for all her trouble. I wished her joy of the future and thanked her heartily for spreading the tale of my moving abroad. But as for Peg's remedy, I threw it away. I had no wish to return to day-time naps and a muddled head. Fresh air and company, I decided, were better remedies than any bottle.

Each morning I walked, and each afternoon I painted and read. When he was free of his work, the captain would accompany me on my jaunts; for as soon as I understood that his gallantry was of the harmless, old-fashioned style, I enjoyed his gentle flirtation. He introduced me to the pleasures of promenading along the pretty gravel walks of St James's Park; and treated me to a daily cup of curds, 'for your good health, madam', at the Milk Stall, where stood a couple of lazily grazing cows.

One February day as we loitered there at our healthful repast, a news-crier ran towards us, followed by a chattering throng. Halting, the crier called his news to gasps of astonishment: the King of France had been murdered by his own people, on that infernal machine, the guillotine. Now the cut-throats of France had declared war on Britain and all of Europe besides. Within days, red-coated militia had been quartered in the city parks, undisciplined lads for the most part. The captain vastly regretted he could not join them, for age allowed him to attack the French only with caustic words.

Amidst these commotions I attended to my small affairs. My new friend showed me where I might buy second-hand clothes, and was made to stand a long while on duty as I rooted amongst the baskets and trestles. With my limited purse I settled on a black woollen mourning gown, not unlike the old-fashioned one I had worn to mourn my mother. I felt this garb to be the surest disguise against troublesome questions, yet I cannot say it fooled the captain. 'Was it a hasty sort of bereavement?' he asked me one day as we strolled to Golden Square. 'After that riding accident – at a stile was it, or another time, a turnpike?' His bright eyes shone as he teased me about my differing accounts of my husband's death.

'I'm afraid it was certainly very hasty,' I confessed with a conspiratorial smile.

I discovered the great sights of our capital, exploring that new institution called the British Museum, where glass cases contain a great many marvels, collected by Englishmen from obscure parts of the world. There I sketched mummified corpses of Egypt, so ancient that those pharaohs lived long before Christ himself. Soon after, I discovered the famed Royal Academy, where I studied the new style in portraits painted with freer, bolder brushstrokes.

Yet if the thick ice of the great shock I had experienced was melting, I cannot claim the detritus of the past was so easily washed away. As I walked I often started at the sight of John Francis across the way or in a passing carriage, only to look a second time and see it was quite another man. On my first arrival I had fancied, like a country bumpkin, that I would find him in the streets as easily as two friends might meet in a small town like Greaves. As the months passed, I began to comprehend the immensity of the capital: spreading parish after parish, a view of church spires and smoking chimneys as far as every distant horizon. John Francis could be anywhere in the city, I told myself, or in Bristol or even America.

Nevertheless, day by day, I eased myself of the drug that my fascination with Michael had been – the nightshade in my veins that had kept me transfixed and insensible. By May-time I breathed in the warm spring air and let unfamiliar sights settle restfully on my eyes. I began to sketch scenes of springtime in the city parks, of greenery and unfurling leaves and new shoots rising in the flowerbeds.

The captain was, indeed, as sharp as a razor. One day, on our usual walk to St James's Park we paused to watch a man taking bets and putting on a lively show using a board, three thimbles and a pea. His trick was to place the pea under one of the thimbles, shuffle them about and invite bets as to which thimble hid the pea. One of the crowd wagered sixpence, then another ninepence. The shuffler goaded him, and soon another fellow made a bet of a whole crown. 'Done!' shouted the shuffler; and lifted his middle thimble. Lo, the shuffler's face was aghast – for the challenger had won his crown. After some laughter at the thimble-man's folly, he offered the crowd a second wager, admitting that his memory was bad, as he had been up all night. He gave us another display of his thimble-shuffling skills, and this time half-a-dozen men vied to lay even larger bets. The highest bidder was a top-hatted gentleman, who boasted that his eye had never left the thimble, and he was confident of making an easy ten bob.

'He may as well hand over his purse and save his time,' muttered the captain in my ear.

I raised my brows; but the captain's prediction came true – when the chosen thimble was raised, the pea had astonishingly disappeared, and moved beneath another. Thereafter all the games were won by the shuffler, or the thimble-rigger, as the captain called him.

'How did you know the outcome?' I asked on our way home.

'It's a trick as old as time. Seen it in Egypt, seen it in India.'

'But how is it done? How does the shuffler always place the pea beneath a thimble no one bets on?'

'Ha, those fellows are as good as conjurors. The trickster's way is to make you see something that was never even there. Think, Mrs Frankland, how can the thimble-rigger be sure to win?'

'By knowing exactly which thimble the pea is under?'

He laughed. 'So what is to stop someone else guessing the right thimble? The odds are only one in three. Come – it's the same method for any conjurer or sharper.'

'I truly don't know. I am poor at guessing.'

'By the time the bets are laid,' he whispered. 'All the thimbles are empty.'

'What? But I have seen the pea go under the thimble!'

'You've seen it go under – but he flicks it out at the back and palms it. Then later, he flicks it back under while you are distracted. It is all done by tricking your eye to look the wrong way.'

'But that must take so much practice.'

'And that is the second way these folk confound the public. You, an honest personage, think it too much trouble to learn such flash-handedness. But look at the thimble-rigger again. How much has he taken this hour? Maybe two pounds already – save for the cut he must give the fellow who won a crown, who is, of course, his accomplice. If he chooses a different place for his table every day, he might earn more than ten pounds a week. So it is worth those hours of practice with the flash-hand technique, wouldn't you say?'

Soon afterwards, the captain was called upon to spend long hours at the Justices' office at Lichfield Street. 'Perhaps you are a criminal on bail?' I teased.

'Perhaps I am. Either that, or a habitual seducer of beautiful young widows.'

'But what is it you do for the Justices? Tell me.'

With some pride, he described their attempts to improve the Watch system and set up an organised band of thief-takers. 'I am sadly too old to be a member of that band of head-breakers,' he quipped. 'For I should enjoy nothing more than to clap up a few of these wicked felons. I am merely a watcher. When the thief-takers want to keep an eye on a fellow – or a woman, of course – they do not want their own visages to be remarked upon. So I sit in a tavern all day, or follow a fellow about the docks. In this alone my white hair is an advantage, Mrs Frankland, for with a few different jackets and caps I might pass for any ancient codger.'

'It sounds dangerous work,' I said – though I was, in fact, wondering how dangerous it was for me to befriend such an upholder of the law.

'It is true that a number of the thief-takers have been injured or even snuffed out – but I believe that's a fair price to pay for saving so many citizens from the scourge of crime.'

Though at last I grew easier in my mind at Glasshouse Street, my body then chose to betray worrying symptoms. Had I ingested a few grains of Michael's ratsbane after all? In the confusion of that evening, who was to say that both glasses might not have been tainted? Or had Michael been slowly poisoning me since I first met him? The fact was that, since December, both my appetite and bodily courses had been in great disorder. Then, in June of that year, I could no longer ignore the swelling of a tumour. Secretly, I found out the address of a respected doctor. I had little hope of surviving such an illness, and for the first time considered writing to Mr Tully to set my affairs in order. I was absolutely decided; if I should die, Michael must not inherit a penny from me.

Dr Dalrymple was a medical man of the grand type, in a red coat and cauliflower wig. But his manner was kindly enough as he bade me lay down while he prodded the swelling. Then, to my consternation, he smiled and said, 'Well, Mrs Frankland, it is indeed a tumour of the benevolent type. And I heartily predict you will be delivered of it within a month or two at most.' Astonished, I let my fingers creep down to the taut dome of flesh and experienced a queasy sense of the miraculous.

'You are happy with the diagnosis?'

'I am, sir. Only rather confounded by the news.'

All I could think was what a terrible irony it would be for me to bear Michael's child. And also, of course, how foolish I had been. I was still, it seemed, quite stupefied by life, not to have understood the clearest of natural signs.

27
London

Summer 1793

~ A Savoury and Nourishing Food at a Cheap Rate ~

Take half a pound or what you have of clean meat, two ounces of rice, a turnip, potato and onion, and mix also parsley and thyme and a proper quantity of pepper and salt. Let it boil an hour or till done, with water and let it be frequently stirred. This dish is very nourishing and well tasting at a very small cost.

A worthy receipt devised by Mrs Emma Macdonald to feed the poor in times of need

The news of the baby changed everything. Michael, however despicable, was my child's father, and I could not allow him to be rid of me, and of his child, so easily. As for his marrying Miss Claybourn, I would see him imprisoned for bigamy if she ever wore that Venice lace. But before I told him about the child, I decided to be more cautious than in the past. Whenever I turned over the tangled events at Delafosse, I always found awkward little knots of confusion. Chiefly, I wanted to know whether Michael was capable of the cruelty Peg accused him of; and if he truly had sent her to the gallows for such a slight crime. Reluctantly, I decided to take the captain into my confidence. We were alone in the downstairs parlour, and the captain was enjoying his evening dram and tobacco by the fire.

'I need your advice, Captain, as a good friend.'

'Good advice is often the enemy of friendship,' he quipped. Then, seeing my solemnity, he made a stealthy motion with his pipe for us to go upstairs. When we reached his landing he said in a low voice, 'We must be very quiet. Otherwise, I fear we may be punished for impropriety. Who knows the vengeance of Mrs Huckle – perhaps a pair of damp sheets, or a pot of cold tea? Hark though, how might we remark the difference?'

I smiled and followed him into his quarters, all as neat as a pin; his few possessions arranged carefully about the room with such exactness they might have been measured with a ruler. There was his pewter tankard, his pipe and tobacco box laid on the table. The walls bore testament to his remarkable career; his red captain's coat hung at the ready, immaculately brushed, with epaulettes and buttons smartly polished. There, too, hung his medal for bravery, laid in a case of leather, his sword shining like a looking glass; and, on the shelf, a pocket pistol, so small it might easily be hid about his person.

'A useful precaution on certain watching jobs,' he said, nodding at the fine silver craftsmanship of his firearm. I reached out for it, but he shook his head. 'In case of urgency I always keep it loaded. It's a good piece at short range.'

'Your wife?' I asked, seeing a delicate miniature of a pleasant, pink-cheeked woman. 'My Emma,' he said gruffly. 'The finest wife a man could have. But gone these twenty years, Mrs Frankland. It is a long and lonely wait for us to be re-united. Now, do sit in that armchair, my dear, and tell me what troubles you.'

So I told him as concisely as I could, a true account of my marriage to Michael – of his at first seeming not to care for me, but to care rather for the money he might raise from my land. In even briefer terms, I told him of a confession made by my trusted housekeeper that Michael had recruited her to help him replace me with his paramour. His plan was that they would then marry and share my fortune.

'This servant. How was she persuaded to carry out your husband's wishes?' He reached for his pipe and lit it with a spill from the fire; a mazy puff of smoke curled before his wise face.

'This is the nub of it. He had a hold over her,' I whispered. 'Years before, upon compulsion, she told me she had stolen some money from his brother, and my husband stood as a witness at her trial. She was transported to Botany Bay, but escaped and returned to England. Then, as ill-luck would have it, he recognised her on the streets of Manchester, and used that secret knowledge to terrorise her.'

The captain wrote down Michael's name, and asked me his mistress's name, too.

'Miss Sybilla Claybourn.'

'And your servant's name? We might take a look at the court case that drew them together.'

'Mary Jebb,' I said.

*   *   *

Two days later, the captain knocked at my door. I gathered my hat and shawl, and together we took a hackney to Newgate Street. He had found a lawyer, and agreed a fee to examine Mary Jebb's case. We thus arrived at the imposing bulk of Newgate, the prison that so terrorised Peg. Across the way stood the Old Bailey session house, where lawyers processed back and forth in wigs and robes.

The lawyer, Mr Bonamy, eyed me with such apathy that I easily perceived it was only for the captain's sake he had agreed to see me at all. Yet to his credit, a copy of Mary Jebb's case lay before him.

'The case was first indicted at the Lancaster Sessions,' he pronounced in a tired, sing-song tone. 'Mary Jebb, spinster, indicted for publishing a false, forged, and counterfeit pound note, knowing it to be such, with intent to defraud. Then, and this is irregular, they admitted a request to be tried at the Old Bailey before a Grand Jury. An expensive decision, given the cost of the lawyer who drew it up.'

'Why would she want it heard at the Old Bailey?'

'The jury could be one reason. It would not be the first time a young woman worked upon the hearts of a group of men. And yes, no doubt it was a shrewd move. A betting man would have said there was a greater opportunity of a pardon here, given the imminent departure of the fleet waiting on the Thames, in readiness to sail to Botany Bay.'

I asked if there was any reference in the case to my husband, Mr Michael Croxon. Wearily, he flicked the pages over, scanning the clerk's small hand.

'Here: Mr Croxon was indeed a witness for the prosecution.'

I glanced at the paper and read:

Mr Croxon was sworn in.

Q. Do you remember the Prisoner approaching you upon any occasion?

Croxon: Yes, I do remember the Prisoner. My brother Peter and I were awaiting the Greaves coach when she approached us with the pretended offer of changing our note for coin.

And so it ran for many pages.

'And may I ask your opinion of my husband's testimony?'

He scanned it and pinched his nose, then scratched his head beneath his wig. 'He was a lucid and most providential witness in the box.'

'So it was his testimony that ensured Mary Jebb was convicted?'

'Yes, yes. Here. "Verdict: Death by hanging". He did his duty as a good citizen. But just as they ascended the gallows, she and three other women were extended the Royal Mercy. In other words, her sentence of death was commuted to seven years' transportation. She then waited here at Newgate, in readiness to board the transport ship.'

'Why was she reprieved?' I asked.

'For the good of Britain, and for the good of the colony, naturally,' he said carelessly, not looking up. 'She was certainly fortunate. I see the judge did in fact direct the jury to her previous misdemeanours: an appearance for theft in '87 and, in the previous year, here's another case of fraud, when indicted for impersonating a gentlewoman. That time she was freed on appeal. She must have had generous friends. Hence the death sentence, given her long and invidious career.'

'I think there must be some mistake,' I said. 'I doubt this is the same Mary Jebb.'

The lawyer looked at me as if I were an imbecile.

'Is there a description of the woman's appearance?' the captain asked.

Mr Bonamy found the prison surgeon's description, taken down when she was first imprisoned. '"Of above medium height, good figure, red hair, distinguishing features: five ink-dots between thumb and forefinger, left hand."'

I shook my head. 'That is Peg – save that I recall no such ink-dots.'

'It is a common spot for gang marks,' the captain said, 'for no one will generally notice it.' I looked at my own hand and understand his meaning; for the little fold beside the thumb is a hidden place. 'It is the sign of a jailbird. The four dots represent the prison cell walls and the fifth the prisoner herself.'

'"And upon her back,"' continued Mr Bonamy, '"an ink engraving of a naked man and woman, viz Adam and Eve beneath an apple tree. Beneath, the motto: 'The Serpent Tempted Me and I Did Eat'."'

'Goodness,' I said, 'I find that hard to believe. But then I certainly did not inspect her naked back when I employed her.'

I was bewildered. Very well, Michael had been robbed by this Mary Jebb, and had taken a part in her prosecution; but I found it hard to reconcile this tattooed creature with Peg Blissett.

The captain asked, 'Is it possible that Mr Croxon and Mary Jebb might have had further relations? Might he, for example, have visited her while she awaited transportation?'

The lawyer shrugged. 'I have no reason to believe so. But the jailer will have an account in the record book. We are quite modern here. Everything is catalogued in ink. Now, to bring matters up to date, I have a Notice here that states this dangerous felon escaped from His Majesty's colony at New South Wales three years past. She was last seen in the company of another felon, a Jack Pierce. The pair are believed drowned somewhere off the coast of New South Wales.' The lawyer looked hard at both of us, and I avoided meeting the captain's eyes.

Boldly, I spoke up. 'And if such notorious felons were to be apprehended here in England?'

He raised his grey eyebrows and I blushed.

'It is only a theoretical question. What would the consequence be?'

'This time no appeal or reprieve would be possible. The death penalty would stand. Such degenerates need to be extinguished. Britain would be well rid of such a wretch.'

*   *   *

After our meeting my friend led me to the tavern on the corner, where we drank some strong spirits. I was despondent. 'I don't know what I'm looking for,' I said. My ten-shilling fee to the lawyer seemed only to have gained Michael great praise – and Peg even greater condemnation.

'It will do no harm to see the jailer's book now we are here,' the captain replied. 'I know Mary Jebb and her type.'

His manner annoyed me. 'Captain, it is my husband we are pursuing. Whatever you menfolk think of Mary Jebb, I believe she is a wronged woman. Women of her class are generally persecuted. She has already suffered brutal punishment.'

'That's what she told you, is it?' my friend said lightly.

'A woman's lot is hard, Captain. Yes, she told me she fell among thieves when a young woman. An orphan, too. Yet my religion says that any soul can be redeemed. It is hard for a man to understand, I suppose, but we grew friendly. She was my ally against Michael. That woman saved my life.'

He nodded, slowly; but I hoped his benign expression was not the well-meaning pity it appeared to be. We dined after that, lingering pleasantly over roast fowl and peas. The captain lit his pipe, and I dallied over a pot of tea.

'Tell me, dear, does your husband admire your skill in painting?' The old fellow blew a smoke ring that drifted up to the blackened ceiling.

'Michael?' I remembered his looking at my pictures only to scoff at me.

'No.'

'Why ever not?'

I was in the habit of speaking very truthfully to the captain; I pressed my fingers to my brow and examined his question. 'I believe he does not especially care for other people's accomplishments.'

'Oh,' the old fellow replied, tamping down more tobacco into his pipe. 'Now why would that be?'

I felt a frown crease my brow. A whole cavalcade of justifications for Michael sprang up in my mind – that he suffered from melancholia, that his parents had not cared for him, that he had been mistreated at school. There were excuses aplenty – but none of them would satisfy a wise old bird like the captain.

'Because,' I said, not knowing at all what my next words would be ... then, suddenly, the phrase bubbled up from nowhere, like a spring rising from the earth. 'Because now I am no longer with him, I believe he can feel no natural connection with any other soul.' The words resonated in the air, chiming with truth, causing a peculiar shift around me. For a moment my breath caught in my throat and I wondered if I would burst into tears – but instead, I burst out laughing. 'That is quite miraculous,' I said. 'That I finally see it, as clear as day.'

The captain leaned back in his chair and stroked his whiskers. 'When you are young, as you are, my dear, it is easy to dress unworthy characters in grand costumes – to believe them to be noble, charming, or deserving of your self-sacrifice. An old fellow like me has a sharper eye. I judge a person upon their actions, and the actions of that most sensitive organ, the human heart. There is a great deal of flim-flam in the world, and the trick is to see through it.' He leaned forward and fixed me with his bird-like eyes, shining from within a web of wrinkles. 'You deserve better than that, Grace. A good soul like you deserves to be cherished by a man who respects and loves you.'

The smile left my lips as he spoke. 'That is difficult,' I said very quietly.

'I understand. But overcoming difficulties is the price of growing up, my dear. Now what about supping up and putting a brave face upon this visit to Newgate? After all, we might still be home by five o'clock for tea; for they cannot imprison us without a warrant.'

Thus fortified, we crossed the way to Newgate prison; a most oppressive mass of stone, rising above us like a tomb of lost souls. The captain knew the means of entry – namely, to bribe the keeper with another crown. From the moment I passed beneath the

Newgate arch, my skin began to itch, and I gagged on the stench; not just of unwashed bodies, but a putrid taint like a long abandoned charnel pit.

We entered a mean sort of office, where an oaf in greasy leather grinned at me with a broken mouth. 'I am from the Lichfield Street Justice's office,' said my friend, in his most commanding voice. 'I am instituting an inquiry on behalf of this young woman, and I need to see your Visitors' Book for the years 1787 and 1788.'

'What a damned shame – them books being put away some while ago, the Devil knows where.'

'Come along, my man, I am sure they can be found.' As the captain said this, he slipped another half-crown across the filthy board.

The man took it and hid it in his clothes. 'That'll get you a sight of the book itself, but if you be wanting, let's say, ten minutes of study, then you's'll be needing one of me private rooms as well.'

'Another half-crown is my limit,' muttered the captain.

'Great deal of trouble, all this.' The jailer yawned, and the gust from his mouth made me shrink back. This time I produced the half-crown. The hateful man leered at me, then waddled off with the coin.

'Nearly there,' said my friend, with a wry smile of encouragement. Alone with the captain, I covered my mouth and nose with my hand and shook my head mutely.

We carried the books to a grubby cell-like room, inside of which was much lewd graffiti, and a great many dubious stains that might have been ancient vomit or blood. I could scarcely breathe, so vile was the miasma of misery.

The captain began turning the pages, passing a finger along each line. We soon learned that Mary Jebb had indeed lived in Newgate for two months in 1787. However, she had not been housed on the common side, but on the master's side, in quarters of considerable luxury. Food had been ordered for her, along with bedcoverings and spirits. 'Who paid for all this?' I asked.

'Well, let's begin with the visitors. Here's one, Humbug Joe. Your guess is as good as mine, but he certainly sounds like one of the thieving fraternity. Ah – here is Charles Trebizond.'

'Who is he?'

'A quite infamous screeve-faker – or, shall we say, false-letter man of Manchester town. A flash cove, a head of a family of thieves. And here he is, your Mr M Croxon. It always astonishes me how free folk are with their names.' With his bony finger, he traced the dates down the page. 'A series of visits. One, two – five in all. And here, see the column: Night, Night, Night. He paid the "garnish", or fee, to use a private cell.'

I felt hot and defensive. 'I don't believe it. Perhaps someone else used his name? Michael would never have spent the night with Peg. He loathes her. And even if there was some – irregularity – which I cannot believe, why would he first have sent her to the gallows?'

'Only they know that,' he said. 'Perhaps they quarrelled?'

'It's nonsense.'

But even as I protested, my friend was copying down all the facts from that incriminating visitors' book. There it stood in black and white. I could not deny that my elegant, fastidious husband had journeyed here to this stinking hell, bribed the jailer, and paid for the rent of a verminous cell, to spend the night with my seemingly devoted housekeeper.

Soon afterwards, a letter arrived from Peg. I opened it with some trepidation, for my former ally had, it must be said, suffered a violent plummet in my opinion since I had met the lawyer. She was undoubtedly an habitual felon, the records proved it. Her words echoed in my mind, that she had feared and loathed Michael – why, she had even talked of the pleasure of seeing him dead. 'Give him a dose of his own medicine,' she had said coldly. 'He deserves it.'

The more I thought of it, the more I knew the true reason I had let her harry and hustle me from my own home. Horror at the scene in the dining room had certainly been a part of it, but how could that overwhelm my duty to care for Michael as he lay dying? No, I think I guessed even then that it was she, and not Michael, who was capable of murder. I thanked God she had not been successful. My thoughts went around and around: had Peg put rats-bane in the water and given it to Michael, then set me up, like a dupe, to take the blame? But then why did she help me escape? Why then let him live? It was incomprehensible.

It was in this mood that I read with extraordinary relief:

My Dearest Friend,

I write to you with heartfelt thanks for your letter, and to let you know how things lie at present. I must tell you I can no longer be doing with nursing the master any more. He is an exceedingly troublesome invalid, and I feel it wrong, mistress, that he who oppressed me so soundly in health should continue to imprison me in sickness. So I have done your bidding, and thanks to your most generous gift, that I never in a thousand years expected, I have left your husband in the care of a decent nurse recommended by Dr Sampson.

For myself, I am now in a most agreeable position over Halifax way, as Housekeeper to a Mr and Mrs Roper, a respectable family who trade in woollen yarn. So thank you mistress, or friend as I will always remember you, for I now have a good sum laid by, and even more valuable to me, my precious liberty. As for your husband, when I left him he was no better cured in body, and still exceeding vengeful in mind towards you. And so, if you will forgive my saying so, we are both best rid of him, most especially you. For you are a better sort altogether than him and should forget this sorry episode and find yourself better companions and a more suitable station in life than as that rascal's wife.

Sending you again every good wish from your,
Affectionate Friend and Servant,
Peg Blissett

I welcomed the news that Peg had left Delafosse, for it put my frantic mind to rest. And being welcome news, it was easier to believe it was the truth, than subject it to long questioning. Perhaps there was also a tiny part of me that was jealous of whatever Mary Jebb and my husband had once shared in that vile cell, and I was happy to see them parted. But the better part of me was glad that she had escaped and would never be hung from the gallows. Indeed, I was so delighted to see the end of the whole episode that I ceremoniously burned the letter in my grate. So long as I never heard of Peg and her troubled history again, I wished her grudging good luck in her new life of modest labour and precious liberty.

The summer months passed in gentle walks and outings. I learned to cook a little, for Mrs Huckle's dinners disagreed with me. I purchased an iron fire dog, and, with the captain's help, started cooking on my fire. I searched out the cleanest meats, vegetables, bright-eyed fish, and country bread, in preference to the chalky white loaves and rancid butters of London. The captain taught me his own way of making a nourishing dish that his wife had made in former days to feed the poor – layered vegetables and meat braised to a delicious solidity. Thus I not only saved myself fivepence a day, for my purse was diminishing at a surprising rate, but learned to feed myself on nourishing hotpots and plain hasty puddings.

While the summer evenings were long, I worked upon infant's clothes stitched from the cheapest roll-ends. I remembered with shame my condescension to Anne, who had spent all her waking hours sewing. With some grief, I realised that news of her infant's birth would be sent to Delafosse, where Michael, I imagined, would cast her letters aside unread. A few times I began to write to Anne, but set my pen down again. As I could not explain my behaviour without frightening and worrying her, I reluctantly decided that no news would be better than bad news.

*   *   *

I also fretted over the Croxons, wondering what they must make of Michael's sudden change of health. Curiosity roused me, until one day I set off to find the address at Devonshire Square where I had been invited to stay with Peter. It was a hot hour's walk from Golden Square, and hard on my feet and aching back. When I did at last find the address, it was a splendid tree-lined square of snow-white buildings, through the windows of which I could glimpse crystal chandeliers and gilded mirrors. I thought number seventeen very much in the Croxons' showy style.

Standing below a tree, I watched the front door all morning, trying to evade a stern footman who came out to me and asked me my business. At last a maidservant emerged from the back and I set off after her to the market. Once she was burdened with goods, I fell into step beside her and offered my help.

'Thank you, miss, but I can manage well enough on me own.' She looked at me with a sidelong glance. 'You want to be sparing your strength in your condition.'

'Did I not see you leave number seventeen earlier? Could you do me the kindness of telling me if Mr Peter Croxon is still in residence?'

'What, 'im? He's long gone. That place is but a lodging house for them as comes to London on visits. They only stayed for a month or so, down from the North.' She gave me another sly glance. 'So what was you after, then?'

'I know Mr Croxon, we both grew up in the same town.'

'Oh, he were a proper well-made gentleman, weren't he now?' She stopped for a moment to set her goods down and give her arms a rest. 'But then it's the 'andsome ones what leaves unwelcome gifts, they say.' This time she jerked her head very pertly towards the swelling of my stomach.

'For goodness' sake,' I protested. 'It's nothing of the sort. In fact I'm married to his brother.'

She grinned unpleasantly, a picture of scornful amusement. 'So you wish you was, my dear. My advice to you, if you know Mr

Peter's address in the country, is for you to apply to him there. He seemed an open-handed sort of fellow.'

I turned and walked quickly away. It was a harsh lesson, I supposed, in how others would see me, alone and shabby with a child straining at the seams of my cheap bodice. I trudged back to Golden Square, horribly conscious of my fall in rank.

As I stitched my infant's linen, I did my best to make a primitive plan of how I might live once the baby was born, should the Almighty allow us both to survive. Much of my land had still been let for grazing, so my annual rents of £300 were due to be paid that summer. I was sure I could live upon that if I was frugal. Once I had settled in a private rented house I would summon the courage to write to Mr Tully about the Marriage Settlement. If I could impress on him the need to keep my whereabouts secret from Michael, I hoped he could arrange whatever allowance was due to me, once we were officially separated.

Delafosse did often surface in my thoughts. One day, after pricking my finger too many times on my clumsy needle, I got out the thimble I had found in the tunnel, that day I first explored it. It was a cheap bit of ironwork that I fancied had hung from a chain. 'For Mother from her Jamie', I read around the rim. Jamie, Jim, Jimmy, I recited to myself. I had heard of no one of that name at Delafosse. *James*. Was that not the name of Mrs Harper's son, the apprentice to whom I had posted five pounds to cover his fees? My instinct was to write at once to Bess Doutty in Pontefract, who might still wait for news of her sister. But what, I asked myself, was of such significance? I had found Mrs Harper's thimble dropped on the floor at her former workplace. It was of no consequence at all.

✺

It became impossible to keep my condition hidden from Mrs Huckle.

'This is a most genteel lodging house, Mrs Frankland,' she protested. 'We cannot have bawling babies and strings of wet clouts all about the place. You will be more comfortable in a house that is – shall we say, a little less select.'

But the truth was, I was already eager to move lodgings, for it was ridiculous to live beneath the petty tyranny of such a woman. 'You may stay one more month at most,' she said, eyeing the panels hastily sewn into my shabby gown. She held her hand out for the requisite twenty shillings.

Angrily, I bustled past her. 'You are indeed correct,' I snapped. 'There must be many more comfortable places than this, I'm sure.'

Once outside in the street, I convinced myself the woman had done me a favour, for it was certainly time to change my situation. Glasshouse Street had served its purpose as a sedate hiding place. It was July, so I determined to withdraw a part of my annual rental allowance. With that money I would buy privacy and safety for myself and the baby. A building mania gripped the capital, and everywhere I saw brick-built houses of the modern style, with sash windows and pillared porticoes of a type that would suit me very well. Taking a hackney to the bank at Fleet Street, I began to anticipate a settled life for myself and my baby here in London.

Though I had dressed in my only decent cloak and hat, it took some mustering of courage to brave the gold-liveried man at the door of Hoare's Bank. I spoke briefly to the clerk and was directed to a fierce-looking gentleman who sat at a vast mahogany table. I told him my true name and that I had a bank account operated by a Mr Tully of Lancaster, and that, as my land rents had recently accrued, I wished to withdraw two hundred pounds. The gentleman bowed, absented himself for a few minutes, and then informed me with stiff politeness that as I had no credentials, he would be obliged if I would attend him again one week hence. I was disappointed, but bowed my head and left.

On my return to the bank a week later I was all eagerness, having found a pretty house with a garden that cost only one hundred pounds per annum. But I had been unable to leave a deposit, since my poor purse by this date carried only copper. I found the same gentleman at the mahogany table, and he in his turn invited me into a magisterial office panelled with dark wood.

'Mrs Croxon,' he said, and I knew at once that bad news awaited me. 'I am afraid I am unable to oblige you in your request.' His tone was not pleasant; he looked upon me as one might a petty irritant. 'The account you wish to draw upon is empty and has been closed.'

'That is ridiculous,' I said. 'I would know if I had closed it.'

He raised his palms in a gesture of exasperation, as if it were all quite outside his hands.

'So where, sir,' I demanded, 'has my land income been sent?'

'It is not for me to say. I may only give you intelligence of the account that was formerly held at this bank. And that, I am afraid, no longer exists.'

By now I was hot in my face and tight-knotted with apprehension.

'I demand that you tell me how it is that an account I have made no instructions upon this last six months has been closed and emptied. Who pray has signed my name for such an instruction? It is your responsibility, sir!'

He shifted in his seat; he did not like my spirit one bit.

'I am merely relaying the facts, madam. Our instructions were received by way of your advisor, a Mr Tully. Might I suggest that you pursue your enquiries with him?'

'I most certainly will.' I stood up, feeling horribly dishevelled and shabby, as well as clumsy from my large girth. In the bank's front office I wrote a hasty note to Mr Tully. I was incensed, I said, that he had closed my account without my direct instructions. I demanded two hundred pounds by return. Once I had paid a sixpence for paper and ink and a tip to the servant for the privilege of his taking it to be posted, I realised I no longer even had the fare for a hackney.

I began to walk back to Glasshouse Street in a fury. I ranted to myself that I was an idiot to expect Michael to have left my account untouched. What a first-rate numbskull I was. Fuelled by annoyance I ploughed on, up road and down alley, until every step was a weary effort. At first I tried to persuade myself that Michael had merely dipped into the money to live on, and simply rearranged our accounts. Yet for Mr Tully to act without my instruction? It was abominable. Then, of course I saw it – Michael had told the notary I had gone abroad, and used that as an excuse to meddle with my money. Why had I not acted sooner to secure my future income? Because I was a prize idiot, I told myself.

To crown my misery, every few minutes a pain nipped at my back. Rousing myself, I looked about for familiar signs of Golden Square, and saw I had unwittingly entered a part of the city quite unknown to me. Gone were the carriages and gated gardens, the bow-fronted shops and flower stalls. The afternoon was passing to early evening, and in the fading light the streets had a mean aspect, the only trade being gin shops and alehouses. I stopped in my tracks and looked back the way I had come. A couple of ragged bystanders whistled softly at me from across the way. I turned about and retraced my steps. But now the blackened alleys seemed to tighten about me, winding this way and that in a labyrinth worthy of Ariadne's thread. I followed a promising lane, but it ended in a dank court, where a brazier gave off a lurid glow; I halted again, looking for a respectable place to enquire the way. Just then a girl of no more than ten years old appeared beside me and slid her hand in mine. Her face was pinched with hunger, and her cut-down woman's gown was torn and matted with mud.

'You lost, missus?' She had a pert expression, but her hand was marble-cold.

'I need directions to Golden Square.'

Though swarthy with dirt, she smiled up at me. 'Come wi' me.'

Together we wound our way through alleys that every moment grew more sinister as the daylight leached away. From behind flimsy walls I heard raucous oaths and howling dogs, and hurried footsteps clattering on the boards.

'Are you certain of the way?' In answer the girl nodded like a puppet, her bony arm pulling me ever onward. The pain in my back was gnawing now, like a biting dog. A vision of my narrow bed at Glasshouse Street danced before my eyes. How much longer could I walk? At last she halted in a benighted court that reeked of foul tanned leather.

'Just tell me ma I'm 'elpin' a lady,' she said, and scampered up a rackety ladder to a sort of hovel, built of collapsing crates. Once alone, my powerful instinct was to turn about and leave, but I was frightened of tripping and falling in the murk. I persuaded myself that the girl's mother would most likely assist me once she saw my condition.

Then all in a few sudden moments, three beggarly characters leaped down from a gallery above my head and swaggered towards me, cursing and harrying me.

'What 'ave we 'ere?' The rogue had one blind eye and a loose-lipped drunken manner. 'A frigate well-rigged and all a-mort.'

'Go away,' I said stupidly, but it was too late, for a bony woman buffeted my elbow, knocking me towards the wall. I staggered backwards. With a sudden blow from the other man, I was knocked to the ground, and felt a searing crack as my head hit the stone cobbles. In my last lucid moments before falling senseless, I felt merciless fingers turning me this way and that, rifling my pockets, stripping me of every last good possession I owned.

28

London

August 1793

~ Water Gruel ~

Take a pint of water and a large spoonful of oatmeal, stir it together; let it boil up three or four times, stirring it often. Strain it through a hair sieve and add a little salt.

Bill of Fare of the Covent Garden Poorhouse

I woke up scarcely knowing where my body ended and the world began, pushed and pulled on a red tide that submerged me in waves of pain. Slowly, I comprehended that I was in a mean, narrow bed beneath rough grey linen. A bloated coarse-looking woman sallied back and forth, puffing on a pipe as she eventually heaved herself down by my side.

'Where am I?' I asked, after the woman gave me a sip of beer.

'The lying-in ward at the Covent Garden Spike. Robbed you was, young missus – found half-naked in the road. You's only here thanks to an old codger what found you.'

She left me alone, and slowly the events of the previous evening returned to me, renewing my anguish. Misery racked me that long day, as I lay stranded in that beggarly place, utterly powerless to assist myself. I reached for my crucifix and found nothing; it had been snatched from my throat. The ring that bore Anne's hair and my wedding ring, both of those were gone too. My skin felt as naked without my talismans as a soft creature cracked from a shell. Bereft, and not knowing if I wished to be alive or dead, I prayed in frantic snatches for the safety of my child. All day the pain tormented me, twisting and racking my body. Was this my fate, I asked myself – to die here among strangers? I had heard once, and quailed at the recollection, that mothers who died in childbed were thrown in the common burial pit, like any stranger to the city.

It seemed a great age later that the midwife returned and took my feverish hand in her hard-knuckled grip. When she ordered it, I screwed up all my strength and gave a mighty push. Again and again I strained and, at last, at the midwife's cry, my baby entered the world.

'A bonny boy,' she announced, as I lay back gasping.

'Is he healthy?' I cried, as I heard a piping squeal.

'A proper handsome little fellow,' she said, and passed him to me.

Indeed he was. His slate-blue eyes met mine, fringed with golden lashes. I held my little son, quite overcome by every detail of him: his fingernails like fragments of mother-of-pearl, his mouth curved like a rosebud, and the down on his head pale gold. In looks he was undoubtedly Michael's son. Then he blinked and looked into my eyes and I lost myself in his fathomless gaze. I thanked God we were both safely delivered from evil-doers. And I vowed that my golden child would not live as a pauper. I would move heaven and earth to regain what was rightly his.

I am not saying that the poorhouse was not a Christian place, for the master, the matron, and assistants were all decent folk; yet there was about the place such a dismal air of want that I battled to stay cheerful. The paupers themselves had lost all independence of mind, for the regulation by ringing bells, shuffling of weary feet, the thinness of the gruel, and the sour smell of illness might have sapped any spirit. The lying-in ward was much used by street girls, born ignorant, and hardened by brutality, who cursed and complained, however kindly they were treated. With scarcely a sigh they handed over their babes, pulled their gaudy frills back on, and crept back to the streets. I urged the timid Irish girl in the next bed to keep her babe, but she was persecuted by a brawny bully-boy who checked on her from the window. 'Can you not get a position and keep your child?' I urged, my heart nearly breaking to see her push her baby away.

'Aw, stow it,' she grumbled at last. 'The parish is more of a chance for 'im than hangin' on my petticoats. If the bawd as I works with gets a sight of him, she'll silence him with Mother Gin.'

*   *   *

Shortly afterwards, word came of the captain; the brave fellow had by good luck been at the Justice's Office that same evening when the watchman reported finding me in the road. He and a band of men set out armed with cudgels and set on those villains who had robbed me, and transported me to the lying-in ward. As for himself, he had taken a terrible blow to the head – so it was with great relief, but also apprehension, that I set off to find the men's ward. I scanned the pitiful row of beds, but could not at first find him amongst the many decrepit fellows. An assistant finally led me to him, and I saw that a great cloth now bound his skull.

'Why, you are setting the new fashion in headdress,' I said cheerily. He managed a wince of a smile.

'Here is someone else to see you.' I pulled little Henry out from under my blanket.

'Well, I'll be damned,' he said, his white-whiskered face reviving at the sight of my infant. 'You have been busy. What a fine brawny chap.' He broke into a fond smile, as elderly persons often will at the sight of babies. 'Many a time I've cursed myself that I let you go off alone. It is all the fault of the Justices' office, keeping me outdoors all night and day.' We exchanged our news, and he told me of his battle with Mrs Huckle to prevent her throwing all my possessions out on the street.

'I must leave that harridan as soon as I am stronger.'

'That would certainly be wise, Mrs Frankland.'

Yet how, now I was penniless, might I find another lodging? With a choke in my voice, I told him of my disappointment at the bank. 'I believe my husband has helped himself to my money.'

He stroked Henry's cheek with his knotted finger, listening keenly. 'You may not like it,' he said at last, 'but it will be best if you do go back to Glasshouse Street for a spell. Just till you return to health. Then we can take a proper look into this case of yours.'

'I should like to, Captain. But I have not a farthing left. I have written to my notary to demand an explanation, but until I see his reply, I have no hopes at all.'

'Mrs Frankland, it will be an honour to assist you,' he said, 'though it is a pity my own funds are not larger. But I could manage a loan of a few pounds.'

I loathed my dependence; but I had no choice but to accept. 'Thank you. I will repay you.'

'I know. Now listen, I have some most interesting information to pass on to you.' The captain pulled a comical face, for Henry was happily exploring the fellow's whiskers.

'I hope it is good news.'

'That is for you to determine, Mrs Frankland. While I was waiting on Justices' business, for a certain felon to appear at his coffeehouse, the time hung mighty heavy. And finding a heap of old newspapers, I read them every line. It happened that a name I recognised jumped out at me in the Notices of the *London News*.'

Here it was, what I had been dreading. 'Has Michael died?' I demanded. So Henry would, indeed, be fatherless?

'No. The name was Sybilla Claybourn.'

'Good God,' I said. 'Don't tell me they are married? It isn't lawful – it can't be.'

'No, it is quite another matter. Here, I have kept it as safe as diamonds, screwed up in the brim of my cap.' At this he unfurled the strip of newsprint, and I read, with increasing bewilderment:

1793. June 17th. Miss Sybilla Claybourn, spinster, after a protracted and tedious illness, in her 89th year. For many decades lived a recluse at Riverslea Park, near Earlby, Yorkshire. Her afflictions of mind were so great that, notwithstanding a good fortune, she knew no true enjoyment in life. Having left no issue this branch of the Claybourns of Yorkshire finishes with her, and the considerable though neglected Claybourn estate will fall to other branches of the family.

'It cannot be the same person.'

'It's an unusual name. Tell me, did you ever meet Miss Claybourn?'

I remembered an elegant woman on horseback, moving at the front of a mass of hunters.

'I think so. Well – I did not meet her – but I saw her. She was quite different from this description: young, fashionable, proud.'

'Think, Mrs Frankland. How was it you got the notion that this Miss Claybourn was your rival?'

'She was our closest neighbour.'

'Yes, I understand that – the newspaper confirms it. But that is not my question.'

When had I first suspected Miss Claybourn? When I found the long black hair? For a long day, after I left the captain to his rest, I puzzled over the matter. There had been that waspish letter from her, my sight of her with the hunt, Mrs Barthwaite's comment, the insights offered by her servant, Sue. Tentatively, I proposed an answer to the captain's question. And one after another of my former assumptions, like a house of cards from which one card is removed, trembled and wavered and collapsed in a great untidy heap.

A few weeks later, when I returned to Glasshouse Street, Mrs Huckle made her opinions exceedingly well known. Most mornings I woke from exhausted sleep to hear her gossiping with the maids on the landing.

'I cannot say what she is doing here. To think they have fobbed me off with a workhouse trull. I've heard such patter as hers before. Turns up all busked up like a lady and then look how matters turn. Next I suppose she'll do a flit and leave me out of pocket.'

Damn her for the dog's mother, I whispered under my breath, an indelicate but apt phrase I had learned from the streetwalkers on the lying-in ward. Then, taking Henry into my arms, I sang to him to cover her voice, and decided I should always be happy, so overjoyed was I with my little man. Sally, Mrs Huckle's maid, was my lifeline, while I awaited Mr Tully's reply. The eldest of seven children, she missed her little brothers and sisters and liked nothing better than to dandle a baby on her lap. Every day she smuggled up scraps for me from the kitchen – for even the scrapings from the other lodgers' plates were a feast to me, after poorhouse gruel. She brought me jugs of good porter too, to help my milk, and pails of hot water to wash myself and my little one's clouts.

Then, at last, Mrs Huckle made her visitation. She told me she had indulged me long enough. She reminded me I had been given notice, and that a number of respectable persons were awaiting my room even now. And there was also the problem, she said, of my being a widow, and yet a new mother. For she could do her sums as well as any scholar, and if my husband had died when I said he had, my baby was not welcome in such a respectable lodging as hers.

I would brook none of her insults. The captain's loan had paid what I owed her, and for a further week's rent besides. 'And when that expires,' I spat, 'no one will rejoice more than I to leave your establishment.' She twisted her mouth in a so-be-it grimace and flounced away downstairs.

In preparation to leave Glasshouse Street, I sorted through my few belongings, racking my brain as to where I might go. While searching for possible employment, I had seen a card in Miss Le Toye's window advertising work for a Fan Painter. Though painting flowers or curlicues would earn me very little, I thought it might allow me to repay the captain and rent a room of the dreariest sort. At the notion of it, my outrage at Michael returned, so I bundled up Henry and set off to visit the postmaster at Golden Square. I believe the poor man pitied me; he even offered me a chair as I waited for the last post of the day. It was a good thing I was sitting, for that day Mr Tully's reply finally arrived.

Dear Mrs Croxon,

It is with some dismay and surprise that I received your letter. Madam, I must wonder if you are quite sane, to give out such contrary instructions. I believe I have acted honourably in all your affairs, for as you will recollect, I advised you in no uncertain terms against your recent actions. I repeat that I am disappointed that you have acted so wilfully against my advice. I trust that you are enjoying the proceeds of the land sale at Whitelow, and am astonished that your grasp of your affairs is so rudimentary that you still expect to collect interest from a property you no longer own. As for the Hoare's account, I have merely followed the instructions you issued on the 5th January. I must protest, Madam, at your tone, and would express my wish that this be an end to our correspondence. I apologise for repeating myself once again, but I am no longer in a position to represent you, the requisite accord between ourselves being absolutely extinguished.

Your servant,
Tully

I believe I might have sunk to the floor had not the kindly postmaster offered me a supporting arm and a cup of sugared tea.

'I am only a little faint,' I said, folding the letter up tighter and tighter, into a horrible hard wad between my fingers. Then, fearing he might question me further, I fled back to Glasshouse Street.

Back in my room I stood and paced. I could not stop the phrase 'I have been ruined' repeating in my mind. Did Michael hate me so much? Did he believe it his right to steal everything I owned? And further, Mr Tully's letter infuriated me, with its inference that I had instructed him myself.

I longed to confide in the captain; to have his wise head advising me, as well as his wiry arm defending me. But his injuries would keep him in the men's ward for another month at least, and then he must convalesce at Mrs Huckle's. On my last visit I had noted his wavering eyes and white, stubbled beard. I could not confide in such a sick man, never mind enlist him. Instead, I let him persuade me to borrow whatever I needed from his chamber.

Tears welled in my eyes at the prospect of Henry living in want. His mother had been a foolish dupe, perhaps, but Henry deserved better from the world. Why should he spend his life being shunted between shabby lodging houses, in the company of demi-reps and drunkards? As I gathered my belongings, a number of loose papers fell to the floor. Resentfully I stared at the portraits of Michael that had once held me spellbound. Then, on a curious whim, I pinned them across my wall as I had used to do at Palatine House. Standing beneath them I felt, as the Bible says, that the scales fell from my eyes. No wonder I had loved Michael best when he was sleeping. Overwhelmingly, I had sketched a man whose sulking mouth and brooding eye revealed profound unhappiness.

I picked up my sketches of Delafosse Hall. There stood the long drive crowded with unkempt trees, the grand entrance as I had first seen it, choked with leaves that rattled in the breeze. I had thought it a living entity then, its sighing breath exhaling like a weary beast. There was the long view of the Hall at dusk, like a stately doll's house with its toy of a woman standing at my studio casement. Was she the lady of the Hall, or a prisoner? I tried to remember my thoughts as I had painted her in a silent, trance-like reverie. Was she intended to represent me, or someone else who had once inhabited the Hall? I could no longer remember. What I did recollect was Michael's despondency over his father's relics. He had said he felt unworthy as a man and that he longed to leave.

Here, beneath, were the sketches I had made after my accident. There were the sinuous limbs of the statues in the summerhouse, once the scene of sensuous pleasure, but since fallen into decay. There was my sketch of Harpocrates, silent in his recess, pointing to the tunnel that led deep beneath the heart of the Hall. The story of Michael's mother and Ashe Moncrieff making their lovers' assignations now seemed unbearably sad. No wonder there had been so many old tales of footfalls at night in the Hall. I thought of my mother-in-law's youthful hopes, casting a blight that still fell on her love-begotten son.

FERREA VIRGA EST, UMBRATILIS MOTUS, I read on the drawing of the tower and its sundial. The York bookseller had translated the motto as 'The rod is of iron, the motion of shadow.' I had felt distaste at the motto that day in York, and the engraving of Death's shadow, descending on the sleeping lovers. Shadows, shadows, I urged myself. What iron figure casts these shadows?

Lastly, I picked up a hasty sketch I had made when ill, after my fall. It was that dreadful scene that had overwhelmed me, of two faceless lovers leaving the tower together. I studied it closely, at the same time resurrecting the event in my inner eye, trying to amplify the scene from every angle. My view had been limited, but even from a back view Michael had not looked at all like the conquering lover; he was slump-shouldered, not even touching the woman.

The black-haired woman, on the other hand, the woman who was neither the lost and faded matron, Mrs Harper, nor the ancient recluse, Sybilla Claybourn, was upright and imperious. The soft swish of metallic jewellery resurrected itself, too; a slinking, chain-like sound. I stared at the drawing, but there was no answer in the grain of the paper or the image flickering in my memory. My head hurt. I took a sip of water from the jug. Beside it stood Mrs Harper's thimble.

Like a distant echo, I remembered the captain saying of the thimble-rigger, 'A good conjurer will get you to see what was never there. It is all done with directing you to look the other way.' With every particle of my intelligence I did my best to turn the story about, inside out and back to front. Who was it cast the shadow? What was it I had seen that was never there?

Then I saw it. And instead of a house of collapsing cards, I saw that same pack of cards new-configured, as if by magic, into a cruel and cunning game.

29

Delafosse Hall

September 1793

~ To Make a Hangi Cooking Pit ~

Dig your pit deep and place your dry faggots inside. Place
inside your firestones, each about the size of a man's fist. Light
your fire and when near to red-hot, arrange the stones neatly
at the bottom using two sticks. Lay on your wet grass and
leaves and over it your kai or food, your raupo and fern roots,
and whatsoever fish or flesh is desired. From a hollow gourd,
sprinkle with water to make much steam, and quickly lay
more green stuffs upon it and bury all within the earth. Leave
all the day, for the hangi pit will never spoil your food.

Traditional cooking method of the Maori people

The hungry ghosts were gathering for the feast tonight. Ma Watson was whimpering for her plum cake. Janey was leering her glass-ragged smile. Brinny couldn't sit still for the weals from her final public flogging. Granny sat nodding in the corner, a dribble of blood staining her chin. And the final one lurked somewhere in a dim corner of the room. Hanging from the ceiling she was, spinning slowly this way and that.

Mary, alone of all of them, had survived. She gazed triumphantly about the glorious dining room. Only she had possessed the crazy mettle to make a bolt for it. Only she now chewed that devilish sweet morsel: vengeance.

'Here's to you, Mrs Grace Croxon.' She raised her glass, slopping a few drops on the linen. 'The most open-handed pigeon ever caught.' She drained the glass of ruby-rich claret. 'Go ahead, help yourselves, girls.' She waved a bountiful hand at the table. The dishes were laid with each dish exactly in its place, like the nine of diamonds on a playing card. Now this is grand, she thought, the white linen well-pressed, the warm light glimmering from a score of candles, the silver plate polished like mirrors. It was a feast in a picture book, a queen's banquet in a fairy castle.

At the centre rose a vast Desert Island moulded from sugar-paste, just as Aunt Charlotte had used to make it. A stockade of liquorice crowned the peak, and a pathway of pink sugar sand stretched to the shore. The whole was surrounded by a sea of broken jelly, swimming with candied fish. First off, she ate the two tiny sugar castaways from the lookout on her island – very sweet and crisp they were, too. She stood to make a toast. 'To you, Jack, my own truelove,' and took a long draught.

Sugarplums next; a whole pyramid to herself, of every colour: raspberry, orange, violet, pistachio. She was eating dinner back to front, and she recommended it heartily. Next, her teeth sank into a sticky mass of moonshine jelly – it was good, very good. Refilling her glass, she made a toast to Aunt Charlotte. 'You old she-toad,' she grinned. 'See you in hell, you hang-in-chains bitch.'

Staggering to the looking glass, she preened herself at her own reflection. She was still a beauty, so long as she had her bits and bobs to dib and dab upon herself. Hold – what was that behind her? A sack-like body swinging low? She turned her head slowly to try to catch it out, but it was nothing at all; only a shadow chased by a draught from the chimney.

Food for the dead. Aunt Charlotte's tales of the Hangman's Supper had always held her spellbound. The finer the supper, the more fast-binding the oath, they said. Tom Rout had worn his pea-green coat and starched ruffles to feast with Jack Dempsey, and invited seven bonny whores besides. And Rob Foster had stopped at every inn on the road to Tyburn to drink his pleasure and say his farewells to the back-slapping crowds.

'But why do they do it, Auntie?' she'd asked, one night by the kitchen fire.

'It's the oldest gift since Eve was a girl. When he dines from your plate, you free the hangman of the black stain of murder,' Aunt Charlotte said.

But would it work? It had worked once before, when she'd fed Piggott on beef and claret the night before she should have swung; she had warded off the hangman's evil. 'Come, take a bite with me,' she called, to the dark corpse that swung at the very edge of her vision. But whenever she stared it full in the eye, it vanished fast away.

That vexatious Harper woman hadn't had the sense she was born with. When Michael had tried to dismiss the woman, the housekeeper had holed herself up in the kitchen with a bottle, making threats to get a coach directly to call on his mother, old Mrs Croxon, in Greaves. Not having a notion what to do next, he had sent for Peg at her lodging house across from the George. She had followed him downstairs and observed the old baggage from behind the kitchen door. 'If I am to go,' the gin-biber had warbled, 'it will only be 'pon Mrs Croxon's word. She gave me a guinea an' I stand 'pon my word.'

'She's a danger to us,' Peg had whispered up the stairs to Michael. 'You go. I'll see her off.'

Once alone she had played the part of a former pot companion from the George. Producing a bottle of Geneva, she coaxed Mrs Harper to the kitchen fireside. Between numerous bumpers, Mrs Harper confided her tiresome troubles: an expensive son, employment that stranded her far from home, her loneliness, her lack of ready coin.

'It's all that handsome young dog's fault,' she hissed loudly, spraying spirituous spittle from a pinched face, as she pointed at the ceiling. 'He is keeping a trull about the place – and 'im about to be married any day. I've heard the filthy pair. Creeping and moaning. Thinks I don't know—'

Just then footsteps shuffled towards them from the passage. Gingerly, Peg pulled her bonnet down over her brow and turned aside from the dying fire. The old mopsy, the one she later knew as Nan, hobbled into the kitchen and helped herself to something from the table.

'This is my friend,' Mrs Harper announced shrilly. 'She 'grees with me.'

Peg kept her head low and her tongue still. Nan mumbled something and disappeared back where she had come from. Once all was quiet again, she took Mrs Harper's arm, leaning in to whisper, 'Got any more tipple down in the cellars? To see me home, like?'

Mrs Harper sniggered in a parody of complicity. 'Tipple? There's tipple all over the place around here.' She lifted a bunch of keys attached by a chain to a grand iron chatelaine fixed at her waist. It made a slithery metallic sound that conjured a ferment of visions in Peg's head: of power over antique locks, of restraining chains and binding cuffs. Her fingers itched to have a closer look at its array of keys, scissors, and knives.

The two women rose, Mrs Harper leaning unsteadily against Peg's side, heady fumes souring the air. Peg's mind was as clear as crystal. While Mrs Harper lit the lantern, she looked about the kitchen for a tool to accomplish her task. Then, almost laughing out loud, she remembered that Mrs Harper was already carrying all she needed hung at her waist. Once the lantern was lit they wove their way merrily to the head of the stairs, and climbed down into a gust of grave-cold darkness.

She broke some more of the Desert Island off and nibbled rock candy and sugar comfits. Devil take it, she could eat to win a wager. Did she have a worm, perhaps? Granny had once paid a half-a-crown for a box of vermifuge pills after watching a quack doctor cure a fellow who retched into a pail. The false worms hidden in the pail were only chicken's entrails; she knew it for a common trick. But as for herself, it was not a worm perhaps but something just as ravenous inside her guts, clinging fast with angry barbs.

Was it the serpent that writhed upon her back perhaps, entwined with those Bible words: 'The Serpent Tempted Me And I Did Eat'? Had it slithered inside her now, devouring her inside out? It was as sly as Old Harry himself. 'The mark of a murderess,' she heard herself say in a leery sing-song voice as she flung herself down on the sofa. She closed her giddy eyes.

෬

Mary had learned that the owner of the tartan gown and bonnet was imprisoned in a nearby hut. She was another *pakeha*, a foreigner, but too valuable to be a *mokai* pet like herself. A band of *pakeha* traders were willing to exchange miraculous muskets for her, the very next day. She worked on this news carefully, stripping and refashioning it, like a bunch of *harakeke* flax being woven into a useful cloak.

That evening she complained of a belly-ache, until Areki-Tapiru gave her a kick and told her she must miss the night's feast. Once alone, she pulled a rush-stemmed rain cloak over her head and crept secretly to the hut where the prisoner was being held. It was easy to tempt the crone who guarded the door with food, a supposed gift from Areki-Tapiru. Once she had taken half the *kai* for herself, the old woman gratefully unlatched the door.

The *pakeha* girl was naked inside a sort of cage of branches. Skeleton-thin she was, with bedraggled brown hair and a pink tear-stained face. The girl appeared remarkably ugly, recalling the tribe's initial bemusement at her own blanched appearance. Hesitantly, she lowered her cape, but the girl was too stupid to even notice her own white skin and red hair.

'*Pakeha* girl,' she said haltingly. 'You want *kai*?' The girl snatched the cold kumara and devoured it. Mary was alarmed to find that her English speech was as rusty as an old lock. She tried again.

'Good evenin', miss.' That sounded mighty odd – but chirpy.

'What is that ye're sayin'?' the girl babbled in – yes, that was it – a Scottish voice. She pushed her snotty face toward the bars. 'Bless ma soul – be you a white woman lurkin' under that heathen costume?'

'Aye,' she said, then wondered at the slippery sound. 'White *pakeha*. Aye, I mean – I am.'

'Ma name is Flora Jean Pilling, an' I pray, if you have an ounce o' goodness in your heart, you will help me flee from these heathen devils!' The girl was trying to poke her pink fingers through the spars and make a grab at her. She backed away nervously.

'My name is—' She racked her brainbox. Her name was Kehua, but that was not right. She groped back into the past, as if burrowing in ancient mud for something long abandoned. 'My name is

Mary Jebb. I was catchered here.' She knew it wasn't quite right, but it worked.

'Och, you poor dear lamb. What suffering you must ha' endured. Ma own dear family were also murthered by these devils. Can you get me away from here?'

'Tonight – bad night. I go talk to *pakeha* fellas,' she said slowly. 'I tell 'em you here.'

'You would do that? Oh, bless you. Thanks be to God for sending you to me.'

'You give me—' What was the word? 'Thing. Token you Flora.'

Flora groped in her tangles of hair, and pulled out a brooch she had hidden there. It bore a tiny painting of a bearded man in a white neck collar, framed by an oval of silver. 'Here, take this. Look – ma father's name.'

'You talk it,' Mary mumbled.

The girl obliged. 'Reverend Henry Pilling. We were sailing to the missionary station at Hokitika on the *Pilgrim*. Father, Mother, little Robert, and me. And here on the back, a Bible verse.' Her speech was hard to follow, but she listened hard, screwing up her eyes and pressing her lips together. Once she'd got the gist, Flora pushed the brooch through the bars with slippery pink fingers.

'We must both pray for deliverance. Hurry now, and send the white folks to fetch me as quick as you can. You are an angel sent by the Lord. God bless you. Go!'

Back at the empty hut, she looked at the brooch. Part of her knew it was *tapu*, a magic stone, an object of power. It had been given to her to guide her future. Another compartment of her mind knew it was a brooch, a clasp to be pinned on a gown. Like turning a rusty key in a lock, she started to move the tumblers in that neglected *pakeha* half of her mind. She counted hours and assembled facts. The making of a scheme was painfully hard, for her reasoning power had shrunk to the size of the *Pa* on the hill. Outside, the singing was still raucous and the dancing had begun.

She pulled on the tartan gown, fastening buttons that nipped her like ants. All she took with her was her flute and the brooch. Throwing the rain cape over her head again, she let herself out of the hut. Keeping far back below the hut eaves, she saw agile silhouettes flickering before the great fire, their voices joined in song. As silent as a rat, she crept down to the sea path, feeling her way, inching forwards.

Halfway down, she glanced back up towards her old *farnow*, at the captors who had for so long been her family. She was surprised to feel the pull of them, as strong even as the pull of Charlie's family of thieves. Pa folk were of the same ilk – as proud as any robber band, quick to laugh and be merry, lovers of the sentimental song and vicious oath. They were superstitious too, running to their *tohunga* priest for their dreams to be unravelled; they were weavers of love spells, casters of curses. She looked back at the Pa, and imagined Areki-Tapiru like a queen tonight on the royal platform.

The orange glow of the campfire looked unearthly, suspended on the hilltop like the first tier of heaven, a world of swelling song and drums and stamping feet. The old song began, *Toia mai te waka* . . . 'Oh, haul away your war canoe . . .' She mouthed the words to each verse – then, as the last chorus died away, the smoky-sweet scent of the *hangi* feast filled her nostrils, so like roast pork that it made your mouth water. The chieftainess had saved her life. It was a bond between them – but in a moment she snapped it, and hurried onwards.

She scrambled down the steep track. Below, the moonlight gleamed like pewter on the rocking sea. There stood the *pakeha* ship, with lamps twinkling in the rigging like netted stars. Her mouth was as dry as dust when she finally reached the beach. She hailed a sailor who was keeping watch at the stores, and, all in a kerfuffle, they rowed her out and helped her up the ladder. She clung to the men quite pitifully as they carried her onto the deck. When the captain appeared, she was mighty relieved at his unsuspecting manner. He took her arm in a kindly, fatherly manner – so she leaned against him, shaking from head to foot.

'Can you speak up, young lady?'

She opened her mouth, and her voice rose like a lark sailing up to the heavens. How could she ever think she'd forget the old patter?

'God bless ye, sir,' she said, in a perfect Edinburgh accent. 'Ma name is Flora Pilling. I was captured by those heathen devils who chase me even now. I pray, sir, dinna let them find me! Let us leave this place at once. Oh, hurry, won't you?'

Her moment of glory over, she let herself be led to a cabin – a cabin with a feather mattress and a flower-patterned jug. Voices muttered around her; that the captain was taking his chance to steal away from those damned heathens with both Flora and the muskets. As she fell asleep on the delicious cotton bolster, she heard muffled oars, and felt a jolt and quiver as the ship began to glide soundlessly away around the bay. By the time she woke again, in a sort of rapture, she could hear the sails snap full of wind, as the ship lifted on the waves like a bird, on course for home, on the long way back to England.

30

Delafosse Hall

September 1793

~ Coloured Sugar Sands ~

*Clarify some sugar and put what quantity you please upon
the fire, with a sufficiency of colouring to produce the tint you
want; boil it till comes to the ninth degree or A Great Plume
or Feather; the surest method is to dip a skimmer in and shake
the hand, if it turns to large sparks that clog together it is done.
Take it off the fire, work it constantly till it returns to sugar
again, and form it into sand by sifting in a sieve. This
coloured sand is a most elegant decoration for a Grand Buffet.*

*A fine French receipt from the scrap box of Mrs Charlotte
Spenlove, much esteemed as it glitters very well in candlelight*

The rain was pelting down as the cart lurched to a halt at Delafosse Hall. I was weary from days of rough travelling, but no longer had the means to pay for even one night's rest at the George. From his sickbed on the men's ward, the captain had insisted I go to his chamber and help myself from what was his – and so, wary of Mrs Huckle, I tiptoed to his door like a thief and groped in a recess for his hidden key. The captain's quarters were as ship-shape and as neat as I remembered them. I took the remains of his savings from where they lay hidden beneath a loose board, making a silent promise to repay him as soon as I might. I paused, too, to admire his red coat hanging to attention on a hook, carefully brushed, with the buttons polished like sovereigns. Here was all that was most precious to him: his medal, his short sword and pocket pistol, and the oval portrait of his late dear wife.

I took what I needed, but even after travelling by the meanest of wagons, by the time I reached Delafosse my purse no longer held the means for me to return to London again. Alighting from the cart, I doubted anyone from Earlby would recognise me; my mourning dress had worn thin and rusty, and my cloak was filthy and torn. My fear of being noticed was of little consequence: I had to understand what had happened – to me, to my husband, and to my money. I had made a few guesses, but could no longer leave the truth undisturbed. However ill he was, I had to speak to Michael, to reach an agreement with him about my own and Henry's future, for my baby's sake.

It was a wet and weary trudge up the drive. At the final bend I halted beneath dripping branches and surveyed my home. Almost a year had passed since my marriage, and the Hall had sunk into even greater dilapidation. The creeper covering the walls was a leafless lacework of black; the roofs had buckled dangerously. The only lights shone from the mullioned first-floor windows, from which I construed that Michael was up and still at dinner. Tucking my bundle up tightly beneath my cloak, I dashed across the lawn to the church-like entrance and pulled the bell. A minute passed, with no answer. I rang again, on and on, blinking away the rain that streamed from my hat into my eyes. At last I heard footsteps, and the wicket door inched open. The maid standing behind it, lantern in her hand, was an utter stranger to me.

'Who are you?' I asked. I knew I must be a pitiful sight, in sodden clothes, with my hair dropping loose in rats' tails.

With an affronted stare, she said, 'The Croxons' maid, ma'am.'

'I need to speak to your master at once.'

'The master's away.'

'Is he convalescing elsewhere?'

'No, ma'am. He's only gone t' village. The mistress is in, mind.' This almost dumbfounded me. But if not Sybilla – well, I made my guess.

I barged my way past her so she had to stand aside. 'Tell her I'll see her at once.'

'What name shall I give?'

'Mrs Croxon.'

'Croxon? Wait here, ma'am.'

It was just as bone-gnawingly cold in that entrance hall as I remembered it from my first arrival. I made a hasty attempt at tidying myself, but the water hung heavy in my skirts, as if I had walked through a freezing stream.

When the servant returned she gave me a peculiar look. Goodness knows who she thought I was; some bedraggled relative of Michael's, perhaps? Climbing the carved stairway, the house seemed even danker and more ramshackle than before. As the maid's lantern sent shadows flurrying along the walls I marvelled at my own courage in returning. So, poor invalid Michael was sufficiently recovered to be abroad in the village? That proved I was correct in at least one of my deductions. But if that was correct, then other, more dangerous implications must follow.

Unlike the rest of the Hall, the dining room was beautifully dressed for a grand celebration. All my best silver was out; a score of candles stood massed in a blaze of gold. Sitting queen-like in my former seat was the black-haired woman, dressed in my green taffeta, with my diamond brooch pinned to the black belt.

'Do take a seat.' Her voice could have passed for genteel if I hadn't known better. 'How pleasant of you to call, Grace.'

I did so, studying her familiar heart-shaped face, looking ill and blotched from drink. 'Good evening, Peg. I cannot say those black locks suit you half so well as your natural red.'

'Oh, this.' She stroked the long tresses, the source of that single inky hair I had once found in my bed. 'I rather like it. Black better suits the night.'

'I trust you are enjoying yourself, with my money?'

'It is very obliging of you.' Her wide mouth stretched as if it were all a great jest. Her gestures were slow, her voice thick with spirits.

'So when is Michael home?'

'Later.' She shrugged. 'Join me, won't you?'

I looked at the mish-mash of sweet stuffs spread over the table; children's trash, dominated by a garish island of paste fringed with sugar sand. 'Not if I were starving.'

'Not good enough for you?' Her manner grew a shade cooler. 'Tell me, have you ever starved, Grace?'

'Almost. These last few weeks.'

'No. I don't mean you have had to wait a few minutes for your supper. I mean starved almost to the death.' She leaned back, and an ugly belligerence hardened her face. 'I suppose it is of no conse-quence that someone like me, a criminal, a convict, might starve? Who cares if my sort are chained up in irons, raped and beaten, or stranded on some savage island?'

'You know,' I said, with sincere force, 'that I always sympathised with you, Peg.'

She chased a dollop of jelly with her spoon. When she had eaten it she asked sullenly, 'Would you eat anything at all, Grace? If you were starved and frightened.'

'I cannot say.' There had, after all, been Mrs Huckle's lodgers' scraps, that I once would have thrown out in disgust. To provide milk for Henry I would have eaten anything – but I was wary of telling her a word of it.

'Me, I've eaten weevils on the transport ship, and caterpillar bugs given me by the black folk in New South Wales – they wriggle in your mouth, but they ain't so bad. And then I ate something much, much worse.' She stared unseeing into the distance as I listened, mesmerised by the sight of her in my chair, in my clothes, eating from my favourite porcelain dish.

'That first night I was captured,' she said, throwing a gulp of wine down her throat, 'Areki-Tapiru gave me roast meat. Smiling she was, coaxing her new pet to eat up. And when I wouldn't eat, she hit me with her bone knife, smack on the head, so that I nearly swooned. I had to decide. Eat it or—' and she mimed a knife, slicing off her head. 'It looked like pork; but it didn't smell right. And when I ate it, I knew right off what it was. I even got it into my head it was the right thing to do. To take Jack's flesh back home, deep inside of me. And that's how I come to be the only one who ever got home. Because I took on his strength. I learned to be strong like that tribe of warriors.'

She pushed the flute across the table. 'I kept the bone. Had it carved nice. All I've got left of Jack Pierce.'

I looked at the yellowing bone. Horror and pity threatened to overwhelm me. I could no longer look at her without revulsion. The thought of every mouthful of Peg's food I had ever eaten made me want to retch. 'I'm sorry,' I whispered.

'That's it, Grace.' She put her head tipsily to one side. 'Unlike that husband of yours, I believe you might be. Though you were a trial at times. All mope-eyed over that milksop.'

'Well, that did not stop you in the end, did it?' I burst out. 'Forged a letter to Mr Tully, I presume?'

She snorted with laughter, affecting exasperation. 'The time it took to find the key to that writing box of yours, and make a skeleton copy. You led me on a merry dance.' She gazed about herself triumphantly. 'What have you ever done to deserve all this?' She spread her palms in a gesture at all the fashionable furniture I'd bought, the silver plate, the Turkey carpets. 'It's a lottery, ain't it? Why should you get all this and not me? Why shouldn't I have it?'

I wondered how I had ever thought her handsome. She was glitter-eyed now, as bright and ugly as a roused lunatic. My voice was shaky but clear. 'I'll tell you why, Peg. Because no one else wants such a world as you want. Because we cannot steal, pilfer and defraud. There have to be laws to protect the weak.'

'The weak?' she sneered, leaning back and looking pleased with herself. 'You mean cullies like your husband?'

'I suppose you're going to tell me what happened.' I braced myself.

She narrowed her eyes. 'What, between me and him?' Daintily, she chose a child's crimson confection and chewed it noisily. 'Ah, what revels we've had in the tower since I come here.' Her mouth widened in a mirthless grin. 'A little horseplay, the lifting of his shirt, a teasing with the birch—'

I remembered the scattering of birch twigs in the tower that night, and the air pungent with desire.

'We had a little code about the fire, d'you remember that? I'd be putting the dinner out and say, "Oh, Mr Croxon, the fire won't take, it's cold ash" or "The fire's burning good and hot tonight." If it were a good fire he knew to meet me at the tower. And you,' she hooted with laughter and pointed at me, 'would be sitting there with a face as blank as a china plate.' She pulled a derisory expression. 'Naturally, the fire din't burn bright too often. I learned that from watching the best of whores, how to stoke it up and stoke it up, till he couldn't think of nothing else. Most of the time I didn't even need to touch his cock—'

'Stop it!' I raised my hands to my ears.

'While as for you,' she crowed. 'I had to coax him with promises, just to get him to bed you. Still, he was keen to open your purse, if not your legs.'

'That's a lie,' I cried out. 'He wanted to leave here, to leave you.' I was breathing fast, staring hard into my lap. When I raised my head, she was slicing a fat piece of cake with an over-large knife. 'No,' I repeated more weakly. 'I knew he was in torment. Now I know his tormenter was you.'

She chewed noisily on her cake as she spoke. 'So how do you account for his fine play-acting, then? Bravo, Michael; what a tragical death scene that was. You should've seen your face. You was confounded.'

'Yes,' I said bitterly. 'By a jug of plain water. Then someone explained the thimble-riggers' trick to me – that they make you see what was never even there. There never was any poison, there never was a man-chasing Sybilla Claybourn. They were all figments invented by you to deceive me. I suppose it was you who summoned my husband to the inn on my wedding night?'

She mimicked applause. 'Give the lady a gingerbread. When that gutless brother of his, Peter Croxon, came by the George, he saw me and knew my face at once, from that other time in Manchester. So I told him a few home truths about his big brother and how he dangled on my leash. So dear brother Peter sent for your husband, all in a botheration about me. I only had to lift my little finger to get them all dancing.'

'So Peter did send that letter.' It was horrible to hear it, and I felt myself slump. 'And never told me.'

'They swore a secret oath, did you not know that? If Peter Croxon would only keep quiet about me, your husband would see him right, and let him be the Croxon heir. After all, Michael had your chink to live off, didn't he?'

'And the blood on Christmas Eve, that was some charlatan's trick?'

She laughed coarsely. 'The bag of blood in the salamagundy? One bite and it burst. Then he had more of them, hid in his pocket. Same as any swordfight in the theatre.'

A dark red globe of what I'd seen as beetroot flashed before my inner eye.

Hearing it told like this, I felt myself suddenly no match for Peg. I should rather Michael had died than listen to this catalogue of how he had duped me so callously. I no longer had the will to make demands of anyone. Looking to the door in defeat, I wondered where in the world I might go next.

Just at this worst of moments Henry moved beneath my cloak, kicking against the shawl knotted tightly around my body. I stood up and paced to the window, praying he might settle down so I could leave at once. But whatever I did, it was no use. He began to whimper.

'What you got in there – a ferret?'

I pulled a chair some way from the table, sat down, and unbundled Henry onto my lap, cradling his fragile head beneath my hand. 'Shush, sweetling,' I whispered. I had no choice but to loosen my bodice and set him to my breast.

'That's a pretty infant.' Peg was at once entirely alert. 'Is it Michael's?'

'Of course he is. Not that he deserves him.'

She poured another drink and watched Henry very closely over the rim as she sipped. 'I never had none meself. None ever bred to the full-size; not even with Jack.'

'Well, I'm sorry.'

'It's the price to pay, specially for little girls given over for the pox cure. Once the clapped old fellow's had them, the girls don't breed. A baby would've been summat to remember Jack by. Better than a poxy bone.'

She got up and staggered towards me. Heaving a chair to sit

beside me, she sat down heavily. Startled, Henry pulled away from me and flailed his tiny arms towards her, his eyes darting this way and that.

'Can I hold him?'

'No.'

'Go on. Just for a minute. I'll look after him.'

She was staring at Henry with a round-eyed hungry look. Entranced, she reached out to him, nudging a sticky confection towards his lips. I stood up abruptly and strode away, standing tall, re-tying Henry tightly inside my shawl again. An image sprang before me: of Henry being starved of my maternal milk and fed instead on poisonous sugarplums. That must never, ever, come to pass, I swore to myself. I had lost so much: my standing, my money, even my precious crucifix. Yet now all of those were replaced by Henry, and he was alive. A new courage filled my blood.

'Do you truly believe,' I said with a voice both clear but a little shaky, 'that after you've taken everything else I have – do you think I would hand my child to you? You know what you can do, Peg? Pack up and go. If you go now, quickly, I promise I won't inform on you. I know that your life has been brutal – but I cannot allow you to do this to me and to my son. I came here tonight to tell Michael I want my life back. And I want my money, too.'

As I said this, I took the captain's pistol from my inside pocket and aimed it straight towards her. It was unfamiliar and awkward in my hand; but I knew its aim was true at short range.

She looked dreamily past me; I could not read what she was thinking.

'Did you hear me? Go.' My breath was ragged. Henry began to shift uncomfortably.

At last she stood up unsteadily and looked from me to the pistol.

'Reckon I'm cornered,' she slurred. 'I've had a good run.'

I aimed the pistol at her swaying form. I watched her carefully, reminding myself that she was a mistress of distraction.

'I'll count to three,' I said. 'Then you must be gone.'

She continued to stare at the back of Henry's head, as if fascinated by his fair curls.

'One,' I said, shakily but firmly.

Still she tottered before me in a sort of stupor.

'Two.' When she still didn't move, I said with all the force I could find, 'Peg, I will shoot you.'

She looked up then – slack with resignation. 'Very well, Mrs Croxon. Only give me a gamester's chance, won't you? I should like to go downstairs and fetch some clothes, and a purse, to get me a distance away on the road.'

I hadn't anticipated this; but it did, after all, seem fair. 'Very well.'

'I'll just take a drink to clear me head – then I'll go and pack.'

I kept the pistol aimed upon her. She weaved towards the table and reached for a glass. The next instant a startling boom erupted – I reeled back, crouching over Henry, as a ball of fire exploded across the table; blue flames climbing almost to the ceiling. Later, I reconstructed that with her hidden hand, Peg had flung a handful of sugar sand into the mass of burning candles. By the time my dazzled eyes recovered, the flames had subsided and the air was thick with smoking burned sugar. A shape darted towards me through the smoke; it was Peg, the silver knife flashing in her hand, the sharp blade headed towards me.

I fired the pistol. Its report cracked the air, flashing with sparks. Peg halted, releasing an aggrieved scream, and crashed backwards against the table, sending glasses and crockery smashing to the floor. A blackened hole smoked in the sleeve of my green taffeta, through which Peg's blood pulsed bright crimson.

'You slippery bitch!' she screamed, and, clutching her arm, steadied herself and rushed at me again with the blade.

I dodged backwards. All my instincts were to protect Henry, to keep him from danger. Clumsy with panic, I lost my grip on the pistol. It clattered to the floor. So I did the only thing I could think of. I ran for the door.

31

Delafosse Hall

September 1793

~ To Preserve Meat in a Cold Larder ~

The most prized meats may best be preserved by hanging upon a meat-hook, so long as it is arranged not to touch any other carcass. So long as the air is kept very chill yet moist, with ample ventilation to keep the meat as sweet as possible, it will be dry-preserved and age most tender.

The Housekeeper's Closet Revealed, 1788

It was as well that Henry was bound tightly against my body, for I hurtled down those stairs with the fear of the Devil at my heels. But on the final flight I heard voices below me and almost stumbled with fright. Crouching behind the carved balustrade, I listened with a thumping heart. It was Michael's voice, though I could not distinguish his words.

The maid answered him, 'Aye, Croxon it were. Family, is she?'

'Croxon? What age was she?'

From high above, I heard Peg calling: 'Michael!' I was trapped between them. As Peg began a noisy descent from the dining-room landing, I dashed around the corner and threw myself unsteadily onto the deserted Long Gallery. Once out of sight, I pressed myself flat against the cracked wainscoting, listening intently. A few feet away Peg passed me by, clambering down to the hall.

'Lock every door and window. Jess, go through the house and seal every way out. Don't just gawp, get a move on.' A moment later she hissed, 'Your wife's here. Look, the bitch has shot me. She wants everything back.'

Michael mumbled in a cowed tone I scarcely recognised. 'What shall I do . . .' A low reprimand followed and the sound of a sharp slap.

'She must not leave. Do you comprehend me? Go and make sure Jess does her duty.'

Silence fell again. It would be a waste of time trying the great entrance door, for I had heard the key being turned, with its familiar rusty groan. Banging and footsteps rang out from distant regions of the house. I made an effort to calm successive waves of panic that threatened to fix me to the spot. If all the doors were locked, the only means of escape I could muster was the tunnel to the summer-house. Scarcely daring to breathe, I took infinitely careful steps down the stairs and across the hall, then tiptoed down the servants' backstairs, until I could just see Nan and the two sisters scouring pots at the kitchen table. I stood as still as a statue, as clattering from upstairs confirmed the search continued. When at last Nan stood to stoke up the fire I cautiously gave her a signal. At first she gaped, then grinned with delight. Raising my finger to my lips, I directed her to be silent, and signalled that she must distract the sisters. She was not as crack-headed as Peg had insisted, for soon afterwards she disappeared, and a cacophony of Nan's screams rose in accompaniment to the frenzied squawking of chickens. With wild oaths, the two sisters ran after her to round up the flock of escaped poultry; and in that brief spell, I grasped a lantern and headed down to the basement.

Once underground a new fear struck me, for the maze of passages was not as straightforward as I remembered. I scurried from a storeroom, to a chamber full of vats, groping the damp walls as I dipped under one archway and then another. Where I had pictured the tunnel to the summerhouse, I ran straight into a dead end. I turned back, panting, remonstrating with myself and forcing myself to think more clearly. Maybe the tunnel was a left-hand turn from the cold larder? Holding the lantern high before me, I retraced my steps. Then, at only fifty or so paces from the tunnel opening, a sound made me stop stock still. Behind me, a stone rattled. The shuffle of footsteps grew louder in the dark.

'Grace? I know you're there.' I almost dropped the lantern as Peg's voice rang out, so close to me I could hear her breath. I turned around as quietly as I could. But she was not yet upon me, for her lantern shed only a diffused glow in the distance. Henry stirred, and a tiny sigh escaped from the depths of my cloak. Please, please, sleep, I prayed. For the first time I comprehended fully the risk of my returning here. Who would notice if I disappeared for ever?

Even the captain might never discover my end, buried here in the dank and darkness. I cared not a jot for myself now, but Henry – Henry must be saved from Peg. I again envisioned his future without me, an existence in which Peg petted him with poisonous caresses. That woman must never have my son.

Ahead of me stood the tunnel to the summerhouse. Dimly I remembered that it had taken at least fifteen minutes to walk the entire way in suffocating blackness. More vividly I remembered that visitation of terror I had heard in the dark: the sound of a woman running; of whimpering, panting dread. I had a powerful conviction that it was a warning I must heed; that to have Peg at my back in that pitch-dark place did not bear contemplation. To the left was an archway, leading to an empty cavern; to the right was the cold larder, where I reckoned there must be many hiding places. Praying I might evade Peg, I stepped inside the larder. Once inside I used the habit learned from daily sketching to commit the scene instantly to my inner eye. It was a large rectangular room, furnished with metal cages containing joints of bacon and so forth. In the centre stood a butcher's block for cutting joints. Feathered game birds were strung up from the ceiling. Behind them, against the far wall, were a row of carcasses, two or three deep, hung on hooks attached to rails. I snuffed out my lantern and set it down gently in a corner. With no better plan save that once Peg had passed the larder, I might retrace my steps upstairs, I slipped into a narrow space behind the nearest of the carcasses. From the smoothness of its pelt and the metallic stink of blood, I supposed it was a slaughtered deer.

I stood very still, urging her to pass the door. But instead the light of her lantern grew stronger until it shone like a golden beacon onto cages and carcasses.

'Are you there?' Peg's voice sounded very loud in the cave-like room. 'You can't hide. I can see you.'

I knew she could not see me at all, for the dead creature hid me well. My pulses roared in my ears as I tried to dissolve into the darkness. At last, with a vexed tutting sound, she turned on her heels and moved off down the tunnel. Cold sweat broke out on my face. I allowed myself to release a long breath.

Then, perhaps because I at last stood still and no longer rocked him, Henry woke up. With a stab of apprehension, I felt his tiny fists flail against me. I groped inside my cloak and tried to connect his mouth to my breast. But instead of sucking, he moved his head awkwardly this way and that. Then my poor baby took a deep breath and uttered a high-pitched wail that reverberated against the stone walls. I rocked and patted him, but his crying only diminished to a nerve-scouring grizzle. Why had I not run away while I could? I wanted to weep, too. Then miraculously, Henry found his fingers and silently began to suck them. I pulled the shawl tightly around me, so he lay spread-eagled against my beating heart.

It was too late. Peg's light returned, illuminating raw meat and dead pairs of eyes. I could sense Peg rather than see her; she moved very quietly about the far side of the room, opening and closing the doors of the cages.

'Is that my little boy?' she said from the other side of the larder. 'Where have you hidden him?'

I risked retreating backwards, pushing past a sticky, raw carcass. I expected at any moment to feel the hard wall behind me.

'I can see you. And hear my little boy.'

Could she see me? The lantern beam swung ever closer, hurting my eyes. Behind the raw carcass was another, this one wrapped in cloth. My hand groped backwards, hopelessly praying to find some means of escape – a door, a cupboard, anything. Then I glimpsed a second tiny light behind Peg. In the outline of the door a bent-backed figure hovered in silhouette. It was Nan. Though only a frail little woman, her light brought me a grain of comfort. I was no longer alone with Peg.

'You will never leave,' Peg crooned in my direction. 'For I am you, Grace Croxon.'

One of her hands held the lantern, while the other lay stiff and useless against her side. She set the light down on the butcher's block, and with her one good hand, took out the knife.

'So you will soon be dead.'

Pinpoints of fear prickled over my skin. Warily, she began to search, edging ever closer to the rack of hanging meats where I was hidden.

Terror drove me backwards. I pushed myself behind the cloth-covered carcass. My scrabbling fingers found something peculiar. A disc of bone? No. A button. I explored further. A piece of what felt like lace. My hand reached backwards and – could it be? – was clasped by another human hand – only this hand was as cold as the grave. I stifled the scream that threatened to burst from my throat. Instead, barely able to breathe, I explored further. I found a mass of wiry human hair. Glad of my tallness, I reached around the corpse and found the iron hook that suspended what I suddenly knew with absolute certainty was Mrs Harper's gown. Then, I held that poor soul's corpse in front of me like a shield.

I knew my plan would only work if I waited until Peg stood just before me. I held my nerve, and my breath, as she swung the carcass of venison aside. Now she was no more than a few paces in front of me. I saw her pale hand reach forward, grasp the next blood-raw carcass and pull that aside. In a moment she would discover me.

Let her see what is not there, I prayed. Her distance from the weak beams of the lamp was in my favour, as was her injury and intoxication. There she stood, only inches in front of me; leaning forward, her head questing this way and that. A skull-like shadow masked most of her face. The glint of her eyes widened in triumph as she saw before her a woman in black that might have been me, her head bowed, cowering before her. Peg swung back her good arm and struck with the knife as I clasped the corpse before me, like a sandbag absorbing the blows of a cutlass. Blow after blow fell upon us. Even though Mrs Harper's poor body took most of the force of Peg's attack, still her fury almost knocked me backwards. But I thought of Henry, hidden beneath my cloak and discovered the strength of a lioness. All about us the smell of death was stifling; a sweet but foul putrescence. Then at last Peg exhaled a victorious groan, stood back, and dropped the knife.

'Now where's my little boy,' she sighed, looking about herself as if waking from a drunken sleep.

With vicious speed I threw Mrs Harper's body towards Peg. What she thought when that cadaver sprang at her from the darkness I will never know. She screamed, as if in horrified recognition, her hands raised to her face. Clumsily, she tripped backwards onto the stone flags and tumbled with a loud gasp and crack. Sprawling on the floor, she tried to kick the corpse away. In the corner of my eye, I saw Nan creep into the room. Then, as casually as if she were butchering a rabbit, Nan retrieved the knife from the floor where Peg had dropped it.

'No!' I cried. Peg was still groaning, half-stunned from her fall as Nan rose over her, the knife wavering in her palsied hands. With all that old woman's strength she drove the blade fast into her tormentor's chest, with a wet noise like a butcher at his block. Peg made an unnatural choking sound and her head arched backwards. Then her face froze in death; her eyes glassy, her mouth fixed open. My adversary lay felled with my gown ridden high to her knees and one shoe half-off, like a drab collapsed in an alley.

I crumpled to the floor, my breath in hoarse rushes, cradling Henry, who protested as I hugged him and kissed his precious face.

'Come here, Nan,' I said, once I grew a little calmer. She came over to me and we gripped hands, both of us trembling like leaves. Her poor bruised arm reached out and touched Henry's head like a talisman. 'I heard the bairn cry,' she said in a tremulous voice. 'And I weren't going to let that she-devil near him.' Looking over her shoulder at the rumpled horror of Peg's corpse, she said, 'That were the best day's butcherin' I ever done.' Then I laughed bitterly, for I could not believe such a terrible test of my strength had ended.

* * *

Footsteps approached from the passage. It was Michael, wild-haired and pale, like a wraith of the man I had married. Nevertheless at the sight of him, the man I had once loved, the father of my new child, I felt a sudden shameful need for him. I called to him and opened my arms. But he had eyes only for Peg, lying splayed on the floor. He knelt at her side, breaking into unmanly sobs of a kind I had never heard before. I watched his cheeks grow wet while I attended to Henry. So Peg had won this final battle. Only after a long spell did he even notice me.

'That baby.' He approached me, thin and hollow-eyed. 'Is it mine?'

I felt near to expiring with weariness. 'What? Like the money and the land, you mean? Yours? No, I don't believe he is, in that sense. I gave birth to him alone. And I'll care for him alone. You'd better get rid of her.' I pointed at Peg's corpse.

'But where?' he asked, in a self-pitying tone. I looked at him with disgust.

'Just think of somewhere to bury her. Unless you want me to send for a magistrate? I want my son to know nothing about this, ever.'

A clinging drizzle fell, but the long night was ending: a luminous smudge was growing at the eastern horizon. As I drove the pony trap through the gloom, nothing looked or felt quite real – yet a febrile energy pushed me continually onward. I was dimly aware of a deadness in my fingers and toes, and the sensation of floating through the muffled landscape. The fear that had beaten against me like a frantic bird was subsiding. I had never felt more resolute.

'Why did you sell my land?' I asked my husband in a tone as frigid as the air.

'That was her idea.'

'Naturally it was.'

'Most of the money is in my strongbox upstairs. I shall give it back to you.'

'Of course you will. You stole it.'

Michael began to jabber, attempting to explain himself. 'You cannot know what it was like – you cannot. That first time I met her, something extraordinary happened. After she fleeced that pound note from Peter – I was angry, but it was more than that. She ran away, and at first I lost her. I found myself inside a mansion. It was like falling into an enchanted world. Red and green lanterns lit my way, and a fountain ran with wine. And the devil was in me to find that girl.

'She was up on the roof, hiding in the lines of laundry. I cornered her against a wall and she threw Peter's pound note at my feet. "Take it," she said. "Now let me go."'

I glanced at him, a hunched outline beside me.

'I didn't want to let her go. The way she pressed herself against the wall; her head back, her throat open, her eyes penetrating mine. She knew me better than I knew myself.'

He fell silent, and I knew he relived the enchantment of that moment. 'Go on,' I demanded, wanting to hear him, but also wanting to end this torture of not knowing, at last.

'She lifted her skirt to her knees, laughing in that throaty way of hers. I grasped her skirts in my fists and lifted them higher. Then, from nowhere, a slap stung my face. I reeled back. She was laughing at me, at my discomposure. "You deserve a slap, you filthy devil," she said. I was so angry I reached out to shake her, to pull her to me. This time she whispered in my ear, "I know a private place. I'll show you who is mistress." And she grasped my hair, jerked my head back, and made me look into her face. She was as strong as an Amazon. "You may serve me only if you swear to obey me." And there it was. She knew the clockwork of my soul– how to make it run faster, make it spin, make it stop dead and tremble.

'However hard I battled against this – this vice, Peg understood me. I told you, it began with that monster at school. At first he protected me from other boys, from bullies, he let me make free in his apartments. Then he began to whisper of cruelties, of lewdness

– no. I cannot speak of it. And never, ever, of what he did to me. I tried, truly I have tried to conquer it. But for solitary years I'd longed for such a fierce mistress as her. She hit me again, and I was hers.

'"Where is this private place?" I asked.

'"Where is it, *Mistress*," she insisted.

'Then, to my eternal frustration, we were interrupted by that magistrate and his constable. I was in an agony. And that damned magistrate wouldn't let up, goading me to charge her.'

'And Peg?'

He muttered quietly, 'It was not very pleasant, you know. She begged me. Said she would be hanged.' His voice grew strident. 'I thought it would be better for the law to have her. At least that way I could save myself.'

'Oh yes? You would have seen her hanged. Yet when she was reprieved you visited her? In that vile cell.' I was near to spitting with fury.

'She begged to see me before she was transported. But when I saw her it was again like falling through that trapdoor into another world. I paid to be alone with her. I was helpless. Pain, pleasure – I lost all reason.

'She had hopes of a retrial; there was some crooked lawyer involved. But it worried me, it would attract unwelcome attention if I suddenly changed my testimony. I realised that all I had to do was never go back to her. The law would pack her off to Botany Bay, and that would be the end of it. Seven years was such a long time that I persuaded myself she would never come back. So the day I was supposed to visit her, I found a tavern and got dead drunk instead. God help me, I paid for that.

'A few weeks later I got that token in my post. Love token? It was a curse. Every day it pressed like an iron weight upon my mind. I fell into despondency, only my parents prevented me from taking my life. Still I hoped, I prayed, that she would never return – for no one ever did return from Botany Bay, did they? But three years later, she found me again and I knew it was the end. She hunted me down; lay in wait for me here, in the empty hall, at Delafosse. Those weeks before you came – I surrendered to my true nature. I'd have beggared myself for her. You do understand, I was in her hands; I wanted to be at her mercy, her willing servant. She wasn't a kind mistress. She told me about Moncrieff, she heard some servant gossip, laughed at my misery – until I had to destroy that room that taunted me with its hypocrisy.'

He looked over, towards me, his eyes huge and beseeching. 'But Grace, I wouldn't let her hurt you. Once she'd got the key to your box and your money, I begged her to leave you unharmed. That charade at Christmas Eve – it was a favour to you, she thought it amusing to let you live, so long as you changed your name and never came back.' He pulled a dark bottle from his pocket and took a long draw.

'What is that? A mind-fogging potion of hers? Don't you see how she has destroyed you?' I snatched the bottle from him and threw it hard onto the road where it smashed with a satisfying crock.

Michael glanced back at where it had landed and said plaintively, 'I'll try, Grace. Now I've come to my senses again. Thank God you are home. We'll settle down again. I'll be respectable again, a good father to Henry.'

He smiled at me, a weak ridiculous smile; but at my shrivelling glance, his next words died on his tongue.

'Once you have done what you need to do, Michael, I wish never to see your cowardly face again.'

The gate to Whitelow pastures hung from its post. The rain still fell across the ruined landscape, in quivering grey sheets. A quagmire of mud stretched before us. The pleasant green pastures of my land had been destroyed, first by the attempt to build the mill, and then by the arsonists' efforts to destroy it. The charred ruins of a few low walls were all that remained. Fearful of the gig's wheels sinking, I halted beneath a dripping tree and we both alighted.

Michael doggedly fetched Mrs Harper's ruined body, wrapped

in a meagre blanket. Old and new wounds punctured her shrunken frame, and her once-modest gown hung in ribbons. For a moment her poor withered face hung upside down, and to my perplexity, I believed I recognised her.

'Peg did give her a chance,' he mumbled sheepishly. 'But the fool wouldn't do the sensible thing and leave. I asked Peg to make her go away, but the Harper woman was obstinate. And then she went in search of liquor in the basement . . .'

His voice trailed away. We set off, Michael swaying as he hauled Mrs Harper's corpse across the mire. A rectangular foundation pit, large enough for the engine's housing, came into view.

'Ah,' I said, splashing behind him through drenching puddles, 'the scene of our great fortune.'

A path ran around the pit, where workers had abandoned heaps of earth and tools, and even a rusting wheelbarrow. Ponds and rivulets glimmered in the ceaseless rain; the ground was as dark and sticky as pitch. Michael edged forward to the bank of mud. Some dozen feet below us, the pit contained a sump of filthy water. I stood behind him, as close as I dared, and uttered a prayer for the poor woman. Then Michael tied a large stone to her skirts and lifted her high, swung her back, and then cast her forth. She tumbled awkwardly, poor soul, into the coal-black waters beneath. There was barely a splash as her body sank. 'That's good,' he muttered. 'She's sinking at once.'

We returned together to the gig to fetch Peg's body. Both of us were drenched. Michael's hair dripped long with rainwater; his coat was sodden, his lean bones stood jagged, his eyes were huge. Halfway back to the pit he stumbled and dropped Peg in the mud, and the blanket that covered her fell away. The wound to her chest had left an oval stain across my gown where the knife was still embedded. He lifted her tenderly in his arms and trudged on.

At the lip of the pit he halted again, panting for breath. I took a last look at Peg as she lay ungainly in his arms. The false raven tresses were, of course, merely horsehair, and now hung clotted with mud. Her eyes stood open in a glazed resentful stare. She was a grotesque mannequin, no longer animated by whatever chameleon spirit had played at being Mary, or Peg, or whichever character most suited her purpose. I waited for Michael to cast her away, but instead, he lifted her in his arms and passionately kissed her open mouth. He was sweating, his skin oyster damp; the old handsome features bleary and raw-eyed. Then, turning to me, he glared with streaming eyes. 'You! You have ruined everything. Why did you ever come back?'

I started back, shielding my face, my own hot tears blurring my vision.

He sank to his knees, cradling her lolling head; I felt he wanted to roll, swine-like, in filth. I had seen enough.

'I am going,' I called, and began to step heedlessly back through the sucking ground, dully aware of Michael's eternal facility to crush me. I was already some thirty feet nearer to the gig when I looked backwards to see if he was following me. He was not. Still he knelt over Peg's corpse like a tragic lover, filthy and distraught.

Even those events we mark clearly with our own eyes can deceive us; I had learned that lesson well from Peg. If memory is, as the ancients say, a tablet of wax marked with a stylus, what happened next was gouged so deep that the wax itself was near destroyed. Propelled by disgust, I again set my head down and picked my way back to the gig through ankle-deep puddles. I started as a sound rang out, a wordless scream that split the air – anguished, terrified, miserable. In the moment in which I turned, I heard a long, splintery splash of water. I looked dimly about through the sheets of rain. The edge of the pit lay empty – both Michael and Peg had vanished from this earth. Stupefied, I scanned the landscape for them, convinced that my eyes betrayed me. Then I ran back to the pit through sucking mud, my lungs bursting. By the time I reached the rim I found nothing moving, save two conjoined rings, slowly dilating in the water. 'Michael!' I screamed at the empty air, wondering if this was some final, cruel trick the pair had played on me. I grasped a stick and threw it feebly into the water. Nothing surfaced. I stood stunned as the rings of water expanded ever more slowly, until the black surface at last grew still. Had Michael leaped after his lover in a fit of despair? I did not know. I could no longer set one rational thought before another. I was alone, shaking and sobbing in that graveyard of dreams.

The dismal sounds of morning broke around me. A few birds awakened and uttered lonely calls. The horse shook a flurry of rain from his coat, jangling his harness. I was so wet and cold that I wondered how I might ever peel off the second skin of my bloodied mourning gown. Then, like a long-forgotten vision, I remembered Henry waiting in the kitchen with Nan, and that I could feed him in bed with a good hot fire before us. The rain was already washing away our footprints in the churned earth. The coming day would discover no sign of the night's events. I returned to the pony cart and turned it around for Delafosse.

32

London

Summer 1796

~ Orange-flower Sugarpaste ~

Chop and pulverise your orange-flowers and pound them with
gum dragon dissolved in a glass of water. Add a glass of
orange-flower water and as much sugar as is necessary to
bring it to a supple paste consistence, and mould as you will
into small cakes, flowers, lozenges, as you will.

The Professed Cook, or The Modern Art of
Cookery, Pastry and Confectionary Made
Plain and Easy by Bernard Clermont

I spent almost a month at Delafosse, in a state of exhausted half-life. I let Nan care for little Henry and me, all the time keeping the fire in my chamber banked up high, and the curtains drawn. Dear Nan brought me caudles of egg and brandy, game jellies, and herb-rich stews. Except to dismiss the sisters from the kitchen, I didn't leave my chamber at all.

I felt I must sleep for a hundred years, safe in some pocket of lost time, before I could wake and find the world alive again. And each time I woke to feed Henry, the memories that blazed in my mind – the glint of a knife-point in the darkness, Mrs Harper's icy hand-clasp in the larder, and Michael's wordless anguish as he vanished from this world – those images dissolved slowly away, like crimson scars fading to new pink skin. No constables or magistrates came knocking at my door with unanswerable questions. The new owner of Whitelow did not demand to search the foundation pit. I would have liked to hibernate there in my old chamber, in the blue tester bed beneath crewel-work tulips, with the bed curtains wrapped tightly around us.

'He should be baptised, mistress,' Nan said, winding bands of linen tightly about Henry's wriggling form.

'One day. In my religion he should wait until he chooses to be baptised himself.'

'That's a shame. I never did get to showing you this.' Nan pulled a paper parcel from her apron and handed it to me. Inside was a miniature cradle, smaller than my hand, painted to look like wood. It contained a tiny peg-sized baby, swaddled in bands. At first I thought it was made of yellowing ivory, but it had a powdery texture.

'Is it made of sugar?'

'Aye. It's a device for a christening cake. I fancied the little one might 'ave it.'

I looked at it closely; it had the look of an antique from a bygone age. 'It's very old. And beautiful.'

'This come with it. You 'ave a look. I never did learn how to read me letters.'

I opened a fading, yellowed paper. As I read it out loud to Nan, my eyes stung with pity: poor Hannah Croxon had made such efforts to give Michael a good and free life.

Again I picked up the tiny figure of a baby; only this time it struck me as a crude depiction of a human being, like a tiny corpse in a shroud.

'And now he's dead,' I said. 'That beautiful baby she rescued.'

Nan's milky eyes looked up into my face, sagging mournfully in their great web of wrinkles. 'Mr Michael?' She had never asked me why he hadn't returned.

'Yes. He died with her. I think he chose to.' I held out the crib to her. 'I can't take it, Nan. Even though he was Henry's father. I want to break the link now.'

Nan ran a mottled fingertip along the length of the sugar figure. 'After I got this from Miss Hannah, I allus knew the bairn were safe,' she said. 'I never even knew he come back here.'

I didn't tell her I guessed someone else had known and had used that knowledge cruelly. Tenderly she wrapped the sugar baby up again in its manger of dusty paper.

A letter arrived, giving Michael notice of the end of the twelve-month's tenancy at Delafosse. With it was enclosed an advertisement for the property's sale, stating that the land and house were expected to command £1,000. Michael's strongbox contained more than that sum; almost £3,000, or half of the £6,000 my land was worth.

I drew back the curtains on a window-rattling, wind-whipped

autumn; the trees were shedding flurries of ochre leaves. Across a pearly sky, a flock of swallows crisscrossed in agitated arcs. I leaned forward on my elbows and wondered at myself. It was not only Michael that I was cured of; I had fallen out of my dream of living at Delafosse; with its untameable acres and incurable decay. I made plans to depart.

The only letter I wrote was to Mrs Barthwaite, informing her I was sorry I could not pursue our acquaintance as I was leaving Earlby for good. My health, I wrote, was not strong enough to withstand the damp northern winters. That one letter, I surmised, would inform the entire neighbourhood of my departure.

I burned Peg's things, and Michael's too. The monstrous hoard of food I found in the basement was given to the church to distribute to the poor. I took only my own goods, and what I thought would prove useful of the new furniture. Beyond that, I wanted nothing that carried the taint of my time at Delafosse Hall.

∽

My house in London is newly built, upon land that was once an orchard. It has crisp rectangular walls, and stands hugger-mugger in the crowded heart of the square. I chose it for its high arched windows that flood my parlour with light from floor to ceiling. From here, I can watch a ceaseless cavalcade of passers-by, carriages, horses and wagons, that cheer me with their incessant reminder that life drives ever onwards. The house is modest and secure; only four narrow floors radiating from the elegant curlicue of a staircase. I want to hug the freshly-plastered walls tightly in my arms; it is a house I can never get lost in.

The captain is well-contented with his quarters, a modest suite of rooms overlooking the stables. I promised him a life of ease, but he will not hear of such idleness. He spends each morning overseeing the stables, and the management of our provisions, too. He has assisted me with matters of business, the deposit of my money at a bank at interest, and the purchase of our home; proving an altogether kindlier advisor than that bulldog, Mr Tully. Then, his duty done, my old friend sets off in his scarlet coat for his day's perambulations. He has never quite recovered from that savage blow to the head, his hearing is declining, and his back is not so straight, but he is the happiest of fellows, saluting passers-by smartly, and jesting with mop-twirling maids from the neighbouring houses.

Today I have the whole of a summer's afternoon before me; and down here in the kitchen, I am indulging a whim to learn to bake.

'Why, it's what you'd call perfect, ma'am,' says Sal, my maid-of-all-work, as we unpack my first ever fruit cake from its brown-paper wrapping. It is of modest size, but well fed with brandy, covered with almond paste, and has a top layer of snowy sugar icing as smooth as white glass.

Sal is another welcome refugee from Mrs Huckle's. Nan would not come south with me, so I settled an annuity on my unlikely saviour. After expressing a hankering to return to her birthplace in Skipton, she lives there now in a doll-sized almshouse, where I hope she may happily end her days.

'Mama, for me?' warbles Henry, toddling across the room, his stubby fingers reaching for the cake.

'Tomorrow.' I playfully bat his fingers away. 'Here. Try a sugar rose petal.' He chews tentatively on the sugar paste, then rolls his eyes in mimicry of bliss. In part I have learned to cook because I still cannot trust a stranger's food to pass Henry's lips. I do not suspect my servants of ill will, quite the contrary; it is only my belief that we sometimes give our trust too easily. And Henry is the gold-crowned sun of my universe, a giggling infant whose world is a bounty of small miracles. Now he tugs at Sal's sleeve, bursting to show her his peg-soldier, whittled and painted by the captain, standing guard at the gate to the yard. I nod at her to follow him, and return to the beautification of my cake.

There had been a method to bake fruit cake amongst the receipts I found in Peg's quarters at Delafosse; written inside that book of hers titled *Mother Eve's Secrets*. For an unthinking moment, I thought I'd found something of worth amongst Peg's hoard. She had always been a fine pastrycook, her puddings dripping with hot syrup, her desserts as light as sugared clouds, her tea-board a never-ending array of ratafias, cakes, and tarts. As for the rest of our roasts and savouries, Nan told me of those deceptions. Peg had made that frail woman little more than a whipped slave; I still chastise myself for my blindness.

I turned over a few of Peg's pages, and yes, there were her glorious desserts, scribed on grease-blotted pages. But there were others too: *A Nostrum for Eternal Youth* (one halfpenny to make, ask two shillings of each gull), *Mother Watson's Elixir* (to be hawked for any remedy), and *A Love Potion Generally Fobbed to the Lonely*. Over the page was a sinister diagram: *A Sure Mesmeric Method to Gain Influence Upon Another*, that contained crude drawings of eyes, staring at each other with dotted lines between them. And at the back were potions that made the hairs on the back of my neck rise – *A Narcotic for Natural-Seeming Sleep, Use of Sassafras to Confuse the Reason, An Usquebaugh to Provoke the Fever of Lust, A Mighty Strong Venom to Procure a Rapid Death.* I dropped the book like a red-hot coal. Then lifting it nimbly in a cloth, for I did not want to touch it, I threw it in the fire. I watched the greasy papers ignite in wild flame, then shrivel to flakes of charcoal. I am indeed fortunate to be alive.

I blink as I look about my kitchen, driving away memories of the underground labyrinth of Delafosse. My smart iron cooking range throws out a steady, warming heat. Blue and white Willow Pattern china fills the wooden shelves. I have bought freshly printed cookery books, copper moulds, and iron pans, and every new-fangled whisk, mill and jigger.

Sal and Henry return with a gust of warm garden air and I settle down to create miniature roses from sugarpaste using tiny ivory spatulas and crimpers. I will have no antique tester bed crowning my cake, only a posy of flowers: symbols of beauty and growth, each year new-blossoming. I let Henry paint the broken pieces with spinach juice, while I tint my flowers with cochineal and yellow gum. As a pretty device I paint a ladybird on a rose, and think it finer than Sèvres porcelain.

At ten o'clock tomorrow, I will marry John Francis at St Mark's Church, across the square. As Sal and I rehearse our plans for the day, pleasurable anticipation bubbles inside me like fizzing wine. We will return from church for this bride cake in the parlour, then take a simple wedding breakfast of hot buttered rolls, ham, cold chicken, and fruit, on the silver in the dining room. Nan has sent me a Yorkshire Game Pie, so crusted with wedding figures of wheatsheafs and blossoms it truly looks too good to eat. We have invited few guests, for I want no great show, and instead will have bread and beef sent to feed the poor. And at two o'clock, we will leave with Henry for a much anticipated holiday by the sea, at Sandhills, on the southern coast. John Francis has promised Henry he may try sea-bathing, while I have bought stocks of cerulean blue and burnt umber to attempt to catch the sea and sky in watercolour. I have no vast trousseau, but have indulged myself in a robe of embroidered silk, and a Spanish hat, with the brim fashionably tipped and garnished with ribbons.

It is a year now since John Francis tapped my arm in a crowd at the Royal Academy Exhibition of Paintings. I was at first grateful merely to find a friend, being still mistrustful of strangers and spending every evening alone once Henry was in bed. On closer acquaintance, I found John was not at all romantically melancholic and is certainly no Renaissance angel in looks. Instead, his clear and honest eyes, his firm opinions and hidden ardour suit me just as well as when I was sixteen and we roamed the moors above Greaves. He is down-to-earth and sensible, a shrewd sea merchant in these embattled times, and a tender and eager lover. It took many weeks before I could confess to him that Michael had died. When I did, John reached for me and wrapped me so tightly in his arms that a great dam-burst of emotions overwhelmed me. I wept into his shirt as he stroked my hair and murmured that he loved me. Michael had trained me to tiptoe around his moods, as though my bare feet circled shards of glass. I am still astonished to speak freely and not be punished by sharp retorts; rather I am listened to with attention and respect.

John and I spoke often of marriage, for before God I am a widow and he a bachelor. There are crowded London parishes where our banns might be read by a careless clerk, who would never question the word of two respectable persons. But without proof of Michael's death I still dreaded the Croxons one day observing us on the street and demanding I give an account of Michael and his whereabouts.

'I shall tell the Justices the truth, that Michael died,' I said. It was John who made myriad objections – that I might be held to account for concealing a murder, and that my life might be blighted by scandal. 'And think of Henry,' he said soberly. 'Spare him from one day learning of his father's transgressions.' There was a further reason too, one that I often repeated to myself. How could I allow Nan to be tried for murder? What, in fact, is justice? I had always believed that justice should follow the most rigid rules, but now I concede it is a cumbersome tool; it can destroy more than it protects.

Even unmarried, I was nevertheless the happiest I had been in all my life. For I knew that loving John Francis would not destroy me; I am still my true self, only stronger, and in our private moments ineffably more tender.

Then, last year, the captain knocked at the parlour door and swept off his cap, a worried expression pinching his cheery face.

'I am afraid I have discovered this, Mrs Frankland.' He handed me a recent copy of *The London Times*:

CORONER'S INQUEST: MYSTERIOUS TRAGEDY OF THREE PERSONS FOUND DEAD IN LAKE

On Saturday night an inquest was held at the George public-house, Earlby, Yorkshire, before Montague Sheldon Esq, coroner for the District of Halifax, respecting the death of three persons found at 2 o'clock on Wednesday afternoon at Whitelow Pastures whilst the lake was being drained.

'Should I leave, ma'am?' The captain raised his white eyebrows.

'Yes, please,' I whispered, and covered my mouth as if I feared to utter a word; as if my life was at that moment being set upon weighing scales. I knew at once that these quiet days living under a fictitious name were stolen time. The next few minutes would decide whether my future held misery or happiness. I devoured the newsprint rapidly:

The coroner began by stating that the three bodies were in such a wretched state of decomposition that they had been reduced to skeletons, which greatly hampered his inquiries. In an attempt to understand this most cruel and mysterious affair, the coroner called forth a number of witnesses.

I glanced through these particulars, gleaning from them that a terrified labourer had unearthed:

. . . something white and fearsome crouched in the mud. Upon a general search of the area, three bodily remains had been uncovered and carried to the George, along with a number of unidentified objects found with them. Upon the coroner's direction, these were cleaned by a Mr Enderson, a local numismatist of some renown. The items were displayed by the coroner and, though affected by their long immersion, were described with care:

'a gold pocket watch bearing inside it the inscription Michael George Croxon, 4th April 1783 and stopped at a quarter to seven o'clock.'

'No,' I whispered. Not for almost three long years had I thought of that pocket watch; a gift to Michael from his parents upon his coming-of-age.

I rose and poured myself a tot of spirits from John's decanter. Quaffing it so fast it burned my throat, I continued reading the account as fast as I could:

> *. . . about 19 shillings in loose change of silver and copper, a knife with a bone handle about 10 inches in length, a silver crucifix on a chain, and a set of keys upon an iron chatelaine inscribed EJH, entangled fast with the chain of the gold pocket watch. Also a disc of copper pierced as if to be worn, but despite Mr Enderson's attempts to remove an amount of verdigris, time had entirely eroded the inscription upon its face.*

Next my eye was caught by an ominous word – 'Delafosse'.

> *Elias Claybourn Esq stated that he was the present owner of the land at Whitelow. In April 1795, following a case at law, he had inherited Riverslea Hall, which bounded Whitelow Pastures. He had then purchased Whitelow Pastures from Mr Thomas Crossfield, Farmer, and also Delafosse Hall and its park. Thereafter he had demolished Delafosse Hall with a view to building a modern country residence for his own retirement. Mr Claybourn attested that he had no acquaintance with Mr Michael Croxon, but understood he had been a tenant of Delafosse Hall some years earlier.*

So there it was – the whole tale was surfacing as if from a stagnant pond – the tale of Michael and the Hall. Next was the surgeon's report:

> *Surgeon Ralph Coleman attested that he had examined the remains of the three persons and ascertained the following: the first body was of a male, of about 5 feet 8 inches. The second was a female of about 5*

feet 6 inches. The third unknown female was about 5 feet tall and from an examination of the pelvic bones, bore evidence of having given birth to an infant. A silver crucifix upon a chain was discovered about her neck.

I turned the page and saw another name. Peter Croxon. They had called Peter as a witness – my fate hung in my brother-in-law's hands. With a pang I recollected with what coolness we had parted, the day he had visited me at the summerhouse.

Peter Arthur Croxon, gentleman, of Bleasedale Hall, stated that he was the younger brother of the deceased, who was thirty years of age when last seen alive, and had been a tenant at Delafosse Hall in 1792. Mr Michael Croxon had become the owner of Whitelow Pastures through marriage to Miss Grace Moore of Greaves . . .

So there at last – my name stood boldly in print in a newspaper. My heart racketed horribly at the sight.

. . . and had been intent upon building a cotton mill upon the land. He further stated that following a nocturnal arson attack upon the site of the mill, his brother had fallen into low spirits and become discouraged. The witness had last seen the deceased in November 1792, when they had quarrelled, the deceased being the victim of a melancholic disposition. The witness confirmed that the deceased was the eldest son of a reputable family from Greaves, Lancashire, but to their immense subsequent regret, the Croxon family had ceased relations with him at that time.

Upon questioning from the coroner, the witness confirmed that the gold pocket watch was certainly his brother's, given to him as a gift by his parents. He did not believe either of the two female bodies to be Mrs Grace Croxon, the wife of the deceased. It was common knowledge that Mrs Croxon had suffered ill health and left the neighbourhood to convalesce. The witness confirmed that on his last visit to Delafosse Hall, Mrs Croxon had already vacated the property and had written to him of her safe arrival on the south coast. Sadly they were no longer in contact after such a length of time, but he could assure the coroner as a gentleman, that he had no reason to believe Mrs Croxon to have been in any respect involved in this affair.

I jumped up, unable to contain my gratitude. Peter had perjured himself to protect me. How I regretted my suspicious nature and ill will to him. Peter had proved a true friend. And Peter, I noted in passing, had indeed claimed Bleasedale Hall and married Miss Brighouse. I read on:

Upon further questioning about the two unknown women, Mr Peter Croxon said that it was speculation, but he did believe his brother had formed an irregular attachment to his housekeeper, but could not remember her name. The witness confirmed that his brother's housekeeper did wear such an iron chatelaine at her waist, but the initials EJH meant nothing to him. With regard to the identity of the second unknown female, he had no notion whatsoever who she might be.

Only one more column of newsprint remained, and I read it greedily.

These were all the material points of evidence which Mr Sheldon summed up with great precision and perspicuity, deducing that the probability was that the deceased male was Mr Michael George Croxon, formerly of Delafosse Hall. It was however unfortunate that the two unknown females could not be identified.

The coroner affirmed that a dramatic feature of the case was the presence of the large kitchen knife in the vicinity of the bodies. However, given the long period of immersion and loss of flesh, all the usual tests of cause of death by surgeon's examination were fruitless. It

445

was at this late date impossible to say if the knife had played a part in the death of any of these unfortunate persons. Certainly none of the three appeared to have been robbed, as money and valuable goods were still found beside their persons.

In summing up the coroner said that there had been much speculation about this mysterious and dreadful tragedy, but that it was not his job to repeat scurrilous rumour against agitators and radicals; only to sum up the facts. One most unfortunate aspect was the erosion of the inscription on the copper disc, for it might well have provided a means of identity. He was therefore forced to advise the jury that the evidence was so slight that it was impossible to give a certain verdict of the cause of death of any of the deceased. In this light the jury gave a unanimous verdict of 1. Michael George Croxon – Death by Misadventure 2. First Female Unknown – Death by Misadventure 3. Second Female Unknown – Death by Misadventure. Accordingly the coroner issued his warrant for the burial of the bodies in a Christian manner.

I finished reading with a giddy sense of freedom. I would forever be grateful to Peter. A more vindictive man might have insisted I be found, and made to give my testimony on oath. I sat a long while, marvelling at what I'd read.

Someone knocked gently at the door. It was the captain, looking very anxious.

'What do you say, Captain? You have had more time than I to digest the meaning of all this.'

He set his hand to his chin and mused. 'The Devil only knows what murderous exchange took place between your husband and your servant.' He looked at me with a scrutinising gaze and I nodded, affecting agreement. 'My opinion is that he threatened her with recapture, and they argued – there was a tussle and both fell in the water. Or perhaps it was an unholy pact to end both their lives? As for the other woman, I reckon she was entirely unconnected.'

'How clever you are,' I said.

'Howsoever it fell out, it's certainly for the best. Those three souls can now receive a Christian burial. And you, if you do not mind my saying so, are free to do as you will. Though it might be a good time,' he added with a sly grin, 'to consider a change of name.'

৶

Only later that night, alone, dreaming of black water flooding my eyes, my nose, my throat, was I haunted by a particular phrase. I got up and scoured the newspaper again. It confirmed that Michael's watch chain had become tangled fast with Peg's chatelaine – again, I heard Michael's terrible scream. Michael had not taken his own life. Even in death Peg had seized upon him in revenge.

And also there in print were the initials engraved on the chatelaine by its unfortunate owner – *EJH*, whose thimble had been torn from its hook during God knew what struggle underground in the dark.

In my parlour are hung the best of my portraits, prettily framed and suspended from blue ribbons. The portrait I made of John Francis when a youth is much admired, as are sketches of Henry as he grows older, embellished with locks of hair fixed in curls under glass. Beside them are Mother and Anne, making a well-loved collection.

There are other pictures I keep out of sight: those of Michael and Peg are packed away in a trunk. Anne's sampler is there too, for though her needlework deserves to be displayed, its celebration of my marriage to Michael does not. As for my painting of Delafosse Hall at dusk, I think it the strangest painting I ever made. I used to ask myself: who is that woman who stares from the window? A figment, or perhaps a symbol of my former loneliness?

On dull autumn days, when even at noon a pock-faced moon hangs high in the sky, and the sun is so hazy it scarcely sheds sufficient light to merit the description of day – then I think I know her. As I bend over paint and paper I strain to hear the rhythmic sweeping of an old-fashioned broom, swishing across the wooden boards. At such times I don't look up. I am almost certain, but not quite sure, I might see her then.

Of course, I did see her at Delafosse; a middle-aged woman with mouse-like greying hair, dressed in the respectable black of a widow. She stood at the fringes of groups of servants, in the dusky corners of rooms, or in the muffling darkness of the basement. I believe I heard her too, by some freak of nature, in the dripping darkness of the tunnel, running for her life.

I have no recollection of painting her into the window of Delafosse Hall: a solitary figure, waiting and watching in that vast memory-haunted building; fixed and unable to leave. I pray she is at rest now, in a Christian grave, saved from the opaque black waters at Whitelow. As an anonymous gesture I settled a sum on orphaned James Harper of Pontefract.

Bless you, Eleanor Jane Harper. I remember your sad smile of encouragement across the grey light of the landing, your colourless eyes meeting mine, and the icy returning pressure of your hand clasping mine when we finally met in the flesh.

These are troubled days we live in. The mood in the country is still uneasy – this war with France makes every man mistrust his fellow, spreading rumours of revolution and spies. But these shores have withstood the Terrors of France, and as we move towards a new century, we harbour hope that better days will come. And one final message did reach me from those extraordinary years. At first the letter had been sent to Delafosse, where the new owner had not known what to do with it; so it was forwarded to Nan at Skipton. Finally, the minister who helped me pay her annuity sent it to my London address.

I had thought often of Anne but had only braved a letter once, to tell her I was safe and a mother. Not even that one letter had reached her, for here was her own enquity bearing many stains, postmarks, and creases. With some trepidation, began to read, bracing myself to hear a tale of starvation and depravity.

> *Greenbeck Farm*
> *Parramatta*
> *New South Wales*
> *5th February 1795*

My dearest Grace,

I am surprised not to hear from you for so long, and hope all is well with you? Or have our letters been lost at sea? Rumours reach us of shipwreck and mutiny on board those frail vessels that traverse the globe with our precious communications. I pray that this, of all my letters, will reach you, for I have not forgotten my promise to be a good correspondent. Often as I touch the ring you gave me, embellished with your own precious hair, I recollect my visit to Delafosse and the pleasures of York in your company. I wonder how Michael is, and whether you are still improving the Hall? I wonder too, if you have yet been blessed with children?

With what joy I can tell you of a wonderful improvement in our circumstances since that first unhappy account I sent you. We have moved to Parramatta town, a most pleasant place on the river, some sixteen miles from Sydney Cove. Our region has for the first time returned miraculous harvests of wheat and maize; indeed the summer here is so long that two crops of vegetables are often harvested. Soon Jacob will be Minister and we make plans to build a church, a modern wooden building with a meeting room where I hope to hold classes for the women and children. Yet I confess, to you alone, Grace, that I think Jacob has found a greater calling in agriculture than in the ministry. Last year the Governor granted us thirty magnificent acres here on the river, and our home, though constructed only of wood, and painted white with pipe clay, is one of the finest in this neighbourhood. We keep goats, pigs and poultry — did you ever picture me as a farmer's wife? And our dear children have a fine and free existence: Robert is a sturdy fellow of almost two years now, and my youngest baby, Grace, is a little sweetheart who I trust will be just as clever and good as her namesake in England. I should never have anticipated it, my dear friend, but I am content here. When I recall those apprehensions I had, and your brother-in-law's warnings, I do not believe God could have been more generous in his gifts.

Grace, I must tell you that here, where there is more open land than could ever be imagined back in the seething alleys of England, we have seen the most remarkable reformation of the hardest criminals. Our own nearest neighbour was once a convicted cracksman, as the locals name a house-thief, but now his farm is an exemplar from which we all gratefully learn. And this man and his family are good and peaceable people, who I believe needed only new hope and the trust of others to flourish.

But enough, I am running through my paper and I still have a most interesting account to give you. When we were in York you asked me to search out a convict named Mary Jebb. I can tell you she was a party to a most infamous escape from Sydney Cove some four years past. In mitigation, she and her fellow escapee, Jack Pierce, did escape the colony at a time of great crisis, when the population suffered most terribly from famine, illness and by all accounts the most awful notions of abandonment by the mother country. The two of them stole a boat and at dead of night sailed away, no doubt intending to sail north to the Dutch Indies or even China. For many years they were forgotten, but I can now supply the end to this tale.

A few weeks past, a whaling master named Captain Hogan came into town with news of a certain tribal chief of his acquaintance across the straits in the savage lands of New Zealand. Having become acquainted with these peoples, Captain Hogan found himself a guest at a grand feast of a Maori tribe. It was at that feast he noticed a woman with the white skin of a European but able only to speak the Maori tongue. At close quarters he observed how proudly she wore her feathered cloak and bone ornaments, and was the wife of a warrior and mother to a brood of his pale-skinned children. In despair he spoke in English, then tried a little French and Dutch. He wondered if she had been a whaler's wife, or a planter's daughter, shipwrecked or otherwise stranded in that land. Then the tale of that infamous couple's escape came to his mind. 'Mary Jebb,' he repeated slowly. The change in the woman's countenance was extraordinary. She grew pale and muttered wildly, as if hearing words of extraordinary power. So moved was the whaling captain by her plight that he spoke secretly to her, offering her a passage back to the Colony should she so wish it, endeavouring to persuade her to rejoin her own Christian race. But at the frequent repetition of her name, the former convict clung to her adopted tribe and would under no persuasion be parted from them. And so she lives a pagan still, and is talked of in the colony as a byword for moral degradation. Captain Hogan informed me that when he tried to teach her to once again speak her own name she no longer possessed the skill. Try as she would to repeat the letter 'M' she made a jumbled mess of 'Mary'. And also of 'Jebb', which she could not utter at all. And soon in frustration she spat in his face and stormed away in anger.

When I reached the end of the letter I felt for a moment the hard ground of my certainties shift – could there be two Mary Jebbs? I inspected the chain of my reasoning: the Old Bailey trial confirmed I had known a red-haired convict named Mary Jebb. Her own account of her escape with Jack had always rung as true as the gospel. And there also stood as evidence the twin copper discs of the matching Penny Hearts. The ground beneath my feet felt firm again. So if I had known Mary Jebb, who was the white woman Captain Hogan failed to rescue? Peg had once spoken of freedom bought by an exchange of muskets, I recalled.

Another character had been involved – that was it – a mission-ary's daughter.

I will never know her name, but wonder if everywhere Mary Jebb and her cast of false characters went, she left a discarded twin – a real Peg Blissett, formerly an alderman's cook, and a nameless missionary's daughter abandoned to a heathen tribe. And of course, a discarded Grace Croxon, mistress of Delafosse Hall. For a moment I experience a sisterly connection with that warrior's wife, who chose to stay at the ends of the earth. We have both survived, but not as we used to be – we are no longer gullible sleepwalkers. We have both clung to the mastheads of our selfhoods and not let go, while Mary Jebb raged about us like a tempest. And now we are both changed and cannot turn back into our former selves. Our victory is too hard won.

Is it possible to ever know such a character as Mary Jebb? Each time I thought I knew her, I poured my credulous trust into a figure of iron, casting a host of shadows. And when she wasn't playing parts? I remember the vicious murder of Mrs Harper. It is the echo-ing unlit stage between Mary's public performances that frightens me most.

I recollect the coroner's remark on that corroded Penny Heart that refused to give up its secret to the end. Perhaps we are all born with a blank heart, and choose which lines are etched upon it. Mary incised hers with vengeance, but the mordant waters dissolved it away. Sometimes I even pity her. Mortality stalked her with a scythe in hand, and felled her at her moment of sweet revenge.

With five bright chimes the church across the square rings out the hour. In seventeen hours I will gladly marry John Francis. I have found my true love again, and we must snatch what remains of happiness in our span of days. I think of that sundial on the tower at Delafosse: the long shadow cast by a shape unseen, relentlessly circling the dial. In time the iron rod will rust, and the brass-bound face will crumble. Time devours all things: love and murder and secrets. And though the sun sinks, and the golden numerals fade, we must believe that our own fragile hearts will guide us, like pin-pricks of starlight through the approaching night.

Acknowledgements

This novel was inspired by the Penny Heart tokens created by convicts as keepsakes, to be left behind with loved ones when the British government transported them to 'the ends of the earth', as the Antipodes were described. Coins were generally engraved with the convict's name, length of sentence and a sentimental verse or message. Much of the imagery and choice of words signifies a vibrant working class subculture also expressed on the convicts' skin in elaborate tattoos; it was surprising to me to find that as many as twenty-five per cent of female convicts put on trial in mainland Britain carried such 'personal marks'. Though pain at separation is the overwhelming emotion expressed on convict tokens, anger, defiance and contempt are also found. Peg's use of a token to express a vow to return and take revenge is however, my own invention. On a few occasions I have blurred the chronology of history to write this fiction, but in the larger backdrop of crime, punishment and the position of women, I have tried to be true to the times.

A great many books, articles, people and experiences helped me in the writing of this book but the following deserve a special mention:

Michele Field & Timothy Millet, *Convict Love Tokens: the Leaden Hearts the Convicts Left Behind* (Wakefield Press, 1998)

Roy Porter, *Quacks: Fakers and Charlatans in Medicine* (NPI Media, 2003)

Amanda Vickery, *The Gentleman's Daughter: Women's Lives in Georgian England* (Yale, 2003)

Prudence Bebb, *Life in Regency York* (1992) *and Shopping in Regency York* (1994) (Sessions of York)

E P Thompson, *The Making of the English Working Class* (Penguin History, 1991)

David Sekers, *A Lady of Cotton: Hannah Greg, Mistress of Quarry Bank Mill* (The History Press, 2013)

Laura Mason, *Sugar-plums and Sherbet: The Prehistory of Sweets* (Prospect Books, 2003)

Elizabeth Raffald, *The Experienced English Housekeeper* (Southover Press, 1996 [first edition 1769])

Stephen Hart, *Cant - A Gentleman's Guide: The Language of Rogues in Georgian London* (Improbable Fictions, 2014). The author's online database of Cant was also invaluable: http://www.pascal-bonenfant.com

Watkins Tench, *A Narrative of the Expedition to Botany Bay* (1789) and *A Complete Account of the Settlement at Port Jackson, (1793)* www.gutenberg.org

James Hardy Vaux, *Vocabulary of the Flash Language* (1812) www.gutenberg.net.au

Peg's adventures were in part inspired by Mary Bryant (also known as Mary Broad) of Fowey, England, who escaped from Botany Bay with her husband, William. In a feat of astonishing navigation, they sailed 3254 miles in 69 days in an open boat up the uncharted coast of Australia, before being recaptured in the Dutch East Indies. Mary Bryant was a very different character from Peg and her life can be discovered in an excellent book, *To Brave Every Danger: The Epic Life of Mary Bryant of Fowey* (Truran, 1993) by Judith Cook, or a less authentic but entertaining film, *The Incredible Journey of Mary Bryant* (2005).

Interpretations of the earliest collisions between Maori and Pakeha cultures in New Zealand vary widely. While I found Trevor Bentley's *Captured by Maori: White Female Captives, Sex and Racism on the Nineteenth-century New Zealand Frontier* (Penguin Books, 2004) a fascinating collection of early accounts, I cannot always agree with his conclusions about the positive aspects of captivity.

Parts of this book were written in New Zealand and Australia, where my husband and I lived for almost two years on a mid-life journey accomplished by house-swaps. It therefore recalls our friends in Whakatane and Ohope, our special home for a magical year. Also in New Zealand, thanks go to Nancy King for our Creative Arts Scholarship at the eco-house at Muriwai and The New Zealand Society of Authors for a place on their mentorship programme with Joan Rosier-Jones, whose wise words and dead-lines were always helpful.

The NZSA also guided me towards Peter Beatson, who gave my son and me the opportunity to write at Foxton Beach and to find his article on 'Richard Nunns: the Renaissance of Traditional Maori Instruments'(*Music in the Air*, Summer 2003), about a traditional bone flute. It also led me to the Flax Stripper Museum where I could handle and wear traditional Maori objects. Heritage New Zealand, National Trust of Australia and The National Trust all sparked my imagination, as did the generous network of libraries across New Zealand that offer wonderful materials, wi-fi, comfort-able chairs and the best views in the world.

I would also like to thank the following people for their help and inspiration: Ivan Day, for the opportunity to learn about Period Sugarwork and Confectionary, consult his library and for the online bounty of www.historicfood.com.

Two writer friends, Elaine Walker and Alison Layland, contin-ued to give me invaluable feedback, support and inspiration, and Lucienne Boyce provided advice on the legal situation of married women of property.

A retreat as Writer in Residence at Church Cottage, Clifford Chambers, came at the perfect time, thanks to Sarah Hosking of the Hosking Houses Trust.

For their crucial encouragement and belief in the novel, thanks to all at Andrew Nurnberg Associates, especially Sarah Nundy, and in the novel's early days, Ella Kahn, while Imogen Russell Williams provided invaluable assistance.

Thank you to all at Hodder and Stoughton for encouragement and support, especially Laura Macdougall and Nick Sayers.

And finally, thanks to my son Chris and my husband Martin, both ever ready with their cameras and great ideas.

VOLUME 1: BLOOD AND DROOL

Writer and Artist
MIKE NORTON

Color Artist
ALLEN PASSALAQUA

Letterer
CHRIS CRANK

Cover Artists
MIKE NORTON AND
DOMINIC MARCO

DARK HORSE
BOOKS

Publisher
MIKE RICHARDSON

Editor
PATRICK THORPE

Designer
TINA ALESSI

Digital Art and Production
CHRISTIANNE GOUDREAU

Special thanks to Brion Salazar, Josh Emmons, and iFanboy.

Published by Dark Horse Books, a division of Dark Horse Comics, Inc.
10956 SE Main Street, Milwaukie, Oregon 97222
DarkHorse.com

To find a comic shop in your area, call the Comic Shop Locator Service: (888) 266-4226

First edition: July 2012
ISBN 978-1-59582-972-6
10 9 8 7 6 5 4 3 2 1

Printed at 1010 Printing International, Ltd., Guangdong Province, China

THE INTRODUCTION TO *BATTLEPUG* SHOULD SIMPLY READ, "The idea we all wish we would have had." Or maybe, "I'm so jealous of Mike Norton and his big, dumb, perfect, amazing idea." Or even, "Whatever, it's just a dude on a giant pug. (I hate you, Mom, for breeding me with broken science, resulting in Mike Norton creating a dude riding a giant pug and not me.)" Any of these would work perfectly, but that wouldn't take up nearly enough of the page and I wouldn't get the chance to figure out a way to make an introduction for *Battlepug* be about me somehow. So, I guess I'll expand a bit.

There's a lot of things that make *Battlepug* a special comic. Most would say that a barbarian riding atop a giant dog from a breed so cartoonishly ugly that they cross back over into cute would be enough to make it special. Or that there are giant seals, toads, and Santa Claus all within a few pages of each other. These are great points. But as a cartoonist myself, the story of how *Battlepug* came to life is a real tingle giver. (Yes, tingle giver . . . I'm trying things; go with it.)

As freelance cartoonists, we usually draw things *others* think of. If we have any time left over, we may pull out a sketchbook and doodle a few things just for ourselves. The more successful we become at doing for others, the less we do for us. Eventually we find ourselves drawing Superhero Book X, and that takes up a good chunk of life. Five or six years of that and we've settled into a groove that works well, and all is good with the world. I met Mike when we were both in this zone. We were in our grooves producing fun work on various superhero comics, and all was good with the world.

We started a Drink and Draw in Chicago and got together with fifteen or so cartoonists every Wednesday. It was great because it was a safe zone for us. We could pull out pencils, pens, and brushes and be free to do or say whatever we wanted with the lines in our books. We were the Masters of Shape and the Lords of Narrative in those bars on Wednesday nights. There were no editors to tell us we're too this or not enough that. No reviews would show up online, no message boards to judge us. Just drinks, friends, and art. It was my favorite time.

During these years I was always blown away by Mike's sketches. I knew him as a superhero guy, and we all know he's not too shabby at being the superhero guy. I was being introduced to the other side of Mike's cartooning. Seeing what he did from the gut always got me excited. He played with shape and applied that to a quick wit that always left you wanting more. If only one of his sketches could turn into a sprawling epic, I could get lost in the action and comedy for days. Page after page of Mike's blue sketchbook had these sketches, and I couldn't get enough. On Thursdays we went back to the world where all was good, but I would always think about the ideas we explored that one night a week.

In the years following, Mike put his hand on pretty much every superhero at Marvel and DC. From time to time he and I would get together at my house and talk about some of our potential ideas for the day when we entered the world of creator-owned comics. And then many more years passed again . . . ha ha. Don't judge. One day Mike was asked to do a T-shirt for our buddies at iFanboy. It was one of those rare freelance gigs that carry the "Do whatever you want" job description. So he did do whatever he wanted and created *the* Battlepug image.

If you're getting woozy from my rambling and forget where I was going with this, just take it easy. The end is near.

The creation of *Battlepug* is the most special part to me. After years of drawing classic superhero books, when asked to do whatever he wanted . . . the Mike I knew from the blue sketchbook came out. The guy can draw his butt off, we all know that, but through *Battlepug* he's showing the world the other side. The Mike we all know. He's funny, passionate, young at heart, and obviously has ideas bursting at the seams. Watching artists cross that line from craftsmen to storytellers is exhilarating for me. It's scary to put your ideas—yourself, for that matter—out there in the open. It's much more comfortable behind a guy in a red cape or a scarecrow. They've been around for decades. They'll protect us. But recognizing when *your* idea is ready to stand between you and the world is a talent in itself.

I hope you have as much fun on Battlepug's journey through this book as I did watching Mike as a cartoonist over the years. The story is a blast, the origin of the book's creation is inspiring, and I for one am excited for the years' worth of future stories to come. Go and enjoy this book . . .

. . . And then pretend the idea was all mine.

SKOTTIE YOUNG
The middle of a cornfield, IL
2012

Our story begins many years ago...

...in a faraway land, with the snow tribes of the Kinmundy.

Among them lived a boy and his mother.

A peaceful child with only thoughts of toys and play.

A mother who loved him more than anything.

The other boys of the tribe spent their days learning the ways of the hunt. But the child preferred to play with his dolls.

His father was outraged by this, but the mother stood behind her son.

On the day of the great hunt, the father left with the rest of the tribe's warriors.

They were never to return.

The mother did her best to hide her growing sadness, but the boy could tell she was no longer the same.

The two went on as best they could.

Unfortunately, the worst had yet to come.

The beast laid waste to the village in moments.

The boy and his mother were unable to escape its wrath.

He found himself alone among the wreckage.

His mother was gone.

His home.

His family.

All lost to him.

Amidst the carnage...

...time seemed to stop for the little boy.

His focus drawn elsewhere.

In that moment, the peaceful child with only thoughts of toys and play...

...and a mother who loved him more than anything...

...would now live for only one thing.

REVENGE

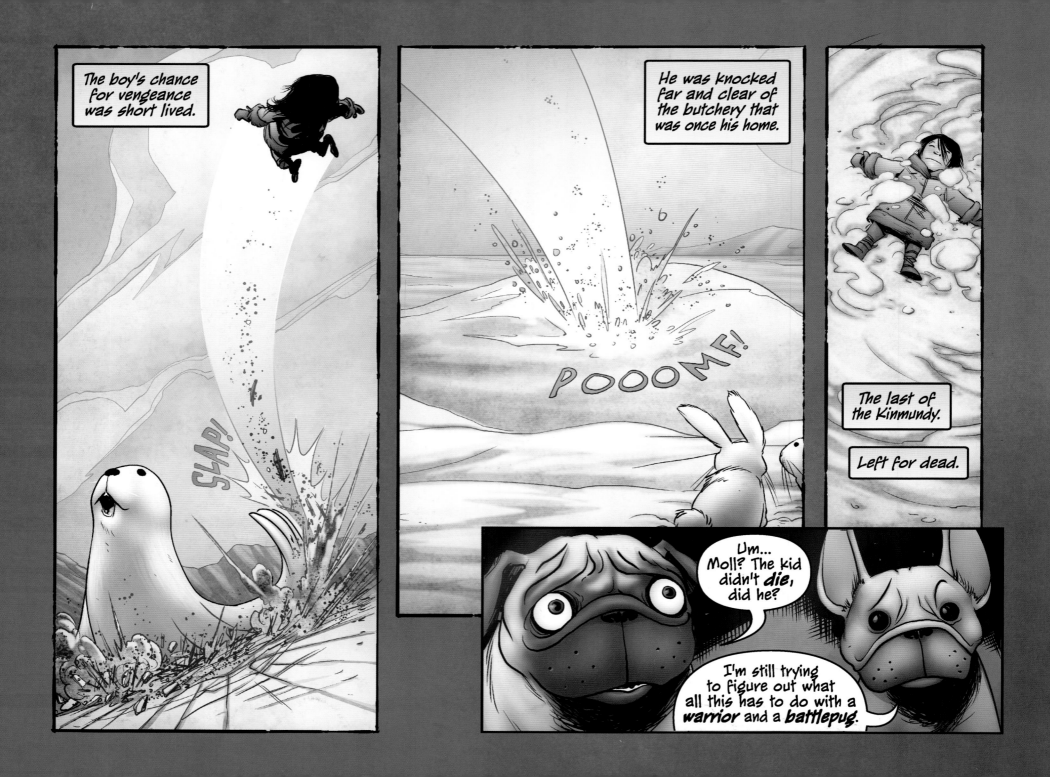

They brought the boy before the king of the Northland Elves to decide his future among them.

Servitude.

But despite longstanding rumors to the contrary, the monarch was not known to his people for his charity.

The child lived a hard and cruel life in his new home.

For years, he toiled for his keepers. His happy life among the Kinmundy now a far-flung memory.

By day he was their slave. By night--their sporting entertainment.

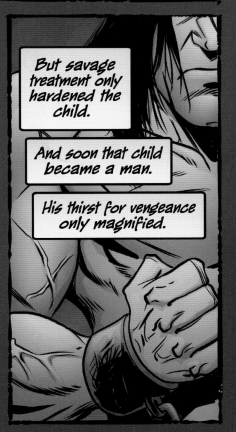

But savage treatment only hardened the child.

And soon that child became a man.

His thirst for vengeance only magnified.

Finally the fateful day arrived...

My lord! We were attacked!

Our glacier outpost was decimated! A giant creature--

A massive beast! It was... *horrible!*

I fear it makes its way here, my lord! We must do something.

Its size... it will destroy all you have worked to build.

The Kinmundian realized this was his opportunity.

If I may, my king.

Set me free...

...and *I* will destroy this monster you fear.

It was the first time he had spoken since he was brought to the Northland kingdom.

The warrior continued into the swamp as the madman rambled to himself.

He decided to find out what had become of Patoka on his own.

And then he did.

Who was this "she" the lunatic spoke of?

What was she?

The warrior faced down the massive beast.

Unafraid.

The beast stared back.

Blankly.

GRAAAAH

FLING!

MISS!

?!?

Exposed to the true danger of the swamp, the warrior wasted no time.

WACK

KRUNCH

SSSTIME FOR NOM NOMSSS!

Scribbly scrabbly!

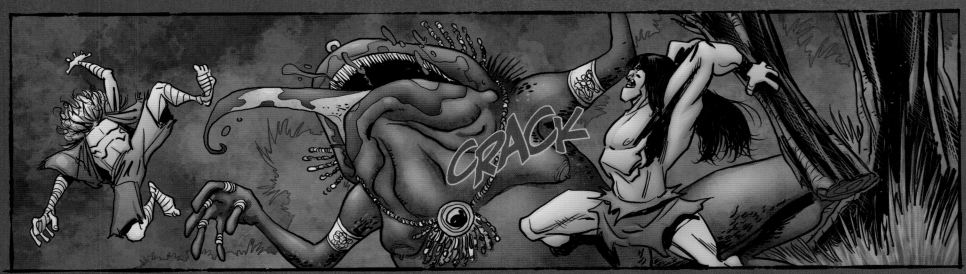

I don't care if the murder of my people *is* the work of sorcery.

I will find the one responsible and I will see him torn asunder!

And there *is* *no* *bond* between me and this... embarrassment of nature!!

schlurp
lick

Magical or otherwise!

If you say so, scrabbly...

If you know of these things, you would serve yourself well to help me find my enemy.

Err...I can do that, scrabbly.

Damn right, you can.

Tomorrow, we make our way to the nearest city and find *our* *own* mage.

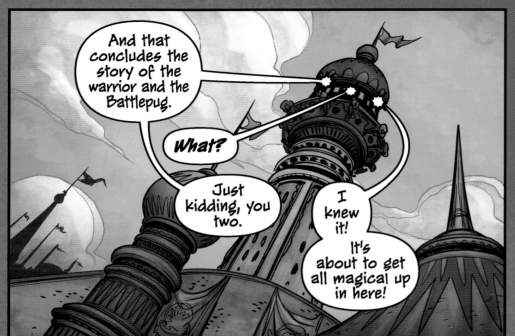

Terrible and grisly, scrabbly!

Told ya, Meaty. You've stuck here.

SKITTER SKITTER SKITTER

SKITTER SKITTER SKITTER

"Magic," eh?

Vermin! I've crushed more formidable creatures with my bare hands! It will be a pleasure to kill you all!

Uh, boss...is this a good idea?

SKITTER SKITTER SKITTER

I don't have time for this.

No! Wait!! What is it with you guys?

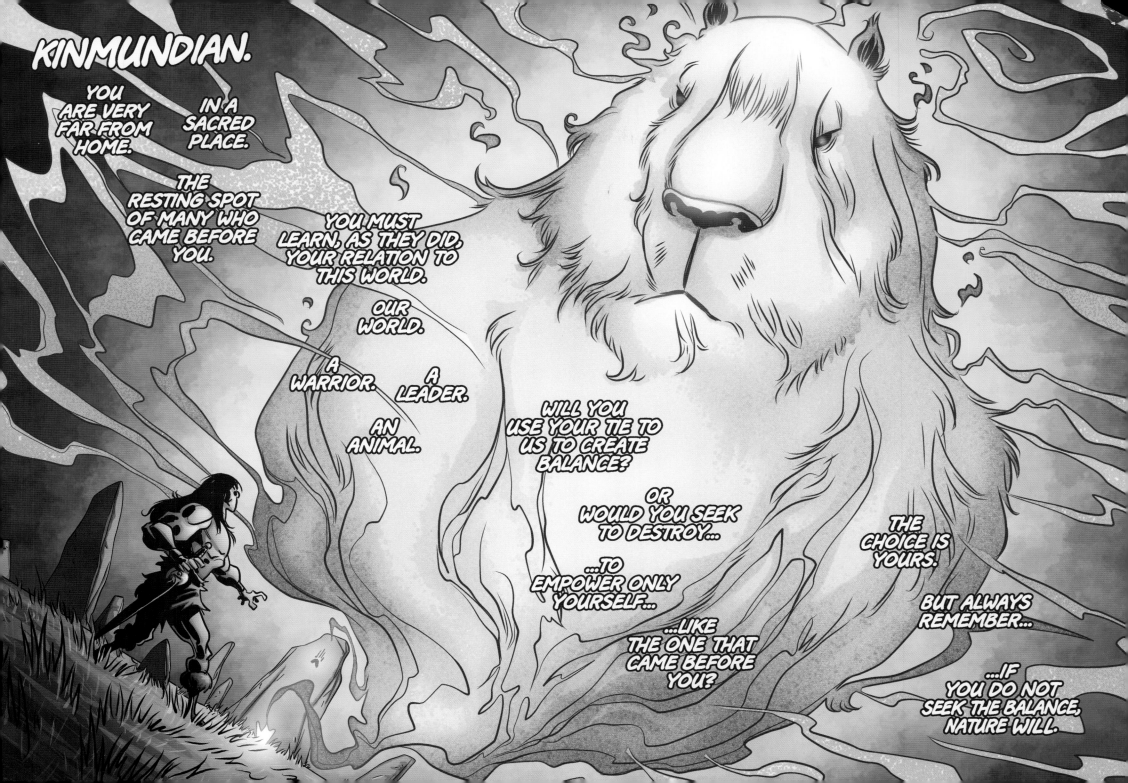

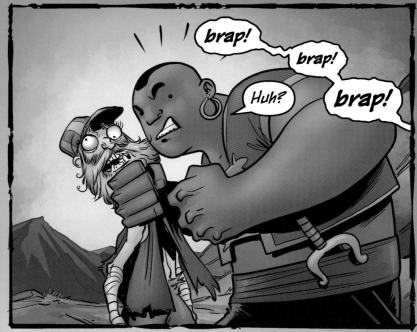

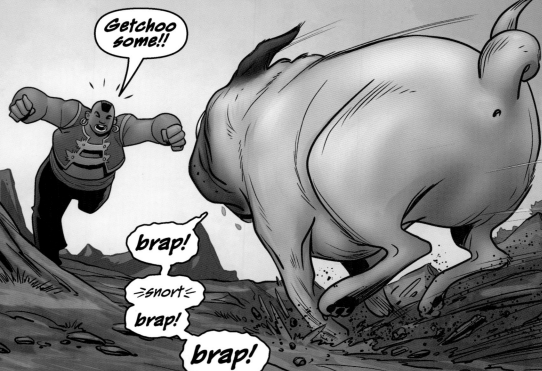

One of Mike Norton's early design sketches of the beautiful and enigmatic storyteller, Moll.

MOLL

BARL!

SCL IT!

COLFAX

And some of the animals we met in this volume—the evil baby harp seal, Colfax, and Mingo.

HAT LIKE CRANK

The genesis of the warrior's eccentric traveling companion, Scribbly.

An early version of the warrior with his critter cohort, the courageous pug.

THE LAST KINMUNDIAN

A design sketch of the Last Kinmundian, the nameless warrior.

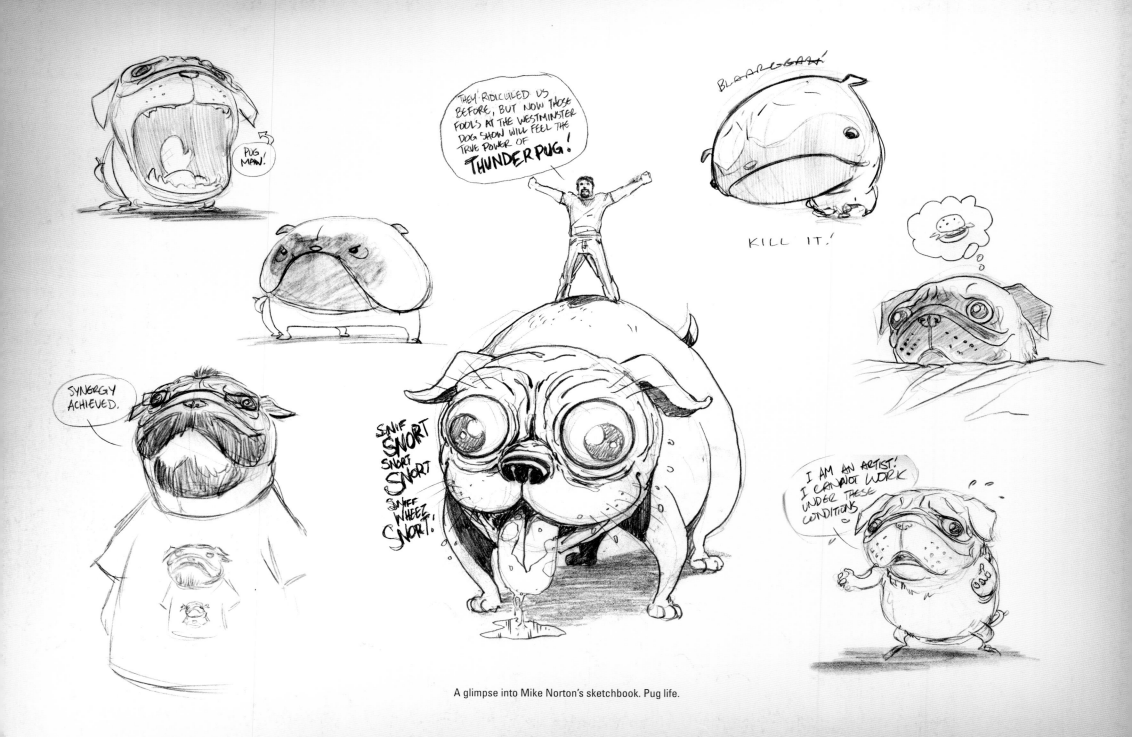

A glimpse into Mike Norton's sketchbook. Pug life.

MIKE NORTON

Mike Norton has been working in comics for over ten years, gaining recognition for projects such as *The Waiting Place* and *Jason and the Argobots*. He's made a name for himself working on books like *Queen and Country*, *Gravity*, *Runaways*, *The All New Atom*, *Green Arrow/Black Canary*, *Billy Batson and the Magic of Shazam!*, and *Young Justice*. He is currently drawing Marvel's *Fear Itself: Youth in Revolt*, and his own weekly webcomic, *Battlepug*. He is also very, very tall.

ALLEN PASSALAQUA

Allen is a professional comic color artist, as well as being involved in promoting culture and art and bringing together the creative community. Combining traditional and pop-culture influences, Allen has been commissioned to create artwork for several national parks, the San Diego Zoo, and the Grand Canyon, has story boarded Emmy-winning commercials, and has worked on various mass-media-outlet projects. His coloring work includes *Justice Society of America*, *Spider-Man*, *Green Arrow/Black Canary*, *Detective Comics*, and many others. He is not as tall as Mike.

CHRIS CRANK

Letterer, musician, and editing pal. Crank is believed to be a myth, and he must let the world think that he is a myth, until he can find a way to control the snotty spirit that dwells within him. Crank once baby-sat Mike's first pug for a whole weekend without damaging him, and he has a podcast with Mike at CrankCast.net.

DARK HORSE BRINGS YOU THE BEST IN WEBCOMICS!

COLLECT ALL OF YOUR FAVORITE ONLINE SENSATIONS, NOW IN PRINT WITH LOADS OF AWESOME EXTRAS NOT FOUND ANYWHERE ELSE!

ACHEWOOD
By Chris Onstad

Since 2001, cult comic favorite *Achewood* has built a six-figure international following. Intelligent, hilarious, and adult but not filthy, it's the strip you'll wish you'd discovered as an underappreciated fifteen-year-old. "I'm addicted to *Achewood*. Chris Onstad is a dark, hilarious genius." –Dave Barry

Volume 1: The Great Outdoor Fight HC
ISBN 978-1-59307-997-0 | $14.99

Volume 2: Worst Song, Played on Ugliest Guitar HC
ISBN 978-1-59582-239-0 | $15.99

Volume 3: A Home for Scared People HC
ISBN 978-1-59582-450-9 | $16.99

PENNY ARCADE
By Jerry Holkins and Mike Krahulik

Penny Arcade, the comic strip for gamers, by gamers, is now available in comic shops and bookstores everywhere. Experience the joy of being a hardcore gamer as expressed in hilariously witty vignettes of random vulgarity and mindless violence!

Volume 1: Attack of the Bacon Robots! TPB
ISBN 978-1-59307-444-9 | $12.99

Volume 2: Epic Legends of the Magic Sword Kings TPB
ISBN 978-1-59307-541-5 | $12.99

Volume 3: The WarSun Prophecies TPB
ISBN 978-1-59307-635-1 | $12.99

Volume 4: Birds Are Weird TPB
ISBN 978-1-59307-773-0 | $12.99

Volume 5: The Case of the Mummy's Gold TPB
ISBN 978-1-59307-814-0 | $12.99

THE ADVENTURES OF DR. MCNINJA: NIGHT POWERS
By Christopher Hastings

What's better than an evil unicorn motorcycle, monster gang wars, a tennis match against a god of destruction, and *bandidos* on velociraptors? Yeah, we couldn't think of anything either!

ISBN 978-1-59582-709-8 | $19.99

WONDERMARK
By David Malki

Dark Horse Comics is proud to present these handsome hardbound collections of David Malki's Ignatz-nominated comic strip *Wondermark*. Malki repurposes illustrations and engravings from nineteenth century books into hilarious, collage-style comic strips. More than just webcomic collections, the *Wondermark* books have been praised for their magnificent design and loads of extra content for casual readers and superfans alike.

Volume 1: Beards of Our Forefathers HC
ISBN 978-1-59307-984-0 | $14.99

Volume 2: Clever Tricks to Stave Off Death HC
ISBN 978-1-59582-329-8 | $14.99

Volume 3: Dapper Caps & Pedal-Copters HC
ISBN 978-1-59582-449-3 | $16.99

AXE COP
By Malachai Nicolle and Ethan Nicolle

Created by five-year-old Malachai Nicolle and illustrated by his older brother, the cartoonist Ethan Nicolle, these *Axe Cop* volumes collect the hit webcomic that has captured the world's attention with its insanely imaginative adventures, as well as the *Axe Cop* print-only adventures. Whether he's fighting gun-toting dinosaurs, teaming up with Ninja Moon Warriors, or answering readers' questions via his insightful advice column, "Ask Axe Cop," the adventures of Axe Cop and his incomparable team of crime fighters will delight and perplex even the most stoic of readers.

Volume 1
ISBN 978-1-59582-681-7 | $14.99

Volume 2: Bad Guy Earth
ISBN 978-1-59582-825-5 | $12.99

Volume 3
ISBN 978-1-59582-911-5 | $14.99

DARK HORSE BOOKS